Lockheed Constellation

Graham M Simons

AIR WORLD

Lockheed Constellation
A History

First published in Great Britain in 2021 by Air World Books,
an imprint of Pen & Sword Books Ltd,
Yorkshire - Philadelphia

Copyright © Graham M Simons
ISBN: 9781526758866

The right of Graham M Simons to be identified as Author of this work has been asserted by him in accordance with the Copyright, Designs and Patents Act 1988. A CIP catalogue record for this book is available from the British Library All rights reserved.

No part of this book may be reproduced or transmitted in any form or by any means, electronic or mechanical including photocopying, recording or by any information storage and retrieval system, without permission from the publisher in writing.

Typeset in 11pt Times by GMS Enterprises
Printed and bound in India by Replika Press Pvt Ltd

Pen & Sword Books Ltd incorporates the imprints of Air World Books, Pen & Sword Archaeology, Atlas, Aviation, Battleground, Discovery, Family History, History, Maritime, Military, Naval, Politics, Social History, Transport, True Crime, Claymore Press, Frontline Books, Praetorian Press, Seaforth Publishing and White Owl.

For a complete list of Pen & Sword titles please contact:

PEN & SWORD BOOKS LTD
47 Church Street, Barnsley, South Yorkshire, S70 2AS, UK.
E-mail: enquiries@pen-and-sword.co.uk
Website: www.pen-and-sword.co.uk

Or

PEN AND SWORD BOOKS,
1950 Lawrence Roadd, Havertown, PA 19083, USA
E-mail: Uspen-and-sword@casematepublishers.com
Website: www.penandswordbooks.com

Contents

Acknowledgements		4
Introduction		5
Chapter 1	Project Origins	7
Chapter 2	On the Drawing Board	23
Chapter 3	Early Days	41
Chapter 4	Rivals in the Skies	83
Chapter 5	Around the World	105
Chapter 6	Development	131
Chapter 7	Enter the Supers	149
Chapter 8	In the Navy - and Beyond!	183
Chapter 9	The L-1049H	231
Chapter 10	Constellation Swansong - The Starliner	239
Chapter 11	Genocide that was Biafra	251
Chapter 12	Last of the Summer Wine...	281
Apprendix I	Variants	299
Appendix II	Survivors	303
Bibliography		308
Index		311

Acknowledgements

A book of this nature would not have been possible without the help of many people and organisations too numerous to individually mention. I am indebted to many people and organisations for providing photographs for this story, but in some cases it has not been possible to identify the original photographer and so credits are given in the appropriate places to the immediate supplier. If any of the pictures have not been correctly credited, please accept my apologies.

I would however, like to offer my special thanks the Fellows, Members and Associates of the Worldwide Society of Civil Aviation Enthusiasts (WSCAE) - many of whom work in the global aviation industry as flight or ground crew or indeed 'on the spanners' - for letting me have free access to their collections, including Dee Diddley, Ameen Yasheed, Wan Hunglo, John Hamlin, Bob Lehat, Kirk Smeeton, Ian Frimston, Carrie Åberg, Simon Peters, Robin Banks, Rick O'Shea, Hugh Jampton, Peter Clegg, Hank Warton, Matt Black, David Lee, Bill Armstrong, Emma Dayle, Dr Harry Friedman, Jack Malloch, and Trymore Simango.

Thanks also go to the executors of the estate of the late Klaas Jurjen Prins, Brian Cocks, Martin Mace, Laura Hirst, Charles Hewitt, Matthew Potts, Harriet Fielding, Amy Jordan, Lori Jones and all at Pen & Sword.

Finally, and by no means least, my special heartfelt thanks to my wife Anne.

Introduction

It would be difficult to exaggerate the debt which modern airliner development owes to two factors: the United States' belief in the benefits of airline competition - along with the political and regulatory climate which has always seen to it that such benefits accrue to the travelling public - and, more particularly, the competitive requirements of the US transcontinental routes from New York through Chicago to Los Angeles or San Francisco. From the early 1930s onward, the three major US transcontinental airlines and their predecessor companies had been engaged in an increasingly strong battle for transcontinental traffic, not only between themselves but also with the railroads. The goal which each airline sought of reducing its coast-to-coast time over that of its competitors and cutting the number of stops, led United Airlines, American Airlines and Transcontinental and Western Airlines (later Trans World Airlines) to sponsor not just one but a whole series of highly successful transport aircraft from the drawing-boards of Boeing, Douglas and Lockheed.

Too often there is a tendency outside the USA to think of America's dominance in airliner manufacturing and sales as being due solely to the size of the home markets its industry enjoys; less apparent advantages are the pace of re-equipment and technological advances which a highly competitive environment makes possible - even before the war this was of genuine benefit - and, to use the industry's jargon, the plurality of native user demand resulting from the number of competing airlines, and the broader specification writing that goes with it. Whether a type is sponsored by an individual airline, as the Lockheed Constellation was by TWA, or collectively by several carriers, like its contemporary the Douglas DC-4, the value to US manufacturers of the feedback of operating experience and ideas for improvement from a number of vigorously competing user airlines has been, and is, immense, whether in developing stretched versions of the existing airframe or writing the specification for its successor, as well as in the more everyday business of defect rectification and the introduction of minor modifications.

The Constellation, true to the Lockheed tradition for sleekness of line, upheld the maxim that what looks good is good. When it first went into airline service, the Constellation surpassed every other transport aircraft in almost every aspect of performance and introduced such advanced features as pressurisation, hydraulic power-boosted controls, reversible-pitch airscrews and high-lift Fowler flaps. And as the type was developed by successive increases in weight, power, fuel capacity and payload, it achieved the unique 'triple crown' among post-war piston-engined airliners - operation of the first non-stop North Atlantic and US transcontinental services and the first round-the-world service.

Primarily intended for international and domestic trunk routes, when it was displaced as first-line equipment by the jets in the 1960s, it demonstrated its qualities in the hands of many smaller airlines, charter and supplemental carriers in areas far off the beaten track and in operations of sometimes dubious legality. These included flying in support of oil-drilling operations in Alaska, flying arms into the Yemen and Biafra, a number of smuggling ventures to South American countries. In particular, the Biafran airlift, primarily maintained by Super Constellations, was a remarkable performance in terms of reliability considering the military and operational hazards involved and the lack of any major maintenance and overhaul facilities in the area.

It was among the very first transports to test a collision-warning radar and weather radar, and its outstanding design qualities were well demonstrated during the vital part it played in defence of the continental USA in the role of airborne early warning and radar picket. Significant excrescences like the dorsal and ventral radomes, and the earlier Speedpak freight container had little effect on its handling characteristics and early warning/special electronics versions continued to be developed, while some one-off modifications of early warning aircraft for such jobs as oceanographic research and radiation measurement have done.

Few, if any aircraft have been flown with so many radome configurations as the Constellation, ranging from the WV-2E's saucer-shaped dorsal radome and no ventral radome to the ventral radome only on some one-off research aircraft.

Different engines presented no difficulty and the prototype flew by conventional piston engines, a Turbo-Compound and an Allison turboprop at the same time! Although stressed for conversion to turboprop and flown as a test-bed for such powerplants, the Super Constellation never went into production with turboprops, and in the final production model with the new thinner larger-span wing, the airframe development potential ran ahead of its engines. Had the pure jets not dominated the scene in the 1960s the basic Model 1649A airframe would doubtless have been developed into turboprop versions and, as such, would undoubtedly have given the long-haul Bristol Britannia turboprop a run for its money.

Writing this book has proved to be challenging - reading it may be the same. The difficulties, as usual with much of my work, springs from the differences of the so-called 'common language' British and Americans share. Color becomes colour, program becomes programme, and of course, American phrasing is often different from English. Then there is the dreaded use of plane instead of aircraft; I don't care what anyone says, a plane is a cutting tool used to smooth wood in my books!

This brings me to the conundrum of whether to use imperial or metric units of measurement. Invariably there are times when I must use both, but by and large my writing rules are simple: the aircraft was designed using imperial units, I use imperial measurements. I am English, so I write in that language; however, as a sign of respect to that nation, if I am quoting an American, I use their spelling and phrasing.

Another difficulty is that for much of this book two independent storylines are in place - the chronology of the Constellation, which in itself is somewhat convoluted, and the commercial and political events that were swirling around it, especially in the early days. Inevitably this has produced a disjointed main storyline, which I have tried to at least partially resolve by telling the story in a series of almost stand-alone chapters. Unfortunately it does mean that some photographs do not mesh into place with the main body text.

Speaking of photographs, many have been supplied by my good friends in the Worldwide Society of Civil Aviation Enthusiasts - some of whom have been taking and collecting since the 1950s and all freely admit that of the many hundreds of images I have used in this book, some are lacking in quality by today's standards At the time of writing in 2020, we have all been spoiled by the ability to take hundreds of pin-sharp digital images whenever and wherever we want. Some readers, I am sure, are not even old enough to remember the days of 'Instamatic' camera with twelve shot cartridge films that were in use when I saw my first Constellation. These images were often printed on horrible 'orange-peel' textured paper, that when scanned, often appear out of focus! Even with a thirty-five-millimetre camera, the cost of film, processing and printing meant that images had to be rationed. Many of the pictures used are from personal collections; some are repairs of company promotional material, a few are from newspaper cuttings pasted in albums without credit. All, however, are historic in the sense that they show aspects of the story.

An outstanding example of piston-engined airliner design at its peak, the Constellation lived up well to the dictionary definition of its name as 'a group of fixed stars, or an assemblage of splendours or excellences'.

Graham M Simons
Peterborough, December 2020

Chapter One

Project Origins

From the early 1930s three major US transcontinental airlines were engaged in a battle for traffic on routes from New York through Chicago to Los Angeles or San Francisco. The struggle was not only between themselves but also with the railroads. The goal sought was to reduce coast-to-coast time and reduce the number of stops. It led United Airlines, American Airlines and Transcontinental and Western Airlines to sponsor not just one but a whole series of highly successful transport aircraft from the drawing-boards of Boeing, Douglas and Lockheed.

Whether an aircraft type was sponsored by an individual airline, as with the Lockheed Constellation by TWA, or collectively by several carriers like its contemporary the Douglas DC-4, the value to manufacturers of feedback from operating experience and ideas for improvement from several vigorously competing user airlines was immense. It was equally valid whether in developing stretched versions of the existing airframe or writing the specification for its successor.

Starting with the Vega of 1927, Lockheed produced a line of single-engined, small-capacity transports of exceptionally clean aerodynamic design for the period. The high-wing Vega was followed by the parasol-wing Air Express designed for Western Air Express, the low-wing Sirius Mailplane, the two-seater Altair and the seven-seater Orion of 1932, the latter being the first production transport aircraft to have a retractable undercarriage. As well as operators in the USA, Orions were used by Swissair, and an increasing number of other European airlines followed and bought from Douglas and Lockheed up to the outbreak of the Second World War.

The Lockheed Company came on hard times following the 1929 stock market crash, a condition exacerbated by its failure to produce new types of aircraft following Northrop's highly successful, record-setting Vega, Sirius, Altair, and Orion designs. Five years passed without the development of a new kind of aircraft, something that could be fatal in an industry that lives on advances in technology. Finally, Lockheed, with only four people remaining on the payroll, found itself in the hands of federal bankruptcy receivers. The company struggled on, but in April 1932, a federal receiver took inventory, valued the assets, and offered them for sale.

Robert E Gross, Walter T Varney and Lloyd Stearman bought Lockheed on 6 June 1932 for $40,000. Gross became chairman and treasurer; Stearman, president; Carl Squier, who early on had distinguished himself selling Lockheeds, became vice president of sales; and Hall L Hibbard, a graduate of the Massachusetts Institute of Technology and assistant chief engineer for Stearman-Varney Aircraft, became vice president, chief engineer, and a member of the board. About a year later, Clarence L 'Kelly' Johnson, who was to become one of the pre-eminent aircraft designers of all time, joined Hibbard's staff.

Hibbard's engineering department produced a series of high-speed, twin-engine transport designs that restored Lockheed's leadership position. Included was the piston-powered Model 10 Electra, the first of a line of twin-engined transports built to the new formula of all-metal construction with retractable landing gear, flaps and variable-pitch props. The six-passenger Lockheed 12, of which 114 were built followed in 1936 and the eleven-passenger

Robert Ellsworth Gross (b. 11 May 1897, d. 3 September 3, 1961) Gross was born in Newton, Massachusetts. He attended St. George's School, Newport and graduated in 1915. In 1932, a group of investors led by Robert and his brother Courtlandt S. Gross bought the Lockheed Aircraft Company from the bankrupt Detroit Aircraft Corporation, renaming it the Lockheed Aircraft Corporation. Robert Gross served as the corporation's president from 1934 to 1956.

Model 14 Super Electra in 1937, the latter being the first aircraft in airline service to feature fully-feathering propellers, as well as underfloor freight holds and two-speed superchargers. A total of 112 Model 14s were built, as well as a hastily-designed maritime reconnaissance version, known as the Hudson, which was the first US type to be ordered in quantity by the Royal Air Force and saw widespread war service with Coastal Command and other Allied air forces.

The Model 18 Lodestar, of which 625 were built, was a development of the Model 14 that seated three more passengers. The Lockheed twins were complementary to, rather than competitive with, the larger 21-passenger DC-3, and sold to many smaller operators all over the world, as well as to larger airlines for their multi-stop feeder routes.

Lockheed had searched several years for a large transport development project suitable for commercial marketing and proposed a four-engine design, the Excalibur, in about 1937. It resembled an oversized Lockheed Electra and was capable of flying thirty-two passengers 2,000 miles at speeds from 250 to 275 mph.

Lockheed's L-44 Excalibur design had started off as a twenty-passenger airliner with a single fin and rudder and a gross weight of 27,500 pounds. It later grew to seat 26-30 passengers with the characteristic twin fins and rudders. Pan American Airways showed interest in the Excalibur. Still, they wanted more speed and capacity, and under their influence, it grew into its final form with triple fins and rudders and a deeper fuselage, similar in shape to the Lodestar. It was slightly smaller than the Boeing 307, with a wing of a 95-foot span and 1,000 square foot area, a nosewheel undercarriage, triple fins and rudders with fabric-covered control surfaces and the same engines as the 307 - four 1,000 horsepower Wright Cyclone GR-I820-G205A radials driving Hamilton Standard Hydromatic airscrews. Up to thirty-six passengers could be

Hall Livingstone Hibbard (b. 25 July 1903, d. 6 June 1996) was an engineer and administrator of the Lockheed Corporation beginning with the company's purchase by a board of investors led by Robert E. Gross in 1932. Born in Kansas, he received a bachelor's degree in mathematics and physics at the College of Emporia in 1925. He graduated from the Massachusetts Institute of Technology two years later. He worked for Stearman as a draftsman, before joining Robert Gross' Viking Flying Boat Company. He served on the board of the newly revived Lockheed Corporation and led the design departments as chief engineer.

seated in a pressurised cabin not very much larger than that of the DC-3 - 30 feet long, 7 feet high and 9 feet 2 inches wide - while baggage and freight compartments totalled 400 cubic feet. The two-spar wing had improved Lockheed high-lift flaps installed, and intended to use a retractable shock-absorbing tail bumper for emergency use in such cases as the nose being raised too high for take-off. The nosewheel was steerable, and there were brakes on all three wheels.

The fuel tankage was 1,200 US gallons - or 500 US gallons less than the 307 - while the loaded weight at 40,000 pounds was 5,000 pounds less than that of the Boeing design, having grown somewhat from its original 27,550-36,000 pounds.

The estimated performance was appreciably faster than the 307, a maximum speed of 294 mph at 15,300 feet and a cruising speed of 247 mph at 12,000 feet, although the Excalibur would have had a shorter range. A projected 40-passenger version was studied under the designation L-144 but, in the end, the Excalibur did not get beyond the project stage, despite a provisional order for two placed by South African Airways when it ordered twenty-nine Lodestars for domestic and regional routes in April 1940.

Lockheed considered discussions with Juan Trippe's Pan American Airlines and built a mockup, but the project was dropped. Lockheed's attention was focused on the gathering war clouds in Europe; but its keen interest in entering the large transport market at the earliest possible time did not abate.

The Douglas DC-3 was evolved from the DC-2 to satisfy an AAL requirement for modern sleeper aircraft to replace its old fleet of berth-equipped Curtiss Condor biplanes. Because the DC-2 was too narrow for berths, Douglas proposed to widen the fuselage and increase the maximum operating weight to accommodate twenty-one rather than fourteen day passengers.

Around the same time that Lockheed was working on the Excalibur project, across the

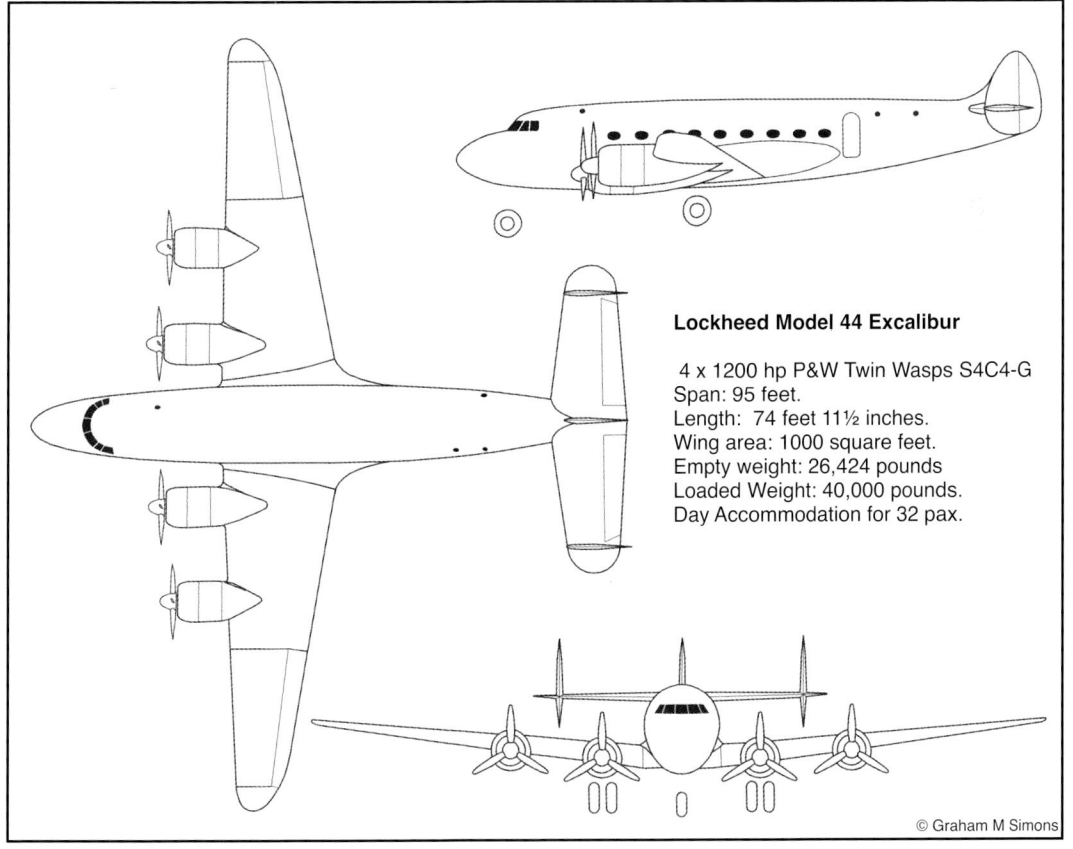

Lockheed Model 44 Excalibur

4 x 1200 hp P&W Twin Wasps S4C4-G
Span: 95 feet.
Length: 74 feet 11½ inches.
Wing area: 1000 square feet.
Empty weight: 26,424 pounds
Loaded Weight: 40,000 pounds.
Day Accommodation for 32 pax.

© Graham M Simons

Atlantic in the United Kingdom, the British Air Ministry, eager to encourage the development of British commercial land machines, issued a pair of specifications for new airliners.

Enter the Fairey FC.1

In typical British tradition, a committee was established in November 1937 under the chairmanship of Lord Cadman to examine the state of British civil aviation and to investigate, in particular, charges of inefficiency in the Air Ministry and within Imperial Airways, then Britain's primary international airline. The report, published in March 1938 pointed out with some asperity that British constructors, with lucrative military orders at their doors had shown '...little disposition to embark upon the costly venture of producing modern civil machines in a speculative attempt to re-enter the lists' against other countries, in particular the USA, which had gained the initiative.

The report recommended a form of State assistance as a stimulus. The Air Ministry should, the Cadman report said, get together with the airline operators and the constructors, specify requirements, ask for design proposals and select the most promising of each type for development and production.

With remarkable promptitude, specifications were prepared and issued. The report of the Cadman Committee had been completed on 8 February 1938, and seen in advance of official publication by the Director-General of Civil Aviation and others concerned in the Air Ministry - an outline specification for the long-range aircraft was quickly agreed and a constructor chosen.

The short/medium-range project was a more difficult proposition - not only because the British aircraft industry would be starting almost from scratch on such a type, but because it would be competing in a market in which the USA had a long and successful lead with, in particular, the DC-2 and DC-3. The specification and the resulting aircraft would need to show a marked improvement in characteristics and performance in relation, for instance, to the DC-3 and Lockheed 14.

By 17 May 1938, the draft specification was complete, and suitable possible constructors chosen. Copies of the specification (15/38) and a covering letter were sent to Sir W G Armstrong Whitworth Aircraft, the Bristol Aeroplane Company, Fairey Aviation, General Aircraft and Vickers (Aviation). The letter explained the proposed financial assistance, with contributions to prototype development and production tooling, and asked for delivery dates, rates of production and the financial contribution likely to be required. An important proviso in the rearmament circumstances of the time was that the effort 'must not be allowed to interfere with urgent work on designs for RAF aeroplanes'. Tenders were required within seven weeks.

Vickers refused the invitation more or less immediately and Armstrong Whitworth refused in July because of the proviso. Fairey, General Aircraft and Bristol accepted with Folland Aircraft being included later.

By mid-August, the Directorate of Civil Research and Production - a new department recommended by the Cadman Committee) had made a technical comparison of the four 15/38 designs analysing them also by fitting each 'on paper' with Taurus engines, tricycle undercarriages and similar tankages. Not unexpectedly the performances and weights turned out to be very similar, except in the matter of speeds, with, on overall technical merit, the GAL.40 in the lead.

These were still only paper aeroplanes, and initial technical merit was not the only criteria. Both the Director-General of Civil Aviation, Sir Francis Shelmerdine, and the new Director of Civil Research and Production, Major C J Stewart, were very much in favour of getting Fairey into the civil aircraft manufacturing business. Furthermore, Alan C Campbell Orde, operations manager of the most likely home customer, British Airways, had made it clear at the first selection meeting on 9 August that his airline would find it difficult to justify reliance on any but a large and experienced constructor - which left a choice between Fairey and Bristol.

British Airways had been formed late in 1935 in a merger sponsored by Whitehall Securities and Erlangers, the merchant bankers, of United Airways, Hillman Airways and Spartan Air Lines. British Continental Airways, who were competing over similar routes, joined

British Airways in August 1936. The original merger followed the report of a 1935 committee set up under Sir Warren Fisher to study British international and particularly European air services.

The committee recommended that one or more airlines in addition to Imperial Airways should receive Government financial aid and be given specific spheres of influence. Imperial Airways, the 'chosen instrument' whose primary responsibility was for the Empire routes, agreed to relinquish concessions north of a line London-Berlin. As the second 'chosen instrument' British Airways developed services, with a subsidy, to Hamburg, Copenhagen, Malmo and Stockholm, as well as night-mail services alongside Germany's Deutsche Lufthansa between London and Berlin. The airline also operated an unsubsidised service to Paris alongside Imperial Airways and had been chosen to develop a subsidised service to South America, via West Africa. As there were no suitable British aircraft for these services, the airline bought US aircraft - first, Lockheed 10A Electras and later Lockheed 14s - as well as Junkers Ju 52s for the Berlin night mail. British Airways was, therefore, an obvious customer for the 15/38, as well as the long-haul 14/38 to operate the proposed South American service.

A difficulty was to arise. The Cadman Committee had recommended the development of services in Europe by a strengthened British Airways in close liaison with Imperial Airways - but the Government chose to merge the two airlines into what was to become BOAC, and announced the decision in November 1938. So British Airways was then no longer a free agent in the choice and purchase of new equipment.

By October, only Fairey and GAL were in the likely running. It had been agreed, inter-departmentally, that neither GAL nor Folland should be selected. Fairey had meanwhile been pressing for two prototypes and later in October agreed to build these at the cost of £225,000, plus powerplants and associated equipment which would be provided on embodiment loan, and up to £100,000 for jigs and tools, and the Ministry had promised an order for twelve at the cost of not more than £80,000 each. A provisional contract on these lines was agreed

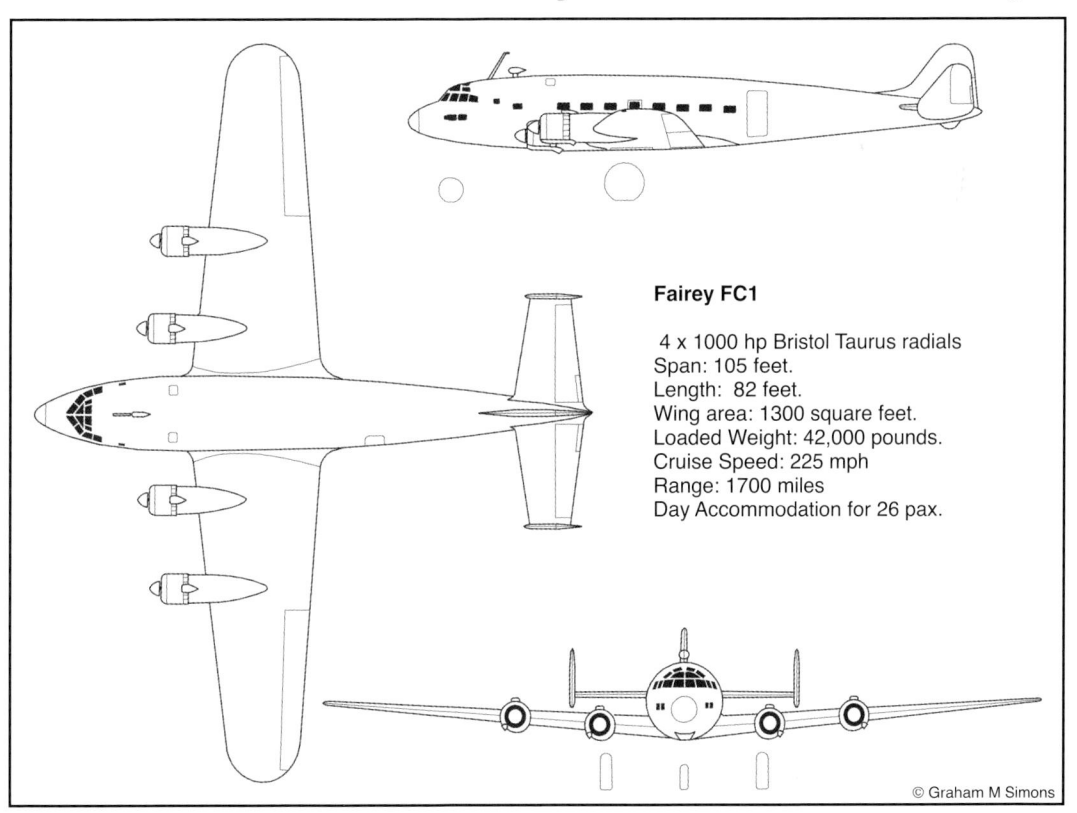

Fairey FC1

4 x 1000 hp Bristol Taurus radials
Span: 105 feet.
Length: 82 feet.
Wing area: 1300 square feet.
Loaded Weight: 42,000 pounds.
Cruise Speed: 225 mph
Range: 1700 miles
Day Accommodation for 26 pax.

© Graham M Simons

on 12 November and signed on 30 November, but it was not until 23 February 1939 that production details were agreed, with a maximum basic price per aircraft of £76,250, a fixed profit on each of £3,750, and with Fairey carrying any additional costs but receiving up to thirty per cent on any savings made on the agreed maximum cost price.

By then British Airways' equipment-ordering stalemate for the planned merger with Imperial Airways had been overcome. Imperial disliked the FC1 because of its high wing loading at 35 pounds per square foot and Fairey's lack of civil-aircraft manufacturing experience and had accepted the fact that the new airline would continue to need about twelve aircraft of the type and the Air Ministry had agreed to be responsible for the order, which was placed officially on 4 March 1939.

The FC1 was by then a very different aircraft, in important technical detail, from that originally proposed. At the selection meeting on 9 August 1938, Campbell Orde, for British Airways, had said that the concept must be updated and technical pressure from the airline was maintained up to and after the order had been placed. A nosewheel undercarriage and a pressurised cabin, with engine-driven blowers maintaining sea-level conditions up to 3,000 feet, were demanded. In spite of Ministry wishes to use British ancillaries, Campbell Orde insisted on what he called 'experienced' equipment such as a Sperry autopilot, Hydromatic propellers and Goodrich de-icers. He asked for, and got, four engine-driven generators, emergency battery-charging equipment, a fuel-jettisoning system and cockpit-operated control locks.

Engineers and designers tend to come up with very similar solutions to a problem, so in many respects it is not surprising that the FC1 looked much like the Model 44.

All of which meant weight increases; the originally proposed 42,000 pounds gross weight limit had long been exceeded, even for the short-haul version, and had reached 44,000 pounds by February 1939 and more than 45,000 pounds by August. The detailed performance requirements remained more or less as originally drafted, though those for range/payload were changed. These became a no-allowance range of 750 miles with 26 passengers plus an 'occasional' four, whatever that meant, and a crew of five, with tankage sufficient for 1,700 miles with ten passengers and a crew of six - including two stewards in each case. The final specification, drafted in August 1939, included such things as cabin noise-level limits of 72 decibels at maximum cruising speed, cabin temperature minima of 16°C at an outside-air temperature of minus 30°C and specific power, speed, attitude and ground-run limitations for blind approaches.

The use of Taurus engines for the home market was generally accepted throughout the negotiations, but even as early as February 1939 the Wright Cyclone was being considered for aircraft being offered abroad. Not only was this engine likely to be more readily accepted worldwide, with its background of civil use and comparatively high inter-overhaul hourage, but it was considerably less expensive - £2,400 by comparison with £3,800 for the Taurus, which then had a time between overhall of only 400 hours. By mid-year it was being proposed that the second prototype should be fitted with Cyclones.

To achieve long-range, the aircraft was designed for efficient cruising with the engines at half power. This required careful streamlining, both for the shaping of the fuselage and also for careful surface finishing. Drag was reduced by the small size of the wings and their high wing loading of thirty-two pounds per square foot. This would otherwise make the aircraft challenging to handle, especially with a high landing speed, but this was countered by the new development of the Fairey-Youngman flap, a device that was patented in 1941. These flaps were large, around one-third of the wing chord. Their movement went in two phases, controlled by a linkage; firstly the flap lowered below the wing and approximately parallel, making the aircraft almost a sesquiplane. This gave improved lift, but with little extra drag, and was used for landing. The flaps could be extended further for landing, now rotating downwards to thirty degrees as a slotted flap. With the use of flaps, wing loading was reduced to the equivalent of twenty-five pounds per square foot and also gave a gain in lift coefficient of around thirty-one per cent.

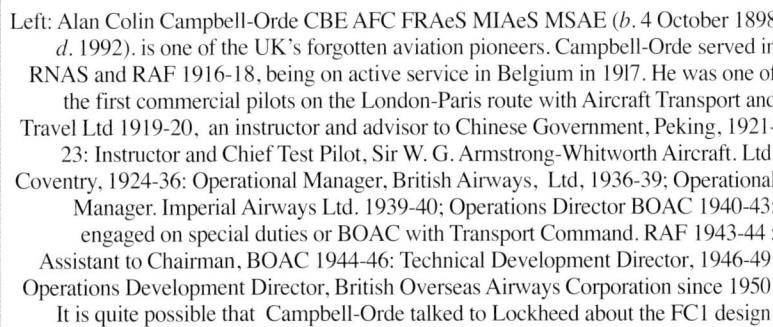

Left: Alan Colin Campbell-Orde CBE AFC FRAeS MIAeS MSAE (*b*. 4 October 1898 *d*. 1992). is one of the UK's forgotten aviation pioneers. Campbell-Orde served in RNAS and RAF 1916-18, being on active service in Belgium in 1917. He was one of the first commercial pilots on the London-Paris route with Aircraft Transport and Travel Ltd 1919-20, an instructor and advisor to Chinese Government, Peking, 1921-23: Instructor and Chief Test Pilot, Sir W. G. Armstrong-Whitworth Aircraft. Ltd, Coventry, 1924-36: Operational Manager, British Airways, Ltd, 1936-39; Operational Manager. Imperial Airways Ltd. 1939-40; Operations Director BOAC 1940-43: engaged on special duties or BOAC with Transport Command. RAF 1943-44 : Assistant to Chairman, BOAC 1944-46: Technical Development Director, 1946-49. Operations Development Director, British Overseas Airways Corporation since 1950. It is quite possible that Campbell-Orde talked to Lockheed about the FC1 design.

Above: The Fairey FC1 got as far as the mock-up stage at the Hayes, Middlesex, facility before it was cancelled.

Right: the flightdeck contained the very latest American instrumentation.
(both Alan Campbell-Orde Collection)

The Fairey-Youngman flap and its initial downward parallel movement were superseded for other aircraft by the Fowler flap as in the Constellation, which too had an initial parallel action, although rearward sliding.

The outbreak of war on 3 September 1939 put an end to this attempt by Britain to make up for five-years of neglect of the short/medium-haul civil market. The prototype and production orders for the FC.l were officially cancelled on 17 October 1939.

There was a common, albeit tenuous thread that linked the two designs. The FC.1 was intended for British Airways; the Operations Manager for British Airways was Alan Campbell Orde, who was heavily involved with British Airways obtaining several Lockheed 10s and 14s. It is not beyond the realms of possibility that Campbell Orde mentioned British Airways' requirements to Lockheed - they did a design study, as did Fairey Aviation and came up with a very similar design with almost matching design parameters. Whether there was any actual cross-over, or one design influenced the other, we shall never know.

Enter TWA

Douglas kept TWA fully apprised of the DC-3 programme and offered good delivery positions. TWA, sceptical of the airliner's performance at numbers of high-altitude airports, reluctantly concluded that it was underpowered for TWA's western routes and did not order DC-3s at the outset.

The DC-3 first flew from Clover Field, Santa Monica, on 17 December 1935. Captain D W 'Tommy' Tomlinson flew it on 6 January 1936 and noted that the take-offs were sluggish, which seemed to confirm TWA's airport performance estimates. Tomlinson reported his findings and TWA lost interest. It proved to be a costly error. A series of engine modifications and improved propellers corrected the performance deficiency. By the time TWA renewed its interest, valuable delivery positions were lost to competing airlines. Jack Frye ordered ten sleeper DC-3s and eight day machine versions, introducing TWA DC-3 services on 1 June 1937, ten months after AAL had done the same.

William John 'Jack' Frye was an aviation pioneer in the airline industry. Frye founded Standard Air Lines which eventually took him into a merger with Trans World Airlines (TWA) where he became president. Frye is credited for turning TWA into a world-class airline during his tenure as president from 1934 to 1947.

Frye began flying lessons in 1923 with instructor Burdett Fuller at Burdett Field in Los Angeles. Frye joined Fuller in the '13 Black Cats', an aviation stunt team for the movie industry. Frye became good friends with two student pilots at Fuller's, Walter Hamilton and Paul E Richter. Frye, Hamilton, and Richter pooled their money together and formed Aero Corporation of California in 1925. They bought out Fuller's flight school and did everything from flight instruction, banner towing, charter flights and crop dusting. Hamilton, who had been a mechanic for the Duesenberg Motors Company, ran their aircraft maintenance operation. Frye held Transport Pilot Certificate number 933 and Richter held Transport Pilot Certificate number 501. In 1926, Los Angeles aerial police ticketed Frye for flying less than 1,000 feet above the city.

Frye, Richter, and Hamilton's new goal was to enter the scheduled airline business, so on 3 February 1926, Standard Air Lines was formed as a subsidiary of Aero Corp. Standard Air Lines initially flew single-engine Fokker F-7 aircraft from Los Angeles to Tucson with a stop in Phoenix. Within a year, they extended their route to El Paso. In 1929, Standard purchased Fokker F-10A aircraft. Frye and Richter took one of their tri-motors and set a commercial aircraft altitude record of 22,680 feet.

Western Air Express bought controlling interest of Aero Corp in early 1930, but still operated Standard as a separate airline. When Western Air Express merged with Transcontinental Air Transport (TAT) in July 1930 to form Transcontinental and Western Air (T&WA), the government forced Western to sell Standard to American Airlines as part of the deal due to its southern route into Texas. However, Frye elected to stay with T&WA and was made Vice President of Operations, Richter became Vice President of Western Division, and Hamilton became Maintenance Superintendent. After the reorganisation caused by the Air Mail Scandal of 1934, Frye became president of T&WA. It eventually became Trans World Airlines (TWA) and was known as 'The Airline Run by Flyers'.

The airline suffered near disaster after its reputation was hurt in 1931 when Notre Dame coach Knute Rockne died on a T&WA Fokker F-10 tri-motor. In 1932 Jack Frye, representing T&WA, sought a better aircraft and in response to this and other requests, Douglas Aircraft Company developed the Douglas DC-1 Transport twin.

In February 1934, Jack Frye and Eddie Rickenbacker, President of Eastern Airlines, set a transcontinental record of thirteen hours four minutes flying the Douglas DC-1 in a publicity stunt for the new airliner. In May 1934, Frye broke his record by flying a Northrop Gamma from Los Angeles to Newark in an elapsed time

Above: D W 'Tommy' Tomlinson (b. 28 April 1897, d. 7 January 1996). He was Jack Frye's engineering specialist and was to become TWA Vice President of Engineering.

Below: Captain Paul Ernest Richter Jr. (b. 20 January 1896, d. 15 May 1949) Richter became Executive Vice President in 1938. After Frye resigned from TWA due to a dispute with owner Howard Hughes in 1947, Richter was offered the position of President but decided to resign as well.

of eleven hours and thirty-one minutes. In 1937, Frye and Richter founded 'Conquistadors del Cielo' (Conquerers of the Sky), an annual gathering of top airline executives at a dude ranch in Wyoming.

In 1939, desiring greater control of their airline, Frye and Richter approached industrialist and film producer Howard Hughes to buy into the company, following Hughes' approach to Frye in regard to aviation investments. Hughes' interest was aircraft, and his initial involvement was the development and financing of the Lockheed Constellation for TWA.

The DC-3 - successful though it was on coast-to-coast services - was not a long-haul airliner and so in mid-1935, discussions started between Douglas, the 'Big Four' domestic airlines and Pan American Airways (PAA) about a new four-engined airliner for the trunk routes. The following March each of these airlines put up $100,000 towards the design and construction of a prototype and this, the DC-4E, first flew on 7 June 1938. It was evaluated by United Airlines over its routes in 1939 and received Civil Aeronautics Administration certification on 5 May 1939. After extensive evaluation, it did not go into production; the five sponsor airlines thought it too large and had too many advanced technical features which would require extensive development before being put into service. The type was redesigned into the production DC-4, being scaled down a bit in the process and, in spite of its designation, became virtually a new airliner.

Another contender began to take shape in mid-1936, while the DC-4E was still in the design stage, when Pan American Airways and TWA started discussions about a possible airliner development of the Model 299 B-17 Flying Fortress high-altitude bomber which Boeing produced in response to an August 1934 Army bid request. The Boeing 307 Stratoliner, the world's first commercial pressurised transport, was strictly a Boeing-TWA affair. No other airline was involved until after the design was conceived and agreed between the two parties.

The 299 was rushed to completion in less than one year and flown to Wright Field for a demonstration after only minimal testing. It crashed during a demonstration flight, which technically disqualified it from the competition; however, the Army was so well impressed with its capabilities that it placed an order for thirteen Y1B-17 bombers.

Tomlinson, who was well known at Wright Field, was invited to fly a Y1B-17. He did so and was extremely favorably impressed with the performance and potential it offered. He reviewed his evaluation and the B-17 programme with Frye and Richter. They agreed that TWA should explore with Boeing the development of a superior high-altitude over-weather commercial variant.

Jack Frye telephoned Boeing, with the almost immediate result that Fred Collins, Boeing's sales manager, and two engineers were dispatched to Kansas City. Boeing had given some prior consideration to a commercial derivative, which would use YlB-17 wings, engines, horizontal tail, and landing gear. It was obvious that it would be nonsensical to provide oxygen masks for passengers and that the only acceptable alternative would be to pressurise the entire occupied volume. An appropriate purchase agreement and specifications were expeditiously developed following the Kansas City meeting. TWA ordered five Boeing 307 Stratoliners on 29 January 1937.

Ralph Ellinger was transferred to Seattle as the TWA plant representative, and John Guy was promoted to the same position at Douglas, where TWA's DC-3s were being manufactured. Later, after the last DC-3 was delivered in August, Guy joined Ellinger. Tomlinson and others made frequent trips to Boeing to inspect mockups and to critique Boeing's design proposals.

While the 307s were being manufactured, Jack Frye encountered serious problems with a conservative TWA Board of Directors, most of whom lacked foresight and confidence in the future of aviation. The board concluded that Jack had overreached his authority and refused to authorise the expenditure of additional funds due Boeing. During June 1938, John Guy dropped by the TWA office in old Plant No. 1, near the Duwamish River, to confer with Ralph Ellinger. He then proceeded to Plant No. 2 on Marginal Way, where three of the TWA aircraft were in final assembly. He was shocked to see

Above: William John 'Jack' Frye (*b.* 18 March 1904, *d.* 3 February 1959). He became president of TWA and is credited for turning it into a world-class airline during his tenure 1934 to 1947.

Below: Walter 'Ham' Hamilton (*b.* 1902, *d.* 1946). He was one of the founders of the Aero Corporation of California and Standard Air Lines. He was a licensed pilot receiving his Transport Licence at the same time as partners, Jack Frye and Paul Richter. He was Vice President Mechanical Operations TWA.

that all TWA markings had been stripped from the aircraft.

John Guy later explained what happened: 'I immediately contacted the factory supervisor to find out what in the devil was going on, and why the machines had been stripped of TWA markings. He claimed he did not know the reason; the airliners had been stripped during the night on orders from Boeing's top management. I called Ralph right away to see if he knew what was going on. At first he didn't believe me, and, I suppose, thought I'd gone off my rocker.'

'Ralph lost no time in calling Kansas City. He talked to either Jack Frye or Paul Richter - I'm not sure which - who said a Boeing wire had been received that purported to cancel the contract. Ralph was advised that Boeing's position was illegal, that the contract was valid, and that the airplanes were still on order by TWA. He was directed to proceed with inspection and other activities on the basis that the airplanes were still ours. Ralph instructed me to continue to inspect the airplanes, to close out areas, and to write squawks [complaints] as if nothing had happened.'

'At times this procedure became a bit humorous. I would write up squawks and hand them over to Boeing Quality Control for handling. They would insist the airplanes were not TWA's, and I would insist they were. They fixed some things and some they ignored. They used to say, "Johnny, you're working for us as a Boeing inspector." This farce lasted from June until late December.'

The contract required Boeing to deliver the first 307 on 22 December 1938. Because Boeing had stopped work on the TWA airliners, it had been obvious for some time that it could not meet the requirement. On 22 December, TWA notified Boeing it was cancelling the contract for failure to deliver the aircraft. It also filed a $1 million damage suit against Boeing. With that turn of events, Ellinger and Guy gathered up their families and left Seattle.

The Mysterious Mr Howard Hughes

Jack Frye's position with TWA's board, like TWA's position at Boeing, worsened and became critical. Jack's back was against the wall. In the same month that Constellation design started TWA's destinies were to come under the influence of a new principal stockholder, the enigmatic and controversial Howard Robard Hughes. Heir to the multi-million dollar Hughes Tool Co, makers of oil-drilling rig machinery, of which he was to become the sole owner, Hughes had a deep and abiding interest in aviation and some notable achievements to his credit as a designer-pilot. In 1935 he had set up a world record of 352 mph with the Hughes H-1 racing aircraft designed by himself, and two years later established a US transcontinental flying record of seven hours twenty-eight minutes. In 1938 he and four others made a record-breaking round-the-world flight in a Lockheed 14, NX13973, starting from New York on 10 July and flying on to Paris, Moscow, across Siberia via Omsk and Yakutsk to Fairbanks, Alaska and back to New York in ninety-one hours fourteen minutes. He had also hit the public eye as a Hollywood impresario, directing the United Artists' spectacular *Hells Angels* in 1931, and as the sponsor of film stars Jean Harlow and Jane Russell. He was an influence on the Constellation project from the beginning, and in 1938 he acquired a twenty per cent financial stake in TWA at $5 a share, previously controlled by the Lehman financial interests in New York, when Jack Frye, then the airline's president, was seeking fresh capital, obtaining an additional ten per cent in March 1940.

Nowhere on the corporate stationery of TWA did the name of Howard Hughes appear, although, with forty-five per cent of its stock owned by the Tool Company, it was his airline for all practical purposes. Jack Frye, the president of TWA, was a pioneer who had set transcontinental records flying the mail in the Thirties. With Frye running it, and Hughes putting in his many millions' worth of dollars and inventiveness, TWA acquired the image of a flyboy's airline. Always in the forefront of technology, it was the first trunk carrier to outwit the weather with high-altitude flying, and at the start of the war, the only domestic airline operating four-engine transports.

Early in 1947, after the airline had lost money, Frye and Hughes came to a parting of the ways, Frye's resignation allegedly being prompted by Hughes (who by this time held forty-six per cent of TWA's stock) insisting upon a change of management as a condition for helping to re-finance the airline.

With the board problem behind and new funds available, TWA renewed contract discussions with Boeing during June 1939.

Frye dispatched Ellinger and Guy to Seattle to review the status of TWA's 307s. Ellinger worked on engineering and contractual items while Guy inspected the five aircraft and wrote detailed reports on the production status of each. After about ten days they returned to Kansas City and briefed Frye and Richter.

Boeing continued with the 307 programme after the TWA airliners had been set aside because PAA had placed an order for four on 24 March 1937, about two months after the original TWA contract. Boeing tried to sell the five cancelled aircraft and finally found interest at KLM Royal Dutch Airlines.

TWA and Boeing settled their differences sufficiently to permit TWA to place a new order for the five 307s on 23 September 1939. By that time, the first Pan American 307 was in flight test.

A short time after the Ellinger-Guy briefing, Harlan Hull, TWA's popular chief pilot, visited Boeing to fly the 307 and report findings to Frye and Tomlinson. Several KLM personnel were at Boeing to fly on a demonstration flight when Hull arrived for the same purpose. The Dutch had the first flight; Hull accepted an invitation to go along as an observer, although some records show him listed as an alternate co-pilot for the flight.

NX19901 left Seattle-Boeing Field at 1257 local time. At 1312LT, a radio message was transmitted from the airliner to the Boeing Aircraft Company radio station located at Seattle, which message gave the position of the aircraft as being between Tacoma and Mount Rainier at an altitude of 11,000 feet. Some two or three minutes later, while flying at a comparatively slow rate of speed in the vicinity of Alder, the aircraft stalled and began to spin in a nose down attitude. After completing two or three turns in the spin, during which power was applied, it recovered from the spin and began to dive. The aircraft partially recovered from the

Howard Robard Hughes Jr. (b. 24 December 1905, d. 5 April 1976) was an American business magnate, investor, record-setting pilot, engineer, film director, and philanthropist, known during his lifetime as one of the most financially successful individuals in the world. He first became prominent as a film producer, and then as an influential figure in the aviation industry.

dive at an altitude of approximately 3,000 feet above sea level, during which recovery it began to disintegrate. Outboard sections of the left and right wings failed upward and broke entirely loose from the aircraft. Major portions of the vertical fin and portions of the rudder were carried away by the wing wreckage. The outboard section of the left elevator separated from the stabilizer and both fell to the ground detached. The right horizontal tail surface, being held on by the fairing along the top surface and also by the elevator trim tab cables, remained with the fuselage. The number one engine nacelle also broke loose from the aircraft and fell to the ground separately. The main body of the aircraft settled vertically and struck the ground in an almost level attitude both longitudinally and laterally at a point approximately 1,200 feet above sea level. Watches and clocks aboard the aircraft, which were broken by force of the impact, indicated the time of the accident as approximately 1317. The aircraft was destroyed by impact forces and all ten occupants were killed.

It seems that one of the KLM pilots was flying

the aircraft with two engines inoperative on one side, an unauthorised and dangerous manoeuvre. Several witnesses on the ground saw a severe yaw, followed by a roll, and then an uncontrolled descent. The aircraft impacted flat with little forward motion and was demolished.

Following the accident, Boeing adding a large dorsal fin and made changes to the control system. A similar dorsal was added to the B-17's. Because of this tragedy, PAA received only three of the four 307s it ordered.

About the time of the accident, Hughes was anxious to learn more about the upper atmosphere and flew to Kansas City in his stagger-wing Beech to discuss Tomlinson's high-altitude exploits. Frye had warned Tomlinson of Howard's arrival and asked that he make the data available to him.

Tommy described the meeting this way: 'Well, when the man came into my office, I couldn't believe my eyes. He looked like a tramp with long hair and dirty fingernails. He was anything but what I expected to see. He sat down opposite my desk. After some discussion, I was amazed at his knowledge and interest. He knew what he was talking about, and he knew how to ask the right questions. He was pretty damn smart.

'When he finally left, I could hardly wait to get to Jack's office. I said, "I just met with this fellow Hughes for several hours. He asked every question under the sun. Do I really have to put up with him?" Jack looked at me and said, "Tommy, he owns the airline".'

Hughes purchased one of the ten 307s Boeing produced. Without the dorsal fin, it was delivered to Burbank with an experimental licence. Howard intended to break his earlier round-the-world record with this aircraft. Extensive modifications were undertaken by a Boeing crew including the installation of fuselage fuel tanks, special navigation aids, and over-water emergency equipment. The modifications, which required over a year to accomplish, were completed with the installation of the dorsal fin.

The impending war forced Hughes to cancel plans to try for a new record when it became apparent that suitable landing fields and flight paths had become entirely too limited. Later, Howard sold the aicraft to Texas oil magnate Glen McCarthy after replacing the fuselage fuel tanks with a plush interior.

The first, much-delayed TWA Stratoliner, a Model -307B, was delivered on 6 May 1940, nearly two months after PAA had accepted its first 307 - despite the fact that the PAA machines had been ordered months after TWA's. TWA inaugurated a new era in domestic air transportation with its Stratoliners on 8 July 1940 by providing the first coast-to-coast service with pressurised, over-weather aircraft. PAA began its 307 services on 3 June between New York and Colombia, via Barranquilla and Bogota.

TWA's 307s were luxurious. No effort was spared to provide the best state-of-the-art meal

The remains of Boeing 307 NX19901 near Mount Rainier. *(Author's Collection)*

Above: NX19903 in flight, by now fitted with the extended dorsal fin.

Left: the aircraft's interior, with sleeper berths on one side, and seating on the other.
(both Author's Collection)

service and other passenger amenities. The airliners accommodated sixteen passengers in berths arranged across the commodious fuselage, or thirty-three day passengers. They could be flown comfortably at 20,000 feet with the passenger cabin pressurised to 12,000 feet. This permitted the pilot to avoid an appreciable amount of rough air and bad weather; a notable advance over the DC-3s.

Cabin pressurisation was a hit with the passengers but produced maintenance headaches. Perhaps this is not too surprising, considering that the GE engine-driven superchargers were the first such attempt. Modifications helped, but they did not cure the problems.

Another serious 307 operating problem was carburettor icing. Ralph Ellinger explained that TWA made numerous attempts to persuade Boeing to provide improved carburettor air heaters during the development programme. Things reached a point where in addition to arguments with Boeing, demand letters were written. However, TWA's pleadings fell on deaf ears; Boeing insisted that warm under-cowl air was sufficient, choosing to totally ignore TWA's wealth of airline experience.

Shortly after aircraft acceptance TWA unintentionally proved its point in spades. The CAA required proving flights prior to commercial service to demonstrate adequate airline preparations for commercial operations. On one such flight between Kansas City and San Francisco, a TWA 307 under the command of Captain Otis Bryan suddenly lost all four engines from excessive carburettor ice near Pritchett, Colorado. Otis had no choice but to make an emergency power-off landing, expertly executing a wheels-up landing on soft ground. The impact forced the belly cargo doors open; mud was scooped in, filling the bins. The energy thus absorbed slowed the machine and prevented considerable damage. The crew and other TWA employees on board were uninjured. Raymond M Dunn, later TWA's senior vice president and system general manager, was the flight engineer during the Pritchett incident.

TWA quickly designed and installed an exhaust-manifold-muff heat system, which Tomlinson found adequate during flight tests. The drawings were given to Boeing so the same modifications could be made in the other 307s, which they, of course, were without further argument.

After all of TWA's Stratoliners were in service, another near disaster occurred. On 1 January 1941, Captain Harry Campbell took off from Kansas City on a non-stop flight to New York. It was a bitterly cold day. Immediately after take-off, the nose rose sharply in an uncontrollable manner and put the aircraft into a dangerous incipient stall condition. Harry applied full power, pushing forward on the control yoke with all of his strength. He did not have sufficient altitude or power to turn and flew straight ahead through downtown Kansas City, narrowly missing the skyscrapers. He somehow wrestled the airliner back and landed at Municipal Airport. Passengers, shaken by this experience, said they had looked into the fifth-floor windows of the Kansas City Power and Light building.

The cause of this near-disaster was congealing of hydraulic fluid in the elevator control system boost cylinder due to exceptionally cold weather. It was never clear why this condition was not discovered before take-off because the checklist required flight controls to be exercised to the full extent in all modes. The fix was to drill a small hole in the piston to permit the hydraulic fluid to circulate at all times.

After the usual period of debugging that accompanied any new aircraft the 307s earned a reputation for excellent, dependable service and rugged reliability, which remained intact

Taken on 12 March 1940, the picture shows the control cabin of a Pan American Boeing 307.
(Author's Collection)

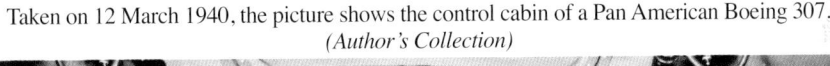

An unidentifiable TWA 307 has the passenger baggage loaded on board. *(Author's Collection)*

throughout their long service history. TWA's Stratoliner services proved to be popular and confirmed what Frye, Richter, and Tomlinson knew all along: flight above the weather was the correct goal, and as soon as technology permitted, further gains would be inevitable. They resolved to keep TWA in the forefront of these developments.

After buying a major share of TWA and saving TWA's Stratoliner programme, Howard Hughes lost no time in sponsoring the development of much larger, highly advanced transports capable of long-range flights at record-shattering speeds.

Airline competition was severe. UAL was squeezing TWA on the north and AAL on the south. Although Charles Lindbergh had done a creditable job pioneering Transcontinental Air Transport's direct coast-to-coast route concerning flight aspects, the route lacked the number of major traffic-generating centres enjoyed by TWA's main competition. For example, TWA had no counterpart cities for Denver, Salt Lake City, Atlanta, or Dallas.

That basic circumstance, which was to limit TWA until deregulation, plus a Board of Directors with myopic aviation vision, had taken its toll by the time Hughes bought in. His new investment needed strengthening. Hughes believed that high-speed, super-deluxe airliners with over-weather, transcontinental, non-stop capabilities - machines that the competition could not come close to matching for years - would do the trick. Hughes also knew that if he influenced prestigious Hollywood stars to fly TWA in such airliners with the attendant well-orchestrated publicity, a larger share of the vital repeat business market and other traffic would also choose to fly TWA.

Because the best payoff would happen if TWA had exclusive use for an extended period of the aircraft he had in mind, and that this effect would not occur should competitive programmes develop, Hughes knew that production of the new airliner must be in secret. During late 1939, before delivery of the first Stratoliner to TWA, Howard called Jack Frye to discuss such a venture. The call lasted over eight hours. They addressed the priority need for the new aircraft to have reliable, high-speed, over-weather capabilities. It was to carry around fifty passengers and 6,000 pounds of cargo in non-stop transcontinental services, and installation of luxurious accommodations, including berths and a private compartment in the rear, would be advisable. By the time Howard's call was over, they had agreed on the airliner's conceptual mission and a list of design objectives. Jack Frye would approach several manufacturers in secret to determine the extent of their interest.

Chapter Two

On the Drawing Board

After Howard Hughes' call, Jack Frye quietly contacted Bob Gross of Lockheed and also Reuben H. Fleet, chief executive officer at Consolidated Aircraft, who had no interest in the proposed venture. Gross, on the other hand, saw this as a tremendous opportunity for the fledgling company he resurrected from bankruptcy only a few years earlier. He jumped at the chance.

The first exploratory meeting was held in Hughes' home on Muirfield Road in the elegant old Hancock Park section of Los Angeles near Wilshire Boulevard. The only people present were Howard Hughes, Bob Gross, Hall Hibbard, and Clarence L 'Kelly' Johnson. All agreed with Johnson that Lockheed should make a fresh start, that no attempt would be made to resurrect and enlarge the Excalibur design.

An extended discussion of Hughes's and Frye's design and operational requirements followed. Hughes strongly emphasised speed, range, and passenger comfort. Lockheed enthusiastically undertook to study how to meet the expressed objectives best.

Hughes required an aircraft capable of carrying 6,000 pounds of cargo and twenty passengers in sleeping berths, at speeds of 250 to 300 mph at 20,000 feet. Even though the Model 44 would meet that requirement, Johnson came to see that the Model 44 would have to be abandoned altogether.

Two different four-engine airliners had been introduced in Europe during the previous year. Both had all-metal construction and featured retractable landing gear. The forty-passenger Armstrong Whitworth Ensign, which served with Imperial Airways, first flew

Artwork showing the final form of the Excalibur design in PAA markings. By now the airliner was fitted with triple fins and rudders and seating for thirty-six passengers.

in January 1938. But a more significant jump in performance came from Focke Wulf, which fielded a smaller design, the twenty-six-passenger Fw-200 Condor. First flown in 1937, the Condor boasted a cruise speed of 230 mph and had a range of 1,000 miles in early airline service. A modified prototype even flew from Berlin to New York nonstop in just under 25 hours. These two designs would surely have an impact on future American transports, but Lockheed, Boeing, and Douglas would look into the future to design aircraft that would fly faster, higher, and farther.

Johnson told Hughes that it would be unsound economics to carry only twenty people when they could accommodate one hundred in virtually the same space.

Here is as good a place as any to deal with a myth circulating for some years that Howard Hughes had designed the Lockheed Constellation. It was not discouraged by Hughes, but certainly was not true. His specifications had consisted of half a page of notes on the size, range, and carrying capacity he wanted. It was not without some encouragement from Lockheed, and Kelly Johnson, for example, did not appreciate someone else taking credit for the Lockheed team's work - that eventually both Hughes and Frye acknowledged the misconception in November 1941. They offered to publish advertisements, but Robert Gross was satisfied that their letter stated: 'to correct an impression prevalent in the aircraft industry the Constellation airplane was designed, engineered and built by Lockheed.'

The next meeting was held at the Beverly Hills Hotel to review Lockheed's preliminary proposal. Jack Frye and Tommy Tomlinson joined the group. A debate occured concerning whether Wright Aeronautical R-2600 engines, which had demonstrated satisfactory service for the military, or the more powerful Wright 3350s, which were then under development for the Boeing B-29 programme should be used. Frye and Hughes favoured R-2600s because they were proven engines. They were wary of 3350s, which were test-stand hardware, unproven in flight. Tomlinson though strongly favoured the 3350s because they were a much better size for the project. Tomlinson had followed test-stand experience with the 3350s and, knowing the immensity and importance of the B-29 programme, was convinced that any bugs would be worked out in good time. He believed the 3350s would provide advisable initial performance margins and permit future growth. Johnson agreed. He considered the power of the R-2600 too marginal and thought that it would limit the design to an unsatisfactory degree. Johnson and Tomlinson prevailed. Lockheed returned to the drawing

Armstrong Whitworth Ensign G-ADSX *Ettrick*, seen at Croydon Airport, London.

A pair of Focke-Wulf FW.200s D-ADHR *Saarland* of Lufthansa and OY-DEM *Jutlandia* of Danish Air Lines. *(both Author's Collection)*

Two views of Robert Gross, the president of Lockheed, seen on the left in the striped suit, with Jack Frye, TWA's president after the signing of the contract for the Constellation. *(Lockheed)*

boards to perfect its offering based on the use of the 3350s.

Lockheed abandoned their earlier studies and concentrated on the new airliner for TWA. They reasoned that it was economically unsound to carry only twenty sleeping passengers when they could accommodate more than one hundred people in the same space with normal seating. The new design was capable of flying transatlantic with the Wright 3350 - the world's largest air-cooled engine - already in development for the military B-29 bomber.

Hughes insisted on complete secrecy. Cyril Chappelet, who was responsible for Lockheed contracts, and Charles Barker, Lockheed's treasurer, met with Hughes at his Muirfield home to finalize a preliminary letter of agreement. Hughes, wearing a bathrobe and slippers, greeted them in the library. He wanted numbers of detail changes made in the letter, which the group drafted on slips of paper. Howard tore into small pieces every scrap of paper they used and threw them into the fireplace to erase any possible evidence of the programme. Because of his concern, the marked-up draft letter was deposited in Cyril's personal safety-deposit box rather than on Lockheed premises. Howard insisted that every precaution be taken to ensure secrecy.

The next meeting occurred several weeks later at the Beverly Hills Hotel to review Lockheed's revised design. The TWA group had been expanded to include Jack Franklin, soon to become TWA's vice president of engineering, and Ralph Ellinger. The design proposal Lockheed presented, except for minor variations that occurred during the course of

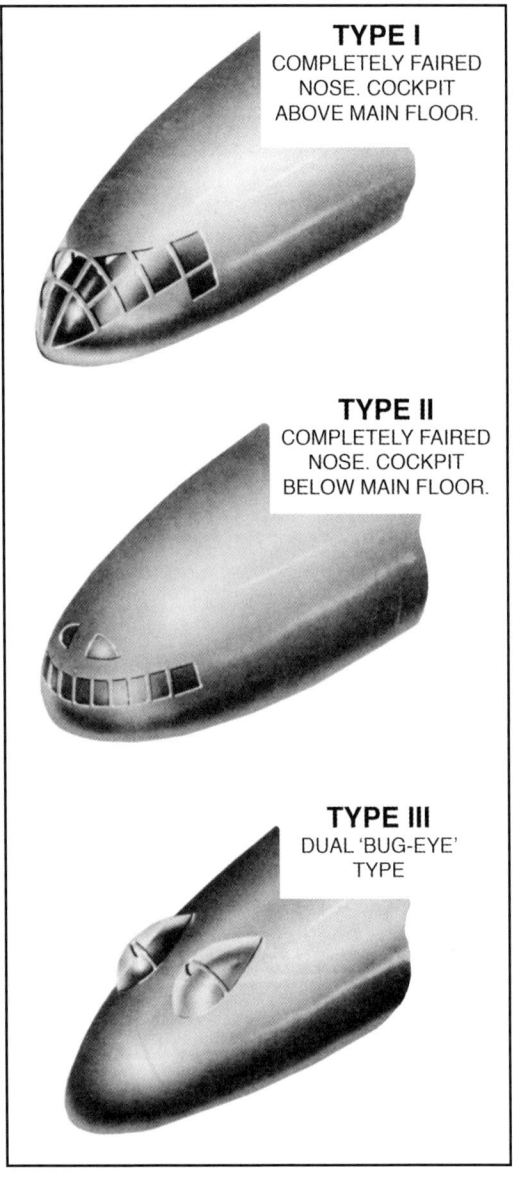

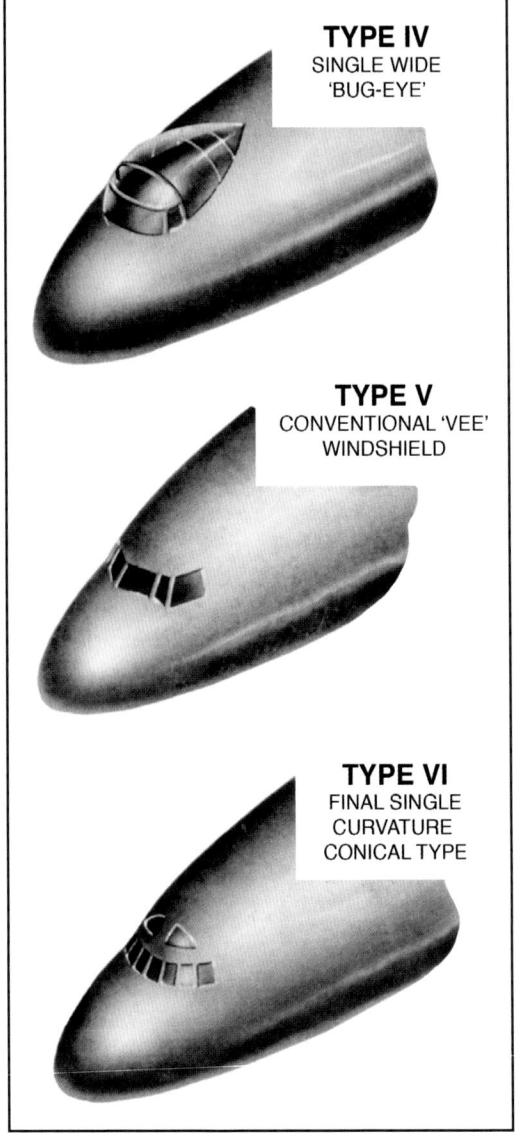

or play ping-pong by the swimming pool. They, like everyone else involved, had been warned of the importance of maintaining absolute secrecy. It was rumoured that Tomlinson and Franklin decided that to avoid security slips during idle conversations they would always refer to Hughes as 'God' and Frye as 'Jesus Christ'. Ellinger adopted the further precaution of simply not saying anything even remotely related to the project for fear that some listener might be able to patch together scraps of information and learn of the programme. He could not be sure what they might already know and did not want to say development, became the Constellation. The sleek, curved-down fuselage, triple tail, fully cowled nacelles, and enlarged P-38 wing with Lockheed-Fowler flaps were all there. Lockheed claimed a phenomenal top speed of 340 mph - better than military fighters of the day - and full mission compliance. A series of meetings followed in one of the bungalows allocated to Howard Hughes at the Beverly Hills Hotel to develop specifications and a contract.

During lax periods between meetings, Tomlinson and Franklin would lounge around anything that might tip them off.

The Constellation design was proceeding well. The new project had a wing span of 123 feet and a wing area of 1,650 square feet, the flush-riveted, stressed-skin wing being a scaled-up version of the P-38 Lightning, but with two main spars and a false spar carrying ailerons and flaps, instead of the P-38's single spar. The Lockheed-Fowler area-increasing flaps were similar to those first used on the Model 14, giving an effective maximum lift coefficient of about 2.6 when extended, with settings for take-off, landing and manoeuvring. The wing was built in seven sections: the centre section, the inner wings carrying the engine nacelles, the outer wings and detachable wingtips. Integral wing tankage for 4,000 US gallons of fuel was provided in the L-049, the wing section being NACA-23 series, of eighteen per cent thickness at the root tapering to twelve per cent - meaning it was NACA 4412 at the tip.

Maximum gross weight was to be 59,200 pounds when the project started, but increased to 68,000 pounds, resulting in a wing loading of forty-one pounds per square foot, though these figures were considerably higher for the first production aircraft. Hydraulic power-boosted controls with manual override were featured as well as thermal de-icing of the wing, tailplane and fin leading edges. The latter feature had been tested by the National Advisory Committee for Aeronautics (NACA) on a Lockheed 12A in 1940; serialled NACA 97, this had been fitted with at least two different types of third, central fin and used for lateral stability tests as well as de-icing trials. The Constellation tail unit was a scaled-up version of those of the Lockheed 12A and 14 with the addition of a third, central fin and rudder; tailplane span was fifty feet and the elevators were metal-covered, although the rudders on the L-049 were fabric-covered.

Unlike that of the DC-4, which was a parallel-section tube, the Constellation's fuselage, of circular cross-section throughout its length, featured a cambered centre-line to give it an aerofoil-like profile in side view. This served both to increase the maximum width of level floor, especially in the nose and tail sections, and to shorten the nosewheel leg by 'drooping' the front fuselage, undercarriage height being dictated by the large airscrew diameter. Lockheed publicity at the time made some play with the supposed aerodynamic advantages of the 'lifting fuselage' but although wind-tunnel tests did indicate some reduction in drag it is doubtful if it amounted to much, and this fuselage shape has been criticised on the score that it prevents full utilisation of the interior space. Its use in the Constellation is an isolated example, and almost all major transport aircraft which followed retained the Douglas parallel-section fuselage - including

The Lockheed Constellation as concived in 1939 with reverse-flow engine cowlings, faired nose and upper level windows for the sleeping berths.

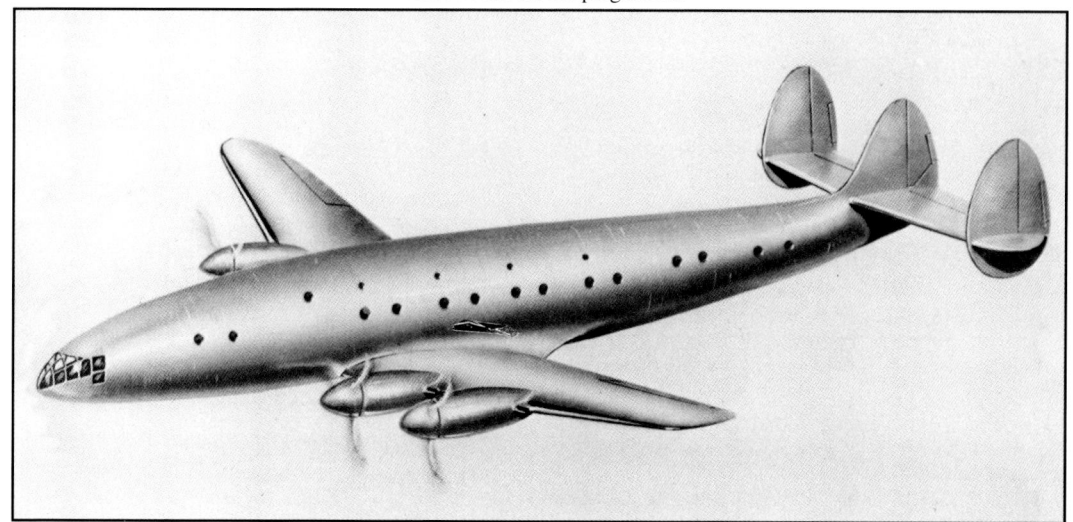

Lockheed's own Electra turboprop which succeeded the Super Constellation series in production. The Constellation's maximum internal diameter of 132 inches allowed space for four-abreast seating in twenty-two inch-wide seats on either side of a twenty-four-inch aisle; later on, five-abreast seating for the higher density coach/economy layouts was to be adopted.

The Excalibur project had featured a conventional stepped windscreen but, doubtless inspired by the Boeing 307 Stratoliner, whose well-streamlined nose shape eliminated the windscreen step, Lockheed studied several windscreen and cockpit configurations to eradicate, if possible, the drag of a step. The first of these was a completely faired nose with transparent glazing, but when it was mocked-up vision for the pilots was found to be bad. The second, also a completely faired nose, this time put the cockpit below the main floor, and was discarded because of its unsuitability for a belly landing or ditching, and also because of the extra drag produced by the larger nose. The third arrangement comprised two small 'bug eyes' for the pilot and co-pilot, a layout which Douglas tried after the war in the C-74 Globemaster, but this was found too claustrophobic for pilots on long flights, as well as creating problems in instrument layout and causing increased drag. The next attempt at a solution was to place both pilots together under a single large 'bug-eye', but this again increased drag and introduced pressurisation difficulties. A conventional 'Vee-type' windscreen was also considered, but the fuselage was too wide to allow an effective design, and the idea was discarded in favour of the final solution, a windscreen with many small panels that gave vision angles equal to those on a DC-3 and involved the least weight penalty. There was a direct-opening panel for clear vision, and an experimental de-icing system was tried, using infra-red rays.

Another innovation was the aerofoil-like fuselage (in side view) of circular cross-section, as opposed to the parallel-section tube-like fuselage of the DC-4. This gave maximum aerodynamic efficiency and increased the maximum width of the flooring for the full length of the fuselage, but also shortened the length of the long nose-wheel undercarriage leg, which was necessary because of the 15 feet 2-inch large diameter three-blade reversible pitch and fully-feathering Hamilton Standard Hydromatic or Curtiss Electric airscrews fitted.

In spite of the fuselage droop the Constellation's nosewheel leg was still a very long one - about nine feet six inches and, unlike those of most later transports in the 1950s, retracted backwards, necessitating an electrically-driven stand-by pump for an emergency extension instead of relying on the slipstream-assisted free-fall gravity method. Cabin pressure differential was 4¼ pounds per square inch, giving a cabin altitude of 8,000 feet at the height of 20,000 feet, there being two

A Lockheed Ventura originally intended for the RAF fitted with a pair of Wright 3350-355 engines known as the 'Vent-ellation' and nicknamed 'Sweater Girl'. *(Lockheed)*

fully-automatic cabin superchargers with manual override control, either of which could maintain the correct air density. Cabin temperature was thermostatically controlled, a refrigeration unit cooling the cabin to 78° F when the outside temperature was 110° F. The undercarriage had dual wheels on all units, the main wheels, with low-pressure tyres, being carried on single shock-absorber struts retracting forwards behind twin doors into the engine nacelles. The steerable twin nosewheel was carried on a single shock-absorber leg with a fairing plate attached to its front which also retracted through twin doors. Dual hydraulic brakes were fitted to the main wheels.

The L-049 Constellation's four Wright R-3350 Duplex Cyclone engines gave it some twenty-five per cent more power than the Douglas DC-4, resulting in a higher speed, longer range and greater payload, not to mention operating costs per seat-mile some twenty-three per cent cheaper than those of the Douglas.

In order to achieve the lowest possible drag, the original Constellation nacelle design had featured a completely enclosed engine with a cooling air intake at the nacelle/wing juncture, the air being turned through 180 degrees to move forward to the front of the nacelle, where it turned through another 180 degrees to circulate through the cylinder fins. These duct bends produced losses, however, and wind-tunnel tests showed that the drag saving over a conventional nacelle with the cooling air inlet at the front was negligible. A similar low-drag cooling system to the one studied by Lockheed had previously been employed in the United Kingdom on the De Havilland DH. 91 Albatross airliner, which first flew on 20 May 1937, powered by four 535 horsepower DH Gipsy Twelve 12-cylinder inverted-vee engines in low-drag nacelles.

The Constellation was first with many design features for passenger airliners. It was the first airliner to have complete power controls - that is, hydraulically 'boosted.' The basic principle of mechanically enhancing the human effort had been used in steamships, cars, and trucks, but the application to aircraft was much more complicated. Lockheed earlier had undertaken it as a long-range research project in anticipation of the greater control problems to come as aircraft performance increased. It was decided early to incorporate the device in Constellation design.

Kelly Johnson: 'I had some difficulty in convincing Robert Gross of the advisability of adding this complexity to the airplane, since other aircraft manufacturers were ignoring it. Why did we need it? But I caught him one day when he had just parked his new Chevrolet in the company garage.

'Bob, you didn't really need power to steer that car, but it makes it a hell of a lot easier, doesn't it?' I never heard another word of dissent about power steering for aircraft.'

A Lockheed Ventura was used as a flying test-bed for the R-3350 engines and this was known as the 'Ven-tellation' to Lockheed engineers when fitted with two 2,200hp R-3350-35s, and also as the 'Sweater Girl' because of its 'big protuberances'! It was found to have a very similar performance to the Constellation, which made it very useful for the latter's test programme, and when this was completed Lockheed sold it to the Wright Aeronautical Corporation for further engine development.

The R-3350s in the Constellation were enclosed in long-chord tapered cowlings, the stainless steel nacelles being completely detachable. They could be changed in thirty minutes, all ducting and controls being grouped at the fireproof bulkhead. In the early models the flight engineer operated the fire extinguisher system on activation of the fire-warning signal. The Constellation was the first airliner with the ability to use reverse pitch, a feature that greatly reduced runway overrun accidents over the years, as well as facilitating operation from wet or icy surfaces.

The flight deck was initially laid out for a crew of five: two pilots with dual controls, a flight engineer's station to starboard behind the co-pilot and facing outward, a radio operator's position behind the pilot facing forward, and a navigator's position and crew rest space separated from the flight deck proper by a bulkhead. This layout underwent some revision over the years, notably with the disappearance

The sleek DH.91 Albatross of 1937, with tightly enclosed Gipsy Twelve engines. *(DH Hatfield)*

of the flight engineer and radio officer from airline crews by the 1960s in favour of an all-pilot complement.

Throughout the negotiation, Hughes' emphasis was on speed, speed, and more speed. Kelly Johnson shared his preoccupation and occasionally took extreme positions. Jack Franklin and Ralph Ellinger considered the artistic lines of the fuselage to be beautiful but far from optimum. They argued strongly for a straight-sided, cylindrical fuselage, pointing out that greater passenger and crew utility, ease of design, and economy of manufacturing would result. They opposed the tiny flight deck because the crew and instrument space would be severely limited and maintenance access extremely difficult. Bob Gross strongly preferred the beauty of the curved-down form, and Johnson opposed the straight-sided fuselage concept, claiming it would cost three miles an hour. Both were adamant, and the now-familiar lines were retained.

Franklin and Ellinger also opposed the installation of powered boost control systems and the extremely complicated wing flap system because of weight and the expected maintenance costs. Again, Lockheed listened but was unyielding. Unfortunately, operating experience would prove Franklin and Ellinger correct. Despite such arguments, however, negotiations progressed surprisingly well, and an acceptable contract and procurement specifications were developed in short order.

One of the practical problems encountered during the negotiation was how to produce the necessary contract papers and maintain complete secrecy. Hughes was suspicious of everyone suggested to handle this aspect. Finally, Tomlinson indicated that his wife, Marge, who had been a court reporter and was

| New TWA Transport Issue See Pages 1, 2 and 8 | # THE TWA SKYLINER | What Are Our Aims? See Page 2 |

Vol. 5, No. 5   Published by TRANSCONTINENTAL & WESTERN AIR, INC.   JUNE 9, 1941

TWA TO BUY FLEET OF AIR GIANTS WILL SPAN NATION IN 8½ HOURS!

Noah Dietrich Is Named New TWA Director

Noah Dietrich, for 15 years Vice-President of the Hughes Tool Company, Houston, Texas, has been elected to the Board of Directors of Transcontinental & Western Air, Inc.

Mr. Dietrich, 52 years old, is widely known in California, Neva-

Noah Dietrich, Vice-President of the Hughes Tool Company, Houston, Texas, who has been named a director of TWA.

da, Arizona, New Mexico and Texas. His business experience includes banking, public utility accounting and many years in the oil industry equipment field in which he now is engaged.

He attended Janesville High School, Janesville, Wisc., and Judd's College at Waukegan, Illinois. For four years he was Cashier of the First State Bank, Maxwell, N. M. He next moved to Los Angeles, where for six years he was engaged in real estate and public utility accounting, serving as Auditor for the Janss Investment Company. The next two years he was engaged in oil production and refining accounting as Chief Accountant for the Pan American Petroleum & Transport Co.

His career also includes two years as senior accountant for Haskins & Sells and five years as Comptroller of Harold L. Arnold, Inc., automobile distributors of California, Nevada and Arizona. He has been connected with the Hughes Tool Company since.

Just in case you have forgotten, or misplaced your form authorizing salary deduction for R. A. F. Benevolent Fund, extra forms are available at the personnel office. Or, contact Newton A. Lieurance or Ed Rose of the Employee Governing Committee.

Mr. Burglar, the Joke's on you—They're dummies

A San Francisco burglar has time on his hands that he can't market.

The TWA office window in San Francisco featured Benrus watches. Recently employees found the window broken when they reported for work and two watches missing. The joke's on the burglar—they were dummies.

TWA Employee Group Launches Drive for RAF

By Newton A. Lieurance, Chairman and Ed Rose, Co-Chairman of TWA's Employee Governing Committee of the R. A. F. Benevolent Fund

President Jack Frye recently was made Chairman of the Airline Division of the Royal Air Force Benevolent Fund of the U. S. A. He, in turn, invited 68 employees of T. & W. A. to serve on a committee to formulate and sponsor projects to raise funds for this worthy cause. Mr. Frye's invitation to the various members of the committee was made strictly on a voluntary basis and the response was 100 per cent.

The employees' committee consists of representatives from every department of the home base at Kansas City and representatives from each station on the TWA System. The committee members at the home base are termed the Governing Committee. Due to the complexity of as large an organization as TWA, it was difficult to formulate projects that would be practical for each station. Therefore, the committee members at other than the home base are more or less patrons to the Governing Committee rather than active members.

Beginning June 1, a concerted drive will be launched by the TWA Employee Committee for the Royal Air Force Benevolent Fund to raise a liberal sum to aid the disabled flyers of Great Britain and the (Continued, Col. 3, Page 8)

New Transport Plane Outstanding Advance In Airline Progress

HOWARD HUGHES   PRESIDENT JACK FRYE

Tomlinson Granted Leave; Franklin, Herre Promoted

Jack Frye, President of TWA, has announced that D. W. (Tommy) Tomlinson, Vice-President in Charge of Engineering, had been granted an indefinite leave of absence to become commanding officer of the Naval Reserve Aviation Base at Fairfax Airport, Kansas City, Kas.

Tomlinson, noted substratosphere flyer and commander in the Naval Reserve, went on active duty at his new post June 2.

Mr. Frye also announced that J. C. Franklin, Executive Assistant and Corporate Secretary, had been named Superintendent of Engineering to assume Tomlinson's duties. Franklin, former superintendent of communications for the company, has been with TWA since its inception.

To accept his new post, Franklin relinquished his position as Corporate Secretary, a post that will be taken over by Paul E. Richter, Executive Vice President. C. W. Herre, Assistant to E. Lee Talman, Vice-President and Treasurer, was promoted to Executive Assistant and Assistant Secretary in the series of appointments.

Franklin has been in aviation since June 3, 1929 when he was employed as Radio Engineer for Western Air Express, being hired by Herbert Hoover, Jr., who then was superintendent of communications for that airline.

In the 1930 merger, out of which TWA was born, both Franklin and Hoover joined TWA in the same capacities they held with Western Air Express. Franklin a short time later succeeded Hoover as superintendent of communications.

A graduate of Stanford University and the Harvard Graduate School of Business Administration, he also knows how to wield a pick and shovel, having handled both on a hydro-electric project at San Francisco back in his university days. He was graduated from Stanford in 1926, majoring in physics (Continued, Col. 5, Page 8)

Hughes-Frye Development of New 57-Passenger 4-Engine Ship Now Under Production

LOCKHEED TO BUILD PLANE

Revolutionary Design of New Airplane Will Assure TWA Leadership in Domestic Airline Field, Frye Says

Development for TWA of the largest and fastest land transport in the world, now under construction at the Lockheed plant in Burbank, Calif., should assure the United States virtual domination in commercial air transportation after the War, according to President Jack Frye.

The development of the plane jointly by Mr. Frye and Howard Hughes, Chairman of the Board of the Hughes Tool Company of Houston, Tex., who holds the present 'round-the-world air record, was announced by TWA's president after a series of rumors concerning the new ship had been published in aviation magazines.

The new plane has four engines, is built for sub-stratosphere flying, and will be able to cross the country in 8½ hours. It has a passenger capacity of 57 plus a crew of seven, and has been tentatively designated as the Lockheed "Constellation." The first model has been in production secretly since the summer of 1939, although practically no information about it has been available to the industry.

"Mr. Hughes and I felt that information on the development of this plane should be protected from leakage to other countries," Mr. Frye explained, "because we believed knowledge of the revolutionary engineering characteristics of the plane would stimulate other nations to attempt to duplicate it.

"This plane has several characteristics which make it the finest (Continued, Col. 1, Page 8)

J. C. Franklin, left, D. W. (Tommy) Tomlinson, center, and C. W. Herre, right.

32

Page 8 THE SKYLINER June 9, 1941

New TWA Transport Plane To Span U. S. in 8½ Hours

(Continued from Col. 5, Page 1)

transport plane ever built. Its specifications require a cruising speed in excess of 285 miles an hour and as a matter of fact, its great speed will allow at least 20 per cent reduction in operating costs.

"Its safety features, size, speed, operating economy and luxury, plus the fact that it is designed for high altitude operation at levels of 25,000 to 30,000 feet, will make it superior to any plane of which we have any knowledge.

"I believe this plane, after the necessary development through actual operation by TWA, will insure this country against any challenge to commercial air supremacy for many years to come. It takes several years to develop a new plane, and I believe the United States is now years ahead of any other country by reason of this plane, whereas if the conception of this plane had been publicized at the outset, this would not have been possible."

The huge ship will be able to cross the United States non-stop in eight and a half hours, cutting five hours from the fastest transcontinental schedules now operated by TWA's Stratoliners, which operate on scheduled 13½-hour flights between Los Angeles and New York.

The flying range of the new plane is so great that it would be able to make the non-stop flight across the country with enough fuel left to fly back to Kansas City. It also would be able to operate on ocean flights from New York to London in 12 hours or from Kansas City to Rio de Janiero in 26 hours with one refueling stop.

The present trip by air from Miami, Fla., to Rio de Janiero requires 56 hours, 55 minutes.

Specifications of the new plane include:

Four Wright Cyclone engines of 2,500 horsepower each, generating 10,000 horsepower at take-off.

Top speed of 350 miles an hour, more than 100 miles an hour faster than the Stratoliner's top speed; and a cruising speed of 283 miles an hour at 47½ per cent of power.

A range of more than 4,000 miles with over 8,000-pound payload, which would bring every point in North America within non-stop operating distance from Kansas City and would permit one-stop operation to any city in the Western Hemisphere.

Supercharged cabins and engines, permitting operation up to 30,000 feet with sea-level passenger comfort.

Operating economy which will reduce seat-mile or ton-mile costs while operating at 47½ per cent of power, by an estimated 20 per cent over present costs of Douglas operation.

The planes will cost approximately $500,000 each, and in terms of present equipment each of the new Lockheeds will be able to do as much work as four Douglas DC-3 planes, or two and a half Stratoliners per hour of operation. Forty of the new planes have been ordered for TWA.

The 2,500-horsepower engines are the most powerful in use on any American-built aircraft, with 18 cylinders and supercharging features that will permit the plane to cruise at 30,000 feet. The present critical altitude of the Stratoliners is about 23,000 feet.

The cabin supercharging represents a development and improvement of the Stratoliner. The cabins will be pressurized to maintain an altitude from 8,000 to 12,000-foot levels while the plane is cruising between 25,000 and 30,000 feet, and sea-level pressure will be maintained up to 10,000 feet.

The present Stratoliner supercharging system begins to function at 8,000 feet, maintaining levels from 8,000 to 12,000 feet while the plane is cruising from 15,000 to 20,000 feet.

T. B. WILSON ENVISIONS AIR CENTER AT PHOENIX

Unlimited possibilities in the development of Phoenix, Arizona, along with the growth of the aviation industry, both in war and peace, were envisioned by T. B. Wilson, chairman of the board of TWA, in an address before the Merchants and Manufacturers Association at Phoenix recently.

"As I visualize the future of Phoenix, I see untold possibilities for a great development in all phases of aviation," Mr. Wilson said. "You already have all the units composing a complete air corps training center and there is no reason why your city should not be destined to become a permanent training base."

Owner of Stratoliner Coin Prizes It More Than Cash

A TWA passenger, mistaking his Stratoliner coin for a half dollar, gave it to the cashier in a KC restaurant to pay for his lunch. The restaurant passed it on to a dairy company, also mistaking it for a half dollar.

Upon discovering his mistake, the coin owner went back to the restaurant, hoping to recover it. He prized it so highly he hunted up the dairy representative and recovered it.

Little Daniel Cupid Has Hit His Stride; Three Airline Marriages Make Headlines

Little Danny Cupid has hit his stride! The result — Three airline marriages which made the headlines:

E. E. Rose, Assistant Sales Manager and System Designer for TWA and Miss Anona Pickard, secretary to C. E. (Chuck) Kaul, District Manager at Phoenix, were married March 16.

"Altar Short Cut Isn't," read a headline announcing the complex wedding of Newt Lieurance, Assistant Chief Meteorologist for TWA and Hostess Sarah Whitcomb at Liberty, Mo.

Stratoliner Captain S. A. Morehouse took advantage of a 10-minute stopover at Boulder City on flight 6 to marry Rachael C. Carrothers Long. Captain "Si" took the Stratoliner on to Albuquerque after the brief but complete ceremony.

TWA Employees' Group Launches RAF Fund Drive

(Continued from Col. 2, Page 1)

families of those who have been killed in action. Every cent of the entire proceeds will be sent overseas. The campaign will last for a period of thirty days beginning June 1.

No doubt, all of you received in your pay envelope for May 15 a letter of appeal from the TWA Committee along with a form authorizing salary deduction. This is TWA Employees' Project and the members of the committee want everyone to give this very serious thought and give at least the equivalent of two hours of their pay. However, this is entirely a voluntary employee action, and those who are not in sympathy with the cause should stand by their convictions. Authorized salary deductions for all contributions will be made on June 10.

Other projects that will be sponsored by the TWA Employee Committee during the month of June are as follows:

Courtesy flights will be offered in a DC-3 for a nominal fee at Kansas City. The expense for operating these flights will be borne by TWA, except that the services of the crew will be donated by the necessary flight personnel.

There will be no further solicitation for this cause in 1941. Other officers of the Governing Committee are P. Redpath, vice-chairman; H. B. Obermiller, secretary and M. W. McQueen, treasurer.

Committee members at each station follow:

New York—John R. Keegan, Ruth Warnock, Harold W. Crowther.
Boston—Vernon C. Kerr.
Philadelphia—David A. G. Mutch, C. E. McCollum.
Harrisburg—J. M. Wulpi, E. C. Ball.
Pittsburgh—R. E. Montgomery, V. J. Stott.
Columbus—L. A. McDonald, Fritz Wolf
Detroit—J. P. Matheson, G. A. Wise.
Dayton—V. L. Gunn, C. T. Sinnard.
Cincinnati—J. C. Stewart, K. A. McGaha.
Fort Wayne—Wm. Pluchel, Worth Johnson.
Chicago—Wm. L. Armstrong, Gano Lightfoot, Alvin E. Corcoran, M. I. Seliger, H. F. Myers.
Indianapolis—W. R. Bunker, E. E. Kelsey.
St. Louis—R. G. Petitte, C. H. Sessions.
Wichita—R. R. Riordan, C. D. Flournoy.
Amarillo—J. D. Harrigan, G. L. Hall.
Albuquerque—G. W. Lusk, F. B. McLeod.
Winslow—J. Kasulaitis.
Phoenix—C. E. Kaul.
Boulder City—W. E. Baker.
Las Vegas—W. T. Evans.
Fresno—H. A. Stancil.
Los Angeles—John E. Guy, Steve D. Welsh, Ernest Kruttschmitt.
San Francisco—Wm. C. McConnell, Ernie Smith, H. G. Andrews.
Kansas City—Ed Rose, R. T. Morrison, Charles S. Hawker, Arnold S. Williamson, William J. Ryan, Kenneth J. Sommerville, H. Poole, Walter Brown, Helen McGarry, Peter H. Redpath, Joe Mountain, Robt. C. Knowles, Earl J. McNaughton, Wm. A. McCurdy, J. H. Clemson, M. W. McQueen, W. H. Simmons, Wm. Brewer, H. B. Obermiller, Meriam L. Furse, John Roche, Roy Stears, Newton A. Lieurance.

Paints Stirring Picture Of Life in Great Britain

J. Chesney Stewart, TWA district manager at Cincinnati, has received a lengthy letter from C. A. Metcalfe, of British Overseas Airways, which paints a stirring picture of the life of the airline representative in England.

His letter tells how a basement room intended for a lounge and restaurant has been turned into an air raid shelter which the airline staff uses during the day when there is an alarm. At night it is turned into a huge dormitory.

Newton A. Lieurance, Chairman of TWA's Employee Governing Committee of the R. A. F. Benevolent Fund.

Thanks for Orchids

Charles W. McGinnis, Regional Manager of the Metropolitan Life Insurance Company, Pittsburgh, Pa., has sent the following letter to Jack Frye, President of TWA:

Dear Mr. Frye:

It certainly was pleasant news to hear of the promotion of Mr. C. J. Templeton, as well as that of Mr. Vincent Stott. Our loss is Chicago's gain and Harrisburg's loss is our gain.

I have known both of these men for many years and, as I said to Mrs. Clemson the other night on Flight 24, it seems to me that in all these years that I have flown with TWA I have seen many men come and go but when they have, they have gone up and not out. This speaks exceptionally well of those responsible for the selection of your personnel.

Kindest personal regards, and may I add "Congratulations and all good wishes."

Carl G. Triest, 9 Rockefeller Plaza, New York, writes:

"I took your flight from New York to Pittsburgh for the purpose of flying east a private plane which had been left there due to fog. The amazing co-operation and help extended by the captain and co-pilot and your LaGuardia and Pittsburgh offices enabled me to take off for New York from Pittsburgh within seven minutes of arrival. Having flown privately for eleven years, I could hardly recover from the shock of having my every wish carried out to the last detail regarding servicing and warming up of this plane."

Benefit by saving the credit union way.

Grant Tomlinson Leave; Promote Franklin, Herre

(Continued from Col. 4, Page 1)

and then attended the Harvard Graduate School.

Herre's early experience was gained in various departments of the Chevrolet Motor Co., at Flint, Michigan, culminating in his transfer to Kansas City as assistant resident comptroller when the Chevrolet Assembly Plant was constructed at Leeds, Mo., in October, 1928. He later was promoted to resident comptroller, holding that position until early in 1932, when he joined General Motors Management Corporation, in connection with dealer accounting. He held that position until December 1, 1932, when he resigned to join TWA, working under F. G. Wilson, Treasurer. He held the positions of statistician and budget officer before holding his post as assistant to Talman. Herre is a native of Saginaw, Michigan.

Tomlinson's high altitude research flying paved the way for the operation of TWA's Stratoliner fleet.

Family Benefit Plan Is Declared Effective

The B. M. A. family benefit hospitalization plan for TWA employees has been declared effective, it was announced by R. G. Bloomer, EMBP head. The traffic department showed almost a 100 per cent enrollment, making it possible to put the plan into effect.

Those who failed to take advantage of the opportunity before the deadline will be required to provide evidence of insurability of each dependent and wives will not be eligible for maternity benefits for 12 months.

Those with the company less than three months can enroll at any time in 30 days following date they become eligible and receive full benefits. Those married recently who desire to apply should do so within 30 days.

What's celestial navigation? Answer: A young man in love who makes his major approaches by the light of the stars.

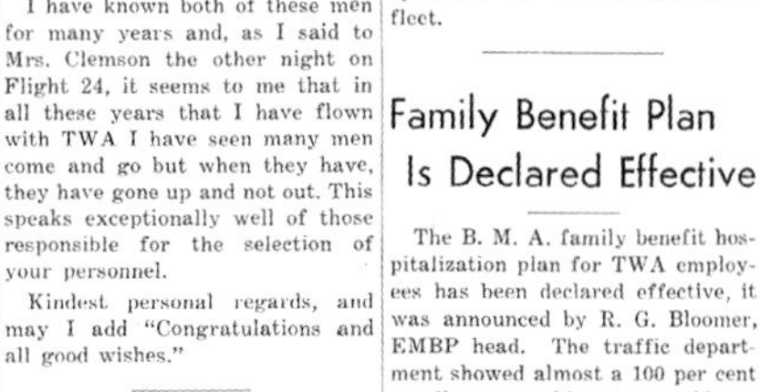

T. B. Wilson, Chairman of the Board for TWA shows his Vice-President of Sales, V. P. Conroy, the value of pulling a rabbit out of his coat when it comes to competition. The Spring sales meeting held at the New York Advertising Club was attended by all the New York Sales Personnel and the District Sales Managers of the Eastern Region. Seated, left to right, are: D. K. Phillips, Station Manager, LaGuardia Field; H. H. Gallup, Superintendent of Operations; William F. McGrath, Eastern Sales Manager; and standing, left to right: W. A. French, Boston Manager; C. E. McCollum, Philadelphia Manager; Conroy and Wilson; I. "Stick" Randall, Assistant to Chairman of the Board; E. O. Cocke, Allegheny Regional Manager and Lee Swigart, New York District Manager.

trustworthy, would be glad to type the agreements. Frye knew her and thought this would be completely acceptable. Hughes and Gross concurred so she moved in, and Tomlinson got to sleep with the secretary.

Howard Hughes read every word of the efficiently prepared contract papers. He wanted a number of language and a few substantive changes made, which Lockheed agreed to for the larger part. The papers were initialled at the Beverly Hills Hotel and formally executed a few days later at Lockheed.

The contract required Lockheed to produce the first forty Constellations for the Hughes Tool Company and to refrain from even committing to sell new Constellations to others until thirty-five had been delivered to Hughes. This arrangement gave TWA about two years exclusivity with the world's fastest, longest-range, and most comfortable transport. The unpressurised Douglas DC-4 and the pressurised DC-6, which was then in the talking stage, could not come close to matching its spectacular performance. Nor could anything else. The Constellation programme gave excellent promise for fulfilling Hughes' and Frye's best hopes for TWA.

Unfortunately for Lockheed, this agreement would also negatively impact the company's relationship with other airlines, most notably American. Kept in the dark about the Constellation, American Airlines would never again buy a commercial aircraft from Lockheed.

Hughes elected to have the airliners, which cost $425,000 each, purchased by the Hughes Tool Company rather than by TWA. His reasoning was simple: if TWA had purchased them directly, banks and financial institutions would have become quickly involved, and secrecy lost because of disclosure requirements. Besides, TWA's then weak financial position, which Hughes quite obviously elected not to reinforce, would never have justified such a large order. It was fortunate for the future of TWA that Hughes had both the financial muscle and inclination to handle the deal - and to do it secretly.

After the papers were initialled, everyone congratulated everyone, and a few bottle corks were popped. Then the negotiating teams left to attend to regular business.

Secrecy - and Mock-Up Mayhem.
It is truly amazing that Lockheed, TWA, and the outside suppliers kept the Constellation project secret. By the time Lockheed found it advisable to announce the Constellation programme, thousands of employees were directly involved. Yet, nothing leaked out during the years required for development. It was all the more remarkable because national security was in no way involved - it has been said that the venture was perhaps the best kept industrial secret of all time.

The secrecy veil was lifted a few months before Pearl Harbor when a visit to Lockheed from the War Production Board was imminent. Because Lockheed was obliged under law to show all work in process, with Hughes' consent it called a special press conference the day before the board arrived. The actual date of this visit is not entirely certain, but what is known is that on 9 June 1941, an article spread over two pages of Volume 5 No,. 5 'The TWA Skyliner' staff magazine revealed not only the existence of the airliner, but also quite an amount of detail.

The announcement and photographs of the Constellation, which appeared in nearly every leading newspaper in the country, electrified the industry. Its long-range, high-speed, and high-altitude capabilities were years ahead - even of anything else on the drawing board. It appeared that TWA would achieve a major lead on its competition because of the foresight of Hughes and Frye and the design genius of Hibbard and Johnson. Hughes was given great credit for his courage and willingness to put a fortune at risk by ordering the first forty Constellations to the account of his wholly-owned company. Without his confidence and determination, the programme never would have materialised.

As soon as technical progress permitted, Lockheed built a full-size mockup of the passenger interior in a shed located in an infrequently used area of the Burbank airport. The mockup was furnished with seats, carefully selected fabrics and upholstery materials, and sample appointments.

It was with great pride that Lockheed presented their labours for approval to Hughes and TWA one Sunday morning - a time selected as the least likely to attract attention. Hughes' passion for secrecy kicked in so, the participants arranged to arrive at the mockup building at fifteen-minute intervals starting at 7am so as to not look like a caravan. Gross, Hibbard, and Johnson were first to arrive, with Frye, Ellinger, and Guy not far behind.

Hughes was last. As he entered the mockup, everyone became silent. Without saying a word, he looked around and deliberately walked the length of the display very slowly. He turned to Bob Gross and said, 'This isn't exactly what I had in mind.'

The Lockheed mouths dropped when he spoke. Howard's reaction surprised the TWA contingent as much as it did Lockheed's. After another pause, he added, 'Bob, I think you should get Raymond Loewy on this.' He then abruptly left, apparently without expecting or receiving an answer from Gross.

Raymond Loewy was a French-born American industrial designer who achieved fame for the magnitude of his design efforts across a huge variety of industries.

He spent most of his professional career in the United States, becoming a naturalized citizen in 1938. Among his designs were the Shell, Exxon and the former BP logos, the Greyhound Scenicruiser bus, Coca-Cola vending machines and bottle redesign, the Lucky Strike package, Coldspot refrigerators, the Studebaker Avanti and Champion, and the Air Force One livery. He was engaged by equipment manufacturer International Harvester to overhaul its entire product line, and his team also assisted competitor Allis-Chalmers. He undertook numerous railroad designs, including the Pennsylvania Railroad GG1, S-1, and T1 locomotives, the colour scheme and Eagle motif for the first streamliners of the Missouri Pacific Railroad, and a number of lesser known colour schemes and car interior designs for other railroads. His career spanned seven decades.

The press referred to Loewy as The Man Who Shaped America, The Father of Streamlining and The Father of Industrial Design, and he had done a creditable job on TWA's DC-3 sleeper interiors. Gross lost no time in getting him on board. During the next several weeks, Loewy developed sample colour schemes and sketches, which Guy handed on to Hughes for approval. However, for reasons unknown, Hughes did not respond. Lacking directions to the contrary, Loewy proceeded with his design efforts.

Sometime later, when Loewy was visiting Lockheed, Hughes asked Guy to arrange for a meeting with him. Loewy had an important meeting in the East with Studebaker the next day, expressed sincere regrets, and said that while he could not meet with Hughes at that particular time, he would be pleased to visit California later at a time convenient for Hughes. John Guy advised the millionaire, who absolutely insisted that Loewy change his plans.

Raymond Loewy (b. 5 November 1893, d. 14 July 1986) an industrial designer, who did a great amount of work for TWA.

Loewy reluctantly did so, with considerable effort and personal embarrassment, only to find that Hughes was too busy to meet with him. When Loewy prepared to leave, Hughes again requested through Guy that Loewy remain. Loewy again acquiesced and shifted plans, and Hughes was again too busy. This happened once again, and Loewy's situation became even more critical. It did not help Loewy's frame of mind that he could talk only with John Guy, not with Hughes.

The three finally met at Hughes' house. After waiting several hours, Hughes came in dragging a large picture of an airliner interior and said, 'Raymond, this is what I have in mind. See what you can do.' John Guy was aghast. After persuading Loewy to stand by for days, the meeting ended almost as soon as it started. To make matters worse, Guy thought the picture looked like an enlarged shot of a standard Douglas interior.

Pan Am gets involved.
Accounts of PAA's entry into the Constellation programme are somewhat contradictory and far from clear. Unfortunately, the principals involved - Howard Hughes, Bob Gross, Jack Frye, and Juan Trippe - have long since died, but it is possible to piece together the story from numerous reputable sources.

Shortly after the Constellation programme became public knowledge, Juan Trippe, PAA's chief executive officer, made clear to Bob Gross that he wanted PAA in the programme. Nothing short of rights to an equal number of airliners would do. Trippe was upset by Lockheed having proceeded in secret with the Constellation after the abandonment of the Excalibur project - a situation to which Gross was sensitive. From Lockheed's spoint of view, getting PAA on board appeared to guarantee the commercial success of the programme.

Juan Terry Trippe was an American commercial aviation pioneer, entrepreneur and the founder of Pan American World Airways, one of the iconic airlines of the 20th century. He was instrumental in numerous revolutionary advances in airline history, including the development and production of the Boeing 314 Clipper, which opened trans-Pacific airline travel, and the Boeing Stratoliner which helped to pioneer cabin pressurisation.

'Juan Trippe is the most fascinating Yale gangster I ever met.' President Roosevelt is supposed to have said to one of Trippe's numerous adversaries, in a moment of pique at his manoeuvring against the President in Congress, adding that, 'In government and in war, you have to use scoundrels.'

Roosevelt was, of course, a Harvard man, and he had taken abuse from Yale, that citadel of isolationism which had fostered the America First movement and produced some of his most vociferous critics, such as Republican Senator Robert A. Taft of Ohio and publisher Henry R. Luce. After Luce's candidate, Wendell Willkie, failed in his challenge to Roosevelt's bid for a third term, the founder of *Time* and *Life* proclaimed 'the American Century', an imperialistic creed by which corporations like *Time/ Life* and Pan American Airways were to disseminate the free-enterprise system about the globe.

In her maiden speech in the House of Representatives Clare Boothe Luce, the publisher's wife, lashed out against an 'open skies' policy for the world's airlines after the war. 'Globaloney,' she called it, trying to force the Administration not to make it the cornerstone of international aviation policy. Suspicion was rampant that Trippe had much to do with the composition of her speech.

It was open versus closed skies, freedom of the air versus the 'sovereignty of American skies' that Clare Luce propounded: the debate was fundamental to the struggle to create a common law of aviation, threatening repetition of the battle waged for hundreds of years to secure freedom of navigation on the seas. Would nationalism restrict rights to the air lanes and access to the airports of various countries, or would open competition be the rule of the skies?

The battle made for strange alliances and permutations of economic philosophies. New Dealers like Berle argued for the widest distribution of commercial air rights and the least regulation of international airlines. Those champions of free enterprise, like the Luces, who regularly attacked

Juan Terry Trippe
(b. 27 June 1899, d. 3 April 1981)

Roosevelt for intervening in the economy, demanded government protection of the airspace above the United States against the carriers of other nations. As a corollary to this, they espoused a single American airline for foreign service, an imperial instrument of trade.

Only one airline carried the American flag abroad: Pan American Airways, the symbol of US economic power all around the world. South American Indians who had never seen an automobile recognized the thunderbird with the Stars and Stripes painted on its tail. Chinese coolies on the wharves of Hong Kong waved to the silver-and-blue flying boats skimming across the harbour.

Pan American Airways camouflaged certain preparations the Roosevelt Administration made for war; island bases in the Pacific, airfields covertly built in South America, an airlift of supplies to the British in North Africa. Pan American Airways transported the President in January to Casablanca, where he and Churchill agreed to exact unconditional surrender from the enemies. The airline carried exiled sovereigns and heads of state, military advisers, diplomats and spymasters on their secret missions.

There was talk of the government taking over Pan American, but it flickered out. Pan American was more useful with an ambiguous status. Not until many years after the war when official documents were declassified and memoirs published would the nature and extent of Pan American Airways' and Juan Trippe's service to the nation be revealed. Yet Adolph Berle said, 'I do not trust Pan American any farther than I can see it.'

Secretary of the Interior Harold L Ickes maintained, 'Trippe is an unscrupulous person who cajoles and buys his way.' According to Ickes, the President described Trippe to him as 'a man of all-yielding suavity who can be depended upon to pursue his own ruthless way.'

Lloyd Welch Pogue
(b. 21 October 1899, d. 10 May 2003),
Chairman of the US CAB.

Why were there such misgivings about so patriotic a man and his company? Was it because of the means Trippe used to acquire the monopoly of the nation's overseas air routes - acting as a master politician at home and an éminence grise of the State Department abroad - the unconfirmed foreign minister of US civil aviation? Or was it the way he had fought to preserve the monopoly by moving heaven and earth to stamp out competition?

In one decade, Pan American Airways had connected the Americas and bridged the oceans from the air. It had transitioned from the era of the barnstormer in leather and goggles to that of the scientific cockpit team. It pushed aviation technology from wooden contraptions with linen-covered wings to sleek metal machines powered by mighty engines.

Trippe was a zealot whose religious faith was commercial air routes, a visionary who saw the future ahead of others and claimed it for Pan American Airways in perpetuity. He was referred to by many as a robber baron and a buccaneer, albeit a gentleman of the species. His most disturbing characteristic was his deviousness. 'If the front door were open, he would go in by the side window,' said one airline executive.

Everyone had stories to tell about Trippe. Lloyd Welch Pogue (b 21 October 1899 d. May 10, 2003), an American aviation attorney and chairman of the Civil Aeronautics Board, believed that Trippe was trying to undermine the Civil Aeronautics Board one way or another because it was under a mandate to see that he had competition. Pogue once dined at the F Street Club where he was seated next to General George C. Marshall and heard Trippe's self-serving message pouring from the lips of the Army Chief of Staff. How had Trippe managed something like that when the War Department was fed up with his shenanigans?

Robert A Lovett's acquaintance with Trippe went way back, as such things did in the

Establishment, to the Hill School and Yale. Several of Lovett's classmates and flying comrades had dealings with Trippe, as large investors and directors of Pan American Airways or as government officials like himself. All were troubled by Trippe's lack of forthrightness. A controversy was bubbling beneath the surface in the War and State Departments over Pan American's handling of the secret airport-development programme in Latin America. For reasons of security and relations with friendly states, the matter had to be kept quiet for the time being. Lovett thought Trippe had outwitted Secretary of War Stimson when the contract was drawn up.

Harry Hopkins had been Secretary of Commerce when he first met Trippe as a member of the Business Council, the powerful group of industrialists who had volunteered to give the Administration the benefit of their thinking. Disgruntled persons were forever coming to Hopkins with tales of Trippe's alleged machinations; the President's Special Assistant brushed them aside, saying that he wanted to hear no more on that subject. Yet in private he expressed the view that 'I have never liked the idea of Pan American having a world monopoly of our airlines.'

Trippe was born in Sea Bright, New Jersey, on 27 June 1899, the great-great-grandson of Lieutenant John Trippe, captain of the USS *Vixen*. Because he was named Juan, he is widely assumed to have been of Hispanic descent, but his family was actually Northern European in ancestry and settled in Maryland in 1664. He was named after Juanita Terry, the Venezuelan wife of his great uncle. Trippe attended the Bovea School and graduated from The Hill School in 1917.

He enrolled at Yale University but left when the United States entered World War I to apply for flight training with the United States Navy. After completing training in June 1918, he was designated as a Naval Aviator and was commissioned as an Ensign in the United States Navy Reserve. However, the end of World War I precluded him from flying in combat. Demobilised from active duty, he returned to Yale, graduating in 1921. While there, he was a member of St. Anthony Hall

Pan American's Passenger Terminal at Miami in 1940. The use of a globe was predominant - as a feature at the airports, and as a design motif promoting the global nature of its aspirations. *(Authors Collection)*

and of the Skull and Bones society. Trippe was treasurer at the first meeting of the National Intercollegiate Flying Association in 1920.

After graduation from Yale, Trippe began working on Wall Street but soon became bored. In 1922 he raised money from his old Yale classmates, selling them stock in his new airline, an air-taxi service for the rich and powerful called Long Island Airways. Once again tapping his wealthy friends from Yale, Pan American Airways, Incorporated (PAA) was founded as a shell company on 14 March 1927 by Air Corps Majors Henry H. 'Hap' Arnold, Carl A. Spaatz, and John H. Jouett as a counterbalance to the German-owned Colombian carrier SCADTA, operating in Colombia since 1920. SCADTA lobbied hard for landing rights in the Panama Canal Zone, ostensibly to survey air routes for a connection to the United States, which the Air Corps viewed as a precursor to a possible German aerial threat to the canal. Arnold and Spaatz drew up the prospectus for Pan American when SCADTA hired a company in Delaware to obtain air mail contracts from the US government. Pan American was able to obtain the US mail delivery contract to Cuba but lacked any aircraft to perform the job and anyways, did not have landing rights in Cuba.

Trippe invested in an airline named Colonial Air Transport, which was awarded a new route and an airmail contract on 7 October 1927. Interested in operating to the Caribbean, Trippe created the Aviation Corporation of the Americas (ACA) on 2 June 1927, with the backing of powerful and politically connected financiers who included Cornelius Vanderbilt Whitney and W. Averell Harriman, and raised $250,000 in startup capital from the sale of stock. Their operation had the all-important landing rights for Havana, having acquired American International Airways, a small airline established in 1926 by John K. Montgomery and Richard B Bevier as a seaplane service from Key West, Florida, to Havana.

In order for ACA to meet its deadline of having an air mail service operating by 19 October, 1927 they chartered a Fairchild FC-2 floatplane from a small Dominican Republic carrier, West Indian Aerial Express. The return

Supposedly Juan Trippe's favourite promotional image, he is seen here standing by an enormous globe, again promoting the aspirational global nature of Pan Americans business. *(Pan Am)*

flight from Havana to Key West, in a Pan Am Fokker F.VII, took place on 29 October, being delayed a day by rain.

Trippe married Elizabeth 'Betty' Stettinius, the sister of United States Secretary of State Edward R Stettinius Jr., in 1928. They had four children, Elizabeth ('Betsy'), John Terry, Charles White, and Edward Stettinius Trippe. By all accounts, Juan Trippe was a highly ambitious and ruthless businessman, who had grandiose plans for Pan Am.

Trippe bought the China National Aviation Corporation (CNAC) to provide domestic air service in the Republic of China, and became a partner in Panagra. In the 1930s. Pan Am became the first airline to cross the Pacific Ocean with the famous Clipper flying boats.

The Atlantic, Gulf, and Caribbean Airways company was established on 11 October 1927 by New York City investment banker Richard Hoyt, who served as president. This company merged with PAA and ACA on 23 June, 1928. Richard Hoyt was named as president of the new Aviation Corporation of the Americas, but Trippe and his partners held strong that Cornelius Vanderbilt 'Sonny' Whitney was made president. Trippe became operational head of Pan American Airways, the new company's principal operating subsidiary.

The US government approved the original Pan Am's mail delivery contract with little objection, out of fears that SCADTA would have no competition in bidding for routes between Latin America and the United States. The government further helped Pan Am by insulating it from its US competitors, seeing the airline as the 'chosen instrument' for US-based international air routes. The airline expanded internationally, benefiting from a virtual monopoly on foreign routes.

Trippe and his associates planned to extend Pan Am's network through all of Central and South America. During the late 1920s and early 1930s, Pan Am purchased a number of ailing or defunct airlines in Central and South America and negotiated with postal officials to win most of the government's airmail contracts to the region. In September 1929 Trippe toured Latin America with Charles Lindbergh to negotiate landing rights in a number of countries, including Barranquilla on SCADTA's home turf of Colombia, as well as Maracaibo and Caracas in Venezuela. By the end of the year, Pan Am offered flights along the west coast of South America to Peru. The following year, Pan Am purchased the New York, Rio, and Buenos Aires Line, giving it a seaplane route along the east coast of South America to Buenos Aires, Argentina, and westbound to Santiago, Chile. Its Brazilian subsidiary NYRBA do Brasil was later renamed as Panair do Brasil. Pan Am also partnered with Grace Shipping Company in 1929 to form Pan American-Grace Airways, better known as Panagra, to gain a foothold to destinations in South America. In the same year, Pan Am acquired a controlling stake in Mexicana de Aviación and took over Mexicana's Ford Trimotor route between Brownsville, Texas and Mexico City, extending this service to the Yucatan Peninsula to connect with Pan Am's Caribbean route network.

Pan Am's holding company, the Aviation Corporation of the Americas, was one of the most sought after stocks on the New York Curb Exchange in 1929, and flurries of speculation surrounded each of its new route awards. In April 1929 Trippe and his associates reached an agreement with United Aircraft and Transport Corporation (UATC) to segregate Pan Am operations to south of the Mexico – United States border, in exchange for UATC taking a large shareholder stake (UATC was the parent company of what are now Boeing, Pratt & Whitney, and United Airlines). The Aviation Corporation of the Americas changed its name to Pan American Airways Corporation in 1931.

Pan Am started its South American routes with Consolidated Commodore and Sikorsky S-38 flying boats. The S-40, larger than the eight-passenger S-38, began flying for Pan Am in 1931. Pan Am operated Clipper services to Latin America from the International Pan American Airport at Dinner Key in Miami, Florida.

In 1937 Pan Am turned to Britain and France to begin seaplane service between the United States and Europe. Pan Am reached an agreement with both countries to offer service from Norfolk, Virginia, to Europe via Bermuda and the Azores using the S-42s. A joint service from Port Washington, New York to Bermuda began in June 1937, with Pan Am using Sikorskys and Imperial Airways using the C class flying boat RMA *Cavalier*.

On 5 July 1937 survey flights across the North Atlantic began. Pan Am *Clipper III*, a Sikorsky S-42, landed at Botwood, Newfoundland from Port Washington, via Shediac, New Brunswick. The next day *Clipper III* left Botwood for Foynes in Ireland. The same day, a Short Empire C-Class flying boat, *Caledonia*, left Foynes for Botwood, and landed 6 July 1937, reaching Montreal on 8 July and New York on 9 July.

Trippe decided to start a service from San Francisco to Honolulu and on to Hong Kong and Auckland following steamship routes. After negotiating traffic rights in 1934 to land at Pearl Harbor, Midway Island, Wake Island, Guam, and Manila, PAA shipped $500,000 worth of aeronautical equipment westward in March 1935 using the *North Haven*, a 15,000 ton merchant ship it chartered for the purpose of provisioning each island where the clippers would stop. PAA ran its first survey flight to Honolulu in April 1935 with a Sikorsky S-42 flying boat. The airline won the contract for a San Francisco – Canton mail route later that year and operated its first commercial flight carrying mail and express freight in a Martin M-130 from Alameda to Manila amid media fanfare on 22 November 1935. The five leg, 8,000 mile flight, arrived in Manila on 29 November and returned to San Francisco on 6 December, cutting the time between the two cities via the fastest scheduled steamship by over two weeks. The first passenger flight left Alameda on 21 October 1936.

On 6 August 1937 Juan Trippe accepted United States aviation's highest annual prize, the Collier Trophy, on behalf of PAA from President Franklin D Roosevelt for the company's 'establishment of the transpacific airline and the successful execution of extended overwater navigation and the regular operations thereof.'

Six long-range Boeing 314 flying boats were delivered to Pan Am in 1939. On 30 March 1939, *Yankee Clipper,* piloted by Harold E Gray, made the first-ever transatlantic passenger flight. The Boeing 314 also enabled the start of scheduled weekly contract Foreign Air Mail service and later passenger flights from New York to both France and Britain.

After the outbreak of War in Europe on 3 September 1939, the terminus became Foynes in Ireland until the service ceased for the winter on 5 October while transatlantic service to Lisbon via the Azores continued into 1941. During the war Pan Am flew over 90 million miles worldwide in support of military operations.

Pan Am's flying boat terminal at Dinner Key in Miami, Florida, was a hub of inter-American travel during the 1930s and 1940s.

Pan Am also used Boeing 314 flying boats for the Pacific route: in China, passengers could connect to domestic flights on the Pan Am-operated China National Aviation Corporation (CNAC) network, co-owned with the Chinese government. Pan Am flew to Singapore for the first time in 1941, starting a semi-monthly service which reduced San Francisco - Singapore travel times from twenty-five to six days.

In 1940 Pan Am and TWA began using the Boeing 307 Stratoliner, the first pressurised airliner in service and the first with a flight engineer in the crew. The Boeing 307's airline service was short-lived, as all were commandeered for military service when the United States entered World War Two.

Gross discussed the matter of Pan American getting involved with a reluctant Howard Hughes, who was finally persuaded to let PAA join the programme on the condition that it operate overseas routes exclusively and was noncompetitive with TWA. This may have been Hughes' ostensible reason for accepting Gross' arguments; however, it seems likely there was more to it.

Howard Hughes was an ambitious and remarkably astute businessman with a unique facility for visualising future opportunities and leaving doors open for their realisation. It seems highly probable that he thought of the possibility of expanding TWA into the international arena, for which Constellations would be well suited, even at that early date. Such gleam-in-the-eye considerations, had they existed, were likely outweighed in his thinking by pragmatic political considerations. For example, he may have believed that the Constellation programme would be more likely to prosper during the oncoming period of heavy war preparations if PAA purchased a sizable fleet. Whatever Hughes' reasoning might have been, one can be absolutely certain that his decision to permit PAA to buy Constellations was arrived at only after exhaustively detailed study and painstaking evaluation of all aspects.

After Gross obtained Hughes' acquiescence, PAA quietly ordered a fleet of twenty L-049s for its Latin American services and ten long-range L-149s with pressurised cabins that permitted high-altitude flying over the Atlantic storms, so matching the quantity ordered by Hughes in 1939. Not long afterward, John G Borger was transferred to Burbank to serve under Bill Del Valle as PAA's chief expediter and liaison agent at Lockheed.

Chapter Three

Early Days

Not long after the Constellation programme became public knowledge, TWA assigned its rights to the forty Constellations to the Army Air Forces because the production of commercial transports had been forbidden. TWA retained the right to repurchase the aircraft when they were no longer required in military service and obtained preferred delivery positions for new production units. The forty airliners on order were designated C-69 transports and configured for carrying troops and cargo on long-range missions.

Before looking at the production and use of the early Constellations, here is as good a place as any to consider the relatively little known Lockheed Model 249. This was the proposed bomber version with four 2,200 hp Wright R-3350-13 engines which eventually became the XB-30-LO.

According to surviving records, the bomber retained the wings and tail surfaces of the Model 049, and was known as the Model 249-58-01. It was to have had a new fuselage with up to six gun turrets - one in the nose, two above and two below the fuselage, and one in the tail - housing ten .50-calibre guns - twinned up in each turret for the nose, dorsal, and ventral emplacements; and one 20 mm cannon for the tail defensive position. It was to be crewed with a complement of twelve. Ventral bomb bays were to accommodate eight 2,000-pound bombs.

The concept originated around 1938, when General Henry H 'Hap' Arnold, the head of the United States Army Air Corps, was growing alarmed at the possibility of war in Europe. Hoping to be prepared for the long-term requirements of the Air Corps, Arnold created a special committee chaired by Brigadier General Walter G Kilner. In its June 1939 report, the Kilner Committee recommended that several new long-range medium and heavy bombers be developed. On 10 November 1939 General Arnold requested War Department and congressional permission to contact major aircraft companies for studies of a very long-range (VLR) bomber. Congressional authorisation was forthcoming, and in January 1940 the Army Air Corps issued a formal requirement for the VLR superbomber.

This specification called for a maximum speed of at least 400 mph and a range of 5,333 miles while carrying a 2000 pound bomb load for half that distance. The super bomber specifications were embodied in a request for data in R-40B. This specification was revised in April to incorporate the lessons learned in early European combat and included more defensive armour and self-sealing fuel tanks.

Lockheed submitted their model 249 design to the Kilner committee for the same requirement that led to the Boeing B-29 Superfortress, the Douglas XB-31 and Consolidated B-32 Dominator. However, on 6 September 1940, a contract was awarded to Boeing to the value of $43,615,095 to construct a pair of prototype B-29s plus and static model. The L-249 never progressed past the design stage, and it appears that only a scale model was built.

Production and facilities
The growth and development of Burbank as an industrial centre, majoring in aviation, was directly linked to the growth and development of the Lockheed Aircraft Corporation in the 1930s. Spurred on to greater achievements by the needs of a nation at war, a greater Lockheed

The Lockheed factory under wartime camouflage - that included the parking lots. *(Lockheed)*

Aircraft final assembly also took place under camouflage netting, as seen here with the prototype L-049 NX25800 surrounded by a number of P-38 Lightnings. *(Lockheed)*

arrived to challenge the future.

At that time Lockheed employed an army of men and women, 100,000 strong, working in more than one hundred geographical locations in eighteen nations on five continents. It operated eighteen manufacturing plants in Southern California; service bases and modification centres in California, Texas, Northern Ireland and England; liaison offices in Washington, New York City, Rio de Janeiro, Cleveland, Detroit and Chicago.

Tens of thousands of war workers, employed by some 3,000 sub-contractors in 300 cities and towns scattered the length and breadth of the United States, shared indirectly in the building of Lockheed aircraft.

The company employed over 2,800 engineers, all seeking out ways to improve its aircraft, designing new and better models, and grappling with the science of advanced aerodynamics. Tests were being made day and night in the Lockheed wind tunnel, one of the largest in the world.

A modern research laboratory, staffed by a battery of specialists, devoted itself to exhaustive exploration of problems of chemistry, physics, structural fatigue, plastics, and an endless number of other subjects.

Lockheed employed close to a hundred experienced test pilots, enough fliers to operate an average airline. Employees of the company were served by a modern, up-to-the-minute commissary which served 60,000 hot meals daily. Lockheed's job-training department, as well as its wartime employee transportation system, was used as a national model for other organisations. Faced with workforce shortages, Lockheed pioneered in the employment of the physically handicapped. It also instituted a programme for the use of boy power, employing youths at a wide variety of jobs during hours which did not conflict with their schooling. Lockheed sent more than 15,000 employees into the armed services.

The Army Air Forces' quotas called for hundreds of Lockheed aircraft per month. Top consideration was given the AAF's demand for more and more P-38 Lightnings. This twin-tailed, twin-engined fighter topped them all as an all-around performer, '...good for any job between ten feet and the stratosphere' the Air Force Public relations teams claimed. It was used as an escort for bombers, an interceptor of enemy aerial raids, as a skip bomber of ships, for tank-busting, ground strafing, as a camera aircraft, and it could tote its own share of bombs over enemy targets when called upon to do so.

Millions of dollars were spent in Burbank since the breaking out of the war in the effort to fool the enemy who might try to drop bombs

Lockheed Model L-249/XB-30

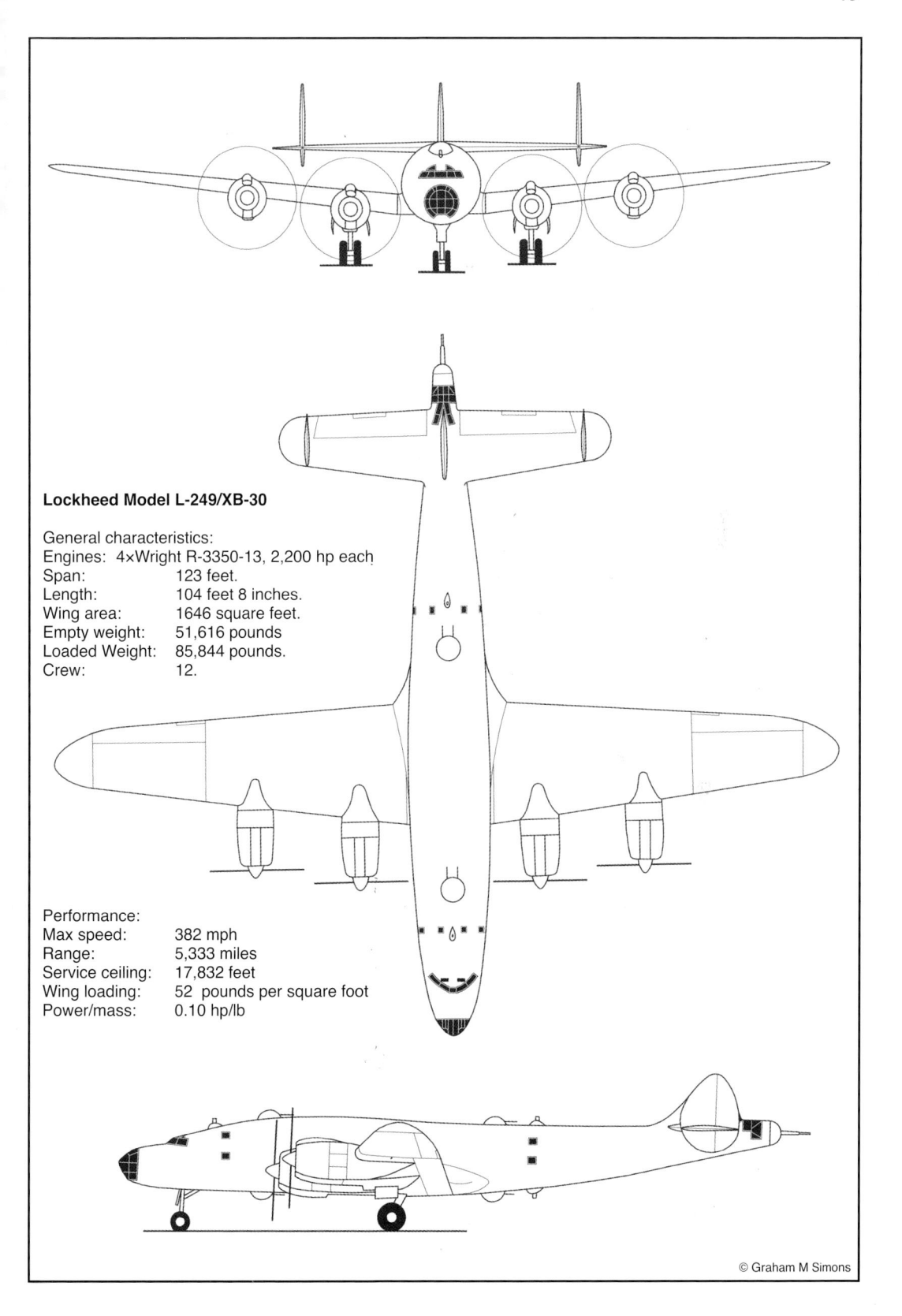

General characteristics:
Engines: 4×Wright R-3350-13, 2,200 hp each
Span: 123 feet.
Length: 104 feet 8 inches.
Wing area: 1646 square feet.
Empty weight: 51,616 pounds
Loaded Weight: 85,844 pounds.
Crew: 12.

Performance:
Max speed: 382 mph
Range: 5,333 miles
Service ceiling: 17,832 feet
Wing loading: 52 pounds per square foot
Power/mass: 0.10 hp/lb

© Graham M Simons

Two views of the test rig vibrating the Constellation's large span wing. The large picture, showing the blurred motion at the tip is clearly a test taking place. The smaller image shows the rig at rest. *(Lockheed)*

from the skies in the hope of putting our war industries out of business. Experts in camouflage spent at least a year in one of the most elaborate efforts in that direction that had been undertaken in any place in the world.

From the air, the territory occupied by the Lockheed Air Terminal and the Lockheed and Lockheed Vega production plants had all of the appearance of a peaceful valley, farmhouses, with more potential buildings resembling apartment houses. The runways at the air terminal had the appearance of fields of grain and other farm crops, with here and there a tree or two to break the monotony. The parking lots where automobiles by the thousand were parked looked like fields of growing alfalfa saturated with an atmosphere of rural bliss and quietude.

In other words, the landscape thirty feet in the air as seen from an overflying aircraft was as different from what it actually was on the surface thirty feet below as it was between a peaceful rural scene and a huge metropolitan industrial centre.

All of these effects were brought about by a lot of false construction on the real buildings, so painted as to have the desired effect from the air. Some of the trees were nothing more than imitation tree-tops sitting on telephone poles. The alfalfa fields covering the automobile parking lots were acres and acres of chicken wire soaked in glue scattered over with chicken feathers. The parklike landscaping on the airfield runways was merely different colours of paint on the surface of the runways.

Underneath this camouflage, together with the other buildings connected with the airport and the industrial buildings were miles and miles of solid concrete air-raid shelters ready for the army of workers should the occasion demand.

As the danger of bombing attack from the enemy waned, it was understood that the camouflage would be removed. An elaborate system of smoke-screen equipment was installed - every few yards in a circle surrounding the airport and industrial plants a half a mile or more from the plants; specially made heaters similar to those used in orchards as a protection from freezing were installed. These were attached by pipe from large drums of oil of a nature found to make the produce the greatest profusion of smoke, so as to bamboozle any enemy bent on bomb raiding.

Lockheed built a number of test-rigs so as to simulate flight conditions in order to study flight conditions in a large-span wing, such as fitted to the Constellation.

Strains were initiated by an out-of-balance wheel journalled in an extension of the main spar and driven by an electric motor at 70 rpm. Lockheed stated that 'the heavy weights simulate the weight of the airplane supported by the wing'. As the wing was not inverted, the load acted primarily as a damper to control the vibrations produced by the motor. The complex vibrations produced by normal smooth airflow, broken air, airscrew buffeting and other factors

The distinctive triple-finned tail unit of the Constellation comes together. This was fitted to the rear fuselage of the aircraft as a single assembly. (Lockheed)

An interesting colour photograph of a number of Constellation fuselages coming together. (Lockheed)

had been studied in flight testing and that the necessary corrections were applied to give a useful result from the dynamic tests.

Two smaller motors mounted on, bearers from the front spar turned suitably unbalanced flywheels at 1,800 rpm to simulate engine vibration. Electronic strain-gauges were applied at all required stations in the structure, and the tests also provided useful data on.the efficiency or otherwise of the integral wing tank construction and sealing.

The Model 049
The 049's wingspan was 123 feet, and its fuselage length 95 feet 1 inch. The top of the Constellation's triple tail rose 23 feet 8 inches above the ground. Total wing area was 1,650 square feet, and 7½ degrees of dihedral was built in for stability. At a gross takeoff weight of 68,000 pounds, the wing loading would equate to 41.21 pounds per square foot. Sweepback of the wings leading edge was slight at 7½ degrees.

The layout of the Constellation was entirely conventional except for the trademark triple vertical tail. It could be argued that Lockheed was going for looks along the lines of their soon-to-be-famous P-38, but the functionality was the real reason. The triple tails would add to yaw stability in engine-out conditions: TWA also wanted the Constellation to be able to fit into its maintenance hangars. A single vertical tail with less structure, weight, and complexity would have been more desirable, but keeping the height of the aircraft down was more important.

The four Wright R-3350-35 radial engines drove three-blade Hamilton-Standard Hydromatic propellers. Capable of being quickly feathered, the 15 feet 2-inch diameter propellers were de-iced by tubes placed on the shank of the propeller that allowed alcohol to coat the blades.

The engine nacelles were works of aerodynamic art. The contour of the nacelles resulted in a uniform increase of airstream velocity over the entire cowling. At extremely high speeds, compression shock waves forming at the nose of the cowl were avoided, yet the air pressure drop inside the cowl provided sufficient airflow for cylinder cooling. The 049's nacelles, cowling, and firewalls were constructed of stainless steel, and the cowling hinged open for ease of maintenance. If a complete engine change was required, the whole unit from the firewall forward could be changed in 45 minutes, according to Lockheed.

Cockpit engine controls were made up of standard throttle, mixture, and priming levers. They were handled either by the pilot or flight engineer. Cables, levers, and pulleys transmitted control lever movement to the firewall pushrods and into the engine compartment.

The wing was built in five sections: the singular stub wing where it joined the fuselage, the two inner wing panels, and the two outer wing panels. Tips with position lights were attached to the end. The stub wing functioned as an attach point for the inner wing panels, which contained the fuel tanks, engine nacelles, de-ice boots, and flaps. Engine firewalls were integral to the nacelles, while the outer wing panels included hydraulically operated ailerons, their control units, and leading-edge de-ice boots.

Right: No, not a bent axle, but a design feature to save nosewheel rubber in tight turns.

Below: extensive Fowler flaps. *(both Lockheed)*

The wet wing used a NACA 23016 airfoil at the root and NACA 4412 airfoil at the tip. Washout towards the tip was a very slight two degrees. The large inner sections of the wing contained two fuel tanks formed by the fore and aft wing spars, solid end ribs, and the skin of the wing. The inner tank had to be subdivided by the main landing gear well, so a fuel tube connected the tanks. A fuel dumping system was incorporated to reduce landing weight.

Fowler flaps gave the airliner excellent low-

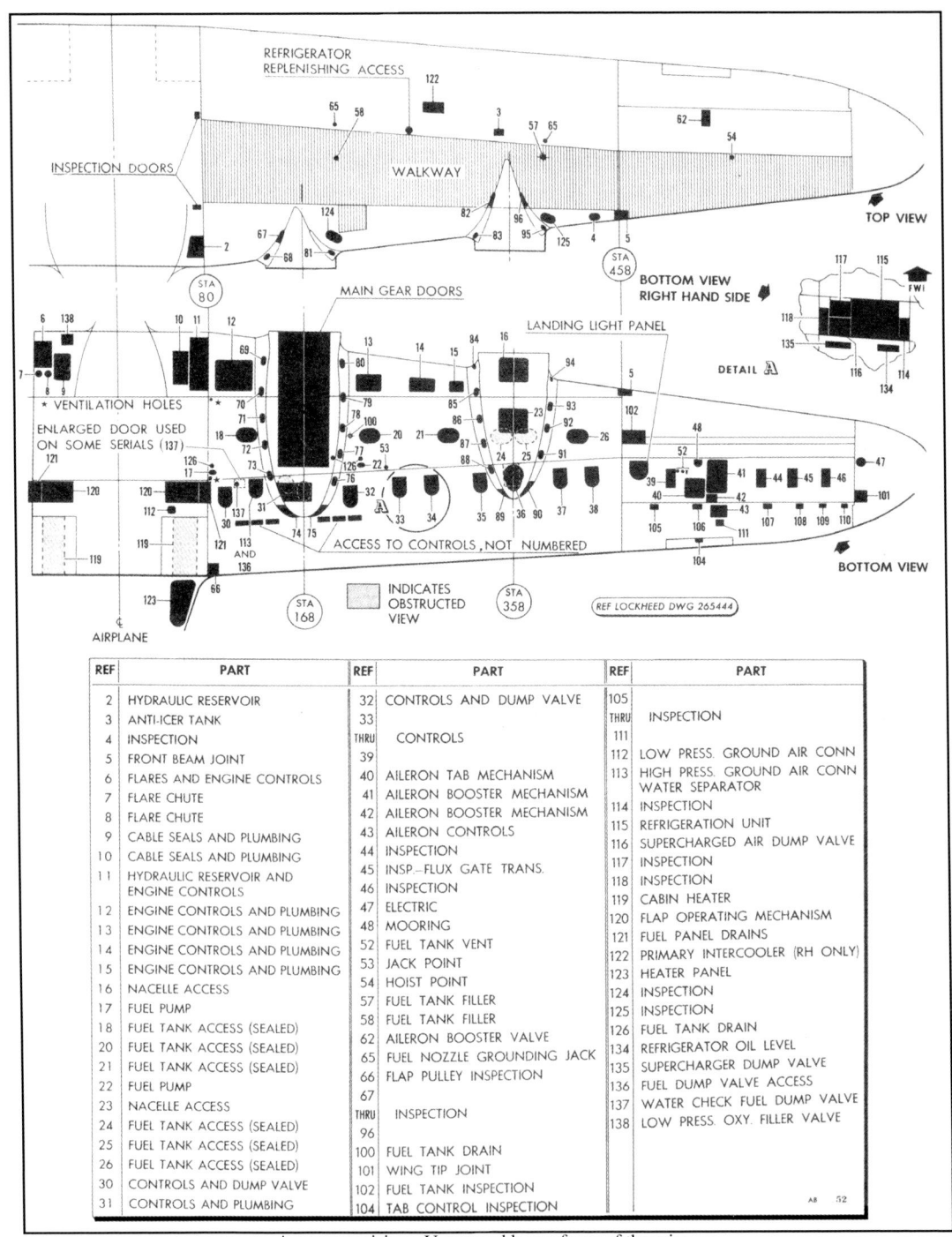

REF	PART	REF	PART	REF	PART
2	HYDRAULIC RESERVOIR	32	CONTROLS AND DUMP VALVE	105	
3	ANTI-ICER TANK	33		THRU	INSPECTION
4	INSPECTION	THRU	CONTROLS	111	
5	FRONT BEAM JOINT	39		112	LOW PRESS. GROUND AIR CONN
6	FLARES AND ENGINE CONTROLS	40	AILERON TAB MECHANISM	113	HIGH PRESS. GROUND AIR CONN WATER SEPARATOR
7	FLARE CHUTE	41	AILERON BOOSTER MECHANISM	114	INSPECTION
8	FLARE CHUTE	42	AILERON BOOSTER MECHANISM	115	REFRIGERATION UNIT
9	CABLE SEALS AND PLUMBING	43	AILERON CONTROLS	116	SUPERCHARGED AIR DUMP VALVE
10	CABLE SEALS AND PLUMBING	44	INSPECTION	117	INSPECTION
11	HYDRAULIC RESERVOIR AND ENGINE CONTROLS	45	INSP.-FLUX GATE TRANS.	118	INSPECTION
		46	INSPECTION	119	CABIN HEATER
12	ENGINE CONTROLS AND PLUMBING	47	ELECTRIC	120	FLAP OPERATING MECHANISM
13	ENGINE CONTROLS AND PLUMBING	48	MOORING	121	FUEL PANEL DRAINS
14	ENGINE CONTROLS AND PLUMBING	52	FUEL TANK VENT	122	PRIMARY INTERCOOLER (RH ONLY)
15	ENGINE CONTROLS AND PLUMBING	53	JACK POINT	123	HEATER PANEL
16	NACELLE ACCESS	54	HOIST POINT	124	INSPECTION
17	FUEL PUMP	57	FUEL TANK FILLER	125	INSPECTION
18	FUEL TANK ACCESS (SEALED)	58	FUEL TANK FILLER	126	FUEL TANK DRAIN
20	FUEL TANK ACCESS (SEALED)	62	AILERON BOOSTER VALVE	134	REFRIGERATOR OIL LEVEL
21	FUEL TANK ACCESS (SEALED)	65	FUEL NOZZLE GROUNDING JACK	135	SUPERCHARGER DUMP VALVE
22	FUEL PUMP	66	FLAP PULLEY INSPECTION	136	FUEL DUMP VALVE ACCESS
23	NACELLE ACCESS	67		137	WATER CHECK FUEL DUMP VALVE
24	FUEL TANK ACCESS (SEALED)	THRU	INSPECTION	138	LOW PRESS. OXY. FILLER VALVE
25	FUEL TANK ACCESS (SEALED)	96			
26	FUEL TANK ACCESS (SEALED)	100	FUEL TANK DRAIN		
30	CONTROLS AND DUMP VALVE	101	WING TIP JOINT		
31	CONTROLS AND PLUMBING	102	FUEL TANK INSPECTION		
		104	TAB CONTROL INSPECTION		

Access provision - Upper and lower faces of the wing.

speed flying characteristics and the ability to land at a mere 77 mph. These hydraulically controlled flaps could extend both down and to the rear, effectively increasing the wing area to lower the stall and landing speeds. Deploying the flaps not only increased the wing area by moving aft but also increased the camber of the wing by moving down 42 degrees. Positions between 0 and 42 degrees could be pre-selected with the flap handle. In case of a hydraulic failure, the flaps could be mechanically cranked down from the cockpit.

Both inner and outer wing panels had plumbing for rubber deicing boots, and the 47-gallon oil tanks for each engine were integral with the inner wing panel structure outboard of the nacelles. The inner nacelles fully housed the main landing gear when retracted, while the

Access provision - Fuseleage

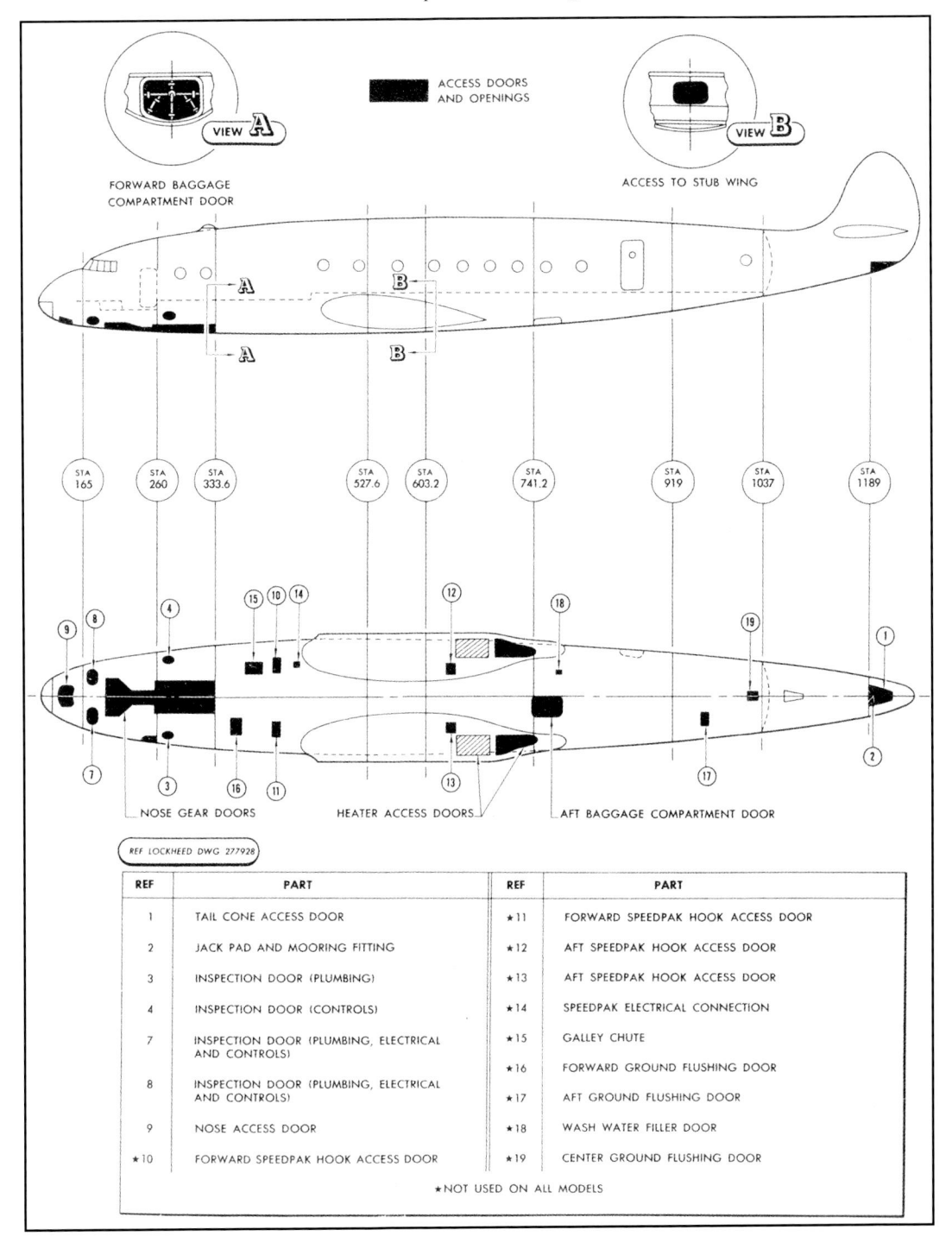

ACCESS DOORS AND OPENINGS

VIEW A
FORWARD BAGGAGE COMPARTMENT DOOR

VIEW B
ACCESS TO STUB WING

NOSE GEAR DOORS
HEATER ACCESS DOORS
AFT BAGGAGE COMPARTMENT DOOR

REF LOCKHEED DWG 277928

REF	PART	REF	PART
1	TAIL CONE ACCESS DOOR	*11	FORWARD SPEEDPAK HOOK ACCESS DOOR
2	JACK PAD AND MOORING FITTING	*12	AFT SPEEDPAK HOOK ACCESS DOOR
3	INSPECTION DOOR (PLUMBING)	*13	AFT SPEEDPAK HOOK ACCESS DOOR
4	INSPECTION DOOR (CONTROLS)	*14	SPEEDPAK ELECTRICAL CONNECTION
7	INSPECTION DOOR (PLUMBING, ELECTRICAL AND CONTROLS)	*15	GALLEY CHUTE
		*16	FORWARD GROUND FLUSHING DOOR
8	INSPECTION DOOR (PLUMBING, ELECTRICAL AND CONTROLS)	*17	AFT GROUND FLUSHING DOOR
9	NOSE ACCESS DOOR	*18	WASH WATER FILLER DOOR
*10	FORWARD SPEEDPAK HOOK ACCESS DOOR	*19	CENTER GROUND FLUSHING DOOR

*NOT USED ON ALL MODELS

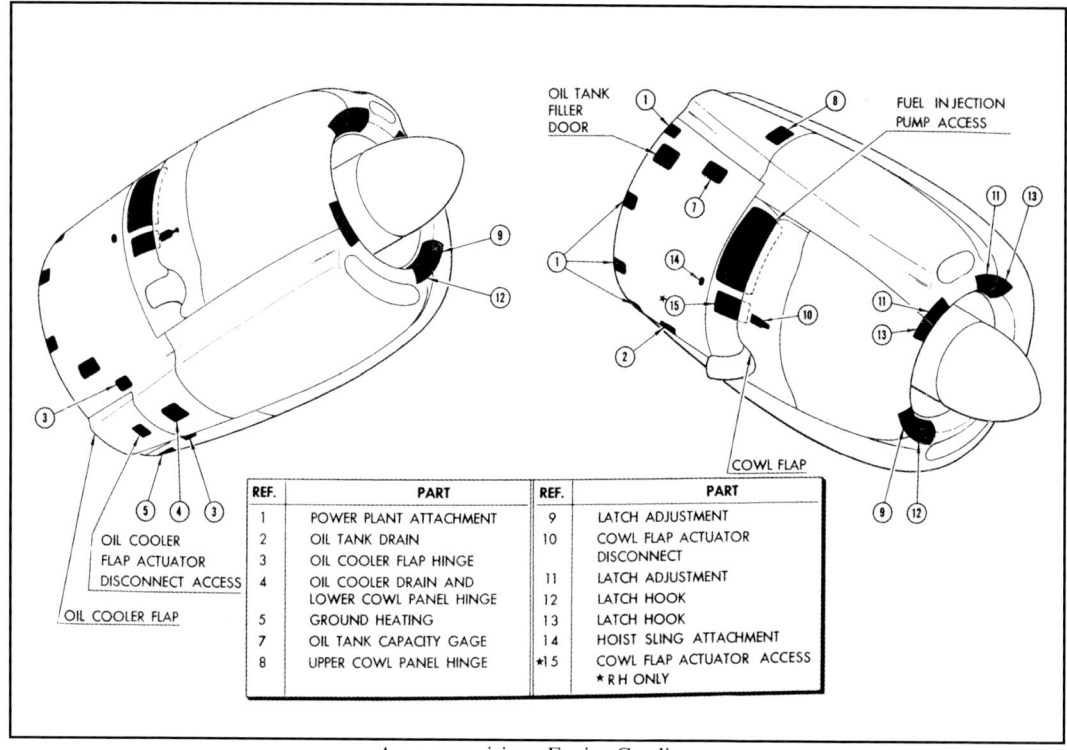

REF.	PART	REF.	PART
1	POWER PLANT ATTACHMENT	9	LATCH ADJUSTMENT
2	OIL TANK DRAIN	10	COWL FLAP ACTUATOR DISCONNECT
3	OIL COOLER FLAP HINGE	11	LATCH ADJUSTMENT
4	OIL COOLER DRAIN AND LOWER COWL PANEL HINGE	12	LATCH HOOK
5	GROUND HEATING	13	LATCH HOOK
7	OIL TANK CAPACITY GAGE	14	HOIST SLING ATTACHMENT
8	UPPER COWL PANEL HINGE	*15	COWL FLAP ACTUATOR ACCESS *R H ONLY

Access provision - Engine Cowling

outer nacelles contained the cabin supercharger units and deicing fluid tanks.

Hydraulically boosted conventional flight controls made the Constellation a docile machine to fly. Since no other aircraft this size had been produced with hydraulic flight controls before, Lockheed built a specific testing system. Four V-8 engines drove four hydraulic pumps to investigate potential problems, and cold boxes were placed around the components to simulate the temperature of high altitude flight. Two hundred hours of rigorous, full-control yoke movement tests were conducted. They proved that Lockheed's design was sound.

There were two 1,500 psi. hydraulic systems. The primary control boost system ran the flight controls, while the secondary system powered the wheel brakes, nosewheel steering, landing gear, and flaps. In the beginning, there was no way to tie the systems together in the event one became inoperative, but this was rectified later by the addition of a cross-over valve. Earlier aircraft were retrofitted.

The unique tail was an all-metal cantilever structure with three rudders and two conventional elevators. Each vertical stabilizer had a fabric-covered rudder mounted on anti-friction bearings and an anti servo trim tab. The outboard vertical stabilizers and rudders were interchangeable. All metal mass-balanced elevators were also mounted on anti-friction bearings and were interchangeable left and right.

An aircraft the size of the Constellation would require a massive landing gear to withstand both the weight of the aircraft and the forces of hard landings and rough runways. Lockheed engineers designed a tricycle landing gear that appeared a bit spindly at first. However, closer inspection revealed a stout, well-built design.

All three landing gear units were hydraulically operated and were fully enclosed when retracted. Each main landing gear leg had a single oleo for shock absorption and a single axle for dual main wheels. Dual tyres (17.00 x 20) were fitted to each main landing gear to evenly distribute the weight of the aircraft on runways and taxiways. The parking and toe-actuated wheel brakes operated multiple disc units on each main wheel. The nose gear was rather long and castored via differential braking during turns. Later examples would feature hydraulic nosewheel steering. The dual nose wheels were canted towards each other where they rested on the ground, which lessened the wear on the tyre on the outside of sharp turns. It was a very practical design that would help keep costs down for the customér.

Wright Aeronautical spent a lot of time developing the R-3350, an engine that would see the Constellation through its service life and power numerous other aircraft designs past the dawn of the jet age. It could be argued that the R-3350 became the most developed radial piston engine in its later 3,700 horsepower Turbo Compound version.

After it was decided an engine of this size would be used, Lockheed kept two powerplants

Access provision - Empenage

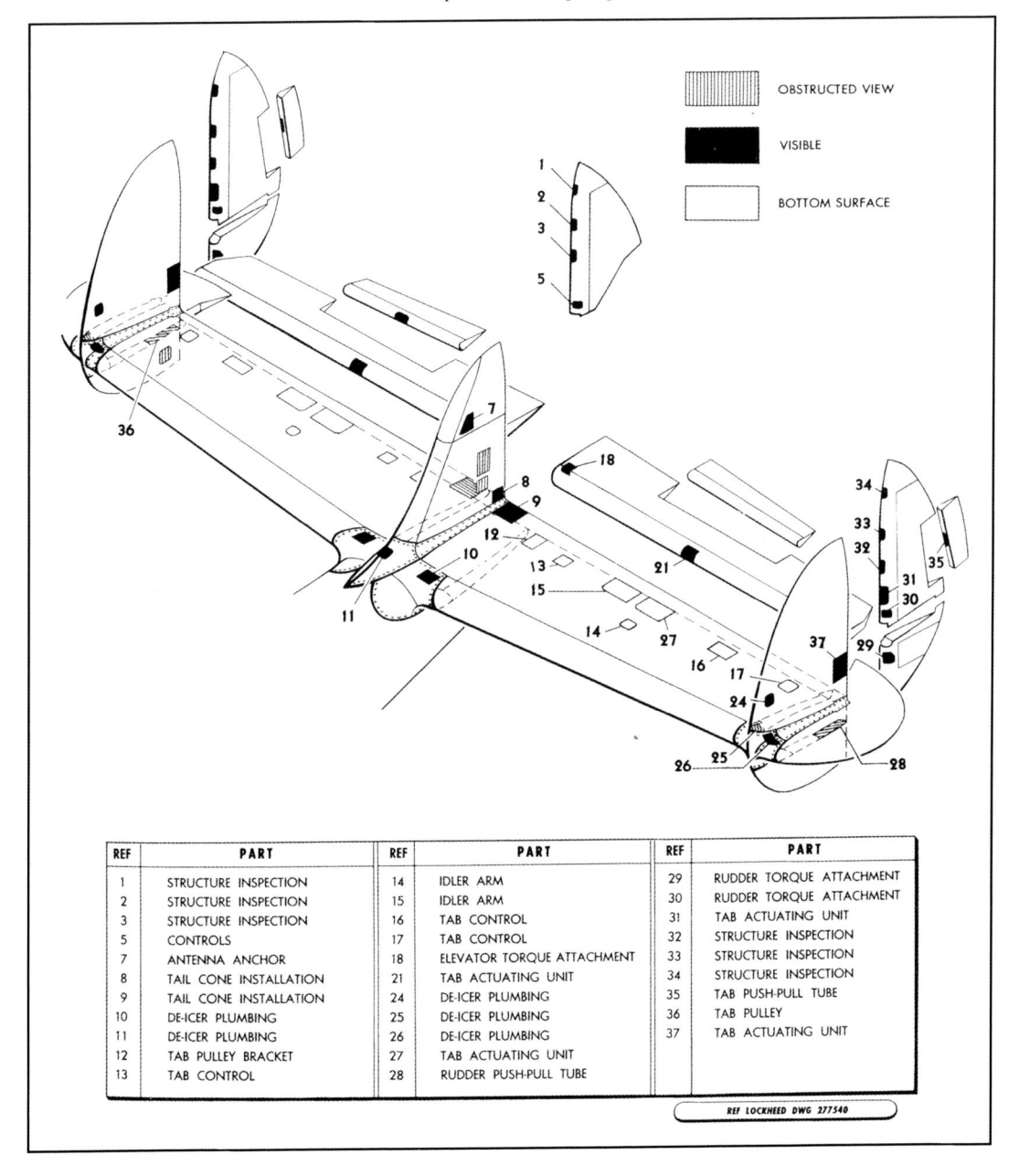

REF	PART	REF	PART	REF	PART
1	STRUCTURE INSPECTION	14	IDLER ARM	29	RUDDER TORQUE ATTACHMENT
2	STRUCTURE INSPECTION	15	IDLER ARM	30	RUDDER TORQUE ATTACHMENT
3	STRUCTURE INSPECTION	16	TAB CONTROL	31	TAB ACTUATING UNIT
5	CONTROLS	17	TAB CONTROL	32	STRUCTURE INSPECTION
7	ANTENNA ANCHOR	18	ELEVATOR TORQUE ATTACHMENT	33	STRUCTURE INSPECTION
8	TAIL CONE INSTALLATION	21	TAB ACTUATING UNIT	34	STRUCTURE INSPECTION
9	TAIL CONE INSTALLATION	24	DE-ICER PLUMBING	35	TAB PUSH-PULL TUBE
10	DE-ICER PLUMBING	25	DE-ICER PLUMBING	36	TAB PULLEY
11	DE-ICER PLUMBING	26	DE-ICER PLUMBING	37	TAB ACTUATING UNIT
12	TAB PULLEY BRACKET	27	TAB ACTUATING UNIT		
13	TAB CONTROL	28	RUDDER PUSH-PULL TUBE		

REF LOCKHEED DWG 277540

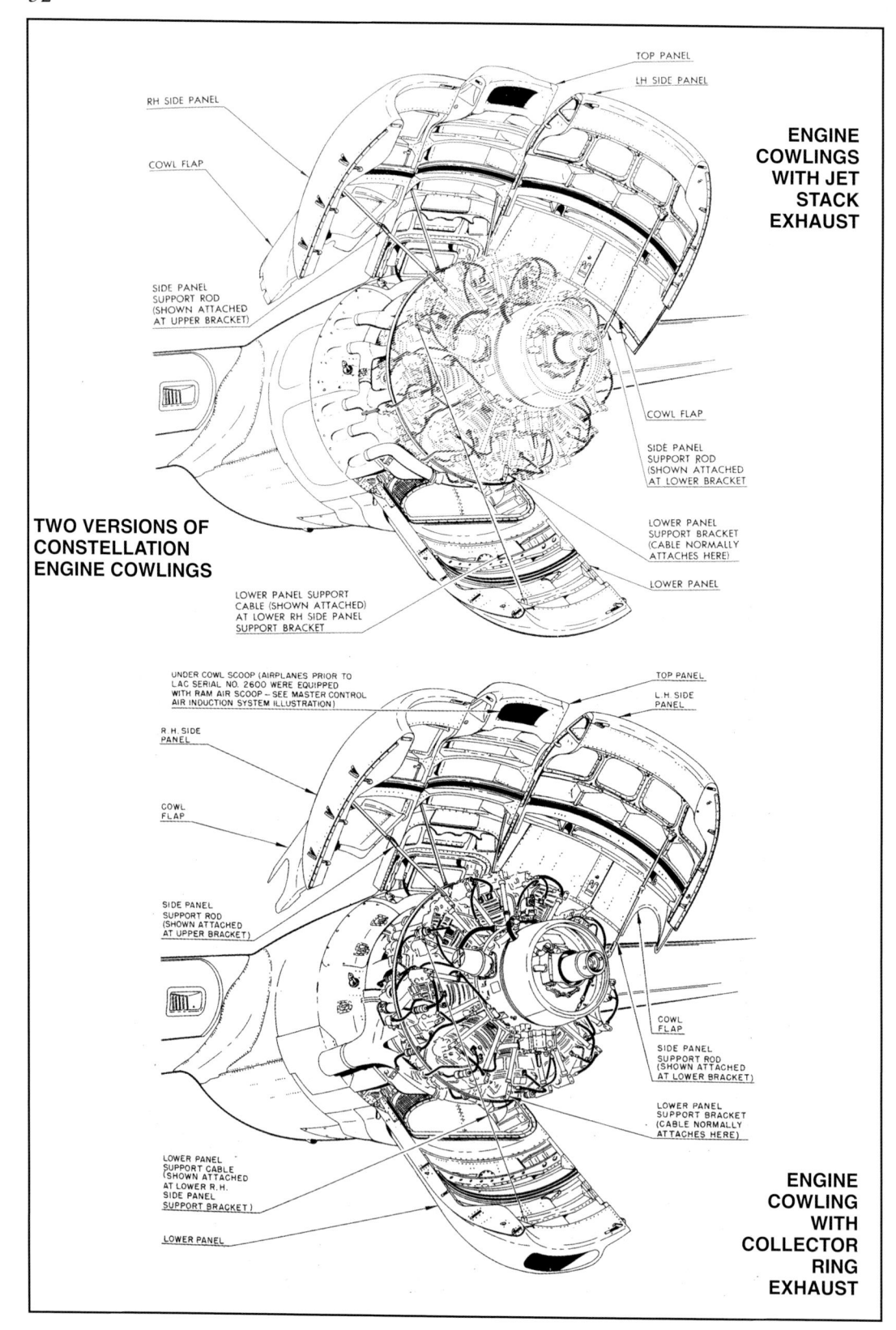

TWO VERSIONS OF CONSTELLATION ENGINE COWLINGS

ENGINE COWLINGS WITH JET STACK EXHAUST

- TOP PANEL
- LH SIDE PANEL
- RH SIDE PANEL
- COWL FLAP
- SIDE PANEL SUPPORT ROD (SHOWN ATTACHED AT UPPER BRACKET)
- COWL FLAP
- SIDE PANEL SUPPORT ROD (SHOWN ATTACHED AT LOWER BRACKET)
- LOWER PANEL SUPPORT BRACKET (CABLE NORMALLY ATTACHES HERE)
- LOWER PANEL
- LOWER PANEL SUPPORT CABLE (SHOWN ATTACHED) AT LOWER RH SIDE PANEL SUPPORT BRACKET

ENGINE COWLING WITH COLLECTOR RING EXHAUST

- UNDER COWL SCOOP (AIRPLANES PRIOR TO LAC SERIAL NO. 2600 WERE EQUIPPED WITH RAM AIR SCOOP — SEE MASTER CONTROL AIR INDUCTION SYSTEM ILLUSTRATION)
- TOP PANEL
- L.H. SIDE PANEL
- R.H. SIDE PANEL
- COWL FLAP
- SIDE PANEL SUPPORT ROD (SHOWN ATTACHED AT UPPER BRACKET)
- COWL FLAP
- SIDE PANEL SUPPORT ROD (SHOWN ATTACHED AT LOWER BRACKET)
- LOWER PANEL SUPPORT BRACKET (CABLE NORMALLY ATTACHES HERE)
- LOWER PANEL SUPPORT CABLE (SHOWN ATTACHED AT LOWER R.H. SIDE PANEL SUPPORT BRACKET)
- LOWER PANEL

Sub-assembly production was a major factor in Constellation manufacturing.

Lockheed had factories in Burbank, Beverly Hills and Bakersfield, California where components were made and then transported to the Burbank assembly line. A wing root fairing is being shaped here by hydraulic presses in the jig. Cleco fasteners hold the sheet metal in place while workers rivet the pieces together. *(Lockheed)*

in mind for the aircraft: Wright's R-3350 and Pratt and Whitney's R-2800. Albeit still in development, both engines would provide the necessary power for a new generation of transports, bombers, and fighters. As war clouds gathered in the late 1930s, most airframe companies took particular notice of engine development and planned accordingly. TWA's Tomlinson had the foresight to believe that the R-3350 would be developed into a reliable high-horsepower engine, but Lockheed hedged their bets by keeping the R-2800 option open.

Wright's R-3350 engine, a twin-row, 18-cylinder, air-cooled radial engine, was designed in 1936. The first test run occurred in May 1937, and problems immediately cropped up; however, problems were expected at this stage in the development of a huge new engine. Engineers began to tackle bugs relating to proper mixture distribution, induction system backfires, and later, in-flight fires. Kept relatively secret, the first details of the R-3350 became available in the 1944-45 *Jane's All The Worlds' Aircraft*.

Wright realised that some of the R-3350's teething problems were caused by the General Electric turbo-superchargers that pumped air into the engines. In 1938, Wright designed and produced its turbo-supercharger for the R-3350. Other issues with the R-3350 included the lack of fuel injection, the need for water injection, and better cylinder and induction cooling. These problems were addressed late in the war, or post-war, and directly contributed to the success of the Constellation. The R-3350 became a robust and reliable aircraft engine for both military and civilian applications.

The R-3350-35 Duplex Cyclone was the engine chosen to power the Model 049 Constellation. It provided 2,200 horsepower at 2,800 RPM at sea level. Weighing in at 2,670 pounds, the engine had a diameter of 55.78 inches and a length of 76.26 inches. The 100/130 octane fuel was vaporised in a Chandler Evans downdraft carburettor that automatically compensated for varying air densities by changing the fuel nozzle pressure in response to engine acceleration and power demands.

The front and rear engine cases and

supercharger housing were machined magnesium. The nose section housed propeller reduction gears, front oil pump drive, prop governor pump, distributor drive, and tappets for the front cylinder valves. The supercharger housing contained the impeller, diffuser, drive gearing, and induction passages. The rear of the supercharger housing case included the accessory drives for dual magnetos, tachometer, hydraulic pump, vacuum pump, starter, two generators, and a spare accessory drive. All gears were machined from steel and had hardened teeth. The rear case cover could be removed to provide access for maintenance.

The R-3350 was quickly recognised as an essential engine for the USA. Wright expanded its production facilities to include two entire manufacturing and assembly plants, and licence-built copies from Chrysler's Chicago, Illinois, engine plant.

Wartime chronology

Before looking in detail at the early days of production and test flying of the Constellation, it is worth investigating the protracted overall chronology of events from December 1940 to February 1946.

December 1940: War Department informed Lockheed that all commercial aircraft production would probably be terminated.

January 1941: The War Department urged Lockheed to increase their P-38 programme. It also intimated that the Constellation project was slowing down vital warplane production. Lockheed replied this was not the case, but that to cooperate with the government as much as possible, they would indefinitely postpone production of the Constellation and would engineer and build only three prototypes.

February 1941: Wright Aeronautical Corporation informed Lockheed that the GR-3350 B-version prototype had failed to produce either the promised output power or desired fuel consumption. Wright indicated it would substitute a newly designed C-version, which was being developed for the Boeing B-29 Superfortress bomber. It meant that not only would there be a further delay in engine delivery but that Lockheed would have to engineer an entirely new powerplant installation.

4 May 1941: The Office of Production Management (OPM) notified Lockheed that they did not object to the construction of three prototypes, but any decision on quantity production was deferred. Furthermore, prototype construction must not interfere with military orders. Of the three prototypes, one was to be a Model 49 and one a Model 349.

The Model 349 was a military version of the longer-range Model 149, identical except with a large cargo door and reinforced flooring.

13 September 1941: OPM advised Lockheed that ten additional aircraft could be produced during 1943, but none were to be released to the airlines.

10 October 1941: OPM countermanded their directive of 13 September 1941.

22 December 1941: OPM indicated that production of eighty aircraft could be authorised. However, these would have to meet the specifications of the US government, TWA, and Pan Am. No delivery to airlines was authorised.

20 February 1942: Government notified Lockheed it intended to place a formal contract for 180 Model C-69 (L-49) aircraft.

30 March 1942: Lockheed notified that the government would own all Constellations produced. TWA and Pan Am would operate all aircraft for the government. Production to total 260 aircraft was broken down as follows: fifty Model 49s and thirty Model 349s on airline contract; 180 C-69s on Army contract.

30 April 1942: Army indicated it intended to buy initial eighty aircraft directly.

20 May 1942: Lockheed scheduled first flight of the prototype for 31 August 1942.

20 May 1942: Army inspected prototype Model 49. Percentage of completion of main assemblies was as follows:
• Fuselage and wings, ninety per cent.
• Tail, sixty per cent.
• Tail controls, forty per cent.
• Power plant installation, five per cent.
• Hydraulic system, fifty per cent.
• Landing gear, seventy-five per cent.

21 May 1942: Army issued clarification of government identification of Constellation models as follows:

1. C-69: original civilian order for fifty aircraft (did not include KLM order).
2. C-69A: additional civilian order of thirty aircraft.
3. C-69B: Army order for 180 aircraft (Model 349).

8 June 1942: Lockheed pointed out to the Army how previous government directives resulted in long delays to Constellation programme. Together with financial outlays by Lockheed related to increased military production, meant that they could no longer manufacture the first eighty aircraft for the original price. Because these eighty machines were to be built to Army standards and were to be operated only by the airlines for the Army, Lockheed thought that it could not build them unless a new price per aircraft were determined. Lockheed suggested spreading research and development costs over all 260 aircraft, with new prices to be:
- 50 Model 49s at $408,800 each.
- 210 Model 349s at $583,600 each.

26 June 1942: Army initiated procurement of first 80 aircraft.

2 July 1942: Assistant Secretary of War made the final decision that the original contract between Lockheed and TWA was to be honoured. Remaining 251 aircraft were to be purchased directly by the government. TWA and Pan Am both would have repurchase rights. Contracts for the two airlines, which made up the balance of the first eighty aircraft, were to be assigned to government.

Quite a well-known - and obviously posed picture of the Constellation production line, with workers apparently swarming all over aircraft '34'.

Bulkheads and stringers for a fuselage section are bolted into a jig. Sheet aluminum is then placed over the structure and riveted in place. The jigs ensured each assembly turned out straight and true. Each section of the Constellation was built in this manner. *(Lockheed)*

14 July 1942: Army issued new production breakdown as follows:
1. 20 C-69s of 65,000 pounds gross weight.
2. 30 C-69As of 67,000 pounds gross weight and with a large cargo door.
3. 210 C-69Bs, Lockheed Model 349s of 86,000 pounds gross weight.

This directive dropped all Model 149s from the order.

31 August 1942: Date for first flight of the prototype; flight was delayed.

21 September 1942: First flight of Boeing XB-29 prototype, which was equipped with virtually identical R-3350 C engines. In the next twenty-six hours of test flying of the B-29, there were sixteen engine changes and twenty-two carburettor changes.

8 December 1942: Wright advises Lockheed that it is unsafe to fly either the Constellation or the Ventura Ventellation, both equipped with R-3350s, until specific changes are made.

30 December 1942: The Number 2 XB-29 makes a successful emergency landing with number four engine on fire and with an uncontrollable runaway propeller.

8 January 1943: Constellation prototype makes first flight. Six flights on first day were all completed successfully.

18 February 1943: Number 1 XB-29, with Eddie Allen at the controls, crashes due to engine fire. Eleven on board and nineteen on the ground are killed.

20 February 1943: The C-69 was grounded by Army pending investigation of R-3350 fires.

13 April 1943: C-69 was cleared for further flight testing after engine modifications by Wright.

18 May 1943: Army determines that 210 C-69Bs cannot be produced until early in 1945 due to engine unavailability. The Army considered having only an initial twenty C-69s built. It was believed this would allow an increase of P-38 production as well as free up material for the production of Douglas C-54A aircraft.

3 June 1943: Lockheed agreed to build only three C-69 aircraft, and not more than 10 C-69's per month through 1944, totalling 80 machines.

16 June 1943: Army stated the original contract for a total of 260 aircraft is still in force.

24 June 1943: Army indicated contract to be altered, and 207 C-69B aircraft would now be C-69 model.

August 1943: Army verbally directed Lockheed to stop all C-69 production work and concentrate on the P-38.

6 October 1943: Army confirmed that all Lockheed production personnel assigned to the C-69 project had been reassigned to P-38 assembly line to increase the rate of production.

14 October 1943: Lockheed confirmed verbal agreement of 18 September 1943, to cease all C-69 work except on the first two machines.

17 December 1943: Lockheed indicated the seriousness of delays caused by problems with the R-3350 engine. Pinpoints problems as high-tension ignition cable failure and unscrewing cylinder heads during flight. For these reasons, Number 1 Constellation flew only three months in 1943.

7 April 1944: Army directed Lockheed to cease development of C-69B model and to produce three C-69B aircraft on contract as C-69 aircraft.

17 April 1944: Number 2 Constellation sets a coast-to-coast record.

12 July 1944: Right main landing gear of number three aircraft collapsed during taxiing. The cause was a welding failure. New design using forgings eliminated much welding.

30 August 1944: Lockheed requested aircraft weight increase to improve utility. Recommended 100,000-pound take-off weight, 87,000-pound landing weight, and fuel capacity increase to 5,200 gallons total.

5 September 1944: Ten crews from Air Transport Command (ATC) assigned TDY on West Coast for C-69 transition training.

27 October 1944: Army approved 100,000-pound take-off weight starting with the number 111 machine.

13 November 1944: Crews, now fifteen in number, permanently assigned to West Coast to continue C-69 training.

8 December 1944: Lockheed proposed amending the contract to 101 C-69 aircraft; ten C-69C (100,000-pound) aircraft, and nine C-69 machines on original TWA contract, for a total of 120 machines.

22 December 1944: Army memo indicated that shifting production personnel to the P-38 line had indeed curtailed C-69 production with only ten machines completed as of this date. No more than 120 aircraft were expected to be built for the Army.

2 January 1945: Army proposed to limit production to 223 aircraft. Crews assigned to newly formed 159th AAF Base Unit, the first C-69 squadron.

23 January 1945: TWA's Intercontinental Division assigned the job of testing and proving C-69 by the Army.

3 February 1945: 159th AAF Base Unit disbanded and personnel reassigned.

15 February 1945: Army formally amended contract and reduced total number of C-69s to seventy three.

17 April 1945: Lockheed proposed building last fifty-three machines, out of a total seventy-three, at a fixed price of $706,845 each.

3 August 1945: Lockheed informed that their P-80 jet fighter now had priority over both the P-38 and the C-69.

15 August 1945: Army terminated C-69 contract at fourteen aircraft.

20 August 1945: Army questioned the need for C-69s beyond 1the fourteen C-69s accepted to date. Six additional machines were nearing completion.

20 August 1945: Lockheed removed production personnel from six C-69s under construction and assigned them to number twenty-one aircraft, which was to be delivered to commercial airlines.

23 August 1945: Government reinstated six undelivered aircraft.

27 August 1945: Army terminated fifty more aircraft from the total order.

19 September 1945: Army indicated the intention of retaining twenty C-69s already or about to be delivered .

20 September 1945: All C-69s were grounded as a result of the Constellation accident at Topeka, Kansas.

26 September 1945: Army recommended termination of three C-69D (100,000-pound version) that were still on contract and were in addition to twenty C-69's.

11 October 1945: Investigation of Topeka accident resulted in twenty-eight safety changes by Lockheed on undelivered C-69s.

19 October 1945: Formal cancellation of three C-69D machines (100,000-pound version), leaving a total of twenty on contract, of which fifteen had been delivered.

12 November 1945: Army decided to offer five undelivered C-69s to Lockheed for sale.

23 November 1945: Offer to Lockheed for

On the assembly line, a Constellation fuselage is about to receive one of its wings.

five C-69s made officially.

26 December 1945: Lockheed made a counter-offer to Army for five C-69s, provided it was accepted before 4 January 1946.

27 December 1945: Army terminated the remaining five C-69s on contract, meaning that they had been sold to Lockheed.

21 January 1946: Lockheed indicated that four of Army's fifteen aircraft had been offered to KLM, which were later delivered.

1 February 1946: Army decides to retain the remaining 11 C-69s and use them within the United States.

The prototype takes to the skies

During 1941 and 1942 construction of the prototype went ahead as fast as Lockheed's military aircraft commitments would permit and on 9 January 1943, bearing the registration NX25800, it made its first flight from Lockheed's airfield at Burbank, California.

Kelly Johnson had previously written to Lt Col Bernard D Morley, Air Corps AFF Resident Representative on 1 January 1943 detailing the plans for the first flight, which were approved the next day.

'The flight crew for the first flight will consist of the following personnel: Chief Pilot, Edmund T. Allen; Second Pilot, Milo Burcham; Flight Engineer, Rudy L Thoren; Observer, Kelly Johnson; Mechanic, Dick Stanton. It is proposed that permission be obtained to use the East-West runway at Lockheed Air Terminal for the first take-off. This runway is approximately 4600 feet long, having no obstructions at the west end and a heading which avoids populated areas and provides emergency landing fields, if necessary. The airplane will be loaded to approximately 63,000 pounds on take-off, the center of gravity position of twenty-six per cent, the landing gear extended. This gives a wing loading of 38.2 pounds per square foot and a take-off power loading of 7.15 pounds per horsepower. It is planned to carry 1600 gallons of fuel, equally divided into four tanks and full oil. This provides an initial flight of one and one-half hours at fairly high power and specific fuel consumption plus four hours at maximum endurance plus 100 gallons for take-off and landing. With this fuel load, it is possible to fly over eight hours if necessary'.

'After take-off, it is turning north to go out over the desert for the initial test. Major Shoop has stated that he will be flying a B-17 which will take-off after us to photograph the C-69 in the air. It is proposed that the actual flight plan be discussed with Major Shoop within the next few hours, and it is suggested that any pictures which may be taken in the air be done from a distance of at least 1000 feet, and during the first one-half hour of flying. After that period of time, we will want to check a number of conditions of control and stability, during which time it would not be advisable to have another airplane close behind. The first flight will probably take about one and one-half hours, at the end of which time it is proposed a landing be made at Muroc Dry Lake. It will be possible to retract the landing gear if conditions warrant it. None of the hydraulically operated landing gear doors will be on the airplane the first flight. For the conditions noted above, the minimum take-off distance for the airplane is less than 1000 feet, and the maximum available rate of climb is over 3000 feet per minute. The control speed with one outboard engine out is well under 100 mph, with a zero yaw. After passing over the field the second time, the initial flight climb will be undertaken to 10,000 feet. Photographic records of all operating conditions will be taken continually'.

'At 10,000 feet, manouverability, engines, instruments, and controls will be checked. The landing gear extension will be tested and a number of stalls made with power off, with zero, twenty-five per cent, fifty per cent, and seventy-five per cent flap setting. The landing at Muroc will be made with the seventy-five per cent flap setting, as this condition gives a very low landing speed of 77 mph for the gross weight involved and will not require the pilot to make a landing with the maximum ground effect the first time. Landing gross weight will be close to 59,800 pounds and the landing c.g. position twenty-nine per cent. Enough lead ballast weight will be carried in the airplane to enable the c.g. position to be shifted approximately five per cent for landing, if so desired'.

'A Lockheed truck with a driver and six

Another colour photograph of the Constellation assembly line, with aircraft having their engines hung.

The cockpit of a USAAF C-69, as seen in August 1944. The pilot's panels were identical, with a central panel for engine instruments. *(Lockheed)*

men, plus the airplane tow bar, ladders, and such equipment will be at Muroc at 1.00pm 5 Jan, to provide any necessary work which might be required for the second take-off. If all conditions are right, it will probably be desirable to shoot a number of landings at Muroc before returning to Lockheed Air Terminal.'

The prototype Constellation was the most heavily instrumented test aircraft of the time. In addition to the normal flight and engine instruments, four Automatic Observers were installed to take pictures of flight test instrument panels at half and one-second intervals. Well over 400 parameters were recorded.

The flight crew needed to make less technical observations, which included rating basic handling, climbs and descents, and a stall series. Stalls with flaps up, one-third flaps, two-thirds flaps, and full flaps were completed with very satisfactory results. These tests were somewhat of a non-event due to experience with the P-38 Lightning, but the docility of the stall characteristics would add to future pilot confidence and passenger safety. The Constellation would deliver the speed, but also allow approaches and landings at relatively low airspeeds.

Stability tests followed, and again, the Constellation performed like a thoroughbred. Stability on all three axes was strong, which confirmed wind tunnel data Lockheed had collected earlier in the programme. Steep turns and rapid pitch changes followed to observe control forces and speed changes.

In all, the first Model 049 Constellation made six takeoffs and landings that day, three by Milo Burcham and three by Eddie Allen, setting a record for a new aircraft. Eddie Allen summed up the general satisfaction with the new transport by saying, 'This thing works so perfect you don't need me around here any

Lockheed Model L-049/C-69 Constellation

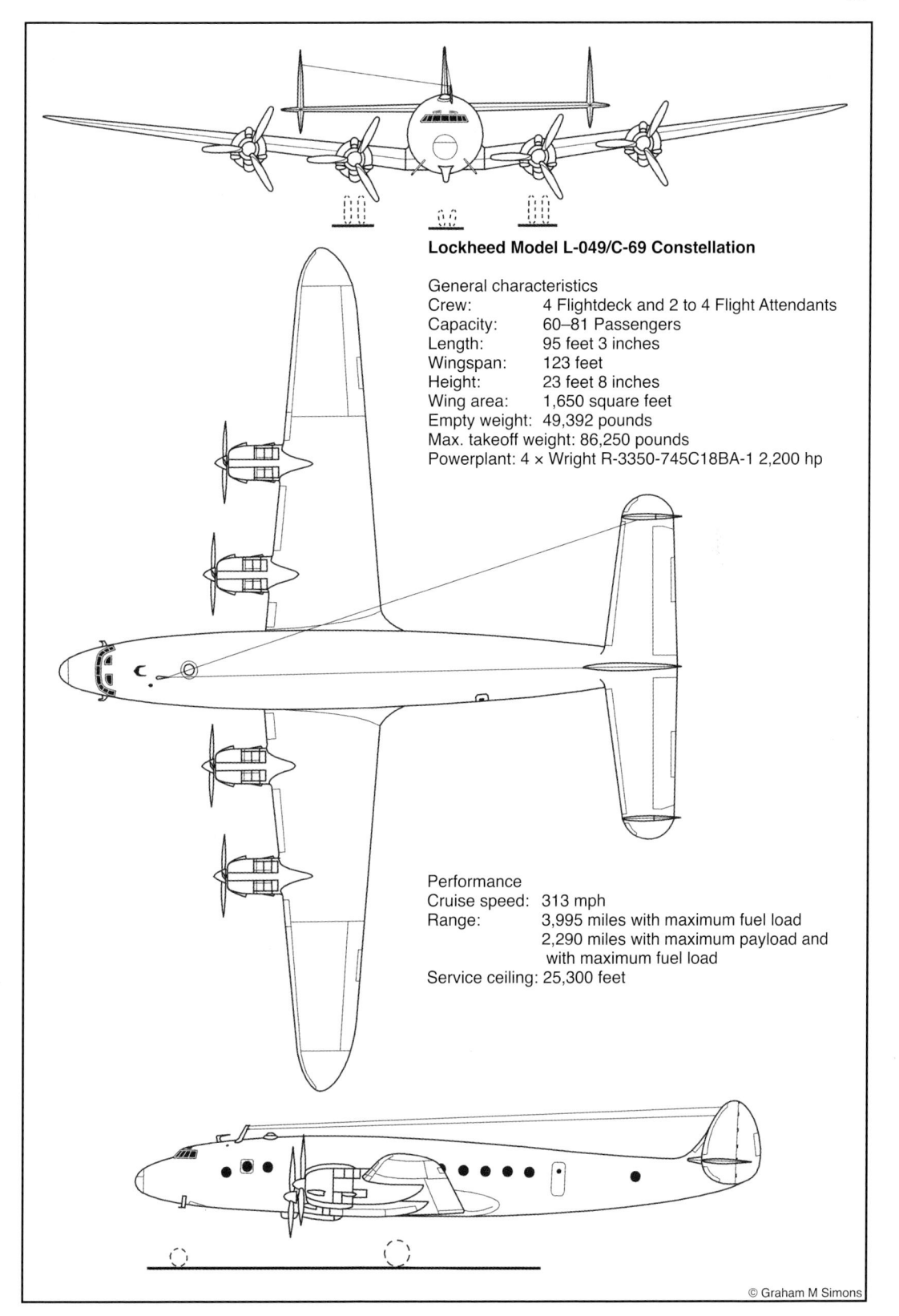

General characteristics
Crew: 4 Flightdeck and 2 to 4 Flight Attendants
Capacity: 60–81 Passengers
Length: 95 feet 3 inches
Wingspan: 123 feet
Height: 23 feet 8 inches
Wing area: 1,650 square feet
Empty weight: 49,392 pounds
Max. takeoff weight: 86,250 pounds
Powerplant: 4 × Wright R-3350-745C18BA-1 2,200 hp

Performance
Cruise speed: 313 mph
Range: 3,995 miles with maximum fuel load
2,290 miles with maximum payload and with maximum fuel load
Service ceiling: 25,300 feet

© Graham M Simons

more.' Some minor changes were made between flights, and several shortcomings were noted. The dullness of the flight test report from the first flight must have contrasted dramatically with the high emotion those involved probably felt. The report stated, 'Everything functioned without incident and with normal characteristics.'

Allen was killed less than six weeks later when the Boeing B-29 Superfortress prototype crashed.

After the first flight of fifty-eight minutes, during which the undercarriage was left down as a precautionary measure, the prototype landed at Muroc Field, now Edwards Air Force Base. The maximum gross weight, initially 68,000 pounds, had been increased during the design stages to 72,000 pounds then to 77,050 pounds and finally to 86,250 pounds by the time the prototype first flew, and flight testing soon showed that the landing weight could be increased from 70,000 to 75,000 pounds. The flight test programme progressed smoothly, the prototype flying with up two tons of water ballast in tanks in the cabin, filled by a four inch-diameter fire hose to simulate various loads and their effect at the different centre of gravity positions. The essential soundness of the Constellation design was demonstrated by the fact that few modifications of any note were incorporated into the production aircraft as a result of flight tests, despite the design's many advanced technical features.

At one stage the hydraulic power boost for the controls was found to be rather too sensitive, but the trouble was soon corrected, and the Constellation was the first transport to go into production with power-boosted controls. This system was designed before stick-force criteria had been established by NACA or the US armed services, and Lockheed conducted its own survey to determine the forces that would be most acceptable to pilots: these were finally set at fifty to eighty pounds on the elevator, one hundred and fifty pounds on the rudder pedal and ten foot-pounds on each aileron. The amount of stick force required under the most critical control conditions for each control surface was then determined, and a wide variety of boost systems and ratios were investigated. The final boost ratios were 9.33:1 for the elevators (ie the pilot's effort on the stick is multiplied 9.33 times by the boost system), 23:1 for the rudders and 26:1 for the ailerons. The prototype featured microswitches on the nose-wheel leg to check the loads upon it and a

In company with a Lockheed Vega, the prototype Constellation XC-69, construction number 1961, and registered as NX25800 is prepared for flight by Lockheed engineers prior to the maiden flight of the aircraft which took place on 9 January 1943, from the Lockheed Air Terminal at Burbank, California, and flown to the Muroc Army Air Base in the Mojave Desert where it made four local flights and then returned to Burbank the same day. The aircraft was inspected, modified and had the nose and main wheel doors fitted in readiness for its seventh flight which took place on 18 January 1943. This colour picture proves that the olive drab and light grey aircraft had the Lockheed 'star' emblem applied to the nose in white and yellow - or was it gold? *(Lockheed)*

Lockheed's Kelly Johnson, left with chief test pilot Milo Burcham in front of the prototype, NX25800. *(Lockheed)*

retractable tail skid under the rear fuselage for tail-down landings, and this was retained on production aircraft.

Flight tests of the prototype showed the Constellation to have an outstanding performance: its top speed of 347mph was faster than any four-engined bomber then in service and comparable with the cruising speeds of contemporary fighters. It met the design goal of one mile per gallon fuel consumption at the high cruising speed of 275mph on only fifty-two-and-a-half per cent power - a good deal faster than most other airliners cruised - while the payload for the design range proved much greater than originally estimated, and the original design specifications were met or exceeded in all respects. In addition, its ample power reserves gave it a very good engine-out performance; it was designed to fly at 15,000 feet with two engines stopped.

The Lockheed C-69

After the Pearl Harbor disaster, both TWA and Pan American had waived their rights to the Constellation in favour of the USAAF, which then took over the type under the designation C-69, the first production aircraft being completed as sixty-three-seat troop transports. A proposed redesign of the C-69 for airline use of July 1943 was designated Model 449. Up to sixteen short tons of freight could also be carried although the C-69's freighting potential was limited by the fact that, unlike the Douglas C-54, it had no special freight doors. The war ended before any C-69 units could be formed, and the type did not see service in either the European or Pacific theatres of operations.

The Army initially increased the C-69 order to fifty, later boosting it to two hundred and sixty transport machines. Still later, when the end of the war seemed imminent, the order was reduced to seventy-three, then finally terminated after only fifteen had been built. However, the Army agreed to accept five additional nearly completed aircraft. The Army Air Force had accorded low priority to the programme, stopping production seventeen times in favour of Lockheed's combat aircraft. Thus, twenty of the forty Constellations Hughes ordered emerged in olive-drab paint rather than polished aluminium and bright red TWA logo - that is, all except the first one, which sported TWA markings.

The prototype was officially handed over to the USAAF on 28 July 1943 as a C-69-1-LO with the military serial 43-10309. The constructor's number was 1961, and it was later converted to the XC-69E-LO variant on being re-engined with four 2,100hp Pratt & Whitney Double Wasp R-2800-34 radials of the same type as fitted to the Douglas DC-6.

Hughes had astutely worked out a deal with

The interior of a Constellation - allegedly the prototype - as seen during construction, looking forward in the cabin from rear bulkhead. The inside surface of pressure fuselage is lined with Kapok Unisorb felt, covered with aluminium foil for heat and sound insulation. *(Lockheed)*

the Army giving TWA jurisdiction over the first Constellation until it was accepted by TWA, after which it was to be immediately turned over to the Air Forces. This arrangement permitted TWA to conduct acceptance shakedown flights. Hughes and Frye decided to fly such a flight while trying for a new transcontinental speed record, hoping to reap favourable publicity from the world's first real view of the new machine.

There were big plans to publicize the introduction of this new transport in service with TWA. Hughes wanted to be at the controls of what would be a record-breaking, cross-country flight carrying press and Hollywood celebrities.

He had earlier established a reputation as a pilot. In fact, Hughes was awarded the Collier Trophy for an around-the-world record flight in 1938. He flew his Model 14 at an average speed of 206 miles an hour over a 15,000-mile route in 3 days, 19 hours, and 9 minutes. Lockheed had not worked with him on that venture, although it was with a Lockheed machine. He had the extra fuel tanks installed on his own.

Hughes would have to be checked out on the Constellation before attempting the cross-country flight, of course. So, before it was delivered to TWA, Milo Burcham, Dick Stanton as flight engineer, and Kelly Johnson took Hughes and Jack Frye on a demonstration and indoctrination flight. Frye was observing, but Hughes was to learn how the airliner performed and how best to handle it.

Lockheed's procedure for checking out a new pilot was to go through the manoeuvres carefully, then have the student follow through on the controls from the copilot seat.

Kelly Johnson: 'We had just taken off from Burbank and were only a few thousand feet over the foothills behind the plant when Hughes said to Milo:' Why don't you show me how this thing stalls?' So Milo lowered the flaps and gear, put on a moderate amount of power, pulled the airplane up, and stalled it. The Constellation had fine stall characteristics, not falling off, and recovering in genteel fashion.'

'Hughes turned to Milo and said "Hell, that's no way to stall. Let me do it".'

'Milo turned the controls over to him. I was standing between them in the cockpit. Hughes reached up, grabbed all four throttles and applied takeoff power with the flaps full down. The airplane was so lightly loaded it would practically fly on the slip stream alone. Hughes then proceeded to pull back the control all the way, as far as it would go, to stall the airplane.'

'Never before nor since have I seen an airspeed indicator read zero in the air. But that's the speed we reached - zero - with a big, four-engine airplane pointed 90 degrees to the horizon and almost no airflow over any of the surfaces except what the propellers were providing. Then the airplane fell forward enough to give us some momentum. Just inertia did it, not any aerodynamic control.'

Not the best of images, but a historic one nevertheless. C-69, number 1961 takes to the skies for the first time.
(Lockheed)

The passenger interior of a USAAF C-69, as seen in February 1945 was pretty spartan, but that was standard for military transports. It appears to be 'three across' on the bench seats, with extra seating down the fuselage side.
(Lockheed)

'At that point, I was floating against the ceiling, yelling, "Up flaps! Up flaps!" I was afraid that we'd break the flaps, since we'd got into a very steep angle when we pitched down. Or that we'd break the tail off with very high flap loads.'

'Milo jerked the flaps up and got the airplane under control again with about 2,000 feet between us and the hills. I was very much concerned with Hughes's idea of how to stall a big transport.'

'We continued on our flight to Palmdale Airport, where we were going to practise takeoffs and landings. That whole desert area was open country in those days and an ideal place for test flying.'

Once back on the runway, Burcham and Hughes exchanged seats. On takeoff from Burbank, Burcham had shown Hughes what the critical speeds were, so Hughes took the transport back into the sky. But he had great difficulty in keeping it on a straight course. He used so much thrust and developed so much torque that the aircraft kept angling closer and closer to the control tower. The Constellation circled the field without incident and came in for an acceptable landing. Then Hughes decided to make additional flights, and on the next takeoff, he came even closer to the control tower, with an even greater angle of yaw. He was not correcting adequately with the rudder. He made several more takeoffs and landings, each worse than the last. He was not getting any better, only worse. Kelly Johnson again: 'I was not only concerned for the safety of all aboard, but for the preservation of the airplane. It still belonged to us. Jack Frye was sitting in the first row of passenger seats, and I went back to talk to him. "Jack, this is getting damned dangerous," I said. "What should I do?"

'Do what you think is right, Kelly,' he said. That was no great help; he didn't want to be the one to cross Hughes. I returned to the cockpit. What I thought was the right thing to do was to stop this. And on the sixth takeoff, which was atrocious, the most dangerous of them all, I waited until we were clear of the tower and at pattern altitude, before I said: 'Milo, take this thing home.'

'Hughes turned and looked at me as though I had stabbed him, then glanced at Milo. I repeated, 'Milo, take this thing home.' There was no question about who was running the airplane program. Milo got in the pilot's seat, I took the copilot's seat, and we flew home. Hughes was livid with rage. I had given him the ultimate insult for a pilot, indicating essentially that he couldn't fly competently.'

'A small group was waiting for us at the factory to hear Hughes's glowing report on his first flight as the pilot of the Constellation. That's not what they heard.'

'Robert Gross was furious with me. What did I mean, insulting our first and best customer? It was damned poor judgment, he said. Hibbard didn't tell me so forcefully that I'd made a mistake because he always considered another person's feelings, but he definitely was unhappy and let me know it. Perhaps most angry of all was the company's publicity manager, Bert Holloway. He had a press flight scheduled that would result in national attention, headlines in newspapers across the country and in the aviation press around the world. Because, of course, the machine would set a speed record. Would Hughes follow through as planned? By that time, I didn't care what anyone else said.

'It was a frigid reception I received next day at the plant. When I explained the situation, that in my judgment I did the only thing I could to keep Hughes from crashing the plane, and then Hughes later agreed to spend a couple of days learning how to 'fly the plane as our pilot would demonstrate, the atmosphere thawed.

'We offered a bonus to our flight crew to check Hughes out in the plane over the next

Five USAAF C-69s Constellations sit on the Lockheed's outdoor finishng ramp at Burbank awaiting delivery, sometime in March 1945. Note the over-wing walkway markings on the aircraft closest to the camera and the lack of spinners on three of the four engines. *(Lockheed)*

C-69-5-LO 42-94538 was used to test the Speedpak freight container. *(Lockheed)*

weekend. Rudy Thoren, our chief flight test engineer, took my place. I never flew with Hughes again; it was mutually agreeable.'

On his next time in the Constellation, Hughes changed his attitude considerably. He followed instructions carefully. He must have made fifty or sixty practice takeoffs and landings over that weekend. In fact, he was flying right up to takeoff time for the cross-country flight.

Many sources suggest that the aircraft Hughes and Frye used for this record-breaking flight was the XC-69 NX25800, which possibly has something to do with their interpretation of the deal Hughes had worked out with the Army giving TWA jurisdiction over the first Constellation for test flights as has already been mentioned. In fact, it was not 1961, but 1962, 43-10310. The aircraft was in full TWA colours and markings with 'The Transcontinental Line' titling, but it carried only the USAAF serial.

Weeks of preparation crystalised early Sunday evening 16 April 1944, when Howard Hughes and Jack Fry decided to depart the next morning as the weather outlook looked favourable. The aircraft had just returned on a flight from Las Vegas, Nevada, and was pronounced mechanically fit. Orders were given to gas up and crew and passengers were instructed to be on board by 3 am.

They departed Burbank at 3:56 am, 17 April for Washington, DC. Jack Frye was in command, Hughes as copilot. At exactly the halfway point to the minute by the flight plan, Jack and Hughes changed places. Also on board were Edward T Bolton, navigator, R L Proctor, flight engineer, and Charles L Glover as radioman.

Leo Baron, the Manager of TWA's Public Information Department, wrote the story up for Volume 8, No.4 of *'The Skyliner'*, TWAs house magazine, dated April 1944. 'Promptly at 3 am the passengers climbed aboard. There were twelve in all: Lawrence W Chiappino, Robert L Loomis, Ed J Minser, Orville R Olson, Lee Spruill and Richard de Campo, all of TWA; Rudy L Thoren, Richard Stanton and Thomas Watkins of Lockheed; Lt Col C A Shoop of the Army Air Forces, S J Solomon, Chairman of the Airlines Committee for US Air Policy and myself.

'The high loading steps were hauled away as the last passenger enplaned. Outside the ground crew completed the last minute preparations as casually as if they were servicing a DC-3 for a routine passenger flight. Across the semi darkened field a few score of onlookers stood in groups of two and three, their attention riveted on the activities about the plane. Word had got around that the Connie was about to leave and newspapermen were on hand to time her take-off.

'Up front the crew took their quarters. Wheel blocks were removed, brakes were released, and twenty husky mechanics pushed the plane backward into a position where the engines could be started. They spun on one by one, churning the air with the roar that echoed dully through the cabin.

'Seatbelts were fastened and in a few minutes

the Connie taxied out to the end of the asphalt runway, which stretched more than a mile through a corridor of dim lights. As Hughes wheeled the big ship about, I felt the tension which no-one else seemed to share. The others were chatting easily as though they were waiting for a cup of coffee and a breakfast roll from a lunch wagon.

'The four 2000 hp Wright Cyclone engines were revved up and almost before we knew it, the ship began to roll. In a matter of seconds, we were off the ground. By the time the last boundary light passed under our wing, we were several hundred feet in the air. "Nice takeoff" someone murmured.

'The climb was smooth and steady. At 15000 feet the plane levelled off. Lights from towns and villages far below us dwindled then faded as we crossed a range of mountains and headed across the desert. Bunks were made up, and most of the passengers sought sleep.

'First to find it was Chiappino, TWA's test pilot in many of the earlier trial flights of the Connie., who was finding that riding as a passenger was a novel pleasure. "Wake me up just before we get to Washington" he grinned as he turned in.'

'Olson, who only three years ago was a chief clerk in TWA's Traffic Department in Kansas City, but who since has amassed more than a thousand hours in the air, scouted around the galley for something to eat. He found ample breakfasts for all aboard. The coffee was cold in the Thermos jugs, but there was an electric heater aboard so that it could be re-heated. Olson designated himself steward for the flight, but no one among the few of us awake were interested in eating at the moment.

'Ed Minser, TWA's chief meteorologist, who had forecast the weather for the flight, peered out of the windows at frequent intervals, looking for landmarks or checkpoints. With slide rule and map he made unofficial computations of speed. Officially, that was the navigators business, but Minser wanted a record of his own.

'He whistled softly under his breath as he sighted Needles, Calif., directly under our left wing. To me, it was almost incredible for it takes eleven hours by the fastest train to cover the distance the Connie had negotiated in less than an hour.

'In a matter of minutes, Minser sighted Kingman, Ariz. Word came back from the

The first-ever Atlantic crossing by Constellation was undertaken by C-69C-1-LO 42-94550, seen here arriving at Orly Airport, when it flew from New York to Paris on 4 August 1945 in the record time of fourteen hours, twelve minutes.

C-69 number 1961 in flight. (Lockheed)

control room over the intercom phone that we were still cruising at 15,000 feet. The skies were cloudless, and the moon glinted sharply against the wings and fuselage. It was a beautiful -night, but a weather front was expected ahead. At the moment, however, it was "CAVU", ceiling and visibility unlimited.'

'The first flush of dawn crept across the skies shortly after five o'clock. At that altitude, Minser observed, we could see the dawn four or five minutes before any groundling who might happen to be about at that hour. It gave one the feeling of viewing a preview of the universe from a ringside seat.'

'Some of the sleepers began stirring in their bunks, and asked about breakfast. Olson and Lockheed's Tommy Watkins set about re-heating the coffee. Cups were handed around, and the talk passed from the flight to other subjects - opening of the big league baseball season the next day, the war, and similar topics.'

'Breakfast was enough to satisfy any hearty appetite. It came packed in boxes - orange juice, fruit, cereal, sweet rolls, coffee and milk.' Loomis relieved Frye at the co-pilot's seat while the latter came back in the cabin to eat. The flight, he reported, was going according to the book.

'The sun was just beginning to lift over the horizon when Minser pointed below. We were passing directly over San Francisco peaks, the highest mountains in Arizona with an elevation of some 12,000 feet. From the ground, these peaks stand like majestic monuments but from where we sat in the sky, they resembled small hills mantled heavily in snow. A few minutes later - in less time than it takes to drink a second cup of coffee - we had passed north of Winslow and veered slightly north of TWA's regular trans-continental course to pick up a great circle route.'

Rudy Thoren, Lockheed's chief flight test engineer, strolled into the control room and emerged a few' minutes later, chuckling. 'Bolton (the navigator) is complaining about his duties,' he reported. 'He says he's getting a stiff neck, turning it from right to left and back again to keep track of the checkpoints we're passing. "I told him that those weren't beacon lights, they're state boundaries".'

'Olson fished a 'crumpled telegram out of his pocket. He had received it just before we left, from his wife in Washington.

'This gave the Western Union people a shock,' he said. The message read: 'Triplets born today, two blonde, one brunette. Mother and babies doing nicely.' 'The clerk who read it thought I was nuts because I laughed about it,' said Olson. 'She didn't know they were puppies.

'We were crossing the continental divide when someone suggested a poker game. There were Olson, Loomis, Solomon and myself. We aroused Chiappino to make it five. Colonel Shoop joined us later. The poker game lasted until we were within fifteen minutes of Washington. Let it be said for the record that Olson was the winner by some $37 by the time we called it quits, and that should buy a lot of dog bones. I dropped $18, but will forever be grateful to the Connie, because had I been on an ordinary transport, flying from Los Angeles to Washington, I would have lost $86.45 by Minser's slide rule.'

'Over Northern New Mexico we began to pick up Weather. Skies grew thick and only occasionally did we sight the ground. As we passed over the higher mountain peaks, updrafts of air caught the Connie and bounced her a little but she rode sturdily through the turbulence wifh no discomfort to her passengers. It was like a battleship biting its way through heavy seas.

'Off to the North, we sighted a conical mountain, unfamiliar to most of us.'That's just south of Durango, Colorado,' said Minser, who knows the United States topography like most people know their way to their favorite drugstore.

'We were climbing now to get on top of the overcast. The mountains and mesas below were blotted out from view. Before long, we were riding along on the top of a solid overcast with a dull blue sky above us. We were not to see the ground again until we were crossing southern Ohio near Cincinnati. At 17,500 feet on instruments we leveled off again, which just cleared us over the cloud formations.

'Light icing conditions were encountered over Kansas. We climbed still higher to get out of it and reached 18,500 feet near Chanutel Even at that level, more than three miles above sea level, we were as comfortable as though we had our feet propped up in our living room. Outside, the temperature was below zero but owing to our cabin supercharger we were comfortable in our shirt-sleeves while Olson won hand after hand. That was our only complaint.

'We passed south of Kansas City, TWA's

Constellation production at Lockheeds Burbank facility shows various stages of fuselage completion. As the fuselage was finished it was turned 90 degrees and mated with wing panels, outer wing panels, the tail and engines. As the major components were added, the aircraft would proceed down the line and out the door at the far end. This shot shows how the centre-section wing was built integral with the fuselage. *(Lockheed)*

headquarters base',and reported our position over Butler, 60 miles to the south. St. Louis was quickly beneath as, but no one saw it, so thick was the overcast. Not until we were approaching Cincinnati did we break into the open and see the rolling Ohio countryside below through the scattered clouds. It was here that we reached our top speed as the plane was borne along in the arms of a favourable wind. The exact speed cannot be told, but it was enough to impress the most sceptical.

'According to plan, the descent should have now begun but because of thunderstorm conditions reported over the Alleghenies, it was delayed until we reached the Ohio river. Frye, who had taken over the controls somewhere in Eastern Kansas, began nosing the plane down gradually and it was at this point that I had the first sensation of speed I had ever felt in an airplane. At 7,000 feet, the ground seemed to be moving by as swiftly as it does to a train traveller staring 100 yards beyond the window.

It was at this juncture that someone in the cabin decided that there was a chance to reach Washington in less than seven hours. 'If we make it in ten minutes, we'll come in under the wire,' he said.

'Watches were consulted and for the first time in the trip, there was a noticeable feeling of tense excitement aboard the plane. Passengers began pulling for the crew, exhorting them mentally to greater speed. No one knew if the men up front were aware of the precious minutes that were slipping by. No one went up front to ask.

'Chiappino, who had flown this course

Left: Howard Hughes in the Captain's seat of a L-049.

Below: With Jack Frye in the Captain's seat and Hughes flying co-pilot, 43-10310 departs the Burbank Air Terminal for Washington DC on 17 April 1944.
(Lockheed)

many times, was as excited as the rest of us.

"Can you see the river?" he kept asking across the aisle. He was talking about the Potomac, which winds about one end of the Washington National Airport. When it was finally sighted, there was a shout of triumph from the passengers. The plane quickly passed over one section of Washington, circled Alexandria, Va., and after a wheeling turn, dropped down on the airport, six hours and 58 minutes after leaving Burbank.

'Most surprised of all at the elapsed time was Hughes himself when he emerged from the cockpit a few moments later.

"I forgot to wind my watch," he said.

As with everything, politics crept into the story, and differing views were recorded. Some accounts exist that a number of Army officials, including General Henry H. 'Hap' Arnold, were reportedly chagrined and unhappy with the flight, especially because the aircraft had become a glamorous billboard for commercial publicity purposes, a circumstance deemed inappropriate considering stringent wartime conditions. Apparently, they also thought that the intent, if not the letter, of the contract, had been violated. Their frame of mind did not improve when Hughes and Frye spent several days demonstrating the new machine to high government officials, including the entire Civil Aeronautics Board.

TWA's *'The Skyliner'* reported it differently.

'Public attention was focused upon the Connie's flight during the day, and when the plane reported its position over Cincinnati at 12:48 pm, (EWT) it was apparent that all transcontinental records would be bettered by several minutes.

'When the Connie streaked over the airport, more than 2500 persons, including newsreel and radiomen, photographers, and press representatives were gathered on the observation deck and loading ramps.

'Lined in front of the TWA hangars were more than 1,000 of TWA's intercontinental division employees who lifted a cheer as the plane taxied past them toward the terminal.

'Awaiting to greet the flight crew were Secretary of Commerce Jesse Jones, Oswald Ryan, Edward Warner, Harllee Branch and Josh Lee, members of the civil aeronautics board, and Col. Frank Collins, commandant of the airport.

'There was no mistaking the graceful ultra-streamlined transport when it first appeared through the haze and circled the airport at pursuit plane speed. As it banked steeply for its runway approach, it afforded the cheering crowd an excellent demonstration of manoeuvrability'.

Frye glided to a perfect landing, taxied across the field, rolled past rows of hangars and finally wheeled to a stop at Gate 12.

'The roar of its four 2200 horsepower Wright engines was noticeably more powerful than any others in the field, and the Constellation's size dwarfed other planes in the vicinity. Even the Constellation's unloading docks set with fifteen steps towered above others on the ramp.

'Spectators cheered as Frye and Hughes stepped from the plane to the unloading dock where they posed for cameramen. Descending to the field, they were surrounded by the reception committee and reporters.

'Frye reported the plane had "handled like a dream" during the entire trans-continental crossing over the course, of approximately 2400 miles between Burbank and Washington. The course as planned originally was 2296 miles, but slight deviations were made due to weather conditions and winds encountered en-route. Built to fly faster, farther, and with bigger loads than any other land transport now in production, the giant plane averaged more than 330 miles per hour using only normal cruising power.

'Able to carry one hundred fully equipped soldiers as a war-time transport, the Constellation was placed under a military armed guard upon its arrival in Washington. The day following its arrival was reserved for inspection by members of the armed forces, and the succeeding two days guests of TWA who had been cleared by the war department were invited to examine the plane's interior. Special flights were operated for ranking military leaders, members of Congress and the Cabinet, the CAA and CAB.

'Prominent among those who were taken aloft in these inspection flights were chief of air staff Maj Gen B M Giles; Maj Gen Harold L George, Commanding General of the Air Transport Command; Secretary of Commerce Jesse Jones; Charles I Stanton, civil aeronautics administrator; L Welch Pogue, chairman of the Civil Aeronautics Board; Rear Admiral Emory S Land, chairman of the maritime commission; Rear Admiral Howard Vickery, also of the maritime commission; William A M Burden, assistant secretary of commerce; and Donald M. Nelson, WPB; Robert P Patterson, undersecretary of War, and Charles E Wilson, WPB, aircraft division.

'Another visitor was Gen H H Arnold, Commanding General of the US Army air forces, who was shown through the plane by Hughes and Otis Bryan, vice-president of TWA war projects.'

'A week of intense activity centering around the Constellation served as an anticlimax to its arrival in Washington. Congratulatory telegrams and thousands of requests to inspect the giant transport poured into TWA's Washington offices. Included among the people who were able to inspect the interior of the airliner were more than 2500 members of 'official' Washington.'

'Among the first women to inspect the plane's interior, fitted now for army use with seats which can be converted to litters for wounded, was Mrs. Woodrow Wilson, wife of the late President.'

'The first woman to fly as a passenger aboard the new transport was Jacqueline Cochrane, noted woman pilot and now Chief of the Wasps.'

'Alben W. Barkley, of Kentucky, majority leader of the senate, and Harry S Truman, of Missouri, chairman of the senate special committee to investigate the national defense program, were among a group of US Senators who were given a special flight on Saturday.'

'Hughes piloted the plane on the senatorial trip, and a box luncheon was served as the Constellation cruised over Washington for an hour and a half.'

Two of these senators would have an impact on Howard Hughes' life soon after, Ralph Owen Brewster and Homer Ferguson.

'Other prominent guests on the short inspection hops included Maj Gen Lucius Clay of the army service forces; Maj Gen Bennett Meyers of the air forces; and Civil Aeronautics Board Members Josh Lee, Oswald Ryan, Edward Warner, Harllee Branch. C Edward Leasure, chief trial examiner of CAB, and Roy Martin superintendent of air mail service of, the post office department, also were taken aloft.

'Impressed with the transport's flight performance was a group of thirteen press representatives who strolled about the plane as they soared 10,000 feet above the capitol at more than 300 miles per hour on a test flight.

'The Wright Aeronautical Corporation, builders of the engines for the Constellation, was host to Frye and Hughes, and other members of TWA at a reception Tuesday night.

'On Wednesday evening, TWA held a reception in the presidential ballroom of the Hotel Statler, which was attended by nearly 2,000 guests.

'There was no official ceremony when the Connie was turned over to the army, but the many TWA mechanics, painters, and cleaners who prepared this greatest of all land transports for delivery to the armed forces treated her with affectionate and thorough care.

'As the Constellation left Washington, the local TWA employees knew she would play a great part in bringing the Allies a speedy victory.'

The aircraft was painted in regulation olive-drab after the demonstration flights and turned over to the Air Forces.

The impact of the war on Hughes's grand game plan was devastating and tragic for TWA. The multiyear competitive advantages foreseen at the programme outset were substantially lost because of the war. Indeed, TWA was unable to deploy Constellations in commercial services until February 1945.

Of the first production batch originally laid down for TWA at Burbank, twenty were completed for the USAAF as C-69-I-LO and C-69-5-LO transports (L-49-10) and one as a C-69C-1-LO, the last two being C-69-10-LOs which were allotted USAAF serials but were sold to TWA at the end of 1945 instead of going into military service. Of the remaining eighteen, four were sold to TWA after the war,

43-10310 seen airborne, just before the record-breaking Burbank to Washington DC flight. *(Lockheed)*

having been refurbished to commercial standards, six went to BOAC and the rest to other operators, ultimately three to EL AL and two to Capital Airlines, except for one broken up, one that crashed at Topeka, Kansas, on 18 September 1945, following a nacelle fire, and one used as a static test airframe at Wright Field. The Topeka accident, in which the C-69 was being flown by a Pan American crew for USAAF Air Transport Command, resulted in all C-69s being grounded for modifications to the fuel system.

War surplus C-69s were sold off very cheaply, at least four for a mere $20,000 each, and two others went for only $40,000 each - an amazing bargain for a very modern and almost brand new four-engined airliner with only a few hundred hours flying time. By way of comparison, the selling price of Constellations built for the airlines in the early post-war years was to range up to $1,000,000 apiece.

Shortly after VJ Day in 1945, the prototype was declared surplus and was acquired by Howard Hughes from the US War Assets Administration at a sum believed to be only $40,000. It was sold without a certificate of airworthiness and was first re-registered NC25800, later becoming re-registered NX6700. From then until 1949, 'Old 1961', as it was later to be known to Lockheed employees after its constructor's number (which became 1961-S in L-1049 form), hardly flew at all, totalling less than 100 hours in the hands of Howard Hughes and his pilots. Early in 1950 Hughes sold it back to Lockheed for rebuilding into the L-1049 Super Constellation prototype. Meanwhile, although all production was earmarked for the military, Jack Frye and Howard Hughes had given the travelling public a headline-catching foretaste of post-war Constellation travel by flying the first production aircraft in TWA livery, carrying three other crew members and twelve passengers, from Burbank to Washington non-stop on 17 April 1944 in the record transcontinental time of 6hr, 57min, 30sec, the aircraft being handed over to the USAAF on arrival in Washington. Two more C-69s were delivered in October 1944, and almost all of the others at intervals through 1945, followed by a few in 1946. Sub-assembly and fabrication of Constellations was undertaken at Factory A adjoining the Lockheed Air Terminal at Burbank. This had been the plant of the former Vega Aircraft Corporation, formed in 1937 as an affiliate of Lockheed, which became a wholly-owned subsidiary in 1941 and was absorbed into Lockheed on 30 November 1943. Final assembly of Constellations was undertaken at the main Lockheed Factory B.

By 1 January 1949 ten C-69s remaining on the USAF list - most of which had already been sold to civil operators - had been redesignated ZC-69 and ZC-69C, the 'Z' prefix denoting 'obsolete' status. Several more C-69 variants were projected but not built.

These were: C-69A (L-49-43-11) with accommodation for 100 troops and a crew of six. C-69B (L-349) with accommodation for ninety-four troops on benches and a crew of six; C-69C-1-LO (L-549) a personnel transport with accommodation for forty-three passengers in

General Henry 'Hap' Arnold, head of the Army Air Corps alongside Howard Hughes at Washington's National Airport after the Constellations record-breaking flight. The two men rarely agreed on anything and according to those who knew the two, tempers often flared up because Arnold was 'part politician' which Hughes despised. Jack Frye was often tasked in the role of mediator. *(via TWA)*

airline-type seats and a crew of six. One, serialled 42-94550, was delivered to the USAAF on 4 August 1945 and orders for forty-nine more were cancelled after VJ Day. The one delivered was given an experimental-category C of A as L-049-46-25 NX54212 and leased to TWA for pilot training from 10 June to 30 July 1946, and in March 1948 it was sold to BOAC as G-AKCE *Bedford*. Two more C-69 variants completed the series. These were: C-69D project, orders for three of which were cancelled after VJ Day, with accommodation for sixty-three passengers and a crew of six; XC-69E-LO, this being the designation of the prototype when re-engined with Double Wasp R-2800-34 radials for comparison as an alternative powerplant to the Duplex Cyclone R-3350s.

The aircraft started as C-69C and C-69D Constellations and cancelled after VJ Day, when most were at an early stage of construction, were completed as L-049s for the airlines, this being the first true commercial version which was certificated by the Civil Aeronautics Board (CAB) (Approved Type Certificate No. 763) on 11 December 1945 after only twenty-seven hours of flight testing. With production underway, competition between Lockheed with the Constellation and Douglas with the DC-6 soon became intense and was to continue as each manufacturer produced new and 'stretched' variants of the basic design. Yet the decision to go ahead with completion of the cancelled C-69s for the airlines, although apparently so logical, in fact, involved big financial risks, even though it kept the work team together and enabled Lockheed to retain

Howard Hughes on the left leads Jack Frye down the stairs after the record-breaking flight from Burbank. *(via TWA)*

some 15,000 employees on their payroll after VJ Day, when most other aircraft firms were laying off men in their thousands. It was a gamble that was eventually to pay off handsomely, even though Lockheed's were to sustain heavy losses in 1946 and 1947.

Into Civilian Service.
With the C-69 in production as a military transport, the end of World War Two found Lockheed in a powerful position among long-haul airliner manufacturers. Lockheed had the edge over Douglas, although the latter was in a much stronger position numerically in the four-engined field by virtue of the many war-surplus C-54s becoming available for conversion to civil use as DC-4s. No other European challengers were yet in sight, post-war four-engined British transport, such as the Avro Tudor and Handley Page Hermes, having proved to be uncompetitive with their US contemporaries.

Hostilities had hardly ceased before Lockheed was able to offer the first true commercial version, the L-49, later to be known as the L-049, to the airlines. Production aircraft had been started as C-69C and C-69D transports but completed as L-049s, the designation L-049 covering those C-69s already completed that had been refurbished to commercial standards. The first Constellation to be built throughout as a commercial aeroplane was completed in 1947, and the 049 - sixty-six of which were built plus seventeen more converted from C-69s - was intended equally for US domestic or long-haul overwater routes, whereas the later L-649 was designed mainly for the former and the L-749 largely for the latter.

Structurally, there was little difference between the military C-69 and commercial 049 models. The all-metal, semi-monocoque fuselage contained crew, passenger, and cargo compartments, and was pressurised to hold an

Saturday 24 April 1943. Sixth from the left is Senator Ralph O Brewster, seventh is Senator Harry S Truman, and eighth is Howard R Hughes. Also in the picture are Senators Arthur H Vandenburg of Michigan; Allen J Ellender of Louisiana; Ernest W McFarland of Arizona; Homer Ferguson of Michigan; Burnet R Maybank of South Carolina; and Theodore Francis Green of Rhode Island. *(Lockheed)*

8,000-foot cabin altitude at an aircraft altitude of 20,000 feet. The pressure differential was maintained by two cabin superchargers operated by the outboard engines. A pressure control unit on the flight engineer's panel controlled pressurisation by regulating the amount of air exiting from the cabin. The atmosphere provided by the cabin superchargers was electrically heated or cooled depending on the desired temperature of the cockpit and cabin.

The pressurised portion of the interior ran from a front pressure bulkhead near the nose cone to another near the tail. Each joint in the pressure vessel had to be sealed, and seals were built into each door, control run, and opening to maintain the cabin pressure. Two large cargo compartments under the cabin floor were also pressurised and could be entered through the cabin or inward-opening doors on the exterior of the aircraft. The forward cargo bay ran from the rear of the nose gear well to the front wing spar. The aft cargo bay began at the rear wing spar and extended to the aft pressure bulkhead. The tail cap of the fuselage was not pressurised and contained the retractable tail bumper and enclosing doors. Later aircraft would have this unnecessary bumper deleted.

Today, the flight-deck of the Constellation is considered cramped but was deemed roomy by 1939 standards. The windscreen was divided into seven different panels. Documents from the era stated that visibility from the flight deck was excellent, but by today's standards, the bracing and small window size blocked a fair amount of sky from the pilots' viewpoint. The captain on the left/copilot on the right layout meant most controls were close to either pilot. The flight engineer had his own panel behind the copilot and was an essential member of the flight crew, often setting power and monitoring the various systems in the aircraft. Standard blind-flying instruments were included. A Sperry A-3 automatic pilot could maintain directional and altitude control of the aircraft.

Behind the crew quarters was a small cargo compartment. The left side of this compartment carried the bulky radio gear,

Crew boarding was not without its dangers!
(via TWA)

while the right side had an enclosed area for cargo. Fire extinguishers and oxygen bottles were located on the forward wall of this area behind a small removable screen. Other interior configurations were available. Even though the Constellation and its peers were designed to accommodate additional crew quarters for international flights and a copious amount of space for large radio and navigation equipment, the better part of the fuselage remained to be filled with fare-paying passengers. Neither Lockheed nor other sources can agree on how many the Constellation could hold. Figures range from twenty-two sleeping berths to eighty-one seated passengers and a crew of seven.

The first Pan-Am 049 flight to depart New York for Hurn in the UK was used as the focal point of an aviation magazine article to discuss interior appointments. Equipped with forty-three passenger seats, it was apparent to the occupants that crossing the Atlantic in an aircraft without the benefit of a sleeping berth or proper attire was a fatiguing situation. As stated in the 15 February 1946 issue of The

It's a pity that almost all of the immediate post-war goings-on with the Constellation were recorded in black and white images, not colour. Above: TWA featured original hand-painted murals in the first class section.
Below: Exciting things were in store for passengers aboard a Constellation - especially at meal times!
(both Lockheed)

Aeroplane, the author pleaded that 'hopefully the airlines' ardour for mass travel will never persuade them to put the seats quite so close together as the long-range bus operators do. We visualise a situation arising in which the operator offering comfort will attract the passengers. There is no question that, on a 17-hour all-night transatlantic flight, sitting up all the time in his clothes leaves a passenger in a condition conducive to nothing else but a nice long sleep between sheets. So we say bunks for overnight flights every time, and you arrive at the other end ready for anything'. This, of course, would not come to be, but the division of cabin classes would eventually evolve.

In addition to the seating accommodations, a galley and two lavatories were also built into the Constellation cabin. An aft galley could be located almost at the end of the cabin and was divided by a passageway leading to the lavatories. The cabin interior contained a thin sheet of perforated magnesium for the ceiling, which also doubled as part of the cabin ventilation system. Grade-A acetate-doped aircraft fabric covered the side panels, and fybertech covered plywood panels served as floorboards. Many interior panels were removable to provide maintenance crews easy access to interior components.

Type Certificate Awarded
The commercial Constellation was awarded Approved Type Certificate ATC-A-763 on 14 October, 1945 by the Civil Aeronautics Administration. However, the Administration required several modifications to improve safety. Among these was an engine fire detection and suppression system, no doubt the result of the R-3350's reputation with the B-29 Superfortress.

The 049A's maximum gross weight was 90,000 pounds and landing weight 77,280 pounds initially, although in the 049D gross weight was increased to 96,000 pounds from November 1946 with minor structural alterations, made progressively through the Models 049B and 049C. Integral wing tankage for 4,000 US gallon was provided in four tanks and the engines were commercial versions of

The galley aboard this Lufthansa Constellation was, in the words of the brochure translated to English 'a kitchen to spoil any housewife'. I'm not brave enough to make any comment on that!
(both Lufthansa)

the C-69's Wright R-33 50-3 5s, designated R-3350-745CI8BA-I and giving 2,200 bhp each for take-off.

The BA-1 version of the Twin Cyclone had a magnesium induction section and backfires sometimes caused this metal to ignite, with uncontrollable results. During flight testing of the fire suppression system, Rudy Thoren, who served as the flight test engineer, rigged a spark plug to ignite a fire in the induction manifold if one couldn't be caused via intentional engine backfiring. When 'normal' backfires failed to produce a fire, Thoren used his device with marvellous results. A tremendous backfire occurred that almost blew the cowling off the aircraft!

Both escape ropes and a flexible rope ladder with fixed rungs were to be installed for passenger evacuation. These were abandoned in favour of the first emergency slides. Inspection of Constellation photos shows, in addition to the cabin doors, two over-wing exits on the left side and one on the right side

Military C-69s were built with eyebrow windows, which were retained on rebuilt aircraft and some new-build 049s. The castoring nosewheel was also kept, which made taxiing difficult if the aircraft was stopped and needed to turn tightly. Twenty-two C-69s and forty 049s would be delivered before this system was changed. Civilian 049s were produced until the 86th example in May 1947.

The airlines bought surplus C-69s from the military and contracted with Lockheed to bring the aircraft up to their specifications. Other operators elected to give up their early 049 delivery positions for later Constellation models like the 649 and 749. Prices for flyaway airliners ranged from $685,000 to $720,000, depending on interior appointments.

Lockheed's Constellation designations comprised the basic model number followed by a second number indicating the variant of R-3350 installed and a third number indicating which Lockheed-designed cabin interior was featured. Thus the Model 649-84-21 was the domestic version with Wright GR-3350-749CI8BD-I radials and accommodation for thirty-eight passengers; the Model 749-79-22 was the intercontinental version with the same model R-3350s and with accommodation for forty-four passengers by day or twenty in sleeper berths for overnight stages, with four more in seats. The suffix '-12' denoted a sixty-four-passenger interior for domestic routes with a crew of two pilots, a flight engineer and two stewardesses. In contrast, the suffix '-24' denoted a fifty-passenger layout in which the seats of each second row could recline to convert to twenty-four sleeper seats or couchettes. This version carried a crew of four, including one stewardess.

By the end of 1945, Lockheed had orders for 103 Constellations, mostly L-049s, with a total value of $75,500,000; besides Pan American and TWA, customers included American Export

TWA's N86515 *Star of Arabia* landing at San Fransisco.

Airlines (which became American Overseas Airlines when it was taken over by American Airlines), Eastern Air Lines (which had ordered L-649s), Air France, KLM Royal Dutch Airlines, Koninklijke Nederlandsch-Indische Luchtvaart Maatschappij (KNILM) and Pan American Grace Airways (Panagra). Northwest Airlines - better known as Northwest Orient - had planned to order five Constellations for its post-war fleet but, instead, chose Boeing Stratocruisers to supplement its DC-4s, while National Airlines of Miami, which had originally intended to order four for the 'plum' New York-Miami route, chose DC-6s instead. KLM's East Indies subsidiary KNILM did not go ahead with its order for four nor was Panagra's order for two proceeded with.

TWA itself had originally planned a fleet of no less than fifty-nine Constellations for domestic and international routes in the first flush of enthusiasm for post-war traffic growth but cut this back by thirty-seven aircraft when the US domestic air traffic bubble burst in 1946 and 1947. During this period US airline managements, faced by financial difficulties and rising costs, cancelled over half of the 610 airliners of post-war design they had on order.

It is ironic that Howard Hughes and Transcontinental and Western Airline put so much into the design and production of the Constellation, only to have Pan Am take the honours of being the first commercial operator of the aircraft. Pan Am's first Constellation flight departed New York for Bermuda on 3 February 1946. Despite this feather in Pan Am's cap, TWA would be known as the Constellation airline. Overall, TWA would operate 188 Constellations in various models. Thirty-one of these would be new or rebuilt 049s.

TWA's first flight with the Connie would occur a scant three days after Pan Am's, departing New York for Paris: Los Angeles to New York service would begin on 1 March of the same year. Constellations would now wing their way across oceans, continents, and into history books.

From a Lockeed sales brochure in 1945. *(Lockheed)*

Chapter Four

Rivals in the Skies

In June 1944 the stage was set for what was a classic example of an unstoppable force meeting an immovable object. Integral to all of it was the use of the Lockheed Constellation. This was when TWA announced that it was seeking a round-the-world air route when it filed an application early in June with the Civil Aeronautics Board in Washington to extend its services 20,000 miles and to bring any point on the world-wide system within thirty-eight hours flying time of Kansas City. It was to be a battle that had its roots some fifteen years earlier.

In the 1930 annual report, Juan Trippe identified the Pan American Airways system as 'a community effort on the part of the American aviation industry throughout the country to operate in the international field'. In this case, 'Community' was a code word of economics espoused by President Herbert Clark Hoover - it stood for various segments of an industry cooperating for the sake of efficiency and self-regulation.

Initially, this 'community effort' was channelled into 'a single company, organized to represent our national interests' in competition with the Europeans for trade in South America. Pan American Airways, a private American enterprise, battled the government-directed airlines of the Old World in the Western Hemisphere. In 1935, Trippe amplified the concept for the bridging of the Pacific. Pan Am was, he stated 'a national air transport institution' representing not only the aviation industry but all segments of surface transportation, and industrial and commercial organizations. By the time war came, he had extended the field of competition to cover the globe. As far as Juan Trippe could ever see, America's air routes to the whole world belonged to Pan American.

With the Roosevelt administration and the Civil Aeronautics Board on a course to destroy Pan Am's monopoly and whittle him down to size, Juan Trippe looked to Capitol Hill, from where help had come in the past, for the CAB was a creature of Congress. A change in the law that defined its authority could make the regulatory agency toe Trippe's line, and frustrate the White House and the executive policymakers. The legislative process, with its protracted hearings and debates, might discourage new candidates for foreign routes and delay the CAB's certification of competitors for Pan American Airways. The board had temporarily put aside a hundred applications for international licences in order to concentrate on war-related transport services. Ideally, Congress could legislate a chosen instrument for international air commerce, such as Pan Am had represented for fifteen years until General Arnold and the CAB interfered. 'There was no law conferring all American aviation on Pan Am', Adolph Berle took comfort in noting. Trippe schemed to correct that omission.

In November 1939, three examples of the Constellation's forerunner, the Lockheed L44 Excalibur; were ordered, but this order was superseded in 1940 by an order for thirty Constellations on 11 June, followed by a further ten six months later.

The first aircraft were to have been delivered early in 1942, but, with the entry of the USA into the war, the order was relinquished to the US government. From January 1945, Pan American flew C-69s on proving trials for the Army Air Force with the airline's Africa-Orient division. A total of approximately 1500 hours flying was accumulated on the type, including many non-stop transcontinental flights between Florida and California. On 23 October 1945, Pan American signed a contract for twenty-two L-049 airliners, although several of the aircraft were transferred to its subsidiaries.

The Senate Commerce Committee was dominated by the Southern Democrats who had been Pan American's staunch allies, though the chairman, Josiah Bailey, had a troublesome habit of keeping an open mind. He had begun to re-examine his commitment to a single international airline.

Bailey's flexibility was counterbalanced by the addition of Patrick McCarran of Nevada to the committee. 'As Britannia has ruled the waves in the past,' the father of the Civil Aeronautics Act declaimed, 'it is my ambition that Columbia should rule the air of the future.' He agreed with Trippe that Pan American was the sole means to that end. Among the six Republicans on the committee, Owen Brewster served Pan American Airways with a curious zeal, considering that the battle over air routes was not a burning concern of his Maine constituents.

The fiercest assault was made with proposals for Juan Trippe's community company. As one President of a domestic carrier remarked, 'It's the chosen instrument in the filmy, seductive allure of one company with all airlines participating.'

Even Trippe's ally, William Patterson of United Airlines, never got the hang of saying 'community company'. He spoke up for 'the chosen instrument' - an understandable gaffe considering Trippe himself used the term and made such transparent alterations in his monopoly plan over the years. Regardless of terminology at any given moment, Trippe persisted in calling for the USA to pit its chosen instrument against the chosen instruments of foreign nations.

In May 1944, McCarran introduced a bill to create 'The All-American Flag Line, Inc.', a private company with a billion dollars in capital, financed largely through the sale of government bonds. All US airlines were to have a share in it, but Pan American owned all the voting stock.

As Berle was conducting the talks with the British that led up to the Chicago conference of 1944 and the CAB was preparing its design for a postwar international route system, the aviation subcommittee of the Commerce Committee scheduled hearings on the bill.

Thousands of pages of testimony from various chosen instrument hearings can be distilled down to a dispute over the nature of competition in the international air lanes. Trippe maintained that it was properly a competition between nations. 'We favor regulated competition in the domestic field which is protected against foreign-flag competition. We do not favor it in the international field between American carriers.' The airlines owned or controlled by the governments of other countries provided all the competition necessary to keep one American-flag airline responsive to the public

Left: Senator Josiah William Bailey [D] *(b.* 14 September 1873 , *d* 15 December 1946) .

Right: Adolf Augustus Berle Jr. (b. 29 January 1895, d 17 February 1971): a lawyer, educator, author, and US diplomat. He was the author of *The Modern Corporation and Private Property*, a groundbreaking work on corporate governance, and an important member of US President Franklin Roosevelt's 'Brains Trust'.

Left: Senator Patrick Anthony 'Pat' McCarran [D] (*b*. 8 August 1876, *d*. 28 September 1954)

Right: Senator Ralph Owen Brewster [R] (*b*. 22 February 1888, *d*. 25 December 1961)

Below: James McCauley Landis (*b*. 25 September 1899, *d* 30 July 1964) Chairman of CAB 1946-1947.

interest. If several US carriers were to jostle for overseas business, the foreigners would play one against another, and the American public would be the loser. Rather than direct their passengers to a native competitor's international flights, the domestic airlines would route them via BOAC, Air France or the Aeroflot, the Soviet national carrier. Did it not make more sense for them to support one US carrier in which they all had an interest?

'It would be a case of the United States setting up a company strong enough so that it could compete on even terms with these great aggregations, monopoly aggregations, that have been reared against us,' he told a doubting Chairman Bailey. By Trippe's reasoning, emulation was the only way to score against a formidable competitor.

Trippe proved to be an exasperating witness. He exhausted the legislators, few of whom did their homework or stayed awake after lunch. They had difficulty following the trail of his reasoning, strewn as it was with half-truths, unverified recollections and distorted statistics.

The Administration depicted the single chosen instrument, in the words of Attorney General Francis Biddle, as '...a virtual guarantee of all of the evils associated with monopoly', from price gouging to technical inefficiency. What yardstick for judging costs and quality of service, what incentive for improvement could there be with one operator?

With Berle personally lobbying the Senators and with the Committee of Seventeen Airlines unleashing a blitz of letters and telephone calls, the McCarran bill expired with the Seventy-eighth Congress. The Senator from Nevada reintroduced it in the first session of the Seventy-ninth, less the provision for government financing. By then, Bailey and Brewster had returned from the Chicago conference; Brewster, who saw himself as leader of the 'anti-Chicago bloc,' was bent on stopping Senate ratification of the interim agreement for an international civil-aviation organization.

In their early June 1944 application for a round-the-world service, Transcontinental & Western Air Inc, filed documents with the Civil Aeronuatics Board in Washington to extend its services 20,000 miles and to bring any point on the world-wide system within 38 hours flying time of Kansas City.

Major cities in the east, midwest and Pacific coast areas would be linked directly with European and Asiatic capitals, including Berlin and Tokyo, by the new route proposal which was filed following the appearance of Jack Frye, TWA president, before the Aviation sub-committee of the Senate Commerce Committee. Frye testified on behalf of demands of seventeen US Airlines that regulated regional competition, and not monopoly, be accepted as basic policy in governing America's international air transport. The Committee, headed by Senator Bennett Champ Clark, of Missouri, had been hearing witnesses on the subject for several months.

In its application, TWA proposed service from Seattle, San Francisco, Chicago, Detroit, Washington, New York and Boston, to ten foreign 'key traffic producing areas in which this country has strong commercial, diplomatic and national defence interests.' It was the first time in the history of the Civil Aeronautics Board that traffic generating areas, instead of individual cities, were used as the basis of a new route application.

The globe-circling network would connect the co-terminals of Chicago, Detroit, Washington, New York and Boston, with Seattle and San Francisco, on radiating schedules, by way of Presque Isle, Maine; Greenland, Iceland, Scotland; London, Paris, Venice, Berlin, Vienna, Budapest, Belgrade, Bucharest, Athens, Istanbul, Cairo, Baghdad, Teheran, Kabul, Afghanistan; Karachi, New Delhi, Calcutta, Mandalay, Burma; Hanoi, Canton, Lanchow, Chungking, Hankow, Shanghai, Tientsin, Peiping, Mukden, Harbin, Manchuria; Tokyo, Attu, Kiska, Dutch Harbor and Anchorage. At San Francisco, the route would connect with TWA's present western terminal.

An alternate route, extending from China across Siberia to Nome, Fairbanks, Whitehorse, Edmonton in Alberta, and then to Chicago, was contained in the application. An express service across the North Atlantic without stopping at Greenland and Iceland was proposed by way of Newfoundland and Eire, or Great Britain. Frye announced that TWA would use Lockheed Constellations, which he and Howard Hughes had conceived several years earlier for just such a service.

Frye said that the big four-engine Constellations would be able to operate between TWA's domestic route to any foreign point on its proposed route in thirty-eight hours flying time.

The ten major traffic generating, or 'key' areas described in the application were the British Isles with fifty-eight cities of upwards of 100,000 population, Central Europe with ninety-two such cities, the Near East eleven, Middle East, eleven; Northeast India, sixteen; South China, twenty-four; Central China, one hundred and two; North China, thirty-five; Manchuria and Korea ten, and Japan thirty-three.

Pointing to the population density in these areas, the airline president said that all have 'normal trade interests' with the United States, that many of them were not served with commercial airline facilities before the war, and that 'none of them received the high standard of service provided US travellers at home.

'The United States, as a great industrial and financial power, will have increasing need in the post-war period for rapid transportation between this country and the other important traffic producing areas of the world,' he said.

On 15 March 1945, Trippe retaliated by filing for domestic routes for Pan American, with plans to use the Constellation on transcontinental services. 'We don't think it's in the public interest, but if the historical policy of

Pan American World Airways L-049-51-26 *Clipper Mayflower* NC88836. Interestingly the aircraft has the construction number 2036 painted under the tail, and the 'C' of the registration crossed out, possibly showing that the aircraft was on test. This aircraft was to make PAA's first overseas flight, to Bermuda on 14 January 1946. *(Lockheed)*

separating domestic and international service is to be changed, then it is essential from a competitive point of view, and from a point of view of equity, that we should operate in the domestic field.'

Trippe cast himself as an advocate of low fares for the average man. Pan Am planned to offer a $100 ticket to Europe. '...but that cannot be achieved unless the American share of the traffic can be concentrated in one carrier, in one united company.' Reduced fares were predicated on economies of scale - larger and costlier airliners; Trippe described 100-passenger machines, 200-passenger ones, such as only an airline in sound financial health could purchase. If more than one US airline engaged in destructive competition for overseas business, none would be solvent, and they would be obliged to turn to the government for 'exorbitant' subsidy. This was ripe, considering it was coming from the champion milker of the Post Office Mail Subsidy who now appeared alarmed about the taxpayer's being 'saddled' with the subsidy burden.

The airlines were to subscribe to Class A voting stock, in amounts proportional to their annual revenues. Pan American was entitled to the maximum twenty-five per cent, American Airlines twelve and a half per cent, United eleven per cent, TWA eight per cent, the remainder going to sixteen other airlines. Carriers with aircraft properties and franchises for overseas service were to sell them to the community company in exchange for Class B voting stock. Only three had such assets - Pan American Airways, Panagra and American Export Airlines - and Pan American would garner ninety per cent of Class B shares.

Trippe also demanded that stock issued for assets be distributed to individual shareholders instead of being held by the three international airlines. This was confirmation enough for the prevalent suspicion that Pan Am would control the community company, and that Juan Trippe would run it. 'Juan Trippe is the only candidate,' a domestic-airline executive declared.

The State Department was troubled by a provision in the bill that implied the community company could strike agreements with foreign countries and then call on the US Government for help. This was a reversion to Trippe's methods the Administration had called to a halt, and that Brewster was trying to restore. One-man commercial diplomacy might have been appropriate when other countries had no airlines to send to the USA the State Department acknowledged, but when reciprocal rights were sought, inter-governmental negotiations were needed for coherence and order.

The hearings were interrupted by the death of Franklin Roosevelt on 12 April, the eighty-third day of his fourth term. Senator Harry S Truman from Missouri then became the thirty-third President of the USA.

Truman was well informed on the airlines in general and Pan American Airways in particular. As the head of an interstate commerce sub-committee, he had worked with McCarran on the civil aeronautics legislation; later, he had presided over the special committee that investigated defence contracts and scrutinized Pan American's record in the secret airport construction. He had voted for the postal appropriation for American Export Airlines. On the record, Truman was opposed to the chosen instrument.

Any doubts about where the new President stood were resolved on 5 July when Truman approved the decision of the Civil Aeronautics Board to administer a larger dose of competition on the North Atlantic than even Trippe had feared. The board certified TWA as well as American Export.

In making the awards, the CAB said it was not considering whether US international air transportation should be rendered by a single company or by a chosen instrument. That policy question had been already settled by Congress in the Civil Aeronautics Act of 1938; the board was proceeding to fulfill its duty, saying that 'No effective substitute for healthy competition as a stimulus to progress and efficiency can be found in monopoly'.

In designing a peacetime route system eastward across the Atlantic to Europe and beyond, the CAB subscribed to Roosevelt's zone concept. The board traced three main traffic flows. Service to Northern Europe was divided between Pan Am, which already had a permanent certificate for Ireland and England,

and American Export, which had been operating the route for the Navy. The board extended it to Scandinavia and then to Moscow. A central route from London and Brussels through the Balkans and the Levant - a term used to refer to modern events or states in the region immediately bordering the eastern Mediterranean Sea: Cyprus, Israel, Jordan, Lebanon, Palestine, Syria and Hatay Province of Turkey - and on to Calcutta was awarded to Pan American. TWA was licensed for a southern route through Mediterranean Europe, North Africa and the Persian Gulf to Bombay.

In light of 'changing and momentous world events,' the CAB said, it was futile to predict future air traffic from the past history of surface transport, and so it was limiting the new certificates to seven years. That the awards were not engraved in stone was of little solace to Pan American for receiving the worst pickings. TWA had a windfall of major terminals - Paris, Rome, Madrid, Athens, Cairo, Jerusalem. Pan American was left with Marseille as a French gateway and was forced to share the London, Frankfurt and Lisbon markets. Although in mid-1945 the board may not have foreseen the descent of the Iron Curtain, Pan Am was to be prohibited by the Soviets from exercising its franchises in Eastern Europe. The grant of six terminals in the USA - New York, Boston, Philadelphia, Chicago, Washington and Detroit - did not include permission for Pan American to operate connecting service between any of them.

The day after Truman signed the certificates, the full Commerce Committee took up the American Flag Line bill. Bailey and Brewster leaned with all their might from opposite sides, and the bill failed in a tie vote to be reported to the floor. The principle of competition, parcelled out at the discretion of the CAB and the President, was effectively preserved.

The Senators from Nevada and Maine roused their colleagues to issue an interim policy report - a highly irregular procedure for legislation that had died in committee. The report was written to imply a recommendation for the community company, and circulated while Bailey was at the bedside of his ailing wife in Raleigh. 'As we used to say in North Carolina, it's the same old coon with another ring around his tail,' Bailey scoffed after he read the document. He deplored the report as a ruse to discredit the CAB and the new President while he was out of the country attending the Potsdam Conference and attempt to influence their decisions about the Latin American routes, which were next on the agenda. His impression that Trippe was behind the mischievous behaviour was confirmed when Brewster flew to Raleigh in the Pan American aircraft to have another argumentative round with him.

Bailey refused to do as Brewster and McCarran asked: to call a meeting of the committee to adopt the report. He stayed in Raleigh and tried to rally the members of the committee with blistering letters.

'I know a great deal about Pan American Airways' activities,' he wrote to Senator George Radcliffe of Maryland, a champion of the airline whom Trippe buttered up with reminders of their common origin in the Eastern Shore, even to saluting him as 'cousin.'

As Bailey observed, 'I thought very favourably of the one company idea myself at one time, but I could not resist the representations of the several departments to which the bill was submitted, nor could I avoid the conclusion that Mr. Trippe of the Pan American was governed very largely by his own selfish interests and that he was entirely too active.'

Bailey advised the Marylander that 'the best thing Pan American officials could do for themselves is to fall in with the established policy, take whatever may be allotted to them' and stop trying to alter the Board's decisions or change the law.

One of Truman's first Presidential decisions was to replace Edward Stettinius as Secretary of State and put him to pasture for a year as United States Representative to the United Nations in New York. Trippe always claimed that having a brother-in-law in the Cabinet was harmful to Pan American because it inhibited him from talking to the Secretary of State about airline matters. Nevertheless, all signs pointed to the welcome mat for Trippe being withdrawn from the White House.

The CAB and the President were

distributing international certificates to the domestic carriers and seemed to be in no hurry to award compensatory internal routes to Pan Am. United Airlines was licensed to serve Hawaii from California (before statehood, gateways to territories were classified as foreign markets), cutting into the only part of Pan American's Pacific operations that showed promise of profitability. United offered a $135 fare from San Francisco to Honolulu; Pan American lowered its fare from $195 to meet United's, corroborating economics-textbook theory about the beneficial effects of competition on the consumer.

The most crushing blow was the award to Northwest Airlines of the Great Circle Route to the Orient via Seattle and Alaska. Northwest had been a military contractor in Alaska and the Aleutians, and it also had an eloquent advocate in Senator Warren Magnuson, a Democrat from the State of Washington who sided with Bailey on the Commerce Committee.

For the same reasons it placed two additional carriers in the North Atlantic, said the Board, it was rejecting Pan American's contention 'that it should remain the sole United States carrier in the Pacific.' The airline's permanent certificate for the central Pacific was extended from Midway to Tokyo - a consolation prize considering that passengers would be asked to travel 1,600 miles farther to the capital of Japan than if they went by Northwest.

Below: The soon-to-be-inconic triple-fins of the Constellation - in this case TWA's NC86516.

Inset right: Noah Dietrich (*b*. 28 February 1889 – *d*. 15 February 1982) was the chief executive officer of the Howard Hughes' business empire from 1925 to 1957. Dietrich continued to oversee and make executive decisions for the Hughes industries as late as 1970.

The CAB deliberated over its Latin American applications for seventeen months before giving Caribbean routes to four of the eleven domestic contenders. Truman was displeased. He wanted competition throughout Latin America, and he sent the decision back for reconsideration, specifying his choice of airlines for each route.

Franklin Roosevelt had said Juan Trippe could not have it all; Harry Truman made sure of that.

Into the middle of all this strode Howard Hughes. He controlled TWA, the airline that was by now set to compete with Pan American halfway around the world, and though his attention was focused on his other business toys during the war years, he still had plenty of pride and money tied up in its future.

Hughes's contributions to winning the war were steeped in controversy. Behind the receptionist's desk in his dentist's office he discovered a pinup girl for the GIs: Jane Russell, a long-legged California beauty with a sulky face and ponderous breasts that defied the law of gravity. Hughes framed her meagre thespian talent in a movie about Billy the Kid, directing and editing it himself. Critics ridiculed *The Outlaw*; the Catholic Legion of Decency proscribed it for lewdness, while a volcano of advance publicity ensured that Miss Russell's photographs adorned the cockpits and foxholes of the Armed Forces.

There was an element of show business in his military-aircraft programme. He hired John W. Meyer, a press agent, to overcome the hostility of Air Corps procurement officers. Meyer's formula for winning over generals and congressmen - caviar, wine, women and free aircraft rides which differed somewhat from Sam Pryor's in style and degree: Hollywood flash versus old boy elegance. The Hughes entertainment site was a twenty-room mansion in Arlington, Virginia; Pan American's, a Federal house on F Street, Washington DC.

Meyer introduced the President's second son to Faye Emerson, an actress, who before long became his bride. Colonel Elliott Roosevelt's strong endorsement of the XF-11, an experimental reconnaissance machine, resulted in a $70-million contract for Hughes Aircraft. In July 1946, long past the deadline for its usefulness in spotting Nazi troop movements, Howard Hughes tested the plane himself and, when one of its propellers malfunctioned, crashed it into a house in Beverly Hills.

Another product of Hughes Aircraft, still not assembled by the time the Japanese surrendered, was the HK-1 Hercules, a 200-ton, eight-engined flying boat made of Duramold, with capacity for 700 passengers. In the final tally, $50 million of Hughes' own money were spent on the project, and another $22 million in losses was borne by the government (*see Howard Hughes and the Spruce Goose*, Pen & Sword 2014, by the same author).

In 1946, the airline was exhibiting symptoms of acute postwar decompression. Passenger and cargo loads contracted, and heavy expenses attended the inauguration of international routes. The price of the Constellations Hughes had ordered from Lockheed before the war increased sevenfold by the time construction on commercial aircraft resumed. With losses accruing at an annual rate of $13.6 million, TWA stock tumbled from $71 to $18 a share, wiping out any chance of raising capital to pay for the aircraft in the equity market.

Dietrich arranged with the Equitable Life Assurance Society for a $40-million loan to be applied to equipment and other capital needs. The haemorrhage worsened, and when he discovered that Frye was using the money to stanch the red ink from operations, he convinced Hughes that he should be fired. Frye blew the whistle in Washington.

In the Administration's view, TWA had proved itself a valuable military tool, too useful to pass out of existence. Its demise would eliminate a competitor on the international routes. In this respect, the airline was a pawn in the running battle over the single company. Never one to miss a trick by putting the knife in, Owen Brewster told James Landis, chairman of the CAB in 1946 and 1947. 'If TWA goes into receivership, it will be a sad but conclusive argument in favor of the chosen instrument.'

TWA's destiny was entwined with that of Lockheed, the builder of the Constellation. If TWA did not take delivery of eighteen

Pan American made great use of department store and travel agent window displays to promote their Constellation services. *(Robin Banks Collection)*

Constellations standing ready in the Lockheed hangars, the manufacturer might well accompany the airline into bankruptcy. The President's Air Coordinating Committee, headed by Landis, accepted responsibility for saving Lockheed.

In late December a meeting to decide the fate of TWA was scheduled to be held in New York among the concerned parties - government, creditors, TWA's Frye - led management and the chronically unpunctual Howard Hughes.

On the morning of New Year's Day, Juan Trippe paid an unexpected visit to Noah Dietrich at his hotel. He drew a gloomy picture of the future of the airlines, which coincided with Dietrich's prognostications and inquired whether Hughes Tool might consider a merger between TWA and Pan American Airways. If Hughes did not want to sell all of TWA, then how about its transatlantic operations? 'We would be glad to consider any proposal you care to make,' Dietrich replied. 'Of course, I would have to discuss it with Mr Hughes.'

The next morning Trippe visited the office

Above and opposite: two views of Pan Anerican World Airways' ship number 2047, registered as NC88847. The picture above is thought to have been taken during final assembly, as 2047 is missing a prop on its port wing, and the Clipper behind it is missing both props and engine cowlings.

PAA were somewhat notorious in naming all their aircraft *'Clipper XXXX'* and then re-naming them at different times. Clearly in this picture both aircraft still need their full names applying. According to some records 2047 (which is the Lockheed construction number) was initially allocated the name *Clipper Hotspur* at its time of delivery on 12 March 1946 and registered NC88847, later N88847. By the time the picture on the opposite page was taken as the airliner runs up its engines for the start of another service, 847 had been named *Clipper Southern Cross*.

of Thomas I Parkinson, president of the Equitable, who was edgy about a possible default on the loan he had made to TWA. After first circling the mulberry bush delivering his canned spiel about the merits of the community company, Trippe said, 'The Equitable may soon be taking additional responsibilities with respect to TWA's management, and in that event, you might be interested in rearranging its overseas routes.' Parkinson's attitude was archly correct. 'The Equitable does not interfere with the management of its borrowers unless they are in default, which has not happened yet with TWA. It is our policy, Mr Trippe, not to discuss with a third party what we might do in those circumstances.'

'I understand,' Trippe replied smoothly, as though Parkinson had not caught him in the unethical act of trying to seize control of a competitor through a back door. As a director of another major insurance company, Metropolitan Life, he was presumed to know better.

'But should the time come when you do have a greater responsibility for the management of TWA,' he said, 'you will find me and the entire organization of Pan American Airways disposed to be very friendly. I simply want to assure you of our desire to be helpful.'

The first airliners for Pan Am

Pan American took delivery of its first Constellation on 5 January 1946. The first

Right: Sam Pryor Jr. (*b*.1 March 1898, *d* 19 September 1986) was born in Ferguson, Missouri. When his father became the general manager of Remington Arms, the family relocated to Greenwich, Connecticut. Sam Jr was sent off to the Taft School, with his brother. In 1917, Sam Jr. enrolled in Yale College. Many of his peers at Yale later were high ranking individuals at PAA. Pryor became executive vice president of Pan American in 1941, and was instrumental in expanding the airline's worldwide service. He was awarded the President's Medal for Merit in 1946 for directing the construction of fifty strategic air bases in Africa and Latin America in World War Two.

overseas flight for the true civilian airliner was from New York La Guardia to Bermuda a few days later on a special charter which took off on 14 January. Shortly afterwards, one left on a cargo charter flight to Hong Kong by way of route-proving, the aircraft returning to San Francisco; Then, on 20 January, the first pressurised commercial North Atlantic scheduled service was inaugurated with a Pan American 049 on the New York - Lisbon route. On 3 February, the first scheduled transatlantic service to Great Britain, to Hurn, near Bournemouth, on the south coast of England via Gander and Shannon, left La Guardia, departing Hurn again on 7 February. The following week, on 12 February, the first New York - England non-stop flight with an airliner was made. Until 31 May 1946, the service to Britain operated to Hurn, with London Heathrow being served from 1 June 1946. By the middle of the year, Connies of Pan American's Atlantic Division were operating daily services from New York to Bermuda and from New York to London (via Gander and Shannon), three times a week to Lisbon (via Gander and Shannon), two of which continued to Monrovia (Liberia) via Dakar and on to Leopoldville (in the Belgian Congo), the other to Natal (Brazil).

Hughes arrived in Manhattan on 7 January almost a week later than expected. A marathon negotiating session, led by Landis, was concluded at the '21 Club', at 21 West 52nd Street, the former Speakeasy where so many affairs of high finance and national interest have been settled. With Parkinson agreeing to subordinate part of the Equitable debt to newer transfusions of funds, Hughes put up $10 million in exchange for a note convertible into one million shares of TWA common stock and the right to get rid of Frye and install his own management. The fresh capital stabilized TWA by enabling it to obtain bank loans and special credits from aircraft manufacturers.

While the meetings to save TWA were going on, Brewster was stirring the ashes of the aviation monopoly legislation. Now the Republicans were at the helm of the committees, and Brewster had on his desk a bill to consolidate and merge the international airlines that had come into being since McCarran had

Passenhger on the wing - a somewhat surreal colour publicity shot from Pan American. *(Pan Am)*

originally tried to cower the CAB.

Hughes was convinced that Trippe and Brewster, who he called 'Trippe's mouthpiece', were out to shaft him. The bill set the cutoff date for ownership of international assets at October 1945 - before TWA had acquired its overseas interests: which meant that it could subscribe to stock allotted to domestic carriers in the community company but would not be compensated for its investment in foreign routes.

Hughes nursed malevolent feelings toward Brewster on another count as well. The first week in February, he was called to Washington to answer questions from the War Investigating Committee behind closed doors, a preliminary to scheduling public hearings on his gargantuan flying boat *(see Howard Hughes and the Spruce Goose*, Pen & Sword 2014, by the same author).

When he arrived in the capital a few days before his appointment, Hughes learned that Brewster was in Kansas City on a speechmaking tour. He telephoned Brewster and said he wanted to see him while he was in Washington. 'If you come back, I'll see that you get to your other engagements'.

At lunch in the Senator's suite at the Mayflower Hotel, they talked mostly about the seaplane. Hughes defended his project. Whether they discussed the aviation bill and a Pan American-TWA merger was later hotly contested. Hughes said they did, and charged that Brewster offered to call off the investigation into the flying boat if Hughes would support the community company and give up TWA's international routes. Brewster and a lawyer who was present at Dietrich's recommendation denied that any such conversation was held.

While he was in Washington, Hughes saw Juan Trippe. The two soft spoken men took each other's measure. Hughes pretended not to understand the overseas-airline business. 'Why isn't there more cooperation between officials of our companies? And why are you pushing this unification of all the international airlines?' - Trippe explained why there was room for only one US flag carrier in the skies. They parted amicably, agreeing to meet again in a month or so when Hughes was again in the East.

On 14 March, a lawyer for the War Investigating Committee went to the Hughes Aircraft plant in California and demanded to see the expense account relating to the Hercules. In New York, Trippe called on Noah Dietrich in his suite at the Waldorf-Astoria and tirelessly recited the case for the chosen instrument.

As he was getting up to leave, he mentioned Pan American's application for a transcontinental route. 'We have operations in the Pacific and in the Atlantic. It is most logical for the CAB to allow us to connect these services. And once we obtain that franchise, it will be an easy step into local service, transcontinentally.' Dietrich inferred from Trippe's velvety statement a threat to TWA's main trunk operations.

Trippe brought up the Brewster bill. 'It's unfair to TWA,' Dietrich said. Trippe replied that he could have it changed. Or so Dietrich and the lawyer from Hughes Tool who attended the meetings claimed - and Trippe denied. During the conversations between the two sides, Hughes or Dietrich had a witness; Trippe went alone.

TWA gears up.
Meanwhile, on 5 July 1945, TWA was granted an international certificate to fly halfway around the world. The following month, on 20 August, the airline signed its first post-war contract for eighteen 049 Constellations, with prior delivery rights on the first twelve aircraft as an acknowledgement for the airline's assistance in development work on the design.

On 14 September 1945, a further eighteen aircraft were ordered, and the order was later updated from the 049 to the 649 type. The announcement by President Jack Frye that a contract had been signed with Lockheed Aircraft Corporation, builders of the Constellation, for a fleet of thirty-six of the giant over-weather transports heralded the inauguration of the World's first 300-mile-an-hour commercial air service.

The Constellation fleet, purchased at the cost of $30,000,000, was be used to establish such service as coast-to-coast flights in approximately ten hours, and New York-to-Europe ocean crossings in less than fourteen hours. This cut four to seven hours off the fastest existing transcontinental flights, and from nine and a half to nearly eleven and a half hours off present transatlantic schedules to Europe.

The Constellations were to be first seen on TWA's North Atlantic and transcontinental routes, Frye explained, because of prior delivery rights gained by TWA's exclusive development of the airliner. The first twelve machines were to be delivered to TWA over a two-month period beginning in October, after which the aircraft would be released to other lines. The delivery schedule called for eighteen airliners to be delivered before the first of the year, for assignment to domestic as well as international service.

'These airplanes will bring about the first reduction in commercial transcontinental schedules since 1940, when TWA pioneered the Boeing Stratoliner,' Frye commented. 'Internationally, the Constellation is the first important advance in over-ocean commercial flying in many years. Besides cutting the time of present transatlantic commercial schedules by more than forty per cent, this airplane will permit a substantial reduction in fares.

'Before the war, it cost $375 to fly from New York to London. During the war, this fare was raised to $672. It subsequently was reduced to $572, where it has remained. This is more than seventeen cents a mile, or nearly four times the rate charged by competing airlines within the United States. TWA will use the Constellation to establish reasonable fares for transatlantic travel, details of which will be announced soon.'

Introduction of the Constellations into regular transcontinental commercial service gave rise to a vast coordinated programme of training, equipment, and engineering changes, considerably expedited because of the early delivery date. Original plans called for delivery of the aircraft no sooner than late spring of 1946.

This programme included such details as engineering changes in the aircraft and instruments at the Lockheed factory and in TWA's own modification shops; the training of stewards and flight engineers on the west coast; designing and ordering of special ramp and shop equipment, and provisioning of the airliner.

On 15 November the first 049 was delivered to TWAs Kansas City facility, carrying the new titling 'Trans World Airline', rather than 'The Transcontinental Line'. The first proving flight to Paris from New York left on 25 November, and, by the end of the year, ten 049s had been delivered.

TWA had taken delivery of its first L-049 on 1 October 1945, this being followed by thirty more plus eight others bought secondhand, and began crew training and route proving for the new type, an Atlantic proving flight between Washington and Paris being flown on 3-4 December by Constellation NC86505, named *Paris Sky Chief* for the occasion, with twenty-three passengers on board. This flew via Gander (Newfoundland) and Shannon (Eire) to Orly Airport, covering the 3,870 miles in a total time of 12 hours 57 minutes at an average speed of 316mph. Pan American, which had ordered twenty-two of these aircraft, had begun 049 Atlantic flights two weeks earlier, on 20 January, and flew its inaugural eastbound Atlantic flight to the UK on 4 February from New York's La Guardia to Hurn airport, near Bournemouth, then serving as the British transatlantic terminal until Heathrow was ready. Calls were made at Gander and Shannon and the aircraft, a Model 049-46-26 NC88833 named *Clipper Bald Eagle,* was commanded by Captain Robert W Fordyce and carried twenty-nine passengers. It returned to New York with a load of thirty-six passengers and two cabin staff in the 43-seat cabin, no sleeping-berths being fitted. At this early stage of Atlantic travel a number of passenger facilities were still lacking both in the air and on the ground; Hurn airport, for instance, had no proper loading steps and its other terminal facilities were still decidedly spartan, while the Constellation itself had, as yet, no humidifier in its cabin pressurisation system.

Two days before TWA inaugurated its Paris service a Constellation piloted by the airline's president and founder, Jack Frye, made a record-breaking transcontinental flight with forty-five passengers to celebrate Lockheed's twentieth birthday, flying non-stop from Los Angeles to New York's La Guardia airport in 7 hours 27 minutes and 48 seconds, covering the great circle course of 2,740 statute miles at an average height of 15,000 feet and an average ground speed of 330 mph. TWA began regular transcontinental services with the Constellation on 15 February 1946 between New York and

Los Angeles, three weeks ahead of American Airlines, which began DC-4 flights over this route on 7 March, followed by United shortly afterwards, also with DC-4s. With its two major transcontinental competitors having to operate the unpressurised and 80mph slower Douglas transport, TWA had a strong competitive lead with the Constellation, and despite the type's grounding through engine troubles, this lead was maintained until the introduction of DC-6s by American Airlines and United a year later. The Constellation's superior speed and range enabled TWA to offer a one-stop New York - Los Angeles schedule of 9 hours 45 minutes eastbound and 11 hours westbound, compared with American's two-stop DC-4 schedule via Washington and Dallas, Texas taking 13 hours 10 minutes eastbound and 14 hours 25 minutes westbound.

1946 saw the inauguration of Constellation services on Trans World's leading domestic and international routes. After a preview flight to Paris from La Guardia from 3 December to 9 December 1945, the first commercial air service from the USA, La Guardia to Paris Orly was started on 5 February 1946; when TWA inaugurated its scheduled Constellation services with Flight 954 using aircraft NC86511. The airliner left La Guardia at 14.21 hours On 5 February, with thirty-six passengers and seven crew, and landed at Orly nineteen hours and forty-six minutes later, at l5.57 hours, local time on 6 February, after intermediate landings at Gander and Shannon. The return flight departed Orly at 23.59 hours on the same day, arriving at La Guardia the following day, twenty-one hours and five minutes later. After a special flight to Rome departing Chicago on 10 February, with two cardinals on board, the first US airline service to Italy left La Guardia on 11 February. TWAs La Guardia - Geneva service was inaugurated on 31 March, and the Paris service extended to Cairo from 1 April. The Lisbon and Madrid route was opened up with Constellations on 1 May. During the early part of 1946, however, with not all the 049s delivered, schedules on all these routes were flown by Constellations on an ad hoc basis - the exception being the daily New York - Paris service via Gander and Shannon, which was always Constellation-operated. On US domestic schedules, proving flights with the 049s were made during early February. 1946, including a record-breaking Burbank-La Guardia flight on 3 February , and the new coast-to-coast schedule with 049s was inaugurated on 15 February using aircraft NC86503 from Los Angeles-Burbank to New York-La Guardia, cutting five hours off the Boeing 307 elapsed time. San Francisco was also later served from La Guardia, and intermediate stops made on some services as more domestic aircraft were delivered. A New York - Chicago service with Constellations was started in April, and by May there were two daily New York-Chicago flights, a daily New York - Chicago - Kansas City flight, and a daily New

TWA's '701' *Star of New York* is NC91201, which first entered service 28 March 1948, and is seen here during an obviously posed picture. The aircraft was re-named *Star of Portugal* and re-registered N91201 a year later. *(TWA)*

York - Los Angeles and San Francisco schedule. On 13 May, a further thirteen 049s were ordered, but the order was later cut back to five aircraft.

From 3 May 1946, a Chicago - New York - Paris - Cairo service was offered without change of aircraft, and by 30 June, nineteen 049s were in operation, eight on international services, nine on domestic services, and two, ex C-69s engaged in pilot training, one aircraft having been lost without injury to passengers when NC86510 ran off the runway on landing at National Airport, Washington, DC on 29 March due to crew error; all twelve on board survived, but the aircraft was written off.

The loss of TWA Flight 513
Then, on 11 July disaster struck. TWA Flight 513, registration NC86513, *Star of Lisbon*, an L-049 Constellation operated by TWA on a training flight crashed near Reading, Pennsylvania. The airliner departed Reading Airport at 11:21, for a local instrument training flight. It climbed to an altitude of 3,000 feet to an area approximately four miles east of Reading Airport, at which time it levelled off to begin practice of instrument approach procedures. Shortly thereafter, the flight crew detected an odour resembling burning insulation, but did not immediately determine the source. At approximately 11:37, the flight engineer went aft in order to determine the origin of the smoke. Upon opening the galley door, he observed that the entire cabin was filled with very dense smoke. The crew immediately attempted to combat the fire with the cockpit fire-extinguisher but were unable to enter the cabin because of the dense smoke and intense heat. The smoke quickly filled the cockpit through the open galley door, rendering visibility extremely poor and making it difficult for the pilots to observe the instruments. The student flight engineer opened the cockpit crew hatch in an attempt to clear the cockpit of smoke, but opening of the hatch increased the flow of smoke from the cabin toward, and shortly thereafter it became impossible to observe any of the instruments or to see through the windshield. The captain opened the window on the right side of the pilot compartment and attempted to fly the aircraft back to Reading

TWA's NC86514 *Star of India* is a backdrop to this picture of a stewardess carrying what appears to be movie film canisters. Note also the letters TWA on one lapel of her uniform jacket. *(TWA)*

Airport for an emergency landing while descending with the engines throttled and with his head out of the side window. With the increased intensity of the heat and denseness of the smoke in the cockpit, it became impossible for the pilots to maintain effective control of the aircraft. At an altitude of approximately 100 feet, two miles northwest of the airport, the captain withdrew his head from the window and attempted to land the aircraft 'blind'. The aircraft contacted two electric power wires strung about 25 feet above the ground, and the left wing tip glanced against scattered rocks and struck the base of the large tree. The aircraft settled to the ground, slowly rotating to the left, as it skidded approximately 1,000 feet across a hayfield, causing the disintegration of the left-wing panel, flaps and aileron. The aircraft continued to yaw to the left and, after having rotated more than 90 degrees, it plunged through trees and telephone poles lining a road bordering the field, coming to rest in a pasture at a point approximately 150 feet beyond the road and pointing approximately 160 degrees from its original heading at the time of initial impact.

The Board determined that the probable

cause of this accident was failure of at least one of the generator lead through-stud installations in the fuselage skin of the forward baggage compartment which resulted in intense local heating due to the electrical arcing, ignition of the fuselage insulation, and creation of smoke of such density that sustained control of the aircraft became impossible. A contributing factor was the deficiency in the inspection systems which permitted defects in the aircraft to persist over a long period of time and to reach such proportions as to create a hazardous condition'. Of the six crew members aboard, five were killed. This accident is memorable for grounding all Lockheed Constellations from 12 July until 23 August when cargo fire detection equipment could be installed.

On 20 September 1946 transatlantic services were resumed with the Connies, with a flight from New York to Paris, and on 2 October 46 daily transcontinental services from New York to Los Angeles were also resumed, under the name, the 'Advance Sky Chief'. Six further 049s were delivered during the remainder of the year, allowing the frequency of services to be increased and more cities added to the Connie network. By the end of the year, there were twelve weekly New York - Shannon - Paris flights and two weekly New York - Lisbon flights. Use of the 'Speedpak' cargo container was first reported in use in Dec 46 on flights between Europe and the Middle East.

Another move from Hughes

In the rarified world of boardrooms and the corridors of Washington DC, Hughes made the next move. From there on, his actions are undisputed. For what went on in his suspicious mind, we have only the word of the accountant who served him for thirty-two years. In 1947, Hughes was eccentric but not appreciably more so than other tycoons. Hughes telephoned Trippe early in April. Could Trippe meet him in the West? He laid down conditions of absolute secrecy. That suited Trippe fine.

They fixed a date to meet on a Saturday, in Palm Springs. Trippe flew out in the B-23, taking his 12-year-old son Charles with him just for the ride. Since Hughes had insisted they meet alone, the pilot was to deposit Trippe and return when he was summoned. Trippe checked into a small inn, and later that morning, Hughes telephoned and instructed him to come to a cottage he had rented in the desert. Noah Dietrich had flown from Houston in his private plane. He had TWA's figures; Trippe had Pan American's balance sheets and income accounts. The discussion got down to the merger immediately. Hughes sat quietly, his 6-foot 3-inch frame slumped in a chair. He let Dietrich draw Trippe out.

'What do you have in mind, Mr Trippe? On what basis do you propose an exchange?' Dietrich asked.

'Well, I think the most logical manner of bringing a merger about would be on the basis of book values,' Trippe said. Pan American's net worth was reported at $13.66 a share, though its stock was selling at around $12.

Dietrich asserted that Pan Am and TWA used different methods of accounting, and therefore an exchange on the basis of the market values of their securities would be the fairest method. The value of TWA was $4.24 a share, but the stock was then trading at around $20, far above the company's net worth, as a result of speculator activity following Hughes's decision to pump more money into the airline.

Hughes stirred himself. He talked about selling TWA completely, but Trippe wanted only the overseas part. He figured it was worth one-fourth to one-third of a combined company.

'Nonsense' said Hughes. 'TWA International is worth almost twice what all of Pan American put together is worth.' 'Why, that's completely out of line,' Trippe rejoined. TWA's foreign business was smaller than Pan American's Atlantic service and not yet profitable.

It was evident from Hughes's outlandish counter-proposal that he was taunting Trippe. According to Dietrich, Hughes had no intention of merging. 'He was simply buying time to plot his strategy against the Brewster-sponsored legislation to freeze TWA out of the overseas market.' Yet Juan Trippe could not be sure.

Trippe changed the subject. 'Why don't you gentlemen read this?' he suggested, handing them a copy of the Brewster bill and a memorandum from Pan Am's public-relations department setting forth reasons to support it. He asked for their position paper, and as Dietrich reached for his briefcase, Hughes snapped, 'I prefer not to give it to you, Mr Trippe.'

Unless they came to an agreement on a merger, Hughes intended to oppose the legislation. 'Let me think about your offer overnight, and we'll meet here again tomorrow at ten...' then left to keep a date in Los Angeles.

The next morning, Hughes was late, as usual, and not in a good mood. They went over the same ground. Trippe suggested they adjourn and re-examine their figures. 'Mr. Hughes, if we can devise a basis for a merger that will be acceptable to you, will you publicly come out in favor of the community-company bill?' Dietrich answered, 'We've taken a position with the other airlines against the bill, and I don't see how we can change that position without looking inconsistent.'

'I agree,' said Hughes. The meeting was over. Hughes was still concerned about the press getting wind of their rendezvous, and he directed Trippe to have his pilot pick him up at a deserted airport near the Mexican border, to which Hughes flew him in his aircraft. A week later, Trippe called on Dietrich at the Waldorf to ascertain whether he and Hughes had arrived at a conclusion. 'None,' said Dietrich. 'I've had no further instructions from Mr Hughes, and I presume that he has no further interest.'

In the spring of 1947, The Chosen Instrument played in both houses of the Eightieth Congress. S.987, a bill to amend the Civil Aeronautics Act and provide for the merger and consolidation of the nation's international air carriers, was introduced in the Senate by Owen Brewster. Companion measures were submitted in the House of Representatives by three Republicans and a Democrat from Arkansas, the home base of Pan American's lobbyist Carroll Cone.

Concurrent hearings were held from April to June, to the exasperation of most involved. No sooner would a witness finish in one chamber than he had to repeat his testimony in the other. With Brewster directing the Senate show as chairman of the aviation subcommittee of the Interstate and Foreign Commerce Committee and with the courtly Southerners absent, the level of civility dropped sharply from what it had been at the 1945 hearings.

Trippe appeared more contemptuous toward the CAB and the unmentioned foe in the White House than he had been two years before. 'Since VE day, a new American international air policy is being tried out; a policy providing for competition between American airlines abroad, domestic as well as international. The facts are that the system is not working well and that [in] a year hence, the situation will become progressively worse.'

The latest modifications in the bill made the community company unmanageable. Hundreds of surface-transport companies and seventeen domestic airlines were to participate, and although a maximum three per cent was set for each subscriber, opponents were sure that in the period of six months Pan American had to dispose of its excess stock, motivated shareholders could band together to amass blocks of shares and install the old management at the head of the consolidated company.

Cued by Brewster, Trippe assured the Senators that this could not happen. 'Pan American Airways disappears as a corporation.' He claimed that the bill made it 'obviously impossible for Pan American to be again designated to represent the United States in overseas air transport. Perhaps three or four of our directors may be permitted to serve on the new board, but the new board will be subject to approval of the CAB.'

Croil Hunter, president of Northwest Airlines, thought he discerned two plots. In 'the mess and confusion,' Pan American would wind up in control of the consolidated company and/or it would sell out to the government at a good price.

Indeed, this model of the chosen instrument was the most attractive for Pan Am stockholders, as it gave them shares in a new company whose financial success was guaranteed by Uncle Sam.

Trippe had made sure that in the bill were a whole range of subsidies to remove the risk from the enterprise: one to pay for construction of new aircraft, another to make it profitable to operate thinly trafficked routes 'in the national interest', a third to protect the company against lower wage and other operating costs of foreign airlines and a special grant to meet the higher subsidies collected by foreign airlines.

If anything ensured rejection of the bill by a Congress bent on economizing after fourteen years of Democratic spending, it was these provisions for financial aid which would have cost the taxpayer dear in administrative expenses alone. Moreover, domestic airlines would be severely disadvantaged. Chairman Landis of the CAB made the point another way: in creating a chosen instrument, Congress would destroy individual airlines, which could not be resurrected in case the chosen instrument proved a failure. 'The only way out would be a government-controlled and government-owned international air transport system - the path to socialism,' he said. The issue Trippe forced Congress to reckon with was one of the few on which a New Deal liberal like Landis and a Republican conservative like Taft could wholeheartedly agree.

The hearings ended and Trippe departed on 17 June 1947 for the triumphal voyage he had been envisioning for twenty years: the inauguration of Pan American Airways' round-the-world service, the first such flight scheduled by a commercial airline.

Without domestic authority, Pan American had to start its round-the-world flights on one coast and terminate them at the other. Flight 001, originating in San Francisco, winged westward over the Pacific Ocean. A passenger boarding 001 at San Francisco Municipal Airport (it didn't become San Francisco International until 1955) and making the entire journey would touch down in Honolulu, Hong Kong, Bangkok, Delhi, Beirut, Istanbul, Frankfurt, London and finally New York. Eastbound Flight 002, originating in New York, hit the same cities in the opposite direction, ending up in San Francisco. An economy-class ticket for the entire journey in either direction cost $2,300, or $4,000 for a couple.

The Constellation left New York La Guardia on 17 June 1947, flying 21,642 miles in an elapsed time of 160 hours, and returning to San Francisco. The airliner called at Gander, Shannon, London, Istanbul, Karachi, Calcutta, Bangkok, Shanghai, Tokyo, Manila, Guam, Wake, Midway and Honolulu. As the flight was not a proper scheduled service, permission was granted to fly across the US continent back to New York, arriving on 1 July.

The mayor of New York, William O'Dwyer and the mayor of San Francisco, Roger Lapham, made speeches predicting that humanity would

TWAs N88518 in flight. *(TWA)*

be brought closer through air commerce, and the National Anthem played.

The regular scheduled 'Round-the-World' flights started on 27 June, once weekly in each direction, but did not call at Shanghai or Tokyo. The Constellations only flew the New York - Calcutta sector, departing New York on Fridays and arriving Calcutta on Mondays. The San Francisco - Calcutta sector was flown by DC-4s. On 29 August 1947, scheduled non-stop New York - London services were introduced with the 749 Connies, but the 'non-stop' nature of the services depended very much on the prevailing weather conditions. At this time Pan American were operating three daily New York - London flights, with one weekly flight continuing to Damascus, one to Calcutta (connecting with the DC-4 Round-the-World to San Francisco), and six weekly flights to Lisbon, via the Azores, two of which continued to Dakar, Accra, Leopoldville and Johannesburg.

Trippe sustained another loss with the overwhelming rejection by the committees in both Houses of the bills to merge and consolidate the international carriers. So the avenue of destruction for Pan American's competitors through Congress was closed. And with it, Pan American's last chance to be the nation's chosen instrument by force of law. If Trippe was disheartened, no one could have guessed it from his demeanour. Everything was business as usual. Those who knew him best understood that Juan Trippe did not acknowledge failure and that when he was ready, he would give them their marching orders. The chosen instrument was his dream, and it could not be taken away from him.

On the afternoon of 6 August 1947, Howard Hughes loped into the Senate Caucus Room. He was forty-two minutes late for his appointment with a subcommittee of the War Investigating Committee.

Photographers' bulbs flashed, newsreel cameras whirred. Reporters, wearing sunglasses against the glare of klieg lights, scribbled furiously. A clatter of applause broke out from among a thousand perspiring spectators, most of them women craning for a glimpse of the capricious millionaire whose romances with filmland's leading ladies were chronicled in the tabloids and fan magazines.

Hughes was cast to play the role of honest knight come to slay a dragon in the nation's capital. He wore his black hair parted in the middle and slicked back, his brush moustache neatly trimmed. A white shirt and double-breasted grey suit overwhelmed his lean body, battered in so many aircraft and automobile accidents. His socks drooped.

Behind a battery of microphones, Hughes raised his hand to be sworn in as a witness. Cupping a hand to a deaf ear, he strained to catch the remarks of the subcommittee chairman, Senator Homer Ferguson of Michigan, and threw a glance of loathing at Brewster, seated on the dais. Then he read his opening lines.

'I charge specifically that during luncheon at the Mayflower Hotel in the week beginning February 10, 1947, in the suite of Senator Brewster, that the Senator told me in so many words that if I would agree to merge TWA with Pan American and would go along with his community airline bill there would be no further hearing in this matter.'

The 'matter' was the investigation, then in its second week, into the military contracts for the uncompleted planes. According to Hughes, Juan Trippe had told him in Palm Springs that he would try to get the Senator to delay both the hearings on the bill and the investigation, pending a merger between the airlines.

The proceedings degenerated into a political circus. Hughes and Brewster staged a sideshow in the newspapers, exchanging calumnies through press releases. Before leaving California for Washington, Hughes issued a statement: 'I worked pretty hard for what money I have, and I didn't make it from airplanes. All in all, in my transactions with the Government, I have made no profit whatsoever.' He portrayed himself as a Texan who kept his word and told the truth, and he threatened to take his story of Brewster's attempted blackmail to the Attorney General.

Brewster counterthrust with an obscure Biblical reference. Reporters were forced to consult their King James versions of the Old Testament to discover, in Chapter VI of the Book of Nehemiah, that the prophet did not let the mischief of his enemies deter him from completing the Work Of God. 'I will welcome and invite the most thorough exploration of this charge by the Attorney General,' and sent a copy of his announcement to the Justice Department.

No evidence of fraud or corruption in the procurement of the contracts for the Hercules and the XF-11 was discovered during the hearings, but there were titillating revelations about the entertainment furnished by Johnny Meyer and another publicist for Hughes. Elliott Roosevelt challenged their expense-account notations and charged that the inquiry was a continuation of 'the smear' of his father by Brewster and Ferguson in the Pearl Harbor investigation.

After Hughes finished repeating to the subcommittee his account of Brewster's menacing offer, the Senator stepped down from the dais to refute him. Brewster stood before his peers and swore to tell the truth. He admitted having talked to Hughes about the merger and about the aviation bill, but never with an intent to 'persecute' him or misuse his investigatory authority. On the contrary, Hughes had tried to 'coerce' him into dropping the investigation by sending one of his lawyers, a former chief counsel to the committee, to tell Brewster he had 'a hot potato' in his hands.

'They were seeking to lay a trap for me,' whined Brewster in a tearful voice. What was Homer Ferguson to do? The investigation had backfired spectacularly, and Republican conduct was being held up to scrutiny. The subcommittee chairman ruled that neither man could cross-examine the other; if they submitted questions in writing, he would relay them.

The next day, Hughes presented his list.

While Howard Hughes was appearing in the Senate Caucus Room, Lockheeds were offering different interiors for their new airliner. *(Lockheed)*

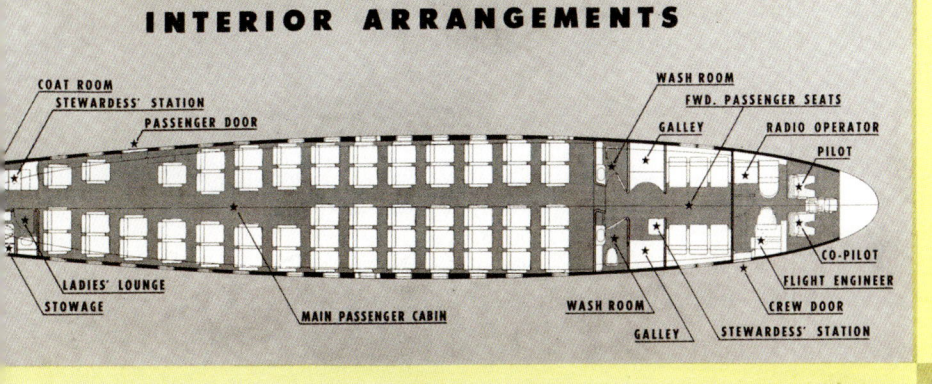

INTERIOR ARRANGEMENTS

Non-Convertible Day

A maximum capacity chair-type interior arrangement which accommodates 64 passengers. Overhead baggage racks are provided at each seat location. Additional under-seat space is available for the stowage of small parcels or brief cases.

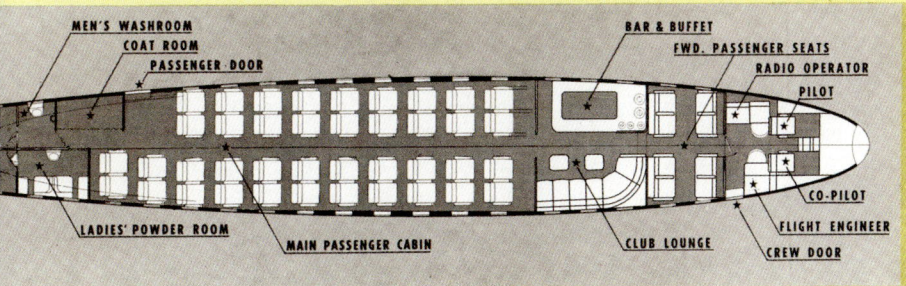

Non-Convertible Club

A deluxe day arrangement for 48 passengers. This interior features a bar-lounge in the forward section of the cabin and is provided with overhead baggage racks and underseat stowage space. (48 passenger seats are exclusive of seats in bar-lounge).

Convertible Day-Sleeper

A maximum capacity convertible interior which provides accommodations for 48 day passengers, or 34 berth passengers. Adequate coat room and stewardess' storage space is featured in this arrangement.

Ferguson read them to his crony. Brewster alternated between defiance and obsequiousness, a seemingly sycophantic, cloying 'umble Uriah Heep vouching for his integrity.

The community company bill was not drawn to favour the stock-holders of Pan American Airways, he said. 'Juan Trippe is a man not interested in making money.' He professed admiration for the president of Pan American, whom he had known for four or five years, though their personal associations were 'very limited'. 'I believe I have been his guest at dinner twice. I believe these are the only times I've ever been in his home. I think he is a very able man.'

He owned up to friendship with Sam Pryor - 'We have a close and very gratifying personal relationship' - but minimized the vice president's bounty. Pryor's generosity to officials was well advertised in gifts of rare bourbon whiskey, tickets to sporting events and other entertainments, and for special friends, the use of his house in Hobe Sound, a Florida retreat for Eastern Old Boys who could not abide the nouveaux riche in neighbouring Palm Beach.

Brewster, a Christian Scientist and a teetotaler admitted that he and his wife had partaken of Sam's hospitality for two Thanksgiving sojourns. 'It's a very modest, bungalow-type place. A small place of five rooms,' he said. 'The Pryors were not there. I paid the cook five dollars a day. I went to the grocery store and bought groceries and the Thanksgiving turkey. I left the place pretty well stocked up with canned goods, as a sort of expression of my appreciation.'

Pan American's house on F Street was also 'very modest', according to Brewster, who compared it with TWA's 'palace' in Arlington. 'It has a toilet on the first floor that is always out of order, more than any other I know.' He claimed to have had no more than three breakfasts on F Street.

Brewster allowed that he had accepted a ride in the Pan American aircraft to see Senator Bailey in Raleigh about the community-company bill. He implicated his fellow Republican Senator John W. Bricker of Ohio as a companion on the TWA courtesy flight to Columbus.

The next day Brewster left for Maine, where he said he was 'gratified at the relatively few skeletons which have been found in my closet.' The hearings were put back on the track of Hughes's military contracts. After a weekend recess, Senator Ferguson startled the audience on Monday morning by suspending the hearings until November and vanishing into hospital to be treated for poison ivy.

Encircled by well-wishers, Hughes turned to the newsreel cameras for his farewell address. 'As soon as Senator Brewster saw he was fighting a losing battle against public opinion he folded up and took a run-out powder,' he said.

The attempt to stain his reputation had failed. Fair play had won out. 'And for that', drawled Hughes, 'I want to thank the people of this country and the members of the press.'

Hughes proclaimed his vindication. A slightly daft tycoon with a Grade B cinematic flair was judged a more credible actor than a greedy politician. Whether Brewster and Trippe threatened Hughes or whether he merely reached an obvious conclusion, their plan to get rid of TWA as an international competitor for Pan American was incontrovertible, and the alliance to further their respective ambitions more than a shade unholy.

The hearings, which were supposed to discredit the Democrats and enhance Brewster's chances of higher political office, confirmed a relationship until then only rumoured between the Senator and Pan American Airways. Although he had five years before his next test at the polls, Brewster's political future and Juan Trippe's chosen instrument were doomed in the Caucus Room.

Chapter Five

Around the World

The First Transatlantic Services
Carrying the largest number of passengers ever to fly between the USA and Europe on one airliner, TWA Constellation NC86511 *Star of Paris* piloted by Capt Harold F Blackburn inaugurated the international service for TWA when it took off from LaGuardia Field, New York at 1:21 p.m., (CST) 5 February and landed at Orly Field, Paris, at 8:57 a.m. the next day.

Strong headwinds held the Constellation to a total flying time for the trip of 16 hours, 21 minutes. Previously, on 3 December, a preview flight covered the distance from Washington to Paris in the record time of 12 hours and 57 minutes. As well as its thirty-six passengers and crew of eight, *Star of Paris* carried a varied cargo of US products, including a mercy shipment of one million units of life-saving penicillin.

The Constellation was christened by Mrs. Jack Frye in brief ceremonies prior to takeoff when 'she released a fog of carbon dioxide from a 'cloud gun' at the ship's sleek silver nose. Ambassador Henri Bonnet of France and Robert Brennan, Irish minister to the US, also took part in the ceremonies dedicating the flight to international peace. Otis F Bryan, vice president-operations of the International Division, represented TWA in the rites at LaGuardia.

The emergency consignment of penicillin was rushed to Paris, then on to Rome, by Dr. John Grieco of The Bronx, New York, in response to a transatlantic telephone call advising him his sister was dangerously ill and in need of the drug.

In announcing the passenger list of the inaugural flight, President Jack Frye pointed out TWA had followed a strict policy of first-come,

Early morning sun glints off this TWA Constellation at Paris-Orly in the late 1940s. *(Dee Diddely Collection)*

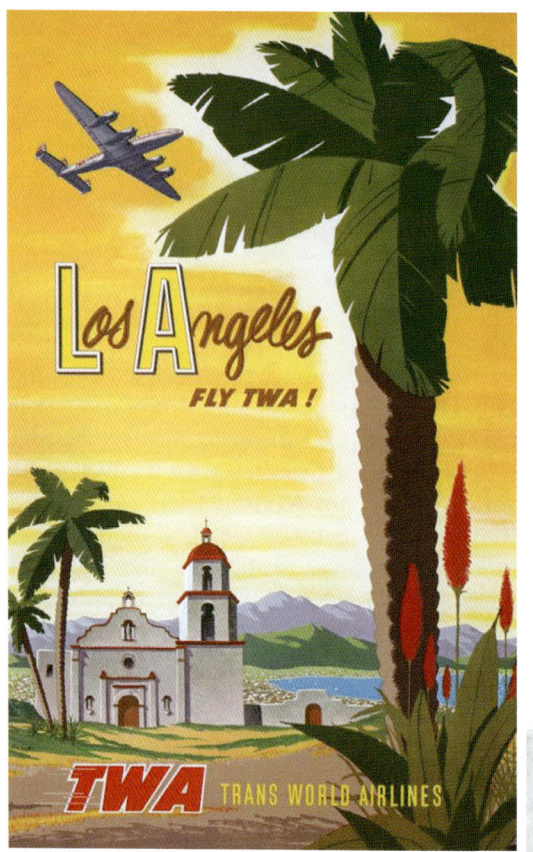

first-served, and that the selection had been based on the priority of application rather than on privilege.

Among the passengers were Joseph Silver, ex-GI, who was going back to marry a girl he courted in Brussels during the war; Lucie Spilo and Robert Ricci, fashion designers en route to Paris spring openings; Ben J. Joseph, Palestine diamond expert; George Herbin, Coty, Inc.; executive Gerard Lorin, returning to his native France to take charge of an extensive 16 mm. movie project for Loew's International Corporation; Henri Doll, a leading French engineer, and a delegation of the French Business Commission.

Scheduled time for the New York-Paris flight was 18 hours. Service, for the time being, was twice weekly, increasing to daily service within the next few weeks.

A few days later, it was time to add another to a long and distinguished list of TWA firsts - the first flight of five cardinals-designate of the

5-6 February 1946: TWA flew its first revenue international passengers on a scheduled transatlantic flight from La Guardia Field, New York to Aéroport de Paris-Orly, Paris. Lockheed L-049 Constellation, NC86511, named *Star of Paris,* under the command of Captain Harold F. Blackburn. Captains Jack Hermann and John M. Calder, Navigator M. Chrisman and Flight Engineers Art Ruhanen, Ray McBride and Jack Rouge completed the flight crew. Purser Don Shiemwell and Hostess Ruth Schmidt were in the cabin along with 36 passengers. *Star of Paris* departed LaGuardia at 2:21 p.m., EST, 5 February. The flight made brief stops at Gander, Newfoundland and Shannon, Ireland, and arrived at Orly Field, at 3:57 p.m., 6 February. The elapsed time was 16 hours, 21 minutes.

Above: In October 1941 KLM - Koninklijke Luchtvaart Maatschappij - Royal Dutch Airlines asked for permission to buy four Model 049 Constellations, but, owing to the wartime situation, permission was refused. In 1943, however, KLM became the first non-US carrier to order Constellations for post-war delivery, the order being formally confirmed after the war on 29 Sepember 1945. On 28 May 1946, the first of KLM's four 049s was handed over, followed during the next three weeks by the three other aircraft. Owing to the grounding of the type in July 1946, however, the Connies could not enter service until later in the year. It was planned to open a twice weekly Constellation service from Amsterdam to New York on about l5 October 1946, but it was November before the 049s entered service on that run.

Left: Such was the image of the Constellation all over the world, it is not surprising that the airliner was linked in with advertising other products, like here with the DKW microbus.

Catholic church from the United States to Rome for their official elevation to their new posts by Pope Pius XII!

The arrival of the prelates in Rome also marked the first US airline service into Italy, only a few days after the inauguration by TWA of the first airline service to Paris.

The five left on 10 and 11 February from Chicago and New York in two TWA Constellations, which carried them via Gander, Newfoundland, Shannon, Ireland, and Paris to the Vatican City in Rome. Aboard *Star of Cairo* which left Chicago Sunday, 10 February were Archbishops Samuel A. Stritch of Chicago and Edward Mooney of Detroit, accompanied by twenty-eight high church and laymen.

The next day the Constellation *Star of Rome* left LaGuardia Field, New York, carrying Archbishops Francis J. Spellman of New York and John J. Glennon of St. Louis and Bishop Thomas Tien of China, first non-Caucasian to be elevated to the post of cardinal in the history of the church. The *Star of Rome* carried a list of thirty-six passengers, including James A. Farley of New York, former postmaster-general, the Very Rev. Robert I. Gannon, president of Fordham University, and former Mayor Joseph J. McKee of New York.

After a mechanical delay at Detroit, the plane bearing Stritch and Mooney spanned the Atlantic in 8 hours and 5 minutes, flying from Gander to Shannon. After a stop there and another at Paris, the *Star of Cairo,* flown by veteran TWA pilot Captain Edward Wells, landed in Rome about noon on 12 February. The cardinals-designate were elevated at rites in the Consistory at Vatican City 18 February.

A day later Capt. Charles O Tate, another long-time pilot, was at the controls of the *Star of Rome* when it left LaGuardia Field with Glennon, Spellman and Tien aboard, landed at Shannon and flew on to Rome after a brief stop in Paris. Aboard the airliners were priceless cargoes of ecclesiastical garments, many of them handed down to the archbishops by their predecessor American cardinals. Each cardinal-elect carried three hundred pounds of additional baggage, comprising robes, vestments and other garments worn by a cardinal in the traditional rites.

Comments of the high churchmen on the flight were uniformly enthusiastic. For Mooney and Glennon it was their first aeroplane ride—and the 83-year-old Glennon, dean of the four Americans, said only the existence of an aircraft such as the Constellation made his trip to Rome for the rites possible. He could not have stood the arduous journey by surface transportation, he explained.

On their arrival in Paris, Archbishop Mooney of Detroit commented: 'A good trip, an excellent trip'. Greeting a friend at Orly Airport, Archbishop Stritch voiced the highest praise for the flying skill of Captain Wells, and said, 'The crossing was smooth, and the ocean resembled glass.' Another member of the party added that '...the ship was so steady one could have played billiards throughout the voyage.'

During the flight, each of the prelates had taken the controls of the big airliner for a short time. The planes bearing the two parties' flew most of the time at altitudes above 20,000 feet, 'over the weather', but the supercharged cabins of the Lockheed Constellations kept the 'inside altitude' at a comfortable sea-level pressure.

Grounding Through Engine Troubles

Although the Constellation was firmly established on the international scene by mid-1946, it was not without its troubles, and fires in the Wright R-3350 engines were a particular problem. Following an engine fire in a Pan American 049 in June 1946, the CAB issued a ruling that the cabin supercharger drive shafts

California Hawaiian Airlines was incorporated in California in 1946. The company was controlled by Colonel Charles C. Sherman and Edna K. Sherman. The airline operated low-fare services from April 1952 until October 1953 between the cities of Los Angeles and San Francisco and Honolulu, Hawaii. In February 1954 CHA and CCA went into voluntary Bankruptcy. California Hawaiian Airlines remerged in 1955 under the same ownership and operations were started in January 1959. In 1960 two 1049s were leased from TWA for charter and MATS contract work. Flights were also made to Europe, mainly Frankfurt during the period June until October 1961. In 1961-62 several 749As were leased in addition to a 1049. After MATS disqualified the airline the interim operating certificate was revoked and the aircraft all returned to their lessors. *(both Kirk Smeeton Collection)*

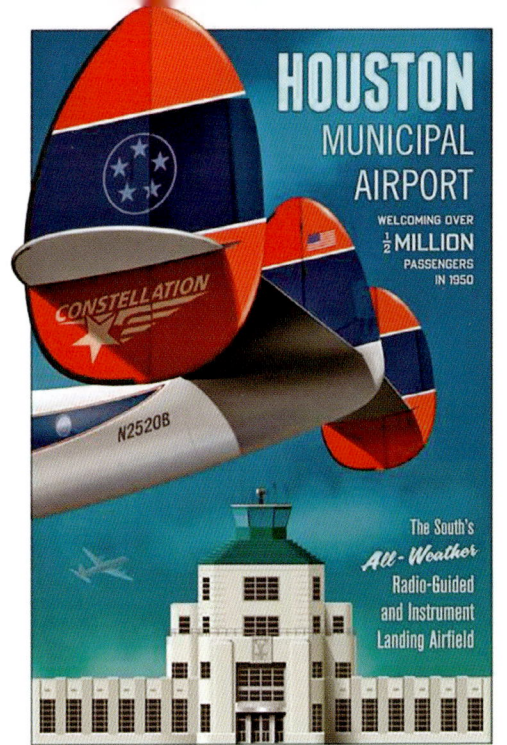

Below: Braniff International Airways operated a pair of L-049s, N2521B seen here. Braniff Airways started operations on the Oklahoma City to Tulsa route in 1928, and added the word 'International' to its title for marketing reasons after services were extended in 1948 from the south of the USA to South America. Two 049s were bought from the Venezuelan Airline LAV in Aug 55, and these were used on the Dallas to San Antonio, Chicago to Dallas and Houston via Kansas City, Wichita and Oklahoma City and the Houston & Dallas to Amarillo First class schedules. In addition, a daily interchange service with TWA (and their 049s) was flown from Houston to San Francisco via Dallas, Amarillo, Las Vegas and Los Angeles until 1 Mar 56, the Braniff 049s operating as far as Amarillo.
(Kirk Smeeton Collection)

Left: The airline, and the Connies distinctive triple fins were used to promote the airports it flew from.

from the outer engines must be disconnected and sealed off. This meant that the aircraft had temporarily to be operated unpressurised, flying at lower altitudes, and without the cabin heating supplied by two superchargers to a pair of Janitrol-type heaters under the cabin floor.

These driveshafts, taken from the two outer engines, were about two feet long, each supercharger being mounted adjacent to the engine, and the troubles arose from the vibration transmitted from the flexibly-mounted engines. The R-3350s had also suffered a number of fires in the induction system, a problem separate from the supercharger drive, and this was finally solved by the installation of direct fuel injection to the engines, although a Bendix direct cylinder fuel injection system had also been available for the Wright R-3350 for some time previously as an alternative.

Following the crash of TWA 049 NC86513 on 11 July 1946 in a hayfield near TWA's training base at Reading, Pennsylvania, after a fire in No 3 engine, the CAB grounded all Constellations, and the type remained grounded until 23 August at a cost of about $50,000,000 for the fifty-eight aircraft involved.

Tests continued to find the cause of this training flight crash, in which all but one of the five crew were killed, and also the cause of the repeated engine fires; there had been 46 cases of trouble with the cabin supercharger drive up to the Pan American 049 fire which had led to its being disconnected. A Constellation had been fitted in May 1946 with direct injection fuel feeds in place of the Bendix-Stromberg injection carburetters in its R-3350s and two-speed superchargers instead of single-speed ones. This commenced a 100 hour programme of test

110

NC90922 *Flagship Denmark* of American Overseas Airlines suffered a minor incident when the right landing gear collapsed when landing on a closed runway at Boston on 3 May 1947. The aircraft was repaired, and later sold to Pan Am. *(Robin Banks Collection)*

flying to prove this new fuel distribution system, which eliminated the carburetter, and thus the seat of induction fires caused by blow-backs, in favour of injecting the fuel into the eye of the supercharger. This also had the advantage of eliminating carburetter freezing. Although the R-3350 had given excellent service mechanically, the induction distribution had never been entirely satisfactory. To solve this problem, Lockheed test flew a Constellation with one engine fitted with ignitor plugs in various parts of the induction system so that fires could be ignited at will, and the system's susceptibility to fires investigated.

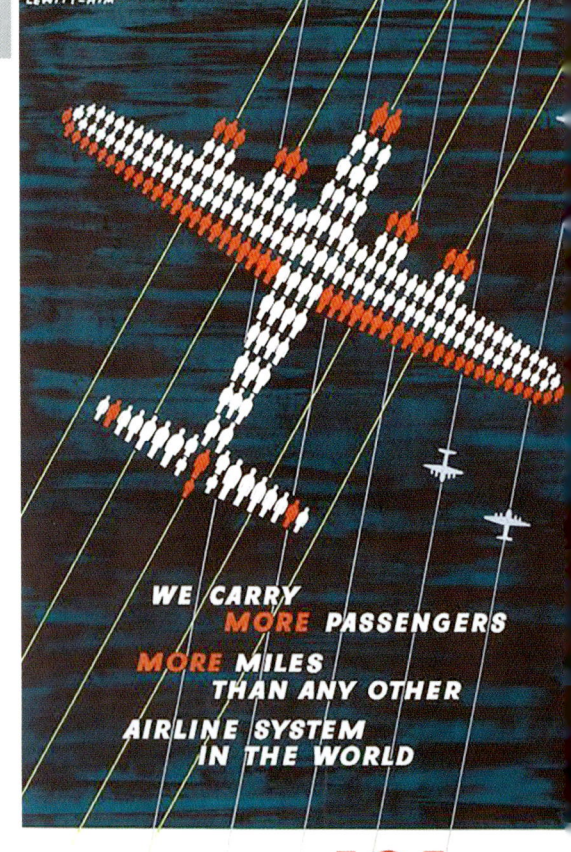

About 150 fires were started on this engine for test purposes and all were successfully extinguished without using the main extinguisher system and without endangering the aircraft. A month or two prior to the grounding, modifications had been approved to the cabin supercharger drive shaft and to the supercharger lubrication system and bearings; several aircraft had been thus modified before the Pan American fire in June, after which some further mods to the drive shaft were approved. The enquiry into the Reading accident concluded that the fire originated as a result of a fault in the electrical system, and the CAB ordered thirty-seven minor modifications to be made to the Constellation, mainly to the electrical system. Direct injection was not specifically required by the CAB although it had become a standard feature on all Constellations, and those not so fitted were being modified retrospectively at the time of the Reading accident.

The engines with direct injection were designated R-3350-745CI8BA-3, and at first one and then all of BOAC's 049s were fitted with the new fuel distribution system. Pan American also fitted its 049s and 749s with a new type of engine analyser that made possible detection and visual presentation of engine faults while airborne, being the first airline to fit its aircraft with such a device. And following the forced-landing of Pan Am's 049 NC88845 *Clipper Eclipse* in Syria on 19 June 1947 after No 2 engine had caught fire and fallen out of the aircraft, it was recommended that methyl bromide be used in place of CO2 in the fire extinguisher system. Pan Am's 049 NC88856 *Clipper Paul Jones* was also fitted with an experimental periscopic sextant for the navigator instead of the drag producing astrodome.

With the introduction of DC-6s by American Airlines and - from May 1947 - by United, TWA's competitors were at less of a disadvantage and the traffic battle settled down to an even fight between TWA and American, with United trailing some way behind in terms of frequencies offered. In September 1947 TWA carried thirty-seven per cent of the passengers on the New York - Los Angeles route, American forty-seven per cent and United sixteen per cent. TWA also put Constellations on the New York-San Francisco route, at first with stops at Chicago, Kansas City and Los Angeles, with a time comparable to United's DC-4s which made only one stop at Omaha (Nebraska). In May 1947 United inaugurated an overnight DC-6 flight on this route with no stop taking 9 hours 55 minutes for the eastbound crossing, and TWA replied on I July by inaugurating a one-stop at Chicago Constellation overnight service to San Francisco taking 10 hours 10 minutes eastbound and 11 hours 40 minutes westbound. This, together with an improved service to and from

In the immediate post-war years the Constellation was seen as a high-prestige aircraft. The sharp-suited Madison Avenue advertising executives made much use of the iconography, such as here for Sinclair Oils and, by inference, Eastern Airlines.

Air France used a large number of Constellations, Here what is thought to be F-BAZJ is about to depart Beiruit Airport in the Lebanon.

Capital Airines advertisement.

HIGH TIME TO SET THE TABLE

Distant cities become suburbs when you fly. You can enjoy so many more pleasant hours at home. Last year more than two million passengers preferred Capital Airlines.

Dependable, friendly service has been a Capital tradition for 26 years. Isn't it High Time you tried it?

Over 500 Flights Daily Between 75 Major Cities

Call your TRAVEL AGENT or ...

Capital AIRLINES

San Francisco via Los Angeles, effectively met United's and American's competition.

Other operators were putting Constellations into service on the Atlantic and other intercontinental routes. The Brazilian national carrier Panair do Brasil, formed as a subsidiary of Pan American and in which the latter still had a forty-eight per cent holding, started operating regular Constellation services to London from Rio de Janeiro on 27 April 1946, calling at Dakar, Lisbon, Madrid and Paris. Panair's Constellations - the initial fleet was three - were acquired from Pan American, which eventually turned over sixteen 049s to the Brazilian carrier, and on 16 April one of these, PP-PCF *Manoél de Borba Gato,* landed at London's newly-opened Heathrow Airport on a proving flight with fourteen passengers. It thus became the first of its type and, indeed, the first aircraft of a foreign airline to land at London Airport, as well as inaugurating the first Brazilian service to the United Kingdom. Panair's Constellations later extended their European routes to include Rome, Zurich, Frankfurt, Istanbul and Beirut, as well as operating the more important ones in South America, such as those to Santiago and Lima. On 20 December 1953 a Panair Constellation completed what was claimed to be the world's longest commercial flight when it flew non-stop between Lisbon and Rio de Janeiro, covering the 4,837 miles in 21 hours 40 minutes. The elegant shape of PP-PCF on the Heathrow apron that

April afternoon was a foretaste of how much more international long-haul air transport was to become now that it was no longer (as before the war) solely in the hands of the USA and a few European countries.

American Overseas Airlines had been the first to operate a scheduled landplane service across the Atlantic, beginning with a DC-4 crossing from New York to Hurn on 23-24 October 1945. AOA's sphere of influence was Germany and Scandinavia, including Finland and Iceland, as well as the UK, and on 23 June 1946, the first of a fleet of seven L-049-46-27s went into service on these routes, followed by eight Boeing Stratocruisers. But in those early post-war years there was not really enough traffic to support three US airlines on the Atlantic, and Pan Am, which had bitterly contested American Export Airlines' entry on this route in 1942, eagerly sought an opportunity to buy out or eliminate AOA. This came about on 25 September 1950, after President Truman, despite TWA's protests, had given approval for Pan Am's acquisition of AOA, so reversing his previous endorsement of the CAB's rejection of this deal. AOA's fleet of Constellations was thereupon taken over by Pan Am.

Air France had meanwhile taken delivery of four 049 Constellations, in June 1946, chiefly for the Paris- New York route on which they began services on 24 June. Still, the French airline's main commitment was to the L-749 and L-749A for expanding its routes to Africa, the Far East and South America. The four 049s were sold to TWA in January and February 1950, following Air France's purchase in December of an equal number of 749-79-46 Constellations from Pan American, which had bought these aircraft to provide extra capacity pending the delivery of its Stratocruisers; Air France had already taken delivery of about half of its L-749s on order.

KLM Royal Dutch Airlines ordered six Model 049s for its long-haul routes from Amsterdam, particularly to New York and to Batavia (shortly to become Djakarta with Indonesian independence) and took delivery of the first, PH-TAU *Utrecht*, on 28 May 1946. KLM had actually placed provisional orders for four Constellations and four DC-4s in 1943, while the war was still on, even though Lockheed could not at this time supply Connies to the airlines. One crashed at Prestwick on 28 October 1948, three were sold to Capital Airlines Inc in the summer of 1950 when they were replaced by 749s, and the remaining two were acquired by TWA. By 1950 Capital had become the fifth largest US domestic airline in terms of passengers carried and its ex-KLM machines joined two other converted C-69s on the more important of Capital's routes in the north-east USA, remaining the airline's first-line equipment until displaced by the Vickers Viscount fleet ordered in 1954, together with some more L-749s acquired from KLM. Capital's 049Es featured a 'Cloud Club Room' lounge forward with seating for eight people, and four-abreast seating for fifty-six passengers in the main cabin, and remained in service until 1960.

A more unusual and exotic interior was featured on the three L-049E Constellations of Cia Cubana de Aviacion SA acquired from Pan American, of which Cubana was a wholly-owned subsidiary before the war and in which Pan Am still had a sizeable holding. The Cuban airline had started a Havana-Mexico City Constellation service on I7 September 1953, and later put these aircraft on to a number of other routes, including Havana-Miami. In 1956 a new management headed by Juan M. Palli Diaz, formerly vice-president and general manager, took over and it was he who suggested that artists from Havana's world-famous Tropicana night club be engaged to help boost load factors on the Thursday evening Havana - Miami Constellation flight, Cubana having lost traffic on this route to other airlines with more modern aircraft to such an extent that more than fifteen passengers each way was considered a good load. Top artists from the Tropicana were hired and the service was named 'The Tropicana Express'. The night club act, complete with drums as well as the piano, was temporarily successful in winning back some of the lost traffic until Viscounts took over the Havana - Miami route in August 1956.

Ana Gloria Varona was a showgirl at the Tropicana and worked some of the Cubana Constellation flights: We hid behind a gold

Below: A Cia Cubana de Aviacion SA postcard, showing one of their Constellations.

In the early 1950s, the airline purchased several L-1049E and L-1049Gs from the U.S. The first, L-1049E, registered as CU-P573 was delivered in early 1953 and was placed in service on Cubana's Madrid route. Cubana was Lockheed's launch customer for the L-1049E. The airliners allowed Cubana to start service to Mexico City, New York City, and to increase frequencies to Madrid via Bermuda, the Azores and Lisbon. With these aircraft, Cubana became the first Latin American airline to establish services to New York. The Viscounts were used for its Miami and Nassau flights, and for domestic services to Camagüey and Santiago de Cuba.

In 1954, the airline became fully Cuban-owned when Pan American Airways sold its minority stake. This marked Cubana's independence as a private Cuban enterprise. Cuban investors were drawn to Cubana by the airline's potential for growth and by its achievements, such as the quality of passenger services, the renovation of its fleet (which was among the most advanced in Latin America), the experience of its crews, and its projected international expansion. An additional attraction was the airline's promotional efforts to cater to Cuba's growing tourism industry, particularly with American travellers.

curtain when the passengers came on board, like we were backstage at a real cabaret. My dance partner Rolando and I were set to put on a live floor show in the front of the cabin. We even had a band from Tropicana with us - a pianist, a bongo player, a drummer, and a trumpet player. The front seats had been taken out so the musicians could all fit in with their instruments. Who knows how they got that piano on the plane?

'The passengers started off with pink daiquiris, and then, as soon as the plane took off, Rolando and I bounded out and started our show. Out we came, singing and dancing. I pranced down the aisles, pulling the Americans up from their seats to dance with me. I was such a happy little thing, pretty, and so young, in my pullover, little sneakers, and bobby socks. The Americans were very good to me. I gave them cards with lyrics, and I got them to sing along with me - old boleros like 'Quiéreme mucho, dulce amor mío . . .'

'We breezed through the airport when the plane landed, jumped on Tropicana's bus, and headed straight to the club. I don't think the Americans had to bother with customs since Tropicana and Cubana de Aviación had a special arrangement. After the show, they were put up overnight at the Hotel Nacional, and then we flew them back to Miami the next day. That's how we brought Nat King Cole to Havana that March, the first of three times he performed at Tropicana. He was tall, so good-looking, a handsome black man. When he headlined at Tropicana, it always filled up to the gills. Those were carefree times'.

Another Latin American operator of 049s was the Venezuelan airline, Linea Aeropostal Venezolana, which took delivery of two on 31 October 1946, followed by two 749s a year later; with these, a direct Caracas-New York service was inaugurated on 21 March 1947, followed by other regional routes in the Caribbean area and, in October 1953, a service to Rome via the Azores, Lisbon and Madrid. LAV's two 049s were sold to Braniff in August 1955.

As TWA took delivery of its L-749s and, later, Super Constellations, its Model 049s were turned over more and more to coach-class domestic services, which had been started early in 1950 with three L-749s seating eighty-one passengers. By 1958 most of TWA's thirty-two 049s had 81-seater coach-class interiors, although some 57-seaters were retained for first-class domestic services. The original 47-passenger layout for a 60-seat had later superseded the Atlantic tourist-class interior for this route, and another layout for thirty-two passengers in reclining seats was for a time featured for 'Sleeper Seat' services on international routes.

Controversy Over BOAC Order

Of all the post-war orders for Constellations, probably none aroused more controversy in their respective countries than BOAC's order for five Model 049-46-25s, announced to the House of Commons on 24 January 1946 by the Parliamentary Secretary to the Ministry of Civil Aviation. To both aviation people and the general public, the order came as a considerable shock, and several prominent aviation personalities expressed themselves forcibly about it.

To the British public, with a strong belief in the war-winning qualities of such aircraft as the Avro Lancaster and De Havilland Mosquito, the Constellation purchase seemed a retrograde step, especially at a time of dollar shortage. Fuel was added to the fire when, a few months later,

Bare-metal Constellations always looked good in my mind. These two images of BOAC's G-AHEL with the sun glinting off the curves I think prove my point!

BOAC ordered six Boeing Stratocruisers. As *The Aeroplane* of 6 September 1946 commented in its editorial:

'As we have frequently pointed out in this paper, if, three years ago, when the Brabazon Committee was planning our production, four Bristol Centaurus engines had been taken and a transatlantic liner built around them, we should by now have a British type larger than the Constellation and not much smaller than the Stratocruiser. But the Powers That Be knew better, so what alternative is there to the present policy if we are not to lose most of our Atlantic traffic to the Americans.'

BOAC's order for Constellations could be defended far more easily than several of its later purchases of American types, for at that time there was really no alternative if their competitive position on the Atlantic was to be maintained. Roy Chadwick's truly dreadful Avro Tudor I was originally intended for this route - and the Constellations were at first envisaged as 'interim' equipment until the Tudors were ready. The Tudor only had accommodation for twelve passengers and would have been much too small to have remained competitive.

In January 1947 the Ministry of Supply in London issued draft specification 2/47 for a medium-range Empire airliner, and ten companies tendered designs. Among them was the Bristol Aeroplane Co, which offered the Type 175. This was the aeroplane which was later to emerge as the Britannia with Bristol Proteus turboprops, although the Type 175 at that stage was a 32-passenger aeroplane with four Bristol Centaurus 662 or 663 radials, and smaller than the Britannia that eventually appeared. But it is interesting to note that Bristol had concluded that the 2/47 specification could best be met by building the Constellation under licence in this country with Bristol Centaurus 662 engines, a scheme which became known as Project Y. Lockheed would have been willing to grant a licence and it was considered that British-built Constellations could have been available at about the same time and for the same price as the Type 175s.

Bristol had some discussions with Lockheed

Two views of BOACs G-ALAN *Beaufort*. The aircraft was originally laid down for Eastern Air Lines, but was transferred to Aerlinte as EI-AAD, but was quickly sold to BOAC in 1948. It is thought these pictures were taken in Australia. *(Matt Black Collection)*.

BOAC's G-AHEJ *Bristol* demonstrates yet another version of the company colour scheme for their Constellations - there were at least three! *(Matt Black Collection).*

as to the possibility of fitting Bristol Centaurus engines in five L-749s which BOAC might also purchase, this scheme was known, somewhat sinisterly, as Project X. In the end, sanction was refused for further dollar expenditure and Projects X and Y were both abandoned while the Type 175 design went ahead.

The first of ten BOAC Constellation proving flights to London's Heathrow airport from New York was flown on 16 June 1946 by G-AHEM *Balmoral* with Capt W S May in command, in the record time of 11 hours 24 minutes non-stop. Regular services to New York began on 1 July, twice-weekly at first, soon stepped up to three a week, and then a daily flight. BOAC's 049s were later put on to other routes and remained in service until the Comet accidents early in 1954 forced BOAC to take drastic measures to restore the capacity lost by the withdrawal of the De Havilland jet. More Stratocruisers had to be ordered and the seven L-049Es then in service

(two more ex-AOA 049s had been acquired from Pan American early in 1953, and a converted C-69C had been bought in March 1948) were exchanged with Capital Airlines in return for seven of the latter's L-749A-79-24s which, with their higher gross weight, had the improved payload/range which was now needed for the Commonwealth routes. The deal, which enabled BOAC to standardise its fleet with the later model Constellations, involved a cash adjustment payment to Capital Airlines of £1,375,000.

BOAC also had the expense of refurbishing the newly-acquired Capital aircraft to its own standards, this work including a change of cabin interior, galleys and associated fittings and the installation of long-range radio. The first ex-BOAC L-049E to leave the UK on delivery to Capital was G-AHEM *Balmoral*, which departed on 8 October 1954, and the seventh was handed over to the US airline at the end of

G-AHEN of BOAC perched in a very undignified position at Filton following it's landing accident.
(Simon Peters Collection).

G-AHEK *Berwick* was built for the USAAF as 42-94555. It is seen here undergoing servicing. *(Authors Collection)*

June 1955.

It may be noted here that the designation L-049E was applied from 1953 to the L-049 with maximum all-up weight increased from 96,000 to 98,000 pounds. Of the original five BOAC 049s one, G-AHEN *Baltimore*, was damaged in a crash at Filton, Bristol on 8 January 1951. It was written off, bought by Mel Adams & Associates, and shipped as deck cargo to the USA where it was rebuilt by Lockheed Air Services International at New York's Idlewild airport using parts of C-69-I-LO 43-10314 (constructor's number: 1966). It was registered N74I92 and on completion of the rebuild was sold to California Hawaiian Airlines Inc, a US charter operator or 'non sked' that specialised in holiday charters to Hawaii. In September 1953 it was sold to EL AL Israel Airlines as 4X-AKD, and the Israeli airline fitted it out to seat sixty-three tourist-class passengers, besides making some changes in the cockpit instrumentation and installing a new cargo compartment.

Before World War Two Imperial Airways operated the London - Sydney service in conjunction with QANTAS Empire Airways. BOAC, the successor, continued this co-operation after the war, but with much larger, faster airliners. QANTAS Empire Airways - QEA - was formed on 16 November 1920 as the Queensland and Northern Territory Aerial Services with a BE.2c and an Avro 504K to undertake air-taxi services and joy-rides. The company started scheduled services in 1922 and operated the Brisbane - Singapore section of the Australia - England air-route in January 1934. A direct service from Australia to England was re-opened in April 1946 as far as Karachi with Liberators and Lancastrians. In October of that year, four 749 Constellations were ordered, followed by an order for four Speedpaks in March 1947. The first Constellation arrived at

Sydney on 14 October 1947 the other three following later that month. On 21 November the first proving flight to London was flown, and then on 1 December, the first through service from Sydney to London operated entirely by QANTAS left Sydney. At that time, this service called the 'Kangaroo Route' was the longest scheduled airline service in the world carried out without a change of aircraft. By February 1948, three return Services from Australia to London were operated every fortnight. A fifth 749 was leased from BOAC in July 1948, and this enabled the schedule to be increased to twice weekly, the service flying from Sydney via Darwin, Singapore (night stop), Calcutta, Karachi (night stop), Cairo and Rome. On the return journey, night stops were made at Cairo and Singapore: Two second-hand 749s were added to the fleet in January 1950 and April 1951: the BOAC aircraft being returned in April 1950. By the middle of 1950, there were three weekly services to London, the third service making additional stops in alternate weeks at

The Henry Dreyfuss-styled interior, with travel-map murals, wood bulkheads and a window-facing 'observation sofa'. It is thought this is a QANTAS machine.

QANTAS Constellation VH-EAC *Harry Hawker* at Eagle Farm, Brisbane in March 1954 during the tour of Australia by Queen Elizabeth II and the Duke of Edinburgh.

QANTAS Constellation VH-EAF *Horace Brinsmead* departs in the background, presumably with Her Majesty on board.

It is believed that VH-EAC was the backup aircraft. Behind VH-EAF is the corrugated iron fence which marks the boundary between Eagle Farm airport and Doomben Racecourse. Note the crown and E II R on the side of VH-EAF

Colombo and Bombay, instead of Calcutta, with an extra stop added at Djakarta on all flights from 1951.

In November 1948, the first survey flight from Sydney to Johannesburg was carried out, but this service, known as the Wallaby Route, was not opened until 1 September 1952, and flew via Melbourne, Perth, Cocos Islands, and, in alternate weeks, Mauritius. In November 1950, a flight was made with a QANTAS Constellation to Japan and back, and, on the return trip, the 749 made the first non-stop crossing from Japan (Iwakuni) to Australia (Darwin). Again, several years were to pass before this route was flown regularly, the first scheduled flight being made in January 1954 with a DC-4. By October 1952, the QANTAS service to London was flown twice weekly via Calcutta, and alternate weeks via Bombay and Colombo. Cairo was dropped from the network, and instead, a call at Beirut was made on all flights, and also at Basra (eastbound) or Bahrein (westbound) if required for load reasons. By mid-1953, a stop at Frankfurt was added on one weekly flight, the stop at Cairo reintroduced on two of the weekly flights, and the night stops had been reduced to one only - at Singapore - on all flights except one of the eastbound, which made an additional night stop at Beirut. From 9 March to 26 March 1954, a specially-equipped Constellation was used by Queen Elizabeth II and the Duke of Edinburgh on their Royal Tour of Australia.

The Israeli Constellations

The three Model 049s delivered to EL AL Israel Airlines in the summer of 1950 came to normal airline service by a devious and incident-filled route in which intrigue and a certain amount of deception were not lacking.

They had been acquired, along with a fourth as surplus C-69s from the USAF by a non-scheduled US operator, Intercontinental Airways, formed by Adolph William 'Al' Schwimmer (*b*. 10 June 1917, *d*. 10 June 2011), a former TWA flight engineer with Zionist sympathies, who had also formed the Schwimmer Aviation Corporation in 1947 to operate Constellation freight services between the USA and Europe. The state of Israel had been proclaimed on 14 May 1948 and it was immediately fighting a war of independence with neighbouring Arab states to establish and assert its identity.

The US State Department and Great Britain imposed an embargo on the supply of arms to Israel, and transport aircraft which could be used for military purposes as well as combat aircraft, both badly needed by the new state in its struggle for survival, came under this ban. This did not, however, prevent a number of attempts by those sympathetic to the Jewish cause to get round the ban and supply the much-needed aircraft. The three Constellations that ultimately went into EL AL service were registered with a Panamanian airline, Lineas Aereas de Panama SA, and, although nominally Panamanian, flew supplies

QANTAS Empire Airways loads another group of passengers for the trans-Pacific service. *(author's collection)*

Left: EL AL's first Israeli flight attendant, Miriam Gold, waves in front of an EL AL Constellation at Lod Airport, 1951. Her flight bag is probably EL AL's earliest one. The Constellation was EL AL's first 'modern' pressurised aircraft, enabling scheduled trans-Atlantic passenger service (as opposed to sporadic charter flights with DC-4s .
(EL AL Archive)

Below: Refuelling a Constellation at Lod Airport, April 1951. Unlike underwing pressure hoses used today, refuelling in the piston-engine era was by overwing gravity methods.
(Israeli Government Press Office)

into Israel from Prague and other places for some months with the Israeli Air Force Transport Command. Al Schwimmer and two other pilots, Sam Lewis and Les Gardner, had planned to evade the arms embargo and fly ten Curtiss C-46s and the three Constellations out of the USA to Israel in 1948. But after the ten C-46s had been flown out and ferried to Lydda the US authorities ordered the three 049s, which were waiting at Milville, New Jersey, to be impounded. However, Sam Lewis managed to take off with one of them and this later damaged its undercarriage in Czechoslovakia on 9 June 1949, but was repaired. Later still it crashed on the seashore about a quarter of a mile short of the Tel Aviv airstrip while attempting an emergency landing. It was subsequently repaired in California and refurbished for EL AL's use. The other two 049s remained in the States for a time and Schwimmer, Gardner and Lewis were arrested and tried on charges of 'conspiracy to violate the Neutrality Act and Export Control Law'. Lewis was acquitted but the other two were convicted and fined $10,000 each. Lineas Aereas de Panama's route licences had been bought by Schwimmer and his associates and one of the 049s, N90829, which became 4X-AKC, did actually appear in this airline's livery late in 1949 but it is unlikely that any of the 049s ever actually operated into Panama.

The three 049s were sold to EL AL in June 1950 and were converted at Burbank to L-249 standard, this being almost the same as a Model 649 and with a maximum gross weight of 100,000 pounds. The interiors were completely refurbished and the flight-deck layout considerably changed. Accommodation for the relief crew was reduced to enable more passenger seats to be fitted, one layout seating up to eighty-five passengers, and others sixty or sixty-six; a sixty-three-seat interior was standardised in 1954 and a fifty-eight-seat version for the Tel Aviv - Johannesburg and New York routes in 1955.

Speedpak cargo containers were bought second-hand for use on the European routes. EL AL's 049s inaugurated a Tel Aviv - London-New York service on 16 May 1951, besides taking over the Johannesburg route and replacing the airline's DC-4s on the European routes.

The EL AL Constellations were temperamental. Mechanical problems were frequent, and a general shortage of spare parts caused numerous delays and schedule disruptions. Often an aircraft would be grounded, perhaps in Iceland or Khartoum, waiting for a scarce replacement engine. One of the airliners was dubbed 'The Turkish Bath' as its air conditioning was 'temporarily' out of order most of its life with EL AL. The cabins were not that well insulated, and the high interior noise level from 'pounding piston engines' made the long flights seem even lengthier.

Published timetables only compounded the

Right: the dramatic royal blue and silver paint scheme of one of EL AL's first Constellations. Capt Sam Lewis (left), a hero in air transport during Israel's War of Independence and later chief pilot of EL AL for many years, is with Pete Rivas, flight engineer. Lewis was with EL AL 22 years, logging 28,000 flying hours. *(EL AL archive)*

problems. They were usually issued late, with numerous errors, and schedule changes were frequent. More importantly, they called for the four machines to be flown between two and four hours per day more than the average utilization of similar aircraft by other airlines. This overambitious plan could not be realised.

Public relations had a hard time. One of their biggest jobs was to convince customers that EL AL was a 'real' airline and not merely an immigrant carrier, for in the early years, most of the company's revenue was derived from such activity. Yet the frequent delays meant that EL AL still appealed mainly to air travellers sentimental about its ties to Israel. They joked that EL AL really was an acronym for 'Every Landing Always Late', and referred to the fleet as the 'EL AL Cancellations'. Nevertheless, during this period, EL AL maintained a flawless safety record, and its load factor was one of the highest of all transatlantic airlines.

A typical weekly flight schedule included two Constellation services to New York - with three to five stops, always including London - one Constellation roundtrip to Paris via Zürich; one Constellation rotation to Johannesburg via Nairobi; one DC-4 trip to Vienna via Rome; and one DC-4 service to Istanbul via Nicosia. A flight between Tel Aviv and New York took between twenty-eight and thirty-three hours, depending on direction and winds.

On 27 July 1955, 4X-AKC was shot down near the Greek frontier, while on a flight from Vienna to Tel Aviv. EL AL Flight 402 was an international passenger flight from London to Tel Aviv via Vienna and Istanbul. For reasons not clear it strayed into Bulgarian airspace and was shot down by two Bulgarian MiG-15 jet fighters and crashed near Petrich. All 7 crew and 51 passengers on board the airliner were killed.

The aircraft's crossing of the western Bulgarian border was registered by an observation post of the Bulgarian military near Tran, and the Air Defence scrambled two MiG-15 jets with pilots Petrov, the pair leader and Sankiisky, by order of the Deputy Chief of Air Defense, General Velitchko Georgiev. The MiGs took off from the Dobroslavtsi airport, and were responsible for the defence of the capital city of Sofia. According to pilots Petrov and Sankiisky, Sankiisky first attempted to warn the EL AL airliner that it was in violation, by shooting signal rounds in front of the Constellation's nose; Petrov repeated the warning. In the meantime, the EL AL airliner neared the southern border of Bulgaria with Greece and the near-border city of Petrich, where it was shot down.

The welcoming reception hosted by the City of New York at Idlewild Airport - now JFK Airport - upon the arrival of EL AL's first scheduled flight to the US, using Constellation 4X-AKA, 1 May 1951. *(EL AL Archive)*

EL AL's ill-fated Constellation 4X-AKC, that was shot down by Bulgarian fighter-jets near the Greek border on 27 July 1955. *(EL AL Archive)*

According to Petrov and Sankiisky, the Constellation initially pretended to follow the instructions and deployed its flaps and landing gear, but then sharply retracted them and changed course for Greece, hoping to escape the fighters. The pilots' account has been disputed; the location of the crash near Petrich - a town several kilometres from the border with Greece - suggested that the EL AL flight had been followed without shooting until its very last minutes over Bulgarian territory. The final shoot-down order was given by Gen. Velitchko Georgiev, deputy commander-in-chief of Air Defense, who was quoted saying 'If the aircraft is leaving our territory, disobeying orders, and there is no time left for more warnings, then shoot it down.' The airliner was hit and then descended, breaking apart at 2,000 feet, and crashing in flames.

The crash took place amid highly strained relations between the Eastern Bloc and the West and was the deadliest involving the Constellation at the time.

The Constellation originated its scheduled weekly flight from London, and departed Vienna's Wien-Schwechat International Airport at 02:53, bound to Tel Aviv's Lod Airport via Istanbul. Why the airliner veered off its intended route was never established, with highly conflicting opinions from Israeli and Bulgarian investigators. One possibility was that, using NDB navigation, thunderstorm activity in the area might have upset the navigational equipment so that the crew believed they were over the Skopje radio beacon, and turned to an outbound course of 142 degrees, but this version is not supported by any factual evidence of thunderstorms in the area. As a result, this version of events is disputed by both the Bulgarian military and current historiographers of Bulgarian aviation. It is firmly established only that the EL AL flight, flying at FL180 strayed off the Amber 10 airway into Bulgarian territory. Bypassing the town of Tran, the EL AL aircraft travelled 120 miles over Bulgarian territory 75 miles from the border it crossed, before being shot down.

At first, however, it was speculated that the aircraft was not brought down by fighters but by anti-aircraft guns from the ground. The next day, the Bulgarian government admitted to shooting down the airliner. They expressed regret and arranged an official inquiry, but would not allow a six-man investigative team from Israel to take part. This latter action has subsequently been criticised both by the Israelis and by Bulgarian sources within the investigation. The Israeli government protested strongly, but it was not until several years later that a marginal sum in compensation was paid.

Two more 049s were acquired by EL AL from Cubana in October 1955, although only one was delivered and given an extensive overhaul, including flight deck and cabin interior modifications, to bring it to the same standard as the other 0493. From December 1957 EL AL's Britannias began to take over as first-line equipment but it was not until 1962 that the last three Constellations in service were sold to Universal Sky Tours Ltd, principal shareholders in Euravia (London) Ltd, which later became Britannia Airways. Sky Tours started 049 operations on 5 May 1962, specialising in the group charter and inclusive tour market.

Sales to Non-scheduled Carriers

The history of non-scheduled airlines - often known as 'non-skeds' in the United States -

records the rise and fall of a uniquely unencumbered sector of what used to be the heavily regulated American airline industry from the end of World War Two to the Airline Deregulation Act of 1978. Often operating in the shadow of huge national airlines, which received federal subsidies and flew scheduled passenger service at costly rates, non-scheduled airlines were generally small companies which could be chartered to transport goods or passengers at an hourly or distance-based charge. Non-scheduled airlines were the first to introduce 'aircoach' fares for civilian air travel in the late 1940s. They brought about the low-rate service offered by almost all airlines operating today. It was a very similar thing that happened in Europe, where they were called 'charter' or 'Inclusive Tour' operators.

The first non-scheduled airlines arose from the industrial and human fallout of the Second World War. The wartime United States aviation industry had, upon the orders of President Franklin Delano Roosevelt, escalated the production of aircraft from a few thousand a year to more than 4,000 each month, and the training centres of the US Army Air Force produced the pilots to fly them. Peace brought these airmen, who often possessed no other skills, back to a country where vast stores of surplus military aircraft were being sold at discount rates to former servicemen. Under the 1938 legislation of the Civil Aviation Authority, the federal agency responsible for regulating civil aviation until 1940, all air carriers providing scheduled air service across states required an official certificate to operate, the Certificate of Public Convenience and Necessity. The certificate demanded compliance with economic as well as safety standards, which meant all certificated companies were subject to the

Skyways of London's G-ANUR seen about to depart from London Heathrow! *(author's collection)*

Capitol Airways of Nashville TN was the largest non-scheduled operator of the Constellation in the USA. Here N4901C is seen at Wilmington in June 1965. *(Robin Banks collection)*

CAA's stringent control over fares, routes, and business practices. Non-scheduled air service, which then referred to light aircraft individually chartered to transport cargo, was exempt.

Snapping up $25,000 Douglas DC-3s, the legendary utility machine which operated in numbers exceeding 10,000 during the war, enterprising pilots established their own freight carriers with ease under the 1938 exemption. A glut of such companies appeared - 2,730 in 1946 alone according to the Civil Aeronautics Board (CAB), which replaced the CAA in 1940. They had such names as Fireball Air Express or Viking Air Lines and commonly were operated by a lone individual with some money given by fellow GIs, or in rare cases a bank loan. For most the romantic venture ended in failure; many former fighter pilots found themselves unsuited to the steady cross-country cruising, the bookkeeping required to stay solvent, and the long-term maintenance. With a safety record up to twenty-five times worse than their scheduled counterparts, the non-scheduled companies faced swift punishment from the CAB, which began widely shutting down operations that were found unsafe or 'financially unfit'. CAB retribution was not the most immediate threat to the non-skeds' continued existence, however, and it soon became apparent there were too few contracts to support the influx of new businesses. Hundreds of thinly financed operations went bankrupt within a few months, and ruthless competition for work turned into suicidal rate slashing as non-sked owners undercut air, rail, and shipping to prices that failed even to cover their fuel costs. Such cut-throat practices and the poor safety record earned the non-skeds an ineffaceable reputation as the aviation industry's seedy underbelly. Savvy non-skeds averted extinction in the late 1940s only by breaching into another market with an innovative service: the aircoach.

Low overhead and fewer regulations allowed the non-scheduled airlines to offer considerably lower fares than the national scheduled carriers, inaugurating the immensely popular aircoach service which attracted millions of Americans unable to afford tickets on the regular airlines. Though the regulatory actions of the Civil Aeronautics Board ultimately extinguished the burgeoning non-scheduled industry, the idea of cheap, efficient air transport endured, and by the passage of the 1978 Airline Deregulation Act, nearly all civil airlines had transitioned to an aircoach model.

Though passenger travel was never intended under the economic regulation exemption enjoyed by non-scheduled airlines, its adoption became essential to their business. Because of their low overhead and few amenities, the non-skeds were able to charge close to forty per cent less than the traditional airlines, with $99.00 fares from Los Angeles to New York versus $159.00 on a standard carrier. Moreover, unfettered from timetables, non-skeds could delay flights until they were full or nearly full, while scheduled airlines had to charge exorbitant prices to ensure profit on half-empty airliners. The non-skeds found a large and willing market for this new service, frequently advertised as 'aircoach' in reference to the established use of 'coach' to mean respectable middle-class travel on trains and ships. Americans who had never flown before could now afford the luxury

Britair East Africa was formed in November 1964 by Captain Marian Kozubski, formerly owner of Falcon Airways Ltd, as a charter company to operate inclusive tours from Europe to East Africa. One 049 was bought in December 1964, and the aircraft started operating on 20 December 1964 from Rotterdam to Nairobi and Mombasa via Malta every three weeks. The tours continued throughout the spring and summer of 1965, together with some general charter work. The aircraft returned to Luton, England, for checks and overhaul. A fleet of four Connies was planned, but the airline suspended operations at the end of the summer of 1965, and only operated the one aircraft G-AHEL, seen here at Luton. *(Matt Black Collection)*

formerly reserved for men of business; non-skeds flourished around population-dense cities with big airports. The west coast experienced a remarkable proliferation of non-scheduled passenger airlines, especially near Los Angeles in places like Burbank or Long Beach where land for a dirt airfield could be cheaply obtained. On the east coast Newark and Trenton in New Jersey were popular hangar bases for non-skeds, and the Miami-Caribbean circuit out of Florida was as trafficked as it was lucrative. One route, from San Juan to New York, facilitated the mass migration of Puerto Ricans seeking opportunity on the mainland who came in numbers exceeding 6,000 each month and settled in squalid conditions in East Harlem. But while the non-scheduled airlines' fares were unmatched throughout the industry, their service quality was frequently unreliable.

The low fare model required that flights be relatively full, and it was a common occurrence when flying on a non-scheduled airline for customers to learn at the airport that their flight had been delayed until the next day so that the airline could sell more tickets. Because most companies had only a few aircraft and just the staff to crew them, delays as a result of weather or mechanical failure could completely incapacitate the airline, forcing it to cancel or postpone flights for which tickets had already been sold. No refunds were given on such tickets, and on one occasion the Burbank police responded to calls from a nearby airfield where an angry crowd of passengers were demanding access to an overbooked flight. Some of the nocturnal non-scheduled carriers attempted to evade landing fees at their destinations by covertly slipping in and out of airports in the middle of the night. However, with the founding of the Aircoach Transportation Association, the trade association and lobbying group of the non-scheduled airlines, stricter policies of etiquette, safety, and consumer protection became standard across the industry. By the close of 1945-46 non-skeds had become a definite presence within the aviation industry, and they found themselves looked upon unfavourably by executives at the old established airlines.

Several TWA 049s were leased to Eastern Air Lines in the winter seasons of 1956-57 and 1957-58 for the Florida holiday traffic. TWA retired its 049s at the end of 1961 and sold twenty-five of them to the Nevada Airmotive Corporation on 31 March 1962, a few more being sold directly to other airlines. During the early 1960s, they were acquired, usually on lease from Nevada Airmotive, by a number of the smaller US non-scheduled carriers, who found the 049 a cheap and spacious aircraft for charter work, combining low first cost with a seating capacity of around eighty and good spares backing. The US 'non-skeds' which acquired 049s sold off by TWA and other carriers included Coastal Cargo, Coastal Air Lines, American Flyers Airline Corp, Imperial Airlines, Magic City Airways, Futura Air Lines, Standard Airways, Consolidated Airlines, World Wide Airlines, Modern Air Transport, ASA International Airlines, Edde Airlines, Hawthorne Nevada Airlines, Pacific Air Transport and Paradise Airlines.

To operators like Modern Air Transport, with five ex-Capital 049s, and American Flyers, which bought two 049s and two L-149s from Delta Air Lines on 1 April 1960, these Constellation fleets were often their first four-engined equipment and an important stage towards the eventual acquisition of jets. But two other 049 operators, Imperial and Paradise, both went out of business after suffering an accident with the type; Paradise had specialised in flying holidaymakers to the Nevada ski resorts.

An ex-Braniff Model 049 acquired by the US 'non-sked' Lloyd Airlines was impounded by the Bolivian authorities at Santa Cruz de la Sierra on 2 August 1961 on suspicion of smuggling while engaged on a charter flight from Miami to Uruguay. A Bolivian Air Force F-5ID Mustang fighter was sent up to intercept it, but the Constellation pilot took a shot at it through the open cockpit window with a revolver and, according to reports, forced the Mustang down!

Lloyd ceased operations after this incident. One of Modern's 049s was sold to a Senor Rymar of Montevideo in June 1965 and leased to the International Caribbean Corporation; it was impounded by the Paraguayan authorities at Asuncion on 9 September 1965, also for smuggling.

The four 049s which American Flyers had bought from Delta had been sold by Pan American to Delta on 1 February 1956, and in the latter's service, two were converted to L-149s. This version was created by fitting the long-range wings of the L-749, whose fuel tanks had a total capacity of 5,820 US gallons, to the Model 049 fuselage. Two of the smaller British independent airlines, Trans-European Aviation and Falcon Airways, operated 049s; the former had acquired one from Cubana, but this was seized at Charlotte, North Carolina, on 27 January 1961 en route to the UK by Jacob Shapiro, who was claiming $750,000 in respect of a hosiery mill he had owned in Cuba and which had been appropriated by the Cuban government. This 049 was never delivered, and Trans-European bought two of Falcon's three ex-Capital 049s. One of these was later impounded in Israel; the other was held at Gatwick for non-payment of landing fees before Trans-European went out of business in 1962. The same fate overtook Falcon, the managing director of which, Captain Marian Kozubski, was a colourful character whose career with Falcon and other airlines had included a number of brushes with airworthiness and safety authorities. He later acquired one of Euravia's ex-EL AL 049s for Britair East African Airways, a Kenya-based charter operator. The Austrian charter operator, Aero Transport, acquired an ex-TWA 049 and later two L-749As. One of their Constellations was grounded at Djibouti in French Somaliland in November 1963 by the French authorities while carrying a cargo of arms for the Yemeni Royalists fighting the

N1880 departs for another service on behalf of Transocean on lease from Dollar Lines. *(Robin Banks collection)*

Formed in 1932 as Woodley Airways, Pacific Northern became the first company in Alaska to be given a CAA scheduled operating certificate. Pacific Northern's main routes were from Anchorage to Kodiak, Bristol Bay and Juneau, and, in 1951, services to Seattle were opened. Pacific Northern operated three leased Constellations in January 1955 for the first class Seattle to Portland and Anchorage routes. In August the CAB renewed the company's US - Alaska routes for an additional five years and authorized the airline to serve Ketchikan. By the end of 1955, the 749As were operating daily non-stop Seattle-Anchorage and Seattle- Portland, and also a daily Seattle to Ketchikan and Juneau route, continuing to Cordova and Anchorage three times weekly, with a second Seattle-Anchorage flight on three days of the week. Two 749As were leased in Nov 56 from Aviation Financial Services Inc. for a while, and the three leased 749As were purchased the same year. 1956 was also the year when Pacific Northern became the first Alaskan airline to carry more than 100,000 passengers in a year. By mid 1957, Constellations were operating three times daily on the Seattle - Anchorage route, with two flights on Sundays, two of the flights operating non-stop, and the third stopping at Ketchikan and Juneau, and with a new point of call for the Connies at Yakutat (three times weekly) in addition to the five-times weekly call at Cordova. Seattle - Portland was served by a five-times weekly flight. Here N1593V is ready to board for another service nothwards.
(Robin Banks collection)

Egyptians, but their more usual sphere of operations was air charter holidays in Europe.

Another little-known territory to be served by 049 was the independent state of Burundi, previously part of the Belgian protectorate of Rwanda-Urundi, adjacent to the Congo. Royal Air Burundi, the national airline, started operations early in 1963, several non-scheduled flights being made between Usumbura, the then capital, and Europe with an ex-TWA 049 registered with Las Vegas Hacienda of Las Vegas, Nevada (the Hacienda Hotel), a US indirect air carrier and tour operator (as the CAB called it) which used several ex-TWA 049s to fly inclusive tour and holiday charter parties to Las Vegas from other parts of the States. Royal Air Burundi ceased operations after a few months, its one and only 049 being flown back to Oakland, California, in the summer of 1963. Several of the Las Vegas Hacienda 049s were later acquired by Lake Havasu City (Lake Havasu Airlines), owned by the firm that bought London Bridge to reopen it in Arizona, one of these being disposed of to another inclusive tour charter operator, Hawthorn Nevada Airlines, for a time in 1968, while two more were sold to Southeastern Skyways Inc in 1970. An ex-Paradise Airlines 049 was leased in 1966 to the Dominican operator Aerovias Nacionales Quisqueyanas for scheduled and charter services from Santo Domingo, and an ex-Capital 049 was acquired in August 1966 by the Chilean charter operator, Transportes Aereos Squella. Another Chilean carrier, Air Chile/Lyon Air or ALA - Sociedad de Transportes Aereos - had operated cut-price services at below IATA (International Air Transport Association) fares from Santiago up the west coast of South America to Havana with an 049 leased from Cubana during 1957-58.

Chapter Six

Development

By the end of 1946 the Constellation was established on the international scene as an outstanding airliner, setting new standards of speed and comfort in international travel and giving TWA and Pan Am such a lead on the US domestic and Atlantic routes as to oblige other airlines, like BOAC and Air France, to order the type to retain their competitive positions.

With the engine troubles that had caused the grounding now behind it -although, like any big radial of this horsepower, the R-3350 still demanded careful handling to get the best out of it - the Constellation could well face the competition of the DC-6s which were now coming off the production line at Santa Monica for United, American, Sabena, KLM and other operators. Weight growth and increased power were the two obvious avenues of Constellation development to which Lockheed had been turning their attention; the prototype's maximum gross weight had been 86,250 pounds and the 049's, originally certificated at 90,000 pounds, had soon gone up to 96,000 pounds and - with the 049E model - to 98,000 pounds. Indeed, it was weight growth rather than fuselage growth that was to be the characteristic and recurrent theme of Constellation development. The Wright R-3350 was at the beginning of its commercial life and, a more recent and more powerful engine than the Pratt & Whitney R-2800 of the DC-6 offered greater potentialities for power increases. Indeed, Lockheed may be said to have pioneered with the Constellation the now common practice of airliner manufacturers in offering progressive increases in gross weight of the same basic model over a period of time, a practice which has really come to the fore with the thrust-growth potential of the modern jet engine.

One feature of the Constellation which might easily, in view of its advanced nature at that time, have given a lot of trouble was the hydraulic power-boost operation of the controls but, thanks to good design and careful rig testing before the prototype first flew, this did not prove to be a problem. The Constellation had exceptional controllability at all speeds, as well as excellent stall characteristics, and it was easy to maintain a heading at low speeds with one or both engines on one side stopped. This was convincingly demonstrated on 19 February 1947, when an Air France Constellation on the New York to Paris route flew over 400 miles - some reports suggest it was 600 miles - to a landing at Casablanca with both starboard engines stopped. An oil leak in the No 4 engine propeller governor unit which drained the engine's front section of oil and caused it to run dry. No 4 propeller windmilled after the engine had been stopped and, grinding on its hub, overheated and projected molten metal particles - luckily there was only a small oil fire. No 4 prop eventually broke from its shaft and hit No 3 engine, chopping off a sizeable portion of No 3 propeller's blades and damaging several cylinder heads, causing vibrations that ceased when No 3 propeller was feathered. The flight was continued on the two port engines operating at 1,250 horsepower, and averaged 150 mph to a safe landing at Casablanca. On another occasion, a Pan Am 049, after a forced landing with engine trouble, was flown across the USA to the west coast for repairs with the offending engine removed and replaced by a fairing.

The Model L-649 Constellation
As the war drew to a close the Wright company had been working out the improvements to the R-3350 that war experience, especially in the Boeing B-29 Superfortress, (see *B-29 Superfortress* by Pen & Sword from the same author) had shown to be necessary and were in a position to produce a new and truly commercial version of this engine. This became known as the GR-3350-749C18BD-1 and gave more power - 2,500 bhp for take-off - than the Model 049s powerplants, as well as having direct fuel injection as standard. In May 1945 Lockheed began design work on the L-649 Constellation, a new version involving a fifty per cent redesign and intended to take advantage of the extra power of the 'BD-1 engines to offer improved payload, a faster cruising speed and greater economy, as well as improved passenger accommodation and a quieter

Eastern's L-649 NC108A in flight. *(Authors collection)*

cabin with better heating, cooling and ventilation. New propellers and an increase in flap deflection were also featured.

The integral wing tankage was increased to 4,690 US gallon and the maximum gross weight rose to 94,000 pounds, or 4,000 pounds more than that at which the 049 had been certificated; the landing weight was now 84,500 pounds. The Speedpak detachable ventral freight container was first used on the L-649 and the first - and as it turned out the only - customer for this particular version was Eastern Air Lines which ordered fourteen, plus a repeat order for seven placed later but delivered as L-749s, for its major routes, in particular the premier New York - Miami holiday route.

Eastern's first L-649 was delivered on 13 May 1947, Eastern having previously evaluated Model 049 NC70000. It is interesting to note that at this time Lockheed actually proposed the 2,400 bhp Pratt & Whitney R-2800-CA15 or the 2,300 bhp R-2800-CA17 Double Wasp as an alternative powerplant for Constellation customérs, following tests of the re-engined prototype designated XC-69E.

Most probably, the object was to win over from Douglas any airlines that preferred Pratt & Whitney to the still relatively untried Wright R-3350 but, in fact, no Constellations were built with the R-2800 engines.

The first of fourteen Model 649s for Eastern was delivered in May 1947 and all were converted to 749s in 1950.

The Model L-749

The increasing post-war interest shown by airlines in long-range transcontinental and overwater flights led to the rapid development of a long-range version of the L-649 and this, the L-749, soon outsold the former variant. It featured an additional 565 US gallon fuel tank in each outer wing to bring the total tankage up to 5,820 US gallons. This location of the extra tanks enabled the maximum gross weight to be increased to 102000 pounds and the landing weight to 87,500 pounds without increasing the spar-bending moment at the wing root, because fuel distribution in the wing and the sequence of its usage by the engines was controlled. There was a small increase in payload, while the range was increased by 1,000 miles carrying the same payload as the 649. The Models 649 and 749 were produced in parallel, the first 749 being delivered to Air France on 18 April 1947, and these two new variants were originally known as Gold Plate Constellations, a name that was soon dropped.

Because the Model 049s had originally been laid down as C-69C and C-69D military transports, the full advantage could not be taken of the possibilities offered by the structural design when installing seats, furnishings and air conditioning, although standards of comfort were well up to what the airlines wanted. To reduce noise and vibration, the cabin walls of the 649 and 749 were mounted so that there was no 'solid' contact with the fuselage skin other than at the cabin windows. Several layers of fibreglass insulation and air spaces provided very effective damping, these layers and the inner layer of fire-resistant fabric being rubber-mounted from the skin. The broadcloth-covered and fully adjustable passenger seats were also designed to reduce vibration and were not flexibly mounted to remove the risk of adjacent seats jamming. The seats could be reclined, or the backs could be folded flat to form a lower berth 6ft 6in long from every two pairs of seats. The upper berths folded down from the walls, from above the windows, and rest bunks forward were provided for the crew for over-water routes although, on domestic routes when a navigator was not carried, the crew rest space was sacrificed in favour of more passenger seats.

Lockheed offered ten different cabin versions to Model 649 and 749 clients, seating from forty-four to sixty-four passengers, and six of these were sleeper layouts. In some layouts, every second pair of seats was reversible either for a party travelling together or for those who preferred to face aft. A typical seat pitch, in the overwater Model 649-79-34 46-passenger interior convertible to twenty-two sleeper berths plus two more in seats, was forty-one inches between centres, with a seat width (excluding arms) of eighteen and a half inches and a central gangway width of twenty inches. On most cabin layouts seating was four-abreast, although a higher density layout, such as the sixty-four-passenger interior, had five-abreast seating for the first seven rows and a correspondingly reduced seat pitch. The improved soundproofing of the 649 and 749 resulted in a cabin sound level of fewer than 93 decibels when cruising at 20,000 feet at sixty-five per cent METO power.

An important consequence of the Reading accident, which had resulted in the Constellation's grounding, was the development of smoke evacuation procedures for all transport aircraft. The drill for the Constellation was now to remove one emergency exit over the wing and to keep the cockpit sliding windows and crew door closed, smoke from whatever cause then being sucked out and the flight deck kept clear of it. In addition, fireproofing standards were established for cabin interior materials and insulation and had to be complied with by all new commercial transports seeking certification by the CAA.

The Speedpak, and early Freight Conversions.
Mention has already been made of the imaginatively-named Speedpak detachable under-fuselage freight container devised by Lockheed to augment the somewhat limited 434 cubic foot capacity of the two underfloor freight holds. The Speedpak was first used on the Model 649. However, it was also employed by several airlines, such as KLM and EL AL, on their Model 049s, and it took advantage of the aircraft's 'lifting fuselage' with its cambered centreline and slightly drooped nose.

The concept of a detachable external cargo container was not new; it had been applied during World War Two to transport conversions of bombers such as the Vickers Warwick and Handley Page Halifax C.VIII.

Eastern's L-649 NC108A seems to have been the one aircraft used for publicity pictures. *(Authors collection)*

Above: details of the Speedpak about to be hoisted up under the belly of this Eastern Constellation. The four lifting cables are just visible, as are the moving wheels.

Right: when slung under a Constellation, the Speedpak could still be loaded and unloaded, as shown in this picture of a baggage handler putting suitcases into this TWA aircraft.
(both Author's Collection)

The Constellation's Speedpak evolved after extensive wind-tunnel tests of various external cargo panniers, and its streamlined shape had no adverse effect on the handling characteristics. Kelly Johnson, speaking in 1984: 'That 'Speedpak', the under-fuselage baggage carrier, was a very good concept and still is. It cost only twelve miles an hour in lost speed because of extra aerodynamic drag, and the passengers' baggage always was right there on landing. I wish we had done more with that; it never really caught on. Of course, airports were nowhere near so busy as they are today.'

When first flight-tested on a C-69, it had a total volume of 400 cubic feet and measured 33 feet long by 7 feet wide by 3 feet deep, with an empty weight of 1,800 pounds. It could carry up to 8,200 pounds of freight and be fitted with special removable compartments which could be off-loaded or loaded at intermediate stops along a long-haul route; the Speedpak's maximum payload of four tons could be carried on stages of up to 1,000 miles. Loading and unloading was by means of a self-contained electric hoist in the Speedpak that lowered it to the ground; this could, it was claimed, be done in two minutes, thus shortening the ground time for handling cargo and baggage. Ground handling of the Speedpak was facilitated by a pair of semi-recessed wheels mounted underneath at each corner enabling it to be moved away from beneath the aircraft. The Speedpak was well suited to freight shipments of high urgency and fairly small dimensions, but its size, and particularly

An Eastern Speedpak is pulled around rear-first by a tug close to NC90821, a Constellation intended for TWA. *(Authors collection)*

its depth, were such that it could not take larger loads that could be manoeuvred through the freight doors of such types as the Douglas DC-4 and DC-6A. And, of course, an external container, however well streamlined, involved extra drag and consequent reduction in speed, unlike freight doors whose only penalty was the weight of the fuselage stiffening around the door cutouts. Thus, the Constellation's true potentialities as a commercial freighter were not to be realised until the L-1049D Super Constellation, with forward and aft freight doors and developed from the US Navy's R7V-1 went into service in 1954. Meanwhile, in 1953, the exclusive worldwide manufacturing rights for the Speedpak had been sold to the French company SECAN (Societe d'Etudes et de Constructions Aéronavales) of Gennevilliers.

To overcome the Speedpak's dimensional disadvantage - and also, perhaps, because by the late 1950s these containers were no longer so readily obtainable - several second-hand L-749As were, in fact, fitted with forward freight doors. One of these was LV-PBH, acquired by the Argentine charter operator Aerolineas Carreras TA in July 1964; this had been operated by Air-India International and later by Aeronaves de Mexico SA. It had undergone a major rebuild in which its rear fuselage (excluding the tail) had been removed and replaced by that of the US Navy's turboprop testbed R7V-2 Super Constellation 131630 together with its rear freight doors, this resulting in a hybrid aircraft. Two of Royal Air Maroc's five L-749As acquired from Air France were also fitted with forward freight doors (at least one of them apparently retained its Speedpak as well) and one of these was sold to the Peruvian operator Copisa (Compania Peruana Internacional de Aviacion SA) in mid-1967.

The British independent Aviation Charter Enterprises, or ACE Freighters as it was popularly known, acquired seven L-749As from 1964 onwards, four of them ex-South African Airways (two of these never had a British C of A issued) and the rest ex-BOAC aircraft which had been modified to incorporate a large rear freight door. Two of these were among a quartet acquired from BOAC by the British independent, Skyways, early in 1959 to replace Handley Page Hermes on the London - Singapore freight service then operated by Skyways under contract to BOAC.

BOAC converted all but one of them for Skyways to have a single upward-opening rear cargo door measuring 6ft high by 10ft wide, in which the passenger door was inset, and stronger freight floors.

They were also used to operate the London-Tunis-Malta route for BEA with a 65-passenger cabin interior, and one was sold to the Austrian charter operator Aero Transport in the summer of 1963, and then to the Luxembourg charter company Interocean Airways SA a year later.

In December 1965 a subsidiary company ACE Scotland was formed. Revenue earning operations commenced on 16 July 1966 with an inclusive tour holiday flight from the ACE Scotland base at Glasgow Abbotsinch to Barcelona and Palma. The airline was equipped with one ex-South African

ACE Scotland's L749A-79-50 G-ASYF seen at Stansted. *(Authors Collection)*

Airways L-749A Constellation. Thereafter regular flights were made from Glasgow to other European destinations including Rome and other flights were made from Gatwick. Ad hoc charter flights took the Constellation to Athens, Jeddah and Tours.

With the Models 649 and 749 well established in airline service, Lockheed continued the pursuit of weight growth and increased allowable payload, and to this end proceeded to review the stress analyses, landing-gear service reports and drawings to evolve the next version.

This was the L-749A in which, by means of a series of small wing and undercarriage modifications, the maximum gross weight was increased to 107,000 pounds and the payload by 5,000 pounds, the maximum landing weight being 89,500 pounds and the zero fuel weight 87,500 pounds. This increase was achieved by fitting brakes of greater capacity, tyres of increased ply rating, stronger main landing gear axles and shock strut cylinders; the wing centre-section and inner wing stubs were also reinforced and the centre fuselage strengthened. The L-749A was revealed in the spring of 1949; the first new Constellation operators to order this variant were South African Airways, which bought four, but by the time these were delivered in 1950 many existing L-749s had been converted to L-749A standard, and during 1949 alone Lockheed issued ninety-eight special kits to operators for modifying their Constellations up to L-749A standard to take advantage of the higher payload.

A similar modification was proposed for the 649 which, by further strengthening of the inner wing and stronger main landing gear shock struts, became the L-649A with a maximum gross weight of 98,000 pounds and a landing weight of 89,500 pounds, the fuel tankage remaining the same. This variant was overtaken in the project stage by Eastern's conversion of all but one of its first fourteen L-649s - which had been lost in an accident - to L-749s in 1950 with the extra outer wing tanks of this model and higher gross weight, the remaining seven aircraft of the repeat order being delivered as L-749s. And not long before the L-749A was revealed, Lockheed announced, in June 1948, that Model 749s due for delivery from the spring of 1949 could be modified to increase the maximum gross weight to 105,000 pounds and the landing weight to 87,500 pounds by a few comparatively minor structural modifications to the inner wings and main landing gear. Most operators, however, preferred to take advantage of the L-749A on which the Speedpak could now be carried at any load factors up to stage lengths of 2,200 miles. Take-off and climb performance at the higher 749A gross weight was not only maintained but actually improved by the use of Curtiss Electric 830 airscrews instead of the Curtiss Electric 8 50s previously fitted, the former resulting in a take-off run of 2,160 feet and the latter 2,450 feet at 107,000 pounds.

Continuing product improvement saw the use of an aluminium plastic Plycor flooring developed in 1949 for the 749 and 749A which resulted in a weight saving of 194 pounds over the previous type of floor. A fireproof coating for the engine oil tanks was also made available, as well as improved brakes and undercarriage hydraulic damping. A new type of

ACE Freighters L749A-79-32 G-ALAL seen at Coventry Airport. *(Authors Collection)*

NACA air scoop under the upper half of each cowling was developed, tipped down so as to exclude dust and rain and the last few L-749As to be built were fitted with 'jet stacks'- a form of exhaust thrust augmentation that reduced back pressure in the exhaust system and added, it was claimed, as much as fifteen miles an hour to the maximum cruising speed, at the expense of an abrupt increase in cabin noise. Jet Stacks could be fitted retrospectively to 749s already built. Performance could also be improved by the fitting of Curtiss Electric Model C6345 three-blade reversible-pitch airscrews which featured automatic synchronisation for the maintenance of uniform engine speeds working independently of the engines' oil supplies, a refinement that made for a quieter cabin as well as improved take-off and climb performance.

Following the crash near Chicago of TWA Model 049 N86511 *Star of Paris* on 1 September 1961 with the loss of all seventy-three passengers and five crew, modifications were made to the elevator boost shifting system on all Constellations and Super Constellations in US airline, Air Force and Navy service. This aircraft had inaugurated TWA's North Atlantic services fifteen years earlier, and it was found that this accident had been caused by the shedding of a bolt from the parallelogram linkage of the elevator boost mechanism, apparently through improper -reassembly during maintenance. The bolt was probably shed during initial climb-out, and its loss would have caused the boost to apply up elevator and the pilots to push hard on the control columns to stop the nose rising sharply. This, in turn, would have reduced, or excluded, any possibility of moving the shift handle of the elevator boost system and, as subsequent tests showed, the likely result was that that part of the tailplane to which the starboard fin was attached, separated from the aircraft before it crashed.

Following a few previous accidents with US Navy and Air Force Super Constellations, the CAB had already recommended a modification to enable the elevator boost shifting system to be operated without restriction, regardless of pilot-applied control forces. Another cause of several previous accidents had been the inability to feather an overspeeding propeller, and this led to the loss of a Linea Aeropostal Venezolana L-1049E Super Constellation on 20 June 1956 on a flight from New York to Caracas. Overspeeding of No 2 propeller had been reported by the pilot, Capt Luis Plata, who was unable to feather it; he turned back for New York but when fifty miles away received permission to start dumping fuel. Shortly afterwards, the aircraft exploded and dived into the sea, killing all the sixty-four passengers and ten crew, and it was believed that the overspeeding prop had come off while fuel was being dumped and that the fuel had ignited. A lawsuit resulted from this accident, and in 1963 damages of $387,387 were awarded to the wife and daughter of one of the victims by a US Federal Judge, who also held United Aircraft Corporation's Hamilton Standard Division negligent in failing to provide a pitch lock which would have prevented the accident.

An Early Airline Radar

An interesting modification test-flown in a TWA Constellation in the summer of 1947 was what might well have been the world's first production collision-warning radar, nearly a decade before airborne radar came into general use in airliners. This was demonstrated in a Constellation by Howard Hughes, whose Hughes Aircraft Co's electronics division had developed and manufactured it after extensive tests.

Flight trials followed in a Douglas C-47 used by TWA for research, the airline's pilots and engineers were very favourably impressed, and there were high hopes that TWA would instal it in all of its 114-aircraft fleet within four or five weeks. Hughes actually announced that it would be made available to other airlines at cost price, estimated at only about $135 (£34), a far cry from the very sophisticated and costly anti-collision radars (around $30,000 each) that were being talked about in the late 1960s when air traffic congestion and near misses had become a major problem.

Such cheapness naturally implied a very basic and simple form of radar, the Hughes set, which weighed only sixteen pounds, being a combined transmitter and receiver operating on frequencies of 420 to 450 megacycles. Two small antennae on either side of the nose sent out pulses at the rate of 40 per second in a cone of nearly 180 degrees included angle in front of the aircraft. The reflection from any object, such as another aircraft, operated warning lights and a bell in the cockpit but did not indicate its direction or height relative to the receiver. The radar could be set to give warnings at various distances, the two settings used on the demonstration model being 2,000 feet and 500 feet, the latter being intended primarily for instrument landings. Although very primitive by comparison with the airborne radars of the mid-1950s, and lacking pictorial presentation of a converging aircraft's path, this Hughes radar of 1947 might well have been developed into something rather more sophisticated which would have met the already evident problem of near misses. Perhaps the real reason why nothing more was heard of it was

Above: A TWA Constellation lands on Runway 31 of Chicago's Midway Airport. *(Authors Collection)*

Left: Tomorrow Today - via TWA. A period advert.

Cessna 170 with a pilot and passenger collided with the airliner, ripping a fifteen foot gash in the forward part of the upper fuselage, in which the Cessna's engine remained jammed. The two occupants of the Cessna were killed, but miraculously none of the twenty-nine people aboard the Constellation was injured. The captain and co-pilot, with a fine display of airmanship, made a safe landing at the USAF base at Mitchell Field in New York State, and, despite the huge hole and some skin buckling, the forward fuselage successfully withstood the strain of the landing.

TWA Flight 154, operated by NC86501 departed San Francisco at 00:45 on 18 December 1949 on an Instrument Flight Plan for New York with one stop scheduled at Chicago. Over Moline, IL, Chicago Air Route Traffic Control cleared the flight to Aurora Illinois and instructed it to hold the west of the Aurora Intersection because of an estimated two-hour traffic delay. Flight 154 reported over the Aurora Intersection at 07:03, and a few minutes later the captain requested a clearance to return to Omaha. This clearance was granted. Seven minutes later, at 07:10, while en route to Omaha the company issued the flight revised instructions to proceed to Kansas City. While en route to Kansas City, the company's Kansas city dispatcher informed the crew that if they returned to Chicago immediately, an approach clearance could be obtained without delay. Accordingly, the flight returned to Chicago, and upon arrival there approach control cleared it to make an ILS approach and to land on runway 13R. At this

that this problem was still thought to be solvable by the 'see and be seen' philosophy.

There had already been several cases of transport aircraft colliding with other aircraft—sometimes escaping with serious damage—and there were many more instances on record of airliners flying into high ground or mountains. The former happened to Pan American L-749 N86530 *Clipper Monarch of the Skies* on 30 January 1949 a few minutes after it had taken off from New York's La Guardia airport on a London flight. At about 4,000ft, a single-engined time the Chicago weather was reported: ceiling 300 feet, visibility 1-1/2 miles with moderate fog and smoke, and wind west-southwest at eight mph. The ILS approach was abandoned at the captain's discretion, and he started another. On this second approach, the aircraft was observed to touchdown approximately 3,200 feet from the approach end of the runway. Pilot Stanley M. 'Toots' Kasper did his best to stop; however, the Constellation just kept hydroplaning down the remaining stretch of blacktop. From this point, it travelled the remaining 2,530 feet of the runway, travelled 875 feet beyond the far end of runway 13R and went through a massive wire fence, crossed a parking lot and struck a billboard and a large ornamental stone pillar before coming to rest. Contact with these structures extensively damaged the aircraft which was eventually repaired.

New Constellation Operators
Pan American's Clipper *Monarch of the Skies* was repaired, and became one of four sold to Air France in December 1949 to replace the 049s the French airline had sold to TWA. And while Lockheed was evolving the weight increases and other improvements to the Models 649, 749 and 749A, the last two versions were going into service not only with satisfied 049 customers like Pan American, Air France, KLM, TWA and BOAC but also with several operators newly established on the international scene. Among the latter were QANTAS and Air-India, for which the Connie was to be the means of establishing a fine reputation in the big league of international air transport. But this ambition was not always fulfilled, as in the case of the Mexican airline

Aerovias Guest SA, which had been founded in 1946 by an American, Winston Guest, in conjunction with Mexican interests. The company had started a Mexico City-Madrid DC-4 service, with stops at Miami (no traffic rights were held here until 1950), Bermuda, the Azores and Lisbon, on 8 January 1948 and three L-749s ordered for this new route were allotted the registrations XA-GOQ, XA-GOR and XA-GOS. The first of these was, in fact, the first L-749 to be built, going into service with Guest in July 1948 and visiting London Airport on the 8th of that month bringing Mexican competitors to the Olympic Games. But the Madrid route did not prove to be a success and, after the frequency had been reduced in the summer of 1951, was suspended completely by the end of that year. Guest was unable to obtain traffic rights to New York because of a long disagreement between Mexico and the USA over a bilateral air agreement, unresolved until 1957 when another

A few years earlier than the picture on the opposite page comes these two newspaper cuttings of NC86501 resting at the end of its landing 'slide' from Runway 13 on 18 December 1949. *(Authors Collection)*

Mexican airline, Aeronaves de Mexico, was given New York rights. This meant that Guest was unable to take delivery of its second and third L-749s, and XA-GOQ was sold after only four months service on the Mexico City-Miami route through Lockheed to Air France, with whom it became F-BAZR.

Miami was the only point in the States to which Guest had traffic rights, and to get around this obstacle a route to Windsor, Ontario - the Canadian city just across the border from Detroit - was opened in 1955 with two L-749As acquired from QANTAS in October and November of that year. The Windsor route proved to be uneconomic and was discontinued in October 1957, the airline continuing Constellation services to Panama and later to Caracas.

Another Constellation operation destined to be short-lived was that of the Irish airline, Aerlinte Eireann, formed in 1947 to operate Atlantic services from Shannon and co-owned with the major Irish operator of European routes, Aer Lingus Teoranta. Five L-749s were ordered for a service to New York, the first of these being delivered on 26 August 1947, but following a change of government policy, the New York service planned for 1948 (thrice-weekly flights to Boston and New York were to have started on St Patrick's Day - 17 March) was shelved, and the Constellations were put on to the Aer Lingus Dublin - London route for a time, from 3 November 1947. But they were really too big for Aer Lingus routes at this stage, and the following summer all five were sold for £315,000 each (£65,000 more than the Irish airline had paid per aircraft) to BOAC, who found themselves in the happy position of getting these, their first L-749s, without any dollar expenditure; they were later modified to 749A standard.

The government of Ceylon also ordered two Constellations in 1947 for the international routes of the newly-formed Ceylon Airways, which soon

London 9 June 1948. The arrival of the first scheduled Air-India service from Bombay, using L-749 VT-CPQ *Malabar Princess*.

Left: Nose detail of the aircraft, showing the profusion of lumps, bumps and wires.

Below: Left to Right: Capt Jatar, F/O Dhuru, Miss McCay, R/o Sule, F/E Desouza, Miss Salway, N/O Mani and Flight Purser Ganesh. (*both John Stroud Collection*)

A detail view of VT-CQR *Rajput Princess* showing the cuffed propellers. From the looks of the tarmac below the inboard engine, the Constellation had already started marking its territory with oil drips! *(John Stroud Collection)*

became Air Ceylon. But this order later lapsed, as Australian National Airways operated two DC-4s under contract for Air Ceylon's Colombo-London service from February 1949, and later from Colombo to Darwin and Sydney. These services ceased in October 1953 and it was not until February 1956 that KLM started a weekly 'Sapphire' service to Amsterdam and London for Air Ceylon with a L-749A, replacing this with an L-1049E Super Constellation in November 1958. The 749A was fitted with twelve 'SleepAir' reclining sleeper-seats and seats for up to thirty-five more tourist passengers.

Perhaps for no other operator did the Constellation and Super Constellation do as much in establishing a reputation as Air-India International - - aided very considerably by the airline's reputation for superlative cabin service epitomised in its advertising by the smiling figure of 'The Maharajah'. Three L-749s were ordered and on 8 June 1948 one of these began the first Bombay-London service via Cairo and Geneva. Initially, the service was once-weekly but more flights were soon scheduled with alternative intermediate stops, and Delhi and Calcutta were added to the international network. A Bombay-Nairobi service was started on 21 January 1950 via Karachi and Aden, not long after delivery of a pair of new 749As, followed by two more a year later. Following delivery of the final pair, Air-India International sold two of its model 749s to QANTAS.

One of the last two 749As acquired by Air-India, VT-DEP *Kashmir Princess*, was the victim of sabotage; it crashed on 11 April 1955 off Sarawak with the loss of fifteen lives while on a flight between Hong Kong and Djakarta carrying a party of Chinese Communist officials and journalists to the Afro-Asian conference at Bandoeng. The culprit was found to be Chow Tse-ming, alias Chou, an airport cleaner employed by the Hong Kong Aircraft Engineering Corporation, who had planted a small time bomb in the 749 in return for a payment, alleged to have been £37,500, made by persons connected with a Kuomintang (Chinese Nationalist) intelligence organisation. Air-India International's remaining three 749s were traded into Lockheed in 1958 for resale to Aeronaves de Mexico after being replaced by Super Constellations. Other Latin American 749 operators were Linea Aeropostal Venezolana, with two, and Avianca of Colombia, which took delivery of two 749As in May 1951 before introducing Super Constellations later, and acquiring three more ex-BOAC and one ex-TWA 749As in 1959.

QANTAS Empire Airways began to make its mark internationally with the 749, four of which were delivered in October 1947 and went into service on the 'Kangaroo' route from Sydney to London on 1 December. This was the first QANTAS service right through to London, previous services having been joint BOAC/QANTAS ones with 'Hythe'- class Sunderland flying boats, QANTAS crews taking over at Karachi for Sydney. Two more 749s were bought from Air-India, and frequencies of London flights were stepped up to four a week, with new stopping-places. On 1 September 1952 a 749 inaugurated the 'Wallaby' route across the Indian Ocean from Sydney, Melbourne and Perth to Johannesburg, via the Cocos Islands and Mauritius, at a once-fortnightly frequency, later alternating with a South African Airways flight over the same route with 749As to provide a weekly service.

QANTAS sold four of its 749s to BOAC in 1954 and 1955 and the remaining two to Guest of Mexico for a total of some £4,300,000 with spares, a price not far from their original first cost in 1947. QANTAS 749s originally seated thirty-eight daytime passengers (and later sixty) with provision for berths, but in June 1950 sleeping berths were removed in favour of baggage racks, as they were from BOAC's 749s on the Australia route, and the berth windows were then removed.

South African Airways' first 749A was delivered on 24 April 1950, and the airline began Constellation services to London on 26 August of that year, and from November 1957 across the Indian Ocean to Perth. To meet BOAC's Comet competition, SAA leased two Comet Is from the Corporation for its 'Springbok' services to London, converting the 749As for tourist-class services. After the 1954 accidents grounded the Comet, the 749As resumed first class services, and two years later were put on the more important domestic routes, like Johannesburg - Durban. Replaced by DC-7Bs, they were put up for sale and cocooned in 1959, but two

1 December 1947: QEA (QANTAS Empire Airways) cover addressed to Hudson Fysh (CEO) flown on the first Kangaroo Route service to London aboard Lockheed Constellation VH-EAD *Charles Kingsford Smith* Captains K G Jackson (Sydney-Karachi) and D F McMaster (Karachi-London). Features silver 25th anniversary vignette and red/black flight vignette. Signed by both Captains.

6 September 1952: Cover addressed to Hudson Fysh (CEO) flown Johannesburg-Sydney aboard VH-EAD *Charles Kingsford Smith* on the first regular air service between Australia and South Africa. Signed by Captains J Connelly (Johannesburg-Perth) and K Jackson (Perth-Sydney). Postmarked Johannesburg 6-IX 52 backstamped on arrival Sydney 9SE52.

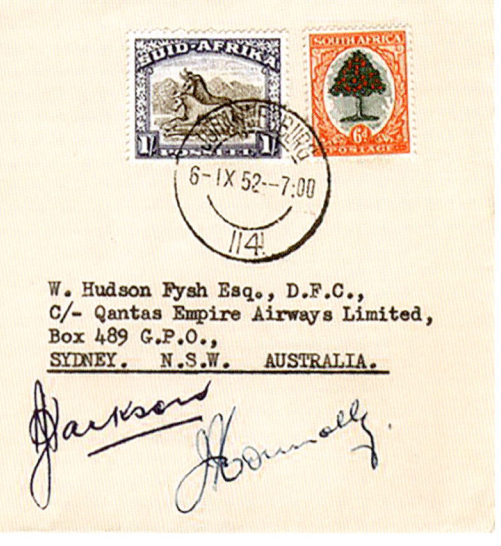

It's almost possible to hear the drone of the engines in this evocative shot of a KLM Constellation as it flies on in the sunshine. *(John Stroud Collection)*

returned to service the following year for low-fare domestic flights, and two more were leased to the South African Trek Airways, in 1961. Trek specialised in low-fare, low-frequency flights to Europe. All four were finally sold to ACE Freighters in 1964.

In the US domestic field, the only new 749 operator was Chicago & Southern Airlines, which took delivery of the first of six Model 749-79-60 Constellations on 1 August 1950 mainly for its routes from Chicago and other midwest cities, Houston and New Orleans to Havana, Kingston (Jamaica), San Juan (Puerto Rico) and Caracas (Venezuela); these Chicago & Southern aircraft were later modified to 749A standard with 'jet stacks' and had accommodation for fifty-seven passengers. Chicago & Southern merged with Delta Airlines of Atlanta on 1 May 1953 and, as a result, three of its 749As were sold to TWA in April and June 1954 and three others to Pacific Northern Airlines, which operated them from Seattle to points in Alaska. Delta acquired four 049s from Pan Am in February 1956.

Capital Airlines purchased seven ex-KLM Model 749A-79-24s which had been traded into Lockheed's from the late summer of 1951 against the Super Constellations the Dutch airline had ordered. Capital placed a contract with KLM at the end of 1951 for the modification and refurbishing of these Constellations to its own requirements, which included the installation of completely new cabin interiors and certain technical modifications to equip the aircraft for US domestic services. All but two of the seven were ferried out from KLM's Schiphol workshops to the States in 1953 but after barely two years' service with Capital they were ferried back across the Atlantic to Britain for refurbishing to BOAC's standards as part of the exchange of 049s and 749As negotiated between the two airlines following the 1954 Comet accidents. At about the same time the Corporation also acquired four 749s from QANTAS and one from Howard Hughes, originally destined for TWA, bringing the total of 749s operated by BOAC up to seventeen. In 1955 these seated sixty passengers in the all-tourist configuration in five-abreast rows of Vickers reclining seats. Two additional cargo compartments could be arranged at the front of the cabin after the removal of six seats on the starboard side.

KLM put into service twenty Model 749-79-338 and 749-79-24s (modified up to 749A standard) the first of which, PH-TEP *Pontianak,* was delivered on 13 August 1947. These were used primarily on the transatlantic routes to New York, Montreal and Curacao and on the service to Djakarta in Indonesia. Their original cabin layout was for forty-six passengers but later an all-sleeper interior with thirty berths was adopted for the 'Cosmopolitan' sleeper service from Amsterdam to New York, while in 1951 a 61-passenger interior was featured on a number of flights carrying Dutch emigrants to Australia.

Air France's 749 and 749A fleet, twenty-four in all, went into service during 1947-51 on routes to Canada and the USA, to the French Caribbean islands such as Guadeloupe and Martinique, to South America, the Far East and Africa, particularly to French West and Equatorial Africa. The fleet included four Model 749-79-46s acquired from Pan American in December 1949; these were Pan Am's only 749s, the airline having gone over to the Boeing Stratocruiser for its first-line equipment of the 1950s. Air France featured a very spacious de-luxe interior for 'The Parisian' service to New York, seating only sixteen passengers in the 749's cabin (replacing a previous 24-berth sleeper interior), and giving them the sort of legroom to be found only in executive aircraft. Three 749s were leased to Air Inter for the latter's domestic routes during April-September 1961 and a few L-1049Gs the following year. Air Vietnam leased 749s from Air France from 1957 for its Saigon-Hong Kong route, later replaced by L-1049s.

TWA was the largest 749 operator with twelve L-749s and twenty-five L-749As supplementing the 049s both on US domestic and the international route through Paris, Rome and the Near East to Bombay. Following the inauguration of Atlantic services in February 1946, TWA's routes were extended eastwards to India, reaching Bombay on 5 January 1947. The original plan had been to continue on to Shanghai in China, linking up there with Northwest Orient Airlines (which had rights to serve a number of cities in China from the USA) to establish a joint round-the-world service. The CAB had awarded TWA a seven-year certificate for the USA - China route on 5 July 1945 and the Bombay-Shanghai portion would have been via Calcutta, Mandalay, Hanoi (then the capital of French Indo-China) and Canton. But the establishment of a Communist regime in place of Chiang Kai-shek and the proclamation of the Chinese People's Republic in September 1949 closed that country to Western airlines, and without through traffic to China services beyond Bombay could not be justified. Although politics at that time thwarted full achievement of the ambition reflected in the airline's title of Trans World Airlines (used as a promotional name from 1946, but in 1950 voted by stockholders as the new name to replace Transcontinental & Western Air Inc), TWA was the most important international as well as domestic Constellation operator. A variety of interiors was featured in its 749 fleet, including a 32-seater 'Sleeper Seat' layout with reclining seats, a 60-seat tourist interior for the Atlantic, an 81-seat layout for US domestic coach routes and a de-luxe 18-berth sleeper layout for 'The London Ambassador' service to London, started on 8 April 1951. Altogether 131 Model 749s and 749As were built, including two PO-IWs and ten C-121 military versions.

Like the Model 049s, the 649s and 749s sold off by the major airlines found a ready market among the smaller non-scheduled carriers, particularly the US 'non-skeds' and European charter operators. Smaller airlines elsewhere, particularly in Latin America, also found them attractive. Eastern Air Lines sold its remaining twelve Model 6493 and five 7493 to the Transit Equipment Co of New York late in 1960 for delivery before 1 January 1961, and Transit later sold them to California Airmotive. Before the sale, Eastern had occasionally leased at least one Constellation to Colonial Airlines which, although dating back to 1928 and with valuable routes from New York to Montreal and Bermuda, had remained a small airline. Both Eastern and National had tried at various times to take it over, and Eastern finally succeeded in doing so on 1 June 1956, thus acquiring the valuable route to Bermuda. A few of the ex-Eastern 649s and 749s were cannibalised for spares or stored and the nose section of one, N110A, was being used as a storehouse for garden tools near Idlewild Airport (later Kennedy International) towards the end of 1961.

Other 649s and 749s were disposed of, usually on lease from California Airmotive, to several of the smaller non-scheduled US carriers such as Standard Airways, Associated Air Transport, Modern Air Transport, California Hawaiian Airlines, Paramount Airlines, Pacific Air Transport, Great Lakes Airlines, Trans-California Airlines and Quaker City Airways (trading as Admiral Airways). Operators like Standard, Associated, Paramount and Quaker City leased their ex-Eastern 649s and 749s out to the other US 'non- skeds' as required. Standard sold N120A on 6 June 1963 to an unusual owner, Casino Operations, which was apparently an associate of Las Vegas Hacienda (the Hacienda Hotel) that operated

Trans-California was a low-cost west coast carrier that briefly used six Constellations for flights between Los Angeles and San Francisco.

several ex-TWA 049s and later itself owned N120A, before it passed on to several more owners. It eventually crashed on a farm near Aracatuba, São Paulo province, Brazil, on 4 August 1969 while on a smuggling flight. Trans-California Airlines used six leased 98-passenger Model 649s and 749s on scheduled low-fare Burbank-Oakland (San Francisco) intra-state services from 1962 but despite a very high passenger seating density - or perhaps because of it - this service could not compete with the Lockheed Electra turboprops of Pacific Southwest Airlines, the major California intra-state operator, and was soon discontinued.

One ex-Eastern 749, N118A, was acquired from California Airmotive by Air Haiti International SA, formed in March 1961 to operate as the designated Haitian flag airline from that country to Miami, New York, San Juan (Puerto Rico) and beyond to points in the British West Indies. Haiti's other airline, Compagnie Haitienne de Transports Aériens (COHATA), was a military airline that flew a domestic network only, and the country had previously relied solely on foreign airlines like Pan American for its international air links .

Air Haiti's 749 was given the Haitian civil registration HH-ABA but the actual owners were the Airline Management & Investment Co, indicative of the foreign interests behind Air Haiti, which later applied, without success, to the CAB for a foreign air carrier permit to operate into the States. The airline's Constellation was lost at sea on 11 November 1961 on a flight from San Juan to Managua (Nicaragua), possibly through sabotage, and Air Haiti ceased operations.

The Constellation was pressed into a military role by one of the several Haitian emigré rebel groups in the States opposed to the oppressive regime of the President, the late 'Papa Doc' Duvalier. From time to time these groups organised 'do it yourself' bombing raids over the capital, Port-au-Prince, usually with any surplus transport they could obtain and without much pretence at accuracy. One of these raids took place on 4 June 1969, when an ex-Pacific Northern Constellation with the false Uruguayan markings CX-BGP, was used to drop several incendiary bombs in the courtyard of the presidential palace. The Constellation was fired on with automatic weapons but flew out to sea, and the bombs were presumably just thrown or pushed out of the passenger entrance door without the benefit of a bomb-sight. A stray bomb set fire to a hut near Port-au-Prince Cathedral, about half a mile from the palace, and one person was killed and another injured in the fire, but the bombs that landed in the palace courtyard did no damage. It is thought that this aircraft was the former TWA 749, named *Star of Virgnia* that was later used in Biafra as 5N-86H.

A day after this raid, the same Constellation landed out of fuel at Gold Rock Creek Airport, on the island of Grand Bahama, with the leader of this latest invasion attempt against Haiti, Colonel René Juares Leon, on board with another of his countrymen, seven Americans and a Canadian. The pilot asked to be refuelled but was refused, whereupon all ten men took a taxi into Freeport at the end of the island, leaving their aircraft unguarded (it was later impounded). They were arrested by the police as illegal immigrants, and it is believed that they were either on their way back from the original raid, having made an intermediate landing at some other Caribbean island unannounced, or were returning from an abortive second raid.

The Dominican airline Aerovias Nacionales Quisqueyanas, next door to Haiti, acquired an ex-Eastern Model 649 from the Peruvian operator Copisa (Compania Peruana Internacional de Aviacion

HI-270 of Aerovías Nacionales Quisqueyana, once the second largest airline of the Dominican Republic.
(Matt Black Collection)

A pair of Cia de Aviacion Trans-Peruana SA Constellations in storage. (Matt Black Collection)

SA) to operate passenger services to San Juan from Santo Domingo and charter flights; Copisa had itself acquired this aircraft from Admiral Airways and the Dominican airline also had a Model 049 leased and a 749. Copisa had acquired its first L-749A, an ex-BOAC aircraft sold to Capitol Airways, from California Airmotive in February 1966. Another came to them from Royal Air Maroc of Casablanca in August 1967 and yet another from Bolivia. With these Copisa operated a service from Iquitos to Maracaibo (Venezuela) and Miami.

Three more 749s were purchased by Trans-Peruana (Cia de Aviacion Trans-Peruana SA) and two other Peruvian operators acquired ex-Eastern Connies. RIPSA (Rutas Internacionales Peruanas SA), which ran cargo flights to Panama and Miami, obtained one from Paramount in September 1966, while LANSA (Lineas Aereas Nacionales SA) took delivery of the first of six 649s and 749s at the end of December 1963, a seventh being bought later for spares and cannibalised. These began operating a domestic network the following month linking Lima with seven other cities, and were later joined by an ex-QANTAS L-1049E Super Constellation on lease. Late in 1965 Eastern took a one third holding in LANSA in return for a technical and managerial assistance contract. In May 1966, following the loss of a 649 in an accident in which all on board were killed, operations were suspended until September while LANSA was re-organised as a completely Peruvian company with the Eastern holding bought out. The domestic routes were then resumed and, on the introduction of four Japanese NAMC YS-I IA turboprops in April 1967, the Connies were gradually phased out.

Aeronaves de Mexico operated three ex-Air-India 749s during 1958-60 pending delivery of its Britannia 302s and two of these were later leased by International Aircraft Services to Miami Airlines, another 'non-sked', which also had a third 749A on loan from Transocean Airlines which, in turn, was leased by Loftleidir of Iceland during July-August 1960. Transocean had been one of the largest US non-scheduled or supplemental carriers during the 1950s and had operated DC-4s, a DC-6A, 749As, L-1049Hs and finally Stratocruisers before it went out of business in 1960. It acquired the first of four 749As and 7493 from BOAC late in 1957, but these were put up for sale at Oakland in 1959. One of these, N9830F, was sold on 31 July 1959, as HL-102, to Korean National Airlines, a private enterprise operator that was succeeded three years later by the wholly Government-owned Korean Airlines. HL-I02 took over the Seoul - Hong Kong route from Korean's DC-4s but this route was discontinued in 1963, only to be reopened four years later with a Super Constellation. HL-102 was sold as OE-IFE to the Austrian charter operator, Aero Transport Flugbetriebsgesellschaft, which also had an ex-TWA 049 and later bought a 749A from Skyways.

Aero Transport ceased operations in the summer of 1964 after one of its Connies had been impounded for debt at Vienna's Schwechat Airport, the company having previously been involved, late in 1963 and quite legally, in flying arms cargoes to the Yemeni royalists fighting the Egyptians. Another concern which had a somewhat chequered career was the US 'non-sked' World Wide Airlines mentioned earlier, which at various times had four ex-TWA 049s, an ex-TWA L-1049A and two former BOAC 749As on

Aero Transport's OE-IFE. *(Matt Black Collection)*

lease. One of the latter had served Capitol Airways, which had three other 749As, having purchased the first from Avianca in 1957; Capitol later built up a fleet of a dozen Super Constellations and went on to operate DC-8 jets. The last US charter operator to acquire a used Constellation was Central American Airways Flying Service of Louisville, Kentucky, to whom TWA disposed of a 749A in October 1967.

By the 1960s used Constellations were being acquired mainly for charter work, but their earlier purchasers in the 1950s had found them every bit as valuable for scheduled services, especially as they were often an operator's first pressurised type. Pacific Northern Airlines acquired three ex-Chicago & Southern 749As from Delta in 1955 after the latter's merger with C & S. These were followed by three more from BOAC and two from TWA, and all were used on PNA's routes from Portland and Seattle to Anchorage and other points in Alaska. Two more ex-KLM 749As were acquired on lease from Aviation Financial Services at the beginning of 1957 but were later returned to KLM as the Constellation fleet built up, and an ex-Eastern 649 was leased from California Airmotive for a year from 8 May 1961. Pacific Northern merged with Western Air Lines on 1 July 1967, the latter operating an extensive network in the western half of the States from Los Angeles. Western then took over PNA's remaining six Constellations but disposed of them all by the end of 1968 when its Boeing 737s were delivered.

Two, N86524 and N86525, later found their way to Africa for the Biafra airlift a few months before the Nigerian victory, the former acquiring the bogus Nigerian registration 5N-86H. Wien Alaska Airlines also acquired an ex-KLM 749A in May 1964 for its Fairbanks-based routes, later changing it's name to Wien Air Alaska and became Wien Consolidated Airlines in April 1968 after its merger with Northern Consolidated Airlines.

Air France disposed of some of its surplus Constellations to its associate airlines in Africa. Air Algérie acquired the first of four such 749As late in 1955, with another leased and began services with them early in 1956 linking the major Algerian centres of population to Paris, Marseilles, Toulouse and other French cities. One of these 749As, F-BAZE, was blown up by the OAS on 26 April 1962 as it stood outside a hangar at Algiers' Maison Blanche airport, but there were no casualties. Air Algérie withdrew Constellation from service in 1963.

One of the Air Algerié machines had an interesting history. It was laid down as a Model 649-79-21, but was completed as Model 749-79-22 for Air France and then converted to a 749-79-46. It flew for Air France as F-BAZJ, then leased to Air Algerie in 1960. A year later it was converted to a special Search and Rescue configuration at Toulouse. The airliner was used by EARS 99 Squadron, Armee de l'Air, with call-sign F-SSFJ on SAR duties.

Five more ex-Air France 749As went to Royal Air Maroc, the first in 1957, and with these the airline inaugurated, on 2 July 1958, services linking Casablanca and other places in Morocco to Paris and other cities in France and neighbouring European countries. Two of the 749As were fitted with forward freight doors, and these operated an all-freight service from Casablanca to Paris non-stop. At the same time, another of the airline's activities was the annual transport of pilgrims to the holy city of Mecca in Saudi Arabia. Two of the 749As were later used for ground training, and the last was sold to Peru in 1967; another had been leased during 1962-64 to the multi-national airline, Air Afrique, which Air France and the French independent UTA had done so much to

The former Air France/Air Algerié Constellion F-BAZT in use by 99 Squadron, Armee de l'Air for Air/Sea Rescue duties. Note the downward-looking observation blister aft of the flight deck.

F-BAZT was transferred to Secrétariat Général d L'Aviation Civile et Commerciale (SGACC) in 1960 and modified for search and rescue duties. It was one of seven ex-Air France L-749As based at Toulouse-Francazai operated by the French Air Force for search and rescue missions before being withdrawn from service in December 1969 and broken up in 1971.

set up. And in 1966 Air France 749A F-BAZL was sold to the Senegal Government as 6V-AAR.

In South America, Constellations took over an old-established flying-boat operation when CAUSA (Compania Aeronautica Uruguaya SA), which had operated Short Sandringhams across the River Plate from Montevideo and Colonia to Buenos Aires since the end of the war, acquired the first of three ex-KLM 749As in February 1963 to replace the Sandringhams, which had become too expensive to operate and maintain, even though they offered a quicker service than landplanes between the city centres.

Other South American acquisitions included a 749A freighter, registered CX-BHC, by a charter operator, Aerolineas Uruguayas SA, and, in March 1964, an ex-KLM 749A by an Argentine company, Aero Transportes Entre Rios SRL, for use on domestic and international freight charters from Buenos Aires. In January 1968, the Bolivian charter operator, Transportes Aereos Benianos SA of La Paz, acquired an ex-Skyways 749A freighter for its cargo flights but sold it later the same year to Copisa. Finally, an ex-TWA 749A was purchased late in 1968 from Aero Tech Inc by the 'Discover America' travel club, one of the many such clubs formed to enjoy the benefit of cheap air travel by operating their own aircraft.

Chapter Seven

Enter the Supers

By the end of 1949, after four years of post-war operations, air transport had been transformed by the rapid growth of international air routes and widespread public acceptance of the new means of travel. Flying was no longer a luxury for the wealthy few, as it had been a decade previously, and no longer was international air transport the preserve of a small handful of operators like Pan American and Imperial Airways.

Already US domestic operators like Capital Airlines had introduced the first coach-class services at cheaper fares, and to the general public, at least, the prospect of mass air travel beckoned invitingly. For manufacturers like Lockheed and Douglas, however, the outlook was far from clear. Both were well aware that stretched versions of their basic Constellation and DC-6 designs would make for reduced costs per seat-mile and so allow lower fare levels, and clearly, there would be a profitable market for such stretched versions. But the question facing both as the new decade dawned was how far into the 1950s would it be before jet airliners like the de Havilland Comet made such stretched versions uncompetitive? The Comet had made its first flight on 27 July 1949 but the jet's operating costs were still rather an unknown quantity, and while their higher speed and cruising altitudes would have obvious passenger appeal, it seemed unlikely that any of the first generation jets would be able to match the low seat-mile costs of piston-engined airliners, especially in the stretched versions. It seemed that there was still time for one more round of re-equipment by the airlines with stretched versions of existing types of aircraft before the jets and turboprops took over.

The Constellation had ample reserves of power, and this had made possible a series of weight and payload increases from the Model 049 to the 749A but, as the projected Models 749B and 849 had demonstrated, more powerful engines by themselves would result in only marginal improvements as the basic airframe was by now volume limited. What was needed was some fuselage stretch to use the extra power promised by the Turbo-Compound to the best advantage, as well as to achieve higher performance for first-class flights and extra cabin length for the high-density coach-class interiors that were going to be increasingly needed.

Flight tests of a L-749 at an all-up weight of 137,000 pounds had indicated the practicability of a 50,000 pounds payload version of the Constellation, and design studies of just such a version, designated L-949, went ahead during 1949. This was intended as a heavy military or civil transport version of the 749 with the fuselage lengthened by twelve feet but otherwise similar to the earlier model. It was to be capable of seating up to one hundred passengers in an air-coach layout or being used solely as a freight carrier, especially in a military role; maximum gross weight was to be 123,000 pounds and the designated powerplants were four 2,250 bhp (maximum take-off) R-3350 Turbo-Compounds. The Berlin airlift and the imminence of the Korean war were to stimulate interest in the type's freight-carrying possibilities and one such all-cargo version of the basic 749, known as the Air Freighter, was proposed at about the same time as the Model 949. It was to be fitted with four 2,400 bhp (maximum take-off) Pratt & Whitney R-2800 Double Wasps and have a total freight hold volume of 3,750 cubic feet. US Navy interest in a freighter subsequently resulted in an order for the R7V-1 Super Constellation with freight doors fore and aft, but it was to be several years later before a civil development for freighting was ordered by Seaboard & Western Airlines.

The Model L-1049A Super Constellation

That a short fuselage Constellation could be successfully test flown at an all-up weight no less than 30,000 pounds greater than that of the L-749A demonstrated the degree of stretch there was in the basic design, and the Model 949 was soon superseded by the L-1049A Super Constellation with a fuselage lengthened by 18 feet 4.75 inches. This increased length was made up of two constant-diameter sections added fore and aft of the spars, the forward section being 128.8 inches long by 139.3

Lockheed Model L-1049G Super Constellation

General characteristics
Crew: 4 flightdeck and 2 to 4 Flight Attendants
Capacity: 65 - 102 passengers
Length: 113.7 feet
Wingspan: 123.5 feet
Height: 24.9 feet
Wing area: 1654 square feet
Empty weight: 73,016 pounds
Max. takeoff weight: 137,500 pounds
Powerplant: 4 x 3,400hp Wright 972TC-18DA-3 trubo-Cyclone compounds

Performance
Cruise speed: 305 mph
Range: 4,140 miles with 18,300 pounds payload.
5,250 miles with 8,500 pounds payload.
Service ceiling: 22,300 feet

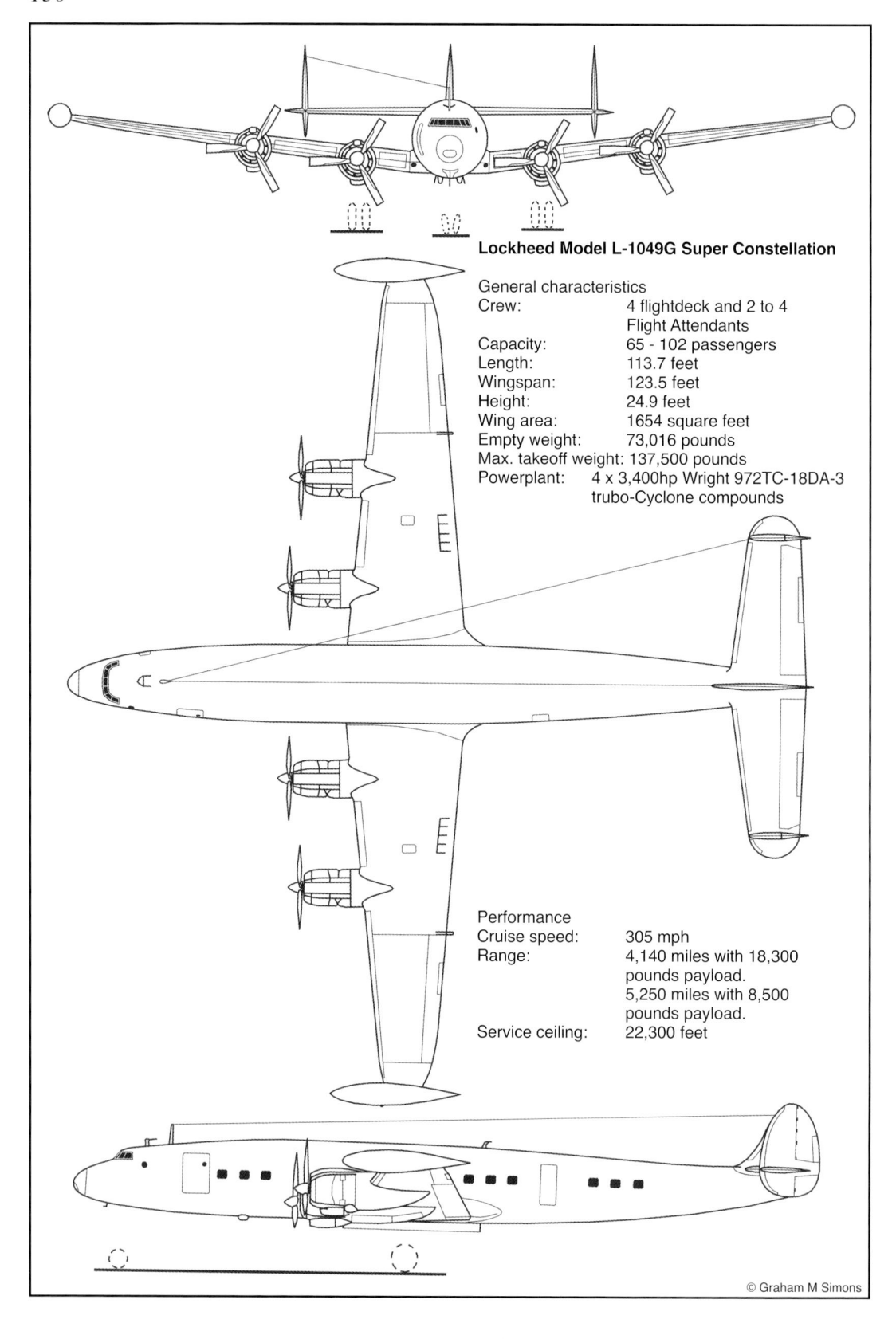

© Graham M Simons

inches diameter immediately forward of the front spar, and the rear section, 92 inches long by 136.6 inches in diameter, added about 55 inches aft of the rear spar. This extra fuselage length resulted in a cabin 56 feet long, 40 feet of which had an inside diameter of more than 127 inches; total length was now 113 feet 4 inches. The circular cabin windows of the short fuselage models were replaced by rectangular windows measuring sixteen inches by eighteen inches, and a new windscreen, made up of seven flat panels three and a half inches higher than before were fitted. To cater for the extra fuselage length and increased cruising speed the structure was strengthened at the cost of very little increase in weight thanks to Lockheed's newly-developed integrally-stiffened skin panel manufacturing techniques. Provision was also made for the installation of centre-section fuel tanks of 730 gallons capacity. Of the twenty-four L-1049As built, fourteen were Model 1049A-53-67s for Eastern Air Lines, and ten were Model 1049A-54-80s for TWA.

The TWA aircraft incorporated the centre-section tanks, whereas those of Eastern only had structural provision for them, and an 88-passenger interior compared with the seventy-five-passenger cabin layout of TWA's aircraft.

The Model 1049A could be regarded as an interim version incorporating the fuselage stretch and more powerful 'conventional' engines pending the availability of Turbo-Compounds and, later on, the hoped-for installation of turboprops when these became available for commercial use. It was powered by four 2,700 brake horsepower Wright R-3350-956CI8CA-1 powerplants, later re-designated R-3350-956CI8CB-1; an alternative version of this engine which could be fitted was the 2,800 brake horsepower R-3350-975CI8BA-1. But the Model 1049A was stressed for the future installation of turboprops of up to 3,500hp such as the Allison T38, which had been used to re-engine the prototype Convair 240 which first flew with these powerplants on 29 December 1950. By now, Eastern were keen to re-engine not only its fourteen L-1049A and sixteen L-1049C Super Constellations with suitable turboprops when these became available, but also the sixty twin-engined Martin 4-0-4s it then had on order. As an Eastern press release of 17 July 1951 stated:

'When the 3250 horsepower combination reciprocating-turbine compound engines are installed, the Super. Constellation's cruising speed will step up to 350 miles an hour and the final conversion to jet power to drive the propellers will advance it well over the 400 mile per hour rating.

'Installation of the jet power plants driving propellers will raise the speed of these airliners (Martin 4-0-4s) also into the 400 miles an-hour class of the Super Constellations.'

Yet for various reasons, and in spite of the much larger military backing accorded to this form of powerplant in the USA than in Britain during the 1950s, a US turboprop for re-engining the Super Constellation was not to materialise in time, and it was left to Napier to set the pace in this field with the Eland. The CB-I engines of TWA's L-1049As were modified slightly from the normal design to simplify

A pair of TWA machines await their passengers. *(via TWA)*

Original Caption: Huge Transport in take-off test - Pulled skyward in steep slant by 10,800 total horsepower of her four jet-stack engines, new Super Constellation transport in use as flying laboratory by Lockheed Aircraft Corporation demonstrates sharp-climb ability in test takeoff at Lockheed Air Terminal, Burbank, Calif. First seven planes of this enlarged transport type are now in service on East Coast (on Eastern Air Lines), with nearly 75 more on order for world airlines and large quantity backlogged for military services. All its government tests were passed months ago, but Lockheed continues to wring out laboratory ship in researching improved flight equipment and designs. On normal takeoff at maximum 120,000-pound weight, Super Constellation gets off ground after about 5400-foot run. At controls during takeoff shown was veteran test pilot Stanley A. Eeltz.

conversion to compound motors if desired by adding an auxiliary unit containing the exhaust-driven turbine to the rear of the engine. And in 1954 TWA requested a number of modifications to their Model 1049As to give a speed increase of approximately 12mph at 20,000 feet under long-range cruising conditions. These included extension of the engine nacelles, elongation of the wing/fuselage fillets, rearward extension of the spinners and improvements to the shape of the cowling, closing of one of the three wing intakes for cabin cooling air and reducing a second intake in size, and removing the wing walkway paint.

The 1049A's fuel capacity was increased to 6,550 US gallons and its maximum gross weight had gone up to 120,000 pounds, which was still some way from the full weight limits of the stretched fuselage. Fin area had been increased slightly to counteract the extra length, and drag reduced by removing a number of external excrescences such as the dorsal astrodome that had featured on earlier models; ailerons were now metal-covered. Cabin pressurisation was improved to maintain a cabin altitude of 5,000 feet at 20,000 feet, and both cabin heating and cooling

Original caption: First wingtip fuel tanks ever to fly on transport aircraft are undergoing tests on Lockheed Super Constellations. This 600-gallon teardrop, being inspected by its inventor, Lockheed Chief Research Engineer Clarence A. (Kelly) Johnson, will be standard on 450-m.p.h. turboprop powered Super Constellations, on order for US Navy. Tiptanks on each wing actually improve plane performance and provide enough extra lift to compensate for the 3900-lb. weight of each, Johnson reported.

capacity were increased. A new electrical system was introduced, as well as a new combination electrical-pneumatic de-icer system featuring an electrically-heated strip located along the stagnation line of the leading edges and small high-pressure pneumatic tubes extending aft to the ten per cent chord line of the wing. More baggage loading doors were also provided, and a fourth optional cargo door could be fitted aft on the Super Constellation, which now had 728 cubic feet of underfloor freight space. Altogether, some 550 design improvements went into the first long-fuselage version.

The Re-Birth of 'Old 1961'
'Old 1961', the prototype Constellation, had been repurchased by Lockheed from Howard Hughes early in 1950 for conversion into the Super Constellation prototype. This was done by cutting the existing fuselage to insert the sections of extra length fore and aft of the wing spars, the circular windows of its original form being retained. Re-registered N67900, 'Old 1961' made its first flight as a Super Constellation at the Lockheed Air Terminal at Burbank on 13 October 1950 and for over a year was engaged in a test programme involving aerodynamic evaluation and development of the control system, powerplant and supercharger development and radio trials. CAA certification trials were completed in only ten weeks, largely with the first two production aircraft for Eastern, N6201C and N6202C. The former had been fitted with six pairs of water-ballast tanks in the cabin for varying the load and c. g. position and the airscrew blades were strain-gauged to measure vibration. The other production aircraft, N6202C, was fully furnished with eighty-eight passenger seats and was used for testing systems such as hydraulics, electrics and air conditioning. The Super Constellation was certificated on 29 November 1951 at a maximum gross weight of 120,000 pounds, or 4,000 pounds more than guaranteed, and met or exceeded all its performance guarantees. Before the prototype flew, sixty-two Model 1049s, valued at $96,041,000, had been ordered by five airlines, and over a hundred by the time the first production aircraft flew, giving Lockheed the largest backlog of orders in its history.

With certification trials out of the way, 'Old 1961' was used to test a number of new features and powerplants intended for future Constellation developments. Early in 1952, it was fitted with two 600 US gallon wing-tip tanks, each with a horizontal stabilising fin at the rear, of the type later to be fitted to the L-1049G and L-1049Es converted to Super G standard, although for these models and military versions the horizontal fins were deleted. They were originally intended to cater for the anticipated higher fuel consumption of turbo-prop engines for use with such versions of the Super Constellation Lockheed at this stage envisaged not only tip tanks but two 500 US gallon under-wing tanks. The tip tanks extended the range, and their endplate effect was aerodynamically beneficial. Later in 1952 'Old 1961' was fitted with the large dorsal and ventral radomes of the US Navy's WV-2 early warning version of the Model 1049, the ventral radome being of greater diameter than that of the previous PO-IW, as well as deeper. In this configuration it was used for aerodynamic tests of the radome shape and the interior was not fitted out like that of production WV-2s.

Shortly before the radomes were fitted, a 3,250 brake horsepower Wright R-3350-972TCI8DA1 Turbo-Compound was test run in the port outer nacelle, and a second engine of this type was later fitted in the starboard outer position; these being the powerplants intended for the L-1049C. After a time the dorsal and ventral radomes and tip tanks were removed and, early in 1954, the' DA-I Turbo-Compound in No 4 position was replaced by one 3,750 horsepower Allison YT-56 turbo-prop which, in its production form, was to power the Lockheed C-130 Hercules military transport. 'Old 1961' made its first flight with the YT-56 on 29 April 1954 and at this stage was flying with a' DA-1 Turbo-Compound in No 1 position and two conventional R-3350s inboard. With the Wright engines, two types of Curtiss Electric and three models of Hamilton Standard airscrew were tested.

The YT-56 drove a three-blade Curtiss turbo-electric propellers with broad-chord blades, and the engine was later modified to resemble the civil Allison 501D-13 turbo-prop which powered the Lockheed Electra. In this form, it completed 207 hours flying time, and when the test programme was completed at the end of 1956, it was replaced by a genuine Allison 501D-13 which first flew in 'Old 1961' in March 1957, with an Aeroproducts 606 four-blade airscrew. Four of these powerplants were later fitted in place of the Pratt & Whitney T-34s in an R7V-2 Super Constellation, which became known as 'Elation' in its new role as a flying testbed for Electra engines and systems. Incidentally, it is interesting to recall that in 1955-56 Lockheed was considering the Rolls-Royce

Above: 'Old 1961', now the Super Constellation prototype with TWA L-749A N6014C *Star of Delaware* as yet unpainted in the background.

Left: three years later the YT-56 was replaced with an Allison 501D-13 turboprop driving a Aeroproducts 606 propeller. The reduction gear was now located below the power section.

Below: 'Old 1961' was fitted in 1954 with a 3,750 horsepower Allison YT-56 turboprop in the No. 4 Position. *(all Lockheed)*

RB.109 Tyne and Napier Eland turbo-props as possible future engines for the Super Constellation despite the massive test and production programme then being planned for the Allison 501.

Like the T-34 installation, the 501D-13 jet pipes exhausted over the wing trailing edges but were of a smaller diameter befitting the less powerful engines. The cowling shape was also different, due to the Allison engine's reduction gearing to the propeller being offset below the power section. With two Convair YC-131Cs of the MATS 1700th Squadron fitted with 3,250hp Allison YT-56s, the 'Elation' took part in an intensive test programme for Allison turboprops, and by July 1958, a year after it had first flown with these powerplants, it had completed more than 750 hours of engine development flying and was averaging a daily eight hours simulated airline flying. Yet despite what was by European standards a pretty massive flight proving programme, the Allison 501D-13 installation in the Lockheed Electra had a chequered career and encountered a considerable amount of engine and structural trouble..

After completing Allison 501 testing for the Electra 'Old 1961' was put into storage and later bought by California Airmotive and eventually broken up. The nose up to the leading edge of the wing was used to repair Air France Model 749A-79-46 F-BAZI which had crashed at Gander, Newfoundland, on 25 August 1954. Its remains were bought by TO Associates, who acquired 'Old 1961's' nose for building on to it, but repairs were never completed although the registration N2717A was allotted to the rebuilt aircraft. Thus ended a remarkably interesting career, for 'Old 1961' was certainly unique in being powered at one and the same time by piston engines, a Turbo-Compound and a turbo-prop.

The Model L-1049D Freighter

A commercial freighter based on the R7V-I would have obvious attractions to those airlines whose volume of freight traffic would justify such an aircraft. The first was known as the L-1049B and Seaboard & Western Airlines - later to become Seaboard World Airlines - placed an order for four of these at the end of 1951 at the cost of some $10,000,000 including spares. This version had a maximum gross weight of 130,000 pounds, but it was superseded by the L-1049D (otherwise identical except for the gross weight being raised to 133,000 pounds like the late production R7V-1s), and Seaboard & Western switched its order to this variant, which had an airframe stressed for an eventual gross weight of 150,000 pounds when re-engined with suitable turboprops. The maximum landing weight was now 110,000 pounds. The 1049D was the world's largest commercial cargo transport when it appeared, and it could carry a payload of up to eighteen short tons on the North Atlantic routes, or up to twenty racehorses in individual stalls with their water, hay and feed. The 1049D's maximum payload was 38,570 pounds, and the total cargo hold volume was 5,568 cubic feet, the main hold being eighty-three feet long. There were fewer cabin windows than on the L-1049C.

The same freight doors and heavy-duty magnesium floor as on the R7V-I were features of the 1049D, which could also incorporate, as an optional 'extra', an electrically-operated mechanical conveyor in the floor to move cargo down the hold. With a maximum full-load speed of fifteen feet per minute, this conveyor could handle items of freight weighing approximately 12,000 pounds or 18,000 pounds loads at twelve feet per minute. The 1049D could also be used as a passenger aircraft, with

R7V-2 BuAer 131631 was re-engined with four Allison 501D-13 turboprops for the Electra test programme, and rapidly gained the nickname 'Elation'. *(Lockheed)*

International Aircraft Services owned N5596A, a 749A when it was fitted with the rear fuselage and freight doors from R7V-2 131630 by Lockheed Aircraft Services. *(Lockheed)*

high-density seating for up to 109 in a coach-class layout, and Seaboard took advantage of this to lease three 1049Ds to BOAC for the New York - Bermuda route during 1955-56. Seaboard had operated the first commercial Atlantic all-cargo flight with a DC-4 on 10 May 1947 and took delivery of its first 1049D N6501C *American Air Trader* on 19 August 1954, three others following in September.

On 19 May 1954, the CAB awarded Seaboard a five-year certificate for a transatlantic route from New York to Germany and Switzerland. The 1049Ds started Atlantic freight charters on 14 September, but scheduled services over this route were not inaugurated until 10 April 1956 because of delay in obtaining Presidential approval and traffic rights. DC-4s were used at first but the 1049Ds took over from 1 December 1956, the US terminals being New York, Philadelphia and Baltimore, with London, Paris, Frankfurt, Hamburg and Zurich the major European terminals. Three 1049Ds were leased to BOAC and flown as 86-passenger aircraft on the New York-Bermuda route from the summer of 1955 to April 1956, after which British West Indian Airways Viscounts took over this route. One 1049D was also leased to Eastern late in 1956 for the New York-Miami holiday traffic, and Seaboard 1049s operated London-New York all-freight services on charter to BOAC from 1958.

One 1049D, N6503C *Paris Air Trader,* was later fitted with wing-tip tanks, and N6501C and N6502C were both modified up to L-1049H/03 standard in the summer of 1956 with the higher gross weight of 135,400 pounds to bring them up to the standard of the five L-1049Hs that Seaboard had ordered. This modification programme was undertaken by Lockheed Aircraft Services International and involved the fitting of two 600 US gallon tip tanks and four 3,250 horsepower Wright R-3350-972TC18DA-3 Turbo-Compounds in place of the R-3350-972TC18DA-1 engines of the 1049D. Subsequently, Seaboard itself increased the gross weight of these 1049Ds to the 137,500 pounds of the L-1049H. In their first full year of operating from 1954, Seaboard's 1049Ds achieved a daily utilisation of nearly ten hours each, and these aircraft also did a good deal of military charter flying.

The First Civil Turbo-Compound
Preceding the 1049D by nearly two years was the first civil Super Constellation with Turbo-Compound engines, the L-1049C with four 3,250 horsepower Wright R-3350-972TC18DA-1 radials. These engines could give 3,500 horsepower each for takeoff with water-methanol injection, and enabled more load to be carried at higher speeds. The maximum gross weight was 133,000 pounds, or 13,000 pounds more than the earlier Model 1049A; the landing weight was 110,000 pounds and maximum zero fuel weight 103,500 pounds. The Model 1049C was offered with a variety of luxury interiors designed by the Henry Dreyfuss organisation to avoid the 'furnished corridor' effect that was becoming increasingly evident in the stretched versions of existing piston-engined airliners. Additional compartmentation was employed to break down this tunnel effect and a new lounge concept was introduced which gave more flexibility in group arrangements for just two people or several. Wood

EC-AMP *San Juan* belonged to Iberia Lineas Aereas Españolas and is seen here in the early colour scheme over the California coast prior to delivery. The aircraft operated Iberia's transatlantic route network from Spain to New York and South America with European summer flights in the early 1960s for subsidiary Aviaco. *(Lockheed)*

panelling was used extensively, incorporating maps and other travel motifs, and direct diffused lighting with controlled intensity and compartment switching was featured in addition to the usual individually adjustable passenger reading lights. Designed to combine serviceability with an impression of luxury, these interiors were known, respectively, as the 'Inter-Continental', seating 54-60 passengers, the 'Siesta' for 47 passengers in a luxury layout, and the 'Inter-Urban' for 106 people in a high-density coach-class arrangement. A lounge seating up to eight people in high-backed chairs or low-backed two-place sofas facing forward or facing each other could be featured, and this could be curtained off from the rest of the cabin. Other interiors could seat 63, 82, 94 or 97 people and, if desired, freight could be carried in the forward part of the cabin.

Like the 1094D, the 1049C was stressed for an eventual gross weight of 150,000 pounds and its fuel capacity of 6,550 US gallons was the same as the 1049A's. The prototype L-1049C, PH-TFP *Atoom*, later to become PH-LKP for KLM, made its two-hour maiden flight on 17 February 1953. Its cabin was filled with test instrumentation and equipment, and it was flown by Lockheed pilots John Fales and C P Nicholson, with P Jensen and J Costa as flight engineers. The Dutch airline had ordered nine 1049Cs, but the last four of these were changed to L-1049Es and a tenth was ordered to replace one that crashed at Shannon on 5 September 1954. A repeat order for three more L-1049Es was placed in mid-1952.

KLM's Super Constellations were fitted with Curtiss Electric 858 props with extruded, hollow steel blades which were interchangeable with the Curtiss Electric 830 blades used on the L-749As of KLM and other operators; Hamilton Standard Hydromatic propellers could be fitted as an alternative. In 1955 a modification to its 1049E propellers was carried out by KLM at its Schiphol workshops to add five miles an hour to the speed, as well as improving cooling both in flight and on the ground. This took the form of extending the blade width down to the boss by means of fillets

EC-ARN of Iberia, seen in a later scheme. *(Lockheed)*

National Airlines' Super G N7133C is seen on a test flight in its 'Airline of the Stars' livery with 'Imperial Club Coach' titling just aft of the cockpit glazing. The picture was taken prior to delivery to the airline in October 1957. *(Lockheed)*

of foam plastic on the blade trailing edge, the blades being subjected to heat, the plastic applied and subsequently hardened in an oven. The process was completed by adding a layer of sheet rubber followed by a coat of paint as a protection against the atmosphere. A special KLM-designed galley was also fitted to its 1049Cs and 1049Es, along with the fitment of loudspeakers instead of headphones for the pilot and navigator. Several interiors were fitted in KLM's 1049Cs and 1049Es, ranging from a fifty-seven-passenger layout for the Amsterdam - Johannesburg route, a fifty-two-seat three-class interior - seven deluxe, thirty first-class passengers and fifteen tourists - for the Amsterdam-Sydney route and a high-density ninety-two passenger 'steerage' interior in four 1049Es for a series of flights carrying immigrants from Amsterdam to Perth in Western Australia.

The L-1049E emphasises that the same process of progressive weight improvements that characterised the Models 649 and 749 was being applied to the Super Constellation, the 1049E being the same as the 1049C with the same maximum take-off weight of 133,000 pounds. The landing and zero fuel weights were still the same as the 1049C's, but the 1049E incorporated all structural modifications except to the landing gear for an eventual take-off weight of 150,000 pounds. Some 1049Es were later modified to 1049E/01 standard with a maximum take-off weight of 135,400 pounds or to 1049E/02 standard with this same take-off weight, and the landing weight increased to 113,000 pounds.

The first production 1049E, YV-C-AMS of Linea Aeropostal Venezolana, made its maiden flight on 6 April 1954 but before the end of that year yet another major variant, the L-1049G, or Super G, had been rolled out and it was not long before seven airlines with thirty-eight 1049Es on order had changed over to this later variant. Several other operators had their 1049Es fitted with the 600 US gallon tip tanks of the L-1049G and modified up to Super G Standard.

These included KLM, which had four of its 1049Es converted from March-June 1956; Iberia of Spain, whose three 1049Es were similarly converted from 1957; Trans-Canada Airlines, which had two of its 1049E-55s modified but not fitted with the tip tanks; and Air-India International, which had its three 1049Es modified. The two remaining 1049Es of Iberia - a third had been lost in an accident on 6 March 1961 - were also converted into freighters in 1963 when they had been finally displaced as firstline equipment by DC-8s. They were also used in the passenger role after this modification on lease to the Spanish independent Aviaco, in particular for holiday charters. A fourth L-1049E was leased by Iberia from KLM from 1 April 1961 to 28 May 1962. Iberia had started Super Constellation services on the Madrid-New York route on 2 September 1954 and later put the type on to its other routes to Latin America and Spanish Africa.

The theme of product improvement started with

the short-fuselage Constellations continued with the 1049 series, mainly through improvements to the production process. From the summer of 1952 the trailing edges of certain wing panels were bonded together with adhesives, thus saving weight, and almost from the start of production 1049s were coming off the production lines at empty weights from 454-942 pounds less than that specified, the average being 658 pounds lighter. A new thermoplastic interior window frame trimming substance called 'Royalite' was among the first of the minor cabin furnishings and finishing improvements made from time to time.

More evident externally was the installation of cloud- and collision-warning radar from the mid-1950s, both retrospectively and in new aircraft off the production line. Two principal types of radar offered for the Super Constellation were the RCA AVQ-10, operating on the 5.6-centimetre wavelength and the Bendix RDR-7 of 3.2-centimetre wavelength, and these could be installed retrospectively by the airline using kits provided by Lockheed. In 1962 Chamberlain Aviation produced two models of its C AIR nose radome for the Constellation, the No 1015 for a twenty-two inch fully rotating antenna and No 201 5X for an eighteen-inch sector scan antenna; both radomes hinged upwards for access to the radar. Weather radar had also been fitted to the C-121A/B Constellations and the two PO-1Ws some time before commercial radars of this kind had been made available.

From 1958, USAF transport aircraft, including C-121s, were fitted with high-intensity collision-warning lights. Following the crash of KLM's 1049E PH-LKY *Triton* at Shannon on 5 September 1954 which was caused largely by an inadvertent undercarriage re-extension shortly after it had been retracted after take-off, and failure to maintain height with the undercarriage down - it was recommended that the warning lights indicating an unlocked or transient condition of the undercarriage be duplicated, and that sufficient emergency lighting for the passenger accommodation be provided.

It was not until being fitted with Turbo-Compounds that the Super Constellation began to realise its true potentialities, even though this engine did run into a number of troubles in service. Of these, the most serious was excessive exhaust flaming and afterburning out of the turbine exhaust hoods of the three 'blown-down' power recovery turbines. Before the engines were modified, the exhaust flames, when the aircraft was climbing, carried right back to the wing trailing edge with adverse effects on structural strength, to say nothing of passenger reaction. Chronic nozzle-box cracking, necessitating many unscheduled removals of turbines and components, together with cooling-cap failures were associated problems continued even with the DA-3 Turbo-Compounds of the Super G. In 1953 various modifications were put in hand to satisfy the CAA, including the addition of a two-inch-wide ring of half-inch armour around each turbine, better cooling and detailed changes giving an increased differential between turbine wheel speed and disc-failure speed. The exhaust flaming problem was not solved until $2,000,000 had been spent which took nine months and hundreds of flight tests, while the introduction of new high-temperature materials helped to reduce the unscheduled removal rate resulting from nozzle-box cracking. By 1956 the longest overhaul time on airline Turbo-Compounds was the 1,400 hours achieved by Air France L-1049Cs, whereas two years before the engine was cleared for only 600 hours between overhauls. Oil sedimentation in the clutches was another snag that had to be overcome, but even with the L-1049G, the engine troubles had not been finally solved.

The 1049 in Airline Service
In spite of the headaches it caused the maintenance engineers, the Turbo-Compound in the Super Constellation had the distinction of powering the first non-stop US transcontinental service, the first eastbound non-stop Atlantic flights, operated by KLM and the first round-the-world service with QANTAS. TWA began L-1049A Super Constellation services on 10 September 1952 and inaugurated the first sustained non-stop transcontinental service - the 'Ambassador' - over the New York - Los Angeles route on 19 October 1953; the westbound flights still stopped at Chicago, but eastbound flights made the coast-to-coast journey non-stop in under eight hours.

TWA's competitive edge over American Airlines DC-6Bs was to be short-lived, for less than six weeks later the latter began Douglas DC-7 services over the same route non-stop in both directions. Eastern Air Lines was the first to inaugurate services with the Super Constellation when it put the 1049A into service on the New York-Miami route on 17 December 1951, and it also ordered sixteen L-1049Cs for its major routes, putting these into service two years later. Five of these were converted into freighters by Lockheed Aircraft Services of Ontario, California during 1959, with big freight doors and heavy-duty floors.

The door dimensions were slightly different from those of the 1049D and R7V-1, the forward door

161
A detailled look at 'D-ALEM' a preserved L-1049 at Munich Airport.
(photos Kirk Smeaton Collection)

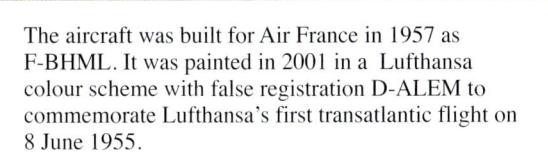

The aircraft was built for Air France in 1957 as F-BHML. It was painted in 2001 in a Lufthansa colour scheme with false registration D-ALEM to commemorate Lufthansa's first transatlantic flight on 8 June 1955.

Above: engine and cowling details. Some Constellations had flaps fitted to the upper air scoops, some did not.

Right: earlier models had a different hydraulic steering system on the nosewheel leg, just above the wheels.

Below: Each wheel of the main landing gear hides a multi-disc braking system.

Left: a detail picture of the tip tank. Highly streamlined, it was similar, but larger than the one originally fitted to the P-38 Lightning.

Below: a general view of the Visitor Park at Munich International Airport. Apart from the Constellation, there is a Douglas DC-3 and Junkers Ju.52.

The main cabin of D-ALEM is used to show videos of Lufthansa's airline operation.

Right: the toilet of the airliner is fully restored, but not to be used by visitors!

Below: the ghostly lines and reflections in this shot of the flightdeck is due to the perspex covering the instruments for protection.

being seventy-two and a half inches high by fifty-six and a half inches wide with the rear door one-hundred and six and a half inches wide by seventy-four inches high. A sixth Eastern 1049C was converted into a freighter in 1963.

It was not as freighters that Eastern's by now nearly obsolete 1049s caught the imagination of the air transport industry and air travelling public in 1961. Instead, it was their inauguration on what was to become the famous 'Air Shuttle' services between Boston, New York and Washington on 30 April of that year. These no-frills 'walk-on' services, although not the first of their kind, were the first really large-scale attempt at a shuttle service, which enabled a cheaper fare to be offered because it cost the airline less to process the passenger.

For the travelling public, the attraction was the elimination of the need to check in about thirty minutes before departure, and the ability to buy tickets on board. The passenger pulled a boarding pass out of a machine and wrote their name and address on it for the load manifest, and when enough passes had been issued for a full load of ninety-five passengers in Eastern's 1049s, the flight was closed out, boarded and dispatched. Back-up aircraft were employed for extra sections of the same flight when there were more than ninety-five people wanting to travel, and on several occasions Eastern laid on a Super to fly virtually empty, carrying only the one or two passengers over the full aircraft load. Even so, Eastern's 'Air Shuttle' prospered over the years, its network was expanded, and Electra turboprops and later DC-9 jets replaced the 1049s; its success was due to a new and welcome emphasis in air transport, on convenience rather than speed.

The First L-1049C Transatlantic Services

KLM was the first to introduce the L-1049C, inaugurating the first transatlantic Super Constellation service with this variant on 15 August 1953, scheduling the eastbound flights non-stop from New York to Amsterdam, and offering for the first time a non-stop Atlantic crossing, albeit in only one direction.

The Dutch airline was followed by Air France, which began L-1049C flights between Paris and New York on 20 November 1953, and by Trans-Canada Airlines which inaugurated L-1049C services on 14 May 1954 from Toronto and Montreal to Glasgow, London, Paris and Dusseldorf. TCA's five L-1049C-55s and three L-1049E-55s featured loudspeakers instead of headphones for the pilots and flight engineer among nearly twenty fairly major and a great many minor modifications; weather radar was fitted from 1957, and later one was used to evaluate the Decca navigational aid. The 1049Cs and two of the three 1049Es were later modified up to L-1049G standard but were not fitted with tip tanks. Air France took delivery of ten L-1049C-55-81 Super Constellations and for their first Atlantic services - named 'The Golden Parisian' - eight two-berth sleeping compartments were introduced, the bunks being removed during the day and replaced by two seats. Other low-density interiors featured during the 1950s included a thirty-two passenger first-class layout, one for twenty-four first-class and thirty-four tourist passengers and, for the 'Eastern Epicurean' services to the Far East, a three-class layout with sleeper, first and tourist accommodation. In 1955 all Air France's Super Constellations were fitted with Kleber-Colombes rubber de-icing boots. From 1961, after they had been displaced as first-line equipment by Boeing 707s, five of the remaining 1049Cs (which by now had been modified up to L-1049E standard) were converted into freighters similar to Eastern's 1049Cs; one of them was leased to Air Cameroun in 1967.

Air-India had already established its name with the Constellation and it ordered two L-1049Cs and three L-1049Es, the first being delivered in January 1954. With these and five L-1049Gs ordered later,

F-BGNI of Air Cameroun. *(Lockheed)*

A misty, hazy, damp Amsterdam Schiphol sometime in the 1950s with a couple of KLM Constellations, a Douglas DC-7C and a Vickers Viscount. KLM flew for many years with the slogan 'The Flying Dutchman' above the airliner's windows. *(KLM)*

the existing pattern of routes from London through Europe to India was expanded eastwards to Singapore via Madras, to Bangkok, Hong Kong and Tokyo and - from 5 October 1956 - to Singapore, Darwin and Sydney. A weekly Delhi - Tashkent - Moscow service was started on 1 April 1959 with Super Constellations, although 707s later took over from the 1049s which, in 1962, were disposed of to the Indian Air Force, except for one retained for a time for pilgrim flights to Mecca.

Weather radar was fitted from 1958 and, like several Model 1049E YV-C-AMS of Linea Aeropostal Venezolana was the first production aircraft of this variant among other operators, Air-India adopted the KLM-designed galley for its 1049s. In November 1955 the lounge in Air-India's fleet was removed and replaced by fully reclining 'slumberette' type seats for nineteen first-class passengers; the interior was now arranged for thirty-one first-class and forty tourist passengers. Air Ceylon's 'Sapphire' service from Colombo to Amsterdam and London was operated by KLM with a L-749A which was replaced in November 1958 by L-1049E PH-LKA *Isotoop*, on lease from the Dutch airline for the next two years; it was later given the Sinhalese registration 4R-ACH and named *Soma Devi*, and after returning from Air Ceylon service it went to Iberia on a lease as EC-AQL *La Confiada*.

Three L-1049Cs formed the fleet of a new national airline, Pakistan International Airlines, which began operations with them on 7 June 1954 on the 'inter-wing' services between Karachi and Dacca, the capitals of West and East Pakistan. On 1 February 1955, PIA's 1049Cs began international operations between Karachi and London via Cairo, with what was then the fastest schedule over the

The Prins family flew KLM from Amsterdam Schiphol in the 1950s.

This sequence of pictures are from one trip...

...when they flew KLM L-1049 Constellation PH-LKB *Positron* to Curaçao...

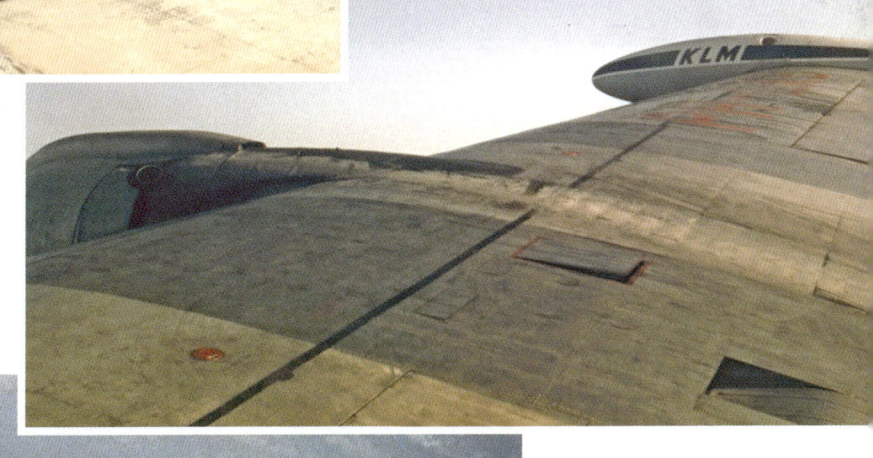

Klaas Prins was an electrical engineering teacher employed by Royal Dutch Shell and was on his first assignment. These pictures were taken over the wing of 'KB, and on the curving approach to Dr. Albert Plesman airport, Curaçao.

Plesman was a director of the Royal Dutch Airlines for the Netherlands and Colonies, and from 1954 following his death the airport was named after him; neverthess, everyone called it Hato Airport after a nearby town!

(*all photos copyright 1957, The executors of the estate of the late Klaas Jurjen Prins*)

BG583 of the Indian Air Force, formerly VT-DJW *Rani of Bijpur* of Air India. The aireliner was operated by No.6 Squadron IAF using the callsign VU-QLG. *(Author's Collection)*

route, and after they were displaced as first-line equipment by Boeing 720Bs from 1962 they were put on to the major domestic routes, and in 1966 began operating domestic night air coach services.

Another major Commonwealth operator of Super Constellations was QANTAS, which ordered four L-1049Cs in 1951 and six more in 19 April 1953; in 1958 all ten were modified up to L-1049E/oI-55 standard, the first one having been delivered on 29 March 1954. They went into service on the trans-Pacific route to San Francisco and Vancouver on I 5 May 1954 as well as on the 'Kangaroo' route to London, and on 14 January 1958 QANTAS achieved the notable distinction of being the first airline to operate a regular, scheduled service around the world when its Super Constellation service to San Francisco was extended on a twice-weekly basis through New York to London to connect there with the 'Kangaroo' services to Sydney through south-east Asia. QANTAS 1049s also took over from 749As the route across the Indian Ocean to Johannesburg on 5 November 1954 and the Sydney-Tokyo route in 19 May 1955. A 1049E was leased to Malayan Airways in 1960 for its Singapore to Hong Kong route.

During 1955 the QANTAS aircraft were modified to carry up to 16,000 pounds of freight and fifty-seven tourist-class passengers with an increased zero fuel weight and some strengthening of the wing root. Other interiors featured were an all first-class layout for thirty-nine passengers and a three-class interior for seven deluxe, twenty first-class and thirty-five tourist passengers; in 1961 QANTAS 1049s seated from thirty-four up to eighty-five passengers. From the start of their life, they had been fitted with RAE counting accelerometers and fatigue meters to gather data on gust intensity and fatigue as part of the Australian aviation research programme. From 1955, following advances in communication techniques, QANTAS dispensed with the radio officer as a crew member. Two L-049E/OI-55s were converted into freighters in 1960 by Lockheed Aircraft Services to supplement the two L-1049H freighters already delivered, and with these an all-freight service from Sydney to London was operated. As the Boeing 707s came into service the 1049s were sold off, the last being delivered to a US dealer on 6 May 1963.

In Latin America, two operators ordered Super Constellations: Avianca of Colombia put three L-1049Es into service late in 1954, plus a 1049G two years later; these were put on to the routes from Bogota to Paris and Frankfurt via Bermuda and Santa Maria in the Azores, and from Bogota to Miami and New York via Kingston or Montego Bay in Jamaica. The accommodation layout was originally for thirty-nine first-class and fifteen tourist passengers that later gave way to a sixty-four passenger layout. One 1049E was later converted into a freighter, and like the other remaining - the third had been lost in an accident on 1 January 1960 - was modified to Super G standard.

Linea Aeropostal Venezolana put two L-1049Es into service in 1954 on its central Atlantic route from Caracas through Bermuda and Santa Maria in the Azores to Lisbon, Madrid and Rome, and also on the routes to Lima (Peru) from Caracas, to Miami via Havana and to New York non-stop.

One of the first operators to order Super Connies, Braathens South American & Far East Airtransport A/S (SAFE) was prevented from taking delivery by government action and had to cancel its order. Formed by the air-minded Norwegian shipowner Ludvig G. Braathen, who in 1937 had applied to operate an Oslo-London air service and the following year planned a transatlantic service with Boeing 314 flying-boats, Braathens began operating DC-4s after the war to Hong Kong and South America on a non-scheduled basis. Early in 1949 the Oslo-Hong Kong route was put on a regular basis when the Norwegian government authorised Braathens to operate over it for a period of five years, and a weekly DC-4 service began in August 1949, two months before SAS started services to Bangkok, and continued until April 1954. Two L-1049Es were ordered in anticipation of Braathens' operating authority to the Far East being renewed, but in mid-1954 SAS had extended its Bangkok route to Hong Kong and Tokyo and the Norwegian government, as a partner in Scandinavian Airlines System, could not license an independent

167

QANTAS Super Constellation VH-EAM *Southern Spray* being christened by QANTAS secretaries Lola Fry and Pamela Cooke with a spray of champagne at Burbank on 4 October 1956.

QANTAS brings you a New Standard of Trans-Pacific Air Travel

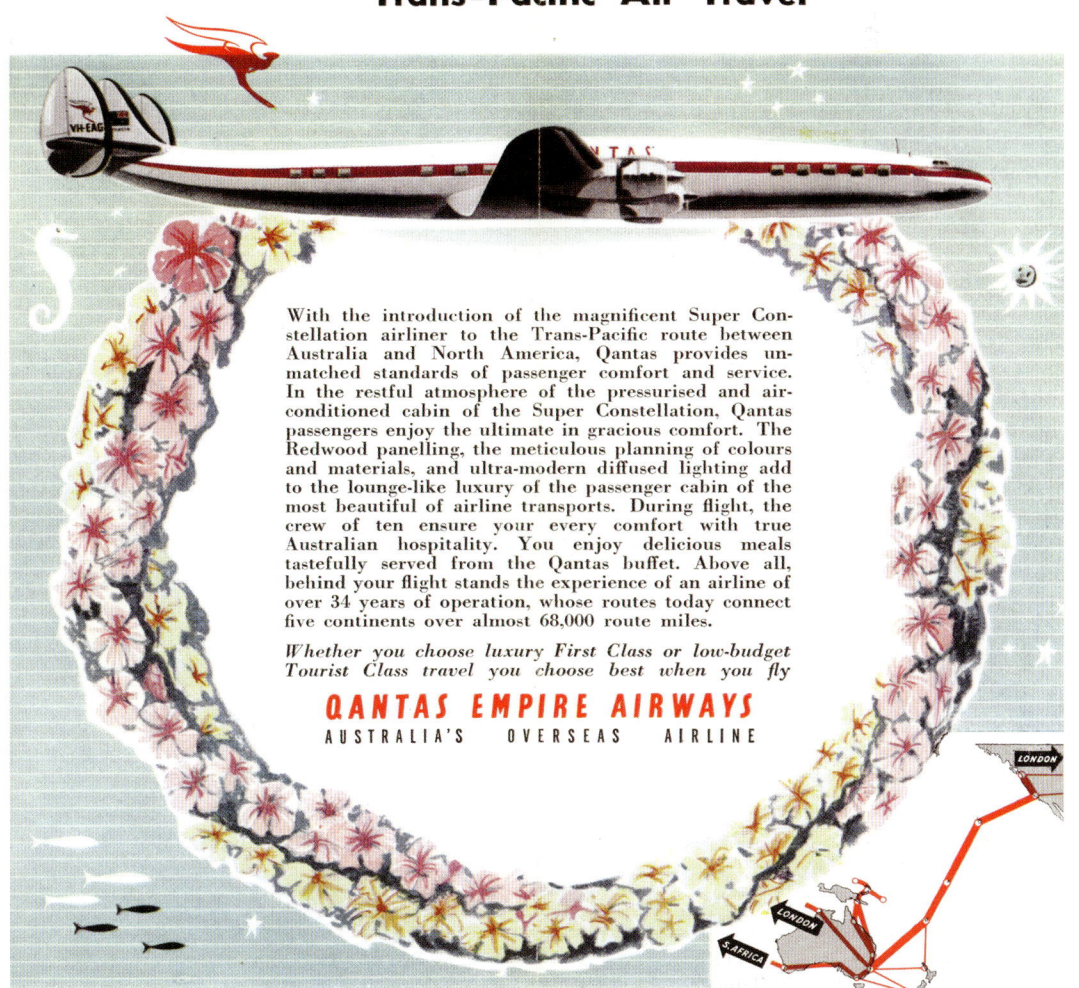

With the introduction of the magnificent Super Constellation airliner to the Trans-Pacific route between Australia and North America, Qantas provides unmatched standards of passenger comfort and service. In the restful atmosphere of the pressurised and air-conditioned cabin of the Super Constellation, Qantas passengers enjoy the ultimate in gracious comfort. The Redwood panelling, the meticulous planning of colours and materials, and ultra-modern diffused lighting add to the lounge-like luxury of the passenger cabin of the most beautiful of airline transports. During flight, the crew of ten ensure your every comfort with true Australian hospitality. You enjoy delicious meals tastefully served from the Qantas buffet. Above all, behind your flight stands the experience of an airline of over 34 years of operation, whose routes today connect five continents over almost 68,000 route miles.

Whether you choose luxury First Class or low-budget Tourist Class travel you choose best when you fly

QANTAS EMPIRE AIRWAYS
AUSTRALIA'S   OVERSEAS   AIRLINE

Immediate Connections to and from Europe and London

airline in competition with SAS on an international route. So Braathens' operating authority was not renewed, its Hong Kong route was suspended and the 1049E order was cancelled, the airline thereafter concentrating on Norwegian domestic services and on charters. Altogether, twenty-four L-1049As and seventy-four L-1049Cs and L-1049Es were built.

The Grand Canyon Accident
The Grand Canyon mid-air collision occurred on June 30 1956, when a United Airlines Douglas DC-7 struck a Trans World Airlines L-1049 Super Constellation over the Grand Canyon National Park. All 128 on board both flights perished, making it the first commercial airline crash to result in more than 100 deaths.

TWA Flight 2, operated by L-1049 Super Constellation N6902C *Star of the Seine*, was crewed by Captain Jack S Gandy, 41, First Officer James H Ritner, 31, and Flight Engineer Forrest D Breyfogle, 37, along with stewardesses Trachine E Armbruster and Beth E Davis.

The service took off from Runway 25 LAX at 9:01 am PDT with sixty-four passengers, including eleven TWA off-duty employees 31 minutes behind schedule caused by minor technical problems. Flight 2's flight plan called for an IFR departure from LAX to Kansas City Downtown Airport, Missouri routing via Green Airway 5, Amber Airway 2, Daggett direct Trinidad, direct Dodge City, Victor Airway 10 direct Kansas City. The flight plan called for a cruising altitude of 19,000 feet with a speed of 270 knots. Take-off time was scheduled for 0830.

After takeoff, TWA 2 contacted the Los Angeles tower radar departure controller and was vectored through an overcast which existed in the Los Angeles area. After reporting 'on top' at 2,400 feet, the flight switched to Los Angeles Air Route Traffic Control Center frequency, 118.9 mcs., for en-route clearance. This clearance specified the routing as filed in the flight plan; however, the controller specified that the flight climb to 19,000 feet in VFR conditions.

Shortly after take-off, TWA's Captain Gandy requested permission to climb to 21,000 feet to avoid thunderheads that were forming near his flight path. As was the practice at the time, his request had to be relayed by a TWA dispatcher to ATC, as neither crew was in direct contact with ATC after departure. ATC denied the request; the two airliners would soon be re-entering controlled airspace (Red 15 airway running southeast from Las Vegas) and ATC had no way to provide the horizontal separation required between two aircraft at the same altitude.

TWA 2 asked for a routing change to Daggett via Victor Airway 210. This was approved. At Daggett, Captain Gandy turned right to a heading of 059 degrees magnetic, toward the radio range near Trinidad, Colorado. The Constellation was now operating 'off airways' – flying in uncontrolled airspace.

United Air Lines Flight 718, a Douglas DC-7 named *Mainliner Vancouver*, was crewed by Captain Robert F Shirley, 48, First Officer Robert W Harms, 36, Flight Engineer Gerard Fiore, 39, along with stewardesses Nancy L Kemnitz and Margaret A Shoudt.

The flight departed Los Angeles International Airport's Runway 25L at 9:04 am PDT with fifty-three passengers on board, bound for Chicago's Midway Airport. The flight plan called for an IFR departure to Chicago via Green Airway 5, Palm Springs Intersection, direct Needles, direct Painted Desert, direct Durango, direct Pueblo, direct St Joseph, Victor Airway 116 Joliet, Victor Airway 84 Chicago Midway. The flight plan called for a cruising speed of 288 knots at 21,000 feet, with a departure time of 0845.

After take-off, United 718 contacted the Los Angeles tower radar controller, who vectored it through the overcast over the same departure course as TWA 2. United 718 reported 'on top' and changed to LA Center frequency for its en-route clearance. This corresponded to the flight plan as filed; however, the controller specified that the climb to assigned altitude be in VFR conditions.

Flight 718 made position reports to Aeronautical Radio, Inc., which served under contract as United company radio. It reported passing over Riverside and later over Palm Springs intersection. The latter report indicated that United 718 was still climbing to 21,000 and estimated it would reach Needles at 1000 and the Painted Desert at 1034.

At approximately 0958 United 718 made a position report to the communications station located at Needles. This report stated that the flight was over Needles at 0958 at 21,000 feet, and estimated Painted Desert at 1031, with Durango next. The DC-7, though still under IFR jurisdiction, was now, just like the Constellation, flying in uncontrolled airspace.

Meanwhile, at 0921, through company radio communications, TWA 2 reported that it was approaching Daggett and requested a change in flight plan altitude assignment from 19,000 to 21,000 feet. Los Angeles Center advised they were unable to approve the requested altitude because of traffic; this was United Air Lines Flight 718. Flight 2 requested clearance of 1,000 feet on top. Ascertaining from the radio operator that the flight was then at least 1,000

Above: L-1049 Super Constellation N6902C *Star of the Seine*, one of the two airliners involved in the disaster.

Left LA Center - the hub of air traffic control in the southern Calfornia area 'sometime in the 1950's'. It was from here that both airliners were supposedly controlled.

on top, LA Center cleared the flight.

At 0959 TWA 2 reported its position through company radio at Las Vegas, stating that it had passed Lake Mohave at 0955, was 1,000 on top at 21,000 feet, and estimated it would reach the 33 degree radial of the Winslow omni range station (Painted Desert) at 1031 with Farrington next. This was the last radio communication with the flight.

Flying VFR placed the responsibility for maintaining safe separation from other aircraft upon Gandy and Ritner, a procedure referred to as 'see and be seen,' since changed to 'see and avoid.' Upon receiving the '1,000 on top' clearance, Captain Gandy increased his altitude to 21,000 feet.

Both crews had estimated that they would arrive somewhere along the Painted Desert line at about 10:31 am Pacific time. The Painted Desert line was about 200 miles long, running between the VORs at Bryce Canyon, Utah, and Winslow, Arizona, at an angle of 335 degrees relative to true north - wholly outside of controlled air space. Owing to the different headings taken by the two airliners, TWA's crossing of the Painted Desert line, assuming no further course changes, would be at a thirteen degree angle relative to that of the United flight, with the Constellation to the left of the DC-7.

As the two aircraft approached the Grand Canyon, now at the same altitude and nearly the same speed, the pilots were likely manoeuvring around towering cumulus clouds, though flying VFR required the TWA flight to stay in clear air. As they were manoeuvring near the canyon, it is believed the

170

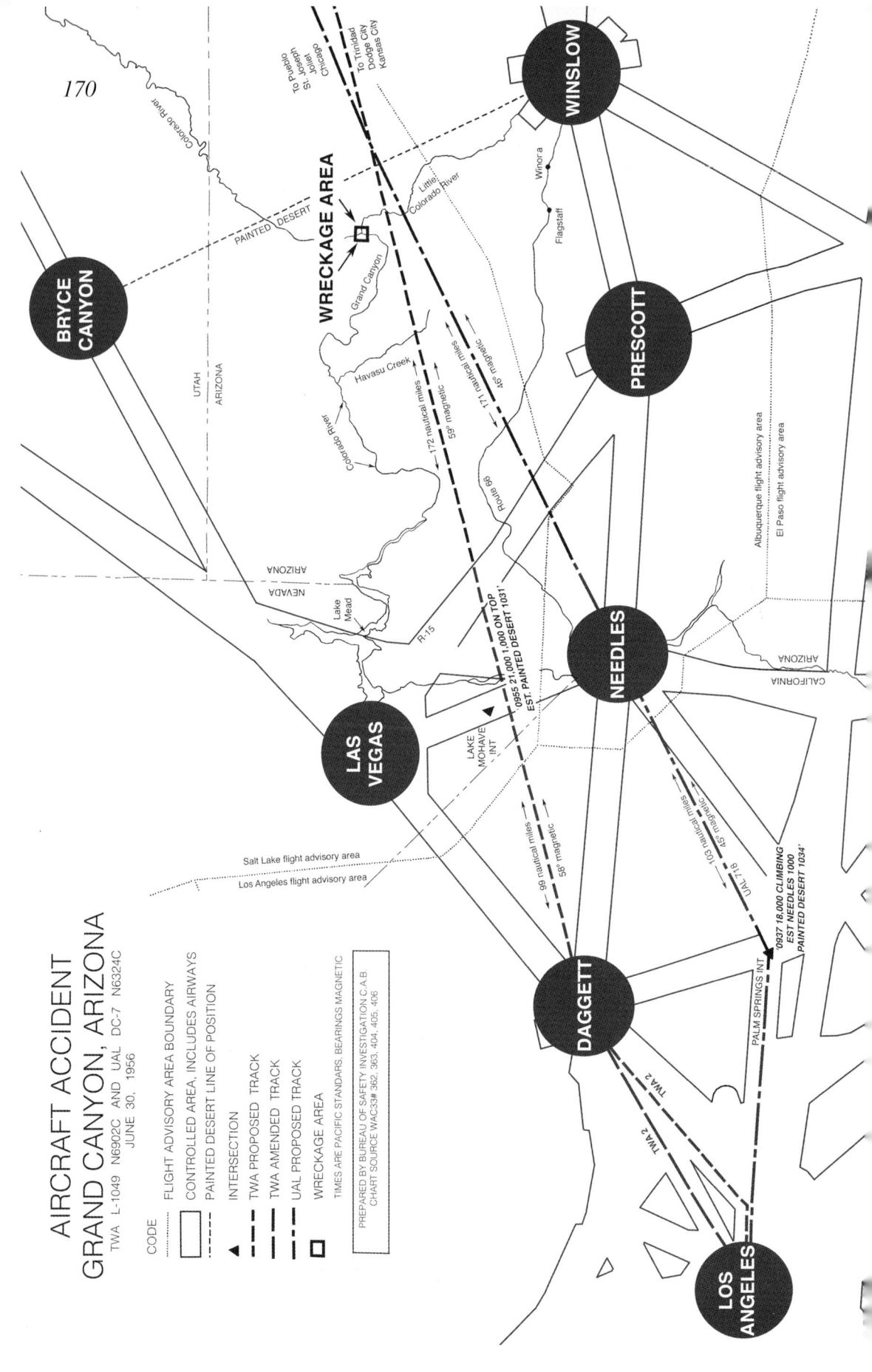

airliners passed the same cloud on opposite sides.

At about 10:30 a.m. the flight paths of the two aircraft intersected over the canyon, and they collided at an angle of about 25 degrees. The post-crash analysis determined that the United DC-7 was banked to the right and pitched down at the time of the collision, suggesting that one or possibly both of the United pilots saw the TWA Constellation before impact and attempted evasive action.

The DC-7's upraised left wing clipped the top of the Constellation's vertical stabiliser and struck the fuselage immediately ahead of the stabiliser's base, causing the tail assembly to break away from the rest of the airframe. The propeller on the DC-7's left outboard, or number one engine, concurrently chopped a series of gashes into the bottom of the Constellation's fuselage. Explosive decompression would have instantaneously occurred from the damage, a theory substantiated by light debris, such as cabin furnishings and personal effects, being scattered over a large area.

The separation of the empennage from the Constellation resulted in immediate loss of control, causing the aircraft to enter a near-vertical, terminal velocity dive. Plunging into the Grand Canyon at an estimated speed of more than 477 mph, the Constellation slammed into the north slope of a ravine located on the northeast slope of Temple Butte. It disintegrated on impact, instantly killing all aboard. An intense fire, fueled by aviation gasoline, ensued. The severed empennage, badly battered but still somewhat recognisable, came to rest nearby.

The airspace over the canyon was not under any type of radar contact and there were neither homing beacons nor 'black boxes' (cockpit voice and flight data recorders) aboard either aircraft. The last position reports received from the flights did not reflect their locations at the time of impact. Also, there were no credible witnesses to the collision itself or the subsequent crashes. The only immediate indication of trouble was when United company radio operators in Salt Lake City and San Francisco heard a garbled transmission from Flight 718, the last from either aircraft. Civil Aeronautics Board accident investigation engineers later deciphered the transmission – which had been preserved on magnetic tape – as the voice of co-pilot Robert Harms declaring, 'Salt Lake, [ah], 718 ... we are going in!' The shrill voice of Captain Shirley was heard in the background as futilely struggling with the controls, he implored the plane to '[Pull] up! [Pull] up!' The bracketed words were inferred by investigators in their report from the context and circumstances in which they were uttered.

After neither flight reported their current position for some time, the two aircraft were declared to be missing, and search and rescue procedures started. The wreckage was first seen late in the day near the confluence of the Colorado and Little Colorado Rivers by Henry and Palen Hudgin, two brothers who operated Grand Canyon Airlines, a small air taxi service. During a trip earlier in the day, Palen had noted dense black smoke rising near Temple Butte, the crash site of the Constellation, but had dismissed it as the brush set ablaze by lightning.

However, upon hearing of the missing airliners, Palen decided that what he had seen might have been smoking from a post-crash fire. He and his brother flew a Piper Tri-Pacer deep into the canyon and searched near the location of the smoke. The Constellation's empennage was found, and the brothers reported their findings to authorities. The following day, the two men pinpointed the wreckage of the DC-7. Numerous helicopter missions were subsequently flown down to the crash sites to find and attempt to identify victims, as well as recover wreckage for accident analysis, a difficult and dangerous process due to the rugged terrain and unpredictable air currents.

Both airlines hired the Swiss Air-Rescue and some Swiss mountain climbers to go to the scene where the aircraft fuselages had crashed. They were

The severed tail of N6902C *Star of the Seine,* after it came to rest deep in the Grand Canyon *(CAB)*

to gather the remains of the passengers and other items. This was given much publicity in US news releases at the time because of the harshness of the terrain where the fuselages came to rest. Due to the severity of the ground impacts, no bodies were recovered intact, and positive identification of most of the remains was not possible.

The collision took place in uncontrolled airspace, where it was the pilots' responsibility to maintain separation. This highlighted the antiquated state of US air traffic control, which became the focus of significant aviation reforms.

The accident investigation was challenging due to the remoteness and topography of the crash sites, the near-total destruction of the two airliners and the lack of real-time flight data. Despite the considerable difficulties, CAB experts were able to determine with a remarkable degree of certainty what had transpired and, in their report, issued the following statement as probable cause for the accident:

'The Board determines that the probable cause of this mid-air collision was that the pilots did not see each other in time to avoid the collision. It is not possible to determine why the pilots did not see each other. Still, the evidence suggests that it resulted from any one or a combination of the following factors: Intervening clouds reducing time for visual separation, visual limitations due to cockpit visibility, and preoccupation with normal cockpit duties, preoccupation with matters unrelated to cockpit duties such as attempting to provide the passengers with a more scenic view of the Grand Canyon area, physiological limits to human vision reducing the time opportunity to see and avoid the other aircraft, or insufficiency of en-route air traffic advisory information due to the inadequacy of facilities and lack of personnel in air traffic control.'

The media covered the accident, and as the story unfolded, the public learned of the primitive nature of ATC and how little was being done to modernise it. The air traffic controller who had cleared TWA to '1,000 on top' was severely criticised as he had not advised Captains Gandy and Shirley about the potential for a traffic conflict following the clearance even though he must have known of the possibility, but he was cleared of any wrongdoing. As Charles Carmody, the then-assistant ATC director, testified during the investigation, neither flight was legally under the control of ATC when they collided, as both were 'off airways'. The controller was not required to issue a traffic conflict advisory to either pilot. According to the CAB accident investigation final report, Page 8, the en-route controller relayed a traffic advisory regarding United 718 to TWA's ground radio operator: 'ATC clears TWA 2, maintain at least 1,000 on top. Advise TWA 2 his traffic is United 718, direct Durango, estimating Needles at 0957.' The TWA operator testified that Captain Gandy acknowledged the information on the United flight as 'traffic received.'

After a series of hearings and investigations, the Federal Aviation Act of 1958 was passed, dissolving the CAA and creating the Federal Aviation Agency (FAA, later renamed the Federal Aviation Administration in 1966). The FAA was given total authority over American airspace, including military activity, and as procedures and ATC facilities were modernised, mid-air collisions gradually became less frequent.

More versions, more operators

With the Super Constellation stressed for the future installation of suitable turboprops and with the commercial Turbo-Compound engined versions now capable of an eventual take-off weight of 150,000 pounds it was only natural that a turboprop flight test programme should be initiated as soon as possible. Airline interest in the new powerplant was evident, and Capt Eddie Rickenbacker of Eastern had visited the UK in 1952 to see Comet and Viscount production and development for himself.

In November 1951 the designation Model 1149 had been given to a proposed turboprop conversion of the Model 1049 and the following year design work began on the first all-turboprop Super Constellation to flight-test the Pratt & Whitney T-34 turboprop for the US Navy. Two aircraft on the R7V-1 production line, BuAer 131630 and 131631, were fitted with four 5,500hp Pratt & Whitney YT-34-P-12 turboprops driving three-blade, broad chord, square-tipped Hamilton Standard Turbo-Hydromatic airscrews of fifteen feet diameter and two feet chord; designated R7V-2, this new variant made its first flight on 1 September 1954. Two more R7V-2s intended for the Navy, BuAer 131660 and 131661, were later transferred to the US Air Force as 53-8157 and 53-8158, being redesignated YC-121F after initially being known as the C-134-LO. The first of these made its maiden flight on 5 April 1955 and for a time flew with its Navy serial but with USAF lettering on the nose.

The YC-121Fs had T-34-P-6 turboprops of 5,700 shp and two 600 US gallon wing-tip tanks to give a total fuel capacity of 8,750 US gallons; there was also provision (as in the R7V-2) for two 500 US gal under-wing tanks, although these were not fitted. Both the R7V-2 and YC-121F had a maximum take-off weight of 150,000 pounds and a payload of up to 36,000 pounds, and could cruise at no less than 440mph, making them the world's fastest propeller-driven transports. At the beginning of 1956, an R7V-2 piloted by R E Wimmer and J F Ware reached a speed of 479mph in a dive, equivalent to the maximum diving speed of the wartime P-38 Lightning fighter; this speed was achieved in the R7V-2 flying from 25,000 feet to 8,000 feet at an angle of approximately twenty degrees at a low power setting as part of a rapid descent test. At about the same time an R7V-2 took off at a record gross overload weight of 166,400 pounds - nearly twice the gross weight of the Constellation prototype thirteen years earlier - as part of a programme, like the diving test, to meet the US Navy's 'extreme emergency' specifications, particularly regarding structural strength. For this overload test, the R7V-2 carried a full fuel load plus 30,000 pounds of water in special tanks inside the cabin, lead ballast totalling 7,800 pounds and 8,214 pounds of test equipment, a disposable load adding up to over 46,000 pounds. In production form the R7V-2 and YC-121F would have had the same interiors as the R7V-I and C-121C, carrying up to 106 passengers overland or 97 over water, or 73 stretcher cases plus four medical attendants, or 36,000 pounds of freight.

Of the two R7V-2s, one was used by Lockheed for performance, stability, control and engine trials and the other for radio, air conditioning, pressurisation, electrical and other systems testing. With the YC-121Fs, they joined four other T-34 testbeds, two Boeing YC-97 Stratofreighters and two Douglas YC-124B Globemasters. Yet in spite of this sizeable test fleet, further development of the T-34 engine into new versions had ceased by 1954 in favour of later designs and this powerplant was already a decade old. Its development for the US Navy had begun in June 1945, but in the end, it only went into production for one aircraft, the Air Force's Douglas C-133 Cargomaster intended to replace the C-124 Globemaster. The T-34 had first flown in the nose of a B-17 Fortress in August 1950, and by the time it powered the Super Constellation it was no longer representative of the latest design practice. A single-shaft engine with a thirteen-stage axial-flow compressor and three-stage turbine, it was now up against the new generation of two-shaft engines with separate high- and low-pressure compressors, exemplified by the Rolls-Royce Tyne, with a higher pressure ratio and hence lower specific fuel consumption.

But in spite of the T-34's age, Lockheed proposed two airline versions powered by this engine, the L-1249A freighter based on the L-1049D, and the L-1249B passenger aircraft similar to the L-1049E. These were to be much the same as the civil Super Constellation except for the powerplants, which were Pratt & Whitney PT2F-Is, a civil version of the T-34 also sometimes known as the Turbo-Wasp and giving 5,500 hp for maximum take-off. The engine nacelle attachment points were to be modified for the new engines, and the undercarriage strengthened for a maximum take-off weight of 150,000 pounds. A maximum speed of 449mph was forecast for the 1249B, with a cruising speed of 368mph at 25,000 feet, and the maximum payload was to be 40,918 pounds. Two 600 US gallon wing-tip tanks would normally have been fitted, with provision for two 500 US gallon under-wing tanks, the wingspan being reduced to one hundred and seventeen feet before the tip tanks were fitted, and increased to one hunded and twenty-six feet with the tanks in place. The range with all four external tanks would have been 4,150

The Lockheed L-049 Constellation F-ZVMV, a testbed used by Turbomeca for their first engines and to test different wings airfoils. The rig in front of the engine is to spray distilled water to test the deicing system of the engines. *(author's collection)*

N6914C, a L-1049H of Flying Tiger Line. This aircraft crashed on 15 December 1965 into Blanca Peak, CO while flying from Los Angeles to Chicago. *(author's collection)*

miles. The Model 1249 could have flown from London to Moscow and back in seven hours, or to Cairo in six hours with a load of 32,000 pounds, or San Francisco or Los Angeles to Honolulu in under six hours, or New York to London in eight and a half hours with a stop at Gander. Had airline interest been sufficient, existing Model 1049s could have been re-engined to become 1249s, but in the end, the latter model was abandoned through lack of firm orders.

Another Super Constellation testbed took to the air in France on 2 March 1971 at the Istres Flight Test Centre with a civil version of the new SNECMA-Turboméca M49 Larzac turbofan mounted beneath the fuselage. This engine, of from 2,300 to 5,400 pounds static thrust was intended for executive jets such as the Dassault Falcon 10 and jet trainers such as the Dassault-Dornier Alpha Jet. SNECMA and Turboméca were responsible for the Larzac installation.

After their test programmes had been completed and the time came for them to be broken up, all four of the turboprop test Super Constellations were partly rebuilt into other Constellations. The rear fuselage (complete with freight doors) of R7V-2 BuAer 131630 had been rebuilt on to the ex-Air-India and Aeronaves de Mexico L-749A LV-IIG (ex-LV-PBH) acquired by the Argentine charter operator Aerolineas Carreras TA in July 1964. After TWA's L-1049G N7121C *Star of Edinburgh* suffered a fuselage failure during a pressurisation test on 24 June 1959, it was fitted with the forward fuselage (and freight doors) of the other R7V-2, BuAer 131631, becoming a L-1049G/H06 in the process and also acquiring the tail unit of the R7V-2. It had been sold to California Airmotive 'as is' after its accident, and they had it rebuilt and then leased it to Trans-International Airlines from 23 April 1961 and later to Standard Airways. By 1963 it had been sold to a firm of car dealers called Bill Murphy Buick Inc, who leased it to the Flying Tiger Line from 1 May 1964 to 28 June 1965.

In 1963 Flying Tiger put into service two 'new' L-1049H Super Connies, made by mating the fuselages of YC-121Fs 53-8157 and 53-8158 to the wings, powerplants and tail units of two surplus Linea Aeropostal Venezolana L-1049Gs, respectively YV-C-AMI and YV-C-AME, which had been sold to California Airmotive. The fuselage of 53-8157 was combined with the rest of YV-C-AMI, the resulting aircraft being registered N173W, and that of 53-8158 with YV-C-AME to become N9749Z and later N174W.

The real reason for this apparently expensive rebuild was Flying Tiger's desire to avoid paying the full going price for a L-I049H freighter -about $500,000 - and having first obtained the two YC-121Fs the airline then acquired the two ex-Venezuelan Super Gs at knockdown prices, the YC-121F fuselages with their freight doors being similar to the L-1049H's. By the time the first of these rebuilt Super Constellations was completed in July 1963, and the second around the end of the year, Flying Tiger had succeeded in producing two serviceable aircraft from four for less than the price of one new L-1049H. The biggest problem in these rebuilds was an adaptation of the electrical systems to a uniform L-1049H standard from the differing systems of two separate models. N174W was sold to Interior Airways of Fairbanks, which operated scheduled and charter services in Alaska, on 21 January 1966 but leased back to Flying Tiger on 1 July of that year and bought back by them on 1 January 1968. It was sold the following year to Murphree Air International and in August 1969 to the North Slope Supply Co of Anchorage for air transport support work in support of oil-drilling operations in northern Alaska. N173W was likewise sold to Murphree Air International on 19 December 1968 and to the North Slope Supply Co the following year.

Perhaps no other single factor can influence the development of a successful aeroplane as much as its engines, and the Constellation was yet another example of a type where successive weight and payload increases were made possible by the engine manufacturers coming up with more power at just the right moment. With the L-1049E, Lockheed had gone about as far as it could in raising the weight without additional power. Still, the Wright company came forward with a new version of the Turbo-Compound, the 3,250 bhp R-3350-972TCI8 DA-3, to power the next version, the L-1049G Super Constellation, or Super G as it was also called. The 'DA-3 Turbo-Compound incorporated oil system changes, superchargers with improved impellers and shell-cast diffusers for improved critical altitude performance, and an increase in METO power from 2,600 bhp to 2,700 bhp in low blower at 2,600 rpm. This enabled the L-1049G's maximum gross weight to be raised to 137,500 pounds, and the landing weight to 113,000 pounds; the maximum zero fuel weight was initially 103,500 pounds but was increased to 108,000 pounds from early in 1956, thus allowing more payload to be carried and greater flexibility in the choice of payload/range combinations over different routes. This zero fuel weight increase was primarily useful to those airlines which needed a combination passenger/ cargo interior with freight carried in the forward part of the cabin, and also came in useful when L-1049Gs, displaced as first-line equipment by the big jets, came to be converted into freighters.

The Super G also featured as an optional 'extra' the 600 US gal wing-tip tanks fitted on the early warning WV-2s and RC-121s, and several L-1049E operators, including KLM, Iberia, Avianca and Air-India, had their aircraft modified to 1049G standard with these tanks, while Trans-Canada had two of its 1049E-5 5s so modified but without the tip tanks. The maximum range of the Super G with these tanks was 4,620 miles with reserves, and the absolute range was 5,840 miles; fuel capacity was increased from 6,550 to 7,750 US gallons. Weather radar, either the RCA AVQ-10 or Bendix RDR-7 sets, could also be fitted, and it increased the fuselage length by thirty-four inches to 116 feet 2 inches. A chordwise type Goodrich de-icer boot installation for the wings and tail was featured. The cabin soundproofing was improved by blankets of a new fibreglass material attached to the inner surface of the cabin skin, an inner wall made of sound-insulating plyboard was introduced, and rubber shock pads on the engine mounts helped to isolate the cabin from noise and vibration. The same range of Henry Dreyfuss- styled interiors as on the L-1049C and L-1049E were available for the Super G, which could seat up to ninety-nine passengers and six crew, and the cabin length was ninety-two feet.

Altogether the Super G embodied one hundred and seven design improvements over the 1049E and the first example, for Northwest Orient Airlines, which had originally ordered six on 20 April 1953, was rolled out in late November 1954. It first flew on 17 December of that year, and the first delivery to Northwest was on 22 January 1955. The order was later reduced to four. The airline put its Super Gs on to the 'Great Circle' routes from the US west coast to the Far East, linking Seattle-Tacoma to Tokyo, Okinawa and Manila via Anchorage, Alaska and also operating first/tourist- class flights between Seattle-Tacoma and Honolulu via Portland, supplementing the DC-6B tourist flights over this route. Later, DC-6Bs took over all the Honolulu services, and the Super Gs operated a service between Tokyo and Seoul, South Korea. When Northwest decided as a matter of policy to reduce the multiplicity of types in its fleet - comprising all four major types of piston-engined airliner, the Super Constellation, the DC-6B, the Boeing Stratocruiser and the DC-7C, as well as the smaller DC-4 - the four Super Gs, after only two years' service with Northwest, were sold 1957, to Linea Aeropostal Venezolana. There they supplemented the two 1049Es and a 1049G already in service, and a sixth Super G, YV-C-AMI, was later acquired. Northwest's 1049Gs accommodated between fifty and seventy-four passengers in

Before the opening of the central terminals including the Queen's Building which would become Heathrow, aircraft parked at what was known as the North Side, more or less alongside the Bath Road. Here Seaboard & Western Airlines' L-1049H, dedicated freight Super Constellation N1006C *Prestwick Airtrader*, is loaded with cargo. The aircraft was operated on scheduled cargo services between New York-Shannon-London, which was extended twice weekly to Frankfurt, with technical stops at Gander.

KLM's PH-LKN undergoing turn-around servicing. (author's collection)

first/tourist interiors divided up into five main compartments, one of which could be used for freight carrying if desired.

Altogether 104 Super Gs were built and the next customer to take delivery after Northwest was TWA, which ordered twelve on 22 October 1953 and eight more in November 1955. These were fitted with both tip tanks and weather radar, trials of the latter being made on three aircraft before equipping the whole fleet. General Electric two-compartment air circulation ovens that enabled sixty meals of pre-cooked frozen food to be prepared simultaneously were featured, and seven hundred pounds of soundproofing was fitted to quieten the cabin. Initially, there was accommodation for sixty-six passengers in three compartments, plus an eight-berth sleeper section and a four-seat lounge, but for the North Atlantic routes the seating was reduced to forty-nine passengers. TWA inaugurated Super G services over the New York-Los Angeles route on 1 April 1955 and put it into service over the Atlantic on its Washington - London route on 1 November 1955, having been forestalled by Lufthansa as the first transatlantic operator of the 1049G.

By the spring of 1956, TWA Super G schedules across the Atlantic had built up to fifty crossings a week in a concentrated effort to take traffic away from Pan American's Stratocruiser and DC-6B services. Pan Am had introduced the DC-7B on 13 June 1955 and the DC-7C on 1 June 1956, the latter giving it a lead which TWA was not to equal until a year later when it introduced the L-1649A Starliner.

Other Super G Operators

Several other transatlantic operators followed TWA in ordering the Super G to supplement earlier 1049 models on their Atlantic and other routes. Trans-Canada Airlines ordered two L-1049G-82s in 1955 and two more in December 1956, while KLM ordered four 1049Gs in 1954 besides taking delivery in June and July 1956 of two ordered by Thai Airways and sold by the latter to the Dutch airline before delivery.

Air France ordered fourteen L-1049Gs in three batches, the first early in 1954. These featured tip tanks but no weather radar. The interiors could be converted in three hours from the thirty-two-seat 'The Golden Parisian' layout to an eighty-one-seater tourist interior, while twenty-four first-class and thirty-four tourist passengers could be carried in a two-class arrangement. One was converted into a freighter similar to the L-1049C freighter conversions, and another was leased to Tunis Air, in which Air France had a forty-nine per cent interest, in 1961. Air France 1049Gs operated a Phnom Penh-Hong Kong route for the Cambodian airline, Royal Air Cambodge, from 11 February 1959 until replaced by 707s in January 1961. Air France Super Constellations also operated a service at sub-economy-type T2-class fares (later a first-class and economy service) for Royal Air Maroc from Oujda in Morocco to Toulouse and Paris to supplement the latter's Caravelle services over similar routes.

Iberia ordered two 1049Gs December 1955 with tip tanks and weather radar, these accommodating a crew of eleven and sixty-three passengers. Also, two of the ex-Thai Airways Super Gs were leased by KLM to Iberia in 1961 and subsequently sold to them on 15 August 1962. Iberia also acquired a third ex-Thai Airways Super G that had been sold to Guest Aerovias Mexico SA by SAS and later leased to Aerovias Panama Airways. Iberia, in turn, leased its 1049Gs to the Spanish independent Aviaco, in which it had a major shareholding, for the inclusive tour holiday charter traffic.

Avianca of Colombia took delivery of a 1049G in October 1955 to supplement its three 1049Es on its routes to Europe and New York, and this was later operated with an eighty-four-passenger layout. Cubana had ordered a L-1049E to supplement its older ex-Pan Am L-049Es, and this was delivered on 22 November 1954, setting up a Los Angeles - Havana record of seven hours twenty minutes on its 2,300 miles delivery flight. Fitted out to seat seventy-four passengers, this 1049E was immediately put on to the Havana - Madrid route via Bermuda, Santa

CU-T-631 was one of three Super Constellations operated by Compañia Cubana de Aviation (CUBANA) on services from Havana, Cuba to New York, Madrid and Mexico City. When the Cuban Government was taken over by Fidel Castro, the US authorities brought in an embargo, with the consequences that the Super Constellations were grounded at Havana for lack of spares and were eventually scrapped.

Maria in the Azores and Lisbon, and also operated the Havana - Mexico City and Havana-New York routes. It was sold to Seaboard & Western after less than two years with Cubana, and in its place, the first of three Super Gs was delivered on 20 February 1956, 1049G services over the Havana - Madrid route beginning on 14 March 1956. Cubana's Super Gs had tip tanks and RCA AVQ-10 weather radar. With Fidel Castro's accession to power in 1959, and Cuba's alignment with the Communist bloc, the services to Miami and New York were abandoned in 1961 and a Havana - Prague Britannia service was substituted for the traditional Atlantic route to Madrid. Russian types such as the Ilyushin Il-18 and Il-14 replaced the Viscount turboprops, which were sold off, and the Super Constellations, which were withdrawn from use.

Eastern Air Lines ordered ten L-1049Gs in September 1955, and these were fitted with a 'Golden Falcon' interior and four-abreast seating for 70-88 passengers; later, from 1962, a 95-passenger layout for the 'Air Shuttle' services was introduced, with a flight crew and cabin staff of five. For these flights, extra windows were fitted aft of the main entrance door. Eastern's ten Super Gs were re-engined from 1956 with 3,400bhp R-3350-988TCI8EA-3 Turbo-Compounds, this being almost the same engine variant as powered the L-1649A Starliner. These later engines were installed for greater engine durability and easier maintenance rather than more power.

Air-India ordered three Super Gs in September 1955 and two later to supplement its 1049Cs and 1049Es. The two latter ones were then converted into freighters, with alternative passenger-carrying layouts, by Lockheed Aircraft Services after they had been displaced as first-line equipment by the Boeing 707 in 1960. With the rest of their Constellation fleet, Air-India's four remaining Super Gs (one had crashed on 19 July 1959) were sold to the Indian Air Force in 1962. QANTAS took delivery of the first of two L-1049G-82-118s on 20 October 1955, these being the two whose delivery positions were released when

VT-DIX was eventually fitted with a cargo door by Air India and sold to the Indian Air Force as BG-579 'D' in January 1962. Here it is seen at Heathrow in July 1961 sporting The Flying Sherpa colours of Air India cargo division.

Flying over the US West Coast before delivery to the airline in early December 1957, PP-VDE displays the classic Varig livery. *(Lockheed)*

Northwest Orient cut back its Super G order from six to four. Two more were ordered in the autumn of 1956, and one was used to test the Loran long-range navigational aid in 1958. L-1049G VH-EAO *Southern Aurora* was sold to Lockheed in 1959 as N9722C but was leased back in 1960 to replace the first 1049G, which had been lost in an accident at Mauritius on 25 August 1960. For this lease it was appropriately renamed *Southern Prodigal*.

Apart from Air-India, there was another Asian carrier, Thai Airways, which twice ordered L-1049G Super Constellations but was never able to start international operations with them. The first two were ordered in the summer of 1953 and, as related previously, were sold to KLM before delivery, this move being made to ease the airline's financial commitments.

Three years later three Super Gs were ordered after the US International Co-operation Administration had given a $2 million grant to the airline and Pan American had started to provide technical and operational assistance. The Super Gs were delivered from July 1957 but remained idle at Bangkok for some months while the airline's international competitive position deteriorated despite the US ICA grant and Pan Am's assistance. Eventually, in 1960, the three aircraft were sold to Guest Aerovias Mexico SA (previously Aerovias Guest). Guest had operated L-749 services to Miami and Madrid, and the Super Gs replaced three ex-SAS DC-6s which had reopened the Mexico City - Madrid route in 1959 via Miami, Bermuda, Santa Maria in the Azores and Lisbon, with the addition of Paris as the European terminal. When Guest was reorganised in 1961, the three Super Gs were sold (after two had been leased for a short time to Aerovias Panama Airways), one to Iberia and two to Transportes Aéreos Portugueses SARL (TAP). These supplemented the three L-1049G-82s ordered by the Portuguese airline in December 1953 and delivered in July and September 1955, complete with weather radar. TAP's Super Gs operated services from Lisbon to Luanda, Angola and Lourenco Marques, Mozambique via Kano, Nigeria and Leopoldville, and were also deployed on the more critical European routes such as Lisbon - London, as well as operating the Lisbon - Oporto domestic route for a time.

Another new Super G operator was the Brazilian

Guest Aerovias S.A. purchased XA-NAF from Thai Airways in September 1959 and used the aircraft on services from Mexico City to Miami as well as transatlantic services via Bermuda or the Azores to Lisbon, Madrid and Paris.

airline Varig - SA Empresa de Viacao Aérea Rio Grandense - named after its home state of Rio Grande do Sul where it was founded in 1927. It had ordered three Super Gs in April 1953 and on 2 August 1955 a Varig 1049G inaugurated a new route from Rio to New York via Belem, Port of Spain, Trinidad and Cuidad Trujillo in the Dominican Republic. Since Varig already operated into Montevideo and Buenos Aires, it could now offer through-service from the Argentine capital to New York, and the initial weekly frequency was increased to thrice-weekly in 1956. The new service to New York soon became popular, and Varig began to make serious traffic inroads into the mighty Pan American, no mean feat for a relative newcomer to the international scene. Varig's Super Gs were displaced as first-line equipment by 707s in 1960 and were put on to the significant domestic and regional routes.

Varig's Super Gs had Bendix weather radar and accommodation for fifty-nine passengers. In June 1956 the airline ordered two L-1649A Starliners for delivery beginning in December 1957. Still, in the spring of 1957, this order was changed to a repeat one for three more Super Gs as Varig preferred to standardise on this version. Varig's five Super Gs (one had been lost in an accident on 16 August 1957) and four ex-REAL L-1049Hs were withdrawn from service in the summer of 1966, by which time they were no longer airworthy. Varig acquired the REAL Aerovias Nacional airline group in August 1961.

Perhaps the best-known of all the new operators who started with the Super G Constellation was the reborn Deutsche Lufthansa AG, the bearer of a famous name in air transport dating back to 1926. Four L-1049Gs had been ordered late in 1953 by its predecessor, Luftag, a provisional stock company, and the first of these was delivered on 29 March, 1955. A New York service from Hamburg, Dusseldorf or Frankfurt via Shannon and Gander for a technical stop was inaugurated on 8 June of that year and, in the following April, the 'Manchester Mid-Western' service linking Manchester direct to Chicago. Paris and Montreal were later added to the Atlantic route. On 15 August 1956 Lufthansa returned to an old sphere of influence with the introduction of a service to Rio and Buenos Aires, with Montevideo and Santiago added later. In September they extended their network to the Middle East, the second batch of four Super Gs, ordered in 1955, having now been delivered. On 1 November 1959, the Super Gs inaugurated a Far East route to Bangkok through Cairo, Karachi and Calcutta. They were superseded by Boeing 707s on the New York services from March 1960 and on the Far East route in January 1961 and were after that progressively replaced on the trunk routes they had initiated.

All eight of the Lufthansa Super Gs had tip tanks but not weather radar and, initially, in 1956, seated sixteen first-class passengers in 'slumberette'seats in two rear compartments and forty-nine tourist class passengers. A forty-passenger first-class interior for the South American route was introduced, as well as a deluxe thirty-two seat interior for the twice-weekly 'The Senator' service to the USA. The latter was aimed at the business traffic over the Atlantic and proved so successful that Lufthansa made 'The Senator' its new standard first-class service on its South American and Far East routes. Lufthansa installed the furnishings, seats and fittings, including the complete galleys, in their Super Gs at Hamburg

Nasantara Airways of Jakarta was issued a licence to operate domestic and international flights for the Indonesian Government. They leased N6916C from Flying Tigers but the aircraft was impounded during the delivery flight in Singapore on 21 September 1968, and not released until May 1969 only to be impounded again at Hong Kong. It was released in June and returned to the airline, but was destined never to operate any services for NAL.

as they were delivered from Lockheed. Initially, while German crews were being trained, the Super Gs were flown by TWA captains with Lockheed flight engineers and navigators from the US 'non-sked' Transocean Airlines.

Lufthansa's Super Gs all had the first-class accommodation removed from April 1963, for operation in an all-economy layout, and several were converted to seat eighty-six passengers for the thrice-daily Hamburg- Frankfurt 'walk-on' air bus service inaugurated on 1 April of that year. The seven remaining Super Gs - one had been lost in an accident at Rio on 11 January 1959 - were grounded in the late summer of 1962 for modifications following the discovery of a fatigue crack in the front spar of one aircraft near the inboard engine nacelle, and were out of service for a few weeks. From late in 1962, the Super Gs were fitted with Mallite EGB (end-grain balsa) laminated flooring in certain areas. One Super G was leased to Seaboard & Western for a time in 1958 and others to Alitalia in 1962 and 1963 for the latter's Milan - Rimini flights. All seven were finally withdrawn from service in 1968.

Psst... Wanna Buy a Second-Hand Connie?

Like the Models 049, 649 and 749, the Super Constellation sold steadily in the second-hand airliner market, although fewer new operators bought used Super Connies than had acquired its predecessor, many preferring the used DC-7s that came on to the market during the 1960s. Most of TWA's ten L- 1049As were in storage in 1960 and the last five were sold to Florida State Tours on 7 August 1964, while Eastern sold eleven of its L-1049As to the Aviation Corp of America in 1968.

The gourmet and glamour of Air France! In 1957, Brian Cocks, the well-known purveyor of aviation books, was employed by Perkins Engines as a machine-tool buyer. His first overseas trip was to Germany to study some gear-hobbing machines. Perkins' travel department booked him for some reason on a flight out of London Airport to Paris, with a connecting flight to Hamburg. Come the day, and Brian turned up at LAP to find himself boarding an Air France Constellation. After take-off, the cabin crew came around and served a five-course meal, complete with wine for each course! Remarkably as the airliner reached the English Channel, whilst the passengers were still on their first course, the Captain made a gentle turn to the right, flying along the Channel and then out over the Bay of Biscay for the next two meal courses before making a full turn around and heading towards Paris for the remainder of the meal!

A Trans-Canada Air Lines Constellation taxies up to the gate at Malton Airport, now Toronto Pearson International Airport.

As before, the various US 'non-skeds' were ready buyers. California Hawaiian Airlines acquired two 1049As from TWA in June and December 1960 (leasing one to Modern Air Transport for a time) but both aircraft were attached in April 1962 because TWA had not received full payment of the purchase price, although a third 1049A was leased from TWA at about this time, and had also been leased to General Airways, another 'non-sked,' in 1960-61. The two attached aircraft were later sold to Florida State Tours. One was subsequently disposed of to an Argentine charter operator, Lineas Aereas Patagonica Argentinas SRL (LAPA), and crashed into the sea on 6 March 1966 south of Lima (Peru) while en route for Asuncion (Paraguay) on what transpired to have been a smuggling flight. LAPA also acquired a L-1049D freighter from Seaboard World Airlines for its non-scheduled freight services. Another ex-TWA Model 1049A was leased by Paramount Airlines from California Airmotive for a month in 1961 and then went to Modern Air Transport (together with a second 1049A) and was then leased to Standard Airways, returning to California Airmotive in January 1964. Standard also acquired an ex-Trans-Canada Airlines L-1049C-55 through California Airmotive on 3 August 1962 and an ex-TCA L-1049E-55 in 1961 from the same source; the latter had previously been leased to Capitol and was sold to American Flyers on 8 April 1964.

Undoubtedly the most glamorous setting for a second-hand Super Connie operation was that of South Pacific Air Lines, which started a weekly service from Honolulu to Tahiti on 2 April 1960 with a 1049A, N6903C, leased from TWA two months before and named *Bounty* after Captain Bligh's famous ship. Until 20 September 1960, the final Bora Bora - Papéeté sector of this route in the Society Islands was operated by the local French inter-island airline, Reseau Aérien Interinsulaire, with a Short Sandringham flying-boat, as Bora Bora was then the only airport available and the new international airport at Papéeté did not open until October 1960. A second 1049A was purchased from TWA on 7 June 1962, but South Pacific ceased operations after agreeing to lease its Honolulu - Tahiti route to Pan American in September 1963.

South Pacific's choice of 1049As instead of the 1049Cs or Es used for long-haul overwater routes was unusual, and second-hand 1049Cs did not lack buyers among the US 'non-skeds'. Capitol Airways, for instance, acquired one - an ex-Trans-Canada Airlines L-1049C-55 - in November 1963, having purchased an L-1049E- 55 and four ex-QANTAS L-1049E/01-55s. Capitol also leased in May 1962 three ex-Seaboard World L-1049Ds, two of which they bought in March 1966. American Flyers also operated, in addition to two ex-Trans-Canada 1049Es, a pair of ex- QANTAS L-1049E/01-55s, one of which had previously been leased to Trans-International Airlines and later operated by LANSA of Peru on lease for a time.

A Canadian charter operator, Montreal Air Services, also purchased an ex-Trans-Canada L-

Lufthansa had eight Super Constellations which inaugurated their transatlantic scheduled services from Europe to North America on 8 June 1955, to South America in June 1956 and the Middle East from September 1956.

1049C-55 in 1964 and an L-1049H the following year. Both were later leased to another Canadian charter carrier, World Wide Airways, but the L-1049C was broken up for spares and the L-1049H returned to Montreal Air Services when World Wide's licence was revoked in August 1965. World Wide had also operated another L-1049 and an ex-QANTAS L-1049E/01-55 acquired in 1964. The latter was subsequently acquired by the Argentine charter operator Aero Transportes Entre Rios SRL, for its freight operations in South America and the same company later acquired an ex-Seaboard World L-1049D freighter and also two L-1049Hs. In 1970 it disposed of its Super Connies but retained its L-749A. Other Latin American purchasers of second-hand Super Constellations included two Panamanian companies, Interamericana Export-Import SA, which bought from International Aerodyne an ex-Iberia L-1049E which was later used on the Biafra airlift, and Aero Fletes Internacional SA, which acquired an L-1049 for its charter work in 1971.

In Europe, the French charter operator Air Frét added an ex-Air France L-1049C and three L-1049Gs from the same source to its fleet, subsequently selling the L-1049C to another French charter operator, Catair, which already owned four other ex-Air France aircraft of the same type, and later a fifth Super G previously operated by Air Cameroun. Air Frét replaced all but one of its Super Connies in 1970 with three Douglas DC-7BF freighters, and one of its Super Gs later went to Phoenix Air Transport, another charter operator.

While most major 1049 operators had to sell off their fleets over a long period, usually to charter operators who sometimes found difficulty in paying for them, Air-India International was luckier in that its Super Constellations - two L-1049Cs, three L-1049Es and four L-1049Gs - were all disposed of in 1962 to the Indian Air Force, except for one kept for a time for pilgrim flights to Mecca. Air-India received about £3 million for the nine aircraft, or over £300,000 each, by no means a bad price when many other Super Constellations had to be stored and eventually broken up because they could not find a buyer.

The Indian Air Force initially used one of its 1049s as a long-haul transport, while the rest of the fleet was allotted to search and rescue and maritime reconnaissance roles. For this, they were later fitted with avionics and other special equipment, and they replaced in No 6 Squadron the venerable Consolidated Liberator GR VI bombers which the Indian Air Force had previously employed on these duties.

Chapter Eight

In the Navy - and Beyond!

Ten weeks before the USSR exploded its first atomic bomb on 22 September 1949, so adding a new dimension to the threat of global warfare, an aircraft specially developed for the US Navy as a flying radar station had made its first flight. This was the PO-1W (later WV-1), and two of these machines quickly demonstrated the soundness of the basic concept of an aerial radar picket able to operate at high altitudes and so overcome the limitations imposed by a curving horizon on the straight-line transmission of unbending radar beams.

So the Constellation went back into uniform again in two new military versions: the C-121A personnel and staff transport (plus the VC-121B variant for VIPs) and the PO-1W for the AEW (Airborne Early Warning) role. This latter was to become the most critical military task of the Lockheed transport, eventually involving the RC-121 and WV-2 Super Constellation variants in around-the-clock surveillance of the North American coastlines and ocean approaches.

The two PO-1Ws built, nicknamed 'Po Ones', proved the basic feasibility of the AEW idea, which enabled detection of surface ships, submarines or aircraft to be extended far beyond anything previously possible. As well as providing a potent tool for detection and long-range sea search, this concept could also be applied to the direction of bomber interceptions by friendly fighters. For these tasks, great range and endurance were essential, and this was achieved in the Super Constellation AEW variants by adding 2,200 US gallons of extra tankage over that of the airline L-1049.

The first PO-1W, serialled 124437, made its maiden flight on 9 June 1949 and was handed over to the US Navy on 5 April 1950. It was later coded XD-9 and went into service with VX-4 special duties squadron like its sister PO-1W, serialled 124438, which was delivered on 12 August 1949. Flight testing proved the Constellation to be a stable platform for the early warning role in spite of the substantial size of the two radomes. A small increase in tail unit area was later found necessary on the PO-IWS to counteract the additional side area of the radomes, the outer vertical surfaces being increased to L-1049 size, but the triple fins and rudders were particularly well adapted to these extra protuberances because the airflow around the outer fins was not disturbed in any way by flow

The first of two U.S. Navy Lockheed PO-1W (BuNo 124437) at the Naval Air Station Patuxent River, Maryland sometime in the early 1950s. The PO-1W made its first flight on 9 June 1949 and was redesignated WV-1 in 1952. *(US Navy)*

One of two U.S. Navy Lockheed PO-1Ws in flight. *(US Navy)*

disturbances around the fuselage. The PO-1W - the suffix 'W' in this designation denoting 'special search' - was redesignated WV-I early in 1952, and the power plants were four 2,500 bhp Wright R-3350-75s.

The WV-Is served the US Navy for several more years while the WV-2 and RC-I21 Super Constellation AEW variants were going into production and squadron service, but in 1958 both WV-1s were disposed of to the Federal Aviation Agency, where they joined three other 749s, two ex-TWA and one ex- Eastern, used by the FAA for flight-checking and calibrating navaids in the Pacific. The first WV-1, BuAer 124437, was registered N119 and 124438 became N120. Both were out of service by early 1965, the former being subsequently registered N1192 and going into storage with the USAF; in 1968 it was re-registered to the FAA. The other WV-I was re-registered N1206 for disposal, and later went to the Schilling Institute of Kansas, which passed it on to Kansas Surplus Property.

For the navaid calibration role, the WV-1s had their dorsal and ventral radomes removed and in place of the AEW interior the cabin was converted to a mixed cargo/passenger arrangement with a flight inspection console forward, a stronger freight floor with tie-down points being featured, as well as a rear cargo door.

Although the two PO-1W radar picket aircraft had proven very successful, the Navy wanted an aircraft with more range and on-station loiter time, more cabin space, and higher payload and gross weights. Kelly Johnson and Lockheed met Navy representatives and brought forth a preliminary design that aroused much interest. Shortly thereafter, the Navy Department placed an order for six prototypes of this design. Known as the L-1049A, it received the Navy designation of WV-2 fleet defence aircraft. The Navy viewed this machine's role as mainly defensive while supporting a fleet operating far off-shore. Its true role was not revealed until considerably later.

Soon after, the Navy asked Lockheed whether a version of their Super Constellation could be used as a long-range aircraft capable of a multipurpose role, carrying cargo, passengers and/or medical litters. The aircraft would have to meet the requirement of rapid conversion to any of the three configurations. It would also need to have a long-range. Again, Lockheed came up with a preliminary design, and this model was identified as the L-1049B.

Not long after the Navy had approved the preliminary design of the L-1049B, it placed an initial order for nine aircraft. Although the L-1049B design was initiated shortly after the L-1049A, the B model would fly and become operational considerably sooner than the A. This was the case because the development, procurement, and manufacture of the B model was considerably simpler and more straightforward than the A, with its highly sophisticated electronic payload. However, much of the airframe, systems, and power plant technology was common to both, and the two designs can be said to have been developed simultaneously.

The realisation of the full potential of this concept had to await the arrival of the Super Constellation with its more powerful Turbo-Compound engines, a longer fuselage and higher gross weight, and development of an AEW (Airborne Early Warning) version of the L-1049 began in 1950. Formerly known as the PO-2W, it was redesignated WV-2 early in 1952. Also in 1952 'Old 1961', by now the Super Constellation prototype, was fitted with the large dorsal and ventral radomes of the WV-2, in addition to its two 600 US gallon wing-tip tanks. In this configuration, it was aerodynamically representative of the production WV-2, although it did not feature the latter's special interior, and was used to check the effect of the large radomes on control and handling characteristics, the ventral radome, measuring approximately nineteen by twenty-nine feet, being larger and deeper than that of the earlier WV-I. In production WV-2s this immense radome contained an APS-20B sea search radar, the eight-foot-high dorsal radome housing the APS-45 height-finding radar antenna.

Speaking of the production WV-2 and RC-121C, Clarence L. 'Kelly' Johnson, Lockheed's chief engineer, said in 1954:

'This airplane constitutes a picket line at our defence perimeter. And it is likely to be the first American airplane in action if this country should be attacked. These flying radar stations can provide as much as three to five hours warning of an enemy attack 'against this country - something we never had before. That's the next best to a telephone warning from the enemy himself.' By flying high to overcome the line-of-sight limitations of radar beams that cannot bend over the horizon, the WV-2 and RC-121C could perform five main tasks:

(i) Detect incoming aircraft from any height from the maximum altitude of jet bombers down to the low over-the-ocean flight of strike aircraft, and fix their course and speed long before they neared their targets;
(ii) Function if desired as a combat intelligence center during amphibious assault operations or fleet actions;
(iii) Direct fighters in aerial combat as they are called up from aircraft carriers or ground bases to intercept enemy aircraft;
(iv) Detect submarines below the surface or ships and call up other aircraft to attack them.
(v) Act as weather reconnaissance aircraft to locate and track weather disturbances, in particular hurricanes in areas like the Caribbean.

Here is aa good a place as any to record that there were numerous forms of intelligence, abbreviated as the suffix 'int'. Signals intelligence appears as Sigint, Communications intelligence appears as Comint, but that can also stand for Combat intelligence, and Elint stands for Electronic Intelligence.

The need for AEW&C units to augment the air defences of the continental USA was identified and emphasized in 1951 by the release of the Charles Report. This report was drafted by personnel at MIT working under an Air Force contract to study the overall air defence picture. The Charles Report, followed by a second report released in August 1952, showed the need for in-depth radar nets located far to the north of potential US targets, with said nets able to provide three to six hours of warning of an impending enemy air attack. Also, due to the long-range capability of the Soviet

'Old 1961, fitted with the dorsal and ventral radomes of the WV-2. *(Lockheed)*

strategic bomber fleet being built around the Tu-95 Bear turboprop bomber, it was shown to be necessary to defend against an end-around sneak attack bypassing the northern radar nets.

The plan began with numerous mainland radar stations coupled with local fighter interceptor units. The number of these radar sites grew to forty-four by 1950. Many of them were woven into a nationwide integrated defence system by 1954. This was expanded by 1957 into a double line of radar sites covering the northern approaches. Following this, military planners came up with a formidable barrier consisting of three separate radar nets.

The first, known as the Pinetree Line, stretched along the US - Canadian border from the Pacific Ocean to Maine and was finished in 1955. The second, the Mid-Canada Line, stretched from coast to coast along the 55th parallel and entered service in 1957. The third, and by far the most expensive line, was the Distant Early Warning (DEW) Line. Built north of the Arctic Circle, it extended from Alaska to Greenland across the northern reaches of Canada. This line also became operational in 1957 at the cost of over $400 million.

Unfortunately, this radar coverage did not give any defence whatsoever against aircraft approaching the US coasts from the northwest or northeast over the ocean approaches. Therefore, in addition to these electronic radar barriers, radar picket ships were to patrol off-shore of both coasts to prevent long-range aircraft from completely bypassing all of the radar nets and reaching the continental United States without any advance warning. Off the Atlantic coast, there were placed three radar stations built on structures, not unlike off-shore oil-drilling rigs, and appropriately named Texas Towers. Finally, further out to sea, the Navy and Air Force were to operate radar picket machines, officially designated as AEW&C aircraft.

The basic concept that envisioned using AEW&C aircraft was simplicity itself, but the realization of that concept was anything but simple

One aircraft, two colour schemes! Above: Lockheed C-121J Super Constellation R7V-1 US Navy (BuNo 131623) of Millington Naval Air Station Memphis, is seen passing through Heathrow Airport, London in 1967 in support of the Blue Angels aerobatic display team that was appearing at the Paris Air Salon.

Below: The same aircraft in 1968 after it became 'Blue Angel Number 8' and was assigned to the team to transport support personnel and equipment to air show locations around the United States.

to carry out. As drawn up in summer 1951, the idea developed by the Air Force saw a need for two seaward extensions of the land-based radar networks.

The original planning envisioned a need for augmenting the basic radar nets because they would not give any real warning of enemy aircraft approaching from the east or west toward the American coastlines, and nets along the coasts would improve this situation only slightly. Thus, the original thinking called for two lines of warning, sometimes called barriers, to be set up off-shore of the two coasts.

Each barrier would be made up of several stations, and at each station an aircraft would orbit in a long race track pattern. The barriers were to be some 800 miles long each and located approximately 225 miles off-shore. A fence might be made up of four or more stations, with the aircraft flying on station some 150 miles apart. This was estimated to provide a ninety per cent coverage. Also, Navy picket ships were to assist the whole operation with their seaborne radar sets.

The barrier was to be an electronic wall some 800 miles long and 5 miles high, with the airborne radar able to detect not only an aircraft moving through at any altitude from near sea level to 40,000 feet but also suspicious ship movements. The theoretical range of the radar sets was 240 miles, and this dictated the distance between stations because a considerable overlap was considered necessary. The actual effective range of radar sets can vary with such factors as weather, the state of a particular radar set, and the size and nature of the radar return. Based on this plan, the Air Force initially saw a need for 56 AEW&C aircraft in late 1951.

The application of the AEW&C concept came about when someone realized the obvious: namely, that an aircraft capable of loitering over a fleet located a considerable distance from land and able to spot attacking aircraft at almost any altitude while they were still up to 200 miles away could perform the same defensive function for a landmass. In this case, the landmass turned out to be the continental USA.

The second part of this concept was the need for more radar barriers further away from the continental coasts, which would provide even greater warning time. This additional need was in part a reaction to intelligence reports indicating a fast-developing Soviet capability to deliver bombing attacks with turboprop-powered long-range aircraft.

Intense rivalry developed between the Navy and the Air Force concerning the proposed new radar picket operations. The Air Force had the primary responsibility for continental air defence, including the proposed radar nets far to the north. The Navy's only clear responsibility at that time was providing some few radar picket ships which would patrol off-shore, and with their radar pinpoint enemy aircraft trying to sneak in very low. Although the Air Force also felt it had a responsibility for the off-shore airborne radar picket operations, the Navy happened to have the right aircraft at the right time.

The solution arrived at provided for the Air Force to staff airborne picket lines some few hundred miles off each coast, while the Navy would handle similar operations considerably further out over the oceans. The Air Force would operate from mainland bases, and the Navy would fly from bases in Newfoundland and the Azores over the Atlantic and Alaska, Midway Island, and the Hawaiian Islands over the Pacific. This arrangement not only satisfied the honour of each service but also created a double line of defence. The only fly in the ointment for the Air Force was that the only AEW&C design that looked promising was already being procured by the Navy.

The Navy's experience with airborne radar was seen as the answer to the threat of air attacks approaching from off-shore. Planners in the Pentagon began looking around for the airframe and hardware necessary to implement a viable airborne early warning system. The Navy had already begun to procure some of the new aircraft for fleet defence purposes, so it was clear that it would make sense, both militarily and politically, to direct the Navy to establish the new barriers located farther out to sea. This was how Lockheed found itself with simultaneous orders for these intricate and sophisticated aircraft from both the Air Force and the Navy, with a competition between the two services for delivery positions to put them into service by 1954.

The planning was based on a twenty-four-hour a day coverage of all barrier stations. The aircraft would have sufficient fuel to remain in the air over twenty hours if need be. Thus, two aircraft each remaining on station twelve hours could fully staff a station. The planners included the need for extra aircraft, for at any one time a certain percentage of the total fleet would always be tied up in training or would be on the ground undergoing major maintenance. Based on this, it was decided that forty machines would be required to staff each barrier fully.

The aircraft that the Navy began talking to Lockheed about in the summer of 1950 became known as the PO-2W but was soon changed to the WV-2. Lockheed gave it the name Warning Star, a name used by all for both these aircraft and the programme. The WV-2 was a direct outgrowth of the PO-1W prototypes.

The Navy had developed a seventeen and a half foot search radar to be mounted inside the envelopes of their non-rigid airships, commonly called 'blimps'. Lockheed representative Henry Rempt recognized the tremendous advantage such a large antenna would provide over the six-foot model then in use on the PO-1W. He suggested that the new 17.5-foot antenna be mounted on the bottom of the new Super Constellation fuselage in roughly the same position as the 'Speedpak'. The engineers at Lockheed thought he was crazy, but after some further consideration, realized that he had come up with the answer to a lot of problems. Thus it was suggested to the Navy that they purchase a new radar picket aircraft based on the newly designed Super Constellation and mount the larger antenna.

Because the effectiveness and range of a radar unit relate directly to the size of the antenna, the new one recommended by Rempt - being almost triple in size - was a great improvement. The use of the new Super Constellation concept, including the Turbo-Compound engines able to lift much higher weights, permitted the Navy to realize an aircraft design that would have more internal space for electronics and crew and a higher fuel load for a much increased loiter capability. The PO-1Ws were already demonstrating what the concept could do in real situations. So it was that in mid-1950, the Navy began contractual talks with Lockheed on the procurement of quantities of the new radar picket aircraft.

By early 1951, the Air Defense Command (ADC) of the Air Force began to pinpoint a need for AEW aircraft to protect ocean approaches. This need was reinforced by the Navy's announcement that radar picket ships that could partially accomplish the same job would not be available before 1954. By mid-1951, a decision had been made that the Air Force go ahead with the procurement of the only AEW aircraft that was then actually available. This, of course, was the Navy WV-2 Fleet Defense Aircraft, which could be used as both an offensive and a defensive weapons system. This decision led in January 1951 to the conversion of the Air Force order for ten C-121C cargo aircraft to RC-121C AEW&C aircraft.

The Air Force asked if they could obtain an aircraft equivalent to the WV-2 in short order. After some investigation, it was determined that the controllers' consoles were going to be a bottleneck. They are the very heart of the system, and the Air Force would not be able to obtain ready-to-operate aircraft until some two years after the Navy machines flew. This was simply unacceptable to the Air Force and precipitated some intense discussions in a desperate effort to solve the problem.

The solution that resulted was an ingenious one. Lockheed would take ten L-1049B Super Constellations that the Air Force had ordered as cargo-passenger C-121 aircraft and rebuild them as the radar picket version. These would carry the same height finder and search radars as the WV-2 Navy machines because these items of equipment were available from the manufacturer. To substitute for the long-lead controller consoles, Lockheed would design and build these consoles themselves. These units, however, would have to be fitted with older scopes, which were smaller than those the Navy was going to obtain. This particular deficiency bothered the Air Force, but a solution was at hand.

Lockheed went to Edwin Land of Polaroid, the inventor of the Land Camera and many other devices. A unit was developed that would take a photograph of the radar scope. Each print carried the image of four sweeps of the radar antenna. The

C-121 Constellation undergoes work on its nose radar at RAF Northolt near London. *(Matt Black Collection)*

189

Right: A pair of Lockheed technicians measure up a C-121 Constellation tip-tank.

Below: The interior of a US Navy R7V-1 is converted for a medical evacuation mission.
(both Lockheed)

film was then quickly developed by the Polaroid instant development system, after which it was projected on a twenty-four-inch circular screen. The radar tracks showed up as four blips, and with the use of filters, the first two blips showed up in green, and the last two were red. This gave the operator an instantaneous picture of the direction of the target. The resulting presentations were considerably brighter than the typical radar scopes. Because the image showed four complete sweeps at one time, it was no longer necessary for the operator to maintain continuous observation of the radarscope.

The L-1049A/W V-2/RC-121D was a unique design in a number of ways. The basic aircraft was identical in its dimensions to all other Super Constellations, except the last model, the 1649A.

The external appearance, however, was certainly different from all other Super Constellations. Above the fuselage, directly over the wing, jutted a majestic plastic radome. This structure housed the APS-45 height finding radar, and measured eight feet high, with a teardrop-shaped cross-section to reduce drag. Directly underneath the wing was attached a bathtub or bowl-shaped radome, built by Zenith Plastics of Los Angeles and said to be the largest plastic part ever manufactured up to that time. It housed the APS-20B search radar and measured some 19 feet by 29 feet by 4 feet deep, with a mere 14 inches ground clearance. In addition to these very noticeable radar housings, the aircraft had the first application of wingtip tanks on a large machine.

The two highly noticeable protuberances on the fuselage led to several nicknames. Kelly Johnson himself made the following comment during a speech in the mid-1950s. He said, 'Speaking of protuberances, these bulges have appeared so illogical to the layman, that we have been suspected of designing an airplane to carry giraffes. The lower radome, approximately 19 feet by 29 feet on the underside, resembles a medium-sized swimming pool. The eight-foot-high dome on the top of the fuselage appears adequate for the upper extremity!'

The WV-2 carried some 12,000 pounds of electronics and associated equipment and its crew, ranging in number from twenty-six to thirty-one, included relief pilots, radar operators, technicians and maintenance specialists.

Apart from the presence of new technology items such as Curtiss-Wright Turbo-Compound engines, the integrally stiffened aluminium skin panels on the wings, and the 600-gallon wingtip tanks, other changes were incorporated. Fuselage and inner wing reinforcing; new, heavier main landing gear; aft cargo door; centre wing section fuel cells; no cabin step; integrally stiffened wing lower surface; a few round windows; and a new oil transfer system. In addition to these items, the fuselage was redesigned to accommodate better the upper and lower radomes, known as the dorsal and ventral radomes; the outer wing was integrally stiffened so as to handle the extra weight of the tip tanks; a fuselage fuel tank was installed for extra range; the wingtip tanks were made standard, although detachable.

Its 3,250 horsepower R-3350-34 Turbo-Compounds and 600 US gallon tip-tanks enabled it to remain in the air for over twenty-four hours if necessary, and there were bunks convertible to couches, a galley with refrigerator, running water and grills for the crew's comfort and sustenance. The cabin was pressurised to maintain an altitude of 10,600 feet while flying at 25,000 feet and liberally soundproofed to minimise crew fatigue. Even the seats had been specially designed to reduce fatigue to a minimum on long patrols. A high degree of self-containment was aimed at, each WV-2 carrying its own complete electronics maintenance shop with extra electronic tubes, spare parts, tools and workbenches for specialist crewmen to make in-flight adjustments and repairs. Details of the strength, speed and number of any enemy attacking force could be transmitted to defending aircraft or missile sites by UHF (ultra-high frequency) radio.

Operational nerve centre of the aircraft was the Combat Intelligence Centre in the central part of the cabin where radar watchers sat, mostly facing aft, at radar consoles engaged in spotting, plotting and directing duties. To the rear of the Centre were five radar search scopes, each with a seat for a crew member, and at the extreme aft end of the cabin there were bunks for the relief crew. Crew members were designated CICO (Combat Intelligence Chief), ACICO I, ACO 2, 3, 4 and 5, height finder, radar operator, ECM (electronic counter-measures) operator, poster, talker and plotter. The radar consoles and plotting tables in the Centre permitted observation of various presentations or segments of the same primary radar picture and work on a variety of search and interception problems, co-ordinating all search information for onward transmission to shore bases, ships or other aircraft, while the auxiliary radar search scopes provided specialised presentations. Both the ventral and dorsal radars were capable of 'seeing' some 200 miles at an altitude of 25,000 feet, and the navigational equipment included APS-42 storm-warning radar in the nose and Loran. The crew worked in two shifts, and to avoid distraction while concentrating on a radar screen, there were only a few circular cabin windows and an internal system of controlled intensity lighting. The maximum gross weight of the WV-2 was 145,000 pounds with a fuel capacity of 7,750 US gallons, the tip-tanks being standard and increasing the wingspan to 126 feet.

As first the Air Force RC-121Cs and then the Navy WV-2s began coming off the Burbank assembly lines, the respective services had to start the complex process that would culminate in operational units carrying out designated missions. However, a number of problems faced both the Air Force and the Navy. The AEW&C programme involved a brand-new weapons system of considerable sophistication. This meant a training programme for operating both the aircraft and its various systems, as well as all the complex and

BuNo 135753, seen on display at a Lockbourne AFB air show in May 1956. Assigned to VW-2 Squadron at Patuxent River NAS, MD, the aircraft was named *'Fricka'*. (Matt Black Collection)

0-30536 USAF Lockheed EC-121D Warning Star in its element - patrolling the skies. *(USAF)*

necessary maintenance.

The two services had highly competent officers to lead their respective programmes, the Air Force assigning Brigadier General Kenneth Gibson to command the newly formed 8th Air Division, and the Navy Captain (later Rear Admiral) Wes Bying to command the Airborne Early Warning Wing, Atlantic.

Although the Navy had placed the earlier orders for AEW&C aircraft, the Air Force played a successful game of catch-up through the strategy of converting their orders for C-121C cargo aircraft to RC-121Cs. By this time, Lockheed was beginning to appreciate the possibility that the total orders for this type of aircraft could amount to very substantial numbers.

The first AEW&C aircraft flying was an Air Force RC-121C in March 1953, with first acceptance by the Air Force in October 1953. Simultaneously, the Air Force established the 4701st AEW&C Squadron at McClellan Air Force Base outside Sacramento, California.

WV-2 deliveries began in 1954 and this version entered squadron service with Airborne Early Warning Squadron One (or VW-I as it was designated) at Pearl Harbor in April of that year; a peculiarly appropriate location since the success of the Japanese attack of 1941 had largely been due to lack of any adequate early warning system against surprise attack.

Now the Navy had to begin operational test flying and procedural developments. Not only was it necessary to write a whole new operational manual on the best uses of the Warning Stars, but the fact was that without sufficient aircraft on hand, neither service could begin to set up even a single offshore barrier.

A month later, in May 1954, the first RC-121D flew, and in June, the Air Force accepted their first one. In August the Air Force began the same type of operational test flights as the Navy from McClellan AFB. This was followed in December by the activation of the West Coast counterpart, the 552nd Wing at McClellan.

The Navy commissioned the Airborne Early Warning Wing, Atlantic, at Patuxent River, Maryland, on 1 July 1955, with the three member squadrons activated on 1 August, 1 September, and 1 October. On 1 May 1956, the wing moved to Argentia NAS, Newfoundland, and on 1 July, the Atlantic Barrier was initiated on a full-time basis. From this date for more than six years, there was never a time when the Atlantic approaches to the continental United States were not guarded by at least one aircraft from either the Navy or the Air Force. Actually, except for the very beginning phase, both of the two Atlantic Barriers had aircraft on station maintaining their vigilance.

While the Navy began its full-time operational AEW flights over the Atlantic, the Air Force began its portion over the Pacific. Each service then initiated its second phase on the opposite side of the North American continent, with the Air Force starting the Atlantic operation from Otis AFB on Cape Cod, Massachusetts, and the Navy starting its Pacific Barrier from Oahu, Hawaii.

Gearing up these operational units proved difficult. The Barrier Patrols had urgency behind them, but at the same time appeared relatively low priority. The Air Force Strategic Air Command and the Polaris programme of the Navy had more immediacy and therefore more immediate funds. Yet the Barrier Patrols were not dissimilar to SAC's operation, in that they, too, were on an around-the-clock basis. Once begun, the barriers had to be correctly manned no matter what the circumstances.

During the initial period of operations, many problems arose. The Turbo-Compound engines were shown to be robust and reliable power plants, provided they were operated and maintained according to the manufacturer's directions. If they weren't, then inflight problems multiplied quickly, and time between overhauls was reduced accordingly.

A second problem was unreliable spark plugs. In time, the failure rate of spark plugs was reduced to an acceptable number, but, as an example, in May and June 1956, just before starting the twenty-four-hour operation of the Atlantic Barrier, the Navy experienced a failure of nearly 2000 spark plugs. Another difficulty that remained for years was that of leaking fuel tanks, for the Warning Stars were not equipped with self-sealing variety!

As it turned out, problems related to the basic aircraft that occurred in-flight did not necessarily cause mission aborts. On the other hand, a serious malfunction with the radar equipment could and did cause aborts, because there was no point in keeping an aircraft on station if its mission of surveillance was impaired. During the first six months of 1957, the Air Force experienced about a three to one ratio of aborts caused by radar malfunctions, as compared to aircraft malfunctions.

There were also problems relating to human factors. The Barrier Patrols routinely required missions lasting up to sixteen hours, sometimes longer. This resulted in serious fatigue problems, especially when severe weather was encountered. A typical crew could be flying every fourth or fifth day, and piling up well over one hundred hours per month. This was in addition to the secondary duties many had to carry out. One solution was that employed by the Air Force, which took a page from SAC's book, and required all crews to undergo a postflight massage and body conditioning period as part of the debriefing. The results were excellent.

Due to the fundamental mission of the combined AEW&C fleet involved orbiting on station within a relatively restricted area, both Air Force and Navy crews found themselves flying a mission within the same storm area. This was in marked contrast to typical point-to-point operations where typically one flew through or around severe weather, but would not be forced to remain in it for an entire sixteen-hour flight. The problem was aggravated by the fact that the Warning Stars normally flew at altitudes of between 12,000 and 18,000 feet. Above this altitude, fuel consumption increased markedly; below this level, radar range decreased. It also meant flying where the very worst icing conditions existed, in addition to often severe and continuous turbulence.

Of the various operating areas used to maintain the Barrier Patrols, the worst was probably the North Atlantic Ocean, extending southeast from Newfoundland. This was the area where the Navy flew its Atlantic Barrier Patrol. The North Atlantic Ocean is generally considered to be the stormiest large body of water in the world, and the weather above it is no better. Thus, when the AEW&C Wing, Atlantic, began flying out of Argentia, Newfoundland, in July 1956, it was confronted by a very special challenge in the form of the weather.

The Warning Stars operated at take-off weights that were very high for the size of the aircraft. The maximum overload take-off weight was 156,000 pounds, and it was common to operate at this figure. At this weight, if a crew lost an engine shortly after take-off, fast action was urgent. They had to reach a minimum altitude, fly to the nearest uninhabited area, dump most of the fuel, and then return to base and land safely. All this while operating the three remaining engines at maximum except take-off power and hoping nothing would let go!

The AEW&C fleets of the Navy and Air Force were used simultaneously as two separate but complementary parts of the complete air defence system. The Air Force staffed patrol lines around 200

131635 was in use at Naval Air Station Keflavik from approximately November 1963 when it was initially named *City of Reykjavik*, but was later renamed *Tinys Little Helper* by 1969. In use with NAS Keflavik until at least November 1970. *(Kirk Smeeton Collection)*

BuNo. 141325, coded MK-325 of VW-13, seen in the snow at Argentia. *(USN)*

miles offshore from each coast, with the Pacific Ocean operation based at McClellan. The Navy manned the Pacific and Atlantic Barrier Lines, both of which were much farther out from the continental United States. The Pacific Barrier Line lay roughly between Hawaii and the Aleutian Islands, with aircraft based in both those locations, as well as sometimes operating from Midway Island. The Atlantic Barrier Line lay between Newfoundland and the Azores with Argentia as the main operating base.

Between the inception of these four air defence lines in the mid-1950s and the gradual reduction and eventual abolition in the mid-1960s, a number of changes took place. The location of the basic lines, as well as the locations of the specific bases, were moved a number of times. Also, the Navy's Atlantic Barrier Patrol was moved in 1961. The operation out of Argentia was replaced with a jawbreaker known as the GIUK Line, which stands for Greenland - Iceland - United Kingdom Line. This line did double duty, because it not only protected the North Atlantic approaches to the American continent but also operated in support of NATO forces and gave warning of aircraft flying toward Western Europe. In particular, it gave warning of Soviet forces operating from northern Russian bases and flying around the northern tip of Scandinavia. One reason for the establishment of this line was the lack of proper radar coverage in the area known as the GIUK gap.

The Barrier Patrols of both services were operated for over six years without let-up. Reliability was nothing short of phenomenal, and together with this tangible proof of superior maintenance, there was built an enviable safety record - a tribute to training and proficiency. Although statistics are not available, it is known that both services accumulated almost perfect safety records in their operation of the Warning Stars.

As a postscript to the Barrier Patrols, this period, roughly 1955-65, coincided with the Cold War reaching new heights of international tension. During this period, the USAF Strategic Air Command (SAC) was maintaining airborne bombers twenty-four hours a day. Simultaneously, the Air Force and Navy were doing precisely the

Lockheed EC-121 Warning Star. They were modified with radar and other electronics used for airborne early warning during the Cold War. Here is the much dayglo-painted 137890 of the Pacific Missile Range *(USN)*

A aerial view of US Navy EC-121Ks at the Military Aircraft Storage and Disposition Centre (MASDC) at Davis-Monthan Air Force Base, Arizona. *(USAF)*

same thing with the Barrier Patrols, although with a much smaller total fleet of aircraft.

But while the SAC operation was generally well recognized by the public, the Warning Stars flew in almost total obscurity. Yet their contribution to the overall security of the United States was hardly less, and their missions almost totally flew in much worse weather, since the Warning Stars could not climb above most of the weather the way the SAC jets could.

Altogether, 141 WV-2s and one WV-2E were built and five separate orders were placed for it to extend production into 1958.

Executive Transports

The ten C-121s ordered by the USAF were serialled 48-608 to 48-617 and were made up of eight C-121A-1-LO personnel and staff transports, one VC-121A-1-LO and one VC-121B-1-LO, the latter being a luxury VVIP and staff transport for the use of commanders-in-chief. The first VC-121B to be built as such, 48-608, was also the first of the C-121s and was delivered to the USAF on 12 November 1948, while six of the C-121As, which as produced had airliner-type seating for between forty-four and sixty-four passengers, were later modified up to VC-121B standard after a few years in service.

General Dwight D. Eisenhower used VC-121A-1- LO 48-610, named *Columbine II* after the state flower of Colorado, his wife's native state when he was commander of SHAPE (Supreme Headquarters Allied Powers Europe) from December 1950 to June 1952. Columbine II was later used by General Alfred M. Gruenther when he took over command of SHAPE from General Ridgeway in 1953, and weather radar was fitted in the nose at a later date. Generals Eisenhower and Gruenther also both used C-I2IA-I- LO 48-614. At the same time, the former *Columbine II* was registered N9970E late in 1955 to the US Department of National Defence and was operated

IGNITION ANALYZERS ON THE C-121s

As with many large piston-engined aircraft of the time, the C-121 was fitted with Ignition Analyzers that looked like small radar scopes. They were used to provide visual means of detecting, loczting and indentifying engine ignition abnormalities. The analyzer could be used on the ground or in flight. Data was presented on a cathode ray tube at the engineers station. The characteristic ignition patterns for each engine could be examined singly or simultaneiously for all cylinders. Any ignition malfunction during engine operation would alter the characteristic pattern and change it's contour. Each pattern could be identified with the number of the cylinder, spark plug or magneto associated with the malfunction.

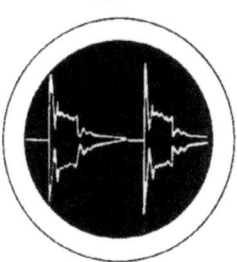

PATTERN 1 - NORMAL PATTERNS - SLOW SWEEP

PATTERN 2 - NORMAL PATTERN - FAST SWEEP

PATTERN 3 - FIRST STAGE OF HIGH-TENSION CIRCUIT (SECONDARY CIRCUIT) HIGH-RESISTANCE PATTERN

PROBABLE CAUSES: LARGE PLUG GAP, HIGH RESISTANCE WITHIN THE SPARK PLUG, DIRTY SPARK PLUG CONTACT BUTTON OR CYLINDER MOUNTED COIL CONTACT BUTTON, DAMAGED CIGARETTE SPRING AT THE SPARK PLUG OR AT THE CYLINDER-MOUNTED COIL, OR ANY ABNORMAL GAP IN THE SECONDARY CIRCUIT.

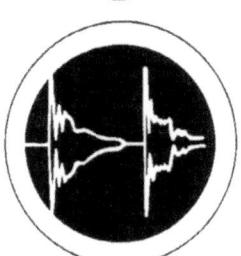

PATTERN 4 - SECOND STAGE OF HIGH-TENSION CIRCUIT (SECONDARY CIRCUIT) HIGH-RESISTANCE PATTERN

PROBABLE CAUSES: LARGE PLUG GAP, HIGH RESISTANCE WITHIN THE SPARK PLUG, DIRTY SPARK PLUG CONTACT BUTTON OR CYLINDER-MOUNTED COIL CONTACT BUTTON, DAMAGED CIGARETTE SPRING AT THE SPARK PLUG OR AT THE CYLINDER-MOUNTED COIL, OR ANY ABNORMALLY LARGE GAP IN THE SECONDARY CIRCUIT.

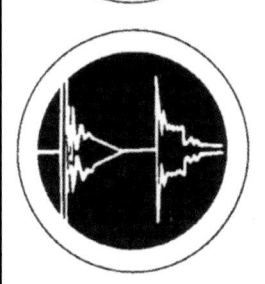

PATTERN 5 - OPEN HIGH-TENSION CIRCUIT (SECONDARY CIRCUIT) PATTERN

PROBABLE CAUSES: AN ABNORMALLY LARGE SPARK PLUG GAP, AN OPEN WITHIN THE SPARK PLUG, MISSING CIGARETTE SPRINGS AT THE SPARK PLUG OR CYLINDER-MOUNTED COIL, OR ANY OPEN IN THE HIGH-TENSION CIRCUIT.

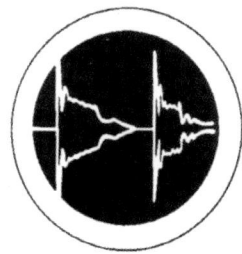

PATTERN 6 - INITIAL FOULING OF SPARK PLUG PATTERN

PROBABLE CAUSES: EARLY STAGES OF SPARK PLUG FOULING DUE TO A FOREIGN SUBSTANCE (LEAD OR CARBON) ON THE SPARK PLUG ELECTRODES. THE CONDITION CAN GENERALLY BE CLEARED UP BY PERFORMING THE RECOMMENDED PLUG DE-FOULING PROCEDURE. (REFER TO SECTION VII, TECHNIQUES, FOR PROCEDURE.)

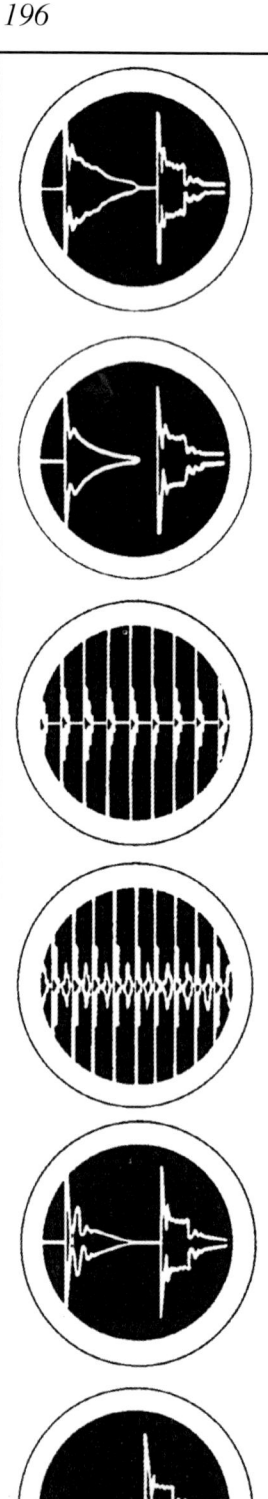

PATTERN 7 - FOULED PLUG PATTERN

PROBABLE CAUSES: SPARK PLUG FOULING DUE TO A FOREIGN SUBSTANCE (LEAD OR CARBON) ON THE SPARK PLUG ELECTRODES. THE CONDITION CAN SOMETIMES BE CLEARED UP BY PERFORMING THE RECOMMENDED PLUG DE-FOULING PROCEDURE. (REFER TO SECTION I, TECHNIQUES, FOR PROCEDURE)

PATTERN 8 - SHORTED HIGH-TENSION CIRCUIT (SHORTED SECONDARY) PATTERN

PROBABLE CAUSES: BADLY FOULED SPARK PLUGS, A SHORT CIRCUIT WITHIN THE SPARK PLUGS, SUCH AS A CRACKED CERAMIC OR CARBON TRACKED CIGARETTE WELL, A SHORT IN THE HIGH-TENSION LEAD OR COIL, A SPARK PLUG LEAD OFF AND SHORTED TO GROUND. IF THE PATTERN APPEARS ON BOTH SPARK PLUGS OF ONE CYLINDER, EXPERIENCE HAS SHOWN THAT THIS CONDITION GENERALLY INDICATES A MECHANICAL FAILURE WITHIN THE CYLINDER. THE METAL PARTICLES FROM THE FAILED PART ARE THROWN AROUND BY ACTION OF THE PISTON, AND PEEN OVER THE ELECTRODES OF THE SPARK PLUG CAUSING A SHORT CIRCUIT.

PATTERN 9 - SHORTED PRIMARY CIRCUIT PATTERN (MAGNETO TO DISTRIBUTOR)

CHARACTERISTIC: EVERY OTHER PATTERN MISSING; THAT IS, NINE NORMAL PATTERNS INSTEAD OF 18.

PROBABLE CAUSES: FAULTY MAGNETO GROUNDING SWITCH OR GROUNDING SYSTEM, THE BREAKER POINTS NOT OPENING, A GROUND PRIMARY COIL OR CONDENSER, OR A GROUND BETWEEN THE MAGNETO AND DISTRIBUTOR.

PATTERN 10 - OPEN PRIMARY CIRCUIT PATTERN (MAGNETO TO DISTRIBUTOR)

PROBABLE CAUSES: THE BREAKER POINTS ARE NOT CLOSING EITHER MECHANICALLY OR ELECTRICALLY BECAUSE OF EXCESSIVE POINT CLEARANCE, OR THE PRESENCE OF A FOREIGN SUBSTANCE INSULATING ELECTRICAL CONTACT BETWEEN THE POINTS. THE PATTERN CAN ALSO BE CAUSED BY AN OPEN IN THE PRIMARY COIL OR BY THE DISTRIBUTOR.

PATTERN 11 - OPEN PRIMARY CIRCUIT PATTERN (DISTRIBUTOR TO COIL)

PROBABLE CAUSES: AN OPEN IN THE LEAD FROM THE DISTRIBUTOR TO THE CYLINDER-MOUNTED COIL OR IN THE PRIMARY WINDING OF THIS COIL.

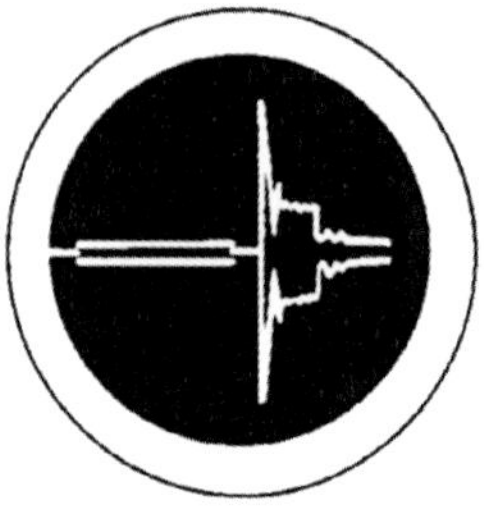

PATTERN 12 - SHORTED PRIMARY CIRCUIT PATTERN (DISTRIBUTOR TO COIL)

PROBABLE CAUSES: A GROUND IN THE PRIMARY LEAD FROM THE DISTRIBUTOR TO THE CYLINDER-MOUNTED COIL OR A SHORT IN THE PRIMARY WINDING OF THIS COIL.

under contract for a short time by Pan American as *Clipper Fortuna*. It later reverted to its military serial and became a VC-121B. Another C-121A also obtained a civil identity when 48-616 was acquired by TWA in 1957 for lease to Ethiopian Airlines (with whom TWA had had a management contract since 1945) both for airline use and as personal transport for the Emperor Hailé Selassie. Re-registered ET-T-35, this C-121A was delivered to Ethiopia on 2 June 1957, complete with a stateroom for the Emperor which could be removed when the aircraft was used for routine airline services. Less than six weeks after delivery, on 10 July, it force-landed fifty miles north of Khartoum with two engines on fire, and although there were no casualties, the aircraft was a total loss.

Of the other C-121A-1-LOs, General Douglas MacArthur used 48-613 during the Korean campaign, when it was named *Bataan*, General Hoyt S. Vandenburg, Chief of Staff of the USAF, used 48-615, named *Dewdrop,* while another, unnamed, was used by General George Marshall. MacArthur's *Bataan* was eventually acquired as a transport by the National Aeronautics and Space Administration for use by the Goddard Space Flight Centre at Greenbelt, Maryland, who operated it with the serial number NASA 422, later registered N422NA, while 48-612 was in use by the US Army in 1967. C-121A 48-611 was named *United States of America,* and the slightly piquant situation arose in the early 1950s of the US Commanders-in-Chief having at their disposal in the C-121s a larger and slightly faster VIP transport than President Truman himself, who was then using a Douglas DC-6 named *Independence.* When Eisenhower succeeded Truman, a C-121A became the Presidential aircraft in early 1953 and was replaced in August 1954 by a VC-121E Super Constellation named *Columbine III*. This was originally to have been R7V-I BuAer 131650 but was completed as the VC-121E. Like the C-121C, the VC-121E featured the rectangular windows of the airline Model 1049s instead of the circular windows of the R7V-I, but the spacing of *Columbine III 's* windows was slightly different to that of production C-121Cs.

The Turboprop Challenge
While several types of US turboprop engines had been designed and run before 1950, some of them very powerful, most did not get beyond the experimental stage and US airline interest in this type of powerplant in the early 1950s could best be described as largely academic. The Wright company had produced the XT35 turboprop of over 5,000hp and flown it in the nose of a Boeing B-17 in September 1947, but abandoned the project when a USAAF contract for the engine was cancelled. They then turned to a civil development of the R-3350 Turbo-Cyclone, or Turbo-Compound as it was later to become known. This had gone into production for several US Navy aircraft, including the Lockheed P2V-4 Neptune patrol bomber, and derived its name from the three 'blown-down' turbines connected to the exhaust ports and in turn directly geared through three fluid couplings to the engine crankshaft, thus converting into useful power about twenty per cent of the available heat energy normally lost through the exhaust gases. The three turbines were equally disposed around the engine on an extension of the rear cover, each being fed by short pipes from six cylinder exhaust ports. Although hardly venturesome in terms of new technology, and subject to some troubles in airline service, the Turbo-Compound was to power both the US contenders in the long-haul transport field, the Super Constellation and the Douglas DC-7, throughout the 1950s. It proved well able to meet the challenge posed by Britain's long-haul turboprop Britannia, and Turbo-Compounds powered the first non-stop North Atlantic and US trans-continental services.

The Turbo-Compound's installation in the L-1049C Super Constellation, preceded by the L-1049A with a more powerful version of the conventional R-3350, led to proposed versions of the Model 749 with these newer powerplants. The first of these, the L-749B, was to have been powered by four of the 2,700bhp Wright R-3350-836CI8CA-I powerplants intended for the L-1049A, and was stressed for the future installation of turboprops; had airline interest demanded it, these engines could have been installed retrospectively in existing 749A and 749 airframes.

The second design study was the L-849 Constellation, a proposed development of the 749 fitted with four R-3 3 50 Turbo-Compounds similar to those of the L-1049C. This version had an all-up weight of 110,000 pounds and a maximum still air range of 5,600 miles with the same 5,820 US gallon fuel tankage of the 749 and 749A. Both the 749B and 849 were overtaken by the Super Constellation proper, as airlines preferred the additional fuselage stretch it offered in addition to the increased power which would not alone have made the 749B and 849 economic propositions.

In Britain, D. Napier and Son Ltd were the pioneers of turboprop re-engining and in 1955-56 had converted a Convair 340 first to two 3,200ehp

Right: US Navy R7V-2 (L-1249) in flight: The L-1249 used Pratt & Whitney T34 turboprop engines in place of the Wright R-3350 radials. *(US Navy)*

YC-121F of the US Air Force. *(USAF)*

NE1.1 Eland turboprops and later to 3,500ehp NE1.6 Elands; a Convair 440 was similarly converted in the States. Airline interest in the Eland for re-engining larger types such as the Constellation quickly grew, Lockheed studied it for use in the Electra and in the late summer of 1957 Panair do Brasil announced their intention of re-engining some of their Model 049 Constellations - eleven was the number reported at the time - with Napier Elands. Napiers estimated that an Eland - powered Model 749 would have a block speed about 50mph faster than the piston-engined type and that though maximum range with the full payload would have been slightly reduced - since no increase in the 749's gross weight would have been practicable - the 749's aircraft-mile cost would be reduced by about four pence over stage lengths of from 300 to 2,000 miles.

In the event, however, the Eland-powered Constellation remained a project. Panair do Brasil's 049s were displaced as first-line equipment by DC-7Cs in July 1961 Napiers were merged with Rolls-Royce, and the Eland was discontinued not long after. Four years later, in 1965, Panair do Brasil was declared bankrupt with debts totalling $62 million. Nine of its 049s had been in storage from 1962-63, one of which had been partly cannibalised and two had been damaged and left unrepaired. These lingered on (except for one) until four years after the airline's collapse, when, in April 1969, six were sold to a firm called Engenav and broken up at Rio's Galeao airport, while a seventh, PP-PDG, was painted in the livery of ASL Arruda Industria e Comercio, though it was not, apparently, ever flown by them. In 1972 it was bought by a São Paulo company called Empresa Amazonense Importacao e Exportacao but crashed on 29 May 1972.

A new quasi-military variant of the Constellation appeared when the SGACC (Secretariat General a l'Aviation Civile et Commerciale), the French Government department in charge of civil aviation, acquired six L-749As from Air France in 1960 and had them extensively modified for air-sea rescue duties two more ex-Air France 749As were acquired in 1964-5 and a third later. Externally the only differences shown by this variant were the four observation blisters, two on each side of the fuselage just behind the crew compartment and two aft just behind the rear entrance door, and some external aerials. No weather or search radar was fitted, but Bendix Doppler and other radio aids facilitated extended searches for crashed aircraft over sea or land, and the aircraft were equipped to drop survival kit containers from the open passenger door using an inclined ramp with rollers. They were operated by the SGACC's SAR section (the letters 'SAR' stand for Search and Rescue or, in French, Section Aérienne de Recherches) but later came under the control of the French Air Force's Commandement du Transport Aérien Militaire (COTAM) and were operated by the Escadron Aérien de Recherche et Sauvetage 99 rescue unit, based at Toulouse-Francazals. They retained their civil registrations,

Early Warning Flight Operations
From 1 July 1956, WV-2s maintained a continuous radar watch of the North Atlantic approaches - known as the 'Barrier Atlantic' - with the first airborne early warning wing of three squadrons

(VW-11, VW-13 and VW-15) rotating between Argentia, Newfoundland and Patuxent River, Maryland. During the first nine months an average of three to seven missions every twenty-four hours were flown from Argentia in some of the worst flying weather in the world but without a single major accident to man or aircraft. Fog and snow conditions were frequent, but gale-force winds were the major problem, take-offs often having to be made in winds of over 60 mph. One night departure was made in a wind speed of 106 mph, and there was an instance of a WV-2 being landed successfully in a 34 mph-crosswind.

USAF aircrews adopted its civil nickname, 'Connie' - the diminutive of Constellation - as reference, USN aircrews used the nickname 'Willie Victor' from the prefix of the USN designation.

The WV-2 had been preceded into first-line service by the US Air Force's version of it, the RC-121C, although US Navy interest in the flying radar picket Constellation had been evident some time before the Air Force's. Ten RC-121Cs which had originally been laid down as C-121C transports entered service with the 552nd Airborne Early Warning and Control Wing in October 1953, and this version was very similar to the WV-2, having a total fuel capacity of 6,550 US gallons without the tip-tanks, although these could be fitted.

Motors were four 3,650hp R-3350-93 Turbo-Compounds, slightly more powerful than the R-3350-343 of the WV-2. The weather radar in the nose brought the total length to 116ft 2in, and the overall height was 27 feet. Like the WV-2, the RC-121C flying at 10,000 feet could cover with its ventral radar a surface area of approximately 45,000 square miles during a patrol, according to Lockheed calculations.

When it was finally superseded by later versions, such as the RC-121D and EC-121H, several RC-121Cs were converted to the TC-121C convertible passenger/cargo version with radar and electronics removed.

The next USAF version was the RC-121D; deliveries began in May 1954, and seventy-two were built in all. The first aircraft went to the Wright Air Development Centre at Dayton, Ohio, for testing and others initially went into service with the 4701st Airborne Early Warning and Control Squadron of the Eighth Air Division at Sacramento, California. RC-121Ds equipped two wings, the 551st Airborne Early Warning and Control Wing at Otis Air Force Base near Boston, Massachusetts, whose thirty RC-121Ds went into service in March 1955, and the 552nd Airborne Early Warning and Control Wing based at Sacramento, California for Pacific guard duties. The RC-121D differed from the RC-121C in having the two tip-tanks as standard and a fuselage fuel tank of 1,000 US gallon capacity to give a total fuel capacity of 8,750 US gallons, sufficient for the endurance of twenty-four hours. The fuselage tank necessitated some rearrangement of the interior and was a departure from the original idea of two 500 US gallon underwing tanks envisaged for the commercial turboprop-powered

55-5267 was built as WV-2/1049A-55-86, mod to 1049A-55-137 for the U S Navy as 141318, being accepted 21 September 1956. Its history is typical of many of the 'Willie-Victors'. To VW-11 Patuxent 6 October 1956. VAH-11 Sanford 10 April 1957. VW-11 Patuxent 11 April 1957. VW-11 Argentia 19 August 1957. To VW-15 Argentia 30 January 1958. VW-15 Patuxent 5 July 1958. Transferred to Storage Facility, Litchfield Park, 15 June 1960. Struck off (Litchfield Park) May 1962, TT:4,391 hrs. Transferred to BUWEPS 25 May 1962. Converted to EC-121H for US Air Force as 55-5267. 551 AEW & CW, Otis 1962/63. Transferred to MASDC, Davis Monthan, for storage 13 November 1969. Scrapped subsequent to September 1976.
This aircraft, by now an EC-121H, carried an extra ton of electronics, including an airborne computer for integration with the SAGE system, and is identifiable by the smaller dorsal radome ahead of the main one.
(authors collection)

Lockheed EC-121: USAF EC-121T 54-2307 is pictured in the static at RAF Mildenhall on 27 August 1978. *(author)*

Super Constellations.

The RC-121D featured new radar consoles with larger viewing scopes for sighting and plotting targets, and for relaxation between watches there were four lounge-type chairs in a crew rest area forward of the Combat Intelligence Centre amidships. There were also eleven bunks available for the off-duty shift, and a galley located in the rear compartment. A particular cooling system was developed for the D-series to relieve the heat generated by some 3,000 vacuum tubes in the aircraft's radar and other electronics; overheating of these had been something of a problem with previous versions. Late in 1957 Lockheed was awarded a $151,536,253 contract for the manufacture and prototype installation of electronic equipment kits in an RC-121D.

In May 1958 the US and Canadian air defence systems had been formally merged into the North American Air Defence Command - NORAD - and one of its most important tasks was the defence of Strategic Air Command bases, particularly from any Russian attack that might come from over the Arctic.

The WV-2s and RC-121s on patrol in the Atlantic or Pacific were extensions of the shore-based radar defences, in particular, the famous DEW line chain of radar outposts stretching from Alaska across northern Canada to Greenland, and following the fringe of the Arctic Circle; the Mid-Canada Line extending across the continent; and the Pine-tree Line, which was more or less on the US-Canadian border. In addition to these shore-based radar chains, there were 'Texas Tower' radar outposts built at distances of up to 200 miles from the US coastline and radar picket ships at sea. Information received from these chains of radar outposts was fed into an electronic weapons control system known as SAGE - Semi-Automatic Ground Environment - which automatically directed fighter squadrons or surface-to-air missiles to ensure that no target is overlooked and no interception duplicated.

The RC-121Ds of the 551st Airborne Early

In Southeast Asia, EC-121 radar aircraft aided in downing enemy aircraft, directed US aircraft to aerial refueling tankers, and guided rescue aircraft to downed pilots. One such machine, now on display at the National Museum of the US Air Force near Dayton Ohio in just about original service condition was nicknamed *Triple Nickel* because of its serial number (53-555). On 24 October 1967, over the Gulf of Tonkin, it guided a US fighter into position to destroy a MiG-21. This action marked the first time a weapons controller aboard an airborne radar aircraft had ever directed a successful attack on an enemy aircraft. *(NMUSAF)*

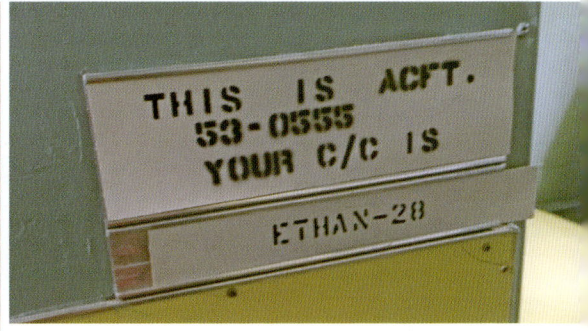

Some interior views of EC-121D 53-555.
(NMUSAF/Dr Harry Friedman)

Warning and Control Wing were converted to EC-121H standard during 1963-64, this version carried an extra ton of electronics, including an airborne computer, to transmit information automatically to SAGE installations on the ground. This version is identifiable externally by a smaller dorsal radome on the forward fuselage ahead of the main one, and the maximum weight went up from the 143,600 pounds of the RC-121D to about 146,000 pounds. The RC-121s of the 552nd Wing operating over the Pacific were not modified to transmit to the SAGE system. The prefix 'E' in the designation EC-121H denoted 'Special Electronic Installation,' and under the new uniform system of US military aircraft designations established by Department of Defence Directive No 4505.6 dated 6 July 1962, the WV-2 became the EC-121K, as the remaining R7V-1s had become C-121Js. Another version, was the TC-121J, a few of which were modified from existing C-121Js.

First Turbo-Compound Version
The outbreak of the Korean war in June 1950 and the USSR's possession of nuclear weapons stimulated two new lines of Super Constellation development; a long-haul cargo and troop transport for the US Navy, designated R7V-1 (or L-1049B), that could mount an airlift across the Pacific, and the WV-2 and RC-121 airborne early warning variants. For the former requirement, the existing maximum gross, landing and zero fuel weights of the Model 1049A were not adequate. The structural design of the latter's wing had been stretched as far as practical and further increases in gross weight meant major structural changes in the wing as well as the extra power of Turbo-Compounds. The wing structure was redesigned so that skin panels and their rib supports could be integrally machined from a slab of 75ST aluminium alloy, thus making it possible to increase the maximum gross weight to 130,000 pounds or 10,000 pounds more than the 1049As, while keeping the landing weight to 110,000 pounds, an increase of 7,000 pounds over the earlier models.

The fuselage structure was redesigned to take large cargo doors fore and aft and a heavy freight floor made up of extruded magnesium planks incorporating cargo tie-down rings, seat attachments and stretcher fittings for casualty evacuation. This floor could take a unit loading of 300 pounds per

The interior of *Triple Nickel* is remarkably complete - Roger Deere and museum staff have done a tremondous job of filling in the few gaps created by equipment that was removed prior to the aircraft being installed in the museum...

square foot, much higher than most other freighter aircraft. The floor was sealed to make it possible to hose down the aircraft's interior - which would have been a useful asset in a Berlin airlift type of operation involving the flying of cargoes such as coal or flour - and the cabin walls were lined with fibreglass and had rings for attaching cargo nets. There were two upward-opening freight doors, the forward one measuring sixty-one and a half inches wide by seventy-six and three-quarters inches high and the rear one hundred and twelve and a half inches wide by seventy-four inches high. The interior could be fitted out to seat up to one hundred and six passengers in rear-facing removable seats stressed to handle 20G or seventy-three stretcher cases, plus four medical attendants. Alternatively, 38,000 pounds of freight could be carried in the all-cargo role, quick convertibility from one role to another being a feature of the interior design.

The prototype R7V-I, BuAer 128434, made its first flight on 12 November 1952 with a flight test crew of nine on board and the following March successfully flew at a maximum weight of 145,000 pounds as part of a test programme for the Hamilton Standard propellers. An initial order for eleven R7V-1s was placed, and the first deliveries were made that same month to the Navy's Fleet Logistics Air Wing for use across the Atlantic and for trans-Pacific operations with the Military Air Transport Service. Altogether, fifty R7V-Is were ordered, thirty-three being transferred to the US Air Force in June 1958 as C-121Gs, those remaining with the Navy being redesignated C-121Js. Late production R7V-Is were delivered with a take-off weight increased to 133,000 pounds. Powerplants were four 3,250 horsepower Wright R-3350-34W Turbo-Compounds which gave a cruising speed of 335 mph.

R7V-I BuAer 131624, named *Phoenix 6*, was specially modified as part of an international research programme into the ecology of Antarctica to catch insects in flight between New Zealand and that continent, being fitted with a special trap to catch the insects without killing them. Two R7V-1s, BuAer 131642 and 131658, which had become C-121Gs with the serial numbers 54-4065 and 54-4076, were acquired as transports by NASA for use by the Goddard Space Flight Centre at Greenbelt, Maryland, which operated them with the respective serials NASA 20 and NASA 21, later

... creating a stunning example of what it was like to go into combat in such an unarmed machine. It's dark, cramped with cables festooned everywhere snaking from open-backed equipment racks to highly complex control consoles.

NASA 420 and NASA 421; they were later registered N420NA and N421NA. Together with two EC-121K Super Constellations and a C-121A, they were used by NASA for satellite ground station calibration and downrange instrument checking, an unspectacular but necessary part of the vast US space programme.

'Flying Saucer' and 'Hurricane Hunter'

On 19 August 1956 a new Version of the WV-2, the WV-2E (later to become the EC-121L) made its first flight; this was Navy tail number 126512, the very first WV-2 built. The aircraft had the very powerful 'flying saucer' APS-70 radar, which featured a thirty-seven foot diameter scanner built by Hughes Aircraft, mounted integrally within a forty-foot dish radome - known as a Rotodome - on top of an extended dorsal radome which still housed the APS-45 radar of the WV-2, though the ventral AN/APS-20 radar and radome had been removed. This superstructure, which weighed nine tons, had a Vickers hydraulic motor to drive the slowly rotating scanner, and it was a tribute to the soundness of the Super Constellation triple fins and rudders that such a very big external shape could be carried without seriously affecting stability and handling characteristics.

The WV 2E radar equipment operated at much lower frequencies, and as a result, gave better performance over the water. Sea waves reflect radar energy, but because the waves are relatively small, the high- frequency, short-wavelength are reflected more than the low-frequency, longer wavelengths. Hence, with the lower frequencies of the WV-2E, much less water return showed on the radar displays, and therefore specific objects on the water's surface or near it became more visible and distinct. The WV-2E could cover an area fifty per cent greater than any airborne radar of its day. The height finder could cover from sea level to 100,000 feet.

Two views of the sole WV-2E to be built, BuAer 126512, later to become EC-121L. The aircraft featured a forty-foot dish radome which contained the slowly rotating scanner. *(both USN)*

205

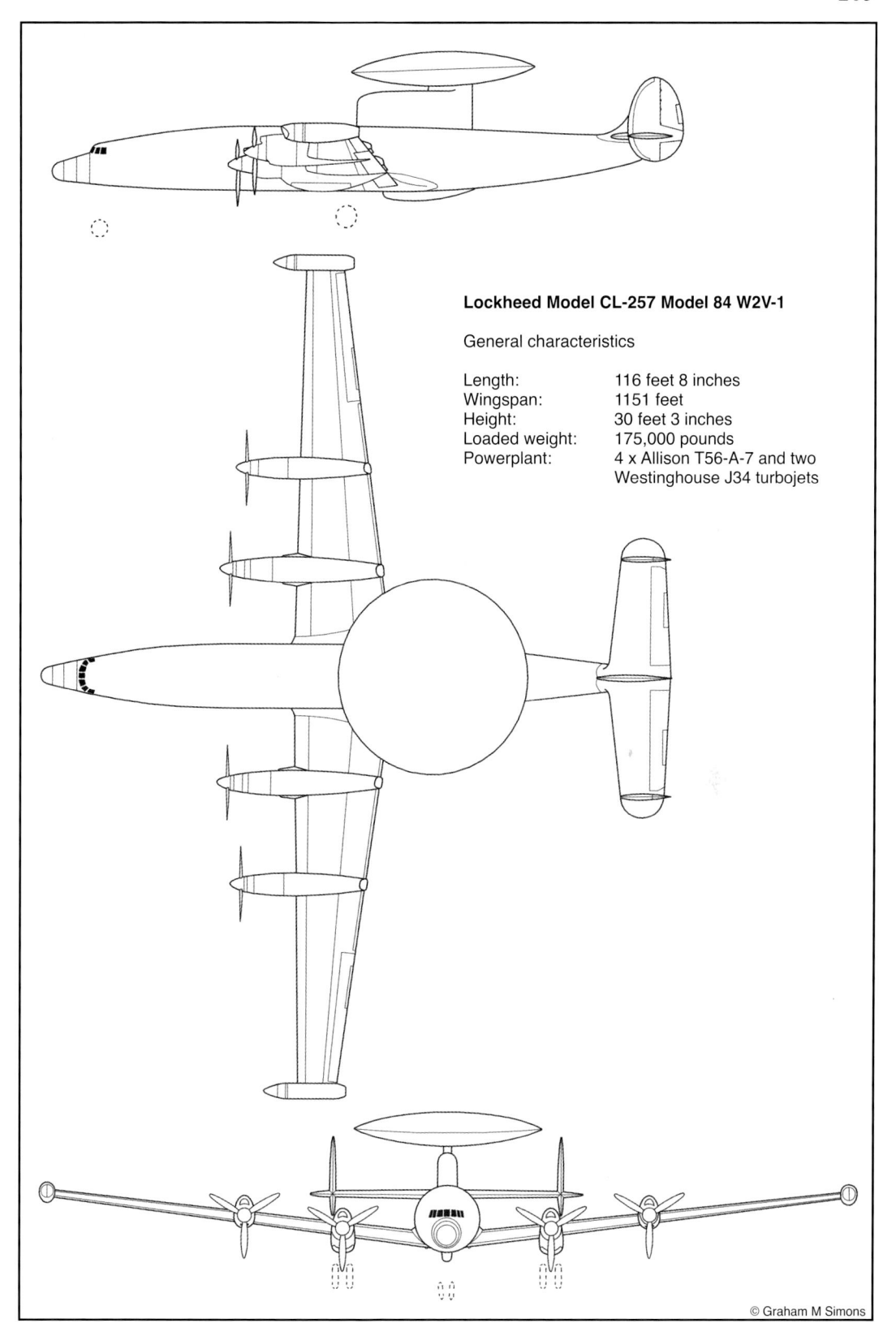

Lockheed Model CL-257 Model 84 W2V-1

General characteristics

Length:	116 feet 8 inches
Wingspan:	1151 feet
Height:	30 feet 3 inches
Loaded weight:	175,000 pounds
Powerplant:	4 x Allison T56-A-7 and two Westinghouse J34 turbojets

© Graham M Simons

Lockheed had produced two earlier proposals for WV-2 developments, the Model CL-257 project, revealed in January 1957, being a new early warning Super Constellation with the same 'flying saucer' radome and APS-70 radar as the WV-2E. Five months later Lockheed were awarded a multi-million dollar contract for the implementation of the W2V-1, a radar picket derivative of the L-1649A Starliner with the latter's new 150 ft span wing and powered by four Allison T-56 turboprops, with two Westinghouse J-34 turbojets in wing-tip pods for cruising at higher altitudes. The disc-shaped dorsal radome of the WV-2E was to have been featured, but with twin fins and rudders, and the maximum gross weight was to have been about 175,000 pounds. The first flight was scheduled for late 1959 or early 1960. Still, only a month after the contract award had been announced, a defence budget squeeze obliged the Navy to abandon the project, and the pre-production engineering phase of the W2V-I was cancelled. However, the Phase One portion of the contract, covering design studies, wind-tunnel tests and the fuselage mock-up, was continued for a time.

Curtailment of US defence spending prevented the WV-2E from going into production, but later the same basic saucer-shape was adopted for several other early warning aircraft such as the carrier-based Grumman E-11B Tracer and E-2A Hawkeye. The APS-70 radar in the WV-2E enabled targets to be picked up at three times the range-limit of the WV-2's APS-45 dorsal radar. With so much of the United States' immunity from attack staked on chains of radar outposts such as DEW line the risk of countermeasures assumed increasing importance. One manifestation of this concern was the WV-2Q (which later became the EC-121M), a version of the WV-2 specially equipped for electronic countermeasures duties but externally similar to the WV-2. Much of the WV-2Q's work was shrouded in secrecy but it may be assumed that the radar and electronics it carried were progressively updated as new countermeasures were developed or new advances in electronics made.

The WV-2 could also be fitted with special equipment for reporting hurricanes and other weather disturbances and in 1955 there appeared the WV-3 (later redesignated WC-121N) 'hurricane hunter', a version of the WV-2 specially equipped for weather reconnaissance and the location and tracking of weather disturbances, in particular hurricanes in the Caribbean area.

The aircraft used were L-1049As, which were Navy WV-2s, but with additional specialised equipment. Even though their activities were divorced from those of the AEW&C squadrons, these aircraft could be quickly pressed into service as AEW&C machines.

Above: NC121K BuNo 145925 NAS Patuxent River, MD as JB-925, complete with emblem named *Paisano Dos* (the second friend).

Right: A closeup of the Roadrunner bird emblem on the Project Magnet NC121K. Note also the flags of the thirty-two countries visited on the oceanic surveys on the nosewheel door. *(both Kirk Smeeton Collection)*

The eight aircraft - known as WV-3s - were ordered by the Navy in 1954 and delivered in the second quarter of 1955. The programme dealt with weather reconnaissance in general and specifically with data gathering on severe tropical storms. These storms are variously known as hurricanes, typhoons, and cyclones, depending on their location on Earth, but they are all the same thing: tropical storms. In the North Atlantic Ocean and Northeast Pacific, they are called hurricanes. But if the same type of disturbance takes place in the Northwest Pacific Ocean, it is known as a typhoon. In the South Pacific and the Indian Ocean, a cyclone is a correct term. Their winds are counterclockwise, and there is usually a small circle of clear, calm air in their very centre, known as the 'eye'.

In 1945 the Navy began flying a limited typhoon-tracking operation in the western Pacific. After the end of World War Two, this operation languished for several years. Then in 1959, this type of reconnaissance began again on a bigger scale. It involved both Navy and Air Force aircraft, and as part of this operation, the eight WV-3s acquired by the Navy were flown for several years well into the 1960s.

The structure of the WV-3 was just about identical to the WV-2, and so was its performance. However, it is interesting to note that official Navy publications indicate that the WV-3 had a lighter empty weight and that its maximum take-off weight 11,000 pounds less. It's possible there is some confusion on this point, because some documents reflect theoretical or design weights, whereas others show actual weights carried during real missions. If this is the case, then it would appear that all L-1049A models, regardless of mission, were generally limited to 145,000 pounds maximum take-off weight.

The WV-3 also carried all of the significant internal equipment found in the WV-2, but also carried specialized meteorological equipment for analyzing the make-up and vital symptoms of large storms. This equipment consisted of vortex thermometers, psychrometers, aneroid barometers, flight recorders, icing rate meters, and a radiosonde. Particular search radar-related items of equipment were omitted from the WV-3.

The WV-3 first went into service with Airborne Early Warning Squadron VW-4 at Jacksonville, Florida, in September 1955. The eight WV-3s or WC-121Ns of VW-4 engaged in what many described as the most dangerous sort of flying in the world - tracking the hurricanes that blow up in the Caribbean to strike Florida and other parts of the southern United States. Only the eight WC-121Ns were built and at least one later went to VW-1 squadron.

Two EC-121Ks based at the Naval Air Test Centre at Patuxent River, Maryland, and named *Paisano Dos* and *Kiwi Special* were also used for a series of survey flights to map the Atlantic. The *Kiwi Special* was used on short-range flights, and *Paisono Dos* (BuAer I45925) was later specially modified into an NC-121K by Lockheed Aircraft Services for the 'Project Magnet' programme of a worldwide oceanic survey initiated by the US Navy Hydrographic Office so as to improve many navigational charts. This involved measuring the intensity and direction of the earth's magnetic field - for which a Vector Airborne Magnetométer was fitted - and the study and measurement of cosmic radiation from outer space. To meet the former requirement the rear fuselage had to be demagnetised, magnetic materials being replaced by stainless steel alloys, aluminium and brass, while the electrical circuits had to be rewired and rerouted to eliminate magnetic fields. The dorsal and ventral radomes and all existing radar were removed from *Paisano Dos*, and new operational stations and other specialised equipment were installed in the cabin for the normal crew of eighteen Navy personnel and four Project Magnet geophysicists. The Vector Airborne Magnetometer was carried in a detachable streamlined fairing under the fuselage. By late 1964 *Paisano Dos* had flown over 250,000 miles on around-the-world flights, surveying all ocean areas along tracks 200 miles apart.

Ocean Research and Satellite Tracking
Also operating out of Patuxent River was EC-121K BuAer 145924, named *El Coyote*, which was specially modified into an NC-I2IK in 1963 by Lockheed Aircraft Services for research by the Oceanographic Prediction Division of the US Naval Oceanographic Office (NAVOCEANO) into such subjects as thermal structure, sea surface temperatures, ocean waves and low-level meteorological phenomena in ocean areas. Modifications included removal of the dorsal radome and the installation of special scientific equipment, including an infra-red sea surface temperature measuring device, air-launched expendable bathy-thermographs, wave-height indicators, radiometers, and temperature-pressure-humidity recorders. Operating in conjunction with ocean station vessels, moored buoys and other research ships, *El Coyote* obtained data from over

Above: another view of NC121K BuNo 145925, this time coming in to land.

Left: NC-121D 56-6956 *Triple Nipple* took its name from the hemispherical domes on the top of the fuselage that contained optical radiation measuring instruments. *(USAF)*

NC121K 145924 was operated by US Navy squadron VXN-8 on ocean survey work from Shannon in Feb 1969. Here *El Coyote* - complete with the Warner Bros. Wile E. Coyote logo on the nose - undergoes work on No.1 engine between missions. *(USN)*

A highly modified EC-121K used by the US Army for missile tracking at the Kwajalein Atoll in the Pacific Ocean.

The aircraft crried an array of cameras and sensors in both the main cargo door, and in a special 'pod' on the roof. *(US Army)*

an area of 100,000 square miles in the course of a single twelve-hour flight. Two EC-121Ks were also used by NASA's Goddard Space Flight Centre, while others were employed on missile and satellite tracking from the Pacific missile range at Point Mugu in California.

Another specially modified Super Constellation was NC-121D 56-6956 *Triple Nipple*, formerly EC-121K 143226, converted to carry the Bendix Corporation's TRAP III airborne radiation measurement system. The modification was carried out by Lockheed Aircraft Services, who delivered this Super Constellation to the USAF Aeronautical Systems Division at Wright-Patterson Air Force Base early in 1964. Purpose of the TRAP III aircraft - the acronym signified Terminal Radiation Airborne Programme - was to scan the skies from a single observation point and obtain visual and precise optical tracking, recording and timing data associated with the re-entry of high-speed bodies, such as space capsules, into the earth's atmosphere. Both dorsal and ventral radomes were deleted, and a large section of the upper fuselage was removed to make way for three hemispherical domes resembling remotely-controlled gun turrets and containing the optical radiation measurement instrumentation. These domes were mounted on a vibration-isolated rigid platform which could be extended clear of the fuselage for maintenance and with built-in walkways extending on each side for servicing. Both the platform and the domes had to leave the cabin pressurisation and flight characteristics undisturbed; there were also two visual sighting stations provided in the aircraft.

Kingpins, Rivet Tops, Commando Buzz, Discos and Batcats

EC-121s were used extensively in Southeast Asia between 16 April 1965 and 1 June 1974, particularly in support of Operation Rolling Thunder and Operation Linebacker/Linebacker II, providing radar early warning and limited airborne control of USAF fighter forces engaging MiG interceptors. Flying orbits over the Gulf of Tonkin and later over Laos, they were the forerunners of Airborne Early Warning and Control aircraft. The USN also used the NC-121 in their Blue Eagle unit from 1965 to 1972. Blue Eagles were television and radio broadcasting aircraft. They were based at NAS Patuxent River and were part of oceanographic squadron VXN-8.

At the onset of Rolling Thunder, the North Vietnamese had an advantage in that their radar coverage could detect most US strike aircraft flying at 5.000 feet or above virtually anywhere in the country, using a system that was difficult to jam. US forces countered with radar ships in the Gulf of Tonkin and a ground site at Nakhon Phanom RTAFB, Thailand, but both systems were line of sight and had serious gaps in coverage.

To increase coverage, the Seventh Air Force requested airborne radar support and the Air

BuAer 135753 was built as a WV-2/1049A-55-86. It went to NAS Patuxent and was converted to a research laboratory in early 1962, before being converted again, this time into an EC-121P, for use by Weapons System Test Patuxent NATC before reverting to an EC-121K. *(Authors Collection)*

Defense Command was directed to set up the Big Eye Task Force. Five EC-121Ds and 100 support personnel of the 552nd AEWCW at McClellan AFB were deployed to Tainan Air Station, Taiwan, with four of the EC-121s sent on to a forward operating location at Tan Son Nhut Air Base, near Saigon, Republic of Vietnam.

The EC-121s were designed for detection of aircraft flying over water and the ground clutter - spurious signal returns off of terrain features such as mountains - caused interference with their radar pictures. The crews were experienced in tracking Soviet aircraft over Cuba and had developed a technique whereby an EC-121 flying at fifty to three hundred feet altitude could bounce a signal from its bottom-mounted APS-95 Search radar off the surface of the water and detect aircraft at medium altitudes out to 150 miles! Operating in pairs, one Big Eye EC-121 flew a fifty-mile race track pattern approximately thirty miles offshore (Alpha orbit), with the orbit's centre at 19°25′N 107°25′E. The second one flew a track at 10,000 ft (Bravo orbit) farther from the coast, acting as a spare for the Alpha EC-121.

This provided a practical detection range of one hundred miles, enough to cover the Hanoi urban area and the main MiG base at Phúc Yên. A major disadvantage of this arrangement, however, was that most MiG contacts were beyond the seventy-mile range of the Big Eye's APS-45 Height Finder radar so that they were unable to provide this information to USAF strike forces. Furthermore, technical shortcomings in the EC-121D's systems precluded either controlling a fighter intercept or identifying a specific flight under attack.

The missions from Tan Son Nhut AB began 21 April 1965, using callsigns Ethan Alpha and Ethan Bravo, which became standard. After refuelling at Danang Air Base, Ethan Alpha made a wave-top approach to its orbit station, where it remained for five hours. Because of the threat of MiG interception, EC-121s were protected by a Lockheed F-104 Starfighters flying MiG Combat Air Patrols (CAPs). If for any reason the MiGCAP aircraft could not rendezvous, the EC-121s cancelled their mission. Airco systems aboard the EC-121 were virtually useless in this profile and the heat produced by the electronics, combined with the threat of being shot down, made Alpha orbit missions in particular very stressful. On 10 July 1965, in its first airborne-controlled interception, an EC-121 provided warning to a pair of USAF F-4C fighters, resulting in the shooting down of 2 MiG-17s. The Big Eye Task Force remained at Tan Son Nhut until February 1967, when the threat of Viet Cong ground attacks prompted a move to Thailand.

In March 1967, Big Eye was renamed Task Force (CETF) and relocated at Ubon Royal Thai Air Force Base. Because of the complexity of the aircraft and its systems along with the large support group it required, CETF was not welcome at the relatively small Thai bases. It moved to Udon RTAFB in July and to its final station at Korat RTAFB in October 1967. Seven of twenty-six EC-121s deployed from Otis AFB and arrived at Korat, on the 19th.

From April 1965 to early 1966 and beginning again in late 1967, the EC-121Ds also controlled a flight of MiGCAP fighters for unarmed support aircraft operating over the Gulf of Tonkin. The EC-121Ds also served as an airborne communications relay centre for strike aircraft to transmit mission results and position reports to Danang Air Control Center; directed operations of fighter escorts, MiGCAPs, Lockheed C-130 Hercules flare ships and A-26 strike aircraft along the North Vietnamese-Laotian border; provided radar and navigational assistance for Combat Search and Rescue missions; and assisted fighters in finding tankers for emergency refuelling.

The government of China in May 1966, formally protested an incursion by a Republic F-105 Thunderchief pursuing a North Vietnamese MiG it subsequently shot down twenty-five miles inside Chinese territory. A US board of inquiry recommended that College Eye also had to monitor the 'no-fly zone' inside the North Vietnamese border with China, to provide alerts to US aircraft nearing the buffer zone and to report border crossing violations by US aircraft. This could not be done from the Gulf so a third orbit, Ethan Charlie, was created in Laos. After tests in June and August, regular missions began 24 August. There were not enough EC-121s or crews to support three orbits twice daily, so the Laotian orbit was only flown every third day, with Ethan Bravo missions canceled on those days. After 13 October 1966, the Charlie orbit was flown every day and the Bravo orbit suspended altogether. In April 1967, four more EC-121s were deployed, two to Thailand on 29 May, making for a total strength of three College Eyes in Taiwan and Thailand.

In April 1967, USAF began fitting its entire EC-121 fleet with QRC-248 IFF transponder interrogators. QRC-248 had been developed to follow Soviet -export aircraft flown by the Cuban Air Force. The SRO-2 transponders installed in Soviet export MiGs enabled Cuban ground-controlled interception (GCI) radars to identify and control their fighters. A testbed EC-121 called Quick Look had flown with College Eye in January 1967 to test QRC-248 and found that North Vietnamese MiGs used the same transponder! QRC-248 accurately discriminated MiG radar returns from the myriad returns picked up during a mission and extended the range of low-altitude detection to more than 175 miles, covering virtually all important North Vietnamese target areas.

By May, all College Eyes had been fitted with QRC-248. Ethan Bravo's mission was changed from that of a backup for Ethan Alpha to being the primary QRC-248 listener. However College Eye was prohibited by the Joint Chiefs of Staff from actively 'interrogating' MiG transponders, following a National Security Agency security policy protecting its 'intelligence sources' (of which the QRC-248 was one) and thus was restricted to waiting for North Vietnamese GCI to interrogate its aircraft. QRC-248 began regular use in July 1967, but by then North Vietnam's MiG force, which had suffered serious losses in May, had suspended its combat ops.

In the last week of August, however, after a period of intensive training and revision of tactics, the MiGs began engaging US strike forces again, scoring a number of kills. Then Seventh Air Force finally obtained permission for the new Ethan Bravo mission EC-121 to actively interrogate with QRC-248 on 6 October. By 4 December, its success outweighed any value in flying the Ethan Alpha orbit, which was discontinued until July 1972.

On 1 March 1968, College Eye callsigns changed to Ethan 01, 02, 03 and 04 in conformity with USAF SOP's. Ethan 03 (Laotian orbit) began 'positive control' (airborne direction) of C-130 flare ship flights and A-26 Invader night interdiction missions along the Ho Chi Minh Trail in Laos on 19 April 1968.

The task force was scaled back in July 1968, to four EC-121Ds and the Rivet Top testbed aircraft to allow for the basing of another College Eye detachment at Itazuke AB, Japan. The name of the task force was discontinued in October 1968, when it was redesignated a final time as Detachment 1 (Rotational), 552nd AEWCW. EC-121 deployments to Southeast Asia were discontinued in June 1970 in the expectation that they would no longer be utilised.

53-0548 was an EC-121D/T, and is seen here stored at MASDC, Davis-Monthan.*(Authors Collection)*

212

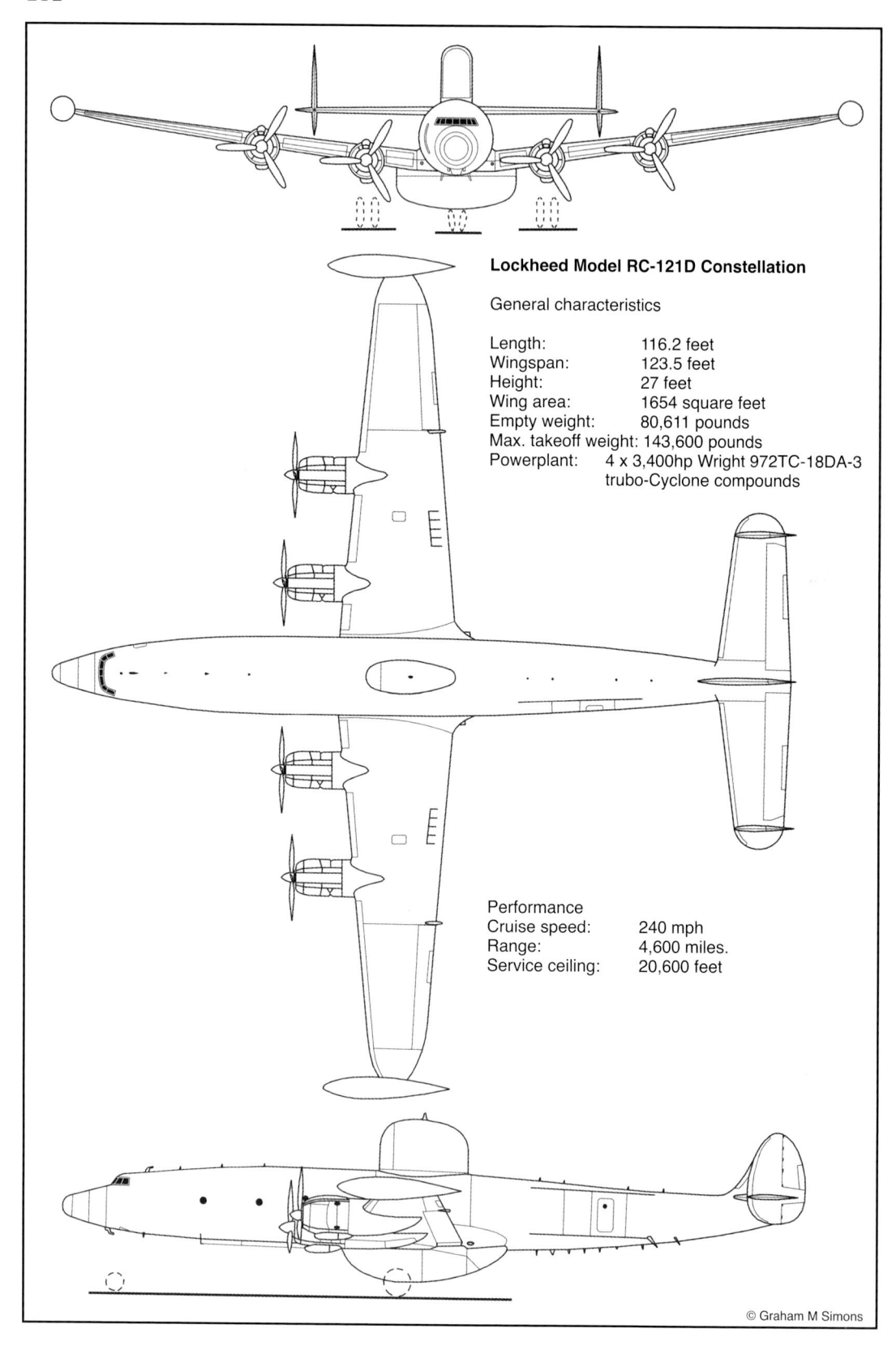

Lockheed Model RC-121D Constellation

General characteristics

Length:	116.2 feet
Wingspan:	123.5 feet
Height:	27 feet
Wing area:	1654 square feet
Empty weight:	80,611 pounds
Max. takeoff weight:	143,600 pounds
Powerplant:	4 x 3,400hp Wright 972TC-18DA-3 trubo-Cyclone compounds

Performance
Cruise speed: 240 mph
Range: 4,600 miles.
Service ceiling: 20,600 feet

© Graham M Simons

Rivet Top

In August 1967, while the College Eye Task Force was still based at Udon RTAFB, another prototype EC-121 variation began operations testing new equipment as Detachment 2 of the Tactical Air Warfare Center. Known as Rivet Top, this modified EC-121K (later redesignated EC-121M) carried the QRC-248 transponder interrogator newly installed in the College Eye aircraft and also had electronic interrogators capable of reading 2 additional Soviet transponders, the SRO-1 and SOD-57. Its electronics were custom built rather than off-the-shelf. Its most important upgrade was the top-secret Rivet Gym installation. This consisted of the addition to the crew of Vietnamese-speaking intelligence specialists manning four voice comms intercept stations able to monitor all comms between the MiGs and their GCI controllers.

Despite this advantage, Rivet Top experienced two problems that reduced its effectiveness. Its operators did not have radar scopes to correlate intercepted conversations with specific flights of MiGs and thus could not determine which US aircraft might be under attack. Secondly, like QRC-248 transponder interrogator, Rivet Gym was an National Security Agency SIGINT asset and subject to even more stringent rules protecting knowledge of its existence. Even when real-time warnings to US aircraft were finally permitted in mid-1972, fighter crews were not made aware of the source of the warnings and because EC-121 radio communications were poor, mandating the use of a radio relay aircraft that often failed, they tended to disregard the credibility of the source.

The Rivet Top prototype moved to Korat RTAFB along with the College Eye Task Force in October 1967. Originally scheduled to return to the USA in February 1968, because of its value it remained at Korat until 1969. Flying daily missions through its testing period, it began flying every-other-day missions over the Gulf of Tonkin after 31 March 1968, when Rolling Thunder operations were sharply scaled back. Rivet Gym installations were back-fitted to all College Eye EC-121s by the end of May 1968.

As later types of early warning and maritime patrol aircraft, and more particularly 'spy in the sky' space satellites, came into service the early warning Super Constellation strength was gradually run down in the the early 1960s; the 551st and 552nd Airborne Early Warning and Control Wings were totalling forty RC-I2IDs and EC-121Hs by 1967.

A number of Navy EC-121s were withdrawn from the Military Aircraft Storage and Disposition Centre for use by the Air Force. EC-121s of the 552nd Wing were used by the USAF over South Vietnam to direct airstrikes against the North from 'safe' air space, and a new role for this version was brought dramatically to public attention - as well as causing some political consternation.

Korean Shoot-down

On 15 April 1969, at 5:00 PM EST (1544Z), a Navy EC-121M reconnaissance aircraft (PR-21/BuNo 135749) of Fleet Air Reconnaissance Squadron One (VQ-1) with a crew of thirty-one, including nine Naval Security Group (NAVSECGRU) and Marine linguists, took off from Atsugi Naval Air Station, Japan on a routine Beggar Shadow SIGINT collection mission over the Sea of Japan.

The EC-121M had been directed to proceed to a point off the Musu Peninsula, where the aircraft was to orbit for several hours along a 120-mile long track, then land at Osan Air Base in South Korea.

137890 was delivered to VW-2, Patuxent and was coded MG-4 by 1958. It then passed Pacific Missile Range, Point Mugu by 1961. Redesignated EC-121K 1962. Modified by late 1960s, with two additional small radomes on upper fuselage in front of large radome, and two additional small radomes on lower fuselage to rear of large radome. It passed to the Pacific Missile Test Center, Point Mugu on 25 April 1975 as seen here. *(authors collection)*

The aircraft commander had been ordered not to come any closer than fifty nautical miles to the North Korean coastline. This particular route had been flown by VQ-1 EC-121Ms for two years without incident, and the mission had been graded as being minimal risk. More than 190 similar missions had been previously flow by Navy and Air Force reconnaissance aircraft off North Korea's east coast during the first three months of 1969, all without incident. Six hours after takeoff, the crew of the EC-121M transmitted a routine radio-teletype activity report at 11:00 PM EST, then disappeared off USAF radar screens at 11:50 PM EST, 90 miles southeast of the North Korean port of Chongjin.

A subsequently declassified Top Secret National Security Agency Report Case No. 60085 painted a different picture. 'Tuesday, April 15, was a day of celebration in North Korea. The year was 1969, and the nation was observing the 57th birthday of its leader, Kim Il-So'ng. His birthday celebration had become the most important national holiday: a day filled with festivals, artistic performances, sports competitions, and academic seminars and debates. The workers and students, freed from their daily routines, were in a cheerful mood as they carried banners and placards of their leader in the numerous parades held during the day. The festive mood, however, changed radically when the crowds became aware of early evening bulletins announcing a 'brilliant battle success'. Birthday cheers were quickly replaced by the familiar shouts of 'Down with U.S. imperialism' and 'Liberate the South'.

The incident that changed the mood of the holiday crowds was the shootdown of a U.S. Navy EC-121 reconnaissance aircraft by a North Korean MIG-21 jet over the Sea of Japan off North Korea's coast. The shootdown, which occurred at 1347 hours Korean time (2347 hours, Monday, 14 April 1969, Eastern Standard Time), claimed 31 American lives. For the second time in 16 months, small, isolated North Korea (referred to as a 'fourth-rate power' by President Richard M. Nixon in his election campaign) had attacked a U.S. intelligence vehicle. This study traces the role the National Security Agency (NSA) played during the crisis situation and in the reevaluation of U.S. intelligence activities which followed.

The shootdown of the EC-121 caused a crisis situation at NSA headquarters at Fort Meade, Maryland. NSA declared a Sigint Alert, BRAVO HANGAR, on the day of the shootdown and maintained it for the remainder of the month. During this crisis period, NSA officials and analysts played major roles in providing answers to questions raised by the Nixon White House, the Pentagon, other US intelligence agencies, Congress, and the press regarding the loss of the Navy intelligence aircraft.

When NSA personnel reported to work during the early hours of that April morning they faced a confusing situation. NSA's role in the mission of the aircraft seemed unclear.

'Although the United States Navy dubbed the flight a BEGGAR SHADOW mission, implying that it was primarily a Comint flight, and thus under NSA authority, the mission of the aircraft was primarily an Elint-directed one [REDACTED] in direct support of Seventh Fleet requirement. The Navy, not NSA had control of the mission'.

'An unfortunate aspect of the EC-121 shootdown was the Navy practice of double-loading the flights for training purposes, allowing the trainees who accompanied these missions to take advantage of transportation to as well as a little liberty in South Korea. This resulted in a loss of 31 men. The normal crew was between 10 and 15. Not only was NSA faced with dealing with the shootdown of a mission that was undertasked but one that was considered overmanned.'

The EC-121M mission had been monitored from the ground by Air Force radar sites in Japan and South Korea, as well as by the USAFSS 6918th Security Squadron at Hakata, Japan and Detachment 1, 6922nd Security Wing at Osan Air Base, Korea (USA-31), which followed the flight by intercepting North Korean air defence radar tracking transmissions. Air Force radars and USAFSS COMINT intercept operators in Korea had detected two NKAF MiGs flying towards the unarmed EC-121 prior to the aircraft's disappearance. In addition, the intercept operators at the USAFSS listening post at Osan, South Korea, who were copying North Korean voice and Morse air defence radio traffic, tracked the flight path of the EC-121 aircraft as well as the intercept course of the North Korean fighters. The NAVSECGRU listening post at Kamiseya in Japan was also intercepting Russian PVO radar tracking of the EC-121M mission, giving NSA two sources of information as to the flight path of the aircraft.

The USAFSS listening post at Osan attempted to warn the aircraft's commander by transmitting a mission abort signal at 11:46 PM EST. But the MiGs caught up with the slow-flying aircraft as it turned for home 90 miles southeast of the North Korean port city of Chongjin, and the MiGs shot the EC-121 down at 11:47 PM EST. All 31

'College Eye' EC-121D 53-0543 in flight. These aircraft were not camoflaged. *(USAF)*

crewmembers were killed, including nine NAVSECGRU cryptologists. The bodies of only two of the crew were ever recovered. The USAFSS listening post at Osan (SIGAD USA-31) issued a CRITIC message on the incident at 5:44 AM GMT on 15 April 1969.

Yet another major NSA role in the EC-121 shoot down crisis was to provide evidence to refute the North Korean claim that the aircraft had come within twelve miles of the North Korean coast. To refute that claim, NSA, in the days following the shootdown, reported detailed tracking information from radar reflections from Soviet, North Korean, [REDACTED TO END OF SENTENCE].

President Nixon used this NSA-supplied information (and caused some consternation at NSA when reporting the source) to refute the North Korean claim that the aircraft had callously intruded upon it airspace.

The President ordered an immediate halt of all aerial reconnaissance missions in the Sea of Japan, but rescinded his order three days later, this time ordering that all peripheral reconnaissance missions off North Korea be accompanied by fighter escorts.

The NSA report continues: 'In contrast to the Air Force ACRP programme, in which NSA played a large role in collection requirements and tasking, the Navy programme was dedicated largely to fleet support. NSA played only a secondary role in these flights. Two Fleet Air Reconnaissance Squadrons - VQ-1 in the Pacific and VQ-2 in Europe - performed the missions. In 1969 the VQ-1 missions

EC-121T on the taxiway at Korat Royal Thai Air Force Base. *(USAF)*

- using EC-121M Comint/Elint and EA-3B Elint aircraft - operated from Atsugi, Japan. They were under the direct operational control of the Commander, Seventh Fleet Admiral William F Bringle. NSA designated USN-39, the Naval Security Group as the responsible station within the cryptologic community for reporting. Because of this responsibility and its close proximity to VQ-1, USN-39 manned the Comint positions on the VQ-1 flights.

The EC-121 flight of 15 April characterized the Navy autonomy. Although the Navy called it a BEGGAR SHADOW mission, thus implying a primary Comint role (with national tasking), its role on that flight was virtually limited to that of an Elint-only operation. While this EC-121 flight was always referred to as a BEGGAR mission, a SAC [Strategic Air Command] message of 26 April 1969 referred to it as the [REDACTED] which was more appropriate as it was the nickname referring to direct support Elint flights. In fact, even the make-up of the large crew on this flight reflected this. Ten members of the crew held the title of Aviation Electronic Technician, signifying them as electronic countermeasures personnel, and thus outside of NSA's Sigint authority. On the ill-fated flight they outnumbered the communications technicians, Sigint personnel assigned to Naval Security Group at [REDACTED TO END OF SENTENCE]

NSA's passive role relating to these flights added to the confusion at Fort Meade on the morning of the shootdown as questions arose over who controlled the aircraft, who tasked the mission, and what it was trying to collect. Even CINCPACFLT, which was in the immediate chain of command of the aircraft, issued seemingly conflicting statements regarding the primary mission of the flight. A CINCPACFLT message of 1 April 1969, for example, gave the proposed VQ-1EC-121 schedule for April. This message listed Comint as the primary task of the (EC,-121 missions, Elint as a secondary task. However, on 16 April (the day after the-shootdown), CINCPACFLT described BEGGAR SHADOW Track 8263 (the track of the ill-fated mission) as designed to optimize Elint collection A DIA memorandum of 18 April further described four EC-121 tracks (including 8263) flown since November 1968 as meeting theatre requirements under the Elint programme. Track 8263 had been flown four times earlier in 1969 as had a similar track, 8261. These tracks were designed primarily to provide intelligence on North Korean radar activities. 'NSA levied no special supplemental Elint tasking that was applicable to the mission.'

According to one source, an NSA review of COMINT intercepts of North Korean Air Force ground-to-air radio traffic from the USAFSS listening post at Osan showed that the shoot-down had resulted from a command and control error between the North Korean ground controller and the fighter pilot. Other NSA intercepts showed that the Soviets were shocked by the North Korean action, so much so that Russian warships were sent to the crash site to help American ships search for survivors.

President Nixon's revelation that NSA had successfully monitored both the North Korean and Russian air defence tracking nets caused both nations to immediately change all of their radio frequencies, operating procedures and cryptosystems in use at the time. It took NSA's cryptologists months to get back to the point where they were prior to Nixon's press conference.

At the end of 1968 Lockheed fitted an EC-I21 with advanced electronic intelligence - gathering equipment as part of the Navy's BLIP (Big Look Improvement Programme), 'Big Look' being the name covering the operations of EC-121s monitoring North Vietnamese surface-to-air missile activity and providing directional information for US aircraft undertaking strikes against radar installations in the North. This EC-121 was fitted with additional sensors, a digital data processor and a more accurate navigational system.

Operation Kingpin

Two EC-121Ds, newly modified with the Southeast Asia Operational Requirement 62 (SEAOR-62) electronics suite but not yet operational as EC-121Ts, were ordered to Korat RTAFB in October 1970. Under the guise of being field-tested, they were accompanied by a C-121G carrying additional crew members, the most experienced 552nd AEWCW technicians and equipment necessary to maintain the new electronics. The SEAOR-62 package was supported by a digital data receiver ground terminal and by radio relay equipment transshipped by separate classified airlift. The EC-121Ts arrived in Thailand from McClellan AFB on 12 November.

The purpose of the deployment was to provide an integrated tactical data display with real-time inputs (similar to the Navy Airborne Tactical Data System equipping E-1B Tracer platforms of Task Force 77) in support of Operation Kingpin, a mission to rescue US prisoners of war held at Son Tay prison. Once at Korat, some equipment was tested for the first time because of emission restrictions in US airspace and the only available manuals and checklists were notes from early flight tests. Even so, both aircraft were operational by 17 November.

On 20 November 1970, two Warning Stars, using the callsigns Frog 01 and 02 respectively, took off 10 minutes apart at 22:00 from Korat to take station at the low altitude Alpha orbit over the Gulf of Tonkin, with Frog 02 as a backup. The seventeen-man crews were advised in the air of the nature of the rescue mission and their role, providing MiG warning and directing USAF F-4 Phantom CAP intercepts. As Frog 01 began its climb to the higher Bravo orbit, it experienced a ruptured oil line forcing the shutdown of one engine. As planned, Frog 02 became the primary aircraft when Frog 01 made an emergency landing at Danang.

The new equipment failed to function properly aboard Frog 02. The ground receivers at the command post in Danang failed to receive data, and the APX-83 IFF processors would not display aboard the aircraft, despite repeated repairs. Their own radar monitors experienced excessive electronic noise, and the jamming of North Vietnamese radars by nearby EKA-3B Skywarriors hindered efforts of the radar technicians to correct the problems. While unable to provide vectoring information to the F-4s escorting the mission, Frog 02 remained on station and relied on its Rivet Top voice intercept capability to provide supplementary data.

Task Force Commando Buzz
The 193rd Tactical Warfare Squadron, Pennsylvania Air National Guard, was tasked to operate Task Force Commando Buzz operation from Korat RTAFB. Purpose of Commando Buzz was to receive the Radio Cambodia programming, then rebroadcast those radio programmes from altitude so all of Cambodia, especially those in fringe areas, could receive the programming. Initially classified secret, the Commando Buzz operation was changed to Top Secret in July 1970.

Upon departure from the US CONUS, the plan was for Task Force Commando Buzz to operate for 179 days. Korat RTAFB was selected because of the presence of the 553rd Reconnaissance Wing with

View of the radar operators in a US Air Force Lockheed EC-121D Warning Star aircraft of the 552nd Airborne Early Warning & Control Wing during the Vietnam War. *(USAF)*

their Lockheed EC-121R aircraft. While the 193rd TWS was mostly self-sufficient, the 553rd Reconnaissance Wing provided the parts supply, as well as ground equipment and personnel from the 553rd AMS, 553rd FMS and 553rd OMS as needed. These maintenance technicians were very familiar with the EC-121 and had shop and test equipment to support Task Force Commando Buzz.

They arrived at Korat RTAFB on 31 July 1970 with their Lockheed EC-121S aircraft. Fifty-eight members of the 193rd TWS came to Korat RTAFB including eleven officers and forty-seven enlisted airmen. Of the fifty-eight members of the 193rd TWS, twenty were aircrew, thirty-eight support personnel. Sources vary on the number of EC-121S aircraft; some sources report at least five aircraft were converted to EC-121S radio relay configuration. Other sources indicate that as many as twelve aircraft were converted to EC-121S configuration.

First Commando Buzz mission was flown on 6 August 1970. The radio relay Task Force Commando Buzz missions were flown until 23 December. By late December the Cambodian government had installed additional ground transmitters, so the fringe areas of Cambodia were now covered adequately by the ground transmitters. The 193rd TWS along with their Lockheed EC-121S aircraft, returned to the CONUS on 3 January 1971.

Disco
In October 1971, North Vietnamese MiGs, operating from forward bases opened after the end of Rolling Thunder, began a campaign to intercept Boeing B-52 Stratofortresses missions over southern Laos. On 20 November, a MiG-21 launched air-to-air missiles at a B-52 that evaded by dropping flares. As a result, Warning Stars of Det. 1 returned to Korat RTAFB to provide radar support by flying the Laotian orbit again, using callsign Disco. Seven EC-121Ts, replacement aircraft for the earlier series, were based in Thailand and contained both QRC-248 and Rivet Top electronic suites.

When Operation Linebacker began on 10 May 1972, Disco was one of two principal GCI radars used by US forces, although it continued to be handicapped by poor radio communications. In addition, its slow turning radar limited its value as a controller of fighters during MiG engagements, while the size of USAF raids during Linebacker nearly saturated its capabilities. However, improvements made in the systems since 1968 enabled the operators to distinguish MiG types and a colour code system for them entered the airops vernacular: 'Red Bandits' (Mig-17s); 'White Bandits' (MiG-19s); 'Blue Bandits' (MiG-21)s, and 'Black bandits' (MiGs low on fuel).

On 6 July 1972, as the result of seven F-4 Phantoms shot down in a two-week period, a second Disco track was initiated. Flown near the former Alpha orbit over the Gulf of Tonkin, its purpose was to gain better low-altitude coverage in the Hanoi area. At the end of the month, Disco was also integrated into what was termed the Teaball control centre, a highly classified system established to collate all signal intelligence on North Vietnamese air activity gathered by all sources, including non-military. Disco became a conduit through which warnings and control vectors were given, but the delay in Teaball acquiring the information and relaying it through Disco - often using an unreliable radio relay KC-135A Combat Lightning aircraft operating under callsign Luzon - cancelled out any value for use in real time. Also, the fact that its existence was kept from US aircrews damaged its credibility. Teaball received direct comms capability but frequently experienced transmission failures. Disco remained the primary backup controller, but its use remained limited because it directly controlled only MiGCAP missions and could only provide its information to strike, chaff and escort forces via the 'Guard' frequency.

On 15 August 1973, Disco EC-121s flew their final combat mission and on 1 June 1974, Det.1 was permanently withdrawn from Southeast Asia. Between 1965 and 1973, the EC-121s flew 13,921 combat missions; more than 98,000 accident-free flying hours, assisted in the shoot-down of 25 MiGs and supported the rescue of eighty downed flyers. No Big Eye, College Eye, or Disco aircraft were lost.

Television from the skies
From 1966 several C-121Js were converted for TV telecasting duties in Vietnam. During the Vietnam War, the United States Navy used Stratovision television technology when it flew Operation Blue Eagle from 1966 to 1972 over the Saigon area of South Vietnam. The television programmes were aimed at two audiences on two channels: one was aimed at the general public and the other was intended for the information and entertainment of US troops who were stationed in South Vietnam.

Stratovision was an airborne television transmission relay system using aircraft flying at high altitudes. In 1945 the Glenn L. Martin Company and Westinghouse Electric Corporation originally proposed television coverage of small towns and rural areas, as well as the large metropolitan centres, by fourteen aircraft that would provide coverage for seventy-eight per cent of the people in the United States. Although this was never implemented, the system has been used for domestic broadcasting in the USA, and by the US military in South Vietnam and other countries.

On 3 January 1966, a Broadcasting magazine article, 'Vietnam to get airborne TV: Two-channel service - one for Vietnamese, other for US servicemen - starts this month', noted:

'Television broadcasting in South Vietnam begins January 21 and it's going to be done from the air. Two airplanes, circling 10,000 to 20,000 feet above the ground, will broadcast on two TV channels - one transmitting Saigon government programs; the other US programs. The project is being handled by the US Navy. Also involved are the US Information Agency and the Agency for International Development. Work on modifying two Lockheed Super Constellations has been underway by Navy electronics experts at Andrews Air Force Base. The project is an outgrowth of a broadcasting plane used by the Navy during the Cuban and Dominican Republic crises when both radio and television were beamed to home in those countries.'

The article went on to report that during the Baseball World Series of October 1965 Stratovision had also been used to bring the games to the troops. The aircraft had picked up Voice of America radio broadcasts from California and relayed the signal to a ground broadcasting station. The Agency for International Development (AID) had purchased through the military Post Exchange Service, 1,000 monochrome, 23-inch television sets modified to operate on a variety of domestic power sources, and which had been airlifted to South Vietnam on 28 December 1965. They were to be put into community facilities around Saigon. AID was also spending $2.4 million to supply a total of 2,500 TV sets to South Vietnam.

The entire project was under the control of Captain George C. Dixon, USN. He claimed to be installing AM, FM, shortwave and TV transmitters on the aircraft which would get their power from an onboard 100 kW diesel-fueled generator. The aircraft would not only relay programmes from film chain kinescopes and video recorders, but they would also have cameras to create their own live programmes.

Ground transmissions would be received from the aircraft on TV sets tuned to channel 11 for Armed Forces Television, and channel 9 for programmes in Vietnamese. On radio the broadcasts would be tuned to 1000 kHz for AM and 99.9 MHz for FM.

On 7 February 1966, *Broadcasting* magazine reported that after working out a number of technical problems, the first show on channel 9 would begin at 7:30 p.m. and feature South Vietnamese Prime Minister Nguyen Cao Ky and US Ambassador Cabot Lodge in a videotaped production, followed by channel 11 at 8 p.m. with General Westmoreland introducing a two-hour programme which incorporated one hour of the Grand Ole Opry filmed in Nashville, Tennessee. After that, the Vietnamese channel would be seen for one and half hours a day and the US channel for three hours daily.

On 8 February 1966 The *New York Times* article *'South Vietnamese Watch First TV Show'* reported that South Vietnamese viewers had to strain their ears because the speakers on the TV sets would need to be amplified if they were going to be heard by a room full of people watching THVN-TV channel 9. The US programming on NWB-TV

54-0159 was built as a C-121C, but was converted to an EC-121S around 1967 as seen here. The aircraft has assorted antennas on the roof, and under the wings *(authors collection)*

channel 11 was Bob Hope in a two-hour special called *Hollywood Salute to Vietnam*, followed by half-an-hour of the Grand Ole Opry and another half-hour of the quiz show *I've Got a Secret*. The regular line-up of shows included *Bonanza*, *Perry Mason*, *The Ed Sullivan Show*, and *The Tonight Show Starring Johnny Carson*.

Four years later, and on the other side of the world, news stories began to appear in the United Kingdom that Ronan O'Rahilly, the founder of the pirate radio ship based service called Radio Caroline, which at that time was not on the air, was about to launch Caroline Television instead.

Lockheed were contacted in August 1970 by a Bruce Maxwell of the London *Daily Mirror* who was seeking to establish the identity and location of the Constellations and their owner. According to The Lockheed Star house newspaper O'Rahilly had been making test transmissions and had sold millions of dollars of advertsing!

His plans called for two Constellations, one in service and one as a relief, which would transmit commercial television programmes to Britain by Stratovision. Although these stories continued for some time, nothing came of the project.

The success of the Navy's R7V-1s stimulated US Air Force interest in a very similar version of the Super Constellation with the same passenger capacity and convertibility to freighting or casualty evacuation. This was the L-1049F or C-121C, the new model suffix letter denoting structural reinforcement for a slightly higher maximum gross weight of 137,500 pounds.

Up to 106 passengers in forward-facing or rear-facing seats or seventy-three stretcher cases, plus four medical attendants, or 40,000 pounds of freight could be carried. However, more typical loads were seventy-five passengers or forty-seven stretcher cases. The folding seats could be stowed in the underfloor holds when cargo alone was carried. Four 3,250 horsepower R-3350-91 Turbo-Compounds were fitted and, unlike the R7V-I, the C-121C had a 50hp Solar Mars gas turbine as an auxiliary power unit to provide a source of power when on the ground. An initial order for ten C-121Cs was placed in 1951 and twenty-three more were ordered in 1954; but the first C-121C did not make its maiden flight until July 1955, as production priority had been given to R7V-Is and RC-121 early warning versions. Later thirty-three R7V-1s were turned over to the USAF as C-121Gs. By 1965 the C-121C was being used mainly by US Air National Guard units in the casualty evacuation role, with ANG squadrons operating a total of fifty-two C-121 Super Constellations.

Incident at the Pole

On 8 October 1970, 131644, a C-121J named *Pegasus* took off from Christchurch, New Zealand. Before departure, the crew was informed that weather conditions at McMurdo Sound station was favourable. Unfortunately, these conditions deteriorated in flight and upon arrival, the crew was unable to locate the runway. A fierce storm was ravaging the air above the South Pole. But they were forced to fly onward, a lack of fuel making it impossible for them return back to New Zealand.

Snow and ice whipped through the air, erasing any and all visibility. *Pegasus* was dropping toward the frozen desert below. In such conditions, the captain decided to make a go-around and during a second attempt to land in zero visibility due to blowing snow, he failed to realize his altitude was too low when the right main gear struck a snowbank and was torn off. The right wing was also torn off and the airliner crashed.

Miraculously, the eighty people aboard the

Four views of 131644 *Pegasus* resting in the frozen wilderness of Antarctica. *(Kirk Smeeton Collection)*

aircraft - sixty-eight passengers and twelve crew - survived the crash with no major injuries. They were all rescued and able to carry on with their Antarctic research largely unharmed.

Pegasus is still there, resting beneath a blanket of snow. Most of the aircraft is usually covered by layers of ice and snow, though people do like to expose it to take photographs or carve their names onto its exterior.

The crash inspired researchers to rename the ice runway and airfield after the wrecked aircraft. However, Pegasus Field closed in December 2014 because of excess summer melt.

The Batcats

During the Vietnam War some forty EC-121s were modified from USN WV-2 and WV-3 early warning Constellations for use with ground sensors to detect enemy troop movements along the Ho Chi Minh Trail and twenty-five were deployed to Korat RTAFB as a part of Operation Igloo White. The resulting EC-121R configuration was nicknamed the Batcat.

The 553rd Reconnaissance Squadron was a detachment of the 551st AEW&C Wing at Otis AFB, Massachusetts. The unit was formally organized at Otis in January 1967, although it existed before then for some months in an unofficial capacity. The Batcats had a unique , at the time highly secret mission.

The North Vietnamese supplied and replenished their units in the very heart of South Vietnam by means of a supply system that used a complex web of trails and roads known as the Ho Chi Minh Trail. This was a network of secondary roads and trails that started in central North Vietnam, ran south to near the North-South Vietnamese border, then curved west into Laos, and then followed the Laotian - South Vietnamese border. At points, branches of the trail curved into South Vietnam. Laos was a neutral country, and therefore the location of the Ho Chi Minh Trail, together with the fact that the vehicles and personnel moved only at night, made detection very difficult. The problem was compounded by the existence of multiple parallel trails, and their location through thick jungle, which provided an umbrella of thick vegetation.

In 1966 the Rand Corporation, a well-known

American think tank, studied the problem of interdiction of the Ho Chi Minh Trail and came up with a concept designed to reduce its effectiveness. The plan involved laying down by parachute, or 'seeding', vast areas of the trail with self-powered sensors. These could be triggered by either noise or vibration, at which time the sensor would broadcast on a discrete VHF frequency whatever it was sensing. Airborne aircraft would receive the broadcasts, pinpoint the sensor location, and call down an airstrike.

Secretary of Defense Robert MacNamara accepted this plan and in 1967 began implementing it. This involved seeding various portions of the Ho Chi Minh Trail in Laos and southwest North Vietnam. Old US Navy sonobuoys, originally designed to be dropped into the ocean to monitor the passage of submarines, were converted for this use. These sensors each had a particular VHF frequency on which they relayed whatever they heard. The sensors came in two types and were battery-powered. Their battery life was supposed to be up to four months of intermittent use, but many operated up to eight months. Whenever the sound or vibration ceased, the sensor turned its transmitter off. They were dropped in place by the Navy using specially adapted Lockheed P2V Neptunes.

The Air Force had the responsibility of monitoring these broadcasts at night, the only time there was much activity on the Ho Chi Minh Trail. It was for this mission that the 553rd Recon Wing was created. The Wing was equipped with converted EC-121Rs, which came out of storage at Davis-Montham AFB, and had originally been Navy WV-2s. These had no search or altitude finding radar, and hence no radomes. They did have special VHF radio receivers, a digital data processor, and a data link. They also had a nose-mounted weather radar, which doubled as terrain mapping radar.

The 553rd had some twenty-five aircraft assigned to it at Otis AFB, of which eight per cent were in SEA at any one time, operating from Korat Royal Thai Air Force Base, Thailand. Their missions involved flying over the general area of the Ho Chi Minh Trail at altitudes of up to 20,000 feet. The altitudes were dictated by the need to receive VHF line-of-sight transmissions from the sensors on the ground even from considerable distances.

There were up to eight monitoring positions in each aircraft, manned by combat information monitors (CIM). There was also a combat information control officer (CICO). The various CIMs would each monitor certain specific frequencies assigned to them. If signals were picked up that sounded promising, the CIM would tell the CICO on the intercom. The CICO, who could monitor all the frequencies on his console, would listen in. He would then try to evaluate the signal and attempt to decide if it meant something worth reporting to intelligence officers back on the ground. To help him in this task, the CICO had large-scale maps that accurately showed the exact locations of all the sensors. If the CICO decided to relay the information back to base, he would do so via the data link, thus permitting the intelligence officers on the ground to evaluate the information in its original state.

The 553rd reached the point where it had five different stations to cover, four over Laos, and one just south of the DMZ. Later, a sixth station was added over the Gulf of Tonkin. Each station would have an EC-121R on it for eight hours at a stretch. Allowing for some two hours flying to the station and two more returning to home base, each crew flew missions of close to twelve hours. So it was that three aircraft were needed per station every twenty-four hours. The stations were 200-300 miles from each other.

EC-121R 67-21475, seen at Otis AFB, Massachusetts, on 17 May 1969. Look closely and you can see the FM radio antennas on the top of the outside vertical stabilisers. *(Kirk Smeeton Collection)*

High angle side view of U.S. Air Force EC-121R 67-21490 of the 553rd Reconnaissance Squadron in flight over Thailand. *(USAF)*

For reasons of safety, the EC-12lRs patrolled their stations at different altitudes, especially if two stations were adjacent. Thus, at one station the aircraft assigned would begin the mission at 16,000 feet, and halfway through go to 18,000 feet. At the next station, the starting altitude might be 17,000 feet, with 19,000 feet as the final altitude. If an aircraft had to abort its mission, and its time on station was past the midpoint, then one of the adjacent aircraft would move to a point where it could cover both areas. In such a case, this machine would climb to 20,000 feet. Naturally, if an aircraft had to abort early in the mission, a backup aircraft would be launched in relief.

Crews were scheduled to fly approximately nine times each month. This meant a crew would fly some 100 hours per month, or 1,200 hours per year, sometimes even more. Each crew was scheduled to fly a twelve-hour mission on Day 1, rest for twenty-four hours, then be on a five-hour alert as the backup aircraft. The next day, or Day 4, they would begin the whole thing over again. Of course, if the backup crew was launched as the replacement aircraft, this meant they were flying with only one day off, rather than two.

By 1967 these were already high-time aircraft, and pretty well worn out. After a few months in South East Asia, things could only get worse, despite the very best efforts of the ground crews, who struggled to maintain the aircraft as best they could.

There were a number of Batcats incidents during the war, with the loss of twenty-two crewmen and four Thai civilians.

The first incident to EC-121R, 67-21476, callsign Howey 92, happened on 21 January 1969. At 0630 EST the aircrew reported to Base Operations at Eglin AFB, Florida, for flight preparation. Clearance was filed to fly from Duke Field (Eglin Aux #3) on a local range mission, land at Eglin (Main Base) for equipment off-load, then proceed to Otis AFB, Massachusetts for termination.

As the accident report stated: 'Initial takeoff was made at 0730 EST. Landing at Eglin (Main Base), takeoff and flight en route to the PAH pattern of Otis AFB was normal. At Otis AFB, Honey 92, attempted three PAR approaches under poor weather conditions. The first terminated in a missed approach. The second approach was terminated before the glide path interception because of deteriorated weather conditions. After being advised that Otis AFB weather had improved, the aircrew began the third approach.

During the latter stages of the approach, at 1814 EST, the aircraft struck the ground 4060 feet from PAR touchdown. At this point, the aircraft entered an area covered by small pine trees. The nose gear and left main landing gear collapsed during rollout over the unimproved terrain. Forward travel stopped 2560 feet from the PAR touchdown point near the extended centerline of the runway. Egress from the aircraft was orderly, though difficult for the personnel in the flight station due to the severe compaction of that area'.

The second accident, on 25 April 1969, happened to EC-121R, 67-21493, callsign 'Batcat 21' crew number 39 from the 554th Recon Sq, Korat RTAFB, was scheduled for a tactical combat mission directed by frag order number 115, mission number 6901. Scheduled mission briefing time was 1315 local, taxi time 1530, and takeoff time 1600, for a flight from Korat to the combat zone and return. Pertinent aircrew positions were: Aircraft commander; (Pilot):Lt Col Heller; Co-pilot: Major Lunsford; Flight Engineer: TSgt Fowler. Mission briefing consisted of a standard 553d Recon Wg

EC-121R, 67-21476, callsign Howey 92 in the weeds following its accident on 21 January 1969.
(Kirk Smeeton Collection)

briefing. Weather briefing, utilising slides and telephone, was standard and contained specific forecast for Batcat 21's takeoff time of intermittent conditions with winds variable in direction at 20 knots with gusts to 35 knots, visibility reduced to two miles in thunderstorms with rain showers and associated dust storm. In addition, due to variable weather conditions, the pilot was advised to contact weather on 344.6 prior to takeoff for updated weather. Special operations briefing presented by the 553d Recon Wg Tactical Operations Center (TOC) Duty Controller contained a number of mission items and specifically included Crew Briefing Instructions, dated 17 April 1969, covering weather conditions during the Southwest Monsoon Season.

Those instructions included a review of the 553d Recon Wg policy of no takeoffs or landings when thunderstorms are in the near vicinity of the airbase. The crew then proceeded to the 554th Recon Sq Squadron Operations Center equipment section to pick up the required crew kits and survival equipment. Pre-flight of the aircraft was normal using the prescribed checklists and Batcat 21 called mission ready at 1449 hours. Programmed fuel load was 8030 gallons and calculated takeoff weight was 132,000 pounds. Batcat 21 started engines approximately 1520 and commenced taxi to run-up position at 1530. After completing engine run-up, Batcat 21 was cleared for takeoff by Korat Tower at 1554 and was advised to contact departure control. Batcat 21 established contact with departure control and requested information on the position, direction of movement and speed of the thunderstorm cell near the base. Departure control advised Batcat 21 that the thunderstorm was over the base and extended twenty miles southwest. Batcat 21 requested a right turn after takeoff and radar vectoring around the thunderstorms.

Batcat 21 was requested to maintain runway heading and departure control would vector the aircraft around the thunderstorms. Prior to becoming airborne, Batcat 21 was advised that he was cleared to turn right to two eight zero degrees. Batcat 21 reported airborne at 1558 and departure control advised the heading was two eight zero degrees and he would radar identify Batcat 21. Batcat 21 acknowledged his vector to two eight zero and a short time later requested to make a right turn if possible as it was very turbulent. Korat departure control approved the request. No further transmissions were received from Batcat 21. The aircraft impacted with the ground approximately 1559, 3.7 miles off the departure end of runway 24 on the 260 degree radial of the Korat TACAN. The impact occurred less than a half minute after the co-pilot's last transmission. Distance from takeoff to impact indicates a total flight duration of approximately two minutes.

According to the accident report: 'Once initiated, search and crash response was excellent. Pedro 33, rescue HH-43B, was airborne at 1624, six minutes after search request was made, and located the crash site at 1629. Upon notification, the tower controller activated the primary crash net. The secondary crash net alert was completed at 1631. Pedro 33 landed at the crash site and, utilizing an airborne relay, established communications with the control tower. At 1632 aeromedical technicians verified there were no survivors. Pedro 33 returned to base, picked up the fire suppression kit and extinguished the remaining fire at the crash scene. Base medical personnel were alerted by the primary crash net, and a flight surgeon with two medical personnel departed for base Operations immediately. The Director of Base Medical services, knowing the second rescue helicopter was inoperative, called the Army flying detachment for helicopter support. By the time the medical personnel arrived at the ramp, the helicopter was ready. The Flight Surgeon, accompanied by the Support Group Commander and one Medical Technician arrived at the crash scene at 1650. The disaster control convoy was formed within thirty minutes and proceeded to the crash site arriving at 1725. In the interim, all necessary personnel for recovery of the bodies and securing the crash area had been ferried to the site via helicopters.'

The third incident, which occurred on 5 September 1969, an EC-121R, 67- 21495, callsign 'Batcat 19', with aircrew number 40, from the 554th Recon Squadron Korat RTAFB, was scheduled for a combat tactical mission directed by 7th AF Frag Order number 69-248, mission number 1334.

According to the official accident report, scheduled mission briefing time was 1400G, taxi time 1600G, and take-off time 1630G for a flight from Korat RTAFB to the combat zone and return.

The weather briefing was conducted by the base duty forecaster utilising slides and telephone; his voice was being piped into the briefing room by means of a speaker system connected through the telephone circuit. This briefing was standard and contained specific forecast data for Batcat 19's take-off time.

Upon completion of the formal pre-mission briefing, the aircrew proceeded to the 554 Recon Sq, Squadron Operations Center (SOC) to obtain, inventory and sign for the required crew mission kits. Each aircrew member then proceeded to the 553rd Wing Life Support Unit and obtained his personal survival gear. From here, the aircrew boarded a crew bus and proceeded to their assigned aircraft to conduct the pre-flight.

Pre-flight duties were normal using the prescribed checklists and no discrepancies were noted. Mission programmed fuel load was 8,050 gallons. Calculated take-off weight was 134,516 pounds with the center of gravity (CG) 24.8% MAC.

Engines were started at 1550G and at 1600G the aircraft was taxied to the runup area. At the completion of engine runup, the crew chief performed a 'Last Chance' walk-around inspection of the aircraft. The maintenance inspection complete, Batcat 19 then called the 553d Wing TOC for his final release to proceed with the fragged mission. Prior to granting Batcat 19 his release, the TOC Duty Controller contacted the duty forecaster to check for any existing significant weather hazards located within the immediate vicinity of the airport. Information received by the Duty Controller was transmitted to the aircraft commander along with the Wing release to contact Korat Tower for take-off.

Take-off was initiated at 1625G. During climbout, the take-off time and estimated time to the assigned combat orbit was passed to the 553d Wing TOC. The flight proceeded as briefed. From time of take-off until reporting leaving the combat area Batcat 19 relayed a total of twelve operations normal reports to the 553d Wing TOC. The flight to and within the combat area was uneventful, except for structural and engine icing which was reported as being light to moderate in intensity. Due to these icing conditions, Batcat 19 changed altitude a total of six times. The aircraft was in actual weather throughout most of the flight.

Batcat 19 reported leaving the combat area 06/0356G for return to Korat with an estimated time of arrival of 0515G. Route of the flight was as planned during the pre-mission briefing.

A Meteorological Watch was issued by Korat base weather station to the 553d Wing TOC by Autowriter at 0411G. The 553d Wing TOC acknowledged receipt by telephone at 0415G. This Met. Watch was transmitted to Batcat 19 with a request that the aircraft commander call TOC when 55 miles out. Shortly thereafter, Batcat 19 passed his maintenance status, reporting only one discrepancy. The Radio Maintenance Technician verified the problem as the DME not 'locking on'. He had changed sets a number of times and finally disconnected one of the antennae. The TACAN was working properly upon return to Korat. The radio operator then requested to secure the High-Frequency radios, and TOC approved. Batcat 19 had reported his position to be one hundred nautical miles from Korat, at flight level ten thousand five hundred feet, and had requested Korat weather. The 06/0431G weather passed by the TOC Controller. Batcat 19 questioned the intensity of the rain and TOC remarked that, 'It's coming down in buckets out there.' The aircraft commander stated that the last report he had was for light rain. He asked for clarification, requested a current weather report and was advised the latest weather report had just been passed to him. In addition, the controller remarked; 'It's raining pretty hard outside.'

The aircraft commander then requested 553d Wing release. He was advised that the 553d Wing Assistant Supervisor of Flying was en route to the Control Tower; that there was nothing significant to report except for visibility and ceiling, and that he was released to Korat Approach Control for 'a descent down to minimums'. Shortly after that, TOC advised Batcat 19 that weather, 'just advised us that it is raining light to moderate'. In addition,

EC-121R 67-21485 over South-East Asia. (USAF)

he was provided with the latest two-hour forecast for Don Muang, Bangkok International Airport. This forecast was transmitted as winds out of the southwest at eight knots, visibility six-plus miles, four eights stratocumulus at thirty-five hundred, three-eights altocumulus at ten thousand, with the ceiling of ten thousand. Batcat 19 then asked the ceiling for Korat. It was passed as eight hundred feet. This was an error made the TOC Controller since the ceiling reported by the weather station at 0431G, 0456G, 0512G and 0527G was eight thousand feet. There were no further radio communications between TOC and Batcat 19.

Batcat 19 made initial contact with Korat Approach Control as he was approximately fifty nautical miles east of the airport. The aircraft received radar vectors and descended to twenty-three hundred feet indicated altitude for a precision radar approach. He was thirteen nautical miles northeast of runway 24 when in position to begin his approach. The aircraft, during the approach, drifted left of course, and at a point between one mile and two miles from Runway 24 executed a missed approach. When queried by the Ground Control Approach final controller as to the cause of the left drift, Batcat 19 reported as 'We were just having a little trouble in the rain out here'.

Batcat 19 remained under radar control, completed a right closed radar pattern, and received vectors to a point approximately eleven miles on the final approach course for runway 24. Unlike the first approach, but with the aircraft commander's concurrence, the approach lights were turned on to maximum brilliance along with the strobe lights.

The second precision approach appeared routine, with the aircraft generally on course, holding slightly above glide path until approximately one nautical mile from touch down. At decision height, the aircraft was dropping down through the glide path. The aircraft initially impacted the approach lights three thousand feet from the end of runway 24 at 0524G.

It then struck the ground and eventually came to rest 1400 feet from the runway. Total flight time was twelve hours and fifty-nine minutes. Air Rescue was advised of the crash and location of the wreckage through the primary crash alert system initiated by tower personnel. The helicopter crew responded immediately, taking-off at 0530G. Upon arriving at the crash site, the helicopter pilot found that it was extremely difficult to locate obstacles in the area due to poor visibility resulting from extremely heavy rain and smoke. Realizing that soft ground and concertina wire would hinder firefighting equipment in reaching the wreckage, the helicopter returned to the ramp where a Fire Suppression Kit (FSK)was obtained. The helicopter then returned to the crash site. The FSK was expended on the forward part of the aircraft fuselage. The helicopter ground crew searched the wreckage for survivors with negative results. Later, four survivors, located northeast of the wreckage were airlifted to the east end of runway 24 overrun where they were transferred to an ambulance. Helicopter operations, with the approval of the Fire Chief, were terminated at 0630G.

Response by fire department personnel was effected at 0525G. Vehicles dispatched to the crash scene included two P-2s, one 011A, two fifteen hundred gallon water distributors, one R-2, and the Assistant Fire Chief's pickup truck. Once it had been determined that the crash site was located off-base, a 530B pumper was dispatched to the scene. Fire equipment was unable to gain access to the immediate crash site because of the terrain, very heavy rain, darkness, concertina wire, a petroleum oil lubricant line and large drainage ditch. Meanwhile, the HH-43B helicopter had arrived at the scene with the suppression kit and had exercised fire control. However, due to the limited amount of extinguishing agent available, the fire could not be extinguished completely.

Fire department personnel gained access to the site utilizing ladders that were placed across the concertina wire and drainage ditch. Nine-hundred fifty-feet of two-and-one-half-inch hose was physically carried from the P-2 to the crash site. Working with the helicopter, firefighters managed to extinguish the fire and evacuate some of the inured. Since communications were not available between the helicopter and ground operations, coordination was effected between the two units by means of Korat Tower acting as a communications relay terminal.

By the time the firefighters physically reached the site, a most of the aircrew members had either been thrown clear or had managed to evacuate the burning wreckage. Therefore, most of the survivors were located by voice contact. The four survivors carried to safety by the helicopter were originally found northeast of the wreckage and some distance away. One survivor was found in a hole with water up to his waist; two were found walking around, apparently in shock. Two bodies were recovered from the wreckage. Five aircrew members were located and assisted away from the crash scene by other rescue personnel along with the recovery of the other two fatalities. Four Thai nationals in the route of aircraft travel were fatally injured. Rescue and crash response was terminated at 0815G.

Batcat EC-121s were camouflaged in standard three-colour Southeast Asia scheme while the College Eye/Disco early warning aircraft were not. BatCat missions were eighteen hours in length, with eight hours on station at one of eleven colour-coded orbits used during their five-year history, three of which were over South Vietnam, six over Laos, one over Cambodia and one over the Gulf of Tonkin.

The Da Nang Glider Incident

In the middle of 1969 Colonel Jack January was assigned as the aircraft commander of Batcat crew 31, 554th Reconnaissance Squadron. On 4 June crew 31 was scheduled for a standard combat mission. Col. January replaced the assigned aircraft commander Banner for this mission. This was Col. January's 18th flight since arriving for duty at Korat RTAFB, with the 553rd Reconnaissance Wing, on 9 April. The aircraft was EC-121R serial number 67-21487. After takeoff, the Lockheed EC-121R was flown out to the orbit area. After arrival at the assigned orbit, the aircraft was placed in cruise condition for a planned eight hours on station. As was the normal practice with the 553rd Reconnaissance Wing, one pilot, either the aircraft commander or the co-pilot, would be in the aircraft commander's seat. The co-pilot's seat was occupied by one of the navigators, and one of the two flight engineers on board would be at the flight engineers station. The off duty pilot, navigator and flight engineer would rest until switching positions with the on-duty crew members. As the aircraft assumed its standard orbit the pilot in the left seat was 1st Lt. Mason Ezzell, and the right seat was occupied by Lt. Hardee one of the navigators for the mission, the duty flight engineer was Sgt. Welch. This mission was flown on the blue orbit near Khe Sanh, at an altitude of 19,000 feet. Khe Sanh is on the northwestern part of Vietnam, not too far south of the DMZ, and a little east of the Vietnam border with Laos.

Shortly after assuming the assigned orbit, all four engines stopped. It is important to understand that the Constellation required hydraulic pressure from an operating engine for the flight controls to operate. With all four engines stopped, there was no hydraulic pressure, and the controls virtually froze. The aircraft began to decelerate quickly, nosing over with the left wing dropping. 1st Lt. Ezzell tried to correct for the unusual attitude, but the controls would not respond because of a lack of hydraulic pressure. 'My first reaction was to grab the hydraulic release lever, just to the side of my right leg, and pull it up to disengage the hydraulic system and allow for manual flying of the aircraft through the cable system. Now I was flying the aircraft without any hydraulic assist, and it was like trying to control a large bull. My concerns were to keep the wings level and maintain control while letting the aircraft continue in a gradual descent, so the aircraft would not stall and go out of control. All this took place in less than a minute, although it seems like a lifetime.' Colonel January was laying down in the bunk immediately behind the flight deck as he was off duty when the incident began.

'Some say Silence is Golden, however, if you are enjoying a nap in a four-engine aircraft, in a bunk behind the flight deck, I say Silence is anything but golden.' Lt. Ezzell had the aircraft stabilized and heading for the coast, but still with all four engines stopped. Col. January entered the cockpit switching places with Lt. Ezzell, while the navigator vacated the right seat and Lt. Ezzell took over as co-pilot. Lt. Ezzell: 'Since we did not know if we were going to have to bail out or possibly ditch the aircraft the crew was notified to now put on their water wings. Now everybody had to take off all their equipment and put the water wings on and then put all their equipment back on. When I rang the bell to let them know that they might have to bail out, we suffered the only injury of the trip. The person who opened the rear door was hit in the head by the door as it popped open. He was not hurt seriously and just had a slight cut.' As Colonel January entered the flight deck, the first visible indication of the problem was that all four feather switch/indicators were bright red.

Each Wright R-3350 engine on the EC-121R was equipped with a three-blade, constant speed, fully feathering, reversible, Hamilton Standard hydromatic propeller. Feathering a propeller means rotating the propeller blades about 90 degrees, so each blade is streamlined with the wind, which gives minimum drag. If the propeller does not feather on an engine giving little or no power, the propeller will windmill, which creates substantial amounts of drag. A windmilling - or non-feathered - propeller on the failed engine of a Lockheed EC-121R can cause so much drag, even with the other three engines operating at normal power, that the aircraft is not capable of maintaining altitude if the landing gear and flaps are down. When an engine was lost, it was most times necessary to reduce the weight of the machine by dumping fuel.

On the Lockheed EC-121R, there were two means to feather a propeller, manually, and through the automatic feather control. The automatic feather control would feather a propeller if the throttle was more than halfway advanced, and the BMEP (torque) of the engine fell below about 104, and the BMEP remained at or below that level for at least 1 ½ to 2 seconds. The reason for the automatic feather control is to feather a propeller quickly when an engine fails at a critical time, especially during take-off. Once the automatic feather control feathered the first propeller, and it didn't matter which propeller was feathered, it automatically disabled itself from feathering any other propeller. Lockheed designed the automatic feather control so it could feather only a single propeller. The second method to feather a propeller on the Lockheed EC-121R was for the flight engineer was to do it manually. All of the feather controls in the EC-121R were located at the flight engineers station. The manual feather control consisted of four push-button switches, each covered with its own plastic guard. To feather a propeller, the flight engineer had to lift the plastic cover and depress the switch for the propeller which is to be feathered. When the switch was depressed, a circuit was made to a DC electric feather motor, which pumped oil to the nose hub of the propeller. The oil pressure forced the blades to rotate to the feather position. At the same time, a red light in the switch was turned on.

The feather switches had three positions, push to feather, neutral, and pull to unfeather. After a propeller was fully feathered, the flight engineer pulled the feather switch back to the neutral position. With the feather switch in neutral, the feather pump motor was deactivated. To unfeather a propeller, the flight engineer pulled the switch out. This activated the feather pump motor again, directing the oil to the rear of the hub where the oil pressure forced the propeller blades to rotate back to the low pitch position. Once unfeathered the feather switch was returned to neutral to turn off the feather pump motor. If an engine was feathered, and later an attempt is made to restore power inflight, the engine was first started with the propeller still feathered. Once the engine was restarted and turning, the flight engineer then pulled out the feather switch to unfeather the propeller. After the propeller was unfeathered, the flight engineer again returned the feather switch to the neutral position which turns off the feather pump motor.

As Colonel January entered the cockpit, he could see all four feather switches with bright red lights on. Looking out the cockpit window, he watched the blades come to a standstill as if at perfect attention. Colonel January: 'My first goal was to prepare the crew for bailout and head for

A Batcat in its lair - a sharks-mouth EC-121 undergoes maintenance. (USAF)

open water, where recovery wouldn't be hampered by the jungle and those pesky enemy troops. 'The flight engineer initiated the standard engine start procedure, starting engine #3first, then #4, #2 and finally #1 in that order. Number 3 engine started without incident and gave the electrical power needed for communications with rescue and other assistance agencies.' With Col. January now flying the aircraft, Lt. Ezzell was sending out May Day and handling the radios. Number #4 engine was then started and gained full power, and #3 propeller returned to the feather position. When #3 engine was restarted again and gained full power, #4propeller returned to the feather position. This sequence repeated numerous times. Number 2 engine was started, then #1 engine and both were left at low power to provide stable electrical and hydraulic systems. 'To my pleasant surprise, neither #1 or #2 propeller returned to the feather position for the rest of the flight.' While the cockpit crew was fully involved in making every effort to achieve stable power, the back end crew prepared for a bailout. This preparation involved finding and putting on your parachute, destroying sensitive material, etc. Little communication occurred between the cockpit crew and the back end crew. Radio contact was maintained with the ground and rescue services, so others were aware of the rapidly changing situation. By now open water had been reached, and there were rescue aircraft flying alongside. Col. January flew the aircraft towards the nearest U.S. airbase, Da Nang. As power was reduced to lose altitude to land, the number of feathering incidents with number 3 and 4 propellers greatly reduced. As Da Nang came into view, an overhead circling approach was made to achieve the final goal, 'the aircraft and crew were on the ground safely.' All four engines were operating before engine shutdown.

A huge effort went into discovering the reasons behind what had happened. An incident review board was appointed by the theatre commander. In addition to maintenance technicians from the 553rd Reconnaissance Wing at Korat RTAFB, and Da Nang, South Vietnam, the Senior Lockheed Research Engineer who originally designed the Constellation propeller system reviewed the problem. Even with all the expertise available the exact reason for all four propellers feathering was never fully identified.

Due to the inability to identify the cause a large number of components were replaced on the aircraft: Engines #3 and #4; Prop feathering pumps on #3 and #4; Prop feathering motors #3and #4; prop governors #3 and #4; propellers #3 and #4; torque switches #3 and #4;spark plugs #1 and #2; plug and receptacle connector #1 at the flight engineers station;prop synchronizing box; both bus sectionalizing relays; all four prop feathering relays; all four-time delay relays; prop feathering switches #1, #3 and #4; and the prop reversingcoordination relay panels #3 and #4 were overhauled at depot and reinstalled.

Even with all the items above replaced some additional steps were taken before the test flights

A very common view from a fuselage window of an EC- 'feathered and stopped'. (USAF)

began. The auto feathering system was temporarily bypassed, and a special panel installed to indicate any unknown attempt to activate the auto feathering system. Two 'no-can-feather' switches were installed in the feathering systems for #2 and #3. Several high speed ground runs were made at Da Nang, South Vietnam. With the ground runs showing no problems it was time to flight test the machine. The flight test crew for the 'Da Nang Glider' was named 'Flight Test Crew 007'. The crew was made up of: Chief of 553rd Wing Safety; Chief of 553rd Wing; 553rd Wing Quality Control/Flight Test Officer; 553rd Wing Stan/Eval flight engineer; 553rd Wing Quality Control/Flight Test flight engineer.

The first test flight was two hours in length and flew around Da Nang, South Vietnam. On the second test flight, the aircraft was returned to Korat RTAFB after a four-hour flight. Eight more test flights were conducted out of Korat for a total test flight duration of twenty-four hours. Beginning with the third test flight, some of the modifications made at Da Nang were deactivated. On the eighth and last test flight, all precautionary modifications had been removed. On 16 September 1969, the aircraft returned to normal reconnaissance operations with Flight Test Crew 007 in the cockpit, and crew 33 in the back end. After much research, it was finally revealed that the identity of The Da Nang Glider was 67-21487, Lockheed construction number 4480, previously Navy Bureau number 143206 before conversion to EC-121R.

EC-121Rs were operated by the 553d and 554th Reconnaissance Squadrons of the 553d Reconnaissance Wing, between October 1967 and December 1970, with approximately twenty Batcats on hand at any time. The 554th RS relocated to Nakhon Phanom RTAFB to fly QU-22 sensor monitors nicknamed 'Baby Bats'. Initially with eleven aircraft, the 553rd RS continued ops for another year, gradually returning aircraft and crews to the USA. The final Batcat mission was in December 1971. The last remaining administrative and support personnel returned to Otis AFB in January 1972.

A requirement for a new category of aircraft to replace the Super Constellation and known as AWACS - Airborne Warning and Control System - was evolved by the USAF and in 1970, in the face of strong competition, the main contract went to Boeing for an eight-engined early warning version of the 707-320 carrying a dorsal 'saucer' radome similar in shape to the WV-2E's. Lockheed had produced two earlier proposals for WV-2 developments, the Model CL-2 57 project, revealed in January 1957, being a new early warning Super Constellation with the same 'flying saucer' radome and APS-70 radar as the WV-2E. Five months later Lockheed were awarded a multi-million dollar contract for the implementation of the W2V-1, a radar picket derivative of the L-1649A Starliner with the latter's new 150 ft span wing and powered by four Allison T-56 turboprops, with two Westinghouse J-34 turbojets in wing-tip pods for cruising at higher altitudes. The disc-shaped dorsal radome of the WV-2E was to have been featured, but with twin fins and rudders, and the maximum gross weight was to have been about 175,000 pounds. The first flight was scheduled for late 1959 or early 1960. Still, only a month after the contract award had been announced, a defence budget squeeze obliged the US Navy to abandon the project, and the pre-production engineering phase of the W2V-I was cancelled. However, the Phase One portion of the contract, covering design studies, wind-tunnel tests and the fuselage mock-up, was continued for a time.

Chapter Nine

The L-1049H

On 29 June 1955 Lockheed announced the L-1049H, a freighter version of the Super G with the same freight doors and heavy-duty, anti-corrosion magnesium floor of the L-1049D. In a matter of hours, it could be converted to a high-density passenger layout by the addition of such things as vinyl interior walls, baggage racks, curtains, reading lights, toilets and a buffet. Up to 118 passengers could be carried, or 104 at a seat pitch of thirty-eight inches with a crew of up to eleven, the passenger seats could be stowed in the underfloor freight holds when the cabin was converted back to freight. The maximum gross weight of 137,500 pounds was originally achieved, the same as the Super G's, but this was increased to 140,000 pounds when the L-1049H went into service with the EA-6 Turbo-Compounds giving more cruising power. Instead of the DA-3 Turbo-Compounds of the Super G, the L-1049H was usually powered by 3,400 bhp limited to 3,250bhp R-3350-988TCI8 EA-3 Turbo-Compounds giving easier maintenance and greater durability; so much so, that Eastern had had its Super Gs re-engined with this R-3350 variant. Tip tanks, as on the Super G, could be fitted and the L-1049H's fuel capacity was the same, giving it a range of 4,313 miles with three hours' fuel reserves as a passenger aircraft, or 3,393 miles as a freighter; a payload of up to 19 short tons could be carried on the North Atlantic routes. A payload of 40,203 pounds of freight could be carried at the 137,500-pound gross weight under the five per cent overload conditions authorised by the Civil Aeronautics Administration, but a more normal payload was 35,118 pounds. The freight holds volume and cargo door dimensions were the same as on the L-1049D, but the L-1049H, unlike the earlier version, retained the same number of cabin windows as the Super G besides having a smaller passenger door inset into the upward-opening rear cargo door. The hold dimensions could accommodate such loads as a seventy-three feet length of ten-inch pipe, or a package measuring forty-two inches wide by five feet high by twenty feet long.

Do you haul passengers... or air freight... or a combination of both?

The Lockheed Super H Constellation does all three — at a profit!

ALL SET FOR 104 PASSENGERS...

Two pages from the Lockheed Aircraft Corporation brochure for the L-10149H, along with a glowing recommendation from Frank B Lynott of Flying Tigers

The first customer for the new version, of which fifty-three were built, was QANTAS, which ordered two L-1049H-82-133s, the first of these, VH-EAM *Southern Spray,* making its first flight on 20 September 1956. QANTAS had two L-1049E/01- 55s converted into freighters in 1960, and along with the 1049Hs, an all-freight service from Sydney to London was operated. The QANTAS order was followed by one from Seaboard & Western Airlines for two, plus three more ordered at the end of 1955. Seaboard had bought a L-1049E from Cubana and in 1958 had leased a Super G from Lufthansa, besides having two of its L-1049Ds modified up to L-1049H/03 standard in the summer of 1956 with a higher gross weight of 135,400 pounds, later increased to 137,500 pounds. Seaboard used its 1049Hs not only for its scheduled cargo services across the Atlantic to cities in Europe and for civil and military charters but also leased them out to other operators to whom the L-1049H's quick convertibility to passenger-carrying was highly valuable. An early example was the lease of 1049Hs to Eastern at the end of 1956 to cater for the extra Christmas holiday traffic on the routes from New York and other cities to Miami, and early in 1958 the Belgian airline, Sabena, leased three 1049Hs for the duration of the Brussels Exhibition. The ex-Cubana L-1049E was leased to the US 'non-sked', Intercontinental Airways, or Intercontinental US Inc, in 1962, which was engaged in world-wide charters in association with the Luxembourg charter carrier, Interocean Airways.

Transtate Airlines, a subsidiary of Intercontinental, applied in November 1963 to operate a New York - Buffalo 'walk-on' service with 84-passenger L-1049Hs but permission was not granted by the CAB. The L-1049E was later leased to TAP of Portugal, which also leased a Seaboard L-1049H during 1958-59, and on 1 June 1965 to Capitol Airways as well as to Aerlinte Eireann. An L-1049H was also leased to Intercontinental by Seaboard, and later to Transtate, and the former also used a second L-1049H.

Seaboard's best-known leasing operation was the provision of two L-1049Hs, plus the L-1049E and flight crews on a mileage basis to the Irish airline, Aerlinte Eireann, which had taken delivery of five L-749s in 1947 to begin a service to New York but sold the aircraft to BOAC after a change of government had caused a deferment of these plans. A new agreement with Seaboard in November 1952 to provide aircraft for an Atlantic service beginning in 1953 also proved abortive

Eastern Airlines N6227C in the 'hockey stick' colour scheme. *(author's collection)*

when the CAB declined to approve for more than two years. Aerlinte's third and successful attempt was timed to coincide with the introduction of IATA economy-class fares over the Atlantic. The Seaboard agreement of 1952 was revised and updated, and on 28 April 1958 a thrice-weekly Dublin - Shannon - New York service was inaugurated with the L-1049Hs fitted out to seat ninety-five passengers. In June, the frequency was stepped up to seven flights a week, reducing during the winter months, and a stop at Boston was added in October 1958.

The L-1049Hs continued this service until, with the introduction by the Irish airline of Boeing 720-048 jet service on 14 December 1960, the lease was terminated. Aerlinte also used the Super G which Seaboard leased from Lufthansa. In the summer of 1962 Seaboard leased seven of its Super Constellations - three L-1049Ds and four L-1049Hs - to Capitol Airways, which, exercising an option to purchase, eventually bought two L-1049Ds and an L-1049H.

Slick Airways, another US scheduled freight service operator, had ordered five L-1049Hs but later postponed this order when mounting losses on its transcontinental freight routes forced it to suspend all scheduled services on 22 February 1958. However, it continued military charter flying and the leasing of aircraft and finally acquired three L-1049Hs from Lockheed ex-storage in 1959, plus two more operated by the Argentine airline Transcontinental SA. Slick resumed scheduled freight services in April 1962, and also operated L-1049H flights across the Pacific under various charter contracts for the USAF Military Air Transport Service. It had three more ex-California Eastern Aviation L-1049Hs on lease from World Airways from September 1963 until the end of 1965. Still, in July of the following year, Slick's financial difficulties became acute. Its fleet, including the L-1049Hs plus an ex-Alaska Airlines one, was acquired by Airlift International, formerly Riddle Airlines of Miami, which later sold one of the L-1049Hs to Bal Trade. Slick had also used an ex-Trans-Canada 1049 for a time, and its 1049Hs were later fitted with the 3,440bhp R-3350-988TCI8 EA-6 Turbo-Compounds giving 150hp greater cruising power.

The US 'non-sked' California Eastern Aviation ordered three L-1049Hs in the spring of 1956, these being originally intended for the newly-started Argentine airline, Transcontinental SA, in which California Eastern had a financial interest, as well as providing technical and operational

Aerlinte Eireann, the predecessor to Aer Lingus, leased four L-1049 Super Constellations from April 1958 for use on the Dublin-Shannon-New York route, inaugurated on 28 April 1958. *(author's collection)*

With full flaps and gear down, CF-PXX, a L-1049H of World Wide Airways comes in to land. *(author's collection)*

assistance. Two 1049Hs were employed by Transcontinental SA to inaugurate a Buenos Aires - New York service via Sao Paulo, Rio de Janeiro and Caracas in September 1958. On replacement by two Britannia 308 turboprops in March 1960, the two 1049Hs were acquired by Slick.

The three California Eastern L-1049Hs were leased to the Hughes Tool Co at the beginning of 1958 for use by TWA for three years at a monthly rental of $45,000 per aircraft, and with these TWA inaugurated a twice-weekly London-New York all-cargo service on 6 October 1959. The California Eastern aircraft were returned in January 1961 and later sold to World Airways. Hughes Tool also leased for TWA's use from February 1958 the two L-1049Hs ordered by Resort Airlines in the spring of 1956 for military contract cargo operations and for inclusive tour traffic, Resort being one of the first US carriers to specialise in the latter type of business.

Resort provided package holiday tours to the Caribbean, and its L-1049Hs were fitted out to seat ninety-six passengers. One was lost in an accident on 24 November 1959, and the other was leased to World Airways just before Resort ceased operations on 1 July 1961. In addition to its leased L-1049Hs, Hughes Tool also ordered four new L-1049Hs for TWA's use, these being sold to Trans-International Airlines in September 1961.

Another South American airline, REAL Aerovias Nacional of Brazil (the initials stood for Rédes Estaduais Aéreas Ltda) ordered four 1049Hs in May 1957. These had seating for eighty-one passengers but could be adapted to a luxury first-class interior, and tip tanks were fitted. Established in 1946, REAL, by a series of mergers and acquisitions of fourteen other Brazilian airlines. It became the largest airline in South America, serving over 200 places in Brazil. The L-1049Hs went into service on routes from Sao Paulo and Rio to Miami and Los Angeles, but perhaps the most interesting of the airline's L-

Capitol International Airways' N1927H seen at Boston. *(author's collection)*

WEIGHT SUMMARY Model 1049H/01

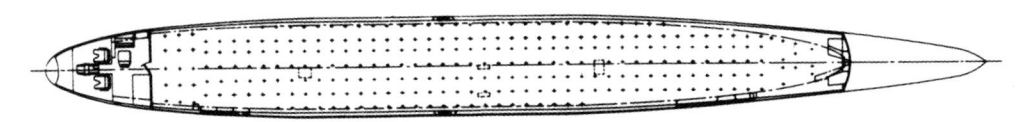

Domestic Cargo Interior

Manufacturers Weight Derivation		
Item		Pounds
Basic Spec. Weight Empty		71,056
+/- to Spec Weight		-1,690
CMC 775 - Prodn Changes		+ 132
CMC 811 - Gross Wht Increase		+ 40
CMC 762 - Prodn Changes For Stripped Cargo Airplane		-1862
Revised Weight Empty		69,366

NOTE: Add 120 pounds to weight empty for EA-6 engines.

Structural Limitations	Pounds
Max Take-off Weight	140,000
Max Landing Weight	118,400*
Max Zero Fuel & Oil Weight	112,200*
Structural Oil Weight	1,200
Max Zero Fuel Weight	113,400*
Structural Payload Limit	40,518

Operating Requirements	Pounds
Revised Weight Empty	69,366
Operating Equipment	2,316
Crew & Crew Baggage (3)	585
System Fuel & Oil	1,113
Winter Equipment	264

	Pounds
Miscellaneous Equipment	154
Cargo Tie-Down Equipment	200
Consumable Oil**	865
Op Weight Empty, Incl Oil	72,547
Weight Limit Payload	40,203
Reserve Fuel (2½ Hours)	5,550
Landing Weight With Reserves +100 Pounds Ground Maneuver Fuel	118,400

*5% Overload Condition.
**Based on 40:1 volume ratio for fuel required, including reserves, at maximum range with full payload.

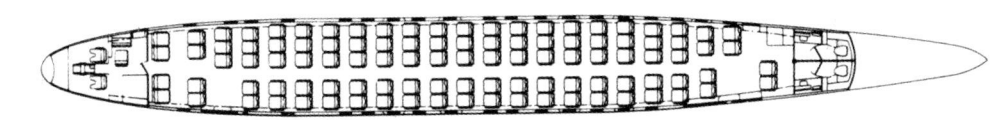

Domestic Coach Interior

Manufacturers Weight Derivation	
Item	Pounds
Basic Spec. Weight Empty	71,056
+/- to Spec Weight	+3,378
CMC 775 - Prodn Changes	+132
CMC 739 - Passenger Facilities	+3,416
CMC 801 - CRAF Provisions & Goodyear Brakes	+119.4
CMC 811- Gross Weight Increase	.+ 40
CCC 6992 - Station 311.8 Window L.H. Side	+ 25
CCC 6986 - Interior Changes	+53.4
CCC 6985 - Fwd Compartment Modification	-408
Estimated Airline Eqpt	.+ 1,996
Pax Seating @ 24 Pounds /Seat	+2,496
Galley Wht vs CMC 739 Allowance	-500

	Pounds
Revised Weight Empty	76,430

NOTE: Add 120 pounds to weight empty for EA-6 engines.

Structural Limitations	Pounds
Max Take-off Weight	140,000
Max Landing Weight	113,000
Max Zero Fuel & Oil Weight	106,800
Structural Oil Weight	1,200
Max Zero Fuel Weight	108,000
Structural Payload Limit	26,412

Operating Requirements	Pounds
Revised Weight Empty	76,430
Operating Equipment	3,958
Crew & Crew Baggage (5)	895
System Fuel & Oil	1,113

	Pounds
Winter Equipment	264
Miscellaneous Equipment	334
Pax & Galley Service @ 13 lbs	1,3S2
Consumable Oil*	1,100
Operating Weight Empty Incl Oil	81,488
Weight Limit Payload	25,112
Pax @ 165 Pounds	17,160
Baggage @ 40 lbs & 3 cu ft/pax	4,160
Cargo	3,792
Reserve Fuel (3 Hours)	6,300
Landing Weight With Reserves +100 Pounds Ground Maneuver Fuel	113,000

* Based on 40:1 volume ratio for fuel required, including reserves, at maximum rangewith full payload.

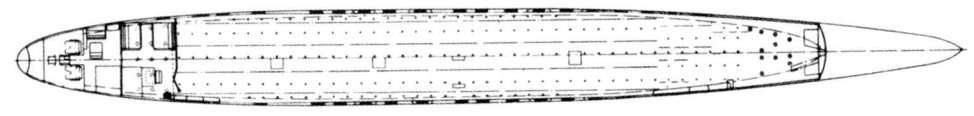

International Convertable Cargo Interior

Manufacturers Weight Derivation	
Item	Pounds
Basic Spec. Weight Empty	71,056
Additions to Specification Weight	+172
CMC 775 - Production Changes	+132
CMC 811 - Gross Weight Increase	+ 40
Revised Weight Empty	71,228

NOTES: If this configuration is used alternately as a pax transport through the installation of CMC 739, add 550 pounds of non-removable facilities to Weight Empty shown above.

Add 120 pounds to manufacturer's weight empty for EA-6 engines.

Structural Limitations	Pounds
Max Take-off Weight	140,000
MaxLanding Weight	118,400*
Max Zero Fuel & Oil Weight	112,200*
Structural Oil Weight	1,200
Max Zero Fuel Weight	113,400*
Structural Payload Limit	38,043

Operating Requirements	Pounds
Revised Weight Empty	71,228
Operating Equipment	2,929
Crew & Crew Baggage (5)	975
System Fuel & Oil	1,113
Marine & Navigation Equipment	202
Winter Equipment	264

	Pounds
Miscellaneous Equipment	175
Cargo Tie-Down Equipment	200
Consumable Oil**	900
Operating Weight Empty, Incl Oil	75,057
Weight Limit Payload	36,593
Reserve Fuel (3 Hours)	6,650
Landing Weight with Reserves and 100 Pounds Ground Maneuver Fuel	118,400

*5% Overload Condition.
**Based on 40:1 volume ratio for fuel required, including reserves, at maximum range with full payload.

International Coach Interior

Manufacturers Weight Derivation		
Item		Pounds
Basic Spec. Weight Empty		71,056
+/- to Specification Weight		+3,616
CMC 775 - Production Changes		+ 132
CMC 811 - Gross Weight Increase		+ 40
CMC 739 - Passenger Facilities		+3,416
AMC 6238*- Hat Rack Sta. 338-392 L.H. Side		+ 28
Estimated Airline Equipment		+1,986
Pax Seating @ 24 lbs / Seat		+2,256
Galley Wht vs CMC 739 Allowance		-270
Revised Weight Empty		76,658

NOTES: 94 passenger seats provided for in weight table listed above.
Add 120 pounds to manufacturer's weight empty for EA-6 engines.
* Formerly referred to as AMC 8570.

Structural Limitations	Pounds
Max Take-off Weight	140,000
Max Landing Weight	113,000
Max Zero Fuel & Oil Weight	106,800
Structural Oil Weight	1,200
Max Zero Fuel Weight	108,000
Structural Payload Limit	24,371

Operating Requirements	Pounds
Revised Weight Empty	76,658
Operating Equipment	5,771
Crew & Crew Baggage (7)	1,285
System Fuel & Oil	1,113
Marine & Navigation Equipment	895
Winter Equipment	264
Miscellaneous Equipment	334
Pax & Galley Service @ 20 lbs	1,880
Consumable Oil*	1,100
Operating Weight Empty, Incl Oil	83,529
Weight Limit Payload	23,071
Passengers @ 165 Pounds	15,510
Baggage @ 44 lbs & 3.3 cu ft/Pax	4,136
Cargo	3,425
Reserve Fuel (3 Hours)	6,300
Landing Weight with Reserve & 100 Pounds Ground Maneuver Fuel	113,000

* Based on 40:1 volume ratio for fuel required, including reserves, at maximum range with full payload.

International Hi-Density Coach Interior

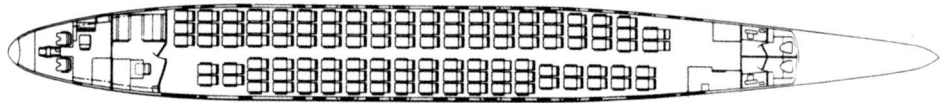

Manufacturers Weight Derivation		
Item		Pounds
Basic Spec. Weight Empty		71,056
+/- to Specification Weight		+5,588
CMC 775 - Production Changes		+132
CMC 811- Gross Weight Increase		+40
CMC 739 - Passenger Facilities		+3,416
Estimated Airline Equipment		+2,346
Pax Seating @ 24 lbs /Seat		+2,616
Galley Wht vs CMC 739 Allowance		-270
Revised Weight Empty		76,990

NOTES: 109 passenger seats provided for in weight table listed above.
Add 120 pounds to manufacturer's weight empty for EA-6 engines.

Structural Limitations	Pounds
Max Take-off Weight	140,000
Max Landing Weight	113,000
Max Zero Fuel & Oil Weight	106,800
Structural Oil Weight	1,200
Max Zero Fuel Weight	108,000
Structural Payload Limit	23,689

Operating Requirements	Pounds
Revised Weight Empty	76,990
Operating Equipment	6,121
Crew & Crew Baggage (7)	1,285
System Fuel & Oil	1,113
Marine & Navigation Equipment	945
Winter Equipment	264
Miscellaneous Equipment	334
Pax & Galley Service @ 20lbs	2,180
Consumable Oil*	1,100
Operating Weight Empty, Incl Oil	84,211
Weight Limit Payload	22,389
Pax @ 165 Pounds	17,985
Baggage** @ 40.4 Pounds/Pax	4,404
Reserve Fuel (3 Hours)	6,300
Landing Weight with Reserves & 100 Pounds Ground Maneuver Fuel	113,000

* Based on 40:1 volume ratio for fuel required, including reserves, at maximum range with full payload.
**Weight limited by 392 pounds from standard baggage allowance of 44 pounds per passenger.

1049H routes was an extension in May 1960 of the Los Angeles service to Tokyo via Honolulu and Wake Island, with an eye to the many immigrants of Japanese origin who had made their homes in Brazil. This was the first direct air service between Brazil and Japan, but it had to be suspended when, in May 1961, Varig purchased a majority holding in Aerovias Brazil, the international division of REAL, later acquiring a controlling interest in the whole REAL Aerovias Nacional airline group. The L-1049Hs then passed into Varig service and were finally withdrawn from use in the summer of 1966.

Another L-1049H customer to use the type in the passenger role was National Airlines of Miami, which ordered four in 1956. Fitted out to seat 109 passengers, and carrying weather radar and tip tanks, they were used on National's routes from the Eastern seaboard cities to Florida and also operated a New York-Miami all-freight service. They were finally retired early in 1962 and sold off late in 1964 to Nordair of Montreal, which used them to operate charters across the Atlantic and to Jamaica; an L-1049H was leased to Eastern Provincial Airways in 1969.

KLM also used its L-1049Hs, three of which it had ordered in 1957, for passenger services, with seating accommodation for 101, later diverting them to all-freight services. Two more L-1049Hs ordered by Trans-Canada Airlines were again used

This L-1049G, c/n 4617, was delivered to the Portuguese flag carrier TAP as CS-TLB in July 1955 and retired in mid-1967. It was sold to International Aerodyne and flown to Miami in September 1967 and registered as N4624 in April 1969. It was sold to Air Cargo Operations Inc in June 1969 and to Leasing Consultants the same month. The aircraft never flew again but was used instead for spares. It was disassembled in October 1969, transported to the Everglades and by September 1971 was placed atop a restaurant at the Oasis restaurant and gas station on the Tamiami Trail. The Oasis was owned by Mr. Earl Ball and four of his closest friends and it was Earl's idea to put the old airliner on top of the building. The restaurant closed and the building was later used as a garage with the aircraft remaining there until early February 1978 when the garage closed. The aircraft was taken about a mile away and cut up for scrap in February 1978. *(Authors Collection)*

mainly for passenger-carrying, and one, CF-TEZ, was involved in an overshoot accident and rebuilt in 1962 using parts of L-1049C-55, CF-TGC, after which it was sold to California Airmotive as N9640Z. The surviving 1049H was sold to Trans-International Airlines through Lockheed in May 1961. Pakistan International Airlines ordered two 1049Hs in mid-1957 to supplement its three L-1049Cs and used them both for all-freight and tourist-class flights on the 'inter-wing' services linking Karachi and Lahore in West Pakistan to Dacca in East Pakistan.

Transocean Airlines, one of the biggest US non-skeds' or supplemental carriers, took delivery of the first of its two L-1049Hs in the summer of 1957 on lease from the Air Finance Corporation, a company formed by Conrad and Barron Hilton of the Hilton Hotels Corporation and Joseph Drown, an independent hotel owner, 'to buy airliners and lease them to airlines preferring rental to an outright purchase commitment'.

Transocean used its L-1049Hs, fitted out to seat ninety-two passengers, on a once-weekly, low-fare trans-Pacific service from Oakland, California to Okinawa via Honolulu, Wake Island and Guam, which was largely patronised by personnel at the US military base on Okinawa. Later, a Transocean L-1049H was leased to Lufthansa for the latter's Frankfurt - New York all-freight service, and an order for four more was cancelled when Transocean went out of business in the summer of 1960. Another financing company in the airline field was the Standard Factors Corporation of New York, which ordered two L-1049Hs late in 1956 for lease to airlines, with an option to purchase.

The largest L-1049H operator was the Flying

Bal Trade's N6933C is prepared for another flight. *(authors collection)*

Eastern Air Lines' L-1049 N6201C. *(Author's Collection from 35mm transparency dated Mar 62.)*

Tiger Line, which ordered ten in September 1955, plus five later. Also, the company leased an L-1049A from TWA for a time in 1960, an ex-Resort Airlines L-1049H from World Airways in 1964, and two ex-KLM L-1049Hs from World in July 1963, which they eventually bought in April 1966. They also acquired an ex-QANTAS L-1049E/OI-55 which they sold to the charter operator, Atlantic Airways of Miami, in 1969, while the 1049A leased from TWA in 1960 later went to Paramount Airlines. Altogether Flying Tiger operated twenty-three Super Constellations bought outright or on lease, by far the largest fleet of these aircraft to be used for freighting.

Flying Tiger used its Constellations for scheduled all-freight services across the USA over a route linking Boston, Hartford/ Springfield and New York to Chicago, Los Angeles and San Francisco, also calling at Binghampton, Philadelphia, Cleveland, Detroit and Minneapolis/ St Paul, with connecting services from San Francisco to Portland and Seattle, this being known as US Airfreight Route No 100. In addition, a good deal of contract charter flying was done, the L-1049Hs flying for the MATS across the Pacific from San Francisco to Tokyo, Okinawa and Manila via Wake Island and Honolulu, and across the Atlantic carrying Jamaican emigrants to Britain, student groups, convention delegates and numerous other group charters. As many as 120 passengers have been carried at a time in an L-1049H flight, although a more typical interior seated 99-114 passengers for the trans-Pacific flights and 118 for transatlantic charters, the interiors were quickly convertible for freighting and featured General Electric galley equipment.

The EA-3 Turbo-Compounds that powered Flying Tiger's 1049Hs were converted to the EA-6 versions after delivery to give 150hp greater cruising power, and the original solid dural airscrews were replaced by Hamilton Standard hollow-bladed airscrews which saved six hundred pounds of weight on each aircraft. The EA-6 Turbo-Compounds enabled the maximum gross weight to be raised from the original 137,500 pounds to 140,000 pounds, the higher gross weight adding about 300 miles more range on US domestic flights by allowing 2,500 pounds more fuel to be carried, and payload to be increased from 37,000 pounds to 39,500 pounds on overwater flights such as San Francisco - Honolulu. The first L-1049H approved for the higher gross weight was delivered to Flying Tiger in the spring of 1957, and on 11 March an L-1049H carried a record commercial air freight load of 41,746 pounds of general cargo from Newark, New Jersey to Burbank.

An L-1049H was leased to Lufthansa in 1960, and two more to Trans-International Airlines on 14 November of that year by Lockheed, one being bought by TIA on 1 March 1964, but both were repurchased by Flying Tiger on 30 September 1966. L-1049H N69I9C was leased to Korean Airlines on 14 April 1966 as HL-4002, this operator having previously leased a L-749A from Transocean for the Seoul - Hong Kong route, which was discontinued in 1963. The L-1049H was used by Korean mainly for charter work and was returned to Flying Tiger on 4 December 1967.

Chapter 10

Constellation Swansong - the Starliner

By the early 1950s the continual process of stretching the basic Constellation and Super Constellation designs through a series of versions of increased fuselage length, payload and range had brought transport aircraft design within reach of a long-desired goal.

Already KLM had started operating Super Constellation flights non-stop eastbound from New York to Amsterdam from August 1953, thus offering for the first time a non-stop Atlantic crossing, although not in both directions. In 1954 both Douglas and Lockheed started the design of what were to be their final models in the piston-engined line, both specifically designed for non-stop all-the-year-round operation of the North Atlantic route in both directions, with sufficient fuel capacity to cope with the strongest westerly headwinds without loss of payload.

The designation Model 1349, not used for superstitious reasons, was a radical one, involving a completely new and redesigned wing of 150-foot span with integral fuel tankage for

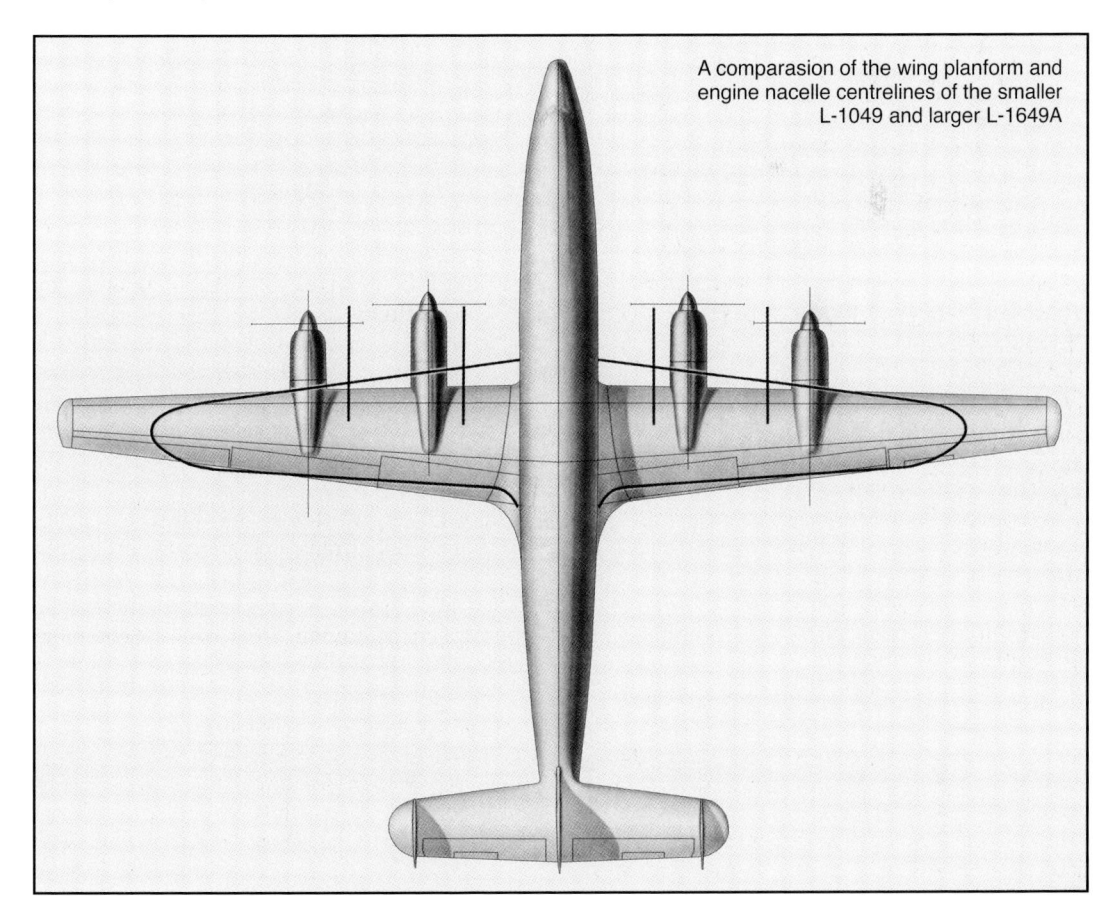

A comparasion of the wing planform and engine nacelle centrelines of the smaller L-1049 and larger L-1649A

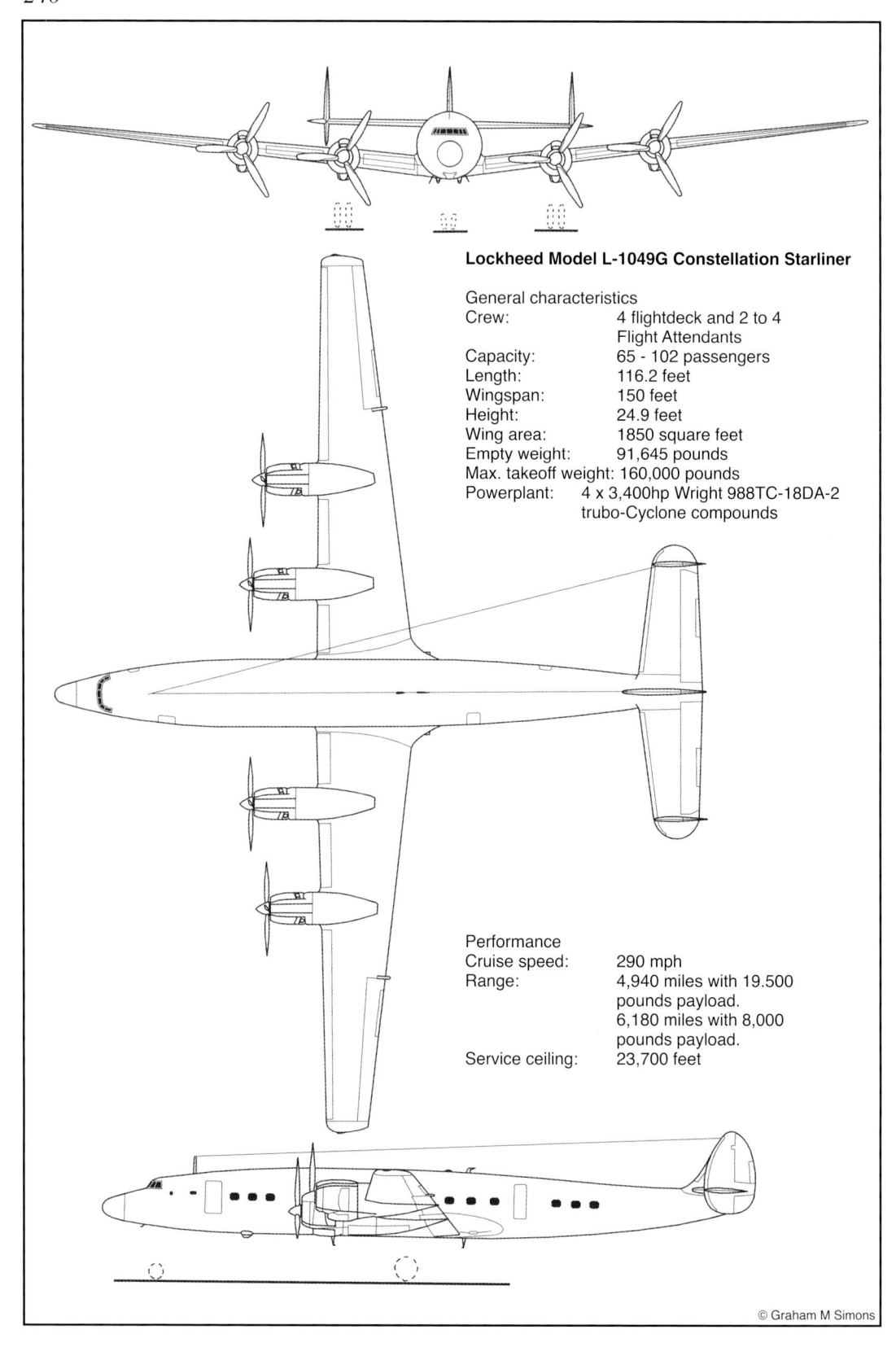

Lockheed Model L-1049G Constellation Starliner

General characteristics
Crew: 4 flightdeck and 2 to 4 Flight Attendants
Capacity: 65 - 102 passengers
Length: 116.2 feet
Wingspan: 150 feet
Height: 24.9 feet
Wing area: 1850 square feet
Empty weight: 91,645 pounds
Max. takeoff weight: 160,000 pounds
Powerplant: 4 x 3,400hp Wright 988TC-18DA-2 trubo-Cyclone compounds

Performance
Cruise speed: 290 mph
Range: 4,940 miles with 19.500 pounds payload.
6,180 miles with 8,000 pounds payload.
Service ceiling: 23,700 feet

© Graham M Simons

One of four Starliners purchased new by Lufthansa, D-ALER, delivered to the airline in Ianuary 1958, displays its lines during a service flight to New York. After five years with Trek Airways of South Africa, the aircraft was withdrawn from service in 1969 and after less than a year in storage, was broken up in May 1970. *(Lufthansa)*

9,600 US gallons, more than twice that of the L-049. Wing area was increased by 200 square feet to 1,850 square feet, the aspect ratio was 12.15 instead of the 9.7 of the earlier wing, and thickness/chord ratio was reduced to provide laminar flow as far as possible.

The complete redesign of the wing, coupled with the non-availability of its originally intended turboprop powerplant, meant that the L-1649A Starliner, as the production version was known, was later than the DC-7C by a year in entering North Atlantic service, and sales suffered.

The L-1449, the first new wing version, was intended to be powered by four Pratt & Whitney PT2F-I turboprops, the civil version of the T-34 tested in the R7V-2 and YC-121F. A number of turboprop powerplants were also considered, including the Rolls-Royce RB.109 - the Tyne - the Pratt & Whitney T-52, which never went into production, the Allison T-56 and the Bristol BE.25, later to be named Orion, a very promising new two-shaft engine of very low fuel consumption. The two British engines had not been test flown, and anyway US airlines would have preferred an American turboprop, while to have chosen the civil version of the Allison T-56, which also powered the Lockheed Electra turboprop on which design work began in 1955,

Lufthansa's Alpha November gets refuelled and checked over. *(Dee Diddely collection)*

would have potentiall affected sales of the Electra. So it was that development delays in producing a civil version of the Pratt & Whitney T-34 led to the abandonment of the L-I449 project early in 1955. The 1449's cruising speed was estimated at 432mph at 20,000 feet at a weight of 150,000 pounds, and the maximum still air range at 5,300 miles with a 16,460 pounds payload. Its maximum take-off weight would have been 177,000 pounds, more than twice that at which the Constellation prototype had made its first flight twenty-one years earlier. Maximum landing weight would have been 123,000 pounds, and the wing loading 94.3 pounds per square foot.

Although it remained a project, the 1449 accounted for a great deal of the design work on new features, particularly the new wing that later went into the L-1649A. The wing, with a significant exception, was to be constructed of sizeable integrally-stiffened skin panels up to thirty-seven feet long and measuring from 1¾ inches to ½ inches in thickness, the largest machined panels so far built for a transport aircraft. A single integrally-stiffened sheet skin ran from the root to the tip between the spars on both upper and lower surfaces, and between the spars, the whole wing comprised a vast torsion box used for fuel tankage as far as the outer engine nacelles.

There full-depth tank-end wing ribs form the

Not only did TWA's Skyliners roam the world, but so did their advertising!

The coast to coast sticker, supposedly for the company's internal transcontinental service was spotted, of all places, in a storeroom window of the Stoa Atalos Museum in the centre of Athens, Greece!

The Polar Route sticker was even further from home, being spotted in a travel agents window in Melbourne, Australia!

Above: One of TWA's 'Jetstreams' - or L-1549 Starliners - appears to be being readied for a MATS flight.

Right: a fashion statement' from the 1960s - a metalised paper dress, called the Alcoa Dazzler as worn by this model leaving a TWA Starliner.
(both author's collection)

ends of the four-tank fuel system, very closely spaced ribs being a characteristic of the wing structure. Each half-wing was continuous from the aircraft's centre-line to the tip, and on the Model 1649A the single skin panel between the spars was replaced by five twenty-four inch panels top and bottom at the wing root, adjacent sections being joined by double rows of rivets. The wing trailing edges and flaps were revised, the tailplane chord slightly increased to reduce the thickness/chord ratio to a point comparable with that of the wing, and the tailplane span increased. The wing leading edge sub-structure was arranged to hinge upwards as far as the outer engines to provide access to various interior services, and on the 1449 de-icing would have been by hot air bled from the turboprop compressors. The control surfaces were hydraulically boosted by a new model of Eclipse-Pioneer hydraulic booster similar to the units used on the company's C-130 Hercules.

With the new wing went main undercarriage legs of improved design and considerably more massive construction to cater for the higher gross weights and to allow their use as a speed brake at indicated airspeeds of up to 269 mph; the nose leg was also strengthened. The Model 1449 would have featured the standard Super Constellation fuselage lengthened by fifty-five inches to give a length, with weather radar fitted, of 120 feet 9 inches, and typical cabin interiors were a sixty-seat first-class layout with a four-seat lounge or seventy first-class on the US domestic routes or an eighty-nine seater all-tourist interior, the capacity payload being 20,000 pounds.

A month after the design of the L-1449 had begun, development started of the L-1549, very similar to it and likewise featuring the new wing and Pratt & Whitney PT2F-I turboprops. The fuselage, however, was to be 10 feet 9 inches longer than that of the Super Constellation without weather radar, giving an overall length of 124 feet 4 inches. The proposed maximum gross weight now went up to 187, 500 pounds, the Model 1549 being the heaviest Constellation variant projected, with the wing loading being slightly over 100 pounds per square foot.

Accommodation for sixty to seventy-five first-class passengers or up to ninety tourists would have been provided, although more could have been carried in a high-density layout making use of all the available extra fuselage length. A payload of about 18,000 pounds could have been carried over 4,000 miles at 410mph at 30,000 feet, but this was not considered a sufficient advance over the existing Super Constellation variants to have made the L-1549 a commercial proposition. This, together with delays in the development of the T-34/PT2F-I turboprop, led to its being abandoned along with the Model 1449 early in 1955.

ASA International Airlines, or Aerovias Sud Americana Inc, which operated scheduled freight services from Miami to Central and South America, and which had suspended operations in July 1965 when a bankruptcy petition was filed, was planning to resume operations in 1966 with three L-1649As converted into freighters and re-engined with turboprops, as well as three Boeing 727QC jets. But nothing came of these plans as ASA International was unable to restart operations, in spite of Airlift International acquiring a forty-two per cent financial stake in it.

Following the demise of the Models 1449 and 1549, work began in earnest in May 1955 on the L-1649, later designated L-1649A, and known at first as the Super Constellation, then renamed Super Star Constellation and later, from March 1957, the Starliner. The earlier name had been dropped because it was thought to be too long, though TWA called its 1649As Jetstream Starliners to capitalise on the publicity appeal of the word 'jet', if only obliquely. The L-1649A was claimed by Lockheed to have the greatest range of any airliner and to be able to fly from Paris to New York in nearly three hours less time than the DC-7C when carrying the same payload. It was also claimed to be 70mph faster than any other piston-engined airliner at ranges of over 4,200 miles, and capable of bringing every European capital within non-stop reach of New York. In place of the PT2F-I turboprops intended for the 1449 and I 549, the I649A reverted to Turbo-Compounds, being powered by four 3,400bhp R-3350-988TCI8 EA-2 engines mounted 5 feet 2½ inches further outboard from the cabin than previous models. Cabin noise was further reduced by choice of an airscrew reduction gear ratio of 0.355 instead of 0.4375 and larger diameter - 16 feet 10 inches instead of 115 feet 2 inches - low tip-speed Hamilton Standard airscrews.

Two types of Hamilton Standard airscrew were offered for the 1649A, the Model 43H60/HA17A3-4 with hollow dural blades and the Model 43H60/6993-B4 with solid dural blades, the former giving a weight saving of 680lb per aircraft but costing nearly twice as much as the other version. Initially, TWA chose the hollow-blade model but soon replaced them by the solid-blade version after running into problems with the nylon foam core material of the hollow blades.

No, you're not seeing things - 24 March 2019 and a restored Starliner, N8083H is 'parked up' in Times Square NYC on it's way to JFK Airport to be transformed into a cocktail lounge at the newly refurbished TWA Flight Center hotel. *(author's collection)*

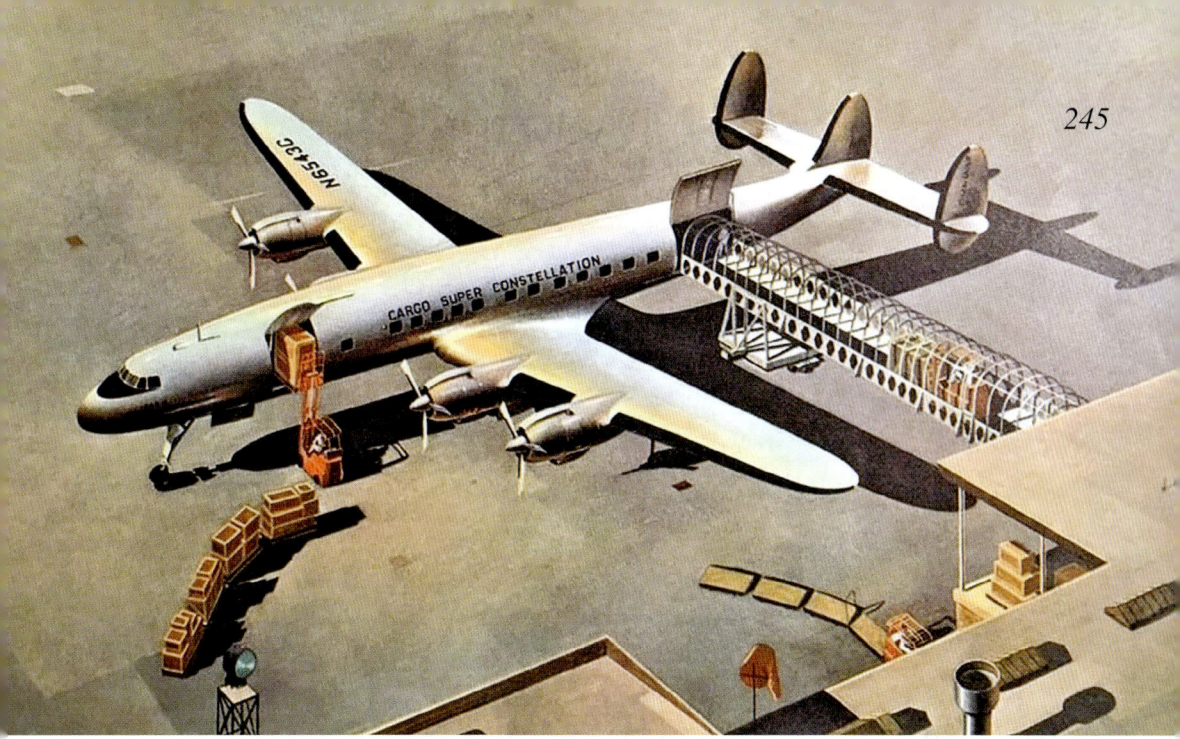

True, this is not a Starliner, but it is from the same timeframe when Lockheed were considering the use of Air Bridges as a more direct way of loading freight with forklift trucks. *(Lockheed)*

Air France chose Curtiss Electric airscrews for its L-1949A fleet. Cabin soundproofing was further improved by the addition of 900 pounds of insulating material and this, together with the synchrophasing of the airscrews, helped to achieve a cabin that was even quieter than that of the Model 1049G.

With its design emphasis on the range rather than the payload, the 1649A could carry fifty-eight to sixty-four passengers in a four-abreast first-class layout or thirty-two in a deluxe interior or up to ninety-nine coach-class, a typical mixed interior seating twenty-six first-class plus forty-five tourist passengers. A payload of 17,000 pounds could be carried over a still-air range of 5,300 miles at a cruising speed of about 350mph.

Unlike the Models 1449 and 1549, the 1649A featured no fuselage stretch, the length with weather radar installed being 116 feet 2 inches. The total fuel capacity was 9,600 US gallons.

There were two fully independent hydraulic systems, each operating at 3,000 pounds per square inch, and for the control surfaces Eclipse-Pioneer hydraulic control boosters similar to those on the C-130 Hercules. Stronger main undercarriage legs as schemed for the Model 1449 were incorporated, and Goodyear Tri-Metallic disc brakes could be fitted. The 1649A's maximum gross weight of 156,000 pounds was less than that of the 1449 or 1549 projects, and the maximum landing weight was 123,000 pounds, the space-limited payload being 17,130 pounds on US domestic routes or 16,428 pounds on international routes. The zero fuel weight was 116,000 pounds, and maximum gross weight was later increased to 160,000 pounds.

The flight deck was laid out for two pilots, a radio officer to port facing aft and a flight engineer to starboard, with a navigator's position to port further aft, separated from the rest of the crew by a bulkhead. Opposite the navigator was a crew rest area with a settee or two rest bunks, and the basic crew arrangement was not very different from that of the L-049.

The 1649A prototype, appropriately registered N1649, was rolled out on 19 September 1956 and made its first flight on 11 October from Burbank, California. The flight was of fifty minutes' duration, and Roy Wimmer piloted the aircraft with Herman R.' Fish' Salmon as co-pilot. The second aircraft - the first for TWA - was used in the eighty-six-hour flight-test programme before test flying for CAA certification got underway, and the cabins of both aircraft were full of test instrumentation. A third aircraft was used as a static test airframe. The prototype made 130 flights totalling 165 hours over a period of fifty-one days to qualify for its CAA certificate, and early flights revealed a hydraulic problem, causing sub-standard brake operation, which was put right by the redesign of a pump.

Air France called their L-1649s 'SuperStarliners' and provided an incredible service to all on board. Here F-BJBK is seeing flying along the Californian coastline on a pre-delivery test flight.

AIR FRANCE

The first deliveries to TWA, which had ordered twenty-five, were made in April 1957 and the airline had ten by 14 June. The next major customer, Air France, whose original order for twelve had been reduced to ten, took delivery of its first 1649A on 9 July 1957, this aircraft flying non-stop from Los Angeles to Paris in the record-breaking time of 17 hour 11 minutes for the 5,800-mile journey. Air France's 1649As were fitted with RCA AVQ-10 weather radar and company-designed tourist seats.

Air France called its 1649As SuperStarliners, and equipped the airliners with three-class interiors; thirty-four tourist seats, twelve first-class Sky-lounge sleeper seats and eight Pullman-style sleeping-berths, which could be converted to forty-four Sky-lounge seats and six berths for the new trans-Polar route from Paris to Tokyo via Anchorage, Alaska which the airline inaugurated on 10 April 1958.

In March 1956 two other European carriers, Deutsche Lufthansa and Linee Aeree Italiane (LAI) of Italy each ordered four L-1649As; LAI's were to have been named *Roman*, *Ambrosian*, *Vesuvian* and *Sicilian* and to have operated what would have been the world's longest non-stop airline service from Rome to New York, a distance of 4,280 miles, taking twelve hours eastbound and fifteen hours thirty minutes for the westbound crossing. LAI was due to receive its first 1649A in October 1957 and had specified Hamilton Standard airscrews with solid Dural blades. At this time there were still two separate Italian airlines for the major international routes, LAI, in which TWA had a forty per cent interest - which may have influenced its choice of the 1649A - and which operated a European network

AIR FRANCE

presents the finest of all long-distance aircraft: the *SuperStarliner* Lockheed 164

and to the Middle East and the important Rome - New York route, and Alitalia, in which BEA had a thirty per cent interest, operating European routes and to South America, East Africa and South Africa. But it was becoming increasingly clear that Italy's air transport interests were not best served by two separate airlines and with the prospect of having to finance the purchase of jets in a few years time a merger became logical. This came about when LAI was formally liquidated in August 1957 and the new airline, Alitalia-LAI, was incorporated on 1 September and took over LAI's operations on 6 October. Alitalia had ordered DC-7Cs before the merger, and so the LAI 1649As were added to TWA's fleet. TWA surrendered its financial interest in the airline, and BEA eventually sold its interest in Alitalia in April 1961.

Lufthansa's first 1649A landed at Hamburg on 3 October 1957 after flying 7,000 miles non-stop from Burbank in 17 hours 19 minutes - a dramatic illustration of the extra range conferred by the new wing. Lufthansa put its 1649As, which it called Super Star Constellations, on to

From Air France's stunning publicity brochure for the SuperStarliner comes these images

248

the USA and Canada routes, and also on services to South America and the Near and Middle East. The transatlantic services at first featured a three-class deluxe, first and tourist interior followed later by a deluxe 32-seat interior with which Lufthansa introduced their twice-weekly 'The Senator' prestige service to the USA.

After they were displaced as first-line equipment by the 707s introduced in 1960, two of the Lufthansa I649As, D-ALAN and D-ALUB, were converted into freighters from April

Air France's SuperStarliner brochure provides this double page spread...that not only shows the layout but also the level of service provided.

The *SuperStarliner* sets NEW STANDARD

In addition to its distinctive décor, the interior of Super Starliner features traditional AIR FRA aids to passenger comfort and convenience.

Every possible facility has been provided to make l distance flying a pleasurable experience. On a f lasting several hours, comfort plays an important — and on the AIR FRANCE Super Starliner, no c has been overlooked to insure that passenger being is taken care of.

The sleeping compartments and sky-lounge c are designed for utmost relaxation. Prominent an other installations aboard are individually adjust

1960 by Lockheed Aircraft Services with the upward-opening freight doors fore and aft of the L-1049H and the latter's heavy-duty floor and cargo tie-down points. These were sold, in 1962, to the US supplemental World Airways. The other two 1649As were transferred to Lufthansa's charter subsidiary, Condor Flugdienst, which flew group charter and inclusive tour flights to points in Europe, North Africa and the Mediterranean.

In June 1956 Varig of Brazil ordered two L-649As for the Buenos Aires - New York route for delivery beginning in December 1957, but this order was later changed to a repeat one for three more L-1049Gs as Varig decided to standardise on this version. The 1649As were to have seated 33-45 first-class passengers in a special deluxe 'siesta' interior with eight berths in the rear compartment.

Meanwhile, TWA introduced Model 1649A services, known as 'The Jetstream', across the Atlantic on 1 July 1957. By the end of the month, these were linking New York to London and also Frankfurt, Paris and Rome. A seventy-four-passenger all-tourist interior was featured for the Atlantic services and a two-class interior accommodating thirty first-class and thirty-four tourist passengers for the US transcontinental routes, with a central first-class sleeping compartment with four upper and four lower berths. The 1649As operated the 'Non-Stop Ambassador' from New York to Los Angeles and San Francisco non-stop, as well as a Boston - Los Angeles flight from mid-August, and a Washington - San Francisco service. On 2 October 1957 TWA inaugurated an over-the-Pole 1649A service between Los Angeles and London via San Francisco, three weeks after Pan American had started the same route with DC-7Cs but three years before BOAC's 707s began flying over the Pole between London and Los Angeles. In March 1958 a TWA 1649A achieved the record time of 19 hours 5 minutes on a non-stop London-San Francisco flight with eighteen passengers and ten crew aboard, beating the previous best 1649A time of 23 hours 20 minutes set up the previous October. The cabin arrangement for the US transcontinental flights

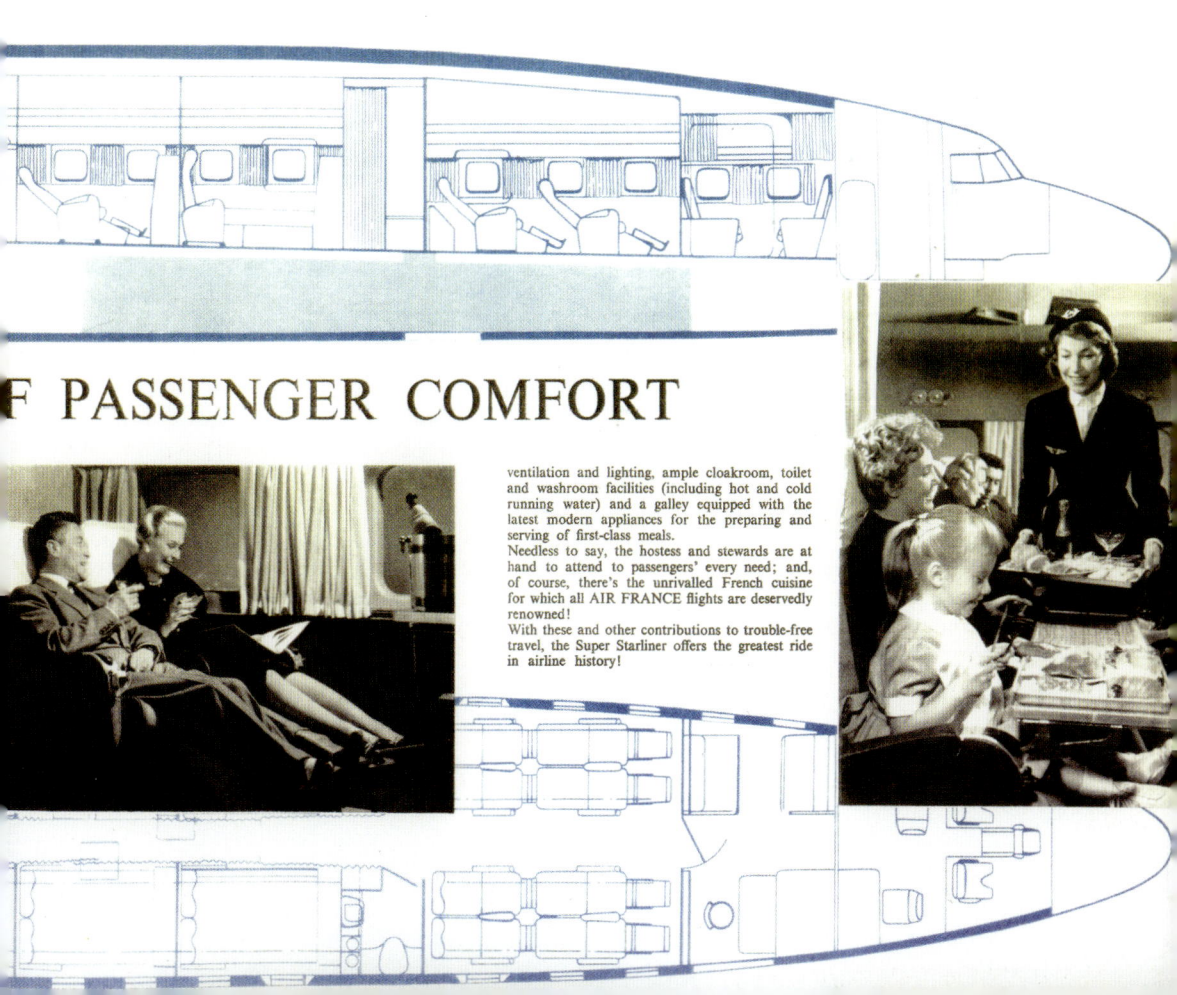

F PASSENGER COMFORT

ventilation and lighting, ample cloakroom, toilet and washroom facilities (including hot and cold running water) and a galley equipped with the latest modern appliances for the preparing and serving of first-class meals.
Needless to say, the hostess and stewards are at hand to attend to passengers' every need; and, of course, there's the unrivalled French cuisine for which all AIR FRANCE flights are deservedly renowned!
With these and other contributions to trouble-free travel, the Super Starliner offers the greatest ride in airline history!

On 28 September 1968 at 1613 local time, L-1649 Starliner N8081H of Willair International Airlines had a little bit of an 'incident'. The crew was completing a local training flight at Stockton Airport, California. Following several uneventful circuits, the crew initiated a new approach. On final, the crew failed to realize his altitude was too low when the right main gear struck a blast pad located 102 feet short of the runway threshold and was torn off. The airplane partially belly landed and slid for a dozen yards before coming to rest. While all eleven occupants escaped uninjured, the aircraft was damaged beyond repair. *(Bureau of Aircraft Accidents)*

was later changed to forty-four first-class and twenty coach-class seats and from 14 October 1957 TWA introduced a new deluxe facility on these flights by converting the first-class section to take thirty-two sleeper seats, a 'Starlight Lounge' being a feature of the US domestic flights.

The 1649A and 1049G transcontinental coach services were also known as 'Golden Banner' services, the name 'Sky Chief' was applied to first-class services on other Constellations, and 'Sky Club' was the name applied to the L-049 Constellation coach-class services, most of these aircraft now being operated with 81-passenger air coach interiors. In 1959, TWA's entire 1649A fleet was operated in an economy/coach-class configuration.

In 1960 six of the Jetstream Starliners were converted into freighters by Lockheed Aircraft Services, with a forward cargo door 4ft 8½in wide by six feet high and a rear door 8ft 10½-in wide by six high, both opening upwards and a strengthened freight floor, the transatlantic cargo payload now being 37,250 pounds. These started to replace the L-1049Hs on TWA's transcontinental and transatlantic freight services from August 1960, and in 1961 six more I649As were converted to freighters. With the introduction of Boeing 707s in 1959, TWA's 1649As were gradually displaced as first-line equipment, the last international service with the type, from Cairo to New York, being flown on 28 October 1961. The 1649A was withdrawn from the US domestic routes the following year, although the converted freighters continued transatlantic cargo flights until 1963 and US domestic services for four years after that. TWA's last flight with any of the Constellation series was made by L-1649A freighter N7315C on 11 May 1967 and its last passenger flight with the type - and last piston-engined flight with any type had been flown between New York and Kansas City on 6 April 1967 by L-749A N6024C *Star of Nebraska*. The year 1959 had seen the peak of TWA's Constellation operations, with a total fleet of no less than 147 in service, made up of thirty-two L-049s, twelve L-749s, twenty-seven L-749As, nine L-1049As, twenty-eight L-1049Gs, nine L-1049Hs and twenty-nine L-1649As. An estimated 50 million passengers were flown in TWA Constellations between 1946 and 1967. In the end, only forty-three L-1649As were built plus the prototype, and despite its ability to operate very long stages such as London- San Francisco non-stop this new wing variant was heavily outsold by the DC-7C.

Chapter Eleven

Genocide that was Biafra

In 1960, Nigeria became independent of the United Kingdom. As with many other new African states, the borders of the country did not reflect earlier ethnic, cultural, religious, or political boundaries. Thus, the northern region of the country had a Muslim majority, being mostly made up of territory of the indigenous Sokoto Caliphate. The southern population was predominantly Christian, being primarily made up of the indigenous Yoruba and Biafra kingdoms in the West and East respectively. Following independence, Nigeria was mostly demarcated along ethnic lines: Hausa and Fulani majority in the north, Yoruba majority in the West and Igbo majority in the East.

Ethnic tension had simmered in Nigeria during discussions of independence, but in the mid-twentieth century, ethnic and religious riots began to occur. In 1945 an ethnic uprising flared up in Jos in which Hausa-Fulani people targeted Igbo people and left many dead and wounded.

Three hundred Igbo people died in the Jos riot. In 1953 a similar riot occurred in Kano. A decade later, in 1964, a political crisis divided the Western Region as Ladoke Akintola clashed with Obafemi Awolowo. Widespread reports of fraud tarnished the election's legitimacy. Western Nigerians especially resented the political domination of the Northern People's Congress, many of whose candidates ran unopposed in the election. Violence spread throughout the country. The domination of the political system by the north, and the chaos breaking out across the country, motivated elements within the military to consider decisive action. The federal government, dominated by Northern Nigeria, allowed the crisis to unfold to declare a state of emergency and place the Western Region under martial law. This Nigerian federal government was widely perceived as corrupt.

In January 1966, the situation reached a breaking point. A military coup occurred during which a mixed but predominantly Igbo group of army officers assassinated thirty political leaders including Nigeria's Prime Minister, Sir Abubakar Tafawa Balewa, and the Northern premier, Sir Ahmadu Bello. The four most senior officers of Northern origin were also killed. Nnamdi Azikiwe, the President, of Igbo extraction, and the favoured Western Region politician Obafemi Awolowo were spared. The commander of the army, General Aguiyi Ironsi, seized power to maintain order. Between twenty and thirty thousand civilians were slaughtered in the tribal and religious genocide.

In July 1966 northern officers and army units staged a counter-coup. Muslim officers named a General from the Angas, an ethnic group in central Nigeria, General Yakubu 'Jack' Gowon, as the head of the Federal Military Government (FMG). The two coups deepened Nigeria's ethnic tensions. In September 1966, approximately 30,000 Igbo were executed in the north, and some Northerners were killed in backlashes in eastern cities.

When, in May 1967, the breakaway state of Biafra under Colonel Chukwuemeka 'Emeka' Odumegwu-Ojukwu seceded from the rest of Nigeria, the country was plunged into civil war, and soon Biafra was in urgent need of food, arms and medical supplies. The word Biafra, by the way, comes from two Igbo words, 'bia' which means 'come' and 'fara' which means 'live'.

The background and origins to this particularly bitter conflict is nothing but a microcosm of a myriad of other 'local wars' that were going on around the world that often involved the use of the Sky Tramps and the Lockheed Constellation.

In January 1967, the Nigerian military leadership went to Aburi, Ghana, for a peace conference hosted by General Joseph Ankrah.

The eastern region of Nigeria was the leading oil-producing area with, at the time, the only oil refinery being in Port Harcourt. The implementation of the agreements reached Aburi fell apart upon the leaderships return to Nigeria. On 30 May 1967, as a result of this, Lieutenant Colonel Odumegwu Ojukwu, the governor of Nigeria's eastern region, declared Eastern Nigeria a sovereign state to be known as Biafra following a unanimous vote by 300 elders of the Ibo people who inhabited the area: 'Having mandated me to proclaim on your behalf, and in your name, that Eastern Nigeria be a sovereign independent Republic, now, therefore I, Lieutenant Colonel Chukwuemeka Odumegwu-Ojukwu, Military Governor of Eastern Nigeria, by the authority, and pursuant to the principles recited above, do hereby solemnly proclaim that the territory and region known as and called Eastern Nigeria together with her continental shelf and territorial waters, shall, henceforth, be an independent sovereign state of the name and title of The Republic of Biafra.'

The federal military government in Lagos led by General Yakubu Gowon retaliated on 6 July by launching land and air attack to crush the rebels and their secessionist dreams. 'The Commander-in-Chief of the Armed Forces of Nigeria has issued orders to the Armed Forces to penetrate the East Central State and capture Ojukwu and his rebel gang,' Radio Lagos reported. Sandhurst-trained Gowon predicted it would be 'a short, surgical police action' that would be completed in a few days. What followed, however, was a genocidal tragedy of horrendous proportions. By the time Biafra was extinguished on 14 January 1970 more than two million Ibos, mainly old men, women and children, had been killed.

From the outset, Nigeria's civil war was presented in simplicities. The Lagos military regime, Prime Minister Harold Wilson's Labour government and Washington all sang from the same hymn-sheet, prepared by the British Foreign Office: Nigeria was a unitary state and its 'Balkanisation' - a favourite description from the lexicon of British Foreign Office demonology - would threaten its future prosperity and encourage secessionist tendencies all over Africa, if not the globe, causing economic mayhem, regional instability and bloody fratricidal warfare. When that started to wear thin, they switched to Cold War rhetoric: the Russians are coming, and we must stop them from gaining a toehold in Nigeria. Of course, Biafra's untapped oil riches were rarely mentioned.

The Biafran lobby was equally sure of the righteousness of its cause: the predominantly Catholic Christian Ibos had suffered pogroms, persecution and discrimination at the hands of the Muslim Hausa-Fulani people from the north and the Yorubas in the west of the country. Following two coups in 1966 - in January and July- the circumstances of the Ibo population became dire: after 50,000 Ibos were butchered in neighbouring states with the connivance of army commanders and police, two million fled home to become refugees in their province. For the Ibos, secession wasn't a diplomatic dance - it was a desperate bid for survival.

The Nigerian naval blockade of Biafra's seaports, which forcefully denied all imports of vital Norwegian stockfish, and the fact that the Federal Army had advanced and captured the cattle-rearing areas of north-east Biafra had a far-reaching effect upon the Biafran civilian population. Stockfish is unsalted fish, especially cod, dried by cold air and wind on wooden racks. The drying of food is the world's oldest known preservation method, and dried fish has a storage life of several years. Cod was the most common fish used in stockfish production, while other whitefish, such as pollock, haddock, ling and cusk, were used to a lesser degree. Stockfish was a major source of protein for the region.

As early as Autumn 1967 there was a realisation within Biafra that the suffering among the population would become a major issue. Three leading relief agencies - the World Council of Churches, CARITAS Internationalis, and the International Red Cross - began to warn that 'a protein deficiency in Biafra was rapidly becoming a serious problem'. The two Church organisations pressured the International Committee of the Red Cross (ICRC) to take action.

By early 1968 reports emerging from inside Biafra spoke of a disturbing situation. They noted a huge rise in civilian deaths due to starvation. These reports originated from relief organisation representatives including several from the International Red Cross man in Biafra, a Swiss businessman named Henrich Jaggi that highlighted a widespread protein deficiency that had already resulted in outbreaks of two associated diseases, Marasmus - undernourishment causing a child's weight to be significantly low for their age - and Kwashiorkor, a form of severe protein malnutrition characterised by oedema and an enlarged liver with fatty infiltrates. Jaggi suggested to Geneva that they launch an international appeal for medicine, food and clothing.

A similar call for aid had also gone out from a group of Catholic and Protestant missionaries. A number had been forced to abandon their missions in the face of the Federal Army advance but decided to remain with the refugees. It was those same missionaries who created a focal point at the Queen Elizabeth Hospital at Umuahia. From that group of missionaries developed a close working relationship between the various religious groups as well as with the International Red Cross.

Initially, the Umuahia group concentrated on

hiring medical staff for hospitals within Biafra and under the control of foreign medical missions. Later, when the amount of aid increased, the group concentrated on organising the flow of relief aid inside Biafra. Under the leadership of three missionary doctors, the World Council of Churches Refugee Relief Operation in Biafra developed and became the effort between the Christian Council of Biafra and the World Council of Churches in Geneva.

Concern for the situation in Nigeria had first been highlighted by the Catholic Church in December 1967 when two Monsignors, George Rocheau and Dominic Conway were asked by the Vatican to undertake, on its behalf, a peace mission to Lagos and Kaduna. The mission also visited the Biafran town of Onitsha but faced difficulty in obtaining diplomatic clearance to travel on either side, especially within Biafra. The two Monsignors visited Lagos for an audience with General Gowon who offered freedom to travel only in areas that the government of Federal Nigeria could guarantee their safety. The authority to travel was aimed at denying the Vatican's representatives access to Biafra. The Bishops of Onitsha, as well as the Biafran people, were angered at what appeared to be a snub, and as a consequence, they appointed Father Anthony 'Tony' Byrne (the Director of Catholic Social Services in Biafra) to travel to Rome and help resolve the overall situation. After several weeks in Rome, Father Byrne succeeded in convincing the Vatican to authorise a visit by the same two Monsignors to Biafra.

It was as if someone had 'poured a welter of outsiders on to the genocide by trying to help, or just help themselves: politicians, journalists, cameramen, philanthropists, doctors, pilots and pundits; along with mercenaries, arms dealers, oilmen, conmen and call-girls. No author could have invented such a cast-list'.

At this point, we need to 'leap forward to go back' as it were and look at a remarkable article called *Werewolves,* surfaced in the January 1971 edition of *Gudok* (Whistle) a Russian newspaper. which began as a small newspaper focused on rail industry news, but grew into a 700,000-circulation daily with an edgy mix of commentary and satire on culture, politics, and society. Gudok's circulation was relatively small but deceptively influential when it first started out, which encouraged creativity and expression as the newspaper's focus on the railway industry shielded authors from some of the ideological hazards of writing for general-interest publications. Inside the article was an introduction to one of the key players in the whole Biarfran Airlift saga, an English translation of the piece was discovered in the CIA files at Langley, marked 'Cleared for Release Date 29 April 2009'

'Are there werewolves in the world? Do not hurry to answer. There are. A portrait of one of them was published in the American magazine *Time*. However, much you looked at him, though, you would not see anything special. "An ordinary man", you would say. To be sure, nothing remarkable. Average height. Middle age, 40 or so. Thin hair, smoothed down. Eyes concealed behind sunglasses. This is an unobtrusive man, one familiar with the nighttime sky over dozens of Asian and African countries. For many years he has specialised in contraband deliveries of arms to various hot spots of our planet. He fills a plane with machine guns and mortars, shells and cartridges, and he flies it to the appointed place under cover of nighttime darkness... But still, why a werewolf? Judge for yourself.'

'One April night in 1966 his airplane crashed over the Northern Cameroons. When the Cameroon police reached the scene of the crash, they did not find any identification signs on the aircraft. But in its fuselage, they found about 1,000 quite recent American automatic weapons. The hero of our tale and four other members of the crew, when driven into a corner, admitted that they had been carrying arms into Eastern Nigeria, whose leaders the previous year had kindled a bloody civil war in that country, proclaiming the so-called 'independent state of Biafra'. It was established that the soldiers of fortune caught red-handed had made dozens of such trips in that direction. It is easy to imagine the

Father Anthony 'Tony' Byrne, the Irish priest who went to Africa as a missionary, and ended up running an airline. *(Simon Peters Collection)*

amount of arms they had carried though!'

'Arms contraband is punished by the most severe penalties by the laws of any country. What sort of punishment did these cut-throats suffer? None! To be sure, a story was trumped up for the public. The press of many countries carried a report to the effect that the owner of the airplane and its chief pilot, as well as one member of the crew had received serious injuries in the crash and soon died in Cameroon hospital. Deadmen, as we know, are not called to account.'

'That would seem to be the whole story. But it had a curious sequel. Some time later the principal dead man happily came back to life and expanded arms contraband by air to truly unprecedented proportions. It is, finally, time to give his name. He is Henry Arthur Wharton, an American. He now has two nicknames: "Hank" and "the leading pirate of Biafra". The second nickname is very significant. Wharton's airplane traveled continuously over the so-called air bridge, which was built between Western Europe and Biafra. At that time Wharton had a very solid enterprise; an entire squadron of Super Constellation airplanes belonging to him was based in Lisbon. Every trip brought Wharton 25,000 dollars in net proceeds.'

'A cult of the criminal at large flourishes in the Western press. The main thing is that he be successful. Wharton was outstanding in this respect. After his "resurrection", it is true. He was caught red-handed several more times, but every time he got away scot-free! Nevertheless, in Liberia, he went behind bars, but he stayed there only a few weeks. On Malta he was arrested for contraband shipments of large lots of narcotics (enough narcotics to "give dreams" to many millions of people). And what happened? He got out of it "Someone's influential hand", *Time* notes, "again helped him".'

'Whose is this "influential hand?" Who is it that rescues Wharton and his colleagues every time?'

'The answer to this question is to be found in the history of Daniel Wolcott, "king of the contribandists", as he is called in the countries of notorious free enterprise. According to the newspapers, for four years Wolcott and his accomplices carried into India on his airplane contraband gold and precious stones worth a colossal sum - 150 million dollars. But he did not only carry gold, and India was not his only destination. Wolcott, like Wharton, for years, delivered arms to the most varied corners of the globe where the CIA was organizing plots and preparing coups d'etat. The very close connections between the king of the contrabandists and the CIA were discovered during Wolcott's trial in Lebanon in 1964. Material evidence confirmed that he was engaged in espionage in carrying .out aerial photography of Lebanese military installations on the assignment of American intelligence. But Wolcott was tried in Lebanon in absentia since he managed mysteriously to disappear. A year earlier he had been tried in Delhi for smuggling weapons. He was present at the trial. And what happened? Through the intervention of the American Embassy Wolcott was: temporarily released on bail not long before the trial, and he naturally took advantage of this. The Indian police managed to catch the king of the contrabandists only three years ago. He is now in prison. But it is not precluded that the CIA is trying to have him released; this agent-werewolf who has combined smuggling with subversion and espionage is very valuable to American intelligence.'

'Indeed, the facts demonstrate that espionage and subversion combined !beautifully with smuggling. Last May the American magazine *Ramparts* published an interesting article which in fact was entitled *"The CIA Is in the Opium Trade"*. How is it doing this? Very simple. The American airlines Air America and Continental Air Service, which are at the service of the CIA, regularly deliver weapons to the commando detachments in the interior of Laos. Here is a typical sketch by the correspondent of the Hong Kong magazine *Far Eastern Economic Review:* "Quiet reigns in Long Tieng, a small town located in an area occupied by the rebels belonging to the Meo tribe. The silence is unexpectedly broken by the noise of motors. When the aircraft lands we read on its silver fuselage the words: Air America. It has brought weapons. The Market in Long Tieng is saturated with opium, which is sold at 50 American dollars per kilogramme'. Arms are delivered here, and the airplanes fly out loaded down with 100-kilogram slabs of opium. Regular American spies, but on the side they are smugglers and organize the production of heroin from opium. They have organized the most up-to-date industrial production of heroin on a high technical level. On one of the islands in the Mekong River, *Rambarts* writes, CIA officials have set up a secret heroin factory. A kilogram of heroin, which costs at least 100,000 dollars on the black market, is obtained from 25 kilograms of opium there. American spies and diversionists are engaged in a very profitable business on the side which is causing envy among American diplomats.'

The blood of many thousands of people is on the

255

Lisbon - Bissau = 2200 miles
Bissau - Ferndando Poo = 1900 miles
Abidjan - Fernando Poo = 875 miles

The general area, with details of the islands and landing strips used in the Biafran Airlift.

hands and conscience of these death merchants. Dollars are flowing into the bottomless pockets of international adventurers, who are highly esteemed by the imperialist intelligence services!

The piece, although from the 'other side' of the Iron Curtain is remarkably accurate, although there are a number of errors and some further explanation is needed.

Long Tieng - also spelt Long Chieng, Long Cheng, or Long Chen - is a Laotian military base located in Xaisomboun Province. During the Laotian Civil War, it served as a town and airbase operated by the CIA. During this time, it was also referred to as Lima Site 98 (LS98) or Lima Site 20A (LS20A).

At the height of its significance in the late 1960s, the secret city of Long Tieng maintained a population of 40,000 inhabitants, making it the second-largest city in Laos at the time, although it never appeared on maps throughout this period. In 1962 the CIA first set up a headquarters for Major General Vang Pao in the Long Tieng valley, which at that time had almost no inhabitants. By 1964 a 4133 feet long runway had been completed and by 1966 Long Cheng was one of the largest US installations on foreign soil, becoming one of the busiest airports in the world.

The article introduces the reader to several people, not least Hank Warton, and gives the impression that the air crash it describes involved a Lockheed Constellation - it did not. Indeed, there was an air crash in Northern Cameroon on 11 October 1966, and Hank Warton was indeed the Captain on board. But it was a Canadair DC-4M that had originally been registered as CF-TFM, not a Lockheed Constellation. At the time of the crash, the aircraft was carrying the false registration I-ACOA and had twenty-four cases of Lancaster sub-machine guns, thirteen cases of magazines for the guns and four cases of clips of bullets on board. It was thought to be Warton's first intended visit to Biafra. It was true, however, that Wharton operated a fleet of Constellations. These aircraft were based at Lisbon, Portugal.

Warton was a fascinating character. Trying to piece together his story is like trying to grab hold of fog. As far as I can tell, Henry Arthur 'Hank' Warton - occasionally spelt Wharton - which was the way he did not like his last name spelt - was born in Gratz, Germany as Heinrich Wartski in 1916. He immigrated to the United States in 1937, joined the US Army in 1941, and became an American citizen. He fought in the Pacific theatre and worked in military intelligence. He was fluent in German and

Henry 'Hank' Warton in front of one of the Lockheed Constellations used in the Biafran Airlift.

Spanish. In 1947 he earned a commercial pilot's licence. Beginning in the late 1940s Warton flew for numerous non-mainline airlines throughout Europe and to developing areas of the world, including Israel and India.

At the end of January 1968, church officials succeeded in reaching Biafra, travelling to Port Harcourt, via Lisbon, aboard one of Warton's Constellations. When they returned to the Vatican and submitted their report to the Pope, the response was immediate. Pope Paul IV commissioned Monsignor Jean Rodhain and Monsignor Carlo Bayer, respectively the President and Secretary-General of CARITAS International, to establish a relief programme for both sides of the conflict. In turn, Father Anthony Byrne was appointed as Director of the CARITAS operation in Biafra, the CARITAS operation on the Nigerian side being co-ordinated by a Lagos-based Director of Operations. The moral obligation of helping to feed hungry people proved to be far greater than the political necessity of maintaining a good relationship with the Federal government.

CARITAS Internationalis, the Catholic agency for international aid, had been formed in 1951 to supply humanitarian aid to areas of acute starvation. In setting up its Biafra operation, Father Byrne first flew to the Portuguese island of São Tomé and Principe to explore the possibility of establishing a relief base there. In geographical terms, the island was not ideal, but it was politically secure and diplomatically independent of Federal Nigeria. The Spanish island of Fernando Póo was better situated geographically but the sympathetic attitude shown by the Portuguese towards the Biafran cause outweighed the disadvantage of distance. Fernando Póo was also due to gain its independence from Spain; a political uncertainty within colonial Africa.

The Catholic Agency launched its Biafra operation in March 1968. Sixty tonnes of relief material was immediately shipped from Lisbon to São Tomé, the priority being protein-rich food and medicine. The first CARITAS relief flight from São Tomé to Port Harcourt took place during the night of 26/27 March 1968.

The only route from São Tomé to Biafra open to CARITAS was to make use of Hank Warton's irregular arms airlift to Port Harcourt. Father Byrne had therefore met Warton at the Tivoli Hotel, Lisbon and successfully negotiated a deal involving blocks of six charter flights at the cost of $3,800 per flight. Warton also agreed to undertake one free flight for every six 'paid-for' flights.' The Catholic Church airlift had got underway but after Warton had completed just twenty-four flights under this the arrangement, the cost factor caused CARITAS considerable anxiety over the future of its relief programme.

Although Father Tony Byrne was effectively in charge of the São Tomé airlift, much of the groundwork was carried out by another Irish priest, Father Billy Butler. He had been the CARITAS representative at Port Harcourt until its capture by the Nigerian Army in May 1968. On São Tomé Butler was in charge of loading relief supplies onto the aircraft.

With the Biafran death toll climbing at the inexorable rate of over a thousand a day, along with Ibo resistance reduced to an enclave of death, disease and starvation, it is not surprising that 'this nasty little war' was getting reported in the press - and more war correspondents from around the world were screaming for access,. Only a small group of reporters were selected by Markpress, a shadowy public relations agency operating from Route de Chêne 136, Geneva and retained by the Biafran authorities to spread their desperate message to the world's media.

Markpress - whose American CEO was a booted and suited Madison Avenue Advertising Executive called H William Bernhardt, covered the costs of the war correspondents' travel and accommodation. Markpress skillfully 'sold the case' for Biafra. The press were flown out to Lisbon, where their contact was the local office of CARITAS, and wait for further instructions about a flight to Biafra.

Portugal's dictator, Antonio de Oliveira Salazar, who had been in charge since 1932, was a clerical fascist whose Estado Nova - 'New State' in English - regime ruled according to the social and economic principles of various Papal encyclicals and with the iron fist of his all-pervasive secret police, the Policia Internacional e Defesa do Estade. Often the stay in Lisbon was longer than expected. Flights were delayed because the Biafrans were having difficulty paying cash upfront for the charter.

Eventually, the Biafran cash came through, and the war correspondents were told to check out of the hotel and to meet a contact at the international air terminal. It was way past midnight, and the terminal was deserted before they were called to board the aircraft by a couple of surly airport

Hank Warton checks the security of a cargo inside one of his Constellations used in the Biafran Airlift. *(Simon Peters Collection)*

The suave H William Bernhardt - standing behind the teleprinter - directs his team of journalists as how to spread the word about the Biafran war from Geneva. *(Simon Peters Collection)*

officials. A minibus took the small group to the far end of the airstrip, where an unmarked Super Constellation was standing in the semi-dark.

The war correspondents could not believe what they were about to travel in. It was even worse when they boarded. The interior of the aircraft had been stripped and the rows of passenger seats removed. Into the empty fuselage had been packed dozens of timber boxes of arms and ammunition. The clapped-out aircraft, straining under the weight of its cargo and shaking from nose to tail, rose over the city and headed south on its 4000-kilometre journey.

The constant whine of the engines plus the shaking and shuddering of the fuselage made it impossible to sleep. Ten hours later they landed on São Tomé where they refuelled, ate sandwiches and drank some beer. Warton was sparing with information. He wouldn't tell the war correspondents when they were leaving or even where they were going in Biafra. But after he made radio contact with his associates, everyone piled back into the airliner and flew to Fernando Póo, a Spanish island about twenty kilometres off the coast of Biafra. Late that night they were roused from the tin shed which doubled as a passenger terminal to set off on the flight to Ojukwu's stronghold.

The war correspondents questioned Warton as to why they were travelling at night. He wearily replied 'Don't you know the Nigerian army has artillery? They've already brought down a dozen relief planes. We're going in under cover of darkness, and we'll be flying low - about 2000 feet.' It wasn't a comforting message.

They sat in complete darkness peering out of the porthole windows into more darkness. They had been flying for just over an hour when the airliner began to slow and lose altitude. 'Assume a landing position,' Warton said over the intercom. 'Put your hands on your knees and bend forward, placing your head between your legs.' The seconds ticked by. The black void swallowed the airliner as the flight crew lowered the undercarriage. Suddenly the ground below was alive with fairy lights: dozens of hand-held torches formed an avenue on either side of a runway - more like a football field - carved out of the jungle. Warton placed the Constellation on the ground with barely a bounce.

As the cabin lights came on after the airliner stopped, one war correspondent asked one of the young men who emerged from the darkness outside to begin unloading the boxes of ammunition where they were. 'Uli,' was the reply.

The war correspondents were escorted to a makeshift building to be processed, bizarrely, by customs and immigration. All passports received the official stamp: 'Immigration Enugu Airports, Biafra - Visiting Pass Holder of this passport is permitted to enter and remain in Biafra from 22-7-68 until 20-8-68'. It was signed with a flourishing but illegible signature by the state's Chief Immigration Officer. It was a friendly but surreal welcome to the Biafran tragedy.

The Secret Airstrips
Biafra's two main airfields were at Enugu and Port Harcourt; both had tarmac runways and full air traffic communications. Three other landing-grounds existed at Calabar, Owerri and at Ogoja, all of which featured hard clay runways but little in the way of facilities. The loss of Enugu, the Biafran capital, on 4 October 1967 was seen to signal the imminent collapse of Biafran forces.

Two weeks later Calabar was lost to a successful seaborne assault by the Nigerians on 18 October. Port Harcourt survived for a further seven months, but its recapture by Nigerian forces in May 1968 came as a significant blow.

It was the loss of Enugu which prompted the concept of establishing a series of secret airstrips in the Biafran bush, and a team of Biafran engineers began to select possible sites. The easiest option was to produce a traditional bush landing-strip capable of accepting aircraft the size of a C-47 Dakota was by converting stretches of road where they ran suitably straight for a sufficient distance. Development of three sites began at the end of 1967: at Uli, Uga and Awgu.

Awgu was abandoned due to the threat from Nigerian forces advancing from the north during the spring of 1968. At that point effort concentrated upon the second site, codenamed 'Annabelle', just to the south of the village at Uli.

By far the largest of the three projected airstrips, properly known as Uli-Ihiala, became synonymous with the entire Biafran effort to survive. The runway was converted from a stretch of the main Owerri to Ihiala road, consisting of a six thousand feet by seventy-two feet tarmac runway - with the headings 16/34 - achieved by widening the road from its original fifty-nine feet to make it sufficient for operation by Douglas C-47s. After strengthening, the 'runway' could bear a load of seventy-three tons or 167,520 pounds. The taxi-strips were only fifty-two and a half feet wide; tight for an aircraft the size of a Constellation.

With virtually no navaids and in a part of the world notorious for its hostile weather, particularly electrical storms in the heavy rains season, landing a big aeroplane like a Constellation on such a narrow and primitive airstrip was dangerous. The Super Constellations had a mere twenty feet of clearance on either side of the landing gear when using Uli! It was extremely hazardous at the best of times, and even more so under the constant threat of enemy action. It was, as one airlift pilot put it, 'a nice wide road, but a damned narrow runway'.

Initially, although more were added, there were six circular bays, each with a direct link to the taxiway, laid in the adjoining bush on the eastern side of the strip. Installed along either side of the runway was a single line of kerosene 'gooseneck' flares which marked out the extent of the landing area. Green electrical lighting marked out each runway threshold, and a single centreline of red lights marked out the short-final approach at each end. To the north of Uli, a single red light was on the spire of Uli church which jointly acted as an obstruction beacon and a crude navigational aid.

The World Council of Churches made their first relief flight into Uli during the night of 21/22 May 1968, when a DC-7C, flown by British pilot John Phillips, arrived with a mixed cargo of military supplies and relief material. A major threat came not from the Nigerian Air Force MiG-I7 jet fighters and Il-28 jet bombers supplied by Egypt, whose daylight raids could be countered by the airstrip's heavy anti-aircraft defences, but from the six Nigeria Airways DC-3s commandeered by the Nigerian Air Force, four of which were used as night bombers with a crude shute fed by a roller conveyor belt for ejecting bombs out of the cargo doors. Five more DC-3s were later acquired from SABENA for bombing and these aircraft flew almost nightly from Benin City over Uli. Cruising at between 14,000 and 18,000 feet to get above the flak, they would wait for the L-1049s to arrive and warn them on the VHF set that they would be bombed if they continued their approach. The threat was usually enough to persuade the supply aircraft to go back to their bases at São Tomé in the Gulf of Guinea or Libreville in Gabon. Pilots who did attempt to land were apt to find a 220-pound bomb exploding on the runway ahead of them as soon as they switched on their landing lights. The resulting overshoot involved a

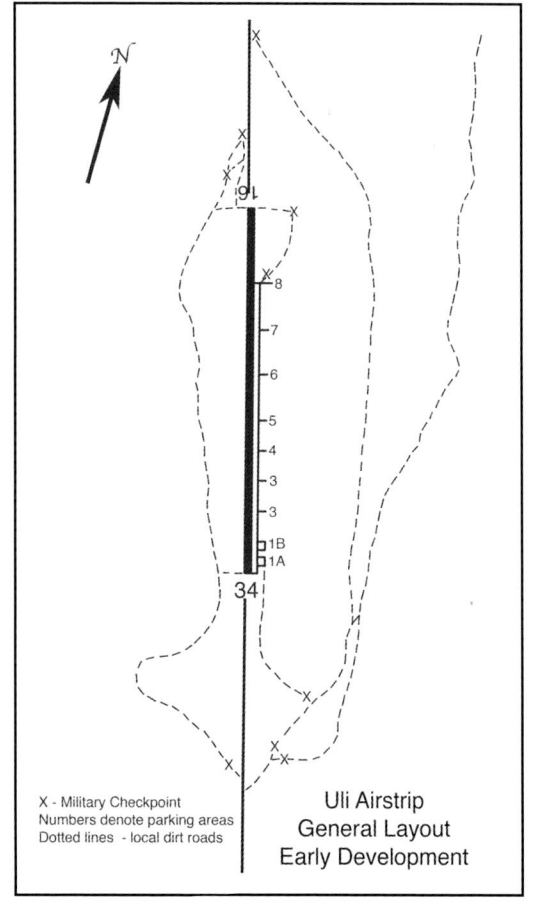

X - Military Checkpoint
Numbers denote parking areas
Dotted lines - local dirt roads

Uli Airstrip
General Layout
Early Development

further hazard as flak from the airstrip was often directed at the supply aircraft in mistake for the DC-3s. Fortunately for Biafra, the DC-3s could not carry bombs of sufficient size to inflict irreparable runway damage. As their endurance was limited, there came a time when the supply aircraft could slip in unmolested and unload their vital cargoes.

Uli may have been big enough and suitably equipped for the initial relief flights, but it lacked many of the facilities needed for the dramatic increase in flights planned by NordChurchAid and aircraft the size of the Constellation. A meeting in Biafra, between the World Council of Churches, NordChurchAid, the heads of the Biafran Ministry of Works and the Biafran Air Traffic Control addressed the concerns. Afterwards, the World Council of Churches representative at Uli, Reverend William 'Bill' Aitken, was tasked with flying to Malmo, Sweden with a 'shopping list' of items required. Electric lighting to replace the remaining kerosene flares which tended to be blown out whenever an aircraft landed or took off; spare parts, for the radio Non-Directional Beacon (NDB) and the VHF Transceivers used by Uli Air Traffic Control; a series of high-intensity fog lamps for placing at the approach to runway 34 given the frequent morning fog that had often forced aircraft to abandon a landing and to return to base. They also wanted additional telephone equipment to link various points on the strip to the tower and a standby generator for the landing lights.

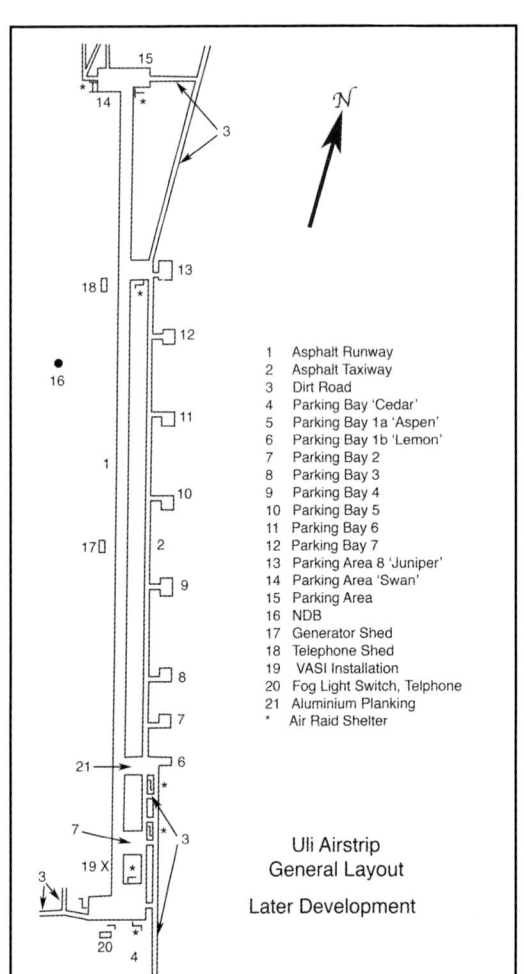

Even in the early days of flights into Uli, there could be fifteen flights a night, all unloaded by teams of fatigue workers under one Biafran officer.

Uga, the second of the three sites selected as a bush airstrip, was quickly developed following the threatened loss of Uli during September 1968. Like Uli, the strip at Uga was converted from a stretch of the main Orlu to Awka road. Instead of creating concrete hardstands, the Biafrans used a form of PSP, a pierced-steel planking system, described as 'perforated aluminium strips'.

By the end of 1968, the strip was declared operational as a secondary strip to Uli and strictly for government and military usage. Uga could only be considered for emergency purposes as the actual landing strip was very uneven and pilots who used it complained about the undulating surface. Uga was very rarely used, even by arms flights which continued to use Uli under the cover of relief flights. It was not until the late-Spring of 1969 after Uli had been subjected to a particularly bad spell of night-bombing that Uga was used more often. Even then, it was pressure from the Churches which brought Uga into more regular use rather than any desire to separate the two commodities of relief and arms.

The first known landing of a regular arms flight into Uga came on the night of 10/11 May 1969 when Jack Malloch flew one of his own DC-7CFs, TR-LOJ, into Uga. With him were co-pilot Clive Halse and Flight Engineer Cliff Hawthorne. None relished the idea of using Uga strip again; the landing surface was not as good as Uli with considerable amounts of loose stone and shingle. The surface proved to be a major hazard, especially when putting heavily-laden DC-7CFs into reverse pitch after landing. Contrary to popular belief, very few flights were made by DC-7s or L-1049Gs into Uga.

Arrival of 'The Grey Ghost'
One Constellation that became quite well known - and lived something of a charmed life - was Biafra's 'Grey Ghost', the former Air France L-1049G F-BGNE which had been inactive at Orly Airport

since its certificate of airworthiness expired on 4 October 1963. In preparation for a sale to the French dealer Etablissements Jean Godet, F-BGNE was taken out of storage on 27 July 1967 and was officially sold on 9 August 1967. Repainted in an overall drab grey-green colour scheme, F-BGNE was restored to the French register on 16 August for ferrying purposes. The next day, the L-1049G was flown to the Biafran capital, Enugu via Lisbon. On its arrival it carried the spurious marks '5N-07G'.

Etablissements Godet was nothing more than a second-hand dealer. Documents lodged with the French authorities by Godet revealed that the aircraft was resold immediately, supposedly to a Portuguese company, but in a manner that suggested two separate sales were made, firstly to Rhodesian Airlines who, in turn, resold the aircraft to Transportader do Ar - Portuguese for 'Air Transport'. Both companies appear to have been part of a 'paper cover' for sale to the Biafran government who allegedly paid some US$350,000 for the aircraft - quite a mark-up considering Air France received only US$84,000 for it.

While Jean Godet reportedly sold the aircraft to the Biafrans he may have retained a degree of responsibility for the airliner's operation and for hiring a crew. From the start, Frenchman Jacques Languillaume made most - if not all - of the flights, including the initial delivery flight from Paris-Orly.

He must have been familiar with the aircraft as he had flown it during his time with Air France. He was also known to the French legal authorities as, at the time of the Biafran operation, Languillaume was the subject of a French police investigation into the financial collapse of SOGESTA, the pension fund for Air France pilots. Languillaume had been formally arrested back in 1966 but released from custody in November pending a court trial. As of August 1967 the trial had yet to commence.

Languillaume's involvement may have been more than just 'doing a job'. There are suggestions that he was given an option by the French government; to either fly on behalf of the Biafrans or face an immediate trial. As with much of the Biafran episode, there is no official evidence or much supportive documentation to prove the Rhodesian connection apart from the fact that Jack Malloch offered one of his own employees, Henry Kinnear, the Flight Engineer's position on the 'Grey Ghost' alongside Languillaume.

That Malloch was offering his own staff positions on the 'Grey Ghost' suggests more than a passing interest. In the event, Kinnear declined the offer so Languillaume's regular crew consisted of two other Frenchmen, co-pilot Roger Fontenau and Flight Engineer Gilbert Kermerecfi.

From 17 August 1967, the overall grey-drab painted aircraft began operating regular flights on behalf of the Biafran government immediately after its arrival. Most of its destinations involved Portuguese, or Portuguese colonial airports, such as Bissau in Guinea, Luanda in Angola as well as São Tomé and, of course, Lisbon. On arrival at Enugu in September with a cargo of Czech arms on board, the airliner was hit by Biafran anti-aircraft fire - it seems no-one told the gunners the Constellation was about to arrive!

Since August 1967 the Biafrans had operated its own L-1049G, the so-called 'Grey Ghost' Super Constellation, '5N-07G'. The Biafrans continued to own the aircraft and control where it flew and what it carried but, from January 1968, Warton took on the role of supplying crews and organising the maintenance. This, as Warton saw it, was part of the monopoly deal negotiated with the Biafrans.

Warton, of course, was paid a fee for managing

One aircraft which operated the Biafra run longer than any others was Biafra's own 'Grey Ghost' Super Constellation 5N07G, which operated the Biafra run for almost two years. It is seen here during its former life with Air France as F-BGNE.

the 'Grey Ghost' but not as much as when operating his own aircraft. For that reason alone '5N-07G' did not undertake a tremendous number of flights during 1968; it spent much of the time at Lisbon where Hank's mechanics would occasionally rob it of parts to keep their own fleet of L-1049Gs serviceable. Then came the wind of change during the summer of 1968.

The French government raised its level of assistance for Biafra at the end of July 1968. Within two months, the question of supplying arms and ammunition would be solved with the appointment of Jack Malloch as a replacement for Hank Warton. But Malloch was not taking over the responsibility for operating the 'Grey Ghost'. That responsibility was being kept by the Biafrans themselves.

The Portuguese Governor of São Tomé, Major Antonio Jorge de Silva Sebastiao, turned an official 'blind eye' to Warton's gun-running activities. The landing fees, sales of fuel and overnight accommodation at the island's one hotel provided a boost for the island's economy. But as the Churches began to raise the awareness of civilian starvation in Biafra so the Governor came under increasing pressure, from both the World Council of Churches and CARITAS to alter his standpoint. They eventually won over his support enough to persuade him to issue an ultimatum to Hank Warton. Fuel supplies would only continue to be made available for arms flights on the assurance that he undertook a proportion of relief flights into Biafra. The Governor also added a condition of his own: that in view of the flight time between São Tomé and Port Harcourt being only one hundred minutes each aircraft could undertake two return flights per night, each of which was capable of carrying up to 10½ tonnes.

The whole Lisbon operation was shrouded in mystery. It eventually became referred to as the 'Phoenix' operation; even the Biafrans themselves used the name 'Phoenix', referring to 'Phoenix Airlines' or 'Phoenix Air Transport' but nobody quite knew the exact name of the company operating out of Portugal. Nor, for that matter, did anybody know who was financing it.

The company had offices in New York and Lisbon, then later at Faro, also in Portugal. The registered address of most of the aircraft was - as with Hank Warton's aircraft - in the Miami area of Florida, USA. The main person connected with Phoenix appeared to be a Jack Crosson; it was regularly suggested that the company had the discrete backing of the CIA - so as to protect American interests in the oil market, should Biafra win the war!

Phoenix's first aircraft, registered to J. Crosson, was another ex-Portuguese Constellation L-1049G that had been stored at Miami, N8338, and this airliner commenced flying the arms airlift from the Portuguese Airforce base at Lisbon on 7 November 1968. Shortly afterwards it received the unofficial Biafran registration 5N-83H. It joined a Panamanian L-1049G Freighter HP-475, which had started flying from Lisbon at the end of September 1968.

The owner of this aircraft remained something of a mystery. Formerly operated briefly by RAPSA - Rutas Aereas Panemenas SA, it is believed to have been purchased by the Biafrans themselves, or was perhaps connected with Phoenix as well.

Towards the end of September reports told of 'N480C' landing at Lisbon on the 25 September. The identity has never been proven and its lack of other markings - apart from a red fuselage cheat-line - ensured that it remained well-hidden.

Throughout the period from the autumn of 1968 to the late spring of 1969, the airlift from Lisbon to São Tomé and Uli was flown regularly by HP-475, 5N-83H and the long-standing 5N-07G. Early in 1969, the arms activities became rather of an embarrassment to the Portuguese authorities at Lisbon, and most operations were transferred to Faro, further to the south.

In July and August 1969, two further Constellation L-749As, were added to the Phoenix fleet at Faro. These were former Western Airlines' aircraft N86525 and N86524, bought from Concare Aircraft Leasing by Robert W. Cobaugh, although after the war was over the remaining aircraft was restored to Jack Crosson. N86525 joined the airlift in late July and N86524 at the end of August. One of the pilots of the 749As was Duncan Baker - later to form his own company Lanzair. In early November 1969, the two 749As received Biafran registrations, 5N-85H and 5N-86H respectively. The Biafran registrations were painted on the aircraft after two FAA inspectors visited São Tomé and discovered the American registrations were being carried illegally. The two aircraft were painted in full blue-grey camouflage colours on the upper fuselage. The aircraft also operated from Arrecife on Lanzarote in the Canary Islands and were joined in June or July 1969 by an ex-Air Fret L-1049G F-BHBI, which was officially sold to a company in Switzerland in November 1969 after its French C of A had expired the previous March!

The high demands made on the aircraft - the minimum of maintenance, flying missions at a high

N1583V had a chequered history, and although a sister machine to some used on the Biafran Airlift, this one did not participate - it had enough adventures of its own! It was impounded by US Customs after it made an emergency landing due to being low on fuel at Grand Bahama Auxiliary Airfield on 4 June 1969. It seems the Speedpak contained eight rifles, two sub-machine guns, some automatic revolvers and hand grenades. The aircraft also wore numerous bullet holes. It is believed this aircraft acted as a decoy or back-up aircraft for the raid on Haiti carried out by N6022C, which later was used in Biafra. *(Matt Black Collection)*

gross weight and making the frequent hazardous and often hard landing on the improvised airstrip at Uli - took its toll on the aircraft. 5N-83H had been withdrawn at Faro during the summer of 1969, and was used for spares. F-BHBI was abandoned at Lanzarote in November 1969, and at the end of November one of the 749As, 5N-85H, was lost with all on board after a triple engine failure over the Sahara Desert.

By the Autumn of 1968 the state of the Biafran economy had seriously deteriorated. When secession was announced in May 1967, Biafra had been able to finance the purchase of armaments and supplies from private arms dealers to fight what was seen as a brief war of independence. But the decision by Lagos to introduce new currency at short notice in January 1968 had rendered valueless millions of old Nigerian pounds still in Biafran hands. It is believed that Biafra's foreign-exchange reserves were exhausted by April 1968 and that by September 1968 the country was bankrupt. So, who did financially support the new operation?

It is known that France used its secret service fund to supply something over £2 million worth of arms and related military assistance over the September-December 1968 period. France saw a unified Nigeria as a threat to French-speaking West Africa. The real prize, however, was the likely gains by French oil interests and the substantial concessions that until then had been enjoyed by British oil companies. These concessions would have become bargainable with a Biafran victory. Therefore, the true funding of the new Portuguese-based operation was probably French, and not, as it appeared to be, American funding, but it could well have been both! In the world of the spooks, it is quite possible that the French financed the whole operation but hired Americans. That way, it would look like a secretly-funded American - for that read CIA - set-up. Of course, the CIA would deny any involvement, they were, after all, still denying any involvement in Vietnam. That would convince everybody it really was the CIA, so it probably was funded by the French!

The Protestant World Council of Churches also used Hank Warton for relief flights into Biafra, the

5N-86H, the former TWAN6022C *Star of Virginia*, seen at Faro, Portugal, sometime after the Biafran Airlift. *(Matt Black Collection)*

first of which had taken place on 22 March 1968 with a chartered L-1049G flying from Lisbon to Port Harcourt. Further flights were organised, but the frequency became increasingly irregular; by July 1968 only six flights had been made by World Council of Churches from São Tomé into Biafra. Two further flights, between Lisbon and Fernando Póo, were also funded by them, the first of which took place on 27 June 1968.

Despite the Governor's support, Father Byrne was concerned at the lack of available space and at the beginning of July 1968, in one of his regular reports back to Rome, he suggested that CARITAS organise its own separate airlift. The response from CARITAS International's Secretary-General, Monsignor Carlo Bayer, was dramatic and unexpected. Byrne was told to immediately fly to Germany and make an appeal on national television for financial aid to support the purchase and operation of their own aircraft. Within hours of the broadcast, the German government had donated eight million Deutchmarks, split equally between the German Catholic agency, Deutscher Caritasverband (DCV) and Das Diakonische Werk (DDW), a German Protestant relief agency.

The World Council of Churches had also been exploring alternative means of getting relief aid into Biafra. While Father Byrne was lobbying the Vatican for action, the World Council of Churches was entering into a contract with an American company, Intercity Airways, to undertake a minimum of twenty-five flights into Uli during August, each flight to carry seven tonnes of relief material or fifty to seventy passengers. On 3 July 1968 Intercity's L-1049H Super Constellation N469C - with Air Mid East titling - flew into Geneva airport for inspection by the World Council of Churches and the application of red cross insignia.

Intercity Airways was managed by American entrepreneur Lucien H Pickett, who had convinced the World Council of Churches that he could break Warton's monopoly of the Uli landing-codes and procedures. This was based on the fact that one of the L-1049H's crew, a pilot named Bell, had previously flown for Warton on the arms airlift from Lisbon. Furthermore, Pickett had claimed that he could undercut Warton's charges and operate a Lisbon to Uli return shuttle for only $10,500.

Like many others who turned up at that time, Lucien Pickett 'had form' as they say in some circles. Pickett first came to the fore in July 1964 when he had operated a single L-1049G Super Constellation, N9642Z, on a series of charter flights within Europe under a company name of 'USAir'. At the end of the year, the aircraft was grounded at Frankfurt for several months but reappeared at Malta, in February 1965, with the false identity '9G-28' and was operated by 'Trans Africa Airlines'. The aircraft had landed to take on fuel before planning an air-drop of weapons to rebels in the Algerian Berber mountains, but delivery never took place. Lucien Pickett, who was on board the L-1049G, was arrested for violating Maltese airspace and later fined.

N469C was being flown by a Canadian pilot, Axel Duch, who joined Intercity after a tour in South-East Asia with Air America. The aircraft was believed to have taken on board a cargo of relief material before its planned flight south.

As is usual with many of these airliners, ownership is not clear, but accounts suggests that it is believed to be owned or operated by Aerolessors Inc from 1966 until 1969, but the US Civil Aircraft Register lists Intertrade Leasing Corp as the owner from April 1967 until January 1970. Records suggest that the airliner arrived at Fernando Póo from Madrid on 26 July 1968 and supposedly remained there until at least 17 August 1968, when it returned to the USA. A few weeks later, when

N469C of Air Mid-East with Angel of Mercy titling seen in the Canary Islands after its visit to Geneva. (Matt Black Collection)

Hank Warton had been 'removed' from the airlift, N469C appeared again, this time flown by Cuban emigre pilots on lease from Aerolessors in Miami. From 23 September 1968 until 13 November 1968, the aircraft was a regular sight at Lisbon on the arms lift, after which it was not seen again.

Pickett later had his aircraft flown to Copenhagen, where he negotiated a new contract with the relief agency DanChurchAid. Under this agreement, Pickett was paid $10,000 before Duch and Bell flew N469C to Madrid to uplift ten tonnes of stockfish. When the aircraft later arrived on Fernando Póo on 22 July 1968, the Air Mid East titling had been replaced with the more prophetic legend 'Angel of Mercy'.

On 8 April 1968, the International Committee of the Red Cross signed a contract with Biafra's primary gunrunner for five flights, each carrying relief material exclusively from Fernando Póo to Port Harcourt, the first flights taking place the same day. Lagos immediately intervened in an attempt to stop the flights. Then, on 18 April 1968, the Nigerian Foreign Ministry issued a written authority to the Red Cross giving permission for relief supply flights to be flown from Fernando Póo to Biafra 'at its own risk'.

Fernando Póo was perfect for flights to Biafra, being about half the distance than from São Tomé, but there were major problems, the worse being that Santa Isabel airport operated only during daylight hours and the island authorities refused to include night opening. Biafra refused to accept any incoming flights, whether relief or arms, outside the hours of darkness and so, on the initial Red Cross flights, Warton's aircraft were positioned from São Tomé to Fernando Póo during the mid-morning for loading of Red Cross relief material before the aircraft was then flown back to São Tomé to await darkness before making the final leg into Biafra, after which the aircraft was usually then routed back to Lisbon, occasionally returning to São Tomé for refuelling.

Public faces, and shadowy figures
It was not long before rumours, tales, stories, myths, legends and just plain lies were doing the rounds as to the activities of the Sky Tramps.

One person who knew Warton, and a number of other 'adventurers' in Africa was Bill Armstrong, the founder of, amongst other airlines, Autair. I wrote long and in great detail about Bill's operations in *'Colours in the Sky, the history of Autair International and Court Line Aviation'* (Pen & Sword 2018).

'To understand Africa and what happened to us, one must go back to the beginning. It is quite true to say we were often under-capitalised. Nevertheless, we made excellent progress, often with assistance and welcome guidance of Eric Knight, founder and Chairman of Lombard Banking.

'In 1956 I negotiated our first contract in Africa - with Rhodesian Selection Trust who wanted to use helicopters for mineral exploration. From this toe-hold, other activities emerged, including setting up a regional base in Salisbury, Rhodesia.

'Rhodesian Prime Minister Ian Smith, (a former RAF officer and pilot, who was politically moderate and locally well-respected) had been locked in talks with UK Prime Minister Harold Wilson regarding independence for Southern Rhodesia.

'Wilson was under pressure from the United Nations and other political groupings to repress what was regarded by many - including many of our Foreign Office 'mandarins' - as the aspirations of rabid colonialists. It did not matter that they were wrecking the lives and destroying the loyalty of many thousands of faithful British citizens!

Smith eventually issued the Unilateral Declaration of Independence (UDI) from the UK and years of sanctions, bush-warfare and terrorism followed.

'Our helicopter work expanded, and with money in hand in 1964, we found ourselves looking at the fixed-wing field again, this time taking over from David Butler's Rhodesian Air Services and forming a successor company, Air Trans Africa - known as ATA - with Captain Jack Malloch as Managing Director, and using DC-3s, 4s and 7s.

'In 1965 I also formed the first national airline of Bechuanaland, shortly to become Botswana, with Dave Morgan as the managing director and Johnnie Gibson as Chief Pilot.'

'Bechuanaland National Airways (Pty) Ltd was established in Francistown on 1 October 1965 as a regional scheduled service passenger and freight airline, with two DC-3s transferred from Autair. Revenue flights started on 15 November linking Francistown with Bulawayo and Livingstone. Other routes were started from Lobatse to Johannesburg, along with Serowe, Gaborones, Ghansi, Serondellas and Maun. By the end of the year, the new company had taken over Bechuanaland Air Safaris. 1966 saw the airline flying a twice-weekly round trip between Francistown and Johannesburg. I have never been able to confirm his exact role, but I do know that Jack Malloch was involved with BNA as well.'

'1964 also saw the creation of Autair Helicopters

William 'Bill' Armstrong, founder of Autair, and his new wife Doreen at their marriage in Nice in 1952. Doreen was to become a future co-director, business partner and secretary. *(W Armstrong archive)*

(EA) Ltd in Nairobi. F W 'Freddie' Wilcox was sent out to manage the concern, which, apart from flying assorted charters, also acted as the Bell Distributor for Kenya'.

John McVicar Malloch, known by all as 'Jack', who Bill Armstrong brought in to manage Air Trans-Africa, was a pioneering aviator who ran numerous clandestine airlines in Africa in the early post-independent years, where he was involved in gun-running against the encroachment of Communism. He actively fought against the UN, yet was in the pay of both the Central Intelligence Agency and the French Secret Service, the Direction Générale de la Sécurité Extérieure, or DGSE. He became well known as the arch Rhodesian sanctions buster who almost single-handedly kept Rhodesia alive through a steady supply of consumer goods, arms and ammunition throughout the years of Rhodesia's UDI.

There were reports that Jack was an 'arms dealer', but I doubt that in the true sense of the words he was. Yes, indeed he was a mercenary, he would carry anything to anywhere on behalf of some pretty shady characters, and certainly some of his cargoes were of a highly explosive or illegal nature, but no-one I have ever spoken with has said he was involved in actual dealing.

Jack Malloch's aviation career was as complex and convoluted as Bill Armstrong's. Malloch was closely involved with Rhodesia's Special Air Service regiment, including having direct involvement in some of that unit's long-range cross border operations. He also became involved with the British military at about the time of UDI and was subsequently involved in some military support flights into the Sudan for Whitehall. There were also clandestine military flights into the Aden desert in the early 1960s delivering weapons for the British SAS in their fight against the Communists.

Air Trans-Africa carried mercenaries to the Congo in 1964 to help the government of Moise Tshombe quell the insurgency of a group of Congolese rebels called the Simba.

It seems that most of Air Trans-Africa's expenses were being hidden from the authorities by the simple expedient of being paid from Malloch's own personal Swiss bank account - furthermore all of ATA's aircraft were not owned by them, but were leased from Autair.

ATA acted as a charter carrier to the Biafran Civil War in Nigeria. During the civil war the C-54 was

Bill's business partner in Africa on a number of ventures was Jack Malloch, seen here during the Biaflan war. He later managed with Bill Armstrong a complex sanctions-busting operation in and out of Rhodesia. On 26 March 1982 he was killed while flying his personal Spitfire F.22 (PK350) north of Harare. To the left is Chris Dixon, one of his many loyal Rhodesian pilots.

Above: N9642Z seen at Amsterdam. *(Matt Black Collection)*
Below: the same aircraft at Malta after it was impounded with '9G-28' on the fuselage and a whited out area on the lower rudder where the original registration was.

impounded and the crew imprisoned for a time in 1967. ATA operated a Lockheed Super Constellation (VP-WAW) under the name of Afro Continental Airways after UDI for a weekly service from Salisbury to Windhoek, and also apprently operated it on a weekly service from Lisbon to Biafra from September 1967 until March 1968. A second machine, the former CS-TLF was purchased in July 1967 for spares use, but this aircraft remained in Salisbury after delivery and never flew for Air Trans Africa.

Aircraft came and went through Autair's Luton base, disappearing southwards into darkest Africa. Noticeable was Douglas C-54 G-ASZT, which appeared briefly under Autair ownership from January to August 1965 before heading for Air Trans Africa.

After Warton was ousted from the airlift in September 1968, Malloch's Super Constellation again appeared on the scene, and from early September until November again made regular flights, this time under Gabonese registry as TR-LNY, flying from Lisbon to Biafra. Jack Malloch's Rhodesian company appeared to be closely associated with the Gabonese company Compagnie Gabonaise d'Affretements. Later, the Super Connie flew from Libreville, in Gabon, to Uli, carrying arms. The L-1049G later appeared in the colours of Afro-Continental Airways.

Warton and Malloch were sometime rivals, and became - as much as they could be, given the nature of their activities - the public face of the Biafran war - Bill Armstrong preferred to operate much more in the shadows.

'The Biafran Job'...
It was during this time that the saga of the liberated banknotes evolved. This is possibly the most difficult story I have ever had to research, simply because there are so many different versions of it! It seems that when Biafra broke away from Nigeria, the Biafran Government' took possession' - or was it that they 'did a bank job'? - gaining a substantial amount of Nigerian currency in the form of banknotes. This money was then used for the purchase of war materials, and to pay for the airlift. Another version of thre story is that they managed to 'divert' a Nigerian Airways aircraft to Enugu.

Whatever the true story, the Nigerians decided to put a halt to this by withdrawing all the currency from use and replacing it with a new issue. This they did in a relatively short period of time, at the

Afro Continental Airways was formed by Jack Malloch of Air Trans Africa/Affretair based at Salisbury Airport to operate the weekly scheduled route to Windhoek, South West Africa. The service did not last long. This Constellation - VP-WAW - was in excellent condition and was used during the Biafra airlift throughout that war. It was later retired to being used as a clubhouse.

end of which all previous Nigerian banknotes were to be declared null and void. A date of 22 January 1968 was set for this. At the beginning of that month, the Biafrans had a considerable amount of cash that they needed to put onto the international currency markets as soon as possible. A plan was made for Jack Malloch and Hank Warton to fly the notes to Switzerland and lodge then in the Biafran's Swiss bank account. This would effectively be converting Niagian pounds into Swiss francs, which could then be used to continue to fund the war.

Here the story takes another twist, for there are three versions of what happened next. One version is that 5T-TAC made one trip to Basle in Switzerland on 6 January, and that 5T-TAF made two trips for the same purpose on 10 and 13 January to offload the remainder of the Biafran's cash into Swiss banks. Another version is that on 12 January two aircraft left Biafra with around twenty tons of Nigerian banknotes in sacks. The story I got direct from Bill Armsytong is that they made it to Switzerland where they cashed in the money. Bill always claimed to have a picture of himself, Jack Malloch and Hank Warton sitting in the back of one of the Constellations on the sacks of money but, despite him promising to let me have sight of it, he never did.

The other version of the story is that the aircraft were turned away from Switzerland because they were Rhodesian-registered, and Switzerland had no diplomatic relations with that country. This is wrong, as the aircraft were all registered in Gabon. Legend has it that they then flew to Lisbon hoping to change the money there, but to no avail. This could have been possible, for Hank Warton did operate a maintenance base there, so he would have been known.

Then a plan was hatched to fly to Lomé in Togo where it would be roaded to Benin and on to Lagos.

At Togo, Jack Malloch and the crew were summarily detained, the money confiscated and the aircraft impounded. They were imprisoned for around five months then, having paid a substantial fine, they were released.

My own view on this episode is that both actually happened, one aircraft made it to Switzerland, and cashed in the money, the other was turned away for some reason, ended up in Togo where those on board were detained.

Not long after this 5T-TAC, piloted by George Robertson and carrying a load of medical supplies from the Vatican, crashed on landing at Port Harcourt and burnt out, although no one was hurt.

Through Bill Armstrong, Air Trans Africa also obtained a fleet of Douglas DC-7C and DC-7CF aircraft (with the assistance of the Rhodesian Government) which were registered in Gabon, when the airline became a major part of the Rhodesian sanctions-busting operations - and also part of the Biafran Airlift. They flew beef to Gabon, from where it was flown out by aircraft of its associate company Affretair. Essential materiels for the Rhodesian security forces were brought into the country on the return flights. Affretair migrated to Zimbabwe after independence, when it replaced Air Trans Africa.

In May 1968, Biafra succeeded in purchasing two ex-Austrian Air Force Magister jets to add to its meagre Air Force. The problem was that the dismantled aircraft was too large to get through the passenger door of Warton's 1049Gs. Having lost his one aircraft with a cargo door, he searched for a replacement and found a 1049D/0l (updated to a 1049H) in Miami which was conveniently registered in Argentina as LV-ILW. The aircraft had been bought by LAPA in l966 but had been stored in a corner at Miami. The aircraft was flown to Lisbon and registered 5T-TAC (the second). Around 23 May, the aircraft made its first flight to São Tomé with the fuselages of the Magisters. Then, early in the morning of 2 June, it left Lisbon with the two sets of wings, together with some ammunition and a few passengers. At Bissau, the pilot informed the passengers that there was some hydraulic trouble. They were off-loaded and later continued to São Tomé in a replacement Super Constellation. The night after the passengers had left, however, (3-4 June) the cargo Super Constellation with its precious load of Magister wings was blown up - thought to have been sabotaged by one of the crew who was bribed by the Nigerians for a reported $56,000.

Towards the end of June 1968 Warton, under threat of losing his Red Cross contract, made a serious effort to resume his relief flight schedule. At 11:00 hours on 28 June one of Warton's L-1049Gs - either '5T- TAH' or '5T-TAK' - flown by Larry Raab, took-off from São Tomé for the short flight to Santa Isabel; it was loaded during the afternoon before departing for Biafra just after dusk to operate the tenth Red Cross relief flight. Later the same night Raab flew the aircraft empty from Uli to Lisbon. The eleventh Red Cross flight took place on the following night when another of Warton's pilots, August 'Augie' Martin, flew '5T-TAG' from São Tomé to Fernando Póo and on to Uli. After unloading its cargo, Martin flew the Constellation back to São Tomé. Warton's plan was for Augie Martin and 'ST-TAG' to solely operate Red Cross flights over the next few nights so as to catch up on the original Red Cross schedule.

Captain August 'Augie' Harvey Martin was born in Los Angeles, California in 1919. In 1938 he graduated from DeWitt Clinton High School, Bronx after the family had moved to New York. He moved back to California to attend San Mateo Junior College during which he financed his first flying lessons, making his first solo flight in January 1940. He attended the University of California Civilian Pilot Training Programme for further flight training and acquired his flight instructor rating. In 1942 he worked for the Navy V-12 Programme at Cornell University before joining the US Army Air Corps in 1943. He was sent to Tuskeegee, Alabama for flight training, where he gained his wings in September 1945. He was honourably discharged in 1946 and attempted to find a job as a commercial airline pilot. He continued supporting his family with odd jobs, aircraft maintenance and part-time flying jobs until 1955, when he was employed by Seaboard World Airlines as a Captain, thus becoming the first African American to hold that post with a scheduled US airline. He was a founding member of Negro Airmen International in 1967.

Just four months before arriving in São Tomé, he had married actress Gladys Riddle Martin, the niece of jazz vibraphone player Lionel Hampton and when Martin landed on Fernando Póo around midday on 30 June 1968 his wife was on board as a passenger. The other two crew members were an American co-pilot, Jesse Raymond Meade, and a South African Flight Engineer, Thomas 'Bull' Brown. Bull Brown was probably one of the most experienced Flight Engineers on the Biafra arms airlift; he had previously flown into Biafra with Jack Malloch's Air Trans Africa but decided to join Warton after Malloch was jailed in Togo and the Rhodesian operation was suspended. Also on board were two representatives of the International Red Cross.

Fully laden with 10½ tons of food and medicine the aircraft took-off for Uli; it arrived overhead about 20:20 hours. The weather over Biafra was bad, with active tropical thunderstorms over much of the area. The runway lights were turned on, as was the standard procedure, and '5T-TAG' was lined-up for a landing. The adverse weather conditions may have caused the crew to misalign the let-down because the aircraft turned onto the final approach at too low an altitude. About 1½ miles south of the airstrip, close to the junction of the Ihiala-Oguta road, the aircraft struck rising ground and all on board were killed.

'Augie' Martin and his crew were the first to die on the relief airlift, and with the wrecked airliner lying within close proximity of Uli, the local Catholic priests saw it a fitting tribute that the entire crew be buried within a new cemetery just outside Uli. The crash brought home to all involved the dangers of operating nightly relief flights into Biafra.

At the start of the Red Cross flights Hank Warton was operating three L-1049G Super Constellations, all of which were being flown with illegal Mauritanian registrations, '5T-TAG', '5T-TAH' and '5T-TAK'.

Captain August Harvey 'Augie' Martin who lost his life in a Constellation crash at Uli.

There can be little doubt that the Red Cross was aware that the registrations were not genuine; the Air Traffic Control officer at Santa Isabel was certainly aware but chose to ignore the fact. The crash of 'ST-TAG' brought the matter into the open, and the authorities on Fernando Póo began to display their irritation to such flights.

When confronted by the Red Cross over the registration issue, Warton promised to have them legally registered. It was Warton's Operations Manager, Bertram Peterson, who undertook to register the aircraft legally. Peterson was able to register a new company, ARCO, in Bermuda and applied for registration of Warton's aircraft. The application was made immediately after the crash of '5T-TAG' and to support the process, the International Red Cross Headquarters in Geneva wrote to the Director of Civil Aviation, Bermuda on 13 July 1968 to speed up the necessary paperwork. When, however, the next Red Cross charter flight flew into Santa Isabel, it was made by a Super Constellation carrying the marks 'N8025'. Furthermore, the crew was able to substantiate this with documentation identifying the marks as indeed being legally registered to a Super Constellation of the North American

Above: '5T-TAF' not long after it was impounded on Malta in 1968. *(Matt Black Collection)*

Below and bottom: the aircraft survived as a Bar after being towed to a location alongside the former Safi taxi-strip at Kirkop. *(Author's Collection)*

Aircraft Trading Corporation, Warton's other US-registered company. The Spanish authorities could do nothing but accept the legality of the aircraft and allowed flights to continue. One assumes they were unaware that the true N8025 had been repainted as '5T-TAC' and also that it had crashed at Port Harcourt during February 1968, an incident which Warton had conveniently never advised the Federal Aviation Agency. From June 1968 onwards each of Warton's Super Constellations at some stage or another carried the registration N8025 daubed on the airliner's rear fuselage whenever the aircraft flew into Fernando Póo!

Warton's aircraft flew from the Portuguese Air Force base, known as Base Airfield No. 1 at Lisbon-Portela, effectively part of Lisbon's main airport, usually departing at 0500 hrs direct to Bissau in Portuguese Guinea, a stage-length of 2,200 miles, reached after about nine flying hours. After refuelling and a rest for the crew, the aircraft then continued to Port Harcourt, which represented another eight hours flying, as the aircraft had to fly at least 150 miles out round the Nigerian coastline to avoid interception by Nigeria's Russian MiG fighters. Total radio silence was maintained from Bissau to Port Harcourt, except for one brief, pre-arranged radio call to alert Port Harcourt of their arrival. From about an hour out from their destination, the aircraft was completely blacked out. Allegedly, Warton charged the Biafrans $22,000 for the round trip from Lisbon to Port Harcourt, while the crews received approximately $1,000 each per round trip.

The cargo consisted of arms, ammunition and medical supplies. Needless to say, the aircraft were operated with the minimum of maintenance, and engine failures, hydraulic failures and burst tyres occurred frequently.

Suitably repainted as 'N8025', Warton positioned '5T-TAH' from São Tomé to Fernando Póo on 15 July to operate the fourteenth Red Cross relief flight. The aircraft took-off almost in darkness and climbed to cruise altitude over the island before turning towards Biafra. As it did so, another aircraft turned onto the same course; it was L-1049G '5T-TAK' operating an arms flight from São Tomé. Given the International Red Cross' insistence on advising Lagos of the flight-times and course then the crew of a crucial arms flight from São Tomé considered it to be fair game to use the Red Cross as protection for the inbound flight.

The impounding of L-1049G '5T-TAF' in Malta, during February 1968 had reduced Hank Warton's fleet to just one aircraft, '5T-TAG', although the numbers were made up with the acquisition of two more former Lufthansa aircraft, which became '5T-TAH' and '5T-TAK'.

There is for me an intriguing epilogue to this story. Following a visit to Malta on 12/13 January 1994 in connection with promoting John Hamlin's *Military Aviation in Malta GC 1915 - 1993* (GMS Enterprises 1994) I had the chance to quickly inspect 5T-TAF during the morning while waiting for a flight back to the UK. Unfortunately, I made the classic error of leaving my camera with my bags back at the *Maltese Times* newspaper office for I had taken exterior pictures on a previous visit and was not expecting anything worth shooting - a definite mistake on my part!

By this time the aircraft was in a pretty sorry state, but I did get a good look around the cockpit and undercarriage bays - the main cabin was, by this time trashed. Inside the cockpit, it was obvious that although a number of dials and gauges had been removed, all of the surviving instruments and many of the electrical switches all around the cockpit were marked with KLM stamps or tags. Where had the airliner gained them?

The aircraft, construction number 4618, was built as an L-1049G-82-81 completed on 15 September 1955 for Transportes Aereos Portugueses (TAP) as CS-TLC. It made TAP's final Super Constellation flight when it landed at Lisbon on 13 September 1967, arriving from Rio de Janeiro. Withdrawn from service with a total time of 23,064 hours in TAP service, the airliner was stored at Lisbon before being sold to International Aerodyne Inc later that same month, although the official change of ownership in FAA files states 3 November. The records show it was sold officially to North American Aircraft Trading Co (H.Wharton) on 8 November although it was taken over at Lisbon in October. The Portuguese registration was cancelled 23 November 1967.

It was re-registered with the unofficial - or fake - 5T-TAF registration in early November and was immediately put into use on the Biafran airlift. The airliner was impounded at Luqa, Malta on 16 February 1968 when the crew made a three-engined landing with a load of aircraft tyres on board. According to the official US FAA files, the aircraft was not flown by H Wharton until May 1970 and that he had tried to put the aircraft on the Mauretanian (sic) register. It was issued the registration N51517 in June or July 1970.

There is no sign whatsoever of any KLM involvement in the history, nor, suspiciously was there any sign of the aircraft identity plate in the cockpit or the nosewheel bay, a common place of putting one and Hank Warton did have a track record of swapping aircraft identities. We've already seen he had done it with 5T-TAC, c/n 4645 that Augie Martin crashed near Uli. Wait a minute - 5T-TAC was the former Iberian EC-ACN - but before that, it was built as PH-LLK of KLM - or was it? Both were 1049Gs, and it's not beyond the realms of impossibility that Warton was playing fast and loose with the identities of the Constellations he owned and that 5T-TAC was 4618 and 'TAF was 4645. As no identity plate has been discovered, we may never know.

'Jesus Christ Airways'
It is now that another 'adventurer' entered the scene. Count Carl Gustaf Ericsson von Rosen was a Swedish pioneer aviator and mercenary pilot. He was a student at Lundsbergs boarding school from 1920 to 1926 and at AB Aeromateriel's flight school in 1929, taking his pilot's licence test in the same year. Von Rosen started his flying career as a mechanic before becoming an aerobatic stunt pilot in a travelling circus, then took the airline pilot exam in 1934.

When the Italians attacked Ethiopia, von Rosen joined the Swedish Red Cross ambulance mission. Then, when the Soviet Union invaded Finland in 1939 in the Winter War, von Rosen quit his job to fly bombing missions for the Finns. He purchased a KLM Douglas DC-2, had it converted to a bomber in Sweden, and made one operational mission in March 1940 against the Soviet Union. That same year, as the Germans attacked the Netherlands, von Rosen with a Dutch KLM-crew flew a DC-3 with Dutch government documents to England and applied for service with the RAF but was turned down, due to the family relationship to Hermann Göring. Carl Gustaf von Rosen went on flying for the Swedish airline AB Aerotransport (ABA) from August 1940 until the end of the war.

Between 1945 and 1956 he worked in Ethiopia as the chief instructor for the Imperial Ethiopian Air Force and was later employed by the Swedish charter airline Transair. The company was engaged by the UN during the Congo Crisis. Von Rosen also served as the pilot for the second Secretary-General of the United Nations, Dag Hammarskjöld. However, von Rosen was grounded by illness when Hammarskjöld was killed in an air crash while mediating in the Congo Crisis.

Disgusted at the suffering the Nigerian government inflicted on the Biafrans and the continuous harassment of international relief flights by the Nigerian Air Force, he hatched a plan in collaboration with the French secret service to strike back at Nigerian air power.

Von Rosen first made a sanctions-busting flight into Biafra on 12 August 1968. He met senior personnel of relief agencies in Biafra with the objective of a developing plan designed to enable the relief airlift to resume, not in the rather haphazard manner of the past, but with sufficient number of aircraft operating at a much-increased frequency. The Swede's plan also called for a fully co-ordinated and well-organised airlift which, as he saw it, only the Churches could effectively mount. Von Rosen put forward two provisions; firstly that the reliance upon Hank Warton for flights to Biafra cease immediately and, secondly, that Von Rosen himself be installed as the Chief of Operations.

At a Red Cross press conference in Geneva, Pastor Mollerup learned of Von Rosen's blockade-breaking flight into Biafra. So did Axel Duch, the pilot of the 'Angel of Mercy' L-1049H, N469C, who was at the same press conference and in

CF-AEN was a survivor of Biafra, when it was used by Canrelief Air. It returned to Canada and was sold to Hellenic Air, who never actually used it. In a previous life it had been N1927H of Capitol International Airways.
(Matt Black Collection)

Not the best of pictures, but it does show Nordair's CF-NAJ on the airlift with Canairelief titling. The triple fins have the Church Aid blue and orange 'fishes' on them. *(Matt Black Collection)*

Geneva to persuade the Red Cross to authorise his aircraft to fly into Biafra. Immediately after the press conference Mollerup and Duch flew up to Malmo to meet von Rosen. They met on 18 August 1968 and discussed the feasibility of a new and independent airlift from São Tomé to Uli. All agreed on a further meeting with representatives of the Danish, Norwegian and Swedish church relief organisations. From the second meeting emerged the formation of an ad hoc air transport organisation to be known as Nordchurchaid and an agreement to charter aircraft was reached under the guidance and leadership of von Rosen.

The question of launching a dedicated relief airlift had first been raised at the World Council of Churches assembly in Uppsala during July 1968 when members discussed the possibility of a joint CARITAS/International Red Cross airlift from Fernando Póo to Uli. The concept was put before the Red Cross in Geneva, but met with a refusal. Instead the Churches developed their own plan and, since large financial donations had been raised in West Germany, the German Protestant (Das Diakonische Werke) and the German Catholic (Deutscher Caritasverband) Churches immediately set about purchasing five surplus Douglas DC-7C aircraft from the German carrier, Sudflug.

While the International Red Cross acted as an 'umbrella' operation from Fernando Póo with aircraft operated under a sub-contract basis with its European agencies, the French Red Cross operated independently from Libreville, in Gabon. The French operation never did attract the publicity gained by the International Committee of the Red Cross in Geneva, something which had great benefits. Indeed the French Red Cross continued to operate from Libreville until the very end of the civil war.

The early relief flights organised by the French Red Cross had involved a Transunion DC-6 and an Air Fret Bristol 170. At the same time elements within the French Government began to urge Air France to release aircrew with current L-1049G ratings for secondment to Libreville. Air France eventually gave in to pressure, and at the end of August 1968, one full crew was released to fly F-BRAD, Air Fret's newly-registered L-1049G Super Constellation, to Gabon. On 7 September 1968, the aircraft departed Orly and staged via Luqa, Malta and Douala in the Cameroons to Libreville where, for at least a month, the aircraft became based. F-BRAD flew regularly to Uli carrying in French arms for Ojuwku. As Hank Warton had done previously with his Super Constellations, Air Fret's 'RAD flew in over Fernando Póo, slotting into the pattern of Red Cross medical relief flights and thereby gaining an amount of protection.

F-BRAD, was undertaking 'training flights' at the same time evaluating suitable routes from Libreville to Biafra, often via Douala where the aircraft refuelled. The only fuel available at Douala was 95/115 octane AvGas, but the L-1049G required 115/145. The lower grade was kept for DC-4s but could be used by the L-1049G as long as the crew operated engines in an 'auto-rich' position. The result was a four-metre long flame out of each exhaust at particular power settings which was frequently visible when overflying Fernando Póo. Not only was the aircraft very visible but the French crew rarely maintained radio silence and on some occasions even reported departure times or estimated arrival times to and from Biafra.

The aircraft made similar calls nightly until at least 1 October as it flew food into Biafra. Often, on return flights from Uli to Libreville, the L-1049G was used to evacuate starving children. The only

CF-AEN with Joint Church Aid titles on the roof and the slogan 'Operated by Canairelief' on the front fuselage.
(Matt Black Collection)

difficulty which threatened the operation was the concern by the Cameroons government in losing its good relationship with neighbouring states if it openly supported flights into Biafra. The L-1049G was taken off the nightly roster during October 1968.

The following year Air Fret's l049G was joined by a second aircraft, F-BHBI also made flights from Paris-Le Bourget and Lisbon to Libreville ferrying arms and supplies. In May 1969, Air Fret's Super Constellations took part in an operation that was to cause repercussions throughout the Western world - the transporting of the Swedish-built MFI-9B Minicons - two-seat armed trainers - from Paris to Libreville, from where once reassembled, they flew to Biafra. Under the leadership of Count Gustav von Rosen, the Minicons carried out their daring raids against Nigerian airfields and other military targets.

It is possible that other French-registered L-1049Gs or L-1049G Freighters, owned by Rene Meyer's Catair carried supplies for Biafra during 1969. F-BGNC and F-BGNG were active in West Africa during this period - the former aircraft was lost in the Cameroons in August 1969. Air Fret's F-BRAD, later sporting the Biafran airlift blue-grey cabin roof camouflage, continued flying on the airlift until at least the end of November 1969, carrying out relief flights for the French Red Cross and other organizations from São Tomé and Libreville to Uli.

The first use of the phrase 'Joint Church Aid' appears to have been used during a two-day meeting in Rome, on 8-9 November 1968. That Rome meeting, at which a number of groups had been invited, including Nordchurchaid and the German Churches, had been arranged by Caritas Internationalis to find ways of increasing the capacity of the relief airlift. A name was needed to represent the various agencies now involved in this project, so the title Joint Church Aid emerged and remained as an umbrella for referring to the joint effort by the various churches and denominations who were airlifting supplies into Biafra. It soon became the common terminology for the São Tomé-based airlift, and when the name appeared on

Another version of the Canairelief - Joint Church Aid USA titles, this time on CF-NAK, see departing São Tomé.
(Matt Black Collection)

the fuselage tops, along with 'the sign of the fish' on the vertical fins often with the initials 'JCA' on items, it's not surprising that some wag nicknamed the operation 'Jesus Christ Airways'.

Jointly formed in November 1968 by the Canadian Presbyterian Church and OXFAM Canada, another constituent member of the Joint Church Aid group was Canairelief. At the same time a company, CanRelief Air Ltd was registered specifically for the purchase and operation of suitable aircraft.

Canadian charter company, Nordair, had placed two of its L-1049H Super Constellations, CF-NAJ and CF-NAM, in storage at Dorval and it was the first of these, CF-NAJ, which was purchased on 13 December 1968 at the cost of $C108,000. The crews were hired almost exclusively from Nordair, but the job of organising spares and clearing all the necessary administrative procedures delayed the departure of CF-NAJ until 17 January 1969 when it finally left Toronto for São Tomé.

Relief flights began on 24 January from São Tomé to Uli, with the single aircraft operating two to three flights per night and being kept serviceable by mechanics during the daytime. From 24 January to 9 February, a total of 28 relief flights were made. On 24 April, the remaining three ex-Nordair L1049Hs were obtained, and delivered in May (CF-NAK and CF-NAM) and July (CF-NAL). The first Canairelief L-1049H, CF-NAJ, wore the Nordair colours and white top, but subsequent aircraft were painted with a dark blue jungle 'camouflage' cabin top prior to delivery, and, once in Biafra, bore the dual titling 'Jointchurchaid-Canairelief', and the

Constellations operated by Biafran Government Forces

Identity	Type/ConNo.	Remarks
5N-07G	L-1049G/4514	Known as the Grey Ghost. Ex-F-BGNE of Air France. Ferried Paris - Lisbon 10.8.67. Abandoned at Lisbon mid-1969 and used for spares. Scrapped.

Constellations operated by Hank Warton on behalf of Biafran Government and German Churches

Identity	Type/ConNo.	Remarks
5T-TAC(1)	L-1049G/4645	ex-EC-AQN. The aircraft was ex KLM PH-LKK and served Iberia from 03.61 to 05.67. Acquired by Warton 29.6.67 and registered to North American Aircraft Trading Corp. 8.8.67. Registered as 5T-TAC early October 1967. It crashed on approach to Port Harcourt, Biafra, in 01.68.
5T-TAC(2)	L-1049D/4166	ex-LV-ILW, operated by Líneas Aéreas Patagónica Argentina. Possibly converted to L-1049H/03 standard. Allegedly purchased May 1968. Ferried Miami - Lisbon 22.5.68. Blown up at Bissau 4.6.68.
5T-TAF	L-1049G/4618	ex-CS-TLC of Transportes Aereos Portugueses (TAP). To International Aerodyne Inc 3.11.67. To North American Aircraft Trading Company 8.11.67. Impounded at Luqa, Malta 16.2.68 with a load of aircraft tyres.
5T-TAG(1)	L-1049G/4642	ex-D-ALOF of Lufthansa. To North American Aircraft Trading Company 8.12.67 and ferried Hamburg-Lisbon same day. German registration cancelled 13.11.67. Crashed on approach to Uli 1.7.68.
5T-TAH	L-1049G/4647	ex-D-ALID of Lufthansa. To North American Aircraft Trading Company 23.2.68. German registration cancelled 29.2.68. Abandoned at Abidjan 28.9.68.
5T-TAK	L-1049G/4640	ex-D-ALEC of Lufthansa. To North American Aircraft Trading Company 8.3.68. German registration cancelled 9.3.68. Ferried São Tomé - Lisbon 20-23.9.68 and abandoned. Broken up Lisbon 1981.

Constellations operated by the 'Phoenix Group' on behalf of ther Biafran Government.

Identity	Type/ConNo.	Remarks
HP-475	L-1049G/4551	Ferried Miami - Lisbon 9/68. named 'Angel of Peace' on airlift. Landed at Abidjan at end of war and abandoned. Impounded 3.70, broken up 1.71.
N8338	L-1049G/4616	ex-CS-TLA Transportes Aereos Portugueses (TAP). To International Aerodyne Inc 25.9.67, but not registered as N8338 until July 1968. Purchased by J A Crosson 21.11.68, but ferried Miami - Lisbon 7.11.68. False registration N83H noted.
5N-83H		To Phoenix Air Transport, named *Endeavour* and re-registered. Withdrawn from use at Faro autumn 1969.
N7776C	L-1049H/4801	Originally VH-EAM of QANTAS. Passed through several operators before being listed as 'owned by Leasing Consultants Inc, Miami'. Ferried Miami-Lisbon August 1969. Later stored at Faro 1.70 - 3.70 when flown back to Fort Lauderdale, FL. Broken up 1973.
N86524	L-749A/2660	Lease-purchased by Robert W. Cobaugh 31.10.69 from Concare Aircraft Leasing Corp and used on airlift from 9/69.

5N-86H		Re-registered. Abandoned at Faro 1/70 and broken up 1979.
N86525	L-749A/2662	Originally operated by Chicago & Southern Airlines. After passing through a number of operators, was lease-purchased by Carolina Aircraft Corp for use on Faro airlift.
5N85H		Re-registered. Crashed in the Oukaimeden mountain range, 70km south of Marrakech 28.11.69 reportedly as a result of 3-engine failure.
N563E	L-1049H/4833	Originally operated by REAL - Redes Estaduais Aéreas Ltda as PP-YSA. To VARIG. Leased by Robert W Cobaugh from Carolina Aircraft Corp for four months from November 1969 (probably to replace 5N-83H). Returned to Fort Lauderdale, Florida, at end of war. Broken up 1975.

Constellations used on NordChurchAid/Joint Church Aid Relief Airlift.

CF-AEN	L-1049H/4821	Canairelief. Arrived São Tomé from Montreal 20.11.69. Dep 25.1.70 to Toronto, arriving 29.1.70.
CF-NAJ	L-1049H/4828	Canairelief. 3 Arrived São Tomé from Montreal 17.1.69. Dep 10.2.69 to Paris for servicing; returned São Tomé 27.2.69. Crashed near Uli 3.8.69.
CF-NAK	L-1049H /4829	Canairelief. Arrived São Tomé from Montreal 2.5.69. Destroyed by bombing at Uli 17.12.69.
CF-NAL	L-1049H/4831	Canairelief. Arrived São Tomé from Montreal 30.7.69 Abandoned at São Tomé.
CF-NAM	L-1049H/4832	Canairelief. Arrived São Tomé from Montreal 2.6.69. Sustained damage at Uli 7.10.69; flown back to São Tomé for spares recovery. Later restored and test-flown 17.1.70 but abandoned at São Tomé.

Constellations operated by French Agencies in Biafra.

F-BHBI	L-1049G/4634	Operated by Air Fret until C of A expired 31.3.69. Stored at Nimes until August 1969 when donated to Biafra by French Government. Abandoned at Lanzarote after emergency landing late-1969.
F-BRAD	L-1049G/4519	Air Fret. Ferried Orly - Luqa - Douala - Libreville 7.9.68. Operated by Air Fret until 11.69.

Constellations operated into Biafra by Jack Malloch

VP-WAW	L-1049G/4685	Operated by Air Trans Africa September 1967 until 17.1.68 when ferried Lisbon-Woensdrecht for overhaul. Impounded but later released and ferried Woensdrecht - Las Palmas - Abidjan 24.9.68 as ZS-FAA. Re-registered TR-LNY and repainted at Abidjan 26.9.68.
TR-LNY		ex VP-WAW, ZS-FAA. Repainted at Abidjan 26.9.68 and ferried Abidjan-Libreville same date. Suffered severe engine trouble at Luanda 13.4.69 and grounded; abortive ferry flight out 1.5.69. Grounded until 6.11.69 when ferried Luanda - Salisbury for major overhaul. No further Biafran involvement.

Other Constellations used in Biafra

N469C	L-1049H/4847	Operated by Air Mid-East July-August 1968. Arrived Fernando Póo 22.7.68 for Biafra flights, but not given permission to operate. Returned Europe and then USA.
ZT-TBV	L-14049G/4581	Originally VH-EAB of QANTAS. To a number of operators, then Lee J Matherne. Noted at Lisbon, March 1968 with false registration ZP-TBV and Transcontinental Airlines SA titles. It was intended for use on the Biafran Airlift. Stored Miami June 1968 in Transcontinental titles less registration.

blue-yellow Jointchurchaid fish symbol. On 9 February, CF-NAJ, then the only one in service, had a narrow escape when bombs were dropped on the Uli runway by a Nigerian Air Force aircraft when the lights were lit briefly for a landing DC-6B. Only quick thinking by the World Council of Churches controller saved the airliner, which was just warming up for take-off. As the L-1049H began its take-off run, the controller rushed out towards the runway, flashing a torch. The captain of the Constellation, Don Merriam, saw the torch, immediately put the props into reverse and applied the brakes, stopping the aircraft a few feet away from the bomb crater on the runway. The airliner was ferried to Europe for repairs, first to Luton, England, arriving on 12 February, but the authorities refused to have anything to do with it, so it continued to Paris and returned to the airlift on 27

The ill-fated 5N-85H which crashed in Morroco. (Ameen Yasheed Collection)

February. During March 1969, 56 trips were completed with the single aircraft.

Then, on the night of 3 August 1969, CF-NAJ, piloted by Don Merriam, crashed into a hillside two miles west of the strip at Uli during a thunderstorm while turning on to final approach to land. All four crew were killed. At the time of the crash, Canairelief had completed 253 trips into Biafra carrying 3,800 tons of supplies. A replacement aircraft - L1049H CF-AEN - was ferried out from Montreal via London and Amsterdam arriving at São Tomé on 20 November. Most of the time, two of the four Canairelief Super Constellations were flying - a shortage of crews and necessary overhaul and repair work prevented more flying. During a night's operations, six to eight trips from São Tomé to Uli were flown by the L-1049Hs.

In the first week of December 1969, CF-NAM was damaged landing at Uli when a bomb exploded on the runway in front of its nose. Two weeks later, CF-NAK landed at Uli on 17 December loaded with food supplies. Just after the three crew had got out, a bomb hit the Super Connie, destroying it almost completely, together with its full load of food. Just before the end of the war, Captain Knox flew into various settlements in Biafra to evacuate the white workers (nurses, doctors, missionaries, teachers, etc.), landing the Super Connie on small, virtually unprepared strips without incident.

The last relief flights by the Canairelief Super Connies were made on 9 January 1970, after which CF-NAL and 'NAM were left at São Tomé awaiting a buyer. CF-AEN was ferried back to Toronto via Las Palmas on 25 January 1970. Canairelief carried out a total of 677 flights on the airlift, the record month being Dec 1969, with 113 trips into Biafra.

During September 1968 Hank Warton was finally sacked as Biafra's principal provider of arms flights, and he was ordered to remove the two remaining L-1049Gs from São Tomé as they were taking up valuable apron space. The first to depart was '5T-TAK' which was flown out empty, and on three engines, on 20 September 1968. Three days

An Associated Press Telex dated July 11 1970 announcing that authorities had found the remains of an aircraft with bodies on board. It was L-749 Constellation 5N85H. (Bill Armstrong Collection)

```
MARRAKECH, MOROCCO, JULY 11 (AP)   MOROCCAN  AUTHORITIES
HAVE FOUND A QUANTITY OF ARMS AND THE REMARKABLY PRESERVED
BODIES OF EIGHT EUROPEANS IN THE WRECK OF AN AIRCRAFT BELIEVED
TO BE ONE ﬀ OF BIAFRASXX GREY GHOSTS...THE GUNRUNNERS THAT
  KEPT SECESSIONIST STATE ALIVE DURING ITS WAR WITH NIGERIA.
THE WRECK OF THE PLANE, WHICH VILLAGERS SAID CRASHED LAST
 NOVEMBER, WAS REVEALED WITH MELTING SNOWS SOME 70 KILOMETERS
 SOUTH OF HERE IN THE OUKAIMEDEN MOUNTAIN RANGE AT AN ALTITDE
 OF 3000 METERS.
 THE BODIES WERE BURIED LOCALLY.  IT WAS SPECULATED THAT
  THE SIX PASSENGERS IN ADDITION TO THE PILOT AND COPILOT
  WERE MERCENARIES.  BUT MORROCCAN AUTHORITIES WOULD NOT SAY
   IF THEY HAD DETERMINED THEIR IDENTITY AND DECLINED TO
   PROVIDE ADDITIONAL DETAILS.  (END)
                                   JULY  11
```

Two views of the remains of CF-NAK which received a direct hit on 17/18 December 1969 from a bomb dropped by a Nigerian C-47. The remains were dragged off to one side of the strip at Uli and abandoned. *(Matt Black Collection)*

later it arrived in Lisbon and where, because of its overall state and condition, it was simply abandoned.

'5T-TAH' was in a worse state and failed to make it back to Lisbon. It too flew out of São Tomé on three engines - the Number 2 prop was feathered - on 28 September 1968. The crew headed for Abidjan where the aircraft landed safely. However, they refused to fly any further and abandoned the airliner then and there.

Hank Warton was said to have suffered a bad heart attack; it was not life-threatening, but he had been forced to move to Switzerland for recuperation. That was the official line for ending Hank's monopoly of arms supplies. But he did not completely sever his link with the Biafran airlift; he still had his contract with the German Churches and continued to operate the four surviving DC-7Cs on the relief airlift to Uli.

Hank Warton's rival, the Rhodesian gunrunner Jack Malloch, had been released from jail in Togo on 5 June 1968. He had been put on a aircraft to Europe from where he made his way back to Rhodesia to assess the damage sustained by his company as a result of his five-month absence.

Several of Jack Malloch's crews had transferred across to Hank Warton's operation. Others had joined legitimate companies operating in southern Africa. Malloch's two aircraft, the DC-4 VP-YTY and the L-1049G VP-WAW, were both at Woensdrecht, Holland where Aviolanda had impounded them in lieu of money owed for overhaul and other maintenance work carried out. But Malloch still had influential friends in high places. There can be few doubts that some of those friends were close to the upper reaches of the Quay d'Orsai in Paris.

Jack Malloch personally brought the L-1049G Super Constellation out of Woensdrecht, with Clive Halse in the right-hand seat. The Rhodesian marks were changed to South African for the ferry flight. As ZS-FAA, the L-1049G departed Woensdrecht on 24 September 1968 and was flown to Las Palmas for an overnight stay. The following day it staged on to Abidjan where the aircraft also took on a newly-allocated Gabonese identity. Then, and as TR-LNY, Malloch, Halse and Hodges positioned the Constellation to Libreville but it was not until the night of 2/3 October that it was first flown into Uli. For a week the L-1049G operated almost

Devoid of titles, CF-NAM waits in the rain. *(Kirk Smeeton Collection)*

nightly on an Abidjan - Uli - São Tomé - Abidjan arms run, the visits to São Tomé necessary for refuelling with high-octane fuel. Jack Malloch was back in business.

During the two and a half years that the Biafran airlift was in operation, a number of other Constellations appeared briefly on the scene, apart from the 'regulars' mentioned in the preceding paragraphs. The first of these was a 1049G Freighter complete with tip-tanks and a very smart brown colour scheme with the bold letters Transcontinental Airlines S.A. on the roof, and the Paraguayan registration ZP-TBV. This aircraft made a brief appearance at Lisbon on 17 March 1968, and, so far as is known, its owner, Lee J. Matherne, tried to bid for some of the lucrative business in arms ferrying that was available at the time. However, since Hank Warton had a virtual monopoly at that time, the aircraft returned shortly afterwards to Latin America and eventually to Miami. Somehow it is not surprising that the aircraft was never officially registered in Paraguay, nor did the airline Transcontinental ever officially exist!

A new model of Constellation appeared late in 1969 - the L-1649A Starliner HP-501. The aircraft had originally been registered in Iceland as TF-ERA for ammunition flights between Lisbon and São Tomé. The Icelandic registration was withdrawn, however, after the intervention of the Federal Nigerian government, and the aircraft only made one trip under its Icelandic registration - to Tel Aviv in Israel for an overhaul in mid-August 1969, returning on 13 September. When the same aircraft was later registered in Panama, it was supposedly owned by a former Warton pilot, Larry Raab. The Starliner flew from Luxembourg to Lisbon on 28 October 1969, returning to Luxembourg on 14 November. It later made an ammunition flight to São Tomé, but never flew on to Uli, probably because the L-1649A's main undercarriage track was wider than an L-1049's and with the width of the main runway only seventy-five feet at Uli, - that is 16 feet on either side of the main wheels - the landing would have been tricky in the dark! On 11 January 1970, HP-501 left São Tomé for Faro, and subsequently ended up at Douala in the Cameroons.

In July 1969, a further L-1049H, N7776C, owned by Leasing Consultants Inc. and flying for the Biafran government - or perhaps the Phoenix group - arrived at Lisbon. From then until the end of the war, the aircraft regularly flew from Lisbon, later Faro, and even from Luxembourg on the arms lift to São Tomé and Uli. At the end of the war, it remained at Faro for several months before returning to Florida.

One further Super Connie, again an L-1049H, made a brief appearance on the airlift. This was N563E, almost certainly leased by the Biafran government from the Carolina Aircraft Leasing Corp. in Florida, and again flown by Larry Raab. N563E arrived in São Tomé on 2 January 1970 with a Sud Alouette helicopter for the Biafran forces on board. The helicopter may have been used in ferrying Biafran officials to safety when the Biafrans were defeated a few days later. The 1049H returned to Florida shortly afterwards.

A number of international relief agencies also flew a variety of transport aircraft, mostly L-1049s, DC-7s and DC-6s, into Biafra, these being left unmolested by the DC-3 bombers when operating into Uli. The Roman Catholic relief agency, Caritas International, chartered L-1049s from March 1968, which operated from São Tomé and were often able to smuggle in two plane-loads a night of medicine and food such as salt, rice, beans and powdered milk. An L-1049 chartered by the Red Cross crashed on landing at night in bad weather on 1 July

CF-NAM and CF-NAL are 'preserved' - if that is the right word - at São Tomé. Both airliners sat abandoned at the airport for thirty years until in 2007 it was announced that both aircraft were to be declared national monuments to commemorate the humanitarian airlift based out of Sao Tome during the Biafran conflict

Both aircraft were to form the centrepiece of an airport restaurant.

By 2018 both aircraft were reported to be under cover and incorporated into the Asas D'Avião Restaurante Santola.

As can be seen from these pictures, a better description would be that the aircraft provide cover for the restaurant!

1968 with a load of 10½ tons of medical supplies, the three crew and one passenger aboard being killed. And on 3 Aug 1969 Nordair L-1049H CF-NAJ crashed at Uli while on charter to Canairelief, operated by the Presbyterian Church of Canada and Oxfam of Canada, while CF-NAK was destroyed by strafing at Uli on 17 December of that year. Nordair's other two L-1049Hs were also chartered to Canairelief, while an ex-Transocean and Capitol L-1049H CF-AEN, formerly N1927H, was used by Joint Church Aid. In this curiously ramshackle air war, with DC-3s being used as makeshift bombers and armed light aircraft by Biafra, it was the airlift above all that enabled Biafra to prolong its resistance and hence its agony. Several airlift L-1049s were abandoned by their owners in Africa or at Lisbon after Biafra's surrender in January 1970.

The 749A 5N-86H had the distinction of flying the Biafran leader out of defeated Biafra. Ojuwku, with his family and high-ranking officials, arrived at Uli towards midnight, on 10 January 1970. Just before 1am on 11 January 5N-86H departed Uli for São Tomé and exile for the leader in Abidjan, on the Ivory Coast, where he arrived on 12 January 1970.

During the period from May 1967 until the end of the war on 12 January 1970, at least twenty-four Constellations took part in the Biafran airlift, on arms flights, relief flights, or both. Five were lost in accidents and two more on the ground, with only four accidents involving loss of life. Due to the nature of the operations carried out, it is impossible to assess how many flights were made, or what the total tonnage carried was. It is, however, testimony to the soundness of the Constellation's design and to the stability of the aircraft in flying and landing with engines and systems unserviceable that so many of these Connies continued flying month after month, especially considering the primitive conditions prevailing at Uli airfield.

Chapter 12

'The last of the summer wine,
A vintage love, a vintage brew,
And now my love this toast I give,
Thank you for being you'.

Bill Owen 1914-1999

Most people find the shape of the Constellation very easy on the eye; some admit to a love affair, others find the shape particularly pleasing. I happily admit to being in the latter group; to me, the Connie has 'personality'!

By the late 1960s, many airports around the world had 'Corrosion Corners' - areas of an airport, usually far away from the main passenger terminals that were hang-outs for dubious charter operators, cargo flyers, bull-shippers and others that would carry out flights for a suitcase full of cash, no questions asked. Airlines that operated out of these places often had one eye constantly on the gate for the local airworthiness inspectors to show up, and employed aircraft mechanics who knew how to wash engines with 100 octane fuel to remove any trace of oil leaks!

These were the haunts of many of the airline industry 'characters'; financially astute if morally bankrupt businessmen who knew a bargain when they saw it come their way. Call them Sky Tramps, Flying Buccaneers or Airmen of Fortune - they often flew anything to anywhere at a price that undercut the company next door.

They could do this because the airliners they operated had been obtained at knock-down prices due to the glut of second or third-hand machines that surfaced globally when the major carriers got rid of their piston-engined airliners with the advent of the jets.

Often these machines were Constellations. Like the earlier Super Constellations, the L-1049G and L-1049H found ready buyers in the second-hand airliner market but as the 1960s progressed jets became more and more essential for the best charter business, and so it was that the later Super Connie variants achieved the greatest prominence - and occasionally a high degree of notoriety in operations such as the Biafra airlift.

Capitol Airways had one of the biggest used Super Connie fleets and acquired its first L-1049G in January 1960. This aircraft was built for Howard Hughes and delivered as long ago as 24 February 1956 but, like most airliners built to the personal order of Hughes, it had done little flying for him and when it was returned to Lockheed, Capitol traded in one of their L-749As in part exchange for it. An ex-

N9751C of Trans-International was a L-1049G, formerly VH-EAD of QANTAS. The airliner passed through a number of operators before being scrapped in July 1968. The scene is typical of 'corrosion corners' scattered around the world. *(author's collection from 35mm transparency dated Jan 69)*

N9412H of Air Nevada is the former Air France L-049A-51-26 F-BAZA that was purchased by the Hughes Tool Co in 1950. Air Nevada was set up in 1970 to fly gamblers in and out of Las Vegas from Hawthorne, Oakland and San Francisco *(author's collection from 35mm transparency dated Feb 1970)*

Transocean L-1049H was bought from the Babb Co, the parent company of Transocean, in April 1959, and two more ex-Seaboard World L-1049Hs several years later. The four ex-Hughes Tool (for TWA) L-1049Hs sold to Trans-International Airlines were leased by them to Capitol in 1962-63, and Capitol also purchased an ex-QANTAS L-1049G that had been sold back to Lockheed in March 1960; this Super G later went to Trans-International and to Standard Airways.

The last of Capitol's Super Constellations were phased out early in 1968 when replaced by Douglas DC-8 jets and the remaining twelve L-1049s in Capitol service, plus an L-749A, were put up for disposal at Wilmington; altogether Capitol had operated seventeen L-1049s and L-749s since 1955. One of the last charter jobs to be undertaken by Capitol's L-1049s was a series of inclusive tour flights out of Berlin on behalf of the Berliner Flug Ring travel agency, three or four of these aircraft being based on Berlin for this purpose.

American Flyers Airline Corp acquired the QANTAS Super G VH-EAO *Southern Prodigal* on lease from California Airmotive as N86682, as well as two more L-1049s from other sources, while another ex-QANTAS Super G went to Resort Airlines in 1959 to supplement the two L-1049Hs it had ordered. In 1968 a new charter operator, called Air Mid-East, was formed with a single Super Constellation and by 1970 claimed to have built up its fleet to eight 115-passenger L-1049s from various sources, six DC-7s and four DC-6s. It intended to specialise in charters throughout the Middle East. Another little-known L-1049 operator was Rutas Aereas Panamenas SA which was operating an ex-Thai Airways and Guest 1049G, HP-467, for Cia Interamericana Export-Import SA. The latter had it on lease from the used-aircraft dealers International Aerodyne of Miami when it crashed just after taking off from Panama City on a freight flight on 30 March 1968, killing the crew of three. The export-import company for whom it was being operated also acquired a second Super Connie, an ex-Iberia L-1049E, from International Aerodyne.

One of Trans-Canada's surplus Super Gs was later involved in a gun-running episode; this was CF-TEX, sold to Douglas as N9642Z and later to California Airmotive. It was leased to Continental Councellors and then, from early 1965, went on lease-purchase to Walter R Von der Ahe of Van Nuys, who at one time was the owner and operator of Van Nuys Skyways and previously an executive with the family business, Von's Grocery Stores. Von der Ahe lease-sold it to a charter operator called United States Airways of

N90816 of Pacific Air Transport was a former TWA L-049. It passed through a number of operators being with PAT from 1966 until 1972. It was finally scrapped in 1988.
(author's collection from 35mm transparency dated Feb 70)

N469C, clearly on lease from Aerolessors Inc, was used by Air Mid-East, apparently here being used to transport animals. Established at New York's John F Kennedy Airport to operate passenger and freight flights in the Middle East in 1968 *(author's collection from 35mm transparency dated Jan 69)*

which very little has ever been discovered. The aircraft had already been in trouble at Gatwick on 22 January 1965 when it was detained for failing to take a charter party of West Indians to Jamaica, but on 2 February it was allowed to leave for Amsterdam, ostensibly on a charter for Trans-Africa Air Coach which had been created to operate low-cost flights to Africa. The Constellation landed at Beek in southern Holland where, after the bogus Ghanaian registration '9G-28' had been painted on the fuselage and false papers provided, it left for Prague to carry a cargo of illegal arms to the Congo. Engine trouble forced it to land at Luqa, Malta, where most of the arms on board were confiscated and the three-man crew fined £300. The aircraft was not released until 29 January 1966 and was then repossessed by Mr Von der Ahe, who had received only one instalment of $10,000 as a down payment on the aircraft from United States Airways; the bogus marks N964 were also applied.

A far more substantial operator was one of the major US supplementals, World Airways, which leased three L-1049Hs from California Eastern Aviation in January 1961, a fourth, an ex-Transocean one, N1880 from the 1880 Corp in the same month, and an ex-Resort L-1049H on 3 May 1961, plus two more leased from KLM in 1962. The ex-California

Above: N6931C is the former California Eastern L1049H. It was leased to Skyways and in service May 1969 at Heathrow Airport. *(author's collection from 35mm transparency dated Mar 69)*

Below: With its white paint starting to show signs of weathering, the former PP-YSC of VARIG, now N565E of Carolina Aircraft Corporation, is seen at Amsterdam.
(author's collection from 35mm transparency dated Mar 70)

L-1049D N6502C seen coming in to land sometime in 1960. The airline was renamed Seaboard World Airlines in 1961. *(author's collection from 35mm transparency dated Feb 61)*

Eastern aircraft went to Slick from September 1963 and later to Airlift International, and the ex-Resort and KLM L-10049Hs went to Flying Tiger, while the ex-Transocean L-1049H later went to Alaska Airlines on lease in May 1964, and then to Montreal Air Services and Airlift International. Alaska also acquired a second ex-QANTAS L-1049H on lease late in 1962.

In the Far East, Air America, which operated a sizeable fleet of small aircraft on quasi-military operations in Laos against the Communist Pathet Lao (Free Laos) guerillas, acquired an L-1049H, N6229C, from Flying Tiger late in 1963 for linking its base at Tainan (Taiwan) to other parts of the Far East. And another ex-Flying Tiger L-1049H was acquired by China Airlines, now the national airline of Formosa or Taiwan, on 24 October 1966 and on 2 December this inaugurated a twice-weekly Taipei-Saigon service. In Indonesia, Nusantara Airlines was formed in 1968 by a group of US and Indonesian businessmen and investors to operate domestic services among the Indonesian islands, as well as limited international services. Plans were made to lease-purchase nine L-1049Hs from Flying Tiger and operations were due to start from Djakarta on 16 September. But Nusantara ran into financial difficulties, its first L-1049H was impounded at Singapore on 21 September and later detained at Hong Kong, and the airline never started operations.

Second-Hand Starliners - and the 'Travel Clubs'
As the 1649A was a stop-gap between the Super Constellation and the big jets, it was not long before the first examples began to come on to the used airliner market. TWA sold four to an Argentine carrier, Trans Atlantica Argentina, in 1960-61 on a lease-purchase basis, the first on 12 September 1960, and with these a twice-weekly service between Buenos Aires and Geneva via Rio de Janeiro, Recife and Lisbon was started, Dakar later being substituted for Recife as a stop. However, as many airlines, such as Aerolineas Argentinas, introduced jets between South America and Europe, it became impossible to operate profitably over this route with piston-engined types, and Trans Atlantica Argentina had to suspend operations on 5 November 1961.

Another TWA 1649A was acquired from a Miami aircraft dealer in the spring of 1964 for long-haul freight charters by the Argentine charter operator, Lineas Aereas Patagonica Argentinas SRL (LAPA), which had also acquired an ex-TWA L-1049A and an ex-Seaboard L-1049D. LAPA soon experienced

CF-NAK, the former National Airlines N7132C of the small Canadian airline, Nordair. It is seen here loading freight at Dorval, Canada in October 1967. This aircraft was destroyed on 17 December 1969 in a bombing raid on the airstrip at Uli, Biafra while being operated by Canairelief.
(author's collection from 35mm transparency dated Jan 68)

economic difficulties and suspended all its flights in September 1965, ceasing operations when its L-1049A crashed off Lima on a smuggling flight on 6 March 1966.

Another ex-TWA 1649A was leased by the Argentine scheduled freight carrier, Aerovias Halcon SRL from May 1968; this airline operated freight services within Argentina, to seven other South American countries and to Miami. Yet another ex-TWA 1649A was acquired in 1966 on lease from Passaat of Miami for one flight by Aerovias Condor de Colombia Ltda - (Aerocondor), which operated scheduled domestic services and to Aruba, Curacao and Miami, but this crashed on 18 December 1966 on the approach to Bogota's El Dorado airport.

Air France leased a 1649A to Air Afrique in October 1961 and two more from 18 April 1962, the latter being re-registered in the Ivory Coast as TU-TBB and TU-TBA and returned to Air France on 28 May and 7 June 1963. Air Afrique was the multi-national airline of eleven then newly-independent former French African states to which both Air France and the French independent UAT provided technical assistance and aircraft. The South African carrier Trek Airways, which specialised in the operation of low-fare, low-frequency services from South Africa to Europe, acquired two ex-Lufthansa 1649As from World Airways Inc in February and March 1964, and operated them on scheduled flights from Johannesburg to Luxembourg, having been made the designated South African carrier on this route, for which Luxembourg was now the main European terminal.

Trek's flights were routed through Windhoek, Luanda (Angola) and the Cape Verde Islands to circumvent the anti-apartheid ban on South African aircraft overflying their territories imposed by the black African states in the summer of 1963, and the 1649A's extra range enabled this new routeing to be flown with a full payload; the Windhoek stop was later dropped. A co-operative agreement was signed with the Luxembourg airline, Luxair, for joint operation of the 1649As from April 1964, Luxair operating a connecting Luxembourg-London flight with the 1649As, all three of which were re-registered in Luxembourg. On 7 May 1965, Trek began a once-fortnightly 1649A service on behalf of South African Airways from Johannesburg to Perth via Mauritius and the Cocos Islands. This alternated with SAA's DC-7B service over the same route to provide a weekly South African frequency to match the weekly QANTAS Electra service to Johannesburg; the Trek 1649A flights over the Indian Ocean route continued until September 1965. The 1649As, operated as ninety-eight seaters, were replaced on flights to Luxembourg by a leased Britannia from June 1968, but a 1649A operated the onward flight to London until 30 September of that year; later a 707 replaced the Britannia and the 1649As were used for charter flights from South Africa.

TWA leased two 1649A freighters to Alaska Airlines during 1962-63 for the latter's MATS contract charter work, Alaska finally buying them both on 31 December 1963 and a third, for spares, in March 1965 to supplement its L-1049Hs. After 1965 the 1649As were also used for certain scheduled services such as those between Anchorage and Fairbanks, and both the Alaska aircraft, plus a third ex-TWA 1649A freighter, were disposed of in 1969 to the Prudhoe Bay Oil Distributing Co of Anchorage, one of the companies associated with the big oil-drilling operations in northern Alaska. Prudhoe Bay later turned over one of these 1649As to Red Dodge Aviation, a subsidiary of Flying W Airways.

The travel clubs that sprang up in the States in the mid-1960s to provide cheap air transport for their members in the piston-engined airliners now made obsolete by jets made good use of the 1649A as well as the earlier model Constellations.

This was a phenomenon that first appeared in the United States in the mid-1960s, encouraged by the

Trek Airways' ZS-DVI was the former Lufthansa L-1649 Starliner D-ALOL. It is seen here at Johannesburg in May 1969. It survives in the South African Airways Collection.
(Bill Armstrong collection from 35mm transparency dated June 69)

N179AV, a L-1649 of Air Venturers, a US Travel Club, seen here at London Gatwick. The aircraft survives at Kermit Weeks' Fantasy of Flight Museum in Florida painted in its original Lufthansa colours.
(Kirk Smeeton collection from 35mm transparency dated June 67)

availability of large, long-range, piston-engined transport aircraft at a reasonable price. An 'Air Travel Club' was a group of individuals who, because of a common interest in seeing their own country or the rest of the world, joined together, each contributing a share of, for example, $100 and a monthly or annual sum, which allowed them to take part in the cheap travel (in the early '60s this was up to fifty per cent cheaper than regular air-fares) in their 'own' aircraft. A similar thing occurred in the UK under the title 'Affinity Group Charters' which allowed such groups to charter, but not own their own aircraft.

In the USA travel clubs were originally licenced under the FARs (Federal Aviation Regulations) for general aviation. However, in late 1968, the FAA, seeing a large number of four-engined aircraft used for such purposes, was anxious to ensure a proper level of safety. To solve this, they required the airliners to be certified, as with other operators of large aircraft - both commercial operators and supplemental air carriers - under FAR Part 123 - the regulations under which the travel clubs were allowed to operate.

The most commonly used aircraft in the 1960s were Constellations and DC-7s of various models. Most travel clubs employed full-time executives to coordinate activities, and of course, had full-time qualified commercial pilots and maintenance personnel. They were regarded as non-profit making organizations and were therefore exempt from State and Federal taxes. Membership of an Air travel club could vary from as little as five hundred people to several thousand, and, in the 1960s, each club averaged about three trips of around thirty-five hours flying time per month, though there were obviously very considerable variations.

World Samplers Travel Club acquired N7321C, an ex-TWA machine, through a dealer in November 1965 and had previously leased the one that later crashed with Aerocondor of Colombia besides using a Model 049, the other one being registered to the Association of Flying Travel Clubs in 1967. Another travel club, Flying Ambassadors, was operating an ex-TWA 1649A N7302C in 1966, and an unexpected buyer of one of TWA's Jetstream Starliners was the Moral Re-Armament organisation, an international moral and spiritual movement that developed from American minister Frank Buchman's Oxford Group. Buchman headed MRA for twenty-three years until his death in 1961, although the organisation survived him. The MRA bought N7314C on 10 December 1965.

The airline did not keep it for long, for in 1966 it was in use by the International Travel Club, which gave the airliner its tongue-twisting name of *Supercalifragilisticexpialidocious* from the 1964 *Mary Poppins* movie. There appears to be no truth in the rumour that on the other side it was painted with

Starliner N8181H in the gorgeous red and gold scheme of Willair International. The aircraft suffered undercarriage collapse at Stockton, California on 10 June 1968 and shortly after was scrapped.
(Kirk Smeeton collection from 35mm transparency dated May 68)

Coming out of a menacing Floridian sky is HI-515 of AMSA - Aerolineas Mundo SA.
(Kirk Smeeton collection from 35mm transparency dated May 87)

the name *Dociousaliexpisticfragicalirupus!* It later went to another travel club known as Holiday Wings, and was painted with the legend 'West Texas Flying Clubhouse'.

One of the ex-Lufthansa 1649A freighters used by World Airways went to a travel club called Air Venturers on 3 March 1966, but in October of that year, it was leased to the Lebanese all-freight carrier, Trans Mediterranean Airways SAL, to supplement DC-4s and DC-6s on the airline's cargo services between Beirut and London.

Air Venturers had been formed in 1965 or 1966 and purchased a 1649A in March 1966. One of the early travel clubs, Air Venturers flew its l649A all over the world during the following years, visiting such places as Acapulco, Mexico City, Montego Bay and Europe. The chief pilot was John Connell.

A second 1649A, N7314C was reported in use in June 1967, and the first 1649A was also leased to other operators when not in use by the club, and was later sold to CHS Leasing Corporation and leased back by the club. In 1968, the first aircraft appeared with the additional titling 'Country Club of the Sky', and remained in service until 1970.

World Airways acquired all four of the ex-Lufthansa 1649As on lease, two in July and two in October 1962, to supplement its L-1049Hs. Two of these went to Trek early in 1964, when the contracts on the others expired, one later went to Air Venturers, and the fourth went back to Lufthansa to be finally retired by them in November 1965, eventually ending its days converted into a restaurant at Hartenholm, near Hamburg. Two of the ex-TWA I649As went to a company called Willair International,

One of the Luxair/Trek aircraft, LX-LGY, formerly F-BHBR, became N4796 in July 1969 and was given the Icelandic registration TF-ERA for a single flight to Tel Aviv in the colours of a charter operator called Nittler Air Transport International, although the registered owner was Bjorn Sverrisson. It later left Luxembourg and was registered in Panama as HP-501 in October 1969. Another operator was Air Korea, which acquired 1649A freighter HL-4003 in March 1967 and used it on charter flights in the Far East until operations ceased in August 1968.

One of the ex-TWA 1649As later used by Trans Atlantica Argentina, N7307C, formerly LV-GLI, was returned to TWA early in 1964 and sold by them to the FAA for the low price of $38,000 for a simulated air crash at Deer Valley Airport, Phoenix, Arizona, which was staged on 3 September 1964. The purpose of these tests was to provide comprehensive data to help reduce the hazards of landing and take-off accidents and to study under full-scale, simulated conditions factors affecting passenger survival and evacuation, impact and fire damage and spread. The Flight Safety Foundation made the tests under an FAA contract, and both the DC-7 and 1649A were fully instrumented to record fuel tank pressures, wing and fuselage accelerations and crash loads and stresses. Detailed experiments were designed to obtain data on passenger and crew seat strength and restraint systems, cargo restraint systems and methods of fuel containment. High-speed ciné cameras in the cabin were used to photograph the effect of the impact on seats and twenty-one dummy passengers, while external cameras covered the impact sequence and the rupturing of the fuel tanks.

Some extra window-like squares were painted on the 1649A's fuselage for observation purposes, these stretching right back to the tailplane leading edge and forward over the nosewheel bay, there being a second line of such squares underneath the first on the forward fuselage.

To simulate the crash the 1649A and DC-7 were started, the engines warmed up, and instrumentation switched on. Engine power was then increased by remote control to accelerate the aircraft up to about 140 mph before it struck a series of prepared barriers, the 1649A being guided to the crash site employing a guide rail and an attachment to the nosewheel to ensure that it followed the correct path without any pilots on board; it was, however, just airborne for half a second before impact. The port wing struck an inclined mound of earth intended to provide the progressive destruction of the wing as would occur in a touchdown with one wing too low, the starboard wing then colliding with two telephone wire poles representing trees. The fuselage crashed into a shallow hill sloping at about ten degrees, this slope extending for a distance of one hundred and fifty feet, levelling out for another one hundred and fifty feet and then rising again at an angle of twenty degrees.

Both wings separated from the aircraft, and the fuselage broke in two places. The only fire occurred at impact when engine oil ignited. The prototype gelled fuel containment system, designed to reduce post-crash fires, worked well. Researchers reported that only two of the twenty-one test dummies and one of the three dolls on board would have perished in the crash. These two experiments reflected a growing realization that fatalities in take-off or landing accidents could be reduced if passengers were prevented from colliding with the aircraft's interior structure or furnishings and protected from post-crash fire and smoke. The tests provided valuable data on such matters as fuel spillage; the safety characteristics of the rear-, forward-, and side-facing passenger seats; and the efficacy of passenger-restraining devices.

The aircraft came to rest three hundred feet beyond the wing crash barriers, the fuselage breaking some way aft of the cockpit and again about two-thirds of the way along its length. Later the partly wrecked fuselage, still where it came to rest on final impact, was used for a series of tests on emergency passenger evacuation, beginning on 8 April 1965 with volunteers from the Deer Valley area acting as 'passengers' and selected to reflect the composition of a typical airline flight - fifty-seven per cent male, thirty per cent female, five per cent of both sexes aged sixty or more and eight per cent children under twelve. To achieve the highest realism, passenger injuries were faked, the cabin aisles were deliberately cluttered, and smoke bombs and crash sound effects were added, the breaks in the fuselage from the crash being covered over. Again, remotely-controlled ciné cameras were used both outside and inside the aircraft to record passenger reaction, and various parts of the evacuation process were precisely timed.

Interestingly, when the FAA released footage from the crash to the news media, the Air Transport Association was not happy. Stuart Tipton, the ATA president at that time, complained to then-FAA Administrator Najeeb Halaby that publicly providing the film of the test would 'scare the daylights' out of people already afraid to fly. The FAA argued that the public had been well informed that the footage came from a scientific experiment and not an actual crash. Furthermore, the agency explained, the test showed the FAA's commitment to assuring passenger and crew survival during take-off and landing accidents. Despite ATA's concerns, the public seemed to understand the nature of the test and anxiously awaited the next 'crash spectacular'. On 3 September, FAA and Flight Safety Foundation researchers intentionally crashed a Lockheed Constellation at Deer Valley Airport. The purpose of this and the

From this faded FAA test footage come these stills of the preparation and deliberate crash of N7307C.

In this first image on the right the airliner's nosewheel is connected to the rail that will guide it to the impact point.

Note also the black and white marking that will demonstrate an impact distortion.

Left: the moment of firtst impact as the Starliner's main undervcarriage is wiped off.

Two more stills from the faded FAA test footage of the deliberate crash of N7307C.

It is not the sort of film to be shown as in-flight entertainment!

earlier test, according to FAA, was to measure the forces acting on commercial airliners in a 'marginally survivable' crash so aircraft could be designed for greater safety.

'The Strolling Bones Roadies Van'
The Rolling Stones Far Eastern Tour of 1973 was a concert tour of countries bordering the Pacific Ocean in January and February by The Rolling Stones.

The tour was not associated with any album's release, but effectively was an extension of the Stones' infamous 1972 American STP Tour. The original intent was to play Australia and New Zealand, which had not seen the Stones since February and March 1966, as well as Japan, which had never seen the Stones at all. However, the Stones' 1972 American Tour had drawn worldwide press for its combustive mixture of group decadence and fan riots set amidst jet-set hangers-on. This caused the Stones some serious drama for their Pacific visits in that visas and work permits might be hard to obtain. Accordingly, the Stones scheduled some shows in Hawaii first, as a fallback in case they could not visit certain countries. Hawaiian fans camped out on Christmas night 1972 in order to buy tickets.

The Stones fears were confirmed when on 4 January 1973 Australia's Immigration Ministry let it be known that one of the Stones, unnamed, was banned from entering the country. On 8 January the Japanese Foreign Ministry said Mick Jagger would not be allowed into their country due to his prior drugs convictions.

On 9 January the Australians relented and said the Stones could enter. But first, the Stones announced an 18 January benefit concert at the Los Angeles Forum for victims of the recent 23 December 1972 earthquake in Nicaragua, Bianca Jagger's home country. This event was opened by Santana and Cheech & Chong, and served as the warm-up concert for the Pacific Tour. It raised more than £200,000 in relief funds. Transporting the Stones' sound and lighting gear was a veteran Lockheed 749 Constellation registered N7777G.

Back then, such a tour was breaking new ground and discovering new logistical challenges. Much of the sound and lighting gear had to travel with the group, not because the performers demanded it but because such equipment was not available in the countries on the tour. Taking a tour on the road back then was an 'on the cheap' operation. Their budget determined that the freighter of choice would be a twenty-six-year-old Lockheed Constellation which had been built for the Dutch airline KLM in 1947. Even an aficionado of fine old propliners would have to concede that this once beautiful aeroplane was now best described as decrepit.

The Stones started the tour proper with the three shows over 21 January and 22 January in Hawaii, at the Honolulu International Center with ZZ Top as the opening act. These were Mick Taylor's last shows as a Rolling Stone in the United States until a guest appearance at Kansas City in 1981. Next up on the

N7777G in a previous life as a freighter with Wien Alaska Airlines. (John Bagley/Science Museum)

schedule were a number of shows at the Budokan in Tokyo, running from 28 January to 1 February, for which 55,000 tickets had already been sold. But on 27 January, Japanese officials made a final confirmation of their decision to not let the Stones land; the shows were scrapped and the concert promoter had to refund all the tickets.

The Stones tour of Australasia was promoted by the Paul Dainty Organisation. Arranging transportation for the Stones sound and lighting gear fell to Production Manager, Patrick Stansfield. Enquiries eventually led to Miami, Florida and Air Cargo International which was just one of many companies owned by Lance Dreyer, whose name had become synonymous with the Constellation during the twilight years of an airliner once considered to be the Queen of the Skies. By the time KLM's former PH-TET *Tilburg* was sold to Dreyer's Unum Inc in March 1972 it had already led a hard life with several owners and numerous flights to and from South American destinations with indeterminate payloads.

Air Cargo International provided the aircraft and crew. The airliner was flown into Long Beach by the co-pilot Brooks A. Moore. The Captain, Charlie Rector, joined at Long Beach for the leg to Honolulu. As Brooks had no ticket to fly this aircraft type, the entire enterprise began in violation of FAA regulations, for which Lance Dreyer was cited and eventually fined. Ricky Riccatelli of Buffalo N.Y. was Flight Engineer, and he babied the old girl, replacing cylinder heads between each flight leg.

The tongue and lips logo on both poster and aircraft.

'The design concept for the Tongue was to represent the band's anti-authoritarian attitude, Mick's mouth and the obvious sexual connotations', said designer John Pasche, who started working with the Stones when he was still a student at the Royal College of Art.

The Constellation arrived in Honolulu during the band's two day stand at the Neil Blaisdell Center. All the stage gear had already been freighted to Honolulu with Pan Am. It was time for the band's roadies to work out how to get it all on board. 777G was to carry all the band's music equipment, sound system, and eight 'Super Trouper' arc lights.

N7777G departed Honolulu on 6 February 1973 and arrived at Pago Pago, American Samoa after just over twenty-two hours flying time since leaving Long Beach. On the same day, the Stones departed Los Angeles for Sydney by airline. After a night stop, the Connie departed for Auckland, New Zealand where it arrived on 8 February having crossed the International Date Line. The first Australasian concert by the Rolling Stones was a daytime performance at Auckland's Western Springs Stadium on Sunday 11 February. Later that day, N7777G set off for Brisbane, Australia where the next concert was scheduled for Wednesday 14 February at the Milton Park Tennis Courts which was then the largest venue available.

The day after the Brisbane concert, the Rolling Stones and more particularly the Connie, were in the newspapers for all the wrong reasons. Under the headline 'Stones Worst Kept Secret', the *Brisbane Telegraph* reported that, during a routine search of the Connie, Her Majesty's Customs had found 'a grass-like substance hidden on board.' One could be forgiven for thinking that this was to be expected on an aircraft used previously for transporting livestock but nevertheless, subsequent analysis revealed the substance was indeed six grams of cannabis.

Below: N7777G undergoes maintenance at Melbourne.

Right: reporting the news.

The day after the Brisbane concert, N7777G departed for Melbourne where the next concert was scheduled for Saturday 17 February at the Kooyong Tennis Courts. Two concerts were held on the Saturday with another on Sunday. Adelaide was next on the itinerary with concerts at Memorial Drive Park on Tuesday and Wednesday 20/21 February. All the stage gear was trucked from Melbourne to Adelaide by Comet Transport while the Connie remained in Melbourne for maintenance. Trans-Australia Airlines internal correspondence states that TAA contracted to unload 20,000 pounds of equipment in Melbourne and to perform a one hundred hour service on the airliner. For the purposes of this contract, the owner of the aircraft

STONES' WORST KEPT SECRET

MELBOURNE: It's supposed to be a secret — but the British pop group Rolling Stones is due at Tullamarine Airport at 7 o'clock tonight from Brisbane.

The group left Brisbane early this afternoon. They could make a last minute change of flights — but the tickets are still confirmed for Ansett flight 31 ex Brisbane.

Another worst kept secret is where the Stones' front line troops, Mick Jagger, and Keith Richards, are staying in Melbourne for Saturday's Kooyong tennis courts concerts.

There are 10 bookings for the top performers at an hotel in Exhibition Street, Melbourne.

This morning the Stones rested in a Brisbane motel after a performance in pouring rain last night before 8000 at the Milton tennis courts.

Their sound and lighting gear weighing 11 tons was loaded into a Super Constellation chartered aircraft to fly to Melbourne this afternoon.

When the aircraft arrived in Brisbane from New Zealand on Monday night Customs men found a grass-like substance hidden on board.

Queensland Collector of Customs, Mr. W. Moore said today that analysis revealed the substance as 6 grams, a little more than one ounce, of cannabis.

Mr. Ron Blackmore, a director of the Paul Dainty Corporation which is handling the Stones' 21 day Australasian tour, said from Brisbane today: "No details of the Stones' flight arrangements to Melbourne and their accommodation plans are being given to anybody, not even the media."

Paul Dainty Corporation spokesmen in Melbourne also said that the Stones' movements were a closely guarded secret.

"They might arrive tonight, or they might sneak in tomorrow morning," he said.

N7777G in TWA colours, which is never actually wore in service, at the Science Museum outstation at Wroughton, near Swindon in the UK. *(John Bagley/Science Museum)*

was shown as Sunday Promotions of Houston, Texas (President Lance Dreyer). The contract stipulated that all services rendered would be paid for in cash by the aircraft captain. The one hundred hour service would be under the supervision of the aircraft Flight Engineer who would also sign the aircraft out. TAA worksheets show that the service was carried out from 15 to 18 February. TAA documents also record the allocation of two manhours to paint the leading edges of the fins and tailplane.

On Wednesday 21 February, N7777G positioned empty from Melbourne to Adelaide. After the Stones' second Adelaide concert, the Connie positioned to Perth on 22 February. The Adelaide visit was memorable because of the clash between a local bikie gang and the police! Again the group's equipment was roaded from Adelaide to Perth but N7777G was not exactly empty on this sector. Popular belief has it that the Stones never travelled on the Constellation - this is not quite true. Keith Richards was the only Stone to fly in the airliner and that was on the empty Adelaide to Perth leg. He and his friends fitted it with wall hangings, oriental pillows and diaphanous curtains to give a sort of 'Casbah' look and feel to it. Rumours suggest that surprise surprise, the smoking lamp was lit, and much fine spirits were consumed. Some of the backing band were on board, as were some pretty people for decoration and fun. The cabin must have been hot on the ground and likewise cold at ten thousand feet as the interior had no insulation at all, just a plywood liner to keep the cargo from punching holes in the skin. There are reports that Keith Richards said afterwards that he couldn't believe how loud it was inside. Damning criticism coming from a rock musician!

The Perth concert was held at the famous Western Australia Cricket Ground (The WACA) on Saturday 24 February. The day after the Perth concert, N7777G headed back to Sydney with all the stage gear for the final concerts at Royal Randwick Race Course on Monday and Tuesday 26/27 February.

With the tour concluded, the Rolling Stones departed Sydney on Wednesday 28 February for various overseas destinations. The Connie was loaded up with all the stage equipment and departed Sydney for Nadi, Fiji on 1 March. Another stop was made at Pago Pago and the aircraft finally arrived in Honolulu on 3 March after crossing the date line. After two days for crew rest the Constellation departed for Long Beach on 5 March.

Eventually, N7777G returned to Miami on 4 April and later did the odd charter to the Caribbean and Central and South America. In November 1973, the aircraft went to Lanzair (Channel Islands) Ltd under a lease/purchase agreement. The owner of Lanzair, Captain Duncan Baker, operated several charters within the USA but on 5 December the aircraft departed for Amsterdam via Gander with a load of produce. The aeroplane sat at Amsterdam until 18 February 1974 when it was ferried to Coventry, UK for further maintenance. Lanzair had booked a livestock charter from Dublin to Tripoli on 8 March 1974 but the owners of the aircraft sent its own crew to operate the charter. After the Tripoli charter, the aircraft positioned empty to Dublin where it arrived in the early morning of 10 March. It transpired that this was to be the last flight for N7777G. There then ensued a lengthy legal dispute between the owners, Lance Dreyer's Air Cargo International and the lessee Duncan Baker's Lanzair. This dispute kept the aircraft impounded at Dublin. As so often happens in these situations, while the lawyers fiddled, the aircraft sat at Dublin deteriorating in the weather with the occasional engine run until both parties lost interest in the aeroplane. Duncan Baker's Lanzair resumed operations with Super Constellation N11SR which had once flown for QANTAS as VH-EAB *Southern Horizon*.

By December 1977, with Lanzair having lost interest in 77G - and also N11SR which had been abandoned in Kuwait - the High Court in Dublin lifted its injunction on the aircraft so it could now depart. Although there were expressions of interest from museums and potential operators, none were of substance until March 1982 when the Connie was purchased by Aces High Limited. This company had gained fame from providing aircraft for the fondly remembered television series *Airline*. The show centred around the post-war operation of DC-3s by the fictitious airline Ruskin Air Services. With a second series in prospect, Mike Woodley's Aces High hoped to use the Connie, so with this in mind it was placed on the UK Register as G-CONI in May 1982. Although Aces High painted their name on the Connie, the registration was never applied to the aircraft. While work was continuing on making the aircraft airworthy, the prospect of film work evaporated. Whether it was this development or a growing appreciation of how much the aeroplane had deteriorated after eight years in the weather, any prospect of flight also evaporated.

Fortunately, the historical value of the aircraft was recognised by John Bagley and the London Science Museum and in June 1983 it acquired the airliner for £45,000. Having established that a ferry flight was not economically viable, the aircraft was dismantled and transported by road and sea to the Science Museum's facility at Wroughton where it arrived in August 1983. During the ensuing twelve months, the aircraft was restored to static display standard in the sixties colours of Trans World Airlines but still carrying the registration N7777G.

The Connie Racer

The idea for the Connie Racer had its genesis at the California 1000 Mile Air Race at Mojave on 15 November 1970. Never before had an unlimited race been held over such a long distance on a closed course. The course was laid out in the Mojave Desert around ten pylons with a lap distance of approximately 15 miles. With a planned race duration of 66 laps, the crews of the unlimited warbird racers were faced with a major rethink! Most crews accepted that pit stops would be necessary, while others experimented with 'wet' wings and drop tanks. The most novel entry came from Clay Lacy, the President of the Professional Race Pilots Association, who entered a DC-7B freighter! Lacy reasoned that the DC-7 would possess ample endurance to complete the race non-stop while also generating publicity for the event and for the sport in general. For such a large aircraft to compete, it was necessary to waive the usual 21,000 pound gross weight limitation on unlimited racers. The aircraft chosen was ex American Airlines DC-7BF N759Z which belonged to Allen Paulson of California Airmotive. For the race, the DC-7 was painted with Lacy's usual race number 64 plus the name *Super Snoopy* on the nose.

Inspired by the success of *Super Snoopy* where the DC-7B came sixth out of a field of 20 starters - P-51s, Sea Furies, Corsairs, Bearcats, a P-38 and a B-26 - Allen Paulson entered his 1049G Super Constellation for the 1971 racing season. The idea was for the two greatest piston-engined transports to fight it out around the pylons in an open race.

L-1049G Super Constellation N9723C, which once served QANTAS as VH-EAP *Southern Zephyr*, was prepared for the San Diego race by Allen

N79723C *Red Baron* prior to the abortive attempt at the 1000-mile air race in the Mojave in 1971. It never did get the chance to fly in anger against *Super Snoopy! (Kirk Smeeton collection)*

Paulson In addition to the race number 64c, the Connie carried the name *Red Baron* on the nose and a large black iron cross on the rear fuselage. The aircraft was crewed by Allen Paulson and famed Lockheed test pilot Herman 'Fish' Salmon. The flight engineer was Chuck Mercer, an experienced Lockheed engineer. The *Red Baron* qualified for the race, rounding the pylons at 200 feet, but keeping wide to permit the smaller aircraft to pass inside with minimum risk of encountering its turbulent wake.

There are varying reports of what transpired when race day arrived. One report suggests that several pilots who had been beaten by the DC-7 at Mojave the previous year objected to the presence of the DC-7 and the Constellation, ostensibly on the grounds of wake turbulence, and that both aircraft were scratched. Other reports suggest that Lacy and Salmon elected not to race. Chuck Mercer, the Flight Engineer recalled in August 2005: 'All the pilots of the 'small' aircraft held a meeting the night before the race, and advised Darryl Greenamyer, who was in charge of the race arrangements, that if the two big airliners participated, then they wouldn't! As a result - Fish Salmon and I, together with the *Snoopy* folks, watched the race from the pits. We subsequently enjoyed the big dinner at the Hotel Coronado and the good-natured kidding that took place.'

MATS Connie

Another survivor is an aircraft that was delivered to USAF in December 1948 as C-121A, serialled 48-609. It flew the Westover AFB to Rhein-Main route in support of the Berlin Airlift, before being converted to a VC-121A in 1950 and then flew VIP missions for the remainder of its USAF career.

Retired by USAF and flown to Davis Monthan AFB for storage, in March 1968 the aircraft was one of five VC-121s sold to Christler Flying Service at a Department of Defense auction on 5 May 1970. Registered as N9464 on 10 July 1970 and converted to an agricultural sprayer by Desert Air in Tucson, AZ it went to Les Arrosages Castor/Beaver Air Spray, Inc on 18 April 1979 to become C-GXKO.

Sold to Conifair Aviation, Inc on 30 April 1980 the Constellation was stored at St Jean, Quebec after the 1983 spraying season. Less than a year later, on 31 August 1984 was sold on to John Travolta for $150,000. Registered N494TW it was flown from St Jean to Santa Barbara, CA on September 14-18, 1984 Stored at Santa Barbara, CA, Travolta named the airliner *Star of Santa Barbara*. The machine was sold again, this time to Vern Raburn in July 1987.

Initial restoration began August 1991 with first flight in October 1991. Further work was undertaken during the winter of 1991-92 with another first post-restoration flight in June 1992. It was painted in late 1940s MATS colour scheme and made public debut as 'MATS Connie' at Oshkosh 1992 Airshow. Raburn and his team toured the European air show circuit during summer 1998.

Advertised for sale May 2000 for $1.2M To United Technologies (Pratt & Whitney Division) 22 February 2005 and donated to Korean Air for static display at their training facility at Jeju Island, South Korea and departed Marana Northwest Regional Airport 1 April 2005 on a ferry flight to South Korea. The Constellation was painted in Air Korea colours.

The Breitling Connie

At 9:54 am local time on 26 April 2004, the former 'Camarillo Connie' departed Camarillo CA for probably the last time and headed east for her new home at Basle-Mulhouse Airport in Switzerland. Renamed the 'Breitling Super Constellation', the Swiss-based Super Constellation Flyers Association was to jointly operate the airliner for the next five years on the European airshow circuit with the then-current owner, the Constellation Historical Society. After five years the SCFA planned to purchase the airliner and to continue operating it on the European show circuit.

Francisco Agullo had long dreamed about bringing a Super Constellation back to Europe and flying it on the European airshow circuit. After the MATS Connie's successful tour of Europe during the summer of 1998, it was obvious that operating a Constellation on the Europe airshow circuit would be feasible. Along with Peter E. Kalt and Peter Manzoni, Francisco formed the Super Constellation Flyers Association (SCFA) in June 2000. A number of other Constellations had been investigated and rejected.

Then they looked at C-121C N73544. Operated by the Constellation Historical Society (CHS) and based at Camarillo, California, it had received a 'standard' airworthiness certificate in 1985 and would be allowed to fly SCFA members. Delivered to the USAF in September 1955 as 54-156, it was based at Charleston AFB before serving with the Mississippi and West Virginia ANG. Retired to Davis Monthan AFB in March 1972 the aircraft was transferred to the Smithsonian Institute, which traded it for Boeing 307 N19903. Benny Younesi purchased N73454 in January 1982, and it was stored at Camarillo from 1984 to 1992 when Younesi formed the CHS. Restored to flying condition, the aircraft made its first post-restoration flight on 23 June 1994 and joined the US west coast airshow circuit. It was offered for sale on eBay in January 2002 when a bid of $600,000 was

The MATS Connie in the UK in 1998.

Left: 3 July 1998 at Cranfield, and below on 5 July at Old Warden - Vern Raburn did not land on the grass runway! Its appearance at Old Warden was hastily arranged by the late John Farley of Aero Books, with the assistance of the author!
(author)

received and declined by Younesi. At that time, he was quoted as saying that he would be willing to sell the aircraft for $1,000,000. The SCFA entered into negotiations with Benny in the autumn of 2002 and in December announced to its membership that it intended to bring N73544 to Europe.

Just when things seemed to be falling into place, the project's major sponsor pulled out due to concerns about the financial viability of the project. After several months of additional negotiations with Benny, a five-year lease/purchase agreement was verbally agreed to and the project was back on track. A contract specifying the terms of agreement was signed on 17 December 2003.

Just before the flight to Europe, the Swiss watch manufacturer Breitling signed up as the project's major sponsor and "Breitling Super Constellation" titles were applied to the fuselage. The French fuel company Total also agreed to help out with fuel and their logo was applied to the nose gear doors.

The trip 'over the pond' went well, and on Saturday 8 May, 2004 at 11:30am local time, N73544 landed safely at Basel-Mulhouse Airport in Switzerland where she and her crew were welcomed by a very enthusiastic group of over 1,000 well-wishers and enthusiasts with a water cannon salute performed by the airport fire brigade.

The airliner soon settled down to a highly visible

Beauty in flight! HB-RSC in its element. *(Ameen Yasheed Collection)*

schedule around the airshows of Europe, but there was an end to even the best things. The 14-year-old partnership between the Super Constellation Flyers Association which flies the C-121C Super Constellation HB-RSC and the Swiss watchmaker Breitling was reportedly coming to an end.

Breitling, whose name is strongly associated to aviation, has been a generous donor to many classic aviation projects for years. Breitling was acquired by the British equity firm CVC Capital Partners and was reducing its support for such projects.

Nevertheless, it was Breitling's long-standing support that made it possible for the 3,500 members of the association to acquire, restore and fly the Super Constellation.

The association started looking for new sponsors and ways to continue its operations, and the aircraft should keep flying and offering paid rides in the near future. We hope they will succeed in finding new sponsors and keep this extraordinary aircraft flying. Then, on 29 April 2019, the Super Constellation Flyers Association announced their liquidation, since the necessary repairs to keep HB-RSC airworthy could not be financed. The aircraft, including all of its inventory, was taken over by a group of German investors. It was dismantled and taken by road to Germany where it was placed in storage.

Presidential Icon

No single Constellation drew more attention and was better known throughout the world than was Air Force 37885. Popularly known as *Columbine III*, - simply because it was the third aircraft by this name that Eisenhower had used - 37885 served as the official transportation for VIP personnel and governmental dignitaries during President Eisenhower's administration.

Named after the official flower of Mrs Eisenhower's home state of Colorado, *Columbine III* carried the President during the most of his eight-year-term. Although the aircraft was frequently directed by the President for VIP missions both domestic and foreign, Eisenhower managed to log over 100 hours per year.

This specially-equipped Constellation was developed from a Model 1049C airframe and was dubbed a VC-121E by the Air Force. Powered by four Wright R3350 Turbo Compounds Columbine III supported an incredible complex of communication and navigational instruments. Airborne teletype, air to ground telephones and HF radio equipment allowed the President to remain in contact with Washington at all times from anywhere in the world.

Navigational facilities included LORAN and provisions for the aircraft's navigator to make star sightings. Radar with a looking range of over 200 miles was provided for the aircraft commander, Lt. Col. William G. Draper, to see inclement weather and to make the necessary course adjustment in time to avoid it.

The safety of the chief executive was the uppermost thought of the crew when *Columbine III* was airborne. While on the ground an attachment of eight men closely guarded *Columbine*, and personnel allowed aboard the aircraft were carefully screened to dispel any chance of sabotage. Several armed guards were stationed outside the aircraft at all times while it was on the ground when an executive tour was in progress. All of the guards were adept marksmen and had orders to challenge any unauthorized advance on the aircraft.

Inside *Columbine III*, several unique safety precautions also were taken. Lt. Col. Draper devised a hand-wound scroll checklist that could be more easily read than a paper sheet. Each challenge and response was clearly indicated and no chance was left for a crew member to omit a pertinent item.

Thirty parachutes were stowed forward of the tail on each side of the door. Draper planned for there to be six parachutes for every five persons. This extra precaution was made in case an alarmed passenger preparing for an emergency accidentally pulled the 'D' lanyard and opened the chute in the aircraft cabin. Light luggage, clothes, and miscellaneous gear were also stowed in this compartment, along with first-aid kits, fire extinguishers and fire axes.

Lt. Col. Draper and his co-pilot, Major Thomas W White, flew the aircraft at least three times per week to maintain proficiency and to ensure that it would always be ready on a minute's notice. Scheduled trips for the President were planned several weeks before the flight and the actual routes selected to acquaint the crew with every aspect of the forthcoming trip.

A crew of eleven manned *Columbine III* on all flights carrying dignitaries. A technician from Lockheed accompanied each flight as one of the crew. Two of the eight guards made every flight with the pilot, co-pilot, navigator, radio operator, two flight engineers and two stewards.

The plush VIP interior design for the Columbine III was in warm tones of gray. The 20-foot Presidential stateroom, located in the aircraft's waist, was fitted with two specially built swivel chairs. These chairs were padded with three inches of soft foam rubber and were covered in brown leather. Built to withstand nine times the force of gravity in any direction, these chairs swivelled to face either the couch along the opposite wall or to face the veneer desk on which the seal of the President was embossed.

To the right of the President's chair were two phones - one for communication with Washington and the other for communications with the cockpit. Several instruments were on the wall behind the President which gave him information as to the status of the flight. A small sewing bar was located at the end of one of the couches with a picture of the columbine flower above it. At the other end of the couch, which made into a three-quarter bed, was an AM/FM radio.

Two forward cabins in *Columbine* had seats for sixteen people which could be made into eight berths.

Columbine III on display at the National Museum of the United States Air Force, near Dayton OH.

With the two couches made into beds, the aircraft slept a total of ten.

The lavatory in the ship's tail was large enough to be a dressing room in which the President could freshen up before an arrival. The complete galley featured an electric toaster, a two-burner stove and oven, a soup warmer and a refrigerator. Food from steaks to cold cuts were carried on board. A canister of prepared martinis was also available.

General Eisenhower chose Lt Col Draper as his aircraft commander in 1950. The two men first made acquaintance when Eisenhower was sent by Truman on a European inspection tour of NATO. Draper flew the General round-trip. When elected President in 1952, Eisenhower recalled Draper to be his aircraft commander.

Since Eisenhower had once held a pilot's licence, he considered flying in *Columbine III* a pleasant experience. But for Mrs. Mamie Eisenhower, it was another story. She was worried about her husband's welfare in an aircraft and seldom travelled by air herself. Lt Col Draper undertook the project to try and make her feel at home in an aircraft and after much persuasion and a great deal of instruction, she became the most avid fan *Columbine III* had, aside from her mother.

Colonel William Draper (bottom step, left) with the others of the crew that flew President Eisenhower.

Mrs. John S. Doud, 75-year-old mother of the President's wife, enjoyed flying to the extent that she often went on weekly jaunts that Draper and Thomas took to keep the aircraft in tip-top running order. This practice soon made her a familiar sight at the MATS Terminal at Washington National Airport.

When Eisenhower left the Presidency in 1961, Air Force 37885 was decommissioned as the official Presidential aircraft to make way for Boeing 707s. On January 20, 1961, *Columbine III* had its name removed from under the cockpit and was relegated to become just another member of the Special Air Mission fleet. Because of its unusual communications network, it was often used by the Secretary of Defense.

After decommisioning in 1962, 37885 was painted white and trimmed in bright orange day-glow paint. The airliner was operated by the Military Air Transport Service until being retired from service in April 1966 and flown to the National Museum of the United States Air Force near Dayton OH for permanent display.

The final word
A total of 856 Connies were built, of which 623 were Supers and StarLiners (232 of these were RC-121/EC-121 early warning versions) and design and development of the basic series was estimated by Lockheed to have taken 20,258,118 man-hours to the end of 1955. This represents a sum of over $100 million spent on the engineering aspects alone of the Constellation series up to the end of 1955 at an average cost per working hour of $500, not including various testing and material changes. In 1955 16,800 Lockheed employees owed their jobs to the Constellation programme, apart from many others at Lockheed Aircraft Services engaged in modification and maintenance work.

The price of a Constellation increased as the type was developed, the L-049 costing about $700,000 (£175,000) and later $800,000 (£200,000), the L-749 and 749A costing about $1 million (£250,000) in 1950, and the L-1049G from $1,920,000 to $2,070,000 (£680,000 to £740,000). The 1649A was the most expensive, originally costing about $2,500,000 (£900,000) but later selling at $2,350,000 (£840,000). In 1962, probably the most active year for the used Constellation market, the asking price of an L-049 had fallen to about £40,000, an L-749A £60,000, an L-1049C to about £100,000 and an L-1049G £150,000. The Constellation's low price led it into a number of smuggling ventures and into the hands of not a few under-capitalised and short-lived operators around the world.

So - this was the story. I think it is fitting to let the final word come from the Dictionary. 'Constellation (noun) a group of stars forming a recognizable pattern that is traditionally named after its apparent form or identified with a mythological figure.' It seems to be good enough to describe this Lockheed product in such a way - it truly was one of the classic airliners.

Appendix I

Variants

L-049
The L-049 was the original commercial airliner produced, although some earlier L-049s were begun as military transports and completed as airliners. L-649 aircraft followed, with more powerful engines, but all were soon upgraded to L-749 standard with long-range fuel tanks. 88 L-049, 14 L-649, and 131 L-749 were built, including conversions from earlier models and military versions. First 22 aircraft delivered as C-69 transports, first flight 9 January 1943.

L-149
L-049 conversion to include extra wing fuel tanks for a longer range. Production versions were planned for Pan Am, but none were ever produced.

L-249
Company designation for the XB-30 bomber. Project cancelled in favour of the Boeing B-29.

L-349
Company designation for the C-69B. None built.

L-449
Unknown proposed civilian airliner version.

L-549
Company designation for the C-69C. One built.

L-649
R-3350-749C18BD engines with 2,500 hp each, seating for up to 81, first flight 19 October 1946

L-649A
Reinforced landing gear and fuselage

L-749
6,145 US gal of fuel providing the capability for non-stop transatlantic flights, first flight 14 March 1947

L-749A
Reinforced landing gear and fuselage

L-749B
Turbine powered. Project cancelled due to the absence of a suitable powerplant.

L-849
Planned version of the L-749, which would have had Wright R-3350 TurboCompounds.

L-949
Speedfreighter combi version of the L-849 with an 18 ft 4in fuselage stretch.

L-1049
First production version, 24 built. Fuselage stretched by 8 ft 4 in stretched version offering a maximum capacity of 109 passengers, square windows; all 1049C and later models had Turbo-Compound engines. Some later models had optional tip tanks. First flight 14 July 1951. 579 built, including military versions.

L-1049A
Company designation for the WV-2, WV-3, EC-121D and RC-121D.

L-1049B
Company designation for the R7V-1, RC-121C and VC-121E.

L-1049C
Civil variant of the 1049B for 110 passengers with four R-3350-87TC18DA-1 Turbo-compound engines with 3,250 hp each, 48 built

L-1049D
Freight version of L-1049B with wing and fuselage modifications and a large cargo door, four built

L-1049E
Passenger variant of the 1049D, 28 built.

L-1049F
Company designation for the C-121C.

L-1049G
Advanced variant with four R-3350-972TC18DA-3 engines with higher METO power, ability to carry wingtip fuel tanks, 102 built.

L-1049H
Passenger/freight convertible version of L-1049G with large cargo door, 53 built.

L-1049J
Planned L-1049G with the wings of the R7V-2.

L-1149

A planned Allison turboprop version of the L-1049G and L-1049H.

L-1249A

Company designation for the R7V-2 and YC-121F.

L-1249B

Planned turboprop passenger version of the R7V-2/YC-121F.

L-1349 unidentified. Claims no design with the L-1349 designation ever existed, possibly due to superstitious belief reasons.

L-1449

Proposed turboprop version of the L-1049G with a stretched fuselage and new wing.

L-1549

Planned stretched version of the L-1449.

L-1649A Starliner

Production version, R-3350-988TC18EA-2 Turbo Cyclone engines with 3,400 hp each. Long-range passenger aircraft designed to compete with Douglas DC-7C. The standard radome for the weather radar extends total length by 2 ft 7 in over L-1049 without radome. New thin-section wing with a straight taper, and much larger fuel capacity giving a ferry range of over 6,880 miles, first flight 10 October 1956. 44, including the prototype, were built.

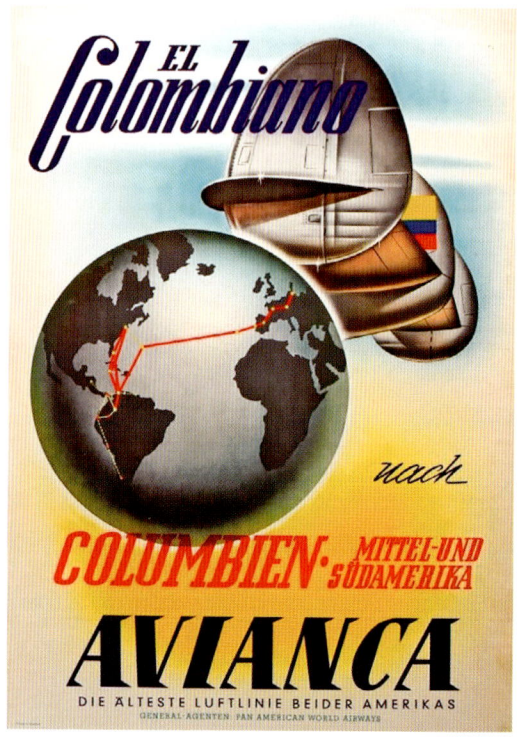

L-1649B

Planned turboprop version of the L-1649A.

L-051

Original company designation for the XB-30 project.

L-084

The XW2V-1 was a planned radar version of the WV-2 with the Starliner's wings for the US Navy. It would have included four Allison T56-A8 engines and missiles for protection against attackers. Considerably different from its predecessors, given the production designation Lockheed L-084.

Military designations

XB-30

Bomber version of the C-69. Was given model designation L-051 and later L-249.

XC-69

Designation for the prototype Constellation. One built. The C-69 was the original military transport version for the USAAF. All aircraft built during World War Two were pressed into military service under this designation.

C-69

Original troop transport version. Almost all of this type were converted into L-049 airliners. 22 were built.

C-69A

Proposed long range troop version of the C-69.

C-69B

Proposed long range troop version of the C-69 designed to carry B-29 Superfortress engines to China. Was given model designation L-349.

C-69C-1

VIP transport aircraft, later designated ZC-69C-1. Only one aircraft was produced. Was given model designation L-549.

C-69D

Proposed VIP transport version.

XC-69E

Prototype XC-69 converted into an engine testbed. It was powered by 4 Pratt & Whitney R-2800 Double Wasp engines.

C-121A

The C-121 was the military transport version of improved L-749 introduced in 1948. Reinforced floor, cargo door in port rear fuselage.

VC-121A

VIP transport aircraft, converted from the C-121A

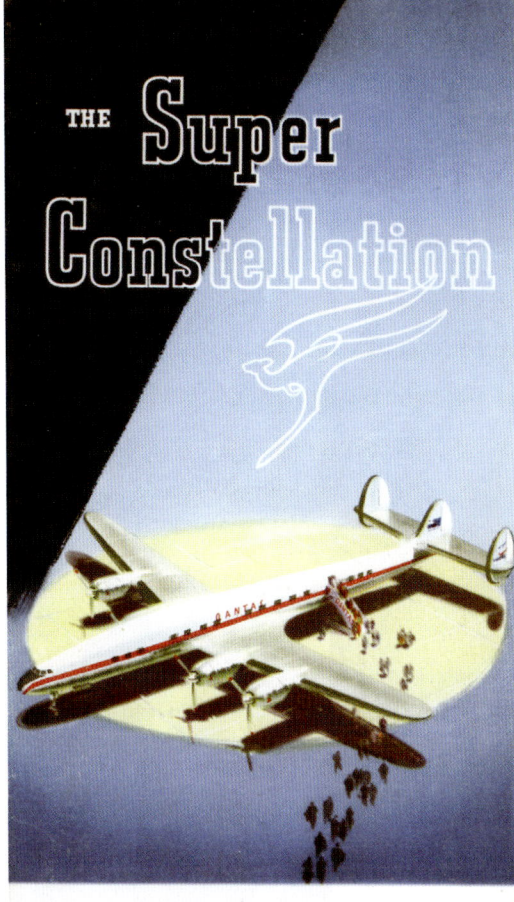

VC-121B
　VIP transport for use by the President of the United States of America.

C-121C
　R7V-1 with R-3350-34 engines with 3,400 hp each, based on L-1049.

JC-121C
　Two C-121C and one TC-121C used as avionics testbeds.

NC-121C
　One C-121C converted for permanent use as a testbed.

RC-121C
　USAF long-range airborne radar analogous to Navy's WV-2.

TC-121C
　Nine RC-121Cs Converted as AEW trainers, subsequently became EC-121C.

VC-121C
　VIP version of C-121C. Total 4.

EC-121D
　Big Eye/College Eye/Disco early warning variant, originally designated RC-121D.

NC-121D
　WV-2 converted to observe high speed objects in the atmosphere nicknamed the 'Tripple Nipple'

RC-121D
　WV-2 with wingtip fuel tanks, later redesignated EC-121D.

VC-121E
　VIP transport for use by the President of the United States of America.

YC-121F
　Two prototype R7V-1 with Pratt & Whitney T34-P-6 turboprops with 6,000 shp each.

C-121G
　32 Navy R7V-1 delivered to USAF.

TC-121G
　Designation given to 9 C-121G converted into trainers

VC-121G
　One C-121G given the role as a temporary VIP Transport.

EC-121H
　42 EC-121D with upgraded electronics

C-121J
　Redesignated Navy R7V-1

EC-121J
　2 EC-121D with upgraded electronics

NC-121J
　7 C-121J modified to send television broadcasts to troops in Vietnam

VC-121J
　4 C-121J converted for VIP use. One served with the Blue Angels.

EC-121K
　Redesignated Navy WV-2 Warning Star

JC-121K
　One EC-121K used as an avionics testbed

NC-121K
　EC-121K used by the Navy

EC-121L
Redesignated Navy WV-2E

EC-121M
Redesignated Navy WV-2Q

WQC-121N
Redesignated Navy WV-3

EC-121P
EC-121K equipped for anti-submarine warfare

EC-121Q
EC-121D with upgraded electronics

EC-121R 'BatCat'
EC-121K and EC-121P equipped to process signals from seismic instruments

NC-121S
Electronic warfare and reconnaissance version

EC-121T
Upgraded radar;

R7O-1
The original US Navy designation of the R7V-1 based on L-1049D, R-3350-91 engines with 3,250 hp each

R7V-1
Re-designation of the R7O-1. Later redesignated C-121J

R7V-1P
One R7V-1 modified for Arctic use

R7V-2
Four prototypes with Pratt & Whitney YT34-P-12A turboprops of 4,140 shp (3,088 kW) each. Two were delivered as YC-121F prototype aircraft (see above).

PO-1W
Two maritime patrol aircraft equipped with search radar based on L-749, later re-designated WV-1.

PO-2W Warning Star
Long-range airborne radar aircraft, R-3350-34 or R-3350-42 engines with 3,400 hp each, based on L-1049, later re-designated WV-2.

WV-1
Re-designation of the PO-1W.

WV-2 Warning Star
Re-designation of the PO-2W. Later re-designated EC-121K.

WV-2E
Experimental version of WV-2 modified to carry a rotating radar dome similar to that of the Boeing E-3 Sentry. Later redesignated EC-121L.

WV-2Q
WV-2 equipped for electronic warfare, later redesignated EC-121M.

WV-3
Eight aircraft equipped for weather reconnaissance. Later re-designated WQC-121N.

XW2V-1
The XW2V-1 was a planned radar version of the WV-2 with the Starliner's wings for the US Navy. It would have included four Allison T56-A8 engines and missiles for protection against attackers. Considerably different from its predecessors, given the production designation Lockheed L-084.

Appendix II

Survivors

C/n 1970 Model 049: on display at the Pima Air & Space Museum in Tucson, Arizona. A former C-69 transport, s/n 42-94549, that was converted for civilian service, and was one of the first TWA aircraft.

C/n 2071 Model 049, : on display at the TAM Museum, located in São Carlos, Brazil. Previously, it served as a children's attraction at the entrance of Silvio Pettirossi International Airport in Asunción, Paraguay. It is painted in the markings of Panair do Brasil.

C/n 2072 Model 049: parked adjacent to a flight school and cafe at Greenwood Lake Airport in West Milford, New Jersey. It was delivered as Air France's first Constellation in June 1946 as L-049 F-BAZA, before being sold to Frank Lembo Enterprises in May 1976 for $45,000 for use as a restaurant and lounge. It was flown to the airport in July 1977, and, along with the airport, was sold to the State of New Jersey in 2000. In 2005, the interior was refurbished for use as a flight school office.

C/n 2081 Model 049: on display in Aerosur livery, on the first ring road in Santa Cruz de la Sierra, Bolivia. It is known as *El Avión Pirata*.

C/n 2503 Model 079: on display with at the Musée de l'Air et de l'Espace located at Paris-Le Bourget Airport 10 km north of Paris. It initially served with Pan American Airways, before being transferred to Air France, with whom it served until 1960. Afterwards, it was used by the Compagnie Générale des Turbo-Machines as an engine testbed until December 1974.

C/n 2553 Model 079: on display in TWA colours at the Large Item Storage facility for the UK Science Museum at Wroughton, near Swindon.

C/n 4544 Model L-1049: on display at the Museum of Flight in Seattle, Washington. It is painted in the markings it carried during its service with Trans-Canada Air Lines from 1954 to the 1960s. After TCA service, it was sold to World Wide Airways and later retired in Montreal by 1965; it was renovated as a restaurant and bar in and around the Montreal area, and sold and moved again to Toronto and used as a convention facility by the Regal Constellation Hotel. It was sold again and stored at Toronto Pearson International Airport. Finally, it was sold to the Museum of Flight, restored in Rome, New York, and shipped to Seattle for display.

C/n 2071 Model 049 : 'PP-PDD' The superbly restored example on display at the TAM Museum, located in São Carlos, Brazil.

Above: VH-EAG *Southern Preservation* was originally built as a C-121C for the USAF, serial number 54-0157, c/n 4176, and was delivered on 6 October 1955 when it was allocated to the 1608th Military Air Transport Wing based at Charleston, South Carolina. On 25 July 1962 it was transferred to the Mississippi Air National Guard and on 14 February 1967 it moved on to West Virginia Air National Guard, where it served for the next five years. The aircraft's last active duty was with the Pennsylvania Air National Guard from mid 1972 until its relegation to storage at Davis Monthan Air Base at Tucson, Arizona in June 1977. It was rescued and restored to flight by the Historical Aircraft Restoration Society Inc (HARS). On 3 February 1996 the airliner arrived in Sydney, Australia.

Below: James Kightly's dramatic picture of a 'fire and brimstone' start-up of VH-EAG at twilight.

C/n 4557 Model L-1049 : on display at the Air Mobility Command Museum at Dover Air Force Base in Dover, Delaware. It is painted to represent a USAF C-121C but was never actually delivered to the air force.

C/n 4604 Model L-1049: on display at the Flugausstellung Hermeskeil, near Hermeskeil, Germany. It is a former Lufthansa Super Constellation and was the actual aircraft that Konrad Adenauer flew into Moscow in 1955 when he negotiated the release of German PoWs.

C/n 4671 Model L-1049: on display near Munich International Airport at Munich, Germany. It is painted to represent Super Constellation D-ALEM, Lufthansa's first long-haul aircraft of 1955.

C/n 4519 Model L-1049: to display by the Amicale du Super Constellation located at the Nantes Airport in Nantes, France. It was delivered to Air France on November 2, 1953, and was upgraded to a L-1049 G in 1956, serving until August 8, 1967, having totaled 24,284 hours under Air France's colours. After retirement, it was sent to Spain, to be registered EC-BEN, briefly flying humanitarian and medevac missions in Biafra. Aero Fret bought it in 1968, brought it back home to France, registered it as F-BRAD, and operated it on cargo hauls until 1974. When the Constellation landed in Nantes one last time to be scrapped, it was ultimately saved by Mr. Gaborit, who revamped it somewhat by his own modest means to finally park it near the terminal, accessible to visitors for a few years, until the Chamber of Commerce and Industry of the Nantes-Atlantique Airport bought it, to contract the Amicale du Super Constellation to undergo a complete restoration of the old aircraft.

C/n 4825 Model L-1049: *City of Miami*: parked on an unused runway at the Rafael Hernández Airport in Aguadilla, Puerto Rico. It was struck by a runaway DC-4 on February 3, 1992, resulting in damage to the right wing and main spar.

C/n 4830 Model L-1049: *Star of America*. Restored to airworthiness by the National Airline

History Museum in Kansas City, Missouri. This aircraft was originally built in 1957, stored for several years, and then delivered to cargo carrier Slick Airways. It was restored in 1986 by the Save-a-Connie, Inc. organization, later renamed as the National Airline History Museum. It was originally painted in red and white with Save-a-Connie, but was later repainted in the 1950s livery of TWA to resemble its original Star of America Constellation.

C/n 1040 Model L-1649: on display in front of the Fantasy of Flight attraction in Lakeland, Florida.

C/n 1042 Model L-1649: Registered ZS-DVJ on display at Rand Airport in Germiston in Trek Airways colours. Used to be at O R Tambo International Airport, South Africa at the South African Airways Technical area. The aircraft is owned by the South African Airways Museum Society.

C/n 1018 Model L-1649: planned to be returned to airworthiness by Lufthansa Technik North America in Auburn, Maine. This aircraft was purchased at auction in 2007, along with c/n 1038, by the Deutsche Lufthansa Berlin Foundation. Lufthansa built a hangar at the airport, which would have allowed the aircraft to be restored indoors. Lufthansa announced in March 2018 that it would be transported back to Germany and further restoration decisions will be made after it arrived. As of the end of 2019 the plan is to restore the aircraft for static display in a museum. According to reports from the USA, the aircraft was dismantled (as apparently was the Ju-52 D-AQUI) without the requisite documentation that would have allowed the return-to-flight work to continue. Stored.

C/n 1038 Model L-1649: This aircraft was purchased at auction in 2007, along with c/n 1018, by the Deutsche Lufthansa Berlin Foundation, and stripped of all usable spares to support the restoration of c/n 1018. The aircraft was subsequently sold and transported to JFK International Airport to become a cocktail bar in the TWA Hotel, a retro-aviation themed hotel built on the former TWA Flight Center.

C/n 4175 Model C-121C, serial 54-0156: Flew with the Super Constellation Flyers Association out of Basel, as The Breitling Super Constellation. Its restoration was sponsored by Swiss watch manufacturer Breitling, and was registered as HB-RSC. Grounded and Stored.

C/n 4176 Model C-121C serial 54-0157: Flies with the Historical Aircraft Restoration Society (HARS) out of Illawarra Regional Airport near Wollongong, Australia. Following its restoration, it was painted in pseudo-QANTAS livery including the QANTAS logo on the tail, and registered as VH-EAG.

C/n 2601 VC-121A serial 48-0609: on display at Jeongseok Airport on Jeju Island, South Korea. It was donated to Korean Air in 2005, and restored to airworthy condition at Tucson, Arizona. It was then ferried to South Korea, where it made its final flight, under its own power, from Seoul to its current location for static display. It has been repainted in 1950s Korean Air colours, and rendered unable to fly by the presence of unserviceable engines.

C/n 2604 L-749A serial 48-0612: on display at the Dutch National Aviation Museum Aviodrome. It was restored to airworthy condition and ferried from Tucson, Arizona, to the Netherlands, where restoration continued. It is now painted in the KLM livery of the 1950s, depicting a KLM Lockheed L-749A. Renamed Flevoland, this is the only airworthy

N749NL seen at Lelystad. *(Stuart Powney)*

example of the short version of the Constellation. However, thanks to Korean Air, which donated two airworthy engines from 48-0609 this aircraft was scheduled to be flying again, but the flights were cancelled. As of 2016, the aircraft is on display in the Aviodrome museum.

C/n 2606 VC-121A serial 48-0614 *Columbine*: on display at the Pima Air and Space Museum in Tucson, Arizona. This aircraft was used by Dwight D. Eisenhower during his role as Supreme Headquarters Allied Powers Europe commander before he became president. It is on loan from the National Museum of the US Air Force.

C/n 4151 VC-121E serial 53-7885 *Columbine III*: Originally to be delivered to US Navy as R7V-1 BuNo 131650 on display at the National Museum of the United States Air Force at Wright-Patterson Air Force Base near Dayton, Ohio. *Columbine III* was used as Dwight D. Eisenhower's presidential aircraft, and was eventually retired to the museum in 1966, where it is now displayed in the museum's Presidential Gallery.

C/n 4174 C-121C serial 54-0155: on display at Lackland Air Force Base near San Antonio, Texas.

C/n C-121C serial 54-0177: on display at the National Air and Space Museum, Udvar-Hazy Center located at Dulles Airport in Virginia.

C/n C-121C serial 54-0180: on display at Charleston Air Force Base near North Charleston, South Carolina.

C/n EC-121K BuNo 137890: on display at Tinker Air Force Base near Oklahoma City, Oklahoma.

C/n EC-121K BuNo 141297: on display at the Museum of Aviation at Robins Air Force Base near Warner Robins, Georgia.

C/n EC-121K BuNo 141309: on display at the Aerospace Museum of California at the former McClellan Air Force Base in North Highlands, California. This aircraft is a former navy aircraft on loan from the National Museum of the United States Air Force. It is painted in the markings of a USAF EC-121 Warning Star.

C/n EC-121K BuNo 141311: on display at the Chanute Aerospace Museum at the former Chanute AFB in Rantoul, Illinois.

C/n EC-121K BuNo 143221: on display at the National Museum of Naval Aviation at NAS Pensacola near Pensacola, Florida.

C/n EC-121 serial 52-3418: on display at the Combat Air Museum in Topeka, Kansas. This aircraft was delivered to the Air Force in October 1954. It served an additional twenty-two years until it was retired and flown to Davis Monthan AFB for storage on 7 April 1976. It June 1981, it was ferried to Topeka, Kansas, with Frank Lang in command.

C/n EC-121 serial 52-3425: on display at the Peterson Air and Space Museum at Peterson AFB in Colorado Springs, Colorado. Previously assigned to the 966th AEWCS at McCoy AFB, Florida, and then the 79th AEWCS at Homestead AFB, Florida. It was the last operational EC-121 and was deployed by the 79th AEWCS to NAS Keflavik, Iceland. It was delivered to Peterson AFB in October 1978.

C/n EC-121 serial 53-0548: on display at the Yanks Air Museum in Chino, California. Stored at Camarillo Airport, from 2000 to 2012, this aircraft

The well-preserved and presented IN 315 on display at the Indian Naval Aviation Museum at Dabolim.

Columbine II was to become the first aircraft to use the Air Force One callsign and the only presidential aircraft ever sold to a private party. The aircraft was ferried from long-term storage in the Sonoran Desert at Marana Regional Airport, Arizona, to the east coast for restoration in March 2016.

made its final flight, to Chino, on 14 January 2012.

C/n serial 53-0554: on display at the Pima Air & Space Museum in Tucson, Arizona. As of 6 April 2014, it is undergoing restoration on its radome.

C/n serial 53-0555: on display at the National Museum of the United States Air Force at Wright-Patterson Air Force Base near Dayton, Ohio, in the museum's Southeast Asia Gallery.

C/n L-1049G IN 315: on display at the Naval Aviation Museum at Dabolim in Goa, India. This aircraft is a former Air India Super Constellation (VT-DHM Rani of Ellora) that was later transferred to the Indian Navy.

WV-1 BuNo 124438 — to airworthiness by Gordon Cole at Salina, Kansas. This aircraft was the first of two WV-1s delivered to the U.S. Navy in 1949. Essentially, it was a prototype for the EC-121 Warning Star that followed. Retired from the Navy in 1957, it served the FAA from 1958 to 1966, before being flown to Salina in 1967 for retirement. It remains parked there, and was last flown in 1992.

VC-121A S/N 48-0610 *Columbine II*: to airworthiness by Dynamic Aviation in Bridgewater, Virginia. This aircraft served as the first Air Force One, during the presidency of Dwight D. Eisenhower, before it was replaced by Columbine III as Eisenhower's primary presidential aircraft in 1954. After a long period of storage at Marana Regional Airport, near Tucson, Arizona, this aircraft made its first flight, since 2003, in March 2016, when it was ferried to Bridgewater for additional restoration.

S/N 48-0613 *Bataan*: to airworthiness by Lewis Air Legends in San Antonio, Texas. This aircraft was used as personal transport by General Douglas MacArthur during the Korean War, and later by other Army general officers until 1966 when it was transferred to NASA. Following its permanent retirement in 1970, it was placed on display at a museum at Fort Rucker near Daleville, Alabama. It was acquired by the Planes of Fame Air Museum at Chino, California in 1992, and overhauled into airworthy condition for a flight to Dothan, Alabama, where it received additional work. After a thorough restoration back to its original configuration with a "VIP interior", it was placed on display at the Planes of Fame secondary location in Valle, Arizona. Then, in 2015, it was sold to Lewis Air Legends, and prepped for a ferry flight to Chino, arriving there on 14 January 2016.

C/n EC-121T serial 51-3417: in storage at Helena Regional Airport in Helena, Montana. Acquired by the Castle Air Museum of Atwater, California in 2014.

C/n C-121J BuNo 131643: in storage at Ninoy Aquino International Airport in Manila, Philippines. It was impounded at the airport in June 1988 and stored in deteriorating condition, but in September 2014, it was secured for removal and static preservation by the QANTAS Founders Outback Museum, Longreach.

Two of the Biafran Airlift machines were abandoned at Sao Tome. Both were Canairelief Ltd aircraft, CF-NAL and CF-NAM. Both were seen still at Sao Tome in poor condition in 2013, but have been cleaned up somwhat. One being used as part of a restaurant and the other now forms part of a house.

Bibliography

Books etc.

Allen, Roy: *Pictorial history of KLM*, Ian Allan, 1978

Anderson, Holmes G: *The Lockheed Constellation - Profile No 120,* Profile Publications Ltd, Windsor, Berkshire.

Bender, Marylin & Altschul, Selig: *The Chosen Instrument Juan Trippe, Pan Am*, Simon and Schuster, 1982.

Berry et al: *The Douglas DC-4*, Air-Britain, 1967

Brooks, Peter W: *The Modern Airliner*, Putnam, 1961.

Corrie, Nicholas J B: *The Connie Breed*; Galago Books, 1993.

Davies, R E G: *Airlines of the United States since 1914*, Putnam, 1972.

Davies, R E G: *A History of the World's Airlines*, Oxford University Press, 1967

Davies, R E G: *Airlines of Latin America since 1919*, Putnams, 1984.

Davies, R.E.G: *A History of the World's Airlines*, 1964.

Draper, Michael L: *Shadows Airlift and Airwar in Biafra and Nigeria 1967-1970*, Hikoki, 1999.

Fahey, J C : *The Ships and Aircraft of the U S Fleet*, Ships & Aircraft, 1958.

Francillon, René: *Lockheed Aircraft since 1913*, Putnam 1982.

Germain, Scott E: *Lockheed Constellation & Super Constellation*, Specialty Press, 1998.

Gill, Frederick W. and Bates, Gilbert L: *Airline Competition*, Division of Research, Harvard Business School, Boston Mass, USA, 1948.

Ginter, Steve: *Lockheed C-121 Constellation*;

Hardy M J: The Lockheed Constellation, David & Charles, 1973.

Henderson, Scott, *Lockheed Constellation in Colour;* Scoval Publishing, 2005

Jane's All The World's Aircraft, Jane's, various

Johnson, Clarence L 'Kelly, with Smith, Maggie: *Kelly - More Than My Share Of It All;* Smithsonian, 1985.

Johnson, Clarence L: *Development of the Lockheed Constellation*, published by Lockheed, Burbank, California.

Luisada, Claude G: *Queen of the Skies The Lockheed Constellation;* Schiffer, 2014.

Marson, Peter J: *The Constellation*, Air-Britain Monograph, published by Air-Britain, Brentwood, Essex, 1969.

Merton-Jones, A C: *British Independent Airlines since 1946*, LAAS/Merseyside Aviation Society, 1976.

Morgan, Terry: *The Lockheed Constellation;* Arco Publishing, 1967.

Rummel, Robert W: *Howard Hughes and TWA*; Smithsonian, 1991.

Simons, Graham M: *Britannia Airways*, Air World, 2020.

Simons, Graham M: *British Overseas Airways Corporation*, Air World, 2019

Simons, Graham M: *Colours in the Sky,* Pen & Sword, 2018.

Simons, Graham M: *Howard Hughes and the Spruce Goose*, Pen & Sword, 2014.

The Lockheed Story; November 1955, published by Lockheed.

The Plane That Grew: Aero Digest, June 1951.

Trans World Airlines: Legacy of Leadership, Walsworth, 1971.

Turner, P St John: *Pictorial History of Pan American World Airways*, Ian Allan, 1973

TWA Skyliner Staff Magazine Vol 03 No. 06 & 07 February/March 1939.

TWA Skyliner Staff Magazine, Vol 03 No.11 August 1939.

TWA Skyliner Staff Magazine, Vol 04 No. 09 July 1940.

TWA Skyliner Staff Magazine, Vol 04 No.10 August 1940.

TWA Skyliner Staff Magazine, Vol 04 No.11 September 1940.

TWA Skyliner Staff Magazine, Vol 05 No.01 November 1940.

TWA Skyliner Staff Magazine, Vol 05 No.02 December 1940.

TWA Skyliner Staff Magazine Vol 05 No.03 January 1941.

TWA Skyliner Staff Magazine Vol 05 No.04 March 1941.
TWA Skyliner Staff Magazine Vol 05 No.05 June 1941.
TWA Skyliner Staff Magazine Vol 05 No.06 July 1941.
TWA Skyliner Staff Magazine Vol 05 No.07 September 1941.
TWA Skyliner Staff Magazine Vol 06 No.03 March 1942.
TWA Skyliner Staff Magazine Vol 06 No.04 April 1942.
TWA Skyliner Staff Magazine Vol 06 No.05 May 1942.
TWA Skyliner Staff Magazine Vol 06 No.06 June 1942.
TWA Skyliner Staff Magazine Vol 07 No.01 January 1943.
TWA Skyliner Staff Magazine Vol 07 No.02 February 1943.
TWA Skyliner Staff Magazine Vol 07 No.03 March 1943.
TWA Skyliner Staff Magazine Vol 07 No.04 April 1943.
TWA Skyliner Staff Magazine Vol 07 No.07 May 1943.
TWA Skyliner Staff Magazine Vol 08 No.04 April 1944.
TWA Skyliner Staff Magazine Vol 08 No.06 June 1944.
TWA Skyliner Staff Magazine Vol 09 No.07 July 1945.
TWA Skyliner Staff Magazine Vol 09 No.09 September 1945.
TWA Skyliner Staff Magazine Vol 09 No.12 December 1945.
TWA Skyliner Staff Magazine Vol 10 No.01 January/February 1946.
United States Navy : US Naval Aviation 1910-1970', NAVAIR OO-8OP-1.
Whittle, J A: *The DC-6 & DC-7 Series*, Air-Britain, 1971.

Reports, Bulletins, Manuals.
Aircraft Production: the Journal of the Aircraft Manufacturing Industry. Vol VIII No. 87, January 1946.
BOAC : Pilot's Handbook, Constellation 749.
Civil Aeronautics Administration : Aircraft Specification No.A-763.
Civil Aeronautics Administration : Supplemental Type Certificates.

To bring things full circle, in the Introduction I mentioned photographs being taken on 'Instamatic' cameras with twelve shot cartridge films that were often printed up on horrible 'orange-peel' textured paper, that when scanned, often appear out of focus! This is one such example, with a pair of Euravia Constellations seen at Luton. The quality may be poor, and I make no apologies for its use, for the image is historic and deserves to appear in a book such as this. *(Bill Armstrong Collection)*

Civil Aeronautics Board : Accident Reports
Clarence L Johnson : The Development of the Lockheed Constellation
Eastern Air Lines : Constellation Flight Manual
Euravia : Constellation Flight Manual
Federal Aviation Administration : Supplemental Type Certificates
Federal Aviation Agency : Aircraft Specification No.6A5
Federal Aviation Agency : United States Civil Aircraft Registers
Hibbard, Hall and Johnson, Clarence L. 'The First Constellation Decade', paper presented at the SAE Golden Anniversary Meeting in New York; Shell Aviation News No 211, January 1956.
International Civil Aviation Organisation : Bulletins & Circulars
Lockheed Aircraft Corporation : Reports
Lockheed Aircraft Corporation : Service Bulletins
Lockheed Constellation Pocket Handbook, September 1951
National Transportation Safety Board : Accident Briefs
National Transportation Safety Board : Accident Reports
Trans World Airlines : Constellation Operating Manual
Trans World Airlines : Operating Manual L-1649A
United States Air Force : Flight Manual C-l21C/C-121G Aircraft

Airline Publicity Material and Published Timetables from the following companies :
Afro-Continental Airways.
Air Ceylon.
Air France.
Air-India International.
Bradshaw Air Guide (1946 - 1952).
British Overseas Airways Corporation.
Capitol International Airways.
Cubana.
Delta Air Lines.
Eastern Air Lines.
Euravia-Skyways.
Iberia.
KLM - Royal Dutch Airlines.
Lufthansa.
Luxair.
Northwest Orient Airlines.
Pan American World Airways.
Panair do Brasil.
QANTAS Empire Airways.
Royal Air Maroc.
Seaboard & Western Airlines.
The ABC World Airways Guide (1954 - 1970).
The Flying Tiger Line.
Trans World Airlines.
Trans-Florida Airlines.
Transportes Aereos Portugueses.
Trek Airways.

Magazines, Newspapers and Periodicals.
Aerial Applicator.
Aeroplane Monthly.
Aeroplane, later Aeroplane & Commercial Aviation News.
Air Enthusiast.
Air Force Magazine.
Air Pictorial.
Air University Review.
Air-Britain Digest.
Air-Britain News.
Aircraft Illustrated.
Airliners.
American Aviation Historical Society Journal
American Civil Aircraft Registers Quarterly Review, formerly *US Register Quarterly*
Aviation Letter
Aviation News
Aviation Week, later Aviation Week & Space Technology
British Aviation Research Group.
Business & Commercial Aviation.
der Spiegel.
Esso Air World.
Flight, later Flight International.
Flypast.
Frankfurter Allgemeine Zeitung.
Humberside Aviation Society.
Interceptor.
L'Aviation Magazine.
LAAS.
le Trait d'Union.
Lockheed Field Service Digest.
Lockheed Log.
Lockheed Star house newspaper 1940-1971.
Lundkvist Aviation Research : Lockheed 049-1649.
Naval Aviation News.
North American Aviation News.
Paris Match.
Propliner.
Shell Aviation News.
Sunday Times.
The Observer.
The Times.
Time Magazine.

Index

A
Abubakar Tafawa Balewa, Sir: 251
ACE (Aviation Charter Enterprises) Freighters: 135, 136, 143
ACE (Aviation Charter Enterprises) Scotland: 135, 136
Aces High Ltd: 293
Admiral Airways: 145, 146
Aer Lingus Teoranta: 140
Aerlinte Eireann: 140, 232, 233
Aero Corporation of California: 14
Aero Fletes Internacional SA: 182
Aero Tech Inc: 148
Aero Transport: : 129, 135, 147
Aero Transport Flughetriebsgesellschaft: 146
Aero Transportes Entre Rios SRL: 148, 182
Aeroflot: 85
Aerolessors Inc: 264
Aerolineas Argentinas: 284
Aerolineas Carreras TA: 135, 174
Aerolineas Uruguayas SA: 148
Aeronaves de Mexico SA: 135, 140, 141, 146, 174
Aerovias Condor de Colombia Ltda (Aerocondor): 285
Aerovias Guest SA: 139, 142
Aerovias Halcon SRL: 285
Aerovias Nacionales Quisqueyanas: 130, 145, 146
Aerovias Panama Airways: 176, 178
Affretair: 268
Afro Continental Airways: 267, 268
Aguiyi Ironsi, General: 251
Agullo, Francisco: 294
Ahmadu Bello, Sir: 251
Air Afrique: 148, 285
Air Algerie: 147, 148
Air America: 254, 264, 284
Air Cameroun: 163, 182
Air Cargo International: 290, 292
Air Ceylon: 164
Air Chile/Lyon Air (ALA): 130
Air Finance Corporation: 237
Air France: 82, 85, 112, 113, 131, 132, 135, 139, 140, 143, 144, 147, 148, 156, 160, 161, 163, 176, 180, 182, 198, 245-248, 260, 261, 273, 282, 285
Air Frét: 182, 262, 273, 274
Air Haiti International SA: 145
Air India International: 135, 139, 141, 142, 146, 159, 163, 174, 175, 177, 178, 182
Air Inter: 144

Air Korea: 287
Air Mid East: 264, 265, 282, 283
Air Nevada: 282
Air Trans Africa: 265, 266, 267, 268, 269
Air Venturers: 286, 287
Air Vietnam: 144
Airlift International: 233, 244, 284
Aitken, Reverend William 'Bill: 260
Alaska Airlines: 233, 284, 285
Alitalia: 247
Allen, Edmund T 'Eddie'; Boeing: 59, 62
American Air Trader: 156
American Airlines (AAL): 5, 7, 14, 22, 33, 87, 97, 110, 131, 160, 293
American Export Airlines: 87, 112
American Flyers Airline Corp: 129, 181, 282
American Overseas Airlines (AOA): 82, 110, 112
AMSA (Aerolineas Mundo SA): 287
Angel of Mercy: 264, 265
Ankrah, General Joseph: 251
Armbruster, Air Stewardess Trachine E; TWA: 168
Armee de l'Air: 147, 148
Armstrong Whitworth Ensign: 23, 24
Armstrong, Doreen: 266
Armstrong, William 'Bill': 265, 266, 268
Arnold, Gen. Henry H 'Hap': 38, 41, 73, 74, 76, 83
ASA International Airlines: 129
ASA International Airlines/ Aerovias Sud Americana Inc: 244
ASL Arruda Industria e Comercio: 198
Associated Air transport: 144
Atlantic Airways: 238
Australian National Airways: 141
Autair: 265, 266, 267
Aviaco: 159, 176
Avianca of Colombia: 141, 166, 176
Avianca: 147, 175
Aviation Corporation of the Americas (ACA): 38, 39, 180
Aviolanda: 278
Avro Lancaster: 115
Avro Tudor I: 78, 115
Awolowo, Obafemi; 251
Azikiwe, Nnamdi: 251

B
Bagley, John, Science Museum: 293
Bailey, Senator Josiah William: 74, 84, 85, 88, 89, 104

312

Baker, Captain Duncan: 292, 293
Baker, Duncan: 262
Balewa, Sir Abubakar Tafawa: 251
Ball, Earl: 238
Barker, Charles: 25
Barkley, Senator Alben W: 74
Baron, Leo TWA: 68
Bayer, Monsignor Carlo: 256, 264
Bechuanaland National Airways Pty Ltd: 265
Bello, Sir Ahmadu: 251
Berle, Adolph Augustus: 36, 83-85
Bernhardt, H William: 257, 258
Bevier, Richard B: 38
Biddle, Attorney General Francis: 85
Blackburn, Captain Harold F;TWA: 105, 106
Bligh, Captain: 181
Blue Angels: 186
Boeing 307 Stratoliner: 8, 9, 16, 18-22, 28, 35, 40, 96, 97
Boeing 314 Clipper: 35, 40
Boeing 707:   163, 166, 177, 179, 250, 285, 297
Boeing 720:   164, 233
Boeing 727:   244
Boeing 737:   147
Boeing Aircraft: 15
Boeing B-17 Flying Fortress: 15, 16, 19, 173
Boeing B.29 Superfortress: 24, 41, 62, 80, 131
Boeing Stratocruiser: 82, 112, 113, 115, 116, 143, 146, 175, 176
Boeing YC-97 Stratofreighter: 173
Bolton, Edward T; Lockheed: 69, 70
Bonnet, Ambassador Henri: 105
Borger, John G: 40
Braathen, Ludvig G: 166
Braathens: 166
Branch, Harlee; CAB: 73, 74
Braniff International Airways: 109, 114, 129
Brennan, Robert: 105
Brewster, Senator Ralph Owen: 74, 77, 84-88, 94, 95, 99, 100, 102-104
Breyfogle, Flight Engineer Forrest D; TWA: 168
Bricker, Senator John W: 104
Bringle, Admiral William F: 215
Bristol Aeroplane Co.:   116
Bristol Brabazon: 115
Bristol Britannia: 116, 146, 177, 197, 234, 285
Bristol Freighter: 273
Britair East Africa Airways: 128, 129
Britannia Airways: 125
British Airways: 10-13
British Continental Airways: 10
British European Airways (BEA):   135, 247
British Overseas Airways Corporation (BOAC):   11, 13, 75, 76, 85, 110, 114-119, 131, 135, 139-143, 146, 147, 156, 157, 232, 249
British West Indian Airways: 157
Brown, Thomas 'Bull':   269
Bryan, Captain Otis; TWA: 20, 74, 105
Buchman, Frank: 286
Burcham, Milo: 59, 62, 63, 65-67

Burden, William A M: 74
Butler, David: 265
Butler, Father Billy: 257
Bying, Captain Wes: 191
Byrne, Father Anthony 'Tony':   253, 256, 257, 264

C
Cadman, Lord: 10
Calder, Captain John N; TWA: 106
California Airmotive: 144, 145, 146, 147, 156, 174, 181, 237, 282, 293
Californian Eastern Aviation: 233, 234, 283, 284
Californian Hawaiian Airlines: 108, 117, 144
Campbell, Captain Harry: 21
Campbell Orde, Alan Colin: 10, 12, 13
Canadair DC-4M: 256
Canairelief: 272, 275, 276, 277, 280, 284
Capital Airlines: 75, 112, 113, 117, 129, 149
Capitol Airways: 127, 146, 147, 181, 232, 233, 234, 272, 280, 281
Caribbean Airways: 38
CARITAS Internationalis: 252, 256, 257, 262, 264, 273, 280
Carmody, Charles: 172
Carolina Aircraft Leasing Corp: 279, 283
Catair: 182, 274
Central American Airways Flying Service: 147
Ceylon Airways: 141
Chadwick, Roy; Avro: 115
Chappelet, Cyril: 25
Cheech & Chong: 289
Chiappino, Lawrence W; TWA: 68, 69, 71, 73
Chicago & Southern Airlines: 143
China Airlines: 284
China National Aviation Corporation (CNAC):   38, 40
Chrisman, Navigator Officer M; TWA: 106
Chukwuemeka 'Emeka' Odumegwu-Ojukwu, Colonel: 251
Churchill, Winston Spencer: 36
CIA (Central Intelligence Agency):   253, 254, 256, 262, 263, 266
Cia de Aviacion Trans-Peruana: 146
Cia Interamericana Export-Import SA: 282
Civil Aeronautics Board (CAB):   36, 73, 74, 87, 88
Clark, Senator Bennett Champ: 86
Clay, Maj Gen Lucius: 74
Coastal Air Lines: 129
Coastal Cargo: 129
Cobaugh, Robert W: 262
Cochran, Jacqueline 'Jackie':   74
COHATA (Compagnie Haitienne de Transportes Aériens):   145
Cole, Nat King: 113
Collins, Col Frank: 73
Collins, Fred: 16
Colonial Airlines: 144
Compania Aeronautica Uruguaya SA: 148
Concare Aircraft Leasing: 262
Condor Flugdienst: 249

Cone, Carroll: 100
Connelly, Captain J; QANTAS: 142
Consolodated Airlines: 129
Consolodated B-24 Liberator: 182
Consolodated B-32 Dominator: 41
Consolodated Commodore: 39
Continental Air Service: 254
Conway, Monsignor Dominic: 253
COPISA (Compania Peruana Internatcionale de Aviacion SA):   135, 146
Cornell, Captain John: 287
Costa, J, Lockheed pilot: 158
Cox, Brian: 180
Crosson, Jack: 262
CUBANA (Cia Cubana de Aviacion SA):   113, 114, 176, 177, 232
Curtess C-46:   122
Curtis Condor: 9

D

Dainty, Paul: 290
DanChuchAid: 265
Das Diakonische Werk (DDW):   264, 273
Davis, Air Stewardess Beth E; TWA: 168
de Campo, Richard; TWA: 69
De Havilland DH.91 Albatross: 29, 30
De Havilland DH.98 Mosquito: 115
De Havilland DH106 Comet: 116, 143, 149, 172
Deere, Roger, NMUSAF: 202
Delta Air Lines: 129, 143, 147
Desouza, Flight Engineer, Air India: 140
Deutscher Caritasvervband (DCV):   264
Dhuru, First Officer, Air India: 140
Diaz, Juan M Pali: 113
Dietrich, Noah: 89, 90, 95, 99, 100
Direction Générale de la Sécurité Extérieure (DGSE):   266
Dixon, Captain George C: 219
Dixon, Chris: 266
Doll, Henri: 105
Doud, Mrs John S: 297
Douglas B-23 Dragon: 99
Douglas C-133 Cargomaster: 173
Douglas C-74 Globemaster: 28
Douglas DC-1:   14
Douglas DC-2:   9, 10, 272
Douglas DC-3/C-47:   8-10, 14-16, 20, 28, 34, 69, 127, 137, 163, 259, 260, 265, 272, 280, 293
Douglas DC-4/C-54:   5, 15, 27-29, 33, 77, 82, 97, 102, 111-113, 120, 122-124, 135, 139, 141, 146, 156, 157, 166, 175, 265, 267, 273, 278, 287
Douglas DC-6:   33, 77, 82, 97, 110, 111, 131, 135, 146, 149, 160, 175, 176, 178, 197, 273, 276, 280, 282, 287
Douglas DC-7:   143, 160, 164, 168, 169, 171, 175, 176, 180, 182, 197, 198, 241, 244, 247, 250, 259, 260, 265, 268, 273, 278, 280, 282, 285, 286, 287, 293
Douglas DC-8:   147, 159, 282
Douglas DC-9:   163
Douglas XB-31:   41

Douglas YC-124 Globemaster: 173
Draper, Lt Col: 296, 297
Dreyer, Lance: 290, 292
Dreyfuss, Henry: 119, 175
Drown, Joseph: 237
Duch, Axel: 264, 265, 273
Duke of Edinburgh: 120
Dunn, Raymond M: 20
Duvalier, 'Papa Doc':   145

E

Eastern Air Lines: 14, 82, 111, 116, 128, 132-136, 144, 145, 147, 151, 152, 154, 157, 160, 163, 177, 180, 184, 231, 233, 238
Eastern Provincial Airways: 236
Edde Airlines: 129
Eeltz, Stanley A: 152
Eisenhower, General Dwight D (later President):   194, 197, 296
Eisenhower, Mamie: 296, 297
EL AL Isreal Airlines: 75, 117, 121-125, 133
Ellender, Senator Allen J: 77
Ellinger, Ralph: 16-18, 20, 25, 26, 30, 34
Emerson, Faye: 90
Etablissements Godet: 261
Etheopian AirlinesL   197
Euravia (London) Ltd: 125, 129
Ezzell, 1st Lt Mason: 227-229

F

FAA: 288, 289
Fairchild FC.2:   38
Fairey Aircraft Ltd: 10, 11
Fairey FC.1:   11, 12, 13
Falcon Airways: 128, 129
Fales, John, Lockheed pilot: 158
Farley, James A: 106
Farley, John: 295
Ferguson, Senator Homer: 74, 77, 102, 103, 104
Fiore, Flight Engineer Gerard; United Air Lines: 168
Fireball Air Express: 127
Fisher, Sir Walter: 11
Fleet, Euben H: 23
Flying Tiger Line: 174, 179, 232, 237, 238, 284
Flying W Airways: 285
Focke Wulf Fw.200 Condor: 24
Fokker F.7:   14
Fokker F.10A: 14
Fokker SV.2:   38
Folland Aircraft Ltd: 11
Fontenau, Roger: 261
Ford Trimotor: 39
Fordyce, Captain Robert W; PAA: 96
Fowler, Tech Sgt: 223
Franklin, Jack: 25, 26, 30
Frye, Mrs Jack: 105
Frye, William John 'Jack':   14-19, 22-25, 33-35, 65, 68, 72-76, 85, 86, 90, 91, 94-96, 105
Fuller, Burdett: 14
Futura Air Lines: 129

Fysh, Hudson; QANTAS: 142

G
Gandy, Captain Jack S; TWA: 168, 169, 172
Ganesh, Flight Purser, Air India: 140
Gannon, Very Rev. Robert I: 106
Gardner, Les: 122
General Aircraft GAL.40:   10
General Aircraft Ltd: 10, 11
George, Maj Gen Harold L: 74
Georgiev, Gen Velitchko: 124, 125
Gibson, Brigadier General Kenneth: 191
Gibson, Johnnie: 265
Glennon, Archbishop John J: 106, 107
Glover, Charles L: 68
Godet, Jean: 261
Goering, Hermann: 272
Gold, Miriam; EL AL Stewardess: 122
Gowon, General Takubu 'Jack':   251, 252, 253
Grand Canyon Airlines: 171
Gray, Harold E: 40
Great Lakes Airlines: 145
Green, Senator Theodore Francis: 77
Greenamyer, Daryl: 294
Grieco, Dr John: 105
Gross, Robert Ellsworth: 7, 8, 23-25, 29, 30, 33-35, 40, 67
Grunenther, General Alfred M: 194
Guest Aeronaves Mexico SA: 176, 178, 282
Guest, Winston: 139, 140
Guy, John: 16, 17, 18, 34, 35

H
Halaby, Najeeb: 288
Halse, Clive: 260, 278, 279
Hamilton, Walter 'Ham':   14, 16
Hamlin, John: 271
Hammarskjöld, Dag: 272
Hampton, Lionel: 269
Handley Page Halifax: 133
Handley Page Hermes: 78, 135
Hardee, Lt: 227
Harlow, Jean: 17
Harms, First Officer Robert W; United Air Lines: 168, 171
Harriman, W Averell: 38
Hawthorne Nevada Airlines: 129, 130
Hawthorne, Cliff: 260
Hellenic Air: 272
Heller, Lt Col: 223
Hells Angels: 17
Herbin, George: 105
Hermann, Captain Jack: TWA: 106
Hibbard, Hall Livingstone; Lockheed: 7, 8, 23, 33, 34, 68
Hillman Airways: 10
Hilton Barron: 237
Hilton, Conrad: 237
HK.1 Hercules: 90, 95, 103
Hoover, President Herbert Clark: 83

Hope, Bob: 219
Hopkins, Harry: 37
Hoyt, Richard: 38
Hughes H.1:   17
Hughes X-11:   103
Hughes, Howard Robard: 15, 17-19, 22-26, 30, 33-35, 40, 64-67, 72-77, 82, 86, 89-91, 94, 95, 99, 100, 102-104, 137, 143, 154, 234, 281, 282
Hugin, Henry: 171
Hugin, Palen: 171
Hull, Harlan: 18
Hunter, Croil: 100

I
Iberia Lineas Aereas Espanolas: 158, 159, 175, 176, 182, 282
Ickes, Harold L: 36
Illyushin Il-14:   177
Illyushin Il-18:   177
Imperial Airlines: 129
Imperial Airways: 11, 12, 13, 23, 39, 149
Indian Air Force: 166
Intercity Airways: 264
Intercontinental Airways: 121, 232
Intercontinental US Inc: 232
Interior Airways: 174
International Aerodyne: 182
International Aircraft Services: 146, 156
International Caribbean Corp: 129
International Red Cross (IRC):   252, 270, 271
Interocean Airways SA: 135, 232
Ironsi, General Aguiyi: 251

J
Jackson, Captain K G; QANTAS: 142
Jagger, Bianca: 289
Jagger, Mick: 289, 290
Jaggi, Henrich: 252
January, Colonel Jack: 227-229
Jatar, Captain, Air India: 140
Jensen, P, Lockheed pilot: 158
Jesus Christ Airways: 272, 274
Johnson, Clarence L 'Kelly'; Lockheed: 7, 23, 24, 29, 30, 33, 34, 58, 59, 63, 65-71, 134, 153, 184, 185, 188
Joint Church Aid: 274, 276, 280
Jones, Jesse; Sec of Commerce: 73, 74
Joseph Ankrah, General: 251
Joseph, Ben J: 105
Jouett, Maj John H: 38
Junkers Ju.52:   11, 162

K
Kalt, Peter E: 294
Kasper, Captain Stanley M 'Toots' ;TWA: 139
Kemnitz, Air Stewardess Nancy L; United Air Lines: 168
Kermerecfi, Gilbert: 261
Kilner, Walter G: 41
Kinnear, Henry: 261
KLM *see* Koninklijke Luchtvaart Maatschappij N.V.

Knight, Eric: 265
Knox, Captainj: 277
Koninklijke Luchtvaart Maatschappij N.V. (Royal Dutch Airlines – KLM): 18, 82, 107, 113, 131, 139, 141-143, 147, 158, 159, 160, 163-165, 175, 176, 178, 236, 238, 239, 271, 272, 284, 289, 290
Koninklijke Nederlandsch-Indische Luchtvaart Maatschappij (KNILM): 82
Korean Air: 294
Korean Airlines: 146, 238
Kozubski, Captain Marian: 128, 129

L

Lacy, Clay: 293
Ladoke Akintola: 251
Lake Havasu Airlines: 130
Lamzair: 262
Land, Edwin, Polaroid Corp: 188
Land, Rear Admiral Emory S: 74
Landis, James McCauley; CAB: 84, 91, 101
Languillaume, Jacques: 261
Lanzair (Channel Islands) Ltd: 292, 293
LAPA (Lineas Aereas Patagonica Argentinas SRL): 181, 269, 284, 285
Lapham, Roger: 102
Leasure, C Edward; CAB: 74
Lee, Josh; CAB: 73, 74
Leon, Col. Rene Juares: 145
Lewis, Sam: 122, 123
Lindbergh, Charles: 22, 39
Linea Aeropostal Venezolana: 114, 137, 141, 159, 163, 166, 174, 175
Lineas Aereas de Panama SA: 121
Lineas Aereas Nacionales SA: 146
Linee Aeree Italiane (LAI): 246, 247
Lloyd Airlines: 129
Lockheed Altair: 7
Lockheed C-130 Hercules: 154, 210, 243, 245
Lockheed Model 10 Electra: 7, 8, 11, 13, 28
Lockheed Model 12 Electra Jnr: 7, 27
Lockheed Model 14 Super Electra: 8, 10, 11, 13, 17, 27
Lockheed Model 18 Lodestar: 8
Lockheed Model 188 Electra: 154, 156, 242
Lockheed Model 249/XB30-LO: 41, 43
Lockheed Model 44 Excalibur: 8, 9, 23, 28, 83
Lockheed Orion: 7
Lockheed P.38 Lightning: 26, 27, 42, 62, 162, 173
Lockheed Sirius Mail Plane: 7
Lockheed Vega: 7
Lockheed Ventura: 28, 29
Lodge, Cabot: 219
Loewy, Raymond: 34, 35
Loftleidir: 146
Long Island Airways: 38
Loomis, Robert L; TWA: 69, 70, 71
Lorin, Gerard: 105
Lovett, Robert A: 36, 37
Luce, Clare Boothe: 35
Luce, Henry R: 35, 36

Lufthansa (Deutsche Lufthansa AG): 11, 80, 161, 162, 176, 179, 182, 232, 233, 238, 241, 246, 248, 249, 285, 286, 287
Lunsford, Major: 223
Luxair: 285, 287
Lynott, Frank B; Eastern Airlines: 232

M

Macarthur, General Douglas: 197
MacNamara, Secretary of Defense Robert: 222
Magic City Airways: 129
Magnuson, Senator Warren: 89
Malayan Airways: 166
Malloch, Captain John McVicar 'Jack': 260-262, 265, 266-268, 278, 279
Mani, Navigation Officer, Air India: 140
Manzoni, Peter: 294
Marshall, General George C: 36. 197
Martin M.130: 40
Martin, Captain August Harvey 'Augie': 269, 270
Martin, Gladys Riddle: 269
Martin, Roy: 74
Matherne, Lee J: 279
May, Captain W S; BOAC: 116
Maybank, Senator Burnet R: 77
McBride, Flight Engineer Ray; TWA: 106
McCarran, Senator Patrick Anthony 'Pat': 84, 85, 88, 95
McCarthy, Glen: 19
McCay, Air Hostess Miss, Air India: 140
McFarland, Senator Ernest W: 77
McKee, Mayor Joseph J: 106
McMasters, Captain D F; QANTAS: 142
Meade, Jessie Raymond: 269
Mercer, Chuck: 294
Merriam, Captain Don: 277
Mexicana de Aviacion: 39
Meyer, John W 'Jonnie': 90, 103
Meyer, Rene: 274
Meyers, Maj Gen Bennett: 74
Miami Airlines: 146
Miles, Maj Gen B M: 74
Minser, Ed J; TWA: 69, 70, 71, 72
Modern Air Transport: 129, 144, 181
Mollerup, Pastor: 273
Mongomery, John K: 38
Montreal Air Services: 181, 182, 284
Mooney, Bishop Edward: 105, 106, 107
Moore, Co-Pilot Brooks A: 290
Morely, Lt Col Bernard D: 58
Morgan, Dave: 265
Murphree Air International: 174

N

National Airlines: 82, 159, 236, 284
Nelson, Donald M; Wright Patterson AFB: 74
Nevada Air Motive: 128
New York, Rio and Buenos Aries Line (NYRBA): 39
Nguyen Cao Ky, Vietnamese Prime Minister: 219
Nicholson, C P, Lockheed pilot: 158

315

Nigeria Airways: 259, 268
Nittler Air Transport International: 287
Nixon, President Richard M: 214, 215, 216
Nnamdi Azikiwe, President: 251
Nordair: 236, 273, 275, 276, 280, 284
NordChurchAid: 260
North American Aircraft Trading Co: 271
North Slope Supply Co: 17
Northern Consolidated Airlines: 147
Northrop Gamma: 14
Northwest Orient Airlines: 82, 89, 100, 144, 175, 177
Nusantara Airways: 179, 284
NYRBA do Brazil: 39

O
O'Dwyer, William: 102
O'Rahilly, Rowan, 220
Obafemi Awolowo: 251
Odumegwu-Ojukwu, Colonel Chukwuemeka 'Emeka': 251, 252, 258, 280
Olson, Orville R: 69
OXFAM: 275, 280

P
Pacific Air Transport: 129, 145, 282
Pacific Northern Airlines: 130, 143, 145, 147
Pacific Southwest Airlines: 145
Pakistan International Airlines: 164, 237
Pan American Airlines (PAA): 9, 15, 18, 19, 23, 35, 36-40, 63, 75, 78, 81-84, 86-102, 104, 108, 110-114, 116, 129, 131, 138, 139, 143, 145, 149, 176, 178, 179, 181, 197, 249, 291
Pan American Grace Airways (Panagra): 39, 82, 87
Panair do Brazil: 39, 111, 198
Pao, Major-General Vang: 256
Paradise Airlines: 129, 1304
Paramount Airlines: 144, 146, 181, 238
Parkinson, Thomas I: 91, 93, 94
Patterson, Robert P; Undersecretary of War: 74
Patterson, William; UAL: 84
Paulson, Alan: 293
Peterson, Bertram: 270
Phillips, John: 259
Phoenix Air Transport: 182, 262, 279
Phoenix Airlines: 262
Pickett, Lucien H: 264, 265
Piper Tri-Pacer: 171
Plata, Captain Luis: 137
Pogue, Lloyd Welch; CAB: 36, 74
Pope Paul IV: 256
Pope Pius XII: 105
Presbyterian Church of Canada: 280
Prins, Klaas Jurjen: 165
Proctor, R L: 68
Protestant World Council of Churches: 264
Pryor, Sam TWA pilot: 90, 93, 104

Q
QANTAS/QANTAS Empire Airways: 118, 119, 120, 121, 139-143, 146, 160, 164, 166, 167, 181, 182, 232, 238, 281, 282, 284, 285, 293
Quaker City Airways: 145
Queen Elizabeth II: 120

R
Raab, Larry: 269, 279
Raburn Vern: 294
RAPSA (Rutas Aereas Panemenas AS): 262
Ratcliffe, Senator George: 88
REAL (Rédes Estaduais Aéreas Ltda) 179, 234, 236
Rector, Captain Charlie: 290
Rempt, Henry; Lockheed: 188
Reseau Aérien Interinsulair: 181
Resort Airlines: 234, 238, 282, 283, 284
Rhodesian Air Services: 265
Rhodesian Airlines: 261
Riccatelli, Rickey, Flight engineer: 291
Ricci, Robert: 105
Richards, Keith: 292
Richter, Captain Paul Ernest: 14, 15, 17, 18, 22
Rickenbacker, Captain Edward 'Eddie'; Eastern Air Lines: 14, 172
Riddle Airlines: 233
Ridgeway, General: 194
RIPSA (Rutas Internationales Peruanas SA) 146, 282
Ritner, First Officer James H; TWA: 168
Rivas, Pete: 123
Robertson, George: 268
Rocheau, Monsignor George: 253
Rockne, Knute: 14
Rodhain, Monsignor Jean: 256
Rolling Stones, The: 289-293
Roosevelt, Col. Elliott: 90, 103
Roosevelt, President Franklin D: 35, 36, 40, 87, 90, 126
Rouge, Flight Engineer Jack; TWA: 106
Royal Air Burundi: 130
Royal Air Cambodge: 176
Royal Air Maroc: 135, 146, 147, 176
Ruhanien, Flight Engineer Art; TWA: 106
Ruskin Air Services: 293
Russell, Jane: 17, 90
Ryan, Oswald; CAB: 73, 74

S
SABENA Airlines: 131, 232, 259
Salazar, Antonio de Oliveira: 257
Salmon, Herman R 'Fish': 245, 294
Salway, Air Hostess, Air India: 140
Santana: 289
SAS (Scandanavian Airlines System): 166, 176, 178
SCADTA: 38, 39
Schmidt, Ruth; Hostess TWA: 106
Schwimmer Aviation Corp: 121
Schwimmer, Adolph William 'Al': 121, 122
Seaboard & Western/Seaboard World Airlines: 149, 156, 157, 175, 177, 180, 181, 232, 233, 269, 282, 284, 285
Sebastio, Major Antonio Jorge de Silva: 262
SECAN: 135

Selassie, Emperor, Hallé: 197
Shapiro, Jacob: 129
Shelmerdine, Sir Francis: 10
Sherman, Col Charles C: 108
Sherman, Mrs Edna K: 108
Shiemwell, Don; Purser TWA: 106
Shirley, Captain Robert F; United Air Lines: 168, 171, 172
Shoop, Lt Col C A: 69, 71
Shorts S.30: 39
Shorts Sandringham: 148, 181
Shoudt, Air Stewardess Margaret A; United Air Lines: 168
Sikorsky S.38: 39
Sikorsky S.40: 39
Sikorsky S.42: 39
Silver, Joseph: 105
Skyways of London: 126, 135, 146, 148, 283
Slick Airways: 233, 234, 284
Smith, Ian, Rhodesian Prime Minister: 265
Solomon, S J: 69, 71
So'ng, Kim Il; North Korean leader: 214
South African Airways: 9, 135, 136, 142, 285
South American and Far East Air Transport: 166
South Pacific Airlines: 181
Southeastern Skyways Inc: 130
Spaatz, Maj. Carl A: 38
Spartan Air Lines: 10
Spellman, Archbishop Francis J: 106, 107
Spilo, Lucie: 105
Spruill, Lee: 69
Squier, Carl: 7
Standard Air Lines: 14
Standard Airways: 129, 144, 174, 181
Stansfield, Paul: 290
Stanton, Charles I: CAB: 74
Stanton, Dick: 59, 65, 69
Stearman, Lloyd: 7
Stettinius, Edward R Jnr: 38, 88
Stettinius, Elizabeth 'Betsy': 38
Stettinius, Elizabeth Betty: 38
Stettinius, John Terry: 38
Stettinius, John White: 38
Stewart, Maj. C J: 10
Stimson, Henry: 37
Stritch, Archbishop Samuel L: 105, 106, 107
Sule, Radio Officer, Air India: 140
Sunday Promotions: 292
Sverrisson, Bjorn: 287
Swissair: 7

T
Taft, Senator Robert A: 35, 101
TAP (Transportes Aéreos Portugueses): 178, 232, 237, 271, 272
Tate, Captain Charles O; TWA: 107
Taylor, Mick: 290
Terry Juanita: 37
Thai Airways: 176, 178, 282
The Flying Sherpa: 177

Thoren, Rudy L; Lockheed: 59, 69, 70, 81
Tien, Bishop Thomas: 106, 107
Tipton, Stuart: 288
Tomlinson, Captain D W 'Tommy: 14, 15, 16, 18, 19, 22, 24, 26, 30, 33
Trans Africa Air Coach: 283
Trans Africa Airlines: 264
Trans Atlantica Argentina: 284
Trans Australia Airlines (TAA): 291, 292
Trans California Airlines: 144, 145
Trans Canada Airlines: 159, 163, 175, 176, 181, 233, 236, 282
Trans International Airlines: 174, 181, 234, 237, 238, 281, 282
Trans Mediterranean Airways: 287
Trans-European Aviation: 129
Transair: 272
Transcontinental Airlines SA: 233, 279
Transcontinental Air Transport (TAT): 14, 22
Transcontinental and Western Airlines (T&WA)/Trans World Airlines (TWA): 5, 7, 14-22, 25, 33-35, 40, 41, 63-65, 68-70, 72-75, 79, 81-83, 85-88, 90-99, 101, 102, 104-106, 108, 111-114, 128-130, 137-139, 141, 143, 144, 147, 148, 151, 153, 160, 168, 169, 172, 174, 176, 180, 181, 184, 197, 234, 237, 238, 242-247, 249, 250, 263, 282, 284, 285, 286
Transocean Airlines: 129, 146, 180, 237, 238, 280, 282, 283, 284, 287, 293
Transportader do Ar: 261
Transportes Aereos Squella: 130
Transportos Aeros Benianos SA: 148
Transtate Airlines: 232
Travolta, John: 294
Trek Airways: 143, 241, 285, 287
Trippe, Charles: 99
Trippe, Juan Terry: 35-40, 83-88, 90, 91, 93, 95, 99-102, 104
Truman, Senator, later President Harry S: 74, 77, 87, 88, 90, 112, 197, 297
Tshombe, Moise: 266
Tunis Air: 176

U
UAT: 285
United Air Lines (UAL): 5, 7, 10, 15, 22, 39, 84, 87, 89, 97, 110, 111, 131, 166, 168, 169, 171, 172
United Aircraft and Transport Corporation (UATC): 39
United States Airways: 282, 283
Universal Sky Tours Ltd: 125
Unum Inc: 290
US Air: 264

V
Valle, Bill Del: 40
Van Nuys Skyways: 282
Vandenburg, General Hoyt S: 197
Vanderbilt, Cornelius: 38
Vanderburg, Senator Arthur H: 77
VARIG (SA Empresa de Viacao Aérea Rio Grandense):

178, 179, 236, 249, 267, 283
Varney, Walter T: 7
Varona, Ana Gloria: 113
Venezuelan Airline LAV: 109
Vickers Viscount: 113, 157, 164, 172, 177
Vickers Warwick: 133
Vickery, Rear Admiral Howard: 74
Viking Air Lines: 127
Von der Ahe, Walter R: 282, 283
Von Rosen, Count Carl Gustav Ericsson: 272-274

W
Walcott, Daniel: 254
Ware, J F: 173
Warner, Edward; CAB: 73, 74
Warton, Henry Arthur 'Hank';   254, 256, 257, 261, 262, 264, 265, 267-273, 278, 279.
Wartski, Heinrich: 256
Watkins, Thomas 'Tommy'; Lockheed: 69, 70
Weeks, Kermit: 286
Wein Alaska Airlines (also Wein Air Alaska and Wein Consolodated Airlines: 147, 290
Welch, Sgt: 227
Wells, Captain Edward; TWA: 106, 107
West Indian Aerial Express: 38

Western Air Express: 7, 14
Western Air Lines: 147, 262, 263
Westmorland, General William Childs: 219
Wharton, Henry 'Hank'; Warton
White, W: 297 Major Thomas
Whitney, Sonny: 38
Wilcox, F W 'Freddie':   266
Wilkie, Wendell: 35
Willair International Airlines: 250, 286, 287
Wilson, Charles E; Wright Patterson AFB: 74
Wilson, Harold, UK Prime Minister: 215, 265
Wilson, Mrs Woodrow Wilson: 74
Wimmer, Roy E: 173, 245
Woodley Airways: 130
Woodley, Mike: 293
World Airways Inc: 233, 234, 238, 249, 283, 285, 287
World Council of Churches: 252, 253, 259, 260, 262, 264, 273, 276
World Wide Airlines: 129, 147, 182, 234

Y
Younesi, Benny: 294, 295

Z
ZZ Top: 289